THE NATURAL HOUSE CATALOG

THE
Natural House
Catalog

EVERYTHING YOU NEED TO CREATE AN
ENVIRONMENTALLY FRIENDLY HOME

DAVID PEARSON

A GAIA ORIGINAL

A Fireside Book
Published by Simon & Schuster Inc.
New York   London   Toronto   Sydney   Tokyo   Singapore

FIRESIDE
Simon & Schuster Building
Rockefeller Center
1230 Avenue of the Americas
New York, New York 10020

A GAIA ORIGINAL
Conceived by David and Joss Pearson

Printed and bound by Dai Nippon Printing Company in Hong Kong
10 9 8 7 6 5 4 3 2 1

Library of Congress Cataloging-in-publication Data
Pearson, David. 1940-
    The natural house catalog: everything you need to create an environmentally friendly home / by David Pearson.
      p.   cm.
    ISBN 0-684-80198-1
    1. Dwellings--Environmental engineering--Amateurs' manuals.
  2. Green products--Directories.   I. Title.
  TH6057.A6P42   1996   95-25220
  690' .837--dc20   CIP

Project Editor	Charlie Ryrie
Research	Caroline Sheldrick
Project Co-ordinator (UK)	Lyn Hemming
Project Co-ordinator (US)	Richard Freudenberger
Design	Adam Banks
	Lucy Guenot
	Kitty Parker-Jervis
US Reader	Carol Venolia
Directory compilation	Helen Bradbury
	Fiona Trent
Project Initiator	Natasha Goddard
Picture Research	Jan Crowley
Managing Editor	Pip Morgan
Production	Susan Walby
Direction	Joss Pearson and Patrick Nugent

This book is printed on chlorine-free SSS paper from Daishowa in Japan

The publishers gratefully acknowledge the co-operation of all those who generously allowed us to reproduce their drawings and photographs. Every effort has been made to contact all the individuals and companies whose illustrations are reproduced in this book, and to credit each picture with the appropriate information. If the publishers have inadvertently mis-credited, overlooked a credit, or reproduced an image without permission, we apologize for any inconvenience.

FRONT COVER PHOTOGRAPHS: *top left:* earth-built house in Napa, California by David Easton and Cynthia Wright of Terra Group; *top right and bottom left:* independent home on Salt Spring Island, British Columbia; *bottom right:* lobby of the Triton Hotel, San Francisco by Michael Moore.

The Author

David Pearson DIP ARCH (London), MCRP (Berkeley), RIBA is an internationally known author, architect and campaigner for ecological design. He has written two previous books, *The Natural House Book* and *Earth to Spirit: In Search of Natural Architecture*, is founder of the non-profit Ecological Design Association, and editor of *EcoDesign* - the Association's journal. A founder member of Gaia International - an innovative group of eco-architects drawn from twelve countries, he is also Director of the eco and healthy building consultancy Gaia Environments. He divides his time between England and North America, and travels and lectures widely all over the world.

The Consultants

Richard Freudenberger, editor and publisher of *BackHome* magazine, has worked in the field of renewable energy and alternative building for nearly twenty years.

Carol Venolia, architect and designer; author of *Healing Environments*; co-founder of the Natural Building Network; editor of *Building with Nature* newsletter.

Debra Dadd-Redalia, expert on environmentally safe and responsible products, consultant, and lecturer; author of many books including *Sustaining the Earth*.

Guy Dauncey, sustainable communities consultant, and writer.

Helmut Ziehe, President of the International Institute of Bau-biologie and Ecology.

CONTENTS

PREFACE

Creating The Natural House Catalog has been an exciting and challenging experience. The idea of the Catalog came out of my first book, The Natural House Book. So many people wrote to me saying that they found the book inspiring and that it had motivated them to use the ideas in their own home. But could I help them further with how and where to get this or that product or material or how to locate a certain organization? Others wrote suggesting and recommending goods they had used or projects I should see. The readers themselves soon made it obvious that what was badly needed was a good sourcing guide as a companion volume. The idea of the Catalog was born!

The Natural House Book also started me off on ever-wider travels, meeting fascinating people and visiting innovative eco-projects and ventures around the world. Some of these experiences are the subject of my second book Earth to Spirit: In Search of Natural Architecture. The lengthy work and research for The Natural House Catalog have introduced me to even wider contacts. The experience has brought many surprises, perhaps the most encouraging of all is the realization of just how much is going on out there, and how many people are involved, in all sorts of ways, in making it happen. The whole field is growing rapidly.

Working on The Natural House Catalog has also renewed my optimism and made me feel the message of a sustainable future is genuinely beginning to make a difference. It has been a pleasure to encounter the sheer enthusiasm and commitment of so many individuals, small businesses, not-for-profit and public and private organizations, both large and small. More than this, all these are steadily accumulating to create the critical mass of ideas, energy, and resources essential for real change.

"Information" and "How-to" are key words today, as more and more people want to take real and practical steps toward solving problems themselves, in their own lives, at home and at work. The convergence of environmental, health, and spiritual concerns continues to influence the marketplace, and a much wider, more attractive, diverse, and affordable range of materials, products and services is available than ever before. The Natural House Catalog has been produced with these developments in mind

The Catalog has been a team effort, and I would like to thank all the consultants and team members for their support and enthusiasm without which the Catalog would not exist. In a project of this kind, although we have done our very best, there are bound to be people, projects, materials and products that have not been included, that could have been. We apologize for this in advance, but cannot claim that the Catalog is entirely comprehensive – it is impossible to be so in the limited space available, with the huge area covered. Now is your chance to get in touch and let us know you are out there.

Make good use of The Natural House Catalog – start today and enjoy it.

David Pearson   August 1995

Man follows the Earth

Earth follows Heaven

Heaven follows the TAO

TAO follows what is natural

Lao Tsu

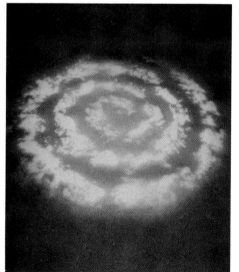

Today, people of North America are more conscious of the environment and their health than ever before. The problems are all too apparent – global warming, ozone depletion, threatened species, pollution and waste – and rapid action is needed to find sustainable solutions. More and more people are now actively joining others in taking positive steps toward an increasingly healthy future. The very best place to take those vital steps is in the home, where we all have some control over our health and environment. Here, through living a more caring and responsible lifestyle, and gradually changing daily consumption habits, individuals and families can help to change the world.

The last two decades have seen great strides forward in developments of materials, technology, and products that provide environmentally-sound and healthy-lifestyle alternatives. When the many alternatives are collected together, as here in *The Natural House Catalog*, it can be seen just what an enormous range and diversity of products and services is now available to the public.

The Natural House Catalog evokes and shares an optimistic vision for a positive future. It stimulates individuals to take practical steps toward this future, while retaining traditional values of

independence, self-reliance, and neighborhood spirit. Everyone, including you, can become inspired and involved and get out there and do it. You don't have to accept what is given to you in the commercial housing market. There are better alternatives and you *can* live a better lifestyle in a natural home. What may appear too complex and out of reach at first will soon seem much simpler, more approachable and affordable once you are armed with appropriate guidance and information. Delve deep into this *Catalog* and follow the advice and information, and your dreams can soon become realities. Don't be put off, start small and simple, then move on to the bigger projects as your experience, confidence,

Opposite: *The high-performance stove supplies back up heat for this solar-powered home in British Columbia.*

This page: *This house in Occidental, California, uses recycled glass blocks to filter light and provide a screen in the* bathroom. *The attractive garden hot tub is made of sustainably forested timber, and solar heated.*

and budget allow. Many of you already use some sustainable and healthy home technology, and the Catalog will also help you to go farther, and develop into other areas. Above all, take it easy, and be sure to enjoy yourself.

Many individuals and families (and organizations) are now living the new lifestyle. Thousands of families are enjoying a life "off the grid" in "independent homes" using solar, wind, and water power, and more are joining them every day. Homemakers all over the United States and Canada are building new homes or retrofitting old ones using environmentally sound and healthy materials. More and more companies, specialists, and organizations are supplying products, materials, systems, and services to meet this fast growing demand.

Need for the Natural House Catalog

But the suppliers are scattered across the United States and Canada, and many are small businesses which may be difficult to find and contact. Homemakers (plus professional designers and contractors) don't always have the time or energy to track them down, and continue, by default, to use harmful products and materials.

Now, The Natural House Catalog provides a huge range of information in one, easily accessible place. Here, at your fingertips, is everything you need to make your natural home. So, whether you are thinking of building in timber frame, adobe, straw bales, brick or stone, for example, or just planning to redecorate or furnish a room, or plant the backyard, the Catalog will guide you

from initial ideas to practical solutions. In the first part of the Catalog, you will find advice, information, and guidance on what to look out for, and what to avoid, plus initial sources of expert and consumer knowhow. Having planned your project, you can turn to the second part of the Catalog for listings of suppliers, products, catalogs, and services.

Do natural or "green" products cost more than conventional ones? Not necessarily, nowadays. Of course you should shop around for the best buy, and the Catalog listings provide you with choices. You should also bear in mind the long-term return on your investment. Photovoltaics, for example, may seem expensive to install, but with rising electricity prices, the free supply from the sun will repay you sooner than you think. Apparently cheaper non-"green" products often also have high hidden costs. These may include depletion of scarce resources, pollution, toxic by-products, and a high environmental toll in transportation. We may not pay for these directly, but they cost us all dearly in the end.

More than products

The Catalog takes a holistic view of all elements that contribute to making the home, placing products and services in the context of the broader perspective and the deeper issues of "green" philosophy. The recurring themes of "green" living – healthy lifestyle, ecological consciousness, and spiritual harmony – are represented throughout the Catalog. In a natural home these need to be interrelated and balanced to make it a truly sustainable, healing, and harmonious place, in tune with Gaia — the living Earth. If any one of these themes — health, ecology, or spirit — is allowed to dominate, an imbalance or distortion will occur which will affect the overall performance of the design. If, for example, energy-conservation (making the home structure air-tight) is not balanced with healthy building (adequate ventilation), the indoor air quality and health of the occupants will be adversely affected. Or, take a garden that is designed harmoniously according to spiritual precepts (Feng Shui), but which ignores composting and water conservation needs; it will be considered environmentally irresponsible and defective.

The new "green" esthetic

Conventional homemakers and professional designers often pose the argument that resource-efficient houses tend to ignore or be insensitive to esthetics and style — form, space, texture, light, and color. But this certainly should not be the case. Environmental, healthy, and spiritual design elements can be successfully integrated with any traditional or modern home design. Used well, their presence will complement and improve conventional designs, making your home more attractive, comfortable, economic, and marketable. This is no passing fashion or shallow application of "eco-chic" style. The new "green" esthetic represents a fundamental and permanent change toward sustainability that will transform not only our homes but everything from domestic products to whole communities.

Consumer guidance and protection

Whereas the steady growth of the environmental, healthy, and spiritual product marketplace is something to be welcomed, there is a downside. This is still a relatively new field with many products and services that could do with a good deal more independent and in-depth scrutiny. Many companies, large and small, have jumped on the environmental bandwagon and marketed new products (or remarketed existing ones) as "green" and "healthy" when they are, at best, untested, at worst, a con. There have been far too many instances of "greenwash"!

How is the consumer to know if the claims are true or false? Labeling programs do exist in some areas, but adequate legislation has lagged behind the marketplace and the development of a comprehensive and reliable independent government-approved "eco-labeling system" (as being introduced in certain European countries) will take some time. Federal and state bodies such as the Environmental Protection Agency (EPA) do already produce helpful advisory information and run educational programs on "green" and health-related issues. Their advice is always worth seeking. In the private sector, help is at hand from a number of national and regional organizations, product-testing organizations, and professional product-and-equipment-evaluation guides. There are also consumer protection organizations such as Coop America who, via their *National Green Pages*, make sure that member companies follow strict codes covering environmental, ethical and fair trading practices. Alternative Trading

Even brick structures are earthquake-proof when built to rediscovered ancient building principles. These Cal-Earth arched domes, usually earth-built, are light, cool, and tranquil spaces.

Organizations (ATOs) can also help you to identify ethnic products from Latin and South America and the "Third World" produced via village cooperatives and other sustainable and equitable means.

In the absence of any nationwide approved labeling system which covers the range of products in the *Catalog*, we have relied on personal recommendation to back-up such labeling and testing as exists in selecting items. However, things are changing all the time and you should always double check for yourself and use your judgment. Your own experience with these products is a valuable part of their development.

part one

EVERYTHING
YOU NEED

Whatever you need to create your natural home – start here. Read up on the basics of how to build and rehab your home, use soft energy, switch to sane electrics and low-energy lighting, create imaginative furnishings and decoration, and maintain your home in non-toxic ways. Find out how to transform your backyard with conserving designs and appropriate planting, or even how to turn your sewage into a water garden! Use the topic pages as starting points, then get further information via the Resources, and ideas from Shoppers features.

You don't need to read Part One from front to back. Start anywhere and dip into whatever chapter or topic catches your interest. For example, you may already have switched to low-energy lighting, or use non-toxic cleaning methods, but would like to branch out into photovoltaics, or permaculture. Wherever you begin, begin today, and let the *Catalog* guide and empower you to create a natural home in harmony with the planet and yourself.

This chapter is about the whole house, its materials and construction, its siting and planning. When faced with creating a house that is environmentally sound and healthy, there is a confusing array of choices. Where should I site the house? Do I use this or that material? What would be the best type of home to build – should it be brick or timber construction, and what about earth and straw-bale? Where can I source the right materials and advice? Should I build a new house or retrofit an older property?

Starting with the home site, this chapter gives you introductory guidance on how to analyze the basic local conditions you will need to work with – climate, soil, and water. Via permaculture, you can transform your garden and backyard into a productive and sustainable asset. Other, less well understood aspects of the site include being sensitive to the subtle ground energies beneath your home, and being aware of the ancient principles of Feng Shui and how they help to orient, lay out, and furnish your home.

Your natural home design should balance the environment, health, and spirit. If you neglect any of these or give undue emphasis to any one over another your home cannot be expected to reach its full potential as a healthy, harmonious, and ecologically sound environment. To reach a balanced approach, follow the practical advice on creating healthy homes plus the inspiring options for organic and spiritual designs.

The choice of building materials and construction methods is very diverse and much will depend on the vernacular traditions of your area, as well as on your budget. Older traditions have often been replaced with newer nationwide anonymous alternatives: a house on the East Coast may be built of much the same materials as one on the West Coast. It is always worth finding out if some of the rediscovered methods such as earth building or straw bales could be used. These may make a more sensible, affordable, and sustainable alternative for you. There can be pitfalls in using natural materials, just as there are with synthetic conventional materials, but proper advice and the latest environment-friendly technology can help you use natural materials wisely.

The growing use of reclaimed materials represents one positive step forward.

Rehabbing or retrofitting an older property (rather than building new), combined with the reuse of as many locally salvaged and recycled materials as possible, is both resource-efficient and affordable. Before buying new products, even if they are billed "green", first look for reclaimed products locally. Every time you do this you will be taking pressure off the environment and saving energy and pollution at the same time.

When you walk into a well-designed natural home, you are immediately aware of something different and special. You feel more alive and positive. The air is refreshing and you can breathe freely; there is plenty of natural daylight and you feel awake; colors, forms, and spaces invigorate and relax you. A natural house is a home fit for all the senses, and a home in complete harmony with you and with the environment.

A timber frame building is an exciting owner-built option. Timber bents, usually cut and crafted elsewhere, are assembled on the ground on site, secured with oak pegs and lifted by a crane and pulleys into place. The raising day is traditionally a big event. Friends, family, and neighbors help raise the frame and join in the celebrations.

FENG SHUI

Meaning literally "wind water", Feng Shui is the ancient Chinese art and science of placement. Akin to geomancy, which is known in many cultures, it aims to bring human beings into a harmonious relationship with the universe through appropriate siting, landscaping, architecture, and interior design. Taoism, on which it is based, seeks harmony by following the "natural" way. Feng Shui locates places of harmony with good ch'i, the vital life force or cosmic breath, and avoids sha, or "noxious vapors". It is an extension of oriental healing practices such as acupuncture, tai chi and meditation, all of which help to balance female Yin and male Yang elements and revitalize the ch'i of body and soul.

Using Feng Shui

Feng Shui is increasingly relevant today. In Hong Kong designers and occupants of public buildings, offices, and homes make use of a Feng Shui consultant to advise on proposals for new buildings and changes to those in use. In fact, without Feng Shui no business or home in the area would expect to have health, prosperity, or good luck. Many of today's Feng Shui skills are devoted to curing modern ills such as noise, pollution, overshadowing, and lack of light — the "noxious vapors" of urban apartments and offices. Among devices used to fend these off are plantings, water features, mirrors, screens, flower arrangements, mobiles, and crystals. Fundamental changes may also be recommended, such as reorienting a room's layout and furniture, adapting rooms to have a greater harmony and symmetry of shape and form, or re-siting various activities in different locations altogether.

Various introductory books and courses are available or you may wish to contact a trained Feng Shui consultant (see Resources, p. 48).

Geomagnetic fields

The Earth has natural terrestrial magnetic fields to which all life has been attuned for eons. Known as the Schumann frequency, the Earth's natural beat is at a rate of 7.83 per second (7.83 Hz). Building biologists (see p. 25) consider that it is essential for our health and well-being to maintain our exposure to this natural frequency. One problem occurs through the many artificial electromagnetic fields (EMFs) in today's homes created by the plethora of electrical circuits and equipment (see p. 93). These are mainly generated by alternating currents (AC) at a frequency in North America of 60 cycles a second (60 Hz), causing continual disturbance to the earth's natural rhythms. Subterranean geological features such as rock fissures, water courses, and variations in rock type and sub-soil also cause natural distortions to the Earth's magnetic field. Areas where these occur are called geopathic zones (geo=earth, pathic=disease). Long-term exposure to these zones (such as sleeping in a bed over them), plus exposure to artificial EMFs, microwaves, and other sources, is claimed to cause geopathic stress. This, added to the other stresses on our bodily systems caused by pollution, can increase the risk of disease, possibly even cancer.

Dowsers and building biologists offer ground surveys and house inspection services that help to locate geopathic zones. They can then advise on the best ways to avoid and protect against them.

▼ **An ideal country site flanked by Yin (tiger) and Yang (dragon)**

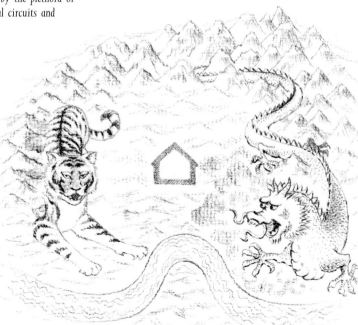

Natural House Book Gaia Books

Wherever you decide to live, ask yourself some detailed questions about the site. As well as finding out about amenities, sources of pollution and noise, and plans and policies for the area, try to build up a profile of the geologic features, soil types, and microclimate. Understanding these factors will allow you to produce a responsive design that works for your particular environment.

The elevation and orientation of your site are important and the microclimate will be affected by its position (for example whether on a hillside or in a valley), by the direction and force of the prevailing winds, by seasonal temperatures, and average hours of sunshine. You must also analyze local vegetation, so that your landscape will be a natural part of its environment. Detailed soil analysis can provide vital information about the geology of your site, and it is important to know your local water courses.

Finding out

Neighbors are a good initial source of information about prevailing weather conditions locally. Local high schools and colleges will probably have weather records, or contact the local weather station for access to their records. Another good source is the local newspaper; find out where their weather information comes from.

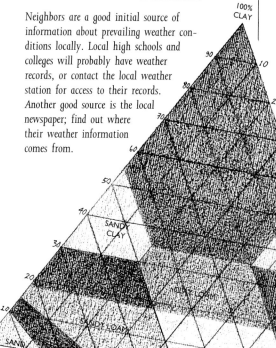

▲ **Understanding your soil allows you to plan planting strategies**

▼ **Check whether the local geology includes adequate groundwater**

Natural Garden Book, Simon & Schuster

Soil analysis

Whether you plan to use the site soil to construct a building (p. 28), to grow food, or to develop into a natural garden, you need to know your soil.

Soil is a mixture of mineral particles, organic matter, air, water, and living organisms. The nature of the underlying rock largely determines the type of soil formed above it by the action of roots, animals, and the weather. Soils can be sandy, clay, or silty, depending on the type of particles.

The acid-alkaline balance, or pH, of the soil is important in allowing plants to absorb mineral nutrients. The lower the pH, the more acid the soil. The best pH for garden plants in temperate soils is 6.5, although 5.5 to 7.5 is adequate for most. Various sampling and testing kits are available to check your soil or you can use a consultant to provide an analysis of nutrients in your soil.

Water analysis

The position of a site in the watershed is of major concern whether you want to harness water for its energy, drink the water, or avoid adding pollutants to any watercourse. Knowing where your water comes from, and where it goes to, is fundamental in planning harmonious construction. You need to discover if there any underground watercourses, and analyze any groundwater problems. It is vital to ensure good drainage for your site.

If there is a water source nearby find out if is it constant, or if you will need to implement water conservation and rainwater collection. You need to test water quality to assess any need for filtration and purification (see p. 77).

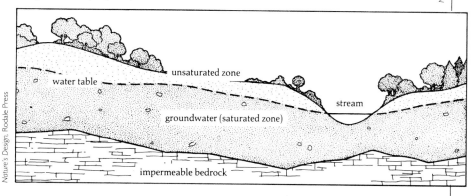

Nature's Design, Rodale Press

PERMACULTURE

The need for small-scale, sustainable agriculture at the end of the twentieth century underlies the principles of permaculture. Pioneered in the 1970s by two Australians, David Holmgren and Bill Mollison, permaculture aims to design "an integrated, evolving system of perennial or self-perpetuating plant and animals species useful to man." Permaculture designs form complete, sustainable, low-energy, high-yield agricultural systems that can be adapted to suit any climate. The system is based on the idea that humans are stewards of the earth and must plan long-term solutions to feeding the population without further damage to the planet. Permaculture is closely related to the Edible Landscape movement.

▲ **A sustainable system maximizes the potential of a small site**

Working with nature

The main principle of permaculture is one of working with, rather than against, nature. Permaculture systems are constructed to last as long as possible, with minimal maintenance. Systems are typically fueled by sun, wind, or water, and produce enough for their own needs and those of the humans controlling or creating them. In this way, they are sustainable. When designing and constructing a permaculture system, make sure the system will store or conserve more energy in its lifetime than you will use in its construction and maintenance.

Plants in a permaculture system should be as diverse as possible. This ensures that invasions of pests never reach epidemic proportions as they can do under monocultural systems. Where possible, maintain local diversity by choosing plants specifically suited to your particular bioregion, and make sure of maximum health and production by opting for companion planting.

Permaculture followers do not just take resources from the environment, they also put them back through positive interaction with nature.

Permaculture design principles

You must work with nature, rather than against it, for you are part of it. Rather than applying chemical pesticides, encourage natural predators. The more we try to fight nature and do things differently, the more nature will fight back. Permaculture believes you should see every problem as its own potential solution. Instead of trying to change something that looks like a problem, see it as a potential benefit and use it as such. If, for example, your site has strong cold winds, use a wind generator and channel the cold air into a cold storage room.

Often the smallest changes have the greatest possible effects. Pollarding and coppicing will produce much more timber than felling trees, and raised beds can be at least as productive as, and less disruptive than, deep digging. Another principle is that the yield of a system is limited only by your imagination and knowledge, not by other people's prescriptions.

You can use observations about other species' effects on habitats and systems to influence your own actions. A properly managed poultry system is a good example of permaculture in practice: the heat naturally produced by chickens might be used to heat a greenhouse to grow fruit and vegetables; chickens will peck out weeds, eat insect pests, and provide eggs and meat. Such a system can be selffueling, self-regulating, and satisfying.

Forest gardening

The principles of forest gardening echo those of permaculture. Widespread in some upland areas of India, a forest garden is a sustainable mini-forest, requiring minimal maintenance and providing fruit, nuts, root and perennial vegetables, and herbs throughout the growing system. It is an intensive and sustainable land use, appropriate for urban or rural areas.

We want our homes and household practices to be in harmony with the environment. Yet an average US household discards 1800 plastic items, 13,000 individual paper items, 500 aluminum cans, and 500 glass bottles annually. As for garbage – calculated over a lifetime, an individual will throw away around 600 times their own weight! Worse, domestic consumption is a linear one-way process which takes from the environment without giving anything back. Clean tap water, used once, is polluted with chemicals and flushed down the drain to distant sewage treatment plants. Valuable energy generated from non-renewable fossil fuels (gas, coal and oil) is wasted powering inefficient lights and electrical equipment, and on heating and cooling under-insulated and poorly weatherproofed homes. Even the materials we use to build and maintain our homes take too much energy to make and transport. We must change from one-way to cyclic processes that reuse and recycle resources and use them with economy and efficiency.

Design for harmony with the planet

Site, orient, and shelter your home to make the best conservative use of renewable resources. Use the sun, wind, and water for all or most of your energy needs and rely less on supplementary, non-renewable energy.

Use "green" materials and products. These should be non-toxic, non-polluting, sustainable and renewable, produced with low energy and low environmental and social costs, and biodegradable.

Use resources intelligently to complement natural mechanisms. Use sensitive and efficient control systems to regulate energy, heating, cooling, water, airflow, and lighting.

Integrate the house with the local ecosystem by planting indigenous tree and flower species. Compost organic wastes, always garden organically, and use natural pest control – no pesticides. Recycle graywater and use low-flush or waterless toilets. Collect, store, and use rainwater (see Chapter Three).

Find out exactly how much energy and water you are using at present, and how much garbage you are throwing away. Survey each room (and the yard) to assess where these resources are being used. List and prioritize your ideas for reducing consumption and waste. Gain advice from utility companies, act on this, and monitor utility bills to check that reductions are being achieved. Remember at every stage to reuse, repair, and recycle.

▼ A sheltered underground house can blend into its environment

Malcolm Wells

What sort of house?

Domes and circular buildings may conserve the greatest amount of materials and heat because they have the least surface area to volume, but small compact homes built in protected locations are also very economical. Even better, homes situated in apartment blocks or row housing will benefit from the shelter and insulation of their neighbors. And, close proximity to workplace and local community activities is a key factor in conserving time, energy, and human resources.

Malcolm Wells

▲ **Earth roofs may sustain natural, maintenance-free, wild gardens**

Eco-homes

Today's "soft energy" technology allows you to unplug from utilities and live in an autonomous or "independent home", (see Chapter Two) or an "Earthship" which provides for all your needs on site. Digging the house into the ground or using earth-sheltered walls and roofs (sod roofs) makes real sense in harsher climates such as hot semi-desert areas or cold northern regions. Designed properly, underground homes are extremely comfortable, have little or no visual impact on the environment, and use minimal energy for heating or cooling.

HEALTHY BUILDING

The National Research Council estimates that around 15% of the US population experiences environmental illness and hypersensitivity to toxic materials and chemicals. The National Academy of Sciences expect this to rise to 60% by 2010. The Environmental Protection Agency has found indoor pollution levels 100 times greater than those outside.

Alfred V. Zamm's *Why Your House May Endanger Your Health* (1980), was one of the first popular books to alert the public to the potential health hazards that lay in and around their homes. He charted the enormous rise in synthetic chemicals since World War II and described how they had permeated almost everything in the home and the environment beyond. He also warned of the explosion in artificial sources of radiation and electromagnetism affecting the home. Since then, concern has grown as studies have confirmed that many homes are indeed unhealthy.

Air pollution

Indoor pollution has many sources. These include air pollution from combustion gases (carbon monoxide, nitric oxide, sulfur dioxide, carbon dioxide) and smoke particles arising from burning fuels in open fires, stoves, furnaces, and cookers. Natural gases can be a problem; in certain areas radon seeps up from the ground and is carried in water and some building materials (see p. 113); ozone is emitted from photocopiers and brush-type motors.

Perhaps the most pernicious are the diverse and growing group of Volatile Organic Compounds (VOCs) which "outgas" (give off harmful vapors at room temperature). These include formaldehyde found in certain interior and building boards, furnishings, carpets, clothing, and bedding, and, until banned, in UFFI cavity insulation. Then come the organochlorines and phenols found in a host of common household items such as synthetic plastic products, carpets and furnishing, stain-resistant and other special finishes, paint solvents, adhesives, wood preservatives, household cleaners, polishes, air fresheners, and insecticides.

Added to this are particles, fibers and dust from asbestos (now banned), micro-organisms (bacteria, viruses, molds, spores, and pollen) in the air, and trace elements from metals such as lead, aluminum, copper, mercury, and cadmium.

Light and water problems

Lack of sufficient natural daylight in our homes and workplaces, especially in winter, and our reliance on artificial light has been shown to contribute to lethargy and depression (see p. 101).

Domestic water is often polluted with toxic chemicals such as chlorine and nitrates and may contain trace elements of metals (see p. 76). Radon gas can be transported through your water supplies and released from tap water far from the original source (see p. 113).

Ventilation

The trend to increased energy efficiency led, at first, to our homes becoming increasingly airtight and sealed off from the outside without adequate ventilation. This allowed high and often toxic concentrations of indoor air pollutants to build up. This problem has now become more generally understood and better ventilation systems are being built into newer homes. But be aware of this hazard in older homes that have been retrofitted and "super-insulated" to make them more energy-efficient. Check that your home allows sufficient ventilation (See also pp. 36 and 64). Keep your house healthy as well as energy-efficient.

Electrostress

These days we are surrounded by electrical equipment, TVs, computers, and microwave cookers. This leads to concern about "electrostress" (the possible harmful effects of our long-term exposure to electromagnetic fields (EMFs) and radiation) from domestic equipment and other sources. The presence of harmful "ground energies" and "geopathic stress" (their negative effects) are becoming more widely recognized when siting a new home and positioning furniture, particularly beds, in a beneficial location (see p. 145). Dowsers using simple divining rods or modern electrical detectors, can give guidance on ground energies; so too can practitioners of the ancient Chinese art of placement — Feng Shui (see p. 20).

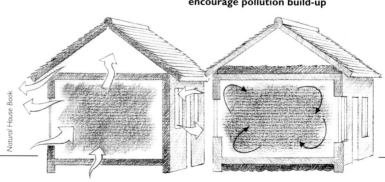

▼ **Modern "sealed" homes may encourage pollution build-up**

Natural House Book

The package of hazards described on the facing page, plus their effects on people, have come to be known as "Sick Building Syndrome". Fortunately, not every home has all these problems. However, you may be surprised to find quite a number of potential health hazards in your home. So what should you do? The basic strategy is to identify potential hazards, and then minimize or eliminate them. Try doing a room-by-room hazard survey of your home yourself. Various publications, including *The Natural House Book* can help you evaluate problems, or you can employ professionals (see Resources p. 48).

◀ Baubiologists practice healthy building for a holistic lifestyle

Clinical ecology

In general, it is wise to lessen your exposure to synthetic chemicals, EMFs and, of course, radiation. Everyone has different reactions to such exposures; some people apparently suffer no ill effects to exposures well over current government permitted limits, while others react violently to only minute exposures. Such variations are the subject of clinical ecology. Some hazards, such as secondary cigarette smoke, asbestos, and radiation, may take years to show their effects. Vital to all this is the level and period of exposure. As the saying goes, "The poison is the dose". So, as well as identifying a possible hazard, you need to know if you, or members of your household, are allergic or chemically hypersensitive to certain substances. If you suffer from persistent allergies, consult a qualified clinical ecologist.

Baubiologie

One of the most interesting developments in the philosophy and practice of healthy building is a movement started by medical doctors in Germany some 20 years ago. Termed "Baubiologie" or Building Biology, it is concerned not only with how buildings and their environments impact on our health, but also with the more positive emphasis of the holistic interaction between human life and our living environment. Every aspect of design and building has been studied afresh and fundamentally reassessed from the point of view of how to build in a healthier way. Fresh air, pure water, natural materials, generous daylight, equitable temperatures and humidity, EMF protection (see p. 93) and beneficial siting to avoid harmful ground energies are all aims of healthy building, Baubiologie-style.

Wider environmental concerns about pollution and waste are also embraced to balance Baubiologie with ecology. These ideas are gaining ground in North America via publications, advisory and educational organizations, and projects.

Creating healing environments

Essential as it is to minimize and eliminate environmental hazards, if this approach is taken too far it can foster a rather negative approach, one preoccupied with problems of pollution and their avoidance. Over recent years, there has been a reaction in North America, and elsewhere, to move beyond this. Many people now prefer to think (and act) in a positive and proactive way about how they can create a home that is not only non-toxic, but one that is harmonious and therapeutic — a healing environment. This involves a personal re-evaluation of the elements of space, form, color, light, scent and sound and the use of their rejuvenating qualities to make your home more life-enhancing for body and soul. A key aspect of this is connecting your home with the natural world by using plants, encouraging wildlife habitats, and acknowledging the seasons (see also Carol Venolia, p. 191).

▼ Light, space, and natural materials are healthy and uplifting

David Pearson

ORGANIC & STEINER DESIGN

The outstanding exponent of organic design in North America is undoubtedly Frank Lloyd Wright. Following in the paths of America's great nature poets and writers such as Emerson, Muir, Thoreau, and Whitman, Frank Lloyd Wright was an ardent lover and observer of nature.

The forces and forms of nature completely captivated him and and emerged as inspirations for his plans, building materials, furnishings, and decorative motifs. Bold spreading cantilevers, arching domes, shimmering skylights, geometric glass designs and delicate patterned screens resemble branching trees, thrusting plant stems, seedheads, and reflections in ponds. The textures and finishes of walls contrast the roughness of rocks, and tree bark with the smoothness of wood grain and river sand. Fallingwater, Wingspread, Hollyhock House and Wright's own Taliesin, among his many other masterpieces, stand as testament to Wright's genius for organic architecture and love of nature.

American organic heritage

Wright has inspired a number of talented American architects and designers. Among the better known are Bruce Goff, Arthur Dyson, Bart Prince, Ken Kellog, and James Hubble plus the Native American Indian architect, Douglas Cardinal. Each has developed a personal interpretation of organic design and created beautiful, unique, and memorable projects. If you want to explore the organic approach, books are available and some architects specialize in this form of design (see Resources p. 48).

Alternatively, you may wish to create and build to your own designs. Get structural advice to ensure that all unconventional roof and wall forms, plus any cantilevers, are adequately constructed and supported. As organic designs are unusual and will probably be something quite new in your area, discuss your plans at an early stage with local government offices to check if special approval will be needed.

Anthroposophic design

A separate root of organic design in Europe and North America is inspired by the anthroposophic philosophy and teachings of Rudolf Steiner. Anthroposophic architects and designers believe that our surroundings affect us physically and spiritually; they can either desensitize us morally and socially or positively support the inner processes of growth that are the foundation of health.

People's physical and spiritual needs are the starting points for a Steiner-inspired building. Designed with love and heart, a building will strengthen our attitude towards life and help our natural self-healing processes. When this approach is developed organically in the building design, it enlivens and delights all the senses - sight, scent, sound, and touch.

Steiner building principles

Straight lines and right angles are thought to constrain and cramp body and spirit so they are avoided or softened by other angles and curvilinear shapes. Organic room shapes are complemented with sensitive contrasting qualities of light. Transparent color glazes also give a special luminous and living atmosphere to the interiors. Pure water and clean air are important, supplied by subtle purification and ventilation systems.

The spirit of water is ever-present in and around the buildings via water sculptures and cascading water "flowforms" (see p. 82). Luxuriant indoor planting, outdoor courtyards, and natural gardens complete these practical and truly holistic organic designs.

▶ **Bart Prince's organic style shown in the Price residence, California**

Alan Weintraub

Besides organic design, there are many ways you can begin your pilgrimage to find and make your spiritual home. The choice will ultimately depend on what has personal meaning for you. You may have strong beliefs centered on one of the established religions. Ecospiritualism has been embraced by some faiths and this may be your natural starting point. Many people feel, however, that the deeper healing and spiritual role of the home was better understood by older cultures and beliefs, and that valuable clues for modern life can be obtained through studying the remains of these cultures.

▲ **A corner of Frank Lloyd Wright's "Falling Water"**

American Indians

Native North American Indian traditions can help us to reach a deeper understanding of our role in nature. To gain insight into their beliefs and lives, and the lessons they can teach us today, visit the many fascinating exhibits, museums and reconstructed buildings in State and National parks and the communities of the Pueblo Indians and the Navajo Nation (see Publications in The Directory, Part Two).

Spiritual influences

The influence of Eastern philosophies and religions as a gateway to inner and outer harmony can be found via practices such as yoga, meditation, tai chi, and acupuncture. Chinese and Japanese cultures continue to inspire the West with the beauty and simplicity of their traditional artifacts, houses and gardens.

Sacred geometry and "divine" proportions derived from European architecture, ancient Hindu vedic building knowledge called Sthapatya-Ved, and Chinese Feng Shui (see p. 20) can all guide us toward more harmonious designs. The inspiring writings of architect and teacher Christopher Alexander also help us see the timeless universality of spaces, forms, and details in building patterns and language.

▲ **Traditionally designed Navajo hogans are still used today**

We should all try to re-sensitize ourselves to the spirit of place. This is equally important when looking at a simple and peaceful garden in town as when considering the earth energy of a mountain vortex in Sedona, Arizona.

EARTH BUILDING MATERIALS

No more than one-third of the world's population live in houses built of industrially-processed materials. By far the majority are sheltered by materials obtained directly from the earth – by stone, rammed earth, wood, or unbaked adobe blocks. Long regarded as primitive, earth building is undergoing a revival. What was a necessity for many has become first choice for many environmentally-conscious architects and builders.

Earth materials have minimal impact during refinement, use little energy, and are free from toxins and pollutants, but check for radon (see p. 113). They can be derived from the building site or close by, reducing the environmental costs of packaging and transport. Minimal processing of materials is needed, so local decentralized production is often possible. This also encourages owner-built housing projects.

Sustainable Architecture

▲ **Adobe is versatile, attractive, durable and easy to work with**

Adobe

Adobe is made from wet mud, or barro, with sufficient clay content to ensure cohesion. The more sand in the mixture, the crumblier the adobe block will be. Some makers add straw to the mixture; this accelerates drying, hinders cracking, and increases the tensile strength of the mud brick. Sometimes bitumen or cement stabilizer are added to resist water erosion.

The wet mixture is molded into blocks by hand or machine, and dried in the sun. After several months of drying in dependably warm weather, the blocks are ready for use and construction with adobe blocks and mud mortar can be rapid. The blocks are generally larger than bricks, typically around 14 x 10 x 4 inches, and each weighs about 35 pounds.

Unbaked earth

Unbaked earth blocks made of turf, laid grass-side down, are used in South and Central America, in Central Europe, Ireland, and the United States, where the turf blocks are called terrones. Another method involves directly quarrying earth blocks from a bank of hard material, a technique called cangahua.

Versatility

A simple earth-walled construction requires only basic construction skills. Earth walls can be left in their natural state, or sealed, plastered, or stuccoed. They are fire, sound, rot, and termite proof, but check local building codes as some areas require "improvements" to rammed earth walls.

Rammed earth

In the rammed earth technique (pisé), earth is rammed into temporary formwork. The mixture should be 70% sand, 30% soil, and a small amount of cement. The earth is allowed to dry, then the formwork is moved upward for the next course. Ideally, each layer should be pounded down with a pneumatic tamper. When the mixture is compressed, the walls become rock hard. Rammed earth looks like rock, and has a density of about 130 pounds per cubic foot. When properly constructed, the walls have ideal thermal qualities, keeping the interior warm in winter and cool in summer. The houses require little supplemental energy for rooms not heated passively by the sun.

Insulated walls

Lighter density mixes, that increase the insulation effect of the earth wall, are also an option. In the German "leichtlehm" (light earth/clay) method, a much higher proportion of rye straw is mixed with clay/earth, sand, manure, and water. This can be rammed or used as a filler in timber-frame walls, covered with timber siding, lime, or clay plaster. Current experiments include dipping straw bales in a clay slurry to make economic thick insulating walls (see p. 37).

▼ **Adobe blocks are easily formed in a simple wooden mold**

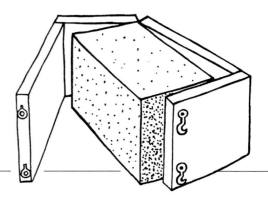

Baked-clay bricks and tiles have been used for over 5000 years. Stronger and more durable than earlier sun-dried earth bricks, they were first employed in Middle Eastern countries as a longer lasting and more imposing outer facing to earth-brick walls.

Baked bricks spread rapidly throughout the world, first as material to build bonded solid walls and more recently, as a facing to cavity walls. Clay bricks and tiles are valued as greatly today as ever for their diverse qualities of warmth, solidity, texture, and beauty. Brick is an incredibly versatile building material, but if you live in an earthquake zone remember that unreinforced masonry is unsafe.

▲ **Roofs, walls, chimneys, facings, all from multi-purpose bricks and tiles**

Glen-Gery Brick Company

Environmental impact

Bricks and tiles have a high "embodied energy" (the total energy expended in extraction of raw materials, production and transport). Although deposits of brick clays appear to be in good supply, open quarries can be a visual and environmental problem. Ideal clays near the ground surface (the traditional source) often become exhausted and alternatives have to be extracted from deeper down. This uses more energy both in the extraction and the processing. Firing in kilns at very high temperatures adds significantly to the energy input and, unless strictly controlled, consequent smoke emissions cause atmospheric pollution.

Clay products are heavy and therefore costly to transport over long distances, so try to source locally-produced products if you decide to use new bricks or tiles. Before buying new, check out suppliers of reclaimed materials.

Durability and reuse

Bricks and tiles are extremely durable. They are capable of lasting many hundreds of years with relatively little maintenance. They can often be salvaged and reused as good quality building materials. Handmade bricks, reclaimed or new, with their subtle mixtures of colors and textures, are always in great demand for new building and renovation.

When reroofing, a large percentage of original roof tiles can usually be saved, and local reclamation centers may be able to offer a matching service for the rest. Even broken bricks and tiles are useful as rubble under concrete slabs or ground up for path and landscape finishes.

Modern insulated cavity wall constructions faced with brick are extremely energy-efficient. Thin brick facing tiles offer economies of cost and material, while choosing larger bricks means you use fewer bricks and less mortar per square foot, and build in less time.

Adaptability

Bricks and tiles suit virtually any design style: colonial to Georgian; Victorian to modern. Open any good brick and tile catalog and you will be surprised at the range of colors, finishes, and special shapes available in extruded, molded, and handmade varieties.

Bricks are also affordable. The relative additional cost between a brick-built home versus a sided home can be as little as 5 per cent. Brick-built homes also generally appreciate faster in value than houses made from timber or earth products, and usually have lower insurance premiums.

If you choose to build with brick yourself, get some instruction first to master the basic skills. Both bricks and tiles lend themselves to fancy designs, but if you opt for patterning it is probably best to have professional help alongside.

STONE

Stone is another ancient and enduring material which can be used and reused for centuries. Impressively solid, or astonishingly delicate, stone buildings have been traditional throughout the ages in many cultures. Medieval stonemasons brought the art of building in stone to an unparallelled state of perfection and grace, as exemplified by the slender soaring columns of 11th century cathedrals.

Stone houses are visually attractive with their solid thick walls and mellow exteriors. Stone is also a preferred landscaping material for many garden features. However, as with so many of our traditional materials, we must be aware of the environmental cost of continued use of stone. Conventional quarrying has already produced many destructive and potentially disastrous consequences.

Disappearing landscape

Large-scale quarrying has meant that whole hills, mountains, and valleys have literally disappeared as millions of tons of stone have been removed for use as building material or as raw materials for cement, aggregate, and road base.

This not only causes irreparable damage to the natural beauty of many wilderness areas but destroys wild species' habitats, forests, caves, sacred sites, and underground water reserves.
Quarrying also produces noise, dust, and polluted water. Public pressure and planning controls have sometimes been successful in restricting quarrying in certain areas of outstanding beauty. This must increase if, like forests, quarries are to be treated as an "environmentally-managed" resource to be operated in a responsible manner with minimal impact.

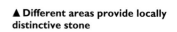

Natural House Book Simon & Schuster

▲ **Different areas provide locally distinctive stone**

▼ **Early stone buildings include magnificent Mayan temples**

Cass Pearson

Using stone wisely

Apart from stone walls and flooring, many lovely features of old stone buildings – mullion windows, door surrounds, roof gables, arches, columns, and moldings – can be reclaimed and reused. Entire stone buildings have even been taken down, the stones numbered, and re-erected elsewhere! If you buy an old stone house, rather than repairing it with new stone, try to source local matching reclaimed stone.

Generally, if you decide to use stone, try to reuse old stone. If you must choose new natural stone, use it as economically and selectively as possible and try to combine stone features with timber, brick, or plastered construction.

For economy of cost and material, you can build "stone style", using stone veneers inside and out to face concrete block cavity walls. A variety of composite blocks are also available which resemble stone in looks and qualities.

Wood is an invaluable natural material for house construction. It stabilizes air humidity and helps ventilation; it filters the air and absorbs sound; it smells good and is warm to the touch; it provides textures attractive to both the eye and skin. In short, wood is good for all our senses. Yet we have destroyed most of the world's natural forests, and are rapidly using up the rest.

Roughly half of the world's wood is burned for fuel, producing carbon dioxide, a "greenhouse effect" gas. Forests in the industrialized world are being damaged by acid rain, pollution, and the clearcutting of old growth forests. In other areas, wood clearance is causing soil erosion and habitat depletion. Worst, the "Earth's lungs", the tropical rainforests, are being cleared to provide western markets with tropical hardwoods and cattle ranchers with more grazing land. We must stop such destructive trends by supporting sustainable forestry and using reclaimed timber.

Responsible purchase

Ask questions about the source of any wood you buy: if your supplier does not have the answers, don't buy. Find an alternative. If you are unable to find a supplier of reclaimed wood, ask one of the organizations below about local outlets. These woods are certified, so insist on seeing the seal of approval before you order. Labels to look for are the Green Cross and the Smart Wood™ symbol.

The regulator for certification is The Forest Stewardship Council (FSC); while principal certifiers are the Rainforest Alliance of New York City, Scientific Certification Systems (SCS) of Oakland, California, and the Rogue Institute of Ashland, Oregon (see Resources, p. 49).

Sustainable forestry

In sustainable forestry the forest ecosystem as a whole remains intact, and the timber that is removed is replaced by natural regeneration. Portable, hand-operated mills are used instead of heavy machinery, so that the forest floor is not destroyed nor soil over-compacted. Logs are sawn where they fall and carried on foot to distribution points. Roads are kept to a minimum. Leaves, brushwood, and sawdust are left as ground cover. Trees are not felled on steep slopes where rainfall will more readily erode soil; and no felling takes place near streams, avoiding water pollution. Trees are felled in the direction causing least damage to other vegetation.

Suppliers of timber produced in these ways also support managed plantations where alternative, non-threatened species are grown, making acceptable alternatives to those tropical hardwoods and native North American timbers endangered by logging. Relevant social and economic issues are also considered: the principle is that the forest will become more valuable to local people standing, rather than wholly felled.

EcoTimber International

▲ **Sustainable logging practices have minimal impact on our forests**

Timber treatment

Most conventional treatment products against rot or pests are toxic either to humans or wildlife. Ask your supplier about non-toxic timber treatment. If you are building from scratch try installing termite sand barriers or use natural pest control (see p. 171).

▶ **Symbols can reassure you of responsible timber purchase**

Smart wood ™

Cedarwood has been used continuously for centuries in North America. To the Indians of the North Pacific Coast cedars were "trees of life". They used the wood for shelters, houses, dugout canoes, and carved totem poles. They wove the stringy bark into blankets and clothing, used the aromatic cedar boughs for bedding, and prepared remedies from the bark. The Western Red Cedar, *Thuja Plicata*, helped settlers to build their cabins and farms. Homeowners have appreciated the natural warmth, earthy colors, and subtle textures of red cedar ever since. Cedar shakes and shingles remain among the most popular natural materials for roof and wall coverings.

A Problem of sustainability

Although cedar shakes and shingles are beautiful, traditional, and practical, there is a growing problem with their sustainable production. The last remains of the great old-growth forests of the Pacific northwest and western Canada are under threat from logging operations and, added to this, the Western red cedar happens to be a particularly slow-growing climax species which does not easily regenerate.

Therefore environmentally-responsible houses should avoid (or minimize) the use of newly-manufactured cedar products. Always check if you can obtain reclaimed cedar products from your local building salvage centers or demolition sites.

▼ **Fancybutt shingles are practical and decorative**

Resource-efficient alternatives

Other options may not have the same charm and attraction as the real thing, but come from renewable and recycled resources which will help to save our ancient forest heritage. These include fiber-cement composite shingles; shakes made with fiber harvested from small diameter and fast-growing species, or fiber reclaimed from wood waste; organic asphalt shingles made with a base of recycled "mixed" waste paper, and roof shingles made from recycled plastic resins (which are recyclable too).

If these products are not appealing or right for the particular situation, then other types of roofing should be considered such as clay tiles, fiber-cement composite slates, and recycled metal roof decking. Look too, for reclaimed roofing materials.

Shake or shingle?

Shingles are sawn and have a smooth surface while shakes are split and have a thicker natural grain and textured look. Shingles can be used on roofs and on exterior and interior walls. They come either square-edged or in many "fancybutt" designs including octagonal, diagonal, diamond, hexagonal, and fishscale which can be combined in an unlimited range of patterns. Thicker split shakes are usually used as roof tiles, giving a roof characteristic strong shadow lines and an attractive rustic appearance.

Shakes and shingles may be used in their natural state, or you can get fire retardant or wood preservative-treated types. Check that treated products are free of any toxic chemicals that could harm wildlife or cause health or pollution problems.

The Cedar Shake & Shingle Bureau (see Resources p. 49) has developed quality and grading standards. Its "Certi" labels certify shake and shingle products made by its membership.

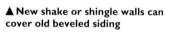

Cedar Shale & Shingle Bureau

▲ **New shake or shingle walls can cover old beveled siding**

Cedar Shake & Shingle Bureau

Boards and sheets began to replace solid wood as a building material as early as the 1930s. Diminishing timber resources and developments in wood and adhesive technology created a host of new, more resource-efficient products that also often proved lighter, stronger, and cheaper than the traditional material. Plywood, particle board, and hardboard quickly became indispensable building products.

Today, a wide range of available boards and sheets suit almost every need. Numerous developments continue to make ever more resource-efficient products. These include oriented strand board (OSB) manufactured from small diameter, fast-growing trees such as aspen or alder; hardboard made from waste wood, and fiberboard from recycled newsprint or agricultural by-products.

Appropriate uses

Externally, plywood is the most common board for sheathing framed structures, but exterior-quality formaldehyde-free medium density fiberboard (MDF) can be used instead. Formaldehyde-free medium board and low-density fiberboard make ideal "breathing" wall constructions (see p. 36) when combined with cellulose, wool or cotton insulation. Alternatively, structural stress-skinned panels can be constructed off-site using OSB outer skins bonded to a foam core (check it contains no CFCs) or other forms of insulation. This reduces on-site labor and produces an energy-efficient wall. Many recycled products are suitable for structural roof decking, sub-flooring, sound control, carpet underlayment and for internal wall paneling (pre-finished with burlap or cork coverings).

Honeycomb and molded panels are also available. Made from 100% post-consumer wood and paper waste and plant fibers, they are also lighter and stronger than conventional plywood, particle and fiberboard alternatives.

New generation products

Although many pressed wood boards and sheets are efficient in their use of resources, there can be a problem from the high levels of formaldehyde-based glue used in the manufacture of particle and fiber boards. Formaldehyde, a suspected carcinogen, can outgas from the boards into the indoor air of the home. To overcome this, there is a new generation of low-formaldehyde or formaldehyde-free boards, some of which use only lignin, the natural bonding agent found in trees.

When choosing products, you need to ensure that they are non-toxic, and always check that any wood products come from a sustainable source and not from North American old-growth forests or tropical rainforests.

▼ Multipurpose boards include MDF, plywood, and particle board

Natural House Book Simon and Schuster

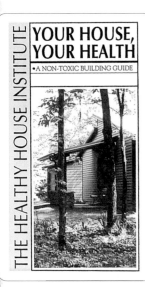

Healthy Home viewing

John Bower, of the Healthy House Institute (IN) takes you around a model healthy home in this VHS video. Packed full of information, this inspiring tour shows you how to build or re-fit in the healthiest ways.

Straw Bale building

Published by Chelsea Green at $25.00, this book tells you all you need to know about straw bale construction - from building houses to retrofitting mobile homes! The authors explain all the advantages of strawbale homes and provide masses of hands-on advice to get you building!

Building bricks

Don't write bricks off as uniform in color or texture! Instead check out the wide ranges of these versatile building materials. Glengery Brick Co offer a huge choice of bricks for different functions. Browse through their catalog at leisure at an early stage to be sure of your choice when you build, add, or renovate.

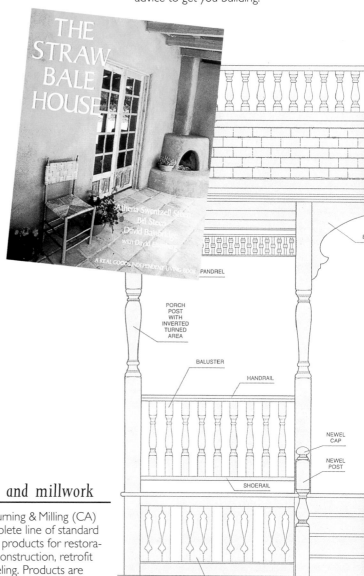

Turnings and millwork

Pagliacco Turning & Milling (CA) offer a complete line of standard and custom products for restorations, new construction, retrofit and remodeling. Products are made from durable sustainably grown redwood which has superb decay and termite resistance.

Magnetic field alert

Magnetic Sciences International (AZ) produce sensitive meters for measuring magnetic fields from power lines, transformers, computers, house wiring, and/or domestic appliances. Easy to use and economical to purchase, these Gaussmeters offer an easy way to safeguard your family's health.

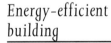

Insulated tempered glass

Promote energy efficiency with versatile insulated glass from Arctic Glass (WI). The tempering means you can use the glass right down to ground level, allowing maximum light and passive solar heat gain throughout your home, or in sunrooms and even workshops.

Energy-efficient building

How often have you ended up at the top of a ladder with that vital tool at the bottom? This need never happen again, thanks to this handy tool and chisel roll from the Shelter Institute (ME). Strongly made with 18 pockets, it is an ideal way to save your energy and work more efficiently!

Design improvements

Any home improvements are possible with the 3D Home Kit from Dan Reif's Design Works (MA)! The kit includes everything from brick, stone, decking, siding, and roofing through interior fittings, all in $1/4$ inch scale, so you can visualize and plan your dream home. Kits even include a scale dog and cat to make the picture complete!

BREATHING WALLS

In the past, our homes had gaps around windows and doors, open chimneys, and little or no insulation. They were often drafty and improperly heated compared to today's standards. Yet, traditional buildings of brick, stone, timber, and plaster could breathe, and few synthetic chemicals existed to pollute the indoor air. Apart from problems with smokey fires, their occupants did have the benefit of plenty of fresh air!

Today the indoor air quality of many homes is under threat from modern energy-conserving practices. As you caulk and weatherproof doors and windows against drafts and block air-infiltration through the structure with polyethylene sheeting, you dramatically reduce the amount of fresh air indoors. Unless you take steps to install adequate ventilation systems, this can quickly lead to a build-up of humidity, pollutants and toxins in the indoor air which cannot escape. Unintentionally, you may be converting your home into a "sick house" (see pp. 24-5).

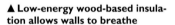

▲ Low-energy wood-based insulation allows walls to breathe

Walls that breathe

Inspired by simpler low-tech building techniques of the past, and confirmed by modern scientific experiments, Building Biologists (see pp. 24-5) have perfected what they call a breathing wall. This relies on the principle of increasing natural ventilation of the interior of the house by allowing controlled diffusion of air and moisture through a structure without losing energy-efficiency. To do this it is necessary to select hygroscopic (porous) and permeable materials such as clay bricks and tiles, timber and building boards, gypsum plaster and lime plaster. Correctly used, these materials absorb and release excess moisture thereby helping to regulate condensation and indoor humidity and expel pollutants.

Tests have shown that a modern breathing wall needs to be constructed of layers of permeable materials on both sides of the insulation, which must also be permeable. Cellulose insulation is ideal, so too, is cotton, wool and straw bale. The construction needs to be appropriate to the climate zone in which you live. In temperate climates, for example, the layers must be graded from those with low permeability (more vapor-resistant) toward the inside, to those with high permeability (less resistant) toward the outside. For temperate areas the permeability ratio of layers, outside to in, should be at least 5 to 1 to be sure to avoid condensation. Check first with "breathing wall" specialists (see Resources p. 49) for the right construction and insulation materials for your area and climate.

▶ Layers of insulation between the wall and interior plasterboard

Airtight walls

Current building science and energy-conservation practice advocate making the shell of the house as airtight and moistureproof as possible. This is done by applying a "vapor barrier" to walls and ceilings on the inside surface of the insulation. This barrier may be made from polyethylene sheeting, aluminum foil, or foil-backed sheetrock. Wall and roof constructions must be adequately vented to the outside to avoid moisture build-up occurring within the structure. Such "interstitial condensation" occurs when water vapor present in warm inside air passes out of the home through an external wall; when this warm air reaches the colder drier air, it cools, reaches saturation point and condenses to form water.

This can be serious as it not only reduces the effectiveness of the insulation but it also encourages fungal growths such as wet and dry rot and can eventually lead to structural decay and collapse. Moreover, the air inside the house will also need ventilating and this usually involves a whole-house mechanical ventilation system plus an HRV (see p. 63). These systems are expensive to install, maintain and run, and can themselves cause problems such as bacteria, micro-organisms, and changes to air ionization.

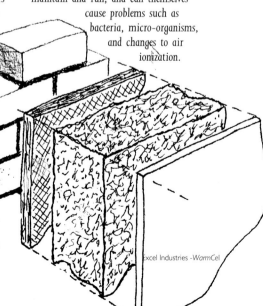

Excel Industries -WarmCel

In a land with few trees but plenty of grass, what do you use to build with? Straw bales, of course! This is exactly what the settlers started to do in the Nebraska Sandhills in the late 1800s. Examples of old straw-bale houses and those built in the 1940s and 50s exist today which still serve as sturdy, warm, and comfortable homes.

Despite isolated attempts to revive the technique, little happened until straw-bale enthusiasts Matts Mhyrman and Judy Knox sparked media interest. In a recent publication Judy stated that straw-bale building "taps into an ancient memory, of a time when we really were connected to the earth. It looks like the earth, sounds like the earth, and it's friendly like the earth. It's not beyond us; the technology is very user-friendly." Now, via publications, hands-on workshops and their own company, Matts and Judy have helped to re-establish straw-bale building as a practical modern alternative construction technique (see Resources p. 49).

▲ **Construction can proceed rapidly from the simplest designs**

▲ **A simply constructed straw-bale home near Tesuque, Arizona**

Building with straw bales

The original Nebraska-style homes were built of load-bearing bale walls (bales stacked in courses and pinned together to support the roof). These are officially approved today in only a few locales. However, non-load-bearing straw-bale walls, which rely on a timber frame to take structural loads have received Code approval in some states, such as New Mexico. With these, you either stack the bales outside the frame or use them as infill between frame members, bedding the bales in adobe mortar. You then plaster both sides of the walls with adobe. If you finish the inside with a coat of lime-rich adobe plaster this will also protect against moisture, fire, and vermin. Insert window and door frames as the bale walls rise.

The cardinal rule is to keep the walls completely dry. So make sure you have good moisture-proof foundations and an adequate overhanging roof.

Pros and cons

Built and protected properly, straw-bale walls need little maintenance and can last for hundreds of years. Consisting of abundant annually-renewable materials,they are highly resource-efficient. Their economy, added to ease of construction, makes the materials ideal for owner-builders. Straw walls over 18 inches thick not only give excellent thermal insulation, with R-values of 40 to 50, they have the beauty of hand-crafted surfaces and textures, plus the value of providing quiet interiors. Certified fire tests have shown straw-bale walls to be surprisingly fire-resistant.

But some questions need answering: What levels of residual herbicides exist in straw and do they present a health problem? Do chemically-sensitive people react when building with straw? Even if dry, is it necessary to do anything else to protect the straw against fungal growth? Before you decide to go with straw, contact the Straw Bale Construction Association for the latest information and results of recent tests into the health and safety of straw-bale building (see Resources p. 49).

WINDOWS

Windows provide light, views, ventilation, and visual character to both the exterior and interior of the home. More recently, low-maintenance and energy-conserving designs have become fashionable for all the best environmental reasons. However, when you consider the design of your windows, you must balance these factors.

Windows made from the newer more thermally-efficient materials, such as metals combined with plastics, may have an unacceptable esthetic impact on visual style (and sometimes market value), especially of older homes. Energy-efficient windows also, by definition, reduce ventilation in houses and, unless adequate alternative means are incorporated, may lead to a consequent deterioration of indoor air quality (see p. 112). Take all these factors into account before you renew or renovate.

David Pearson

▲ **Maximum light encourages both physical and spiritual well-being**

Recycled windows

Apart from sourcing old windows from building material reclamation centers, consider if any of those you are to discard (particularly any with handmade glass) could have a new lease on life as internal windows between rooms or rooms off a sunspace. Bear in mind that windows made of composite materials, such as plastic-coated aluminum, cannot easily be reused or recycled.

Increasing daylight

In cooler climates it is important to bring as much daylight and sunlight into your home as possible — both for general health and for environmental reasons. You can add new windows or increase the size of existing ones via, for example, bay or bow windows, awning windows and, on the sun-facing sides, solar and sunroom windows (see p 61).

To bring daylight deep into your home, install skylights and high-level clerestory windows, or try using a roofmounted reflector and mirrored tube. Increasing window area will often have the added advantage of making rooms appear more spacious and open to fresh views. You can make the most of borrowed light by placing windows in internal walls and doors.

Energy-conserving windows

A fifth to a quarter of the total energy used in the average home is used for extra heating and cooling to compensate for leaky windows. So, whether you are renovating an old home or building a new one, energy-efficient windows must be a high priority. But before you tear out the old ones, see if all or some can be reused either by installing secondary glazing on the inside or by replacing single-pane glass with double glazing. Either course of action should reduce window heat loss by a half and cut energy bills dramatically. If new windows are needed, choose replacement windows in almost any style including casements, sliders, awning windows and, the dominant North American style, double-hung windows.

For maximum efficiency, choose double and triple glazing with various coatings, films, and gas fill (see p. 39). Ensure that gaskets and weatherstripping are included in the frame to prevent air infiltration and that window frame materials and construction also have a high thermal performance. Check if window units have any built-in ventilation devices, known as "trickle" or "weep" vents. The introduction of strict industry performance standards in the '80s monitored by three independent organizations (See Resources p. 49), plus certification and labeling programs, is very helpful when choosing the appropriate energy-efficient replacement windows or window kits for your home.

▼ **Choose design and materials to fit your situation**

David Pearson

Although glass can be considered a sustainable material since its basic ingredients of sand, soda and potash are in plentiful supply, its production does use a great deal of energy. Reuse of existing glass products, recycling of glass jars and bottles plus choosing recycled glass products are all ways to conserve materials and energy.

Glass can be a versatile building material – in sheets for glazing, shelves and table tops, in blocks for walls and partitions, and as fiberglass for insulation. There have been important advances in recent years in the vital area of heat-conserving home glazing (see p. 38).

Reuse, recycling and recycled products

You can reuse glass products in many ways around the home. Try to buy soft drinks, beer and milk from sources which accept return empty bottles for reuse. Also find out if there are stores in your area that offer a refill service.

Recycling centers are now widespread and accessible or you may live in an area with a door-to-door recycling collection program. There is also growing availability of products made from recycled glass — jugs, vases, glasses and candle holders.

▼ **This glass house-front takes full advantage of sunlight and scenery**

Colin Wuishart / Gaia Architects Scotland

Building with glass

Colored glass in windows or doors is especially good to lift the spirits, particularly on cloudy days. Architect Mike Reynolds also makes use of bottles (and cans) as "bricks" in the walls and roofs of his "Earthship" houses in New Mexico. Filled with water and ranged on shelves, bottles can serve as an effective and colorful heat sink in sunspaces or solar sheds. Old windows can find a second life in the backyard as coldframes.

David Pearson

▶ **Use colored glass to add warmth to a quiet corner**

Heat-conserving glazing

For greatest efficiency, double and triple glazing comes with low-emissivity (low-E) coatings on the glass or "Heat Mirror" film suspended between the layers of glass. R-values (resistances to heat transfer) are often given for the glazing by itself, but this can mislead as you need to know the performance of the whole window unit (glass plus frame and weatherstripping).

The National Fenestration Ratings Council (NFRC) has developed a performance rating system, and encourages manufacturers to label all their windows. The system uses U-value (a measure of heat loss rather than resistance to loss). A wood-frame window with single glazing has a U-value of around 1 and a double-glazed, low-E unit rates about 0.4. So far, the most energy-efficient window units available use double "Heat Mirror" film plus argon or krypton gas fill; they have a U value of around 0.1. Remember that window glazing is just one part of a general insulation program (see p. 65).

Ahandsome and durable front door is a matter of obvious pride. Doors made from endangered woods such as mahogany, teak, cedar, and redwood are still much sought after, but there are many equally attractive alternatives available from sustainable North American softwoods and hardwoods.

Before ordering ready-made doors, or the timber to construct your own, check the certification programs (see pp. 31 and 49). If you incorporate glass, try to avoid buying new, and follow the guidance for glass and glazing (see p. 39).

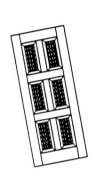

Reuse and recycle

Doors are popular salvage items, available at building recycling and exchange centers. They usually provide a wide selection of interior and exterior doors in materials and styles to suit almost any taste. Reclamation centers are the places to find good solid used hardwood doors made of endangered woods, such as mahogany and redwood, thereby avoiding buying them new and adding to the demand that is destroying both tropical and North American old-growth forests. Also, older doors are often made of thicker section and better quality woods. If you are renovating, you may find doors that match those already in your house. Old doors may have interesting features such as stained glass, leaded lites, unusual moldings, or hardware that can enhance your home.

Good insulation values

Make sure that external doors have adequate R-Values for your area. Rather than replacing older and less energy-efficient doors, add a lobby inside or enclosed porch outside. But however energy-conserving a door may be in itself, it must be well weatherstripped around the frame to exclude air infiltration.

Be aware that as much as 75% of heat loss occurs around the door, not through it! A standard door with only a one-sixteenth-inch-wide gap all round is equivalent to having a 15 square-inch hole in your wall. It is absolutely essential to weatherstrip older doors by caulking them from the inside.

When choosing new, consider pre-hung door and frame units. With these, the door is engineered to fit the frame closely and durable weatherstripping is already pre-fitted. Don't forget the smaller details and make sure that the keyholes have draft covers too.

Low-energy and renewable materials

If you are buying new doors choose materials that are low-energy and low-impact on the environment. Choose doors made from sustainable-source lumber rather than steel, aluminum or plastics. Even better, see if you can source doors made from local lumber (to reduce the toll of transport energy, pollution and costs on the environment). Ironically, you will probably find they will cost more than doors transported half way across the continent or those imported from abroad.

You should avoid metal and plastic doors (and plastic-covered lumber or metal doors) as they use very high-energy and high-impact materials. Only consider using them if they are recycled or if the manufacturer will certify that they are made from high-recycled content metals and plastics.

▶ **This Rudolf Steiner school door incorporates reused glass and metal**

David Pearson

Recycling centers and curbside pickups for cans, bottles and newspapers are becoming the norm. But, beyond this, increased awareness is extending the concept into the reuse and recycling of building materials. A single-family home in North America typically generates between four and six tons of garbage during construction (wood, drywall, masonry, packing, steel, and topsoil). This accounts for almost a quarter of landfill volumes, so there is plenty of scope to cut this dreadful waste.

Whether you are building a new home or rehabbing the one you have, keep thinking "reuse/recycle" when choosing materials. If you are using an architect, interior designer, or builder, ask them to investigate local sources, and specify reclaimed and recycled materials wherever possible.

▲ **Recycling bins have become a common sight in most areas**

Job-site recycling

Although a building site can produce a massive amount of waste, there are many ways this can be reduced and recycled. A number of organizations and local government offices have produced booklets to help builders economize on waste and find recycling facilities (see p. 49). It is always worth dropping in on building and demolition sites to see what's available. This may be the cheapest way to find just what you are looking for (and you could come across some interesting and unusual items you weren't expecting!).

Health and Building Inspectors

Reusing old materials can be hazardous, however. Avoid asbestos (as found in some old insulation, roofing, and flooring) and lead (as in plumbing and old gloss paint you plan to strip). And be aware that some plastic products can offgas.

If you want to reuse old wood for structural purposes, you must first check with the Building Inspector on sizing and grading requirements. Also, you may have to adapt old toilets, faucets, and plumbing to meet local water conservation standards. Check before you start work.

Salvage materials

Throughout this Catalog we recommend you use reclaimed building materials. Ranging from wood to brick, stone to tiles, sinks to toilets, windows to doors, plumbing to hardware, once-used materials can usually meet at least part of your needs. Some companies deal exclusively in salvaging high-quality timber from demolition sites. Old nails and screws are removed, the wood is sorted, re-milled and structurally regraded before shipping to the customer. Post-logging salvage is another useful source. Reclamation, salvage, and material exchange centers are spreading in North America. There is probably one near you — check the Yellow Pages.

Recycled-content materials

An increasing variety of recycled-content materials is now available. This includes composite lumber — cedar waste plus recycled plastics; carpet made from recycled PET bottles; ceramic-style floor tiles from 75% recycled and reclaimed glass; cellulose insulation from recycled newsprint and recycled plastic shake-style roofing. Recycled tires may be used to make tiles.

Decks, railings, and fences may be made from 50% sawdust and 50% post-consumer recycled polyethylene. Steel and aluminum doors and windows can be found with high-content recycled metals, and many ceiling panels contain recycled newsprint and recovered mineral wool. You can even find attractive stone or brick substitutes made with a high proportion of recycled materials, if you can't reclaim the real thing.

Born of the long North American tradition, owner-building is enjoying a renaissance today. If you want a more individual home or simply cannot afford to buy an existing house or apartment, owner-building may be for you. This can range from designing and building an entire house yourself, with friends and family, to buying a kit house and erecting or finishing it yourself.

In addition to determination and commitment, you will need help and advice. It is worth contacting owner-builder organizations and reading practical magazines, but the best beginning is to learn the basic skills. Sign up for hands-on home-building classes, seminars and workshops. If you are interested in communal living, there may be a "CoHousing" (co-operative housing) or sustainable community project you could join.

Community housing

Housing co-operatives and Mutual Housing Associations offer individuals, professional groups, and other housing and food co-ops an opportunity to deposit their savings into the MHA's co-operatively owned credit union or bank.

A MHA can then buy land and place it in a community land trust to ensure continuing affordability of co-op housing built or leased on the land. Even though MHAs have not typically been set up with primarily ecological aims, this could prove a positive dimension for inclusion in future projects.

▼ **The Dollar House - dismantled, resited, rebuilt and retrofitted**

David Pearson

Retrofit

There are a number of ecological disadvantages in building new homes, however energy-efficient they may be in themselves. If, as is often the case, they are built on previously undeveloped land, this leads to even further encroachment of towns and cities. Even when built on developed land, new homes use up considerable resources and energy via new materials and construction. They also cause significant impact on local environments.

The majority of the population lives in older houses and apartments and will continue to do so for the foreseeable future. It is quicker and more resource-efficient to concentrate on repair and renovation of this older stock making use of much of the existing structure and materials. Retrofit, to good ecological standards, should be the priority for most environmentally-aware homeowners. This can be taken to extremes: The Dollar House in Berkeley, California (pictured) was bought for $1, taken apart, moved to a new site and completely retrofitted!

If renovation of an older property is combined with new additions such as sunspaces, and loft and basement conversions, you get the best of both worlds. And, by weatherproofing doors and windows, insulating the structure, and installing new energy- and water-conserving features such as heat exchangers, photovoltaics, solar water heating, wind generators, and low-energy lighting plus low-flow toilets, faucets, and showers, you can achieve just about everything that a new eco-home can offer.

Some retrofit costs, such as solar water heating, will be a little higher than if it was installed as part of the plumbing of a newly built home. But, in general, an ecological retrofit may offer you more — it can give you the technology of the new world combined with the history and charm of the old.

Kit homes have come a long way from the early standard and limited range of styles and designs. Now, kits are available for most conceivable types and styles of home, traditional and contemporary. You can choose timber frame or log homes, rectangular or circular, and for the less conventional, domes, yurts and tipis. Kit homes today can often be arranged or modified to suit individual needs and desires, and to blend in to a variety of locations. Companies usually offer a range of options, and customers can adapt standard models or custom design their own home with the professional help of architectural staff.

Quality materials, factory production, tried-and-tested construction details, and quick erection on site, plus known costs and warranties, all help to make kit homes attractive. When choosing a style and materials, check on energy-efficiency and whether the company applies environmental policies in the choice of materials and factory processing.

▲ **A circular 'eye of heaven' is the central point of a yurt's structure**

Circular homes

Leaky geodesic domes are an abiding image of '60s and '70s alternative living. But now you can choose from many other forms of circular homes as well as watertight domes. One manufacturer markets circular timber homes in sizes ranging from 500 to 2000 sq ft. For more space, these are joined side-by-side or, more economically, "stacked" up to three levels under one roof. The trussed roof spans the whole width of the space to give a spacious open interior and, with no-load bearing walls, allows the owners to arrange interior partitions to suit any floor plan. A range of doors and windows can be placed anywhere around the circle making for extremely versatile home design, adaptable to nearly any setting.

Timber frame homes

Traditional timber frame homes are growing in popularity. Their hand-crafted solid construction and quality finishes are cherished by those who live in them. Some or all of the construction is available in kit form (see p. 44).

Yurts and tipis

Circular nomadic dwelling forms have an ancient history, and always arouse curiosity. Yurts of the Mongol tribes (circular latticework covered by layers of heavy felt) and tipis of the Native American Indians are fascinating for their light yet sturdy structures which give comfort and protection even in the severest weather. Although some are used as homes, many today have recreational uses, or are used as spare rooms, studios, meditation spaces, and workshops.

Log homes

Mention of a log home often conjures up a picture of a small vacation log cabin in the forest. But, increasingly, modern log homes are being chosen as primary residences and are built to similar sizes and levels of amenity as conventional homes. The average size is in excess of 2,000 sq ft and homes in the region of 4,000 to 6,000 sq ft are not unusual.

Log homes are designed to fit a much wider variety of tastes than formerly, including newer, modern styles. For a modern look, one company advises choosing flatter-faced contour logs and square house corners rather than traditional log overhangs. Painted, these styles have a clapboard effect more suited to conventional suburban housing areas.

The natural insulating quality of logs has been enhanced via cavity construction and sheathing filled with insulation materials to give increased energy-efficiency ratings in the region of R30 for walls and R40 for roofs.

▲ **Tipis can provide an ancient solution to modern space problems**

Authentic versions are available as mail-order kits, or you can take workshops to experience old ways of living and help pitch yurts and tipis yourself. Their ease of construction and siting also offers huge potential as attractive temporary housing.

TIMBER FRAMES

"What is essential to timber framing is the integrity of the frame, where the joiner's art takes a pile of raw lumber and turns it into a single whole organism with a life of its own..." enthuses Ed Levin, one of the founders of the Timber Framers Guild of North America.

A timber frame home may conjure up the picture of a series of closely spaced 2-by-4s nailed together to make a frame, covered with plywood, dry wall or plasterboard. Although this is how most of our modern homes are built, there is a traditional option. Until the mid-1800s a different form of timber framing was typical in North America. Stemming from ancient carpentry techniques of the Middle Ages, structures were built using large section solid wood members joined by strong hand-crafted woodworking mortise-and-tenon joints secured by wooden pegs, without using nails.

Shelter Institute

◀ **Timber frames can be bought pre-sawn for self-assembly**

▼ **Raising a timber frame is an exciting and unforgettable experience**

Timber frame revival

In the mid-1970s a number of young idealistic East Coast carpenters started to explore the traditional use of natural materials combined with energy-efficient techniques. The network of carpenters and small woodworking companies that grew out of this subsequently formed, with others, the now large and active Timber Framers Guild of North America. Through conferences, exhibitions, hands-on workshops, newsletters, and advice, the Guild has spread the word and captured the imagination of many homebuilders who want to live in an individual, solid, hand-crafted home.

Today, numerous experienced companies across North America can offer timber frame only or a complete custom design-and-build service for a finished energy-efficient, traditional timber frame home. Check if the company has environmental policies regarding use of sustainable timber, reforestation programs, use of recycled timber, plus minimization and reuse of timber waste materials.

Building a timber frame

Large pieces of carefully selected solid timber are first cut and jointed by hand. These are then laid out on the ground and assembled into "bents" (cross-sectional frames made of posts, beams and rafters). Finally, these are raised by a team of people or by crane and pegged together to form the skeleton of the house. Recalling Amish barn-raising scenes, this is an exciting and rewarding experience for all involved. Once assembled, the frame is covered by various types of stress-skin insulated panels. Choose from a wide variety of exterior finishes including board-and-batten, clapboard, stone, stucco, brick, or a combination of these.

Thistlewood

ECO - Environmental Construction Outfitters

Paul Bierman-Lytle, an architect from New Canaan (CT) was one of the first in North America to pioneer and promote healthy and environmentally sound homes. It all began when Paul began coughing and sneezing and getting headaches during his work as a builder. "We prided ourselves on high-quality homes" recalled Paul, "It never occurred to us that the products were potentially hazardous."

◄ **The interior of the ECO store in New York, an important resource for architects, designers, contractors, and owner-builders**

Since then he has committed himself and his company to pursuing his guiding principles, asking: "Is the house a health hazard to the end user, producers, or installers? Is it a renewable resource? And, is the waste biodegradable?" Via his design and contracting organization, the Masters Corporation, founded in 1980, he has built numerous innovative projects across the United States. His houses are built without synthetics, solvent-based glues, formaldehyde-based plywoods, or wall-to-wall carpeting which harbors dust mites and mold. Instead his home designs specify full-spectrum light bulbs, hardwood from sustainably-forested sources, and resource-efficient heat recovery ventilators. Natural materials decorate the home (see Chapter Seven). Healthy building doesn't have to cost more, it is often a matter of using affordable non-toxic alternatives rather than conventional hazardous material. Even if the initial cost is more, most people are willing to pay the extra to have the satisfaction, pleasure, and security of a truly healthy home environment.

Accessible Products

Through his work Bierman-Lytle became very aware of the difficulty that most architects and builders experienced in researching and sourcing environmentally-sound and healthy construction materials and products. To help overcome these problems he founded Environmental Construction Outfitters (ECO) with Paul Novack and Ira Russack.

ECO now specializes in the design and construction of environmentally sustainable residential and commercial buildings. Its aim is to serve architects, contractors, designers, decorators, and all construction trades such as painters, carpenters, insulators, floorcovering specialists, and cabinet makers. Every product goes through a tough evaluation process and has to meet extremely high environmental and health standards. The headquarters and large showroom, in the SoHo District of New York's Manhattan, have a wide range of products and systems on display, and trained staff can discuss customers' needs. Orders are shipped anywhere in the United States and Canada.

Many well-established building manufacturers and suppliers are at last beginning to provide sound environmental options at affordable costs, accessible through their own channels. Acknowledging this, Paul Bierman-Lytle has recently moved on to develop a computer-based shopping medium as part of The Masters Corporation and is no longer involved in ECO. Via the new concept, the Corporation will be acting more in the capacity of a "broker" for manufacturers.

ECO continues to offer state-of-the-art building products, services, and technologies. The company is a growing and innovative force which is helping to make accessible the materials for healthy and environmentally sound building.

Environmental Construction Outfitters (ECO), 44 Crosby St, New York, NY 10012. Tel: 212 334 9659 / 800 238 5008 fax: 212 226 8084

Deltec home packages

Energy-efficient, low maintenance, and affordable - Deltec panelized houses are easy to erect and beautiful to live in. Home packages range from 500 to 2,000 square feet on one level, or you can stack the units to create an individual home the perfect size for your family's needs.

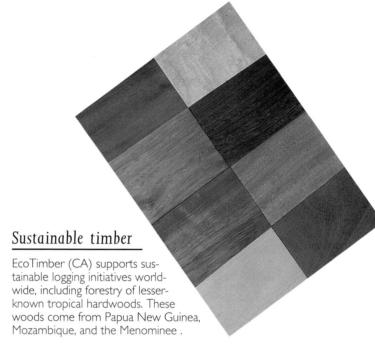

Sustainable timber

EcoTimber (CA) supports sustainable logging initiatives worldwide, including forestry of lesser-known tropical hardwoods. These woods come from Papua New Guinea, Mozambique, and the Menominee .

Wooden arched domes

The arched dome, available from Fourth Dimension Housing (WA), is a 12-sided structure made from 12 curved wooden arches. Earth-friendly, energy-efficient, and adaptable (just take out an arch and insert an extension), these swiftly-erected homes provide flexible housing and a harmonious environment.

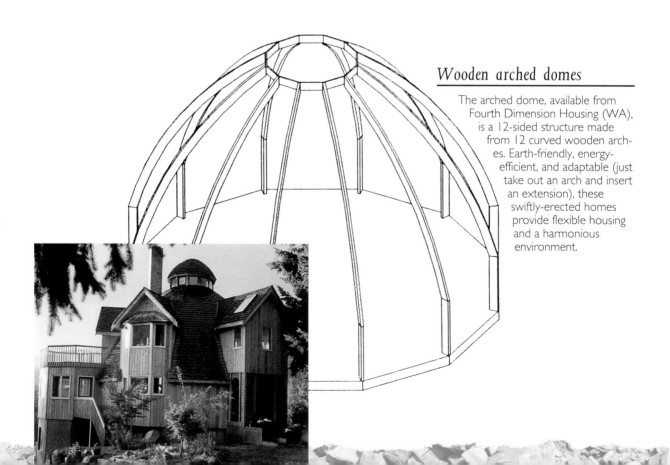

Sew your own tipi

Living Shelter Crafts of Arizona offer beautiful nomadic dwellings in kit form. Tipis and yurts are constructed from quality materials and provide comfortable and functional dwellings for a variety of uses. Living Shelter also offer practical and fun workshops.

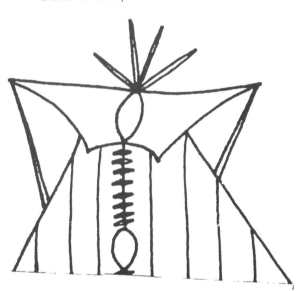

Portable housing

Borealis Yurts (ME) combine traditional design with modern materials, providing lightweight airy structures with ample headroom and a stiff constitution! Their fabric yurts can be packed up, carried off, and replanted, or used as semi-permanent structures.

Solar glazing

Sun-Lite high-performance solar glazing is the ideal choice for direct gain applications, water storage walls, solar attics, and sunspaces. Available from Solar Components Corporation (NH) via their Energy Saver's Catalog, this glazing helps you collect and store the maximum solar energy.

Timber frame homes

Nowadays it takes less than a day to raise the mainframe of a magnificent timber home, from Thistlewood, Ontario. Timbers are pre-assembled on site and secured with oak pegs. The homes are durable, beautiful, and traditional.

RESOURCES

General organizations

American Institute of Architects
ERG Project, 1735 New York Avenue,
NW, Washington, DC 20006
Tel: 202 626 7331 Fax: 202 626 7518

Build Green Program
2395 Speakman Drive, Mississauga,
Ontario, L5K 1B3, Canada
Tel: 416 8222 4111

Builders for Social Responsibility
RR 1, Box 1953, Hinesburg, VT 05461
Tel: 802 482 3295

Center for Resourceful Building
Technology
Box 3413, Missoula, MT 59806
Tel: 406 549 7678

Eco-Design Resource Society
PO Box 3981, Main Post Office,
Vancouver, BC, Canada, V6B 3Z4
Tel: 604 738 9334

Institute for Bio-Dynamic Shelter
86 Washington Road, Waldoboro,
ME 04572
Tel: 207 832 5157

International Institute for Bau-Biologie
& Ecology
PO Box 387, Clearwater, FL 34615
Tel: 813 461 4371 Fax: 813 441 4373

National Center for Appropriate
Technology
PO Box 2525, Butte, MT 59702
Tel: 800 428 2525 Fax: 800 428 1718

Natural House Building Center
RR 1, Box 115F, Fairfield, IA 52556
Tel: 515 472 7775

Rocky Mountain Institute
1739 Snowmass Creek Road
Snowmass CO 81654-9199
Tel: 303 970 3851 Fax: 303 970 3420

The Shelter Institute
38 Center Street
Bath, MA 04530
Tel: 207 442 7938

Siricon
14555, Ouest Boul de Maisonneuve,
Montreal, Quebec, Canada, H3G 1M8
Tel: 514 848 8770 Fax: 514 848 3198

Feng Shui

Natural Habitat, (Valerie Dow)
PO Box 21, Haysville, KA 67060
Tel: 316 788 1793

Melanie Lewandowski
PO Box 536, New Hope, PA 18938
Tel: 215 62 5788

Permaculture

Central Rocky Mountain Permaculture
Institute
PO Box 631, Basalt, CO 81621
Tel: 303 927 4158

Permaculture Drylands
PO Box 133, Pearce, AZ 85625
Tel: 602 824 3456 Fax: 602 824 3542

Permaculture Resources
56 Farmersville, Califon, NJ 07830
Tel: 800 832 6285
(or) PO Box 1173, Cedar Crest,
NM 87008
Tel: 800 874 1641

Home and environment

Planetary Solutions
PO Box 1049, Boulder, CO 80306
Tel: 303 442 6228

Solar Survival Architecture (Earthships)
PO Box 1041, Taos, NM 87571

Sustainable Building Collaborative
815 Southeast Clatsop, Portland,
OR 97202
Tel: 503 235 0137

Environmental Building News
RR 1, Box 161, Brattleboro,
VT 05301
Tel: 802 257 7300 Fax: 802 257 7304

Healthy home

Environmental by Design
PO Box 95016, South Van CSC,
Vancouver, BC V6P 6V4, Canada
Tel & Fax: 604 266 7721

EOS Institute
580 Broadway, Suite 200, Laguna Beach,
CA 92651
Tel: 714 497 1896

Greensource
12 Alfred Street, Suite 300,
Woburn, MS 01801
Tel: 617 933 2772

The Healthy House Institute
430 N Sewell Road,
Bloomington, IN 47408
Tel: 812 332 5073

Natural Building Network
PO Box 1110, Sebastopol, CA 95473

Building with Nature, (Newsletter)
PO Box 4917, Santa Rosa,
CA 95402-4417
Tel: 707 579 2201

Safe Home Resource Guide
24 East Avenue, Suite 1300, New
Canaan, CT 06840
Tel: 203 966 2099

American Society of Dowsers
Danville, VT 05828

Carol Venolia (see p. 191)
Debra Dadd-Redalia (see p. 188)

Organic and Steiner building

James T Hubbell
930 Orchard Lane, Santa Ysabel,
CA 92070
Tel: 609 765 0171

Bart Prince
3501 Monte Vista NE, Albuquerque,
NM 87106

Arthur Dyson AIA
754 P Street, Suite C, Fresno, CA 93721
Tel: 209 486 3582

Malcolm Wells
PO Box 1149, Brewster, MA 02631
Tel: 508 896 6850 Fax: 508 896 5116

Rudolf Steiner Center
9100 Bathurst, Toronto, Ontario,
Canada L3T 3N3

Rudolf Steiner Institute
PO Box 0990, Planetarium Sta,
New York, NY 10024

Earth building materials

California Earth Art and Architecture
Institute (Cal-Earth) (see p. 195)

Friends of Adobe
PO Box 7725, Albuquerque, NM 87194
Tel: 505 243 7801

Rammed Earth Institute
2319-21st Avenue, Greeley, CO 80631

Southwest Solaradobe School (*Earthbuilders Encyclopedia*)
PO Box 153, Bosque, NM 87006
Tel: 505 252 1382

Terra Group, Ltd
1058 2nd Avenue, Napa, CA 94558
Tel: 707 224 2532

Bricks and tiles

Brick Institute of America
11490 Commerce Park Drive,
Reston, VA 22091-1525
Tel: 703 620 0010 Fax: 703 620 3928

Sustainable timber

Rainforest Alliance (Smart Wood)
65 Bleecker Street, New York,
NY 10012-2420
Tel: 212 677 1900

Rogue Institute for Ecology and Economy
Ashland, OR
Tel: 503 482 6031

Forest Stewardship Council
PO Box 849, Richmond VT 05477
Tel: 802 434 3101

Institute for Sustainable Forestry
PO Box 1580, Redway, CA 95560
Tel: 707 923 4719

Scientific Certification Systems
(see p. 198)

Shakes and shingles

Cedar Shake & Shingle Bureau
515 116th Avenue NE, Suite 275,
Bellevue, WA 98004-5294
Tel: 206 453 1323

Breathing walls

Center for Maximum Potential Building
Systems (Max Pot)
Pliny Fisk, 8604 Webberville Road,
Austin, TX 78724

International Institute for Bau-Biologie
& Ecology (see entry p. 48)

Swanson Associates
601 23rd Street, Fairfield, IO 52556
Tel: 515 472 8217 Fax: 515 472 1678

Straw bale construction

Out on Bale (*publications*)
1037 E Linden Street, Tuscon, AZ 85719
Tel: 602 624 1673

Straw Bale Construction Association
31 Old Arroyo Chamiso, Santa Fe,
NM 87505
Tel: 505 989 4400

Strawbale Research Fund and Community
Research Center (CIRC)
PO Box 42663, Tucson, AZ 85733

Glass and glazing

National Fenestration Ratings Council
(NFRC) 1300 Spring Street, Suite 120,
Silver Spring, MD 20910
Tel: 301 589 6372

Canadian Institute for Research and
Construction, Building Materials Center-
20, Ottawa, Ontario K1A 0R6
Tel: 613 993 2463 Fax: 613 952 7673

Owner-building and Retrofit

Center for Resourceful Building
Technology (see p. 196)

National Association of Housing
Cooperatives
1614 King Street, Alexandria, VA 22314
Tel: 703 549 5201

Owner-Builder Center
1516 Fifth St, Berkeley, CA 94710
Tel: 415 848 5950

Innovative Housing, 2169 East San
Francisco Boulevard, Suite E,
San Rafael, CA 94901
Tel: 415 457 4593

Kit homes

Living Shelter Crafts
PO Box 4069, West Sedona, AZ 86340
Tel: 602 230 4283

Wilderness Log Homes
PO Box 902, Plymouth, WI 53073-0902
Tel: 414 893 8416 Fax: 414 892 2414

Timber frames

Timber Framers Guild of North America
PO Box 1075, Bellingham, WA 98227
Tel: 360 733 4001

Now turn to Part Two, The Directory, for more organizations, suppliers and publications

The use of "soft energy" has come a long way since the phrase was coined in the 1960s by Amory Lovins of the Rocky Mountain Institute. With many other experts, he saw the folly of our reliance on conventional "hard energy" sources (coal, oil and natural gas) or "non-renewables". Once used, these resources are gone forever. Lovins knew that the only long-term sustainable way was to transfer to using those energy sources freely available in nature – sun, wind and water – and the "renewables", plants and trees (biomass) that can regenerate. This vision is now becoming a reality as more and more people are switching to use natural resources. Soft energy technology is improving all the time, becoming more reliable, as well as easier to use, and cheaper to buy.

A wide range of components exist to suit almost any home site. You can generate on-site electricity from the sun, using arrays of PVs (photovoltaic cells); from the wind, using windmills; or from water, via small hydropower generators. Your domestic hot water can be heated (or preheated) using solar panels. You may use a combination of "passive" and "active" features to heat your home. Passive features include south-facing windows and sunspaces, thermal walls and floors, insulating blinds, shutters, or drapes. Active solar systems use built-in fans and pumps to enhance "passive" systems and increase flexibility. Many types of efficient and attractive low-emission wood or pellet-burning stoves are available for back-up heating. Heat exchangers can reuse heat from your warm-air and water-heating systems, or can extract heat from the ground. You can reduce air-conditioning costs drastically by cooling your home using a combination of shady vegetation, pergolas, and natural window coverings. Good home insulation is fundamental, and a growing range of natural and reusable alternatives is available.

David Pearson

A combination of these systems can produce an ideal, self-reliant "independent" home which provides all or most of its energy needs directly on the site. This makes it increasingly possible to live in remote areas-far from public utilities but you don't have to go to this extreme; wherever you live in city or country, "soft energy" is now a realistic option. Avoid going overboard immediately on a whole system; begin simply, and upgrade your system as you wish over the years. This will make it realistic in terms of price and allow you (and your family) time to accommodate to a new system and to make any lifestyle changes gradually. Before you buy, take plenty of advice and check if local building approvals are needed. Ask the manufacturer if the products meet national and local codes and exactly what warranty is offered. If possible, visit a similar home installation in the neighborhood and talk to the purchasers. You could also find out before you start if and how you can sell excess electricity to the area utility company.

The greatest contribution to saving world resources comes about through lots of people making small savings rather than the big savings of a committed few. Whatever level of low-energy system you choose, your success, satisfaction and savings will depend on your dedication to a lifestyle that uses energy as efficiently as possible.

David Pearson

A well-sited photovoltaic installation can provide electricity even in cooler climates. This array of photovoltaic cells combines with a wind generator to supply power to a house on Salt Spring Island, British Columbia.

Although situated in an area of high snow-fall, the heavily insulated timber house is autonomous. Built with low-emissivity south-facing windows, most heating is through passive solar gain.

Photovoltaics (solar electricity) is a way of converting sunlight directly into electricity. At the heart of a photovoltaic system are the solar cells. These are mini-generators with no moving parts to wear out or break down. They produce electricity without any combustion, noise, or vibration. Made of wafers of hyperpure silicon, the cells are integrated into lightweight modules (usually 36 at a time to make a 4 square foot module) and sealed in resin between tempered glass and a tough multilayered plastic backing. The whole module is framed in anodized aluminum. A number of modules used together is called an array. Photovoltaics produces direct current (DC) electricity which can be used as it is or converted to alternating current (AC). The amount of power produced will vary depending on the location, season, and weather, but solar cell performance is improving all the time and many will continue to produce electricity in as little as 5% of full sunlight. In winter, and on overcast days, you may also need to use a backup supply generator, particularly when doing intensive electricity-using tasks such as vacuuming or laundry.

Since a solar array is modular, it is easily adapted to almost any power need in any location. It can be fixed directly onto your home, or mounted nearby. It can also grow as your power needs increase and you become less reliant on back-up generator systems. Solar modules are manufactured to endure the harshest weather conditions and most companies will give a minimum 10-year warranty on any module's power output.

Location

Solar cells must have unobstructed sunlight to work efficiently. You will need to adjust the tilt twice a year at the equinoxes. You do not have to be too accurate as 95% power will be gained within 20 degrees of sun direction.

▲ **A passive solar tracker supports this 8 module photovoltaic system**

Pole mounts are good for yards and easy to adjust. One pole can take up to 16 modules. Tracking mounts follow the sun automatically from sunrise to sunset. This can gain you 35% to 50% power in summer but is no help in northern locations where winter sun moves less and the sky may be overcast.

Your system should incorporate a "charge control" (to protect the batteries from overcharging), batteries (12 and 24 volts) and an "inverter" to convert DC power to 120 volt AC. Some equipment includes "integrated systems" which combine charge control, the inverter, digital meters and fuses to make installation far simpler. You will also need a backup generator and battery chargers.

** HOW THE SYSTEM WORKS **

Solar Panel

INVERTER — AC — AC APPLIANCE

DC

DC — BATTERY GUARD — DC — 12 VOLT BATTERY — DC — 12 VOLT APPLIANCE

Sunnyside Solar, Inc

▲ **Transforming sunshine into power through photovoltaics**

Mounting

You can mount your modules on the roof where there are fewer shadows and less chance of theft. But you will have to climb on the roof to make seasonal adjustments. If you are in a snow zone, a nearly vertical setting will help the modules shed snow. Alternatively, if you can find space free from windows it may be practical to fix modules on the south wall. This avoids snow slides and allows easier maintenance. If your system is wall mounted check that there are no roof overhangs which could potentially block the summer sun.

Systems

Many wind power users are linked to the electricity grid, using wind energy when it is available, with excess energy going into the grid and credited against grid supplies used when it is calm. This combination system avoids using batteries, but an average wind speed of 10 mph is considered a minimum. Remote systems which rely on batteries can work satisfactorily on 8-9 mph averages. Wind turbines will run 12, 24, 48, 120, or 240 volt applications, depending on size.

Each wind turbine needs a regulator or controller to prevent battery overcharge. Lights and appliances using DC can be operated directly from the battery, while an inverter is used to convert battery power into 120 volt AC for normal household appliances.

Windmills (or wind turbines) use the kinetic energy of the wind to turn a rotor, and the rotary motion drives a generator. Most have propellers mounted on a horizontal axis and must move to face into the wind; some (like the "eggbeater" Darreius type) are vertical-axis mounted and have the advantage of working whichever way the wind is blowing. A horizontal-axis wind turbine comprises a rotor, a generator, a mainframe, and usually a tail.

Modern rotors typically have two or three wooden or fiberglass blades. The generator is designed specifically for the wind turbine, and usually includes permanent magnet alternators. Moving parts such as gearboxes and belts are subject to wear and damage and should be avoided. The mainframe – the main structure of the windmill – links the moving turbine to the tower on which it is mounted. A tail turns the rotor into the wind.

Aside from any issues of cost, the photovoltaic/wind turbine debate hinges on location; you can use PV even on a site with limited sun, but you need an average wind speed above 8mph to run a wind generator. As wind is strongest and sun weakest in the winter, many soft energy users opt for dual input with PV cells and a wind turbine, both feeding a bank of batteries.

◀ **A typical three-bladed wind generator suits most sites**

▲ **Flagging, or relative deformity of a tree, suggests local windspeed**

Location

A wind turbine needs all the wind it can get. It needs to be positioned at least 30 feet higher than any trees, buildings, walls, or other windproof barriers within 300 feet. Towers may be made of pipes, or from lattice, with guys. Telephone poles can make secure mounts for smaller turbines. Wind turbine makers usually offer towers, and can advise you. In some states, you need permission to erect a tower. In order to decide whether your site has enough wind, find out its average annual wind speed from weather bureaus or airports, remembering that they measure wind speed on the ground and a turbine will be at least 30 feet above it, where the wind is stronger. Other factors are the prevailing wind direction, nearby trees or buildings, the ground surface relief, and the system to be used. Although deformity in tree growth indicates high average windspeed, absence of deformity does not always mean that windspeed is low.

Barelle PNL, D.O.E.

Performance

The power you can produce depends on your site. You need to consider the change in elevation of the stream bed over the length of the property; the minimum gallons per minute flow; the size and type of pipeline if one is already installed; and the distance from the lower end of the creek to the house. Unless you plan to build one yourself, obtain advice on likely output from your hydropower generator supplier. A typical 15 gallons per minute flow from a 2" penstock and 75 foot head produces upwards of 75 watts (5-6 amperes, 12 volts), which compares well with both solar and wind power. Small creeks charging continually produce more power per dollar than any other means.

H ome hydropower is a smallscale version of the huge hydroelectric power generation schemes used successfully in many countries. The main advantage of hydropower over both solar and wind power is its constancy: many creeks run all year round in all weathers. To use hydropower you need a watersource such as a creek with as much head as possible - ie with a high total vertical fall. A water generator uses a small volume of water, raised to high pressure by running downhill in a pipe (a penstock), to spin a wheel at high speed, turning an alternator or generator. This may be a Pelton wheel (diagram) or a cross-flow turbine type. The former is preferable for sites with a high head and moderate flow. If your site has variable flow you may need to dam your watersource.

Water is directed from the penstock through nozzles; a single nozzle generator needs about 40 feet head, and a minimum 2" diameter penstock. Four-nozzle generators need 20 feet of head and a 4" pipe. Each nozzle needs 10-20 gallons per minute. The price of generators is dependent on the number of nozzles, and the efficiency of the alternator. Turbines exist which run on as little as 40 gallons per minute at 5 feet of head, directing the flow through up to four nozzles. You can get power from small branches by using a sensitive, low-duration generator which runs on as little as 2 gallons per minute at 50 feet head, or 12 gallons per minute at 10 feet head.

Output from water generators runs through a regulator to batteries to power DC applications, or you can use an inverter to convert it to 120-volt AC in order to run household appliances.

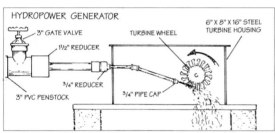

HYDROPOWER GENERATOR

3" GATE VALVE
TURBINE WHEEL
6" X 8" X 16" STEEL TURBINE HOUSING
1½" REDUCER
¾" REDUCER
3" PVC PENSTOCK
¾" PIPE CAP

▲ **A Pelton turbine generator is ideal for high-head, low-flow sites**

◀ **Water wheels preceded today's efficient waterpower generators**

Location

Site your generator at the lowest level practical, as it is likely to need a minimum 25 feet of head. The generator needs a steel housing rarely exceeding 2-3 square feet, but the penstock is made from all-weather PVC.

If the water turbine has to be sited downhill of the house to get sufficient head, you could incorporate a ram pump into your system. This uses the potential energy of the falling water to lift a small proportion of it up to the house for domestic use (see pp. 72-85).

"Tomorrow's farm will produce crops like corn, soybeans, rapeseed, and sunflowers for food and fuel. Farmers will harvest switchgrass and then sell it for feed or to make ethanol. They'll cultivate tree crops for as long as a decade and then harvest them for fiber and energy." This is the vision of the US Department of Energy and the National Renewable Energy Laboratory (NREL) for The American Farm of the future which will grow diverse "energy crops", alongside food crops, to help feed and fuel the nation.

Energy crops are expected both to supply local electricity-generating plants, and to boost the production of ethanol and biodiesel fuels, plant-based oils, chemicals, and biodegradable plastics. The NREL forecasts that, by 2010, energy crops could generate enough electricity to meet the residential needs of 20 cities the size of San Francisco. Renewable plant-based synthetics should also help to reduce the demand for non-renewable synthetics and plastics (made from coal, oil, and gas) used around the home. Plant-based products will have increasing domestic impact on items such as cosmetics, medicines, resins, lubricants, adhesives, paints, wax, solvents, and fabrics. It is to be hoped that any new emphasis on large-scale national production of energy crops will go against the trend toward monoculture farming but will, on the contrary, lead to more diverse and smaller-scale species planting.

A tall native prairie grass, switchgrass is also an energy crop. Its roots extend more than 2 feet into the ground, helping control erosion and build new soils.

The American Farm, US Dept of Energy / 1994

Further developments

Food wastes and animal manures, as well as being composted, can be converted into "biogas" (mainly methane) and alcohol. Biogas can be used in a kitchen stove, and alcohol can be used to run cars, trucks, and farm machinery as an alternative to gasoline or mixed with gasoline to make "gasohol". A methane digester ferments manure to make biogas, while an alcohol still uses a distillation process to make alcohol from crops and crop wastes. A good deal of material, however, is needed to produce a useful amount of fuel, and it is only really feasible for home use in a small community, farm, or group housing project. Do not install a methane digester without consulting other users and experts as improperly set-up methane/algae systems could potentially spread fecal-borne diseases such as cholera, typhoid and dysentery. As a general rule, take advice from local agencies before proceeding with any domestic-level energy fuel options.

Domestic production

At the domestic level there has been considerable research and experiment over the years, especially in developing countries, into the production of energy from organic materials. The simplest form of biomass energy is wood; if you have enough land you could devote some to a fuelwood lot. Coppicing (the sprouting of trees from the cut stump) was the traditional European method of generating the maximum amount of fuel which can be easily harvested on a sustainable basis. Fuelwood must be dry, and burned in a closed stove such as a cast-iron or Franklin stove (see page 57 for more advice). Sunflowers and other species of fast-growing plants may also be desirable biomass crops.

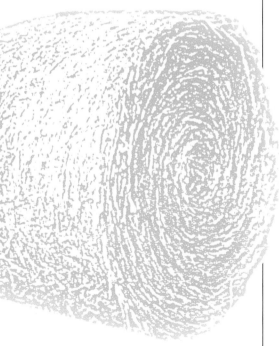

▲ Switchgrass can be harvested in conventional bales like straw or hay

CO-GENERATION

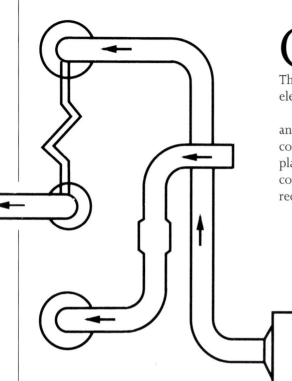

Co-generation is the combination of heat and power to generate electricity and useful heat in a single process. It can be used for water and space heating plus air conditioning. The process makes use of the heat produced in generating electricity rather than wasting it into the atmosphere.

Co-generation can use any fuel: gas, oil, coal – even waste – and typically operates at between 70% and 90% efficiency (as compared with around 35% efficiency at traditional power plants). There are also significant environmental advantages as a co-generation system emits minimal CO_2, thereby helping to reduce global warming effects.

▼ **Current co-generation systems are typically industrial installations**

How it works

A small-scale co-generation unit has an engine, often referred to as the prime mover, which drives a generator to produce electricity. A heat exchanger recovers waste heat from the engine and exhaust gases to produce hot water or steam that can be used for space heating. For optimum performance, a heat/power ratio of between 2:1 and 3:1 is needed. A typical "small" co-generation unit may have an electrical output of 20 kW and a thermal output of 38kW. To be cost-effective this needs to run for at least 4,500 hours per year at full load.

Noise and vibration can be a problem in smaller systems which require anti-vibration mountings and a well-built acoustic enclosure casing around the unit.

Co-generation in housing

Although the use of co-generation in industry and district heating systems is not new, the use of smallscale units for individual buildings is quite recent. These buildings, however, are still large with significant continuous energy demands. They include hotels, hospitals, leisure centers, and offices. Existing systems are only really cost-efficient for such business projects, or for multiresidential sites such as apartment blocks using communal heating. Although co-generation technology and equipment are as yet scarcely viable for homes it may be possible to make individual systems practical by linking the energy needs of several buildings.

It may be worth considering a co-generation system as a means of generating heat and electricity for individual households if you live in, or are involved in the

setting-up of, an eco-community or housing project. It is particularly relevant if there are other on-site activities such as workshops, offices, and nurseries or small schools that will all need heating, cooling, and a power supply. Some individuals have tried home-made co-generation systems in their own homes, but such technology is still experimental.

Before considering what type of heating you need, be sure that you have done all you can to heat the home with solar energy. Ensure that you have weatherproofed windows and doors, upgraded with heat-conserving glazing, drapes, blinds, or shutters, and insulate your home to a high standard. Also check outside. Enhance shelter by planting evergreen trees and shrubs, and by creating earth berms, fences, and walls. Make sure you are making the most of the freely-available heat from the sun and conserving it efficiently so that you need minimal supplementary or back-up heat in cloudy weather.

The next aim is to use environmentally-sustainable fuel, plus efficient and non-polluting heating appliances. It is better to use a renewable fuel such as wood (from a properly-managed source) rather than non-renewable coal, oil or natural gas.

Tulikivi U.S. Inc

▲ **A soapstone oven also provides healthy radiant space heating**

Stoves

Attractive as they are, open-hearth fires are not today's answer because of their low heating efficiency and high emissions. Choose instead from a wide range of current stove designs which burn longer and more efficiently. Environmental Protection Agency (EPA) Phase 11-approved appliances have reduced particulate emissions by around 85%.

Catalytic appliances use similar combustors as those used in vehicles. Wood smoke is burnt at temperatures between 500 and 1,600 degrees F thus dramatically reducing emissions. Heat efficiency is up to 80%. Noncatalytic stoves are also low-emission and about 74% efficient. They ignite volatile gases by balancing incoming primary air below the fuel with secondary air inputs above it, channeled over superheated baffles.

Cookstoves

The traditional cookstove allows you the dual benefits of an oven/cooktop plus gentle and pleasantly-scented radiant heating for the kitchen and surrounding rooms. New models include metal and soapstone ovens, and many classic designs have been updated to meet EPA standards, and can use various fuel options.

Masonry stoves

Used in Europe for centuries, the German kachelofen (tile stove) is gaining in popularity in North America. Known as a masonry stove, it has a firebox surrounded by a brick mass with air channels and a circuitous flue. This helps the masonry surround absorb as much heat as possible, which is gradually released as gentle and continuous warmth over a period of hours to the rooms beyond. The remarkable heat storage design means that only 22-32 pounds of wood burned undampered for 30 minutes to an hour will provide 12-24 hours of warmth. A fire made once in the morning and once at night can give around-the-clock warmth. Masonry stoves are 90-95% efficient, clean burning, and provide radiant and convected heat.

Pellets

Pellet-burning stoves and inserts use the latest wood-burning technology. Small dry pellets made from wood by-products exceed EPA requirements by emitting as little as 0.2 grams of particulate per hour. They burn at 2,000 degrees F and reach 80% efficiency. The pellets are packed in easy-to-store 40-pound bags; good for apartment-dwellers and urban homes. All you do is pour a load of pellets into the hopper, set their feed rate into the fire (dependent on heat output), and the solid-state controls do the rest. Wall thermostats and self-lighting options make the pellet-stove one of the most convenient stoves yet to be designed.

▲ **Wood by-products make convenient and economical fuel pellets**

Sun tracker

This instrument complements the world globe to provide a better understanding of Sun-Earth relationships. Easily set up, it shows you how the sun's path determines the length of day, the seasons, climate, and solar energy worldwide. Available from Suntrak, Indiana.

Solar electric generators

Pre-assembled photovoltaic electric power generators make a very convenient package. This self-contained model comes from Astrodyne of Walpole (MA), and incorporates panels, built-in batteries to store excess power, and microcomputer controls.

Pelton water turbine

The Harris system is an efficient, durable, battery-charging pelton turbine. It is particularly suited to produce usable household power from smaller springs and creeks. Harris Hydroelectric of Davenport (CA) build hydropower generators for a wide range of water sites.

Tile oven

For centuries Europeans have enjoyed wonderful radiant heat produced by tile stoves. They are attractive, use a variety of fuels, and provide space heating and cooking facilities. Various designs are now available in North America through Biofire Inc, of Utah.

Concentrator PV module

Midway Labs Inc. of Chicago really know how to harvest sunlight with their low cost concentrator PV modules. These PVs work like a magnifying glass to focus solar energy. This Powersource™ can get 187 watts of power from a single 4 inch cell.

Rutland windcharger

The Rutland windcharger is distributed throughout North America by Trillium Windmills of Orillia, Ontario. The design combines durable materials with the most up-to-date technology, and will maintain the charge in 12 or 24 volt batteries in any location. This unit can start charging at windspeeds as low as 4 mph, and furls away in strong gales.

Solar pathfinder

Fast, accurate, and easy to use — one 15-minute reading can determine the placement and orientation of solar structures, shading patterns at your site, and sunrise and sunset times each month. This beautiful instrument can provide year-round solar access data in a single reading. It is available from Solar Pathfinder, Hartford (SD).

Whisper windmill

A Whisper wind generator is easily installed and economical. The extra-large propellor diameters optimize average windspeeds of 8 to 13 mph — characteristic of locations where most people choose to live. Manufactured by World Power Technologies of Duluth (MN), dealers exist countrywide.

SOLAR WATER HEATING

Savings without system replacement

Start by looking at your present hot water use and how you can reduce your water consumption (see pp. 73-74). Next, check the hot water tank thermostat setting and reduce this to 120 degrees F. Then, increase the tank insulation and check that all hot water pipes passing through unheated areas are also insulated. You could investigate replacing an old inefficient water heater with a new "demand" water heater (a gas- or electric-fired water heater that needs no water supply tanks). By using these methods you should find that your hot water use and bills are reduced markedly. Ask your local utility company to do a home energy audit and advise on savings and the solar heating option.

Using the free energy from the sun to heat your water sounds attractive. But how many years (the payback time) will it take for the cost of the new system to be repaid by the savings in heating bills? A good investment might pay back in a year or two, whereas a poor investment may not pay back for ten years. Depending on your consumption, and the type of system you choose, a solar water heating system will probably perform somewhere in between. Fitting the system as part of the plumbing of a new home or major retrofit, however, can reduce and absorb installation costs. Rises in utility charges will continue to make solar systems more economically favorable. If you decide to go solar for environmental reasons, or to make your home independent of utilities, you may be willing to take a longer term investment view.

◄ **Options exist to ensure your solar system suits your requirements**

Types of solar heating

A solar water heating system need not be large or expensive. The basic components of a simple system are flat-plate collector panels that use the sun's energy to heat the water, and a solar storage tank to store the heated water. In a direct (open loop) system, the fluid heated in the panels is plain water, which flows directly to the faucet. In an indirect (closed loop) system, the heat-transfer fluid in the panels is treated water or a non-freezing liquid such as antifreeze solution, hydrocarbon oil, or silicone. The heat from these media is exchanged into the solar storage tank and piped as "preheated" water into the existing hot water tank. Supplementary heat, if necessary, can be provided via a standard gas, oil or electric water heater.

A "passive" system usually relies on natural convection to circulate the water between the panels and tank. In an "active" system circulation is via electric pumps.

Installing a system

Although passive systems are simpler and cheaper, they are less flexible as the collector panels have to be lower than the storage tanks to allow for convection. As they risk freezing in cold weather you must make sure they are efficiently insulated with good collector protection, or can be drained in winter. Active systems allow the panels to be above and more remote from the tanks so it is easier to locate them on the roof, and they can operate all year round without freezing.

Before investing in any system make sure that there is an unobstructed site, where the collectors can face true south (or 15 degrees either way). Also check for any potential installation problems and make sure you fulfill building code requirements for the piping, storage tank, and collector roof mounting. Check that any changes to the appearance of the house will be acceptable. Solar collector panels can also be used to provide heat for radiant underfloor heating (see p. 62).

How it works

Orient your glazing as near due south as possible. Panes 20-25 degrees off true south have performance decreased by 5 to 10%. The tilt of panes to the sun is critical to admit as much winter sun as possible, if necessary at the expense of summer sun. The best tilt from the horizontal for overhead glazing is the latitude of the site plus 5-15 degrees. For example, at latitudes of 35 degrees N, slope the roof panes at 40-50 degrees from the horizontal. Provide some operable glazed units to allow ventilation (see p. 64) in the summer. This may be cross-ventilation (horizontal air flow) or stack-effect (vertical air flow), relying on the movement of air from areas of high air pressure to low, and from cool to warmer.

The benefits of passive solar gain are felt by all who add a solarium to their home, but sunspaces add the concept of retaining heat for use elsewhere in the house, or when the sun is not shining. A sunspace can be a living space, greenhouse or conservatory, and requires south-facing glazing, ventilation, thermal-storage mass, air-moving equipment and insulation. The cost of installation is only recovered from savings on heating bills in warm climates, but even in temperate zones the extra space afforded makes a sunspace worthwhile.

Sunspaces are glazed by glass, fiberglass or acrylics; check local codes for requirements on overhead lamination. Fiberglass is translucent rather than transparent and may be preferred when growing food plants, or where privacy is needed. Non-glass materials may turn yellow after three or four years of exposure to ultraviolet (UV) light. Check whether your non-glass material is UV-resistant. The aim in constructing a sunspace pane is to maximize both transmission of light and insulation of heat so look for transmissivity of over 65%. Standard glass transmits 80-85% of the spectrum, absorbing or reflecting the rest. Low-iron glass and many fiberglass products transmit 90-95%. Non-glass materials are shatterproof, lightweight and easy to handle, and are preferable where storm damage or vandalism are concerns.

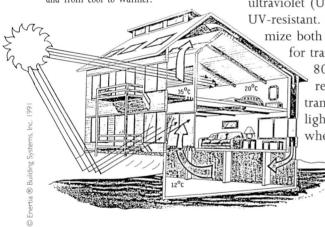

© Enertia ® Building Systems, Inc. 1991

◀ **This house design collects, stores and circulates the sun's energy**

Storing and releasing heat

The flooring in a sunspace should be dark-colored to maximize heat absorption. This heat is then collected in the thermal mass, typically a store of masonry or water tanks below the ground floor. For masonry storage, allow at least 1 cu.ft. of concrete or equivalent for every square foot of south-facing glass, and insulate it underneath and around the sides. Heat trapped in a sunspace can be transferred from the warmest air space via ductwork to the thermal mass. A thermostatically controlled blower draws heat to the duct manifold in the slab. Even without such an air-radiant system you can install through-wall fans to direct heat to other rooms; reversible fans allow heated air to be returned to the solarium at night. Install paddle fans to assist air movement in summer.

Insulating sunspace windows increases R values from R-3 to R-5 to 10. Night insulation can reduce heat loss by up to 75%, but adds little to quad-pane units.

Solar windows

Where a build-on sunspace is impractical, consider a solar window with double or triple glazing, and, ideally, low-emissivity glass. A larger than normal window admits solar heat which is retained by thermal-storage features such as heavy masonry walls, concrete floors, or thick ceramic tiling or additional plaster on conventional walls. Fans can assist heat distribution, and insulated blinds or shutters over the windows are needed at night.

THERMAL WALLS AND FLOORS

A key ingredient of the energy-efficient home is heat storage. Whatever your source of heat, being able to store the heat in the structure of the building is a major part of the equation. When making solar windows, adding a sunspace, or installing a stove, for example, you need to consider how the walls, floors, and internal partitions can become effective heat stores. Heavy masonry such as bricks, blocks, concrete, and earth have good heat-retaining properties. Water containers are even more effective.

There are many ways to incorporate such materials into the interior of the house, either as new construction or as a retrofit. If you add solar windows or a sunspace, for example, try to increase the mass of the existing floors and walls. Lay a thick concrete floor, well insulated below and at the edges, and finish this with clay flooring tiles, bricks, or stone slabs. On the sun-receiving side of the wall add layers of plasterboard or thick wall tiles, or alternatively, build a facing in brick or stone. The more irregular the wall surface the better, as the greater the surface area, the more of the sun's energy will be absorbed.

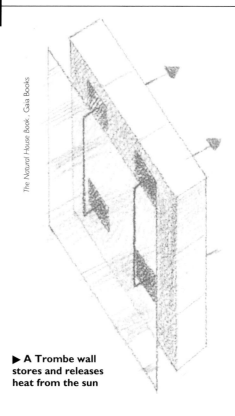

The Natural House Book, Gaia Books

▶ **A Trombe wall stores and releases heat from the sun**

▼ **Solar storage tubes can heat your space and add visual interest**

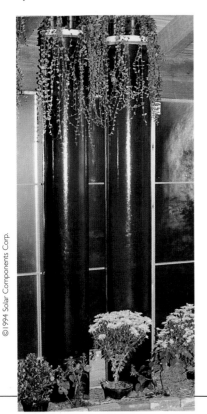

© 1994 Solar Components Corp.

Active systems

You could consider a more complex, "active" system assisted by fans and pumps. Heat from the sunspace or solar collector panels is transferred into a thermal mass of rocks or water tanks beneath the ground floor, and is then redistributed around the home through pipes, vents, or ducts (see p. 61). Your air quality may suffer after running air through rock beds, so check and take action if necessary (see pp. 24-25).

Two other types of thermal walls are Trombe walls, named after Dr Felix Trombe, and water-container walls. Built of heavy masonry material, a Trombe wall has a dark-colored surface toward the sun, covered with glass, with an air cavity in between. Vents top and bottom open by day and close at night to control the heat flow. Water-container walls use either water-filled drums or specially-manufactured "solar storage tubes". One manufacturer has developed the "Solar Attic" concept whereby a series of water-filled tubes, located in the attic space, are heated via roof glazing to produce both full space heating and pre-heated domestic water. The system is designed to have a payback time of under seven years.

Solar storage tubes can become attractive features, located behind sun-facing windows, filled either with clear water or water colored with non-toxic dyes. Where daylight transmission is not desired, the darkest colors will increase solar absorption by 35% over clear-water filled tubes. A water wall can be "fine tuned" on site to balance its esthetic appeal and heat-retaining performance.

Be aware that on hot summer days all thermal walls will need adequate shading to prevent uncomfortable overheating of the home. At night, solar windows will need to be well insulated with blinds, drapes, or shutters (see p. 38). Also, remember that any additional loads caused by heavy masonry or water containers must be properly supported.

Heat pumps or heat exchangers extract heat from one medium and transfer it to another. Most home systems use either air-source heat pumps, which draw heat from the air, or ground-source systems which take heat from the earth or groundwater.

The trend towards tightly sealed superinsulated homes has accelerated the development of air-to-air heat exchangers – now better known as heat-recovery ventilators, or HRVs. Tight homes – those that allow less than half the air to change every hour through the structure, cracks and openings – must have adequate ventilation to avoid build-up of humidity, condensation, and odors. Problem areas include bathrooms, kitchens, basements, hobby rooms, pet areas and spa or indoor pool rooms. It is also necessary to exhaust any harmful concentrations of toxic chemical pollutants that may arise from building materials, adhesives, furnishings, and decoration. Ventilation must also, of course, deal with cigarette smoke.

Richard Freudenberger

Heat recovery ventilators (HRVs)

As part of a mechanical ventilation system, HRVs exhaust warm, stale air from the house while drawing in fresh, colder outside air. Within the heat exchange core, heat is transferred from the outgoing air to the incoming air while keeping each air stream physically separate. The fresh air is automatically preheated or precooled (and humidity-controlled) depending on the season.

HRVs may have controls on the unit or on a separate box. These include a variable-speed control, 24 hour and delay timers, and dehumidistat controls which control the relative humidity of the whole house and localized areas of high humidity. Some systems also have air quality monitors that speed up airflow if certain indoor pollutants exceed preset levels. In very cold weather the condensate can freeze, so check for features which will eliminate frosting problems.

As with any heating or cooling system, an HRV system needs to be designed to suit each house and its occupants. Use the services of a qualified mechanical engineer to design and supervize installation, and to deal with any setup, maintenance, and warranty problems. Alternatively, manufacturers may offer a design service plus approved installers or advice for the do-it-yourself installer.

▼ Integrated systems provide heat, ventilation, and air-conditioning

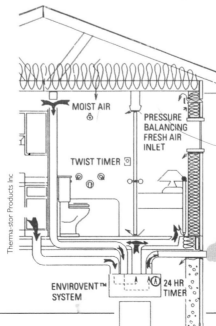

Therma-stor Products Inc

MOIST AIR

PRESSURE BALANCING FRESH AIR INLET

TWIST TIMER

ENVIROVENT™ SYSTEM

24 HR TIMER

▲ Underground tubing with glycol solution collects groundsource heat

Other systems

As an alternative to an HRV, you could consider a ground-source system. Though it is more efficient, installation costs and feasibility often limit this option. To use groundwater, for instance, you will need a well that can deliver at least ten gallons a minute (gpm) to a ground-source heat pump, using a different design to the HRV. A flow rate of 2.5 to 3.0 gpm yields around 12,000 Btu/hr for heating or cooling. To gain heat from the earth, you will need to bury about 1,000 feet of two-inch polybutylene tubing four feet or more underground, filled with gycol solution and connected at each end to a ground-source heat pump. As the ground-loop tubing needs about an acre of land, mostly unshaded, this option is best suited to larger country lots. It is also more feasible, and cheaper, if installed as part of the construction work for a new home.

COOLING, SHADING, AND VENTING

There are many natural cooling devices which can reduce or eliminate your dependence on energy-wasteful conventional air-conditioning systems. It may be possible to use natural vegetation to shade and cool, or you can incorporate various structures during construction. A venting roof will control heat gain, or you could integrate a structure such as a cool tower. This uses the evaporation process to introduce cool air to replace the hot. Even in hot desert areas, houses can remain comfortable with no electrical cooling if built underground, or with thick earth-sheltering. As retrofit, it is simple to add devices such as shades or screens which reduce solar heat gain. Ventilation systems can also be added where necessary.

David Pearson

Shading, screening, and ventilation

Vegetation provides natural cooling, both by creating shade and by cooling the air as the moisture it transpires is evaporated. Trees can be carefully sited to shade the house in summer, while permitting winter sun. Choose trees that lose their leaves in winter and have a full canopy during the

◀ Shutters provide traditional and attractive air-conditioning

summer. Trees shade best when placed on the northeast/southeast and northwest/southwest sides of a house because of the angle of the summer sun. Climbing plants on a trellis grow fast and allow space for air to circulate.

Exterior shading is traditionally provided by overhangs, porches, and awnings. When constructing an overhang, calculate its length to avoid blocking winter sun. An awning, removable in winter, will reduce heat gain on southern windows by 65%. Shutters, exterior or interior, may allow passage of air but eliminate sunlight, while louvers and exterior rolled blinds can be adjusted according to the amount of light required. Solar screens and reflective window coatings and films admit light and air, but reflect the sun's heat by up to 50%.

Stack-effect ventilation is set up by opening windows, clerestories, or permanent vents at the top of the house on the south which release hot air, drawing up cool air from similar vents on the north side at a low level. Vents will draw cooler air from any crawl space under the house, but check for Radon (see p. 113). Connect external areas of high and low pressure for cross ventilation, usually windward and leeward sides of the building.

Building for passive cooling

Designs hinge on three simple facts: hot air rises, wind creates an air pressure imbalance, and moisture increases air density. A cool tower works on the principle that air is cooled as water evaporates. One system (see diagram) uses vertical pads of material at the top of a tower; water passes through them, falls into a tank, and is pumped back up. Air passes through the pads with little resistance and is cooled by the evaporation of the water. This cool, moist air, being heavier than the hot dry air outside, drops down the tower into the adjacent house. It is best to use filtered rainwater rather than tapwater because it contains fewer of the mineral impurities that eventually clog the pads. A home cooled by this method should ideally be open-plan, but if ducts are used make them as wide as possible.

Up to 90% of heat gain through the roof in a passively-cooled house can be eliminated by a vent skin: a metal roof, with radiant barriers, a double-skin construction and vented top ridge. Presently this is a home-build option but one retrofit option is to insert a radiant barrier between the roof and R-19 ceiling insulation. This will soon pay for itself through lowered cooling costs.

▼ A cool tower uses evaporation, circulating air through wet pads

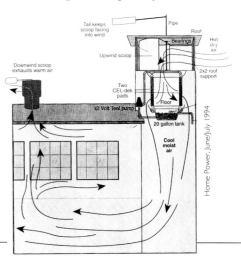

Tail keeps scoop facing into wind
Pipe
Roof
Bearings
Hot dry air
Upwind scoop
Downwind scoop exhausts warm air
2x2 roof support
Two CEL-dek pads
Floor
12 Volt Teel pump
20 gallon tank
Cool moist air

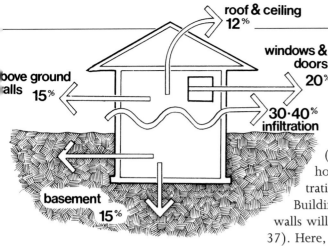

roof & ceiling
12%

windows &
doors
20%

bove ground
alls 15%

30-40%
infiltration

basement
15%

▲ **Without conservation strategies,
your home will suffer high heat loss**

When considering home insulation, you must provide adequate ventilation at the same time, to balance energy-saving with health (see pp. 24-5). The conventional view assumes that the house needs to be completely sealed against moisture infiltration via impermeable vapor barriers. But recently, Building Biologists have put forward a different view – that walls will handle moisture better if they can "breathe" (see p. 37). Here, we summarize the conventional energy-efficient approach. Home insulation both conserves fossil fuels and reduces heating bills. During construction, insulation can be built into the walls, ceilings, and roof, with fuel bill savings of up to 85%. As retrofit, insulation can be added to wall cavities, to the attic or roofspace, or applied to existing walls either internally or externally, with appropriate coverings. Savings of up to 60% can be achieved. Insulating products are rated with an R-value (resistance value) measuring the degree to which they hold captured air or gases (which are poor conductors of heat) and thus reduce channels for heat loss. The higher the R-value per inch, the better the insulation. Current recommended standards for moderate climates (R-12 in walls, R-28 in ceilings) do not recognize fossil fuel depletion or high fuel prices; R-20 and R-32 are better targets.

Insulating materials

Fiberglass is a common insulator but it can have problems – formaldehyde and loose fine fibers. Better are vermiculite and the newer insulating materials – blown cellulose, and rolls and batts of cotton and wool.

Doors and windows

Heat loss through doors and windows is easily reduced. Double-glazing reduces heat loss through windows by a half; triple-glazing by two-thirds. Good weatherstripping around opening doors and windows will reduce their heat loss by 60%. The best is a durable spring metal strip which is slightly pricier than other options, but outperforms and outlasts them. Caulk any gaps in window or door frames inside and out, and cover windows internally with insulated panels, blinds, or shades at night to save 50% of heat loss during winter.

Attics

Batting or blown materials are generally used between the ceiling joists in attics, and a vapor barrier applied to the ceiling below, either with polyethylene sheeting or vapor barrier paint. Ensure adequate ventilation in the attic space.

▶ **Options for super-insulation
ensure an energy-efficient home**

Walls

Existing cavity walls can be filled with blown materials, such as cellulose or loose fiberglass. If space allows, build new frame walls and insulate the new cavity, or apply insulating material in panels to existing walls, then cover with a new vapor barrier and wallboard. A vapor barrier on the moister side of the wall prevents moisture infiltration and consequent fungal attack, but you must also ventilate within the wall structure to allow moisture to escape outside. This is particularly important in basement walls.

Exterior insulation saves the most energy; first a complete vapor barrier is applied around the whole house, then new insulation panels are added, and finally the new house siding material.

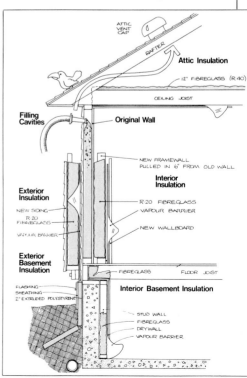

Ecology House

Ceiling fan

Stay cool with a high-efficiency ceiling fan. Simple, effective and economical air-conditioning is provided at a modest price, a fan is easy to install and models exist to suit most home requirements – available from Photocomm, Inc (AZ).

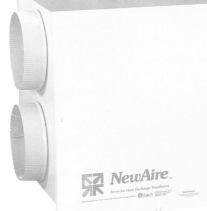

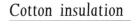

Cotton insulation

Greenwood (SC) have come up with a new low-tech insulation made entirely from reprocessed textiles. This material is highly rated, cost-competitive, and friendly to environment and homeowner alike. Moreover, installation is easy and needs no specialist equipment.

Heat Recovery Ventilator

New Aire™ (WI) heat exchange ventilators exhaust stale air from the home while drawing in fresh outside air. This model incorporates a moisture-transfer feature to eliminate condensate and frosting. It provides quality ventilation for any size home or for individual problem areas.

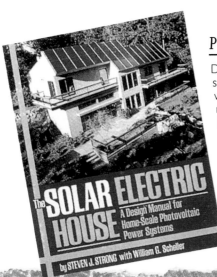

PV design manual

Design a system specifically suited to your own home with the help of this excellent manual from Sustainability Press. Cost-conscious tips and technical advice combine to make this book a must if you are PV-inclined!

Cord caulk

Seal your doors and windows as tight as your refrigerator! Suitable for even the coldest climates, cord caulk from Delta (MA) effectively stops drafts, it is easily applied and just as easily removed and reused.

Solar storage tubes

Make the most of passive solar energy with these Sunlite® water-filled storage tubes. Solar absorption can be maximized by adding non-toxic colorants, making the tubes decorative as well as functional. Available from Solar Components Corporation (NH).

Solar pool heater

You like to use your pool year round but worry about efficient heating? Use a solar pool collector to use energy wisely and economically. A variety of roof, wall or pole-mounted solar pool heaters can be obtained from Aquatherm (NJ).

Reflective insulation

The aluminum foil covering this thick - seven layer – insulation reflects 97% of radiant heat. This insulation, available from Reflectix™ (IN) is effective throughout the home and retards radon as well as vapor.

Sandy Lawrence and Barbara Schickler's house

A growing number of home-owners want to live in an "independent" home, unhooked from local utilities, reliant instead on renewable energy supplies from sun, wind and water. This particular example may be beyond the average intention of most, but well illustrates what can be done by people who think about the future and are committed to living responsibly on the planet.

◄ **Photovoltaic modules on the south side convert solar energy into power. Windows are shaded against high summer sun by overhangs**

Sandy and Barbara wanted a virtually maintenance-free home with almost no energy bills. Looking toward their retirement in twenty to thirty years time, they were prepared to invest in the future now. Their search led them to a five-acre lot in northern Napa Valley, California, with an existing house and swimming pool built toward the rear. This property, with excellent solar orientation and a hill to the west to protect from the heat of the late afternoon summer sun, was ideally sited to use renewable energy.

Intelligent passive-solar design
To make the most of the natural site advantages, the 2,800 sq. ft. house is oriented to maximize south-facing and minimize east- and west-facing walls. The north side is partially buried, with minimal glazing to lessen winter heat loss. South-facing windows are shaded by overhangs from the hot summer sun yet catch the warmth of the low winter sun. The floors on all three levels, constructed of three-inch concrete finished with ceramic

tiles, act as a "passive heat store", absorbing the sun's heat in the day and releasing it into the rooms at night. The main living spaces take up the south side while bedrooms and bathrooms occupy the cooler north side. Well-insulated walls and windows complete this energy-conscious home. Excellent natural daylight to all rooms means artificial light is kept to a minimum but, when needed, fluorescent or compact fluorescent lights are used. The washing machine and refrigerator/freezer are low-energy equipment. Four gas wall heaters supply winter back-up heating.

Renewable Energy System
What distinguishes this home is the size of the renewable energy system installed. Fifty-six photovoltaic modules and two wind generators feed power into a 3,800 amp-hour 24-volt industrial chloride battery bank. This provides energy for the home and pool and runs a submersible well pump to fill water storage tanks. A "powercenter" regulates and monitors

incoming and outgoing energy and charges the battery bank, which can deliver up to five days worth of energy, if necessary. Inverters prevent power surges and ensure steady supplies to sensitive equipment such as computers or CD player. A solar water heating system completes the installation.

Pay-back?
Sandy and Barbara have invested around $50,000 plus installation costs – a sum equivalent to 30 or 40 years of electricity bills at 1994 rates. But if you take account of likely inflation in electricity costs during this time, a pay-back time of 15 to 20 years is more realistic – happily coinciding with their retirement age. Over and above financial concerns, Sandy and Barbara know that they will be living free of energy crises in a house that is in harmony with the land.

Real Goods, (see p. 96) supplied the above system. For information about your nearest Demonstration Home call 800 762 7325

General organizations

Audubon Society
613 Riversville Road,
Greenwich, CT 06831
Tel: 203 869 2017 Fax; 203 869 4437

Rocky Mountain Institute
1379 Snowmass Creek Road,
Snowmass, CO 81654
Tel: 303 970 3851 Fax: 303 970 3420

Worldwatch Institute
1776 Massachusetts Avenue NW,
Washington DC 20036
Tel: 202 452 1999

Nuclear Free America
325 E. 25th Street,
Baltimore MD 21218
Tel: 301 235 3575

Midwest Renewable Energy Association
PO Box 249
Amherst, WI 54406
Tel: 715 824 5166

Great Lakes Renewable Energy Association
11059 Bright Road
Maple City, MI 49664
Tel: 616 228 7159

Natural Resources Defense Council
40 West 20th Street,
New York, NY 10011
Tel: 212 727 2700

Northeast Sustainable Energy Association
23 Ames Street, Greenfield, MA 01301
Tel: 413 774 6051

Citizens for Clean Energy
PO Box 17147
Boulder CO 80308
Tel: 303 443 6181

Photovoltaics

American Council for an
Energy-Efficient Economy
1001 Connecticut Ave NW 535
Washington DC 20036
Tel: 202 429 8873

American Solar Energy Society
2400 Central Avenue, Suite G1
Boulder, CO 80301
Tel: 303 443 3130

Florida Solar Energy Center
300 State Road, no. 401
Cape Canaveral, FL 32920
Tel: 407 783 0300

Solar Technology Institute
PO Box 1115,
Carbondale, CO 81623-1115
Tel: 303 963 0715

Wind power

American Wind Energy Association
122 C Street NW, Fourth Floor
Washington DC 20001
Tel: 202 383 2500

National Renewable Energy Laboratory
1617 Cole Boulevard
Golden, CO 80401
Tel: 303 231 7303

Energy Efficiency and Renewable Energy
Clearing House
PO Box 3048 Merrifield, VA 22116
Tel: 800 363 3732

Biomass

Biofuels Information Center
National Renewable Energy Laboratory
(see entry)

US Department of Energy
Biofuels Systems Division EE-331
1000 Independence Avenue SW
Washington DC 20585
Tel: 202 586 8072

Stoves and tile ovens

Masonry Heater Association
of North America
11490 Commerce Park Drive, Suite 300,
Reston, VA 22091
Tel: 703 620 3171

Solar water heating

Solar Rating and Certification Corporation
Suite 800, 1001 Connecticut Avenue NW
Washington DC 20036
Tel: 202 383 2570

ASHRAE
American Society of Heating,
Refrigeration and Air-Conditioning
Engineers Inc.
1791 Tullie Circle NE
Atlanta, GA 30325-2305
Tel: 404 636 8400

Publications

Energy Saver's Catalog
Solar Components Corporation
121 Valley Street
Manchester NH
Tel: 603 621 1603

BackHome (see p. 190)

Home Power
PO Box 520
Ashland, OR 97520
Tel: 916 475 3179

Energy Source Directory
Iris Communications
258 East 10th Avenue, Suite E
Eugene, OR, 97401-3
Tel: 503 484 9353

Energy Saver's Handbook for Town and City People,
Massachussetts Audubon Society, 1992,
Rodale Press, PA

*The Independent Home, Living well with Power
from the Sun, Wind and Water*, Michael Potts,
1993, Chelsea Green Publishing, VT

Public Citizen (National Directory of Safe
Energy Organizations)
215 Pennsylvania Ave SE
Washington DC 20003
Tel: 202 546 4996

*The Energy-Efficient Home; The Community Energy
Workbook; Reinventing the Wheels;* from Rocky
Mountain Institute Publications (see *General
organizations* entry)

Now turn to Part Two, The Directory, for more organizations, suppliers and publications

To the average modern city dweller, a tap is where water comes from, the drain is where it goes to and rain is a nuisance. To the average layperson, the fact that a region can have severe flooding and a drought in the same season sounds crazy. We have come to take water for granted to such an extent that even in drought-affected regions it often takes statutory regulations to enforce water-saving measures.

The earth cannot indefinitely cleanse and renew polluted natural elements. We must treasure what little clean water we have left, and make provisions to reduce the pollution we are currently pouring into our waterways from our houses, farms, and offices. And we must conserve water whenever possible. Stormwater is a vital resource and measures should be implemented to prevent its waste. Collection also prevents ecological destruction caused by erosion and flooding. You could con-

struct your own miniature wetlands, or choose less attractive but practical options such as plastic drum reservoirs.

We discuss the quality of home water and suggest testing procedures. In some cases purification techniques are necessary, and this chapter suggests appropriate systems. These systems can even allow you to use rainwater runoff for household water. Water wastage in the home must be checked through water-saving devices and sensible water management. Even dirty household water need not be wasted but can become a valuable resource for irrigation. You may even find it is possible to transform your effluent into a garden with wholewater systems and graywater irrigation!

On an individual level we can all act to conserve water and to keep it clean and safe for our own use and for others. We can act at a local level to lessen the effects of both floods and droughts. Community approaches can bear very positive results, as group involvement and identity is often a powerful vehicle for action.

In populated areas public consciousness of a river as a community asset will encourage people to treat the water with respect. You could transform a neglected riverbank or stream by planting the banks and clearing debris, even creating pleasant spaces to sit. Make it a community or school project to name even the smallest branch of a local river or creek – it is easier to rally support for a named local asset. Organize a stream watch program where volunteers could monitor one or more waterways. Recordings might list, for example, flow and turbidity (the amount of mud in it), chemical analysis, and aquatic life. Your findings should form a database to record changing conditions and help in early detection of problems upstream.

Start a local campaign to establish a site for disposal of toxic household waste. Otherwise old paint, motor oils, batteries, and worse will find their way into the watercourse. Find out about local and nationwide programs to clean up community waters (see Resources p. 85). Encourage local involvement at every level, and ask local businesses to sponsor projects. Make it easier for people under pressure to do the right thing by their environment – most will, if given the chance.

In recent years wholewater systems have increased in popularity. A pond and wetland system consists of a primary pond where aerobic bacteria, plus stands of aquatic plants, break down organic pollutants.

Flowforms aerate the water en route to a secondary pond where higher organisms combine with anaerobic bacteria to destroy algae and remaining pollutants.

WATER MANAGEMENT

Our survival is completely dependent upon a good supply of fresh, clean water. Yet we take water for granted, rarely considering implementing measures which would reduce the burden on an already overstrained resource. It is ironic that we find ourselves surrounded by water almost everywhere we go, but somehow there is never enough.

The management of stormwater is a vital but often ignored factor in planning any new home or development. Stormwater is rainfall that does not soak into the ground or evaporate but flows along the surface of the ground as runoff. As land is developed, managing this water becomes a bigger and bigger concern. Various aspects of building add to the increase in stormwater – destruction of established vegetation, land clearing, filling of natural wetlands, and building impervious surfaces such as driveways and roads. You can make responsible choices to manage stormwater runoff, which will protect the environment and often save money at the same time.

Ponds and wetlands

One way to hold stormwater is to construct temporary detention ponds. These come into use during periods of heavy rainfall, to prevent flooding further downstream. Stormwater can be channeled into these ponds, and an outlet structure allows the water to be released gradually after the storm. Detention ponds normally dry out completely between rainy periods.

Retention ponds, on the other hand, are designed to hold water all the time, with the water level rising during storms. The best include shallow areas where wetland plants flourish and help to remove pollutants. A retention pond should always be shallow enough to allow the wind to keep the water mixed and aerobic throughout the pond; otherwise the bottom may become anoxic and result in nutrient release from the sediment, which could add to nutrient runoff in the next storm.

Sediment gradually settles out of the stormwater runoff in retention ponds. This reduces downstream deposits but means ponds need to be dredged from time to time. A well-designed retention pond

can also serve recreational uses, in all but arid areas where evaporation will occur.

Like the shallow edges of retention ponds, constructed wetlands are useful in removing nutrients and other pollutants, and can be an excellent rainwater manager in wetter parts of the country. In fact, they work so well that they may be used in sewage treatment (see p. 81).

Clayton Express

▲ **Traditional-style pumps can pump up rainwater from a holding tank**

▼ **Constructed wetlands clean up stormwater and prevent flooding**

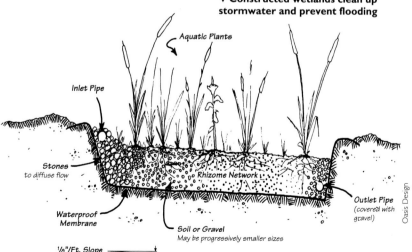

Aquatic Plants

Inlet Pipe

Stones
to diffuse flow

Waterproof
Membrane

Soil or Gravel
May be progressively smaller sizes

Rhizome Network

Outlet Pipe
(covered with gravel)

1/8"/Ft. Slope

Oasis Design

Water storage

However you decide to store your water, your storage system must have sufficient pressure to force the water through your home's pipes. It must also be protected from freezing outside temperatures, and from outside contamination such as animal effluent and agricultural pollution. You may find it necessary to pump water to a freeze-proof or elevated storage site. You can build a storage pond or tank using concrete or a custom made polyvinyl liner. Concrete must be sealed internally to make it watertight. Any tank needs a cover to keep small animals out.

It is possible to build a water storage system using food-grade 55-gallon plastic drums, but you should probably only attempt this if you are a serious back-woods-person!

Collecting stormwater

Even if you have a municipal water supply, or are fortunate enough to have your own spring, creek, or well, you should still collect site rainwater. This has advantages for your household and the environment. Rainwater runoff stored on site prevents additional erosion and flooding problems downstream and allows you to treat the water.

When you are constructing your home try to leave as much of the ground surface as possible undisturbed. If too much land is impacted or covered it may no longer be able to absorb the rainwater that falls on it. Vegetation enhances the ability of soil to absorb rainfall, so protect existing ground cover wherever possible. If trees are destroyed when you develop your site, try to replant disturbed areas as soon as possible to reduce possible erosion.

SIDE VIEW

2 x 6 P.T. BASE
(REST ON GROUND OR BLOCK
AND SHIM AS NEEDED TO LEVEL)

TOP VIEW

2 x 6 P.T. BASE
OR RUNNERS

2'

▲ A home-made storage system uses plastic drums and PVC pipe

BackHome magazine

Environmental Building News

▲ Multiple downspouts take runoff rainwater into a gravel drain

Responsible building

Consider building without conventional gutters as they concentrate rainwater and usually require special measures for management. As an alternative, construct gravel-filled drains at the base of walls. If gutters are installed, include as many downspouts as possible so the flow is distributed over as large an area as possible.

A rooftop rainwater collection can both reduce stormwater runoff and provide useful water for a number of backyard and household uses. Use plastic or fiberglass drums and pipe water to a holding tank.

Filtration systems

Although you must never drink untested water, rainwater can be used in many household applications if you install a filtration system (see p. 77). Sand filters are the most common filters for stored rainwater, but trials using composted leaves are promising. Filtration is mainly to remove sediment, but can also remove pollutants that adhere to sediment particles. Research shows that some compost stormwater filters can remove over 85% of oil, 82% of heavy metals, and between 40-77% of phosphorus.

WATER SAVING

It is a sobering fact that the average American family uses about 263 gallons of water a day. Nor can we assume any longer that water supplies are limitless, as water is a precious resource. We must stop the rapid depletion of our water supplies in order to avoid potentially permanent damage to our ecosystems. Surprisingly, quite small reductions in household consumption could halt these ravages. A low-flow showerhead, for example, can save about 14,000 gallons in a single year for a family of four. Widespread use of such devices would have a real impact on water consumption.

The cost of municipal water is growing, and will continue to rise as water becomes scarcer. If environmental rebuilding is figured into water rates, as it should be, prices will soar. When you save water you also save money.

Water-saving checklist

- Fix all dripping faucets and faulty toilet tanks
- Install a low-flush toilet or a composting model (see p. 75)
- Take short showers rather than baths; in the shower, turn the water off while soaping and shampooing
- Hand wash dishes in a bowl, not under running water
- Use washing machines with full loads only, and on economy cycle whenever possible
- Use rainwater in the garden; mulch beds to conserve moisture
- Wash the car with bucketfuls of water rather than a hose

▼ **Reducing effluent volume helps prevent freshwater contamination**

Water-saving devices

Devices on the market match virtually every home water requirement. Some are economically priced, and all are worth trying. Low-flow showerheads are among the most effective: showers use about 32% of domestic water. With a low-flow showerhead, energy use and costs for heating hot water for showers may drop as much as 50%. A similar fixture for kitchen and bathroom faucets is the low-flow aerator, which reduces water flow by up to 60%.

Most water-using domestic appliances are now available in designs using a minimal amount of water, and washing machines and dishwashers usually have an economy feature.

Consider a waterless toilet if you seriously want to reduce water use (see p. 75). If you retain a traditional style toilet, buy a new appliance conforming to water-saving codes, or decrease the flush water on existing models by installing a toilet dam in the tank. Even a brick in the tank will help.

Fit a toilet sink above the toilet tank. Then you can use clean water in the basin over the tank for handwashing, and reuse the water to flush the toilet. These fit most toilets and are excellent in restricted spaces or for people with limited hand or arm movement.

Ultra Flush

S ince the popularization of the water closet in the 1860s, Americans have happily consigned their natural wastes to the municipal sewage system, or a septic tank, along with gallons of drinking water. A standard toilet uses from 3.5 to 5 gallons with every flush; some use as much as 8 gallons. This waste of precious water, plus the cost and implications of sewage treatment, has prompted a revolution in American toilets.

In 1992 the Comprehensive Energy Policy Act made it illegal to manufacture the traditional water-guzzling toilet. This law mandates a new maximum of 1.6 gallons per flush. There are two main types of ultra low-flush (ULF) toilets; those relying on water pressure in the household pipes to force water into the bowl when you flush, and those relying on gravity.

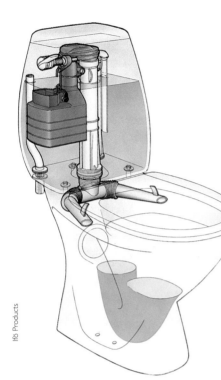

▲ A low-flush toilet with water-conserving tank

Decomposition

The principle behind the composting toilet is the same as in the garden compost heap: aerobic decomposition. Human wastes and other organic matter break down naturally through heat, generated by the compost and a heating element, and oxygen from the ventilating system. The wastes entering the toilet are about 90% water, which is then evaporated as water vapor. Remaining waste material is composted into an inoffensive humus-like substance.

Some models incorporate rotating drums which speed aeration and therefore decomposition. Peat moss and vegetable matter may be added to speed the decomposition process.

Waterless toilets

Some toilets use no water at all. They require no septic system or holding tank, use no chemicals and produce no pollutants. Composting toilets are odorless, easy to maintain, and provide small quantities of composted material which can safely be used in the garden. However, it is not approved or recommended for the vegetable garden.

These toilets have until recently been most popular in sites with no sewage system, no piped water, and seasonal use. Such applications included visitor centers in national parks, or cabins and cottages in remote locations and campsites. Many models are now available for home use.

Most composting toilets use small amounts of electricity for fan-assisted venting and gentle heating. Those specifically designed for remote locations often come with a wind turbine to provide power. Current options include complete self-contained units, or basement composting units with toilet pans situated in bathrooms above. You can buy models which will run on domestic electricity or batteries, or even power-free models.

▲ A basement composting unit is efficient, odorless, and convenient

WATER STANDARDS

In our industrialized country little or no pure water is freely available. Most is contaminated with air pollutants, or with chemicals entering the water system from agricultural run-offs, seepage from landfills, or accidental chemical spills.

Municipal water treatment plants use chlorine to kill bacteria and viruses, but chlorine remains in the water, forming trihalomethanes and even chloroform when it mixes with organic matter. Water may leach lead or asbestos from piping after treatment, or radon gas may be transported in the pipes (see p. 113).

The EPA estimates that 38 million Americans drink water that exceeds the 50 ppb maximum for lead. Clearly the ultimate solution is to remove toxins from the environment so water is again naturally pure for all to drink. In the meantime, however, we must take measures to ensure good water for the household.

Water analysis

If your water comes from a well or spring you may want to have it analyzed. Use a testing laboratory which follows EPA-prescribed testing protocol (see Resources (p. 85). Expect to spend up to $100 for a full analysis, though most will offer different packages.

Water analysis results should express the presence of contaminants in milligrams per liter or parts per million (ppm). Reports should be in writing, and signed. If your water comes from a source on or near farming land you should also test for herbicides and pesticides.

Minimal Tests for Drinking Water

Total hardness • Chloride • Iron • Lead
Sodium •Manganese •Sulfate • Copper
Fluoride • pH • Nitrate
Total dissolved solids • Total alkalinity

Fresh water

One alternative to straight tap water is bottled water, for which there is a huge market. FDA regulations, however, apply only to bottled water transported across state lines; much is treated tapwater. Low-grade bottle plastic can leach toxins into the water, and bacteria can breed in them. Environmental considerations include the transport of this bulky, heavy commodity on the highways, and the wastage of plastic or glass in the bottles.

Various forms of in-home water treatment are described on p. 77. Of these, distillation appears the most environmentally sound, and delivers pure water at less cost over time than bottled water.

Groundwater movement or supply
Intentional input of contamination
Unintentional input of contamination
Freshwater supply

▼ Various common pollutants can contaminate groundwater

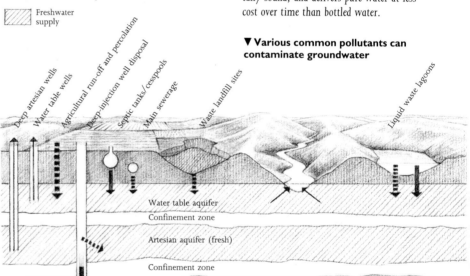

Deep artesian wells
Water table wells
Agricultural run-off and percolation
Deep-injection well disposal
Septic tanks/cesspools
Main sewerage
Waste landfill sites
Liquid waste lagoons

Water table aquifer
Confinement zone
Artesian aquifer (fresh)
Confinement zone
Artesian aquifer (saline)

Natural House Book, Simon & Schuster

Water testing

Before investing in any form of water purification system, test your water. This will show problems and indicate suitable treatments. Some state or county health departments offer limited testing of private water supplies for no charge or a small fee. Contact your health department to see if they offer testing.

Municipal water treatment plants will supply copies of their periodic water analysis; this will tell you, for instance, about chlorine and fluoride treatment, and is a good place to start. Contamination can occur after it has left the water treatment plant, in city water lines or home plumbing, and lead levels are a particular concern. There are home kits for lead testing, or ask a local laboratory.

Carbon filters

Carbon removes impurities from water in two steps: adsorption and mechanical filtration. Adsorption is a natural process in which particles adhere to the surface of a material called an adsorbent. Carbon filters use activated carbon, which has an enormously large surface area. The carbon is normally in a cartridge which will need periodic replacement. Mechanical filtration is a secondary function of the carbon, in which suspended solids are trapped in the carbon bed as water passes through. The longer the water spends passing through the filter, the more impurities will be removed. Block forms of carbon may be more efficient than granules unless your water has a high level of suspended solids which can clog solid carbon.

Because bacteria and viruses thrive in carbon, some manufacturers impregnate their carbon filters with silver, which controls the growth of bacteria. If you choose one of these models, check that silver levels released into the water are below EPA guidelines.

Carbon filters are comparatively low cost, and no water is wasted. But a limited range of impurities is removed, and the filters need periodic replacement.

Three main types of home-based water treatment will remove or reduce different contaminants. Before choosing a system, test your water (see p. 76) to discover which contaminants are present. To be safe, you should never drink untested water.

McCraken Solar

▲ Solar stills are easily erected and inexpensive to maintain

Distillers

In distillation, water is boiled, the steam (water vapor) condensed, and the purified water collected. The water is free from bacteria and viruses, heavy metals such as lead and mercury, and chemicals.

Some volatile organic compounds may remain, so look for a model which incorporates carbon filtration after distillation. This will also prevent any bacterial build-up in the carbon.

Electrically-operated models are widely marketed, but solar-powered "stills" are also available, which will quickly pay for themselves and require no electricity or parts replacement.

▼ Distillation is the simplest method of purification

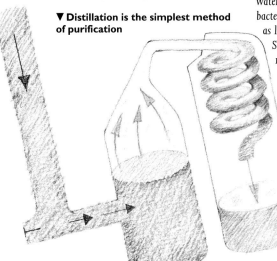

Natural House Book, Simon & Schuster

Reverse osmosis purifiers

There are three filtration steps in this purification system. A mechanical pre-filter, usually made from paper, first removes suspended matter above 5 microns; then the water passes through the primary purifier, the semi-permeable reverse osmosis membrane, which reduces dissolved solids by between 80 and 95%. Finally, after storage, water passes through a carbon filter before discharge at the faucet.

The system requires constant water pressure, and is also temperature-sensitive, so check with the supplier if either of these factors are unusual in your situation. A water softener will be required in hard-water areas.

Although reverse osmosis purifiers offer the purest water, there is an environmental cost. In normal systems, four gallons of water are lost to the drain for every gallon of drinking water produced. The contaminants are not removed from this water, but pass right back into the drain.

Solar still

With a Sunwater™ solar still from McCracken Solar (CA) you can stay on the beach, or wherever you want, indefinitely, while knowing you produce your own completely pure drinking water. Solar panels power the still, which is easy to erect, easy to use, and entirely effective.

Test the water

Use this do it yourself test kit from Environmentally Sound Products (MA) to make sure you are not among the 18% of North Americans drinking water with excessive lead levels. You test at home and send your sample to the EPA-approved lab for a professional analysis.

Biodegradeable tissue

Perfect for use in composting toilets, ask for Liquid Gold rapid-dissolving toilet tissue. It disintegrates speedily without clogging, needs no tissue digesters and keeps systems free-flowing. Sanitation Equipment of Ontario produce ecologically-sound products to help you move to a pollution-free toilet system.

Lowflow showerhead

A lowflow showerhead saves water and energy, and this model from Real Goods catalog (CA) has a satisfyingly vigorous full spray pattern. Also fitted with fingertip flow control, this item exceeds California Energy Commission standards.

Biological toilet

Biological composting toilets are as easy and comfortable to use as regular flush toilets; but they need no water or sewerage, cause neither smell nor pollutiuon, and provide useful compost. Biolet (TX) have several models for permanent or part-time use. Composting Toilet Systems (WA) also provide toilets for a range of situations.

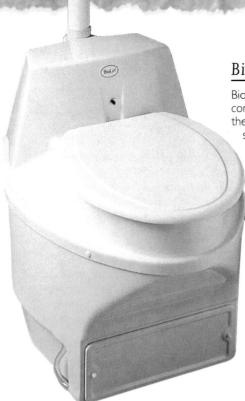

Water pump

The High Lifter from Alternative Energy Engineering (CA) is a light but powerful water pump. Easy to install and maintain, it harnesses the energy from a head of water to drive this water uphill; pistons provide the pumping action and water is the only lubricant.

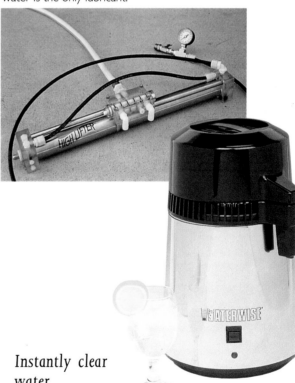

Water purification

The Rain Crystal ™ water purifier gives you laboratory-quality distillation in your own home. It conveniently provides pure drinking water at a fraction the cost of bottled water. Portable and unobtrusive, it is available from Scientific Glass (NM).

Instantly clear water

Waterwise (FL) filters remove up to 99.9% of tap water comtaminants. This tabletop filter combines steam distillation and carbon filtration to produce clean high quality drinking water quickly, wherever you are.

GRAYWATER

Graywater is household waste water that is not flushed down the toilet. It is a valuable source of water for landscape irrigation. First used widely in drought areas, graywater is ideal for garden use at any time – why use water pure enough to drink when plants can tolerate, or even flourish in dirtier water? The best quality graywater sources are showers, tubs, and bathroom sinks, then laundry water. Never collect water that has been used to wash diapers, and avoid graywater from the kitchen because of oily food debris which clogs filters and encourages the spread of bacteria.

Reusing graywater from domestic baths, showers, and laundry rooms is still governed by Health and Safety codes which classify graywater as sewage. This makes its use illegal, but some states apparently ignore this law in drought conditions.

▼ Perforated pipes distribute gray-water to your garden

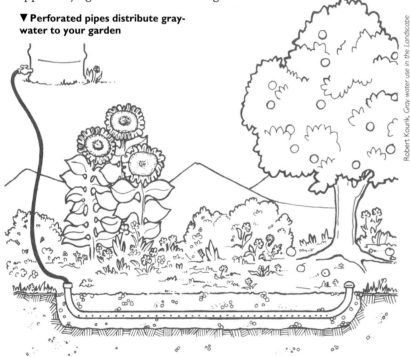

Robert Kourik, *Gray water use in the Landscape*

Distributing graywater

You can distribute graywater through perforated pipes or, in rural areas only, through a sprinkler. Never use graywater in a drip irrigation system, where the water is not used immediately. It would clog the system and cause health risks.

Not all plants like graywater. Soaps and detergents in the water make it alkaline, so acid-loving plants can't tolerate it. Also avoid using it on edible plants except fruit trees or where all edible parts are high above the ground. Garden lawns don't like graywater, the best way to get round this is not to have a lawn!

Plumbing a graywater system

You can pipe graywater straight through an outlet pipe from its source (such as a washing machine outlet pipe) into a holding tank. Otherwise a graywater system needs careful plumbing. Take advice from a qualified plumber and read up about it (see Resources p. 85).

You can use a gravity system if your garden is uphill from your plants, or use a pump. Any pump must run at more than 10 gallons per minute to keep the graywater moving. Graywater must be used immediately to avoid build-up of scum and sediment or bacteria.

Many systems use a surge tank which not only filters incoming water but discharges overflow back into the sewage system. It is vital to prevent a blocked sewer pipe from backflowing into the graywater surge tank. There should also be a device for switching the discharge back to the sewer. This may be necessary during periods of heavy rain.

How safe is graywater?

Properly dispersed graywater is perfectly safe, as the soil's own bacteria can filter and purify dirty water providing a given volume of soil doesn't have to cope with too much at any time. You must never allow it to form puddles or stand, or it will attract mosquitoes, parasites, and possibly even rodents. Improper application of contaminated graywater can spread viruses and bacteria. If you are ever in any doubt about the health of your graywater, return it to the sewage system.

Using graywater means taking full responsibility for a part of the water cycle. If you contaminate your water or misuse it you may get ill, but if you use it properly you conserve water, protect the environment and save money, and your garden will flourish even in drought.

The system

The constructed wetlands in a wholewater system mirror nature by providing aerobic conditions where bacteria and other microorganisms thrive. In a typical system, blackwater from housing (sewage water from toilets) passes through a coarse screen into a series of ponds linked by, or planted with, biological filtering plantbeds. Water from the first pond is enhanced by being channeled through flowforms and then returned to the pond. Semi-treated water then drains into a second pond on a regular cycle. In this pond, remaining biodegradable material is converted into biomass by the activity of microbes. Soluble materials in the waste water are assimilated by plant organisms.

A constructed wetland, where potable water is required as an end product, often features a third pond where further biomass is consumed. The final concentration of suspended solids is low, and water turbidity correspondingly low. This pond supports populations of animals high in the food chain, such as water birds, fish, and beneficial insects. Effluent from the final pond is very low in ammonia and pathogens. Further wetland will reduce the levels of phosphorus in the water.

Such a system transforms polluted effluent into clean, life-giving water. It also provides important wetland habitats to support wildlife populations: These are too often squeezed out of their natural habitats through increasing development of traditional wetlands for agriculture, industry, peat extraction, and housing.

Sewage is conventionally treated by filtration, settling, and chemical means. But you can treat your effluent to obtain clean water and even transform your sewage into a garden. Wholewater systems combine three important elements: ponds, flowforms, and created wetlands. Each of these features is derived from naturally occurring situations, and each has an important role in the cleaning cycle.

When organic matter in sewage enters a pond, huge numbers of aerobic bacteria immediately go to work on it. As they break down the carbon matter, they release mineral nutrients, which support algae. These algae produce, through photosynthesis, the oxygen necessary for further action of the bacteria. Additional oxygenation is introduced by using flowforms (see p. 82) to aerate the water. The third vital element is aquatic planting.

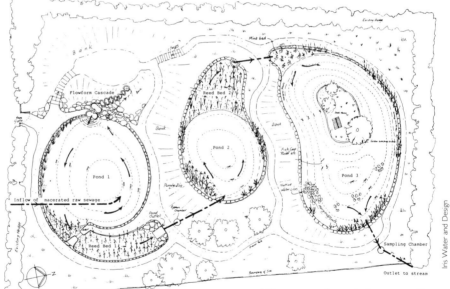

▲ Raw sewage for a whole community can be treated in a "water garden"

Planting wetlands

Wetlands in a wholewater system consist of shallow gravel-lined beds densely planted with chosen aquatic plants. Many wetland plants can transform their surroundings. The common reed is often found in abundance where pollutants are threatening to upset the natural balance in a lake. The roots of reeds offer ideal conditions for

cleaning bacteria to thrive. Yellow iris and water mint exude special antiseptic substances from their roots which help control harmful bacteria.

Other water plants, such as rushes and water hyacinth, have high resistance to toxic chemicals and can even make them less harmful. Such plants can be used as marginal planting in ponds, and in wetlands created between ponds.

FLOWFORMS

Flowforms are functional sculptures often used as part of a system of water treatment. One vital process in water treatment is the exposure of a maximum amount of the water to clean air, to oxygenate it. It is known that water flowing down mountain streams becomes highly aerated, and flowform cascades are designed to reproduce this process in a controlled way. Treated water has enhanced ability to sustain healthy life, therefore benefiting fish and other aquatic life, as well as human users downstream. Flowforms are also visually and aurally pleasing. The rhythmical pulsation of water through a flowform, plus the pleasing sculptural form, bring a soothing atmosphere wherever they are used.

Simon Charter, Ebb and Flow Wholewater Systems

▲ **Use flowforms to enhance a quiet corner of your garden**

Flowform principles

The sculptures are based on forms found in nature, and were developed by John Wilkes, an English sculptor and geometrician. Wilkes worked at the Flow Research Institute at Emerson College (following the work of Schwenck and Schauberger) and studied the archetypal flow patterns in living organisms.

The result of such studies has been the development of the flowform principle of water movement. Water flowing through a shaped vessel is encouraged to take up a figure-eight pattern, and at the same time a "rhythmic pulse". All forms of life, being dependent on water, show water-borne rhythmic patterns, and European studies have shown that rhythmically treated water can better support the organisms necessary for biological water cleaning. In water cleansing systems, these are the aerobic bacteria and micro-organisms living in wetlands and reedbeds.

Flowforms form an integral part of a wholewater cleansing system, combining practical and esthetic functions. They help stabilize effluent to allow aerobic cleaning to take place, and to prevent smell problems. Before installing flowforms as a part of a water treatment system, consult someone with experience in the systems (see Resources p. 85).

Flowform designs

Flowforms are also useful indoors. They maintain air humidity, benefiting both people and plants. They make a healthy addition to most environments, including offices and healthcare facilities, restaurants and schools, as well as homes.

Typically made of softly colored granite or molded concrete, many designs of flowforms are available, ranging from those which cascade down a slope outdoors to self-contained, portable forms which can be housed in a container such as a planter and moved from room to room. You can have designs made to suit the requirements of your own environment.

▼ **Small radial flowforms suit many situations - indoors and out**

Iris Water and Design

▲ **Flowforms link the ponds in wholewater systems**

Ilns Water and Design

Florida House

Born of public worry about use of resources, and potentially draconian planning limitations, the Florida House is a model of sustainable architecture, with emphasis on solar energy and water management.

▶ **Traditional Florida cracker-style architecture is updated with resource-efficient energy and conservation materials and practices**

Early in 1990 a public meeting discussing county water problems was followed by a local referendum threatening to impose a two-year moratorium on all building construction in Sarasota County — symptomatic of a divisive growth/no growth debate. The referendum failed and from that point Michael Holsinger, Sarasota County Extension agent, John Lambie, now President of the Florida House Foundation, and local architect Terry Osborn began planning the Florida House.

Vernacular architecture

By 1992 building work started on a site on the campus of the Sarasota Technical Institute and in April 1994 the house was opened to the public. A cracker-style home typical of oldtime Florida architecture, the Florida House is a look ahead to a time when houses are made with more recycled components, fewer toxic materials, and with plumbing and electrical systems that use less water and energy.

"The emphasis is on environmentally responsible construction without sacrificing livability," says John Lambie. The home offers a total living area of 2,300 square feet. This includes 1,550 square feet of air conditioned space and 825 square feet of outdoor screened porches. It is designed to require only 40-60% of the water used by the average conventional home, and about half the electricity. The house is oriented for best solar exposure without undue heat gain, passive ventilation is via thermal convection, the galvanized metal roof (with ample overhangs) is low-maintenance, covering an R30 insulated and vented attic space. The hot water system is a passive 40-gallon batch-type solar unit and a PV unit on the roof provides back-up electricity to batteries that power low voltage lights and a fan.

Water management

Water conservation features include oversized gutters directing runoff to two 2,800 gallon cisterns at either end of the house. An ozone system treats the stored water, which is kept for irrigation and non-potable household water. Another setup feeds graywater from tubs, sinks, and showers through buried lines to planted areas outside. Landscaping consists of native Florida plants, drought-tolerant species, and edible plants grouped according to their irrigation needs. Mulch is obtained from a local recycler of landscape debris and used liberally on the grounds for water conservation and drought protection.

As well as demonstrating Environmental Landscape Management (ELM), principles of xeriscaping, edible landscaping, micro-irrigation and composting, the grounds demonstrate how to reduce detrimental runoff into the site's groundwater, estuaries and bays.

Project Success

All the conservation measures and equipment promoted by Southwest Florida Water Management have been installed in one house — rainwater cisterns, drought tolerant landscaping, water reuse, plus low-flow plumbing fixtures. The Florida House is a non-profit organization attracting around 5000 visitors a month, and there are plans to work more closely with schools and universities to encourage other groups to build similar houses, and to make the lessons available nationally via the Cooperative Extension Service.

*The Florida House Foundation, 4600 Beneva Road, Sarasota, Florida 34233.
Tel 813 927 2020; fax 813 359 5699*

General organizations

Adopt-a Stream (*stream monitoring*)
PO Box 435, Pittsford, NY 14534-0435
Tel: 716 392 6450

American Rivers (*River saving*)
801 Pennsylvania Avenue SE, Suite 400,
Washington, DC 20003-2167
Tel: 202 547 6900

Clean Water Network
1350 New York Avenue NW, Washington,
DC 20005
Tel: 202 624 9357

Citizens Clearing House for
Hazardous Waste
PO Box 6806, Falls Church, VA 22040
Tel: 703 237 2249

Environmental Defense Fund
257 Park Avenue S, New York, NY10010
Tel: 212 505 2100

Environmental Protection Agency (EPA)
Wetlands, Oceans and Watersheds
401 M Street SW WH-556F,
Washington, DC 20460
Tel 202 260 7166

INFORM (*environmental research and publications*)
120 Wall Street, 16th Floor, New York,
NY 10005-4001
Tel: 212 689 4040

Izaak Walton League of America
1401 Wilson Boulevard, Level B
Arlington, VA 22209-2138
Tel: 703 528 1818

Northwest Environmental Advocates
133 SW Second Avenue,
Portland OR 97204
Tel 503 295 0490

Pollution Probe Foundation
12 Madison Avenue, Toronto, Ontario,
Canada, M5R 2S1
Tel: 416 926 1907

Terrene Institute (*publications*)
1717 K Street NW,
Washington DC 20006
Tel: 202 833 8317

Water standards and testing

American Environmental Laboratories
60 Elm Hill Avenue, Leominster,
MA 01453
Tel: 800 522 0094

National Testing Laboratories
6151 Wilson Mills Road,
Cleveland, OH 44143
Tel: 800 458 3330/ 216 449 2524

Water Test Corporation of America
28 Daniel Plummer Road, Goffstown,
NH 03045
Tel: 800 426 8378

Healthy Environments
PO Box 423, Snowmass, CO 81654
Tel: 303 925 4400

Water testing

Ecology by Design (Audrey Hoodkiss)
1341 Ocean Avenue, Suite 73,
Santa Monica, CA 90401
Tel: 310 394 4146

National Resources Defense Council
40W 20th Street, New Totk, NY 10011
Tel: 212 727 2700 Fax: 212 727 1773

National Small Flows Clearing House
West Virginia University, PO Box 6064
Morgantown WV 26506-6064
Tel: 800 624 8301

Resources Conservation
PO Box 71, Greenwich, CT 06836
Tel: 203 964 0600 Fax: 203 324 9352

Gray water

Robert Kourik (see p. 177)

Wholewater systems and flowforms

Oasis Design
5 San Marcos Trout Club, Santa Barbara,
CA 93015-9726
Tel: 805 967 3222 Fax: 805 967 3229

Iris Water and Design
Langburn Bank, Castleton, Whitby,
N.Yorkshire, YO21 2EU, U.K.
Tel:(+44) 01287 660002
Fax: (+44)01287 660004

Water Research Institute of Blue Hill
Rt 177, PO Box 930,
Blue Hill, MA 04614
Tel: 207 374 2384 Fax: 207 374 2382

Publications

Energy Efficient and Environmental Landscaping
BackHome Books, PO Box 70,
Hendersonville, NC 28793
Tel: 800 992 2546

*Environmental Testing: Where to look, What to Look
for, How to do it, and What Does it Mean?*
Citizen's Clearing House for Hazardous
Waste (see entry)

Water Treatment Handbook
Rodale Product Testing Guide, Northeast
Publishing Inc., PO Box 571, Emmaus, PA
18049

Removal of Radon from Household Water, **also**
Lead and your Drinking Water, EPA booklets
Tel: 202 260 2080

Clean Water Action News
317 Pennsylvania Avenue SE,
Washington, DC 20003
Tel: 202 547 1116

Robert Kourik, *Designing Drip Irrigation for
Every Landscape and all Climates; Gray Water use in
the Landscape* (see p. 177)

Art Ludwig, *Create an Oasis with Greywater,*
from Oasis Designs (see entry)

Now turn to Part Two, The Directory, for more organizations, suppliers and publications

Joss Pearson

What's wrong with electricity? Producing and harnessing electric power has been one of the great wonders of the modern world. At the flick of a switch you can have instant light, power to run almost any equipment, and energy to heat and cool everything from food and drink to whole building interiors. It is an affordable energy source that has brought many benefits to the lifestyles of North Americans. So what's the problem?

Electricity may, in itself, be a wonderful thing but the problems start with how and where it is generated. All conventional methods are environmentally damaging and unsustainable in the longterm, and may be unsafe. Generation using coal and oil exhausts valuable non-renewable fossil fuels, causes atmospheric pollution, and contributes to global warming. Large-scale hydroelectric generation, with its huge dams and reservoirs, destroys wilderness areas, rivers, lakes, and indigenous human and wildlife habitats.

The nuclear power alternative is fading fast because of the associated nightmares of radioactive waste disposal, power plant safety, and security. Although improvements have been made, large fossil-fuel power plants are often grossly inefficient, wasting useful energy as unused heat. Their spread-out regional locations also mean that electricity has to travel many miles from plant to user, often through unsightly grid networks, wasting more electricity in the process.

As well as the environmental problems, newer fears about electricity are being voiced. These concern the effect of electromagnetic fields (EMFs) on the human organism. The potential hazards of continual exposure to EMFs in the home and workplace have not yet been universally accepted. However, some more enlightened authorities have become convinced that preventative action should be taken now. Research by New York Powerlines, for example, has provided convincing evidence to link the increased risk of childhood leukemia to close proximity of their homes to high-voltage powerlines, and in New York State the Education Board has conducted a study of EMFs in state schools. In Sweden new laws are shortly to be implemented along with general consumer guidance about EMFs. Although professional advisory services and testing and protection measures are becoming increasingly available, more research and recognition is urgently needed.

You can move from heavy reliance on an insane electricity supply system to living lightly and responsibly. This chapter will show you how to gain all the benefits of electricity and do more to protect the environment and your health. As described in Chapter Two (Soft Energy), the dream of severing all ties with the power company to live independently has become a reality. You could join thousands of North Americans and be the next to go "off the grid", if you switch to using the modern technology available to produce electricity via freely available sun, wind, and water.

Whatever your power source, conserving electricity is vital. Today, a new generation of energy-efficient equipment, low-voltage lights and appliances that will run off soft energy supplies, plus sensitive and intelligent controls, are available to help you, along with protection measures. Together, these conserving and protective technologies allow you to live with "sane electrics".

In the ideal home environment low-energy lighting is used throughout. In this earth-built house it complements unfinished-style interior decoration; the walls are left uncovered to show the beautiful colors of the natural rammed earth, and floor tiles are made from mixed earth and cement. Appliances throughout the home are low-voltage, and the overall feeling is harmonious, mellow, and completely "sane".

CONTROL SYSTEMS

Keeping the home environment comfortable and balanced is a very important part of any home design. Central heating and air-conditioning have led people to expect comfortable indoor temperatures and levels of humidity in every room of the house regardless of weather conditions and season. But this is good neither for health nor energy-efficiency. You need more variety to keep body and mind vital and stimulated. Lisa Heschong, author of *Thermal Delight in Architecture*, summed up the issue: "Our nervous system is much more attuned to noticing change in the environment than to noticing steady states ... uniformity is extremely unnatural." Moreover, she feels thermally neutral environments design out the potential for "sensuality, cultural roles and symbolism" that make up the pleasures of thermal delight.

High-tech or low-tech?

Today, there are two main approaches to controlling your home environment. One is high-tech and relies on mechanical and artificial methods. This usually involves electrical pumps, fans, switches, sensors, and computer controls. The equipment uses a high level of utility power (unless run by soft energy sources), but the sensitive controls help to save energy overall. However, if high-tech systems go wrong they will need specialist repair and maintenance.

The older low-tech approach uses passive and "natural" controls. Although it is simpler, easier to maintain, and needs no extra energy, it does rely on the occupants' participation in opening and closing windows, doors, shutters, blinds, and vents to control heating and cooling. Indoor plants, bushes, climbers, trees, and water are other natural and traditional ways to moderate temperature and humidity.

A home can be designed to be basically self-controlling using thermodynamic principles such as thermal chimneys (p. 64), thermal walls (p. 62) and "breathing walls" (p. 36). The best strategy is to use low-tech natural controls first, and supplement these with electrical and mechanical controls only when absolutely necessary. For selective use you may be able to use smaller high tech mechanical controls which use less energy. They will also be less costly to repair and replace.

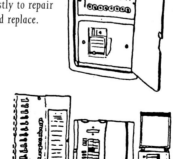

Jade Mountain

▲ **Include a fuse or breaker box as a safety link for your system**

Changing lifestyles

Before modern thermal systems were used, our forebears (and people today in the Third World) would control their immediate environment by altering their habits and moving with daily and seasonal cycles.

In winter, fewer rooms would be used – eating, cooking, and sleeping often all took place in the one room with a stove. In summer, they would wake and work early in the cool of the day and sleep through the hottest part or sit in the shade of trees, ramadas, courtyards, and verandahs to catch the breeze. Modern lifestyles and work patterns make it more difficult to adapt to daily and seasonal changes in this way. Controlling the home environment has gradually passed from the actions of the occupants to the programmed responses of machines. Control systems are getting ever more complex and specialized as they become high tech and computerized.

The interactive home

In this age of information technology (IT), sophisticated computer-controlled homes will become commonplace. Home computers will channel information allowing consumers to monitor and control almost every device in the home.

All electrical equipment – TV (satellite and cable), video, phone, answering machine, fax, will be networked. So too will items such as music systems, security and safety systems, smoke and pollution detectors, kitchen appliances plus all the home's heating, lighting, and air-conditioning. Single multi-wire cables running between every room will not only distribute AC and DC current, they will carry control data to and from equipment micro-chips and sensors, and receive radio and TV signals. Special sockets will allow you to plug in any equipment in any room.

Apart from controlling the home when you are there, interactive systems also let you do so when you are away. If you are going to be home late, for instance, you can tell the house to keep the heating on or record a TV program. You can program each part of the system to suit your tastes and needs to turn lights on when you enter a room and turn them off when you leave, or adjust lighting levels to your personal preferences. You can even use voice commands for selective changes.

Added to this, interactive homes are ideal for home offices since they provide for an advanced integration of business equipment and communication systems both inside and outside the home.

Although an interactive system may cost a little more at the beginning, the higher efficiency of the system will save significantly on electricity. If installed as part of a new house, any extra costs should largely be absorbed.

G P Publishing Inc 1984

Even relatively low-tech homes already include basic controls such as thermostats (to regulate room temperatures) and a time clock (set to switch the system on and off). For energy conservation a basic heating system should include several thermostats, preferably in each room and/or on individual radiators. You must also have a thermostat on your hot water tank, either to turn off the source of heat or to direct the heat elsewhere when the water reaches the required temperature.

To achieve the most sensitive and conserving system, it is worth investing in a mini-computer, programmed to control all heating and cooling systems and maintain indoor temperature and relative humidity at comfortable levels. If you are happy with high-tech solutions, you could even create a resource-efficient computer controlled environment.

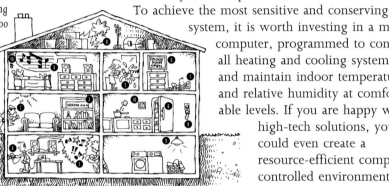

▲ **Interactive systems can control every room in your home**

Soft energy system controls

12 or 24 volt PV (photovoltaic) system controls usually feature a "charge controller" and "meter set". The charge controller regulates the flow of electricity from the PV array to the battery bank. When the battery bank is low the charge controller feeds all the electricity into the batteries. When the batteries are fully charged, the charge controller stops and redirects the supply. At night it prevents reverse flow current from the batteries to the PV array. The meter set is a digital volt/ammeter with an LED readout. It monitors battery voltage, array current, and open circuit array current. It also detects short circuits and troubleshoots the system.

▼ **An inverter can convert DC energy into AC for domestic use**

For a larger PV system, it is best to invest in a fully integrated control system which combines a charge controller, grid fused disconnect (to protect overcurrent to PV array), batteries, inverter and loads plus optional lightning protection, battery temperature compensation, and various system controls and alarms. It all comes in one compact metal box with clearly labeled termination points for quick and easy installation. (Also see Chapter Two - Soft Energy).

Fowler Solar Electric, Inc

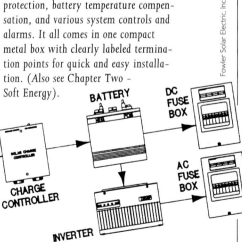

STOVES

Your choice of kitchen equipment will depend on your lifestyle. Before deciding on a specific type of stove or refrigerator, take a step back and look at your dietary habits. Perhaps these could be improved? Eating more fresh, locally-produced and organically-grown produce is good for you and good for the environment. Raw and lightly cooked foods such as salads, fruit, nuts, and lightly steamed vegetables are healthy and save time and energy. A change to a healthier lifetyle can mean less required storage for frozen foods and more for fresh foods and bottled or canned goods. It can also mean you do not need a large stove, and, except in the hottest climates, a small refrigerator/freezer will probably do fine (see also p. 150). Ideally there should be space in all houses for a good-sized cool cupboard, pantry, and/or cellar.

Villager Sun Ovens, Burns-Milwaukee Inc.

▲ **Size doesn't matter where solar cookers are concerned!**

▼ **Hayboxes provide a simple and traditional method of slow cooking**

Stoves

Of all the choices you make when buying a stove, the most important is choice of fuel. As currently generated, electricity produces three times as much CO_2 as natural gas, for the same amount of heat. Natural gas (methane) is the better environmental choice of fossil fuels and figures suggest that switching from an electric stove to gas would save on average 360kg of CO_2 a year. If there is no municipal gas supply, you can use bottled propane or butane as cooking fuel (and see p. 57 for European tile ovens).

If you're using electricity, use efficient cooking methods: a pressure cooker to reduce cooking time; a steamer with two or three tiers, cooking over only one element; using lids on pots and pans, and cooking more than one item at a time in the oven. When buying a new electric stove, ask for electricity consumption figures and avoid "pyrolytic" oven cleaning which uses huge amounts of electricity to superheat the oven to burn off grease and dirt.

Induction cooktops

Save electricity by using an induction cooktop — a smooth-surface top with no exposed electric elements. Cookware is heated as soon as it is placed on the cooktop which cools down and turns off immediately the pots are taken off. The surrounding cooktop stays cool to the touch and will not generate heat if it is turned on accidentally with no cookware on top. Cookware, however, must be made of a magnetic metal such as stainless steel, cast iron, or porcelain-on-steel.

Solar cookers

Popular in the Third World for cooking and pasteurizing water, it is worth making or buying a solar cooker if you live in an area with plenty of sun. All you need is a simple box or shaped stand made of bendable, sturdy, shiny material (sometimes with a glass top). To cook food or boil water, use a black covered pot and rest it on a rope coil, and put this all inside a clear plastic bag in the solar cooker.

Hayboxes and pit ovens

Another traditional device is the haybox, ideal for stews, casseroles, vegetable dishes, and puddings. These are first brought to the boil on another source of heat, then placed in their cooking pots into the thickly insulated box. Cooking is slow and continuous for hours. You can also use a hay box as a cooler.

Even older is the pit oven in which a fire is lit, extinguished when hot, and raked out. Food, typically wrapped in leaves, is placed in the pit, covered with earth, and left for several hours to cook gently. Variations on these two traditional ovens exist in most countries worldwide.

Refrigerators

The US Department of Energy estimates that a typical household devotes 15% of its energy budget to refrigeration and freezing of food. But a new generation of high-efficiency and environment-friendly appliances are available. When buying your next refrigerator or freezer, first consider if you can use a smaller-capacity model than you have at present. Then, check its energy consumption or rating (in Canada look for the lowest EnerGuide number for its size). A very efficient 16 cu. ft. capacity model can consume as little as 16 KWH per month, compared with about 110 KWH for a conventional refrigerator. Ask if the insulation has an R-value rating (R 40 is good) and make sure that insulation and refrigerant are CFC-free.

Today, most new refrigerators have more durable parts than formerly, and they are also recyclable. Some models are available in 12 and 24V DC (for use with solar power), and 120 and 240V AC. Although high-efficiency appliances may initially cost more, they will be cheaper over a ten-year period and are worth the extra investment.

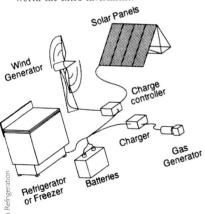

Low Keep Refrigeration

▲ **Combination power sources will run most appliances**

▶ **Equip your kitchen with low-energy, high-efficiency equipment**

David Pearson

Before you invest in equipment to supply soft energy to your home decide how you will use this power. Soft energy sources – photovoltaics, wind, water – supply direct current (DC) through a charge controller to batteries, where it is stored. The power can be used as direct current or, through an inverter, as alternating current (AC).

You may prefer to use DC because even an efficient inverter loses some power in the conversion, or use a combination of both AC and DC. It is common to find systems where DC power from the batteries is used to run lighting, refrigerator, and water pump, while 120V AC from the inverter runs more power-hungry appliances.

▲ **Convert DC to AC via an inverter for any power-hungry appliances**

Using electricity

The consumption of electricity in a home varies according to size, occupation, and lifestyle. *A well-insulated house designed to use solar gain will require little electricity consumption. Electricity is only needed for those appliances modern society has come to find indispensable: washing machines, refrigerators, vacuum cleaners, music systems, computers, and power tools.*

Since the trend towards alternative, off-grid power has grown, so has the development of electrically-powered low voltage equipment. From answering machines to televisions, you can run most appliances on low-voltage electricity. *An increasing range can be run on 12 or 24V DC, and current catalogs include ceiling fans, lighting, refrigerators and freezers, answering machines, shavers, hairdryers, blenders, washing machine, air conditioning units, even TVs, CD players, and VCRs.*

However, most of the appliances which run on 12V DC were originally developed for the RV market, and some products are poorly designed with limited life spans. Choose low-voltage products carefully, especially if they are for long-term use in the home.

▼ **Many 12V DC appliances were originally developed for RVs**

AC/DC combinations

The scale of an installation usually dictates whether you collect and store your power in a 12 or 24V system. You need to work out your total power use in watt-hours. If your needs exceed about 2,000 watt-hours per day, you probably need a 24V system; if less, 12V will do. A higher voltage system is most cost-efficient: it is easier to transmit the electricity, wires can be smaller, and a single charge controller (which controls the flow of power into the batteries) can deal with a higher input wattage. The 12V option is sometimes called "automotive voltage" because of its association with recreational vehicles (RVs). Your choice of equipment will also depend on whether you are wiring your home from scratch or adapting a traditional, on-grid, 120V AC circuitry.

There are good reasons for retaining AC for lighting. Although perfectly good 12V and 24V lights are available, there is a far wider selection of low-energy AC lights, making them cheaper both to install and use. Use lighting efficiently, for example, rather than having a central light strong enough to light the whole room, go for central room lights just strong enough to get by, with more powerful spot lighting where it is actually needed — for reading or working.

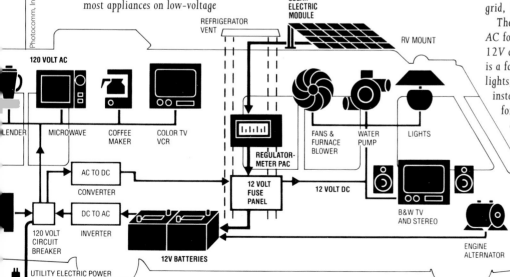

The problem

EMFs are generated by electrical appliances, and most of us are frequently exposed to them in our daily lives. The electrical field of any appliance or installation is measured in volts per meter (V/m), and is readily grounded or earthed. The remaining magnetic field, expressed in milligauss (mG), can penetrate walls and even solid concrete partitions. EMFs have the linear characteristics many of us remember from school experiments with magnets and iron filings. Frequent exposure to strengths of over 1 mG is potentially harmful.

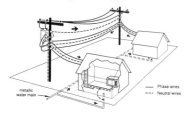

EMF protection

EMFs can pass through walls and floors, but they do not build up, nor can they be transferred to another object. Heat and light are no indication of an EMF, but computers, personal stereos, microwave ovens, dishwashers, and hairdryers are known to produce high EMF readings. Once you know where your EMF high-spots are, you can take precautions.

Companies specializing in EMF testing assert that house-generated fields can usually be corrected by an electrician with little effort and cost. One claims that in 10% of homes with 3.7 mG readings and 1% of homes with up to 19 mG readings, the problem lies with faulty wiring, grounding problems, unbalanced circuits or stray currents on water and gas pipes. EMFs can be reduced by incorporating shielded wiring or even using special supply demand switches so that electrical current is only present when needed.

Recent research and publicity suggest that proximity to electrical cables, and hence to electromagnetic fields (EMFs), can cause serious illness. It is clear that relatively short exposure times even to quite weak EMFs fields cause physical stress, indicated by the release of stress hormones such as cortisone. One of the many effects of stress is reduced immunity, which can allow ever-present viruses and free radicals in the body to develop into illnesses. It has been suggested that proximity to electrical cables can lead to cancers, especially in children. In other cases, stress will lead to headaches, allergies, depression, relationship problems, and even suicide. Once we are aware of the problem, we can identify the EMFs which may be harmful to health, and lessen the risk.

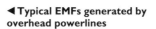

◄ **Typical EMFs generated by overhead powerlines**

► **EMFs from an unshielded VDU (top) and a shielded unit**

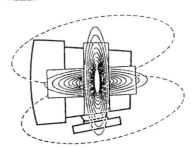

Detecting EMFs

You can get a rough idea of the presence of EMFs by carrying a cheap transistor radio (expensive ones have filters) through the house. Any static picked up by the radio indicates a good possibility of high fields.

More reliable measurement is made using a gaussmeter — you can either hire one to use yourself or employ a testing company. A gaussmeter consists of a sensor and meter. The sensor detects an electromagnetic field and sends an impulse to the meter, which produces a reading. EMFs are site specific: you can only determine your EMF exposure by actually testing in the home.

If you decide to have your home professionally tested, contact the National Electromagnetic Field Technicians Association (see Resources p. 97). Your local electric utility company can also measure your EMF levels. When testing, be sure to have everything switched on, as at peak usage times.

If you buy your own gaussmeter make sure it is made for use in North America where the power distribution network is 60 Hertz. (European meters will be calibrated for 50 Hertz.) Most meters measure only a single axis, showing the field in one direction at a time. If you choose this type of meter remember to turn the meter probe in all directions. Some multi-axis meters are available.

SANE ELECTRICS

No sweat biking

Join the electric vehicle revolution now with an easily-installed ZAP (Zero Air Pollution) electric power assist. Lightweight permanent magnet motors support gel-cell rechargeable batteries. Recharge the batteries by using your bike as an exercise trainer, or plug in to a solar charger. Available from the Real Goods catalog (CA).

PV load controls

Whatever your energy source, your control system needs to be perfectly reliable. Specialty Concepts (CA) design and produce a comprehensive range of PV controls, ensuring effective charge control and sophisticated system monitoring and load control.

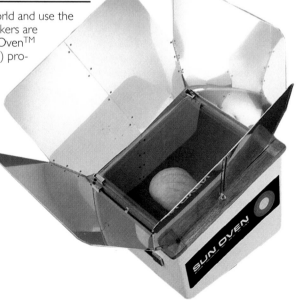

Solar cooking

Take a tip from from the Third World and use the sun to cook your food — solar cookers are ideal for many situations. This Sun Oven™ from Ethel and Ken Farnsworth (ID) provides cheap, clean, and efficient cooking, is rugged and safe, and cooks entirely with energy from the sun.

Counter low-level radiation

Cook's Amazing Diodes, from Ener-g-Polari-t products (AZ) help combat electromagnetic radiations from home and office appliances. Put them in your pocket, or place diodes on electrical appliances to counter harmful energies. These little appliances offer a simple solution to a common health hazard.

Portable solar panels

Even used to power portable computers on research projects in the hinterlands of Antarctica, KIS solar panels really can provide you with efficient solar power any place. But these systems aren't only for Arctic explorers – Keep it Simple Systems (MT) produce a wide range of solar devices so you can harness energy straight from the sun. And their range keeps expanding all the time so you really can just "plug and play"!

Low-energy refrigeration

Probably the world's most efficient refrigerator, the Sun Frost (CA) uses high quality insulation plus an efficient passive cooling system. Ideal for PV power sources, it will also significantly reduce energy consumption in a home using utility power.

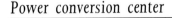

Power conversion center

Ask your local supplier for this advanced inverter, from Trace Engineering (WA). With three microprocessors and bi-directional power topology, this inverter combines features that previously existed only in separate products. It delivers sine wave power without compromise, in all conditions.

Save power, save money

Fit your refrigerator or washer with a GreenPlug from Green Technologies (CO), and save energy and money. These small electronic devices use built-in computer circuitry to reduce electricity usage and prevent energy waste. Thoroughly tested, GreenPlugs are highly recommended for all older appliances.

John Schaeffer and Real Goods

From small beginnings – battery-powered lightbulbs – John Schaeffer has gone on to inspire Americans about the benefits of "off the grid" electricity and renewable energy, and built a multi-million dollar business.

▶ **The interior of a Real Goods store in California - selling energy-saving products**

After graduating from Berkeley in 1971, John Schaeffer moved up to Mendocino County and became an "urban refugee". Some friends of his had bought 290 acres there and he lived in a remote commune where everyone built their own houses, drilled wells, and hiked in with everything. One day, he bought some 12-volt light bulbs in a nearby town, and rigged up a little ceiling fixture, using his car bettery to power the lights. Suddenly, Schaeffer was the "rebel" with light and television in an electricity-free commune.

From 12-volt to $12 million

By 1978, John had opened a store in Willets in N. California selling wood-stoves, gardening supplies, chicken wire, and alternative energy supplies. This grew into a second store in Ukiah and a third in Santa Rosa. They proved extremely successful and turned over around $2 million in the first few years. After he sold out to a partner and went to live in Indonesia, the business went bankrupt. 1986 saw John's return to rescue the business, and he invested his last $3,000 in relaunching the company with a mailing list and a basic 16-page catalog. Sales picked up and, today, Real Goods has

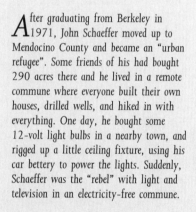

become one of the greatest success stories in the renewable energy field with a team of over 120 staff and annual sales of $12 million.

Business and Education

In addition to the Real Goods' Catalog whose solar products have helped to take 20,000 homes "off the grid" over the years, the company has a strong educational emphasis. Publications include **Real Goods News** and the **Solar Living Sourcebook**. On a recent organized Tour of Independent Homes, 10,000 people visited homes with solar appliances supplied by Real Goods to see, first hand, what living independently was all about. In an interview for E Magazine, Schaeffer said: "Our idea was to get a house in every region so people could travel a few hours at most, and walk into one of these homes." The aim is to select about 100 homes countrywide as permanent Real Goods' demonstration homes. One important part of the business is the Institute of Independent Living. Here, "hands on" workshops held in several States help people plan and assemble renewable energy systems suited to their individual needs and their specific home environment.

New Directions

The recently developed Real Goods' Snowbelt Energy Center has heralded a new venture to develop ten regional renewable energy centers throughout the country in the next four years. Perhaps the most exciting project of all is Real Goods' new headquarters and sustainable design center on a 12 acre site at Hopland, California. Schaeffer hopes will make Hopland the "sustainable capital of California". Visitors are welcomed to the center to take part in its activities and to see the organic orchard and garden, and biological sewage treatment facility They can travel by electric shuttle bus to the local wineries and even stay on in a "solar bed and breakfast".

With all his success, however, Schaeffer still retains his 70s rebel quality. "Send our sons to fight for oil, or let the sun give us energy at home?" was the catalog slogan printed at the time of the Gulf War. "Everyone told us we were crazy to come out criticizing the war," recalls Schaeffer," yet it was one of the most successful catalogs we've ever had."

For more information contact: Real Goods, 966 Mazzoni St., Ukiah, CA 95482-3471. Tel: 800 762 7325

General organizations

American Council for an
Energy-Efficient Economy
1001 Connecticut Avenue, NW 535,
Washington, DC 20036
Tel: 202 429 8873

American Solar Energy Society
2400 Central Avenue, Suite G1,
Boulder CO 80301
Tel: 303 443 3130

Iowa State University of Science and
Technology Electric Power Research Center
111 Coover Hall, Ames, IO 50011-1045
Tel: 515 294 8057 Fax: 515 294 8432

E Source
1033 Walnut, Boulder, CO 80302
Tel: 303 440 8500 Fax: 303 440 8502

National Center for Appropriate
Technology
PO Box 2525, Butte, MT 59702
Tel: 406 494 4572

National Electromagnetic Field Testing
Association (NEFTA)
628-B Library Place, Evanston, IL 60201
Tel: 708 475 3696

The Rocky Mountain Institute
1739 Snowmass Creek Road,
Old Snowmass, CO 81654
Tel: 303 970 3851 Fax: 303 970 3420

Solar Technology Institute
PO Box 1115, Carbondale, CO 81623
Tel: 303 963 0715

EPA Public Information Center
820 Quincy Street North West
Washington DC 20011
Tel: 202 829 3535

Worldwatch Institute
1776 Massachusetts Avenue, NW,
Washington DC 20036
Tel: 202 452 1999

State Energy Offices

Alabama	800 392 8098
Alaska	800 478 4636
Arizona	800 352 5499
Arkansas	501 682 1370
California	800 772 3300
Colorado	800 632 6662
Connecticut	203 566 2800
Delaware	800 282 8616
District of Columbia	202 727 1800
Florida	904 488 6764
Georgia	404 656 5176
Hawaii	808 548 4150
Idaho	800 334 7283
Illinois	217 785 2800
Indiana	800 382 4631
Iowa	515 281 5145
Kansas	800 662 0027
Kentucky	502 781 7653
Louisiana	504 342 4594
Maine	207 289 6000
Maryland	301 974 3751
Massachusetts	617 727 4732
Michigan	800 292 9555
Minnesota	800 652 9747
Mississippi	800 222 8311
Missouri	800 334 6946
Montana	406 444 6697
Nebraska	402 471 2867
Nevada	702 687 4990
New Hampshire	800 852 3466
New Jersey	800 492 4242
New Mexico	505 827 5950
New York	800 342 3722
North Carolina	800 662 7131
North Dakota	800 247 1493
Ohio	800 282 0880
Oklahoma	405 521 3173
Oregon	800 221 8035
Pennsylvania	800 692 7312
Rhode Island	800 828 5477
South Carolina	800 851 8899
South Dakota	605 773 3603
Tennessee	800 342 1340
Texas	800 643 7283
Utah	800 662 3633
Vermont	800 642 3281
Virginia	800 552 3831
Washington	800 926 9731
West Virginia	800 642 9012
Wisconsin	608 266 8234
Wyoming	307 777 6079

Publications

Appropriate Technology News, Jade Mountain, PO
Box 4616, Boulder, CO 80306-4616

Electromagnetic Fields in Your Environment
EPA Public Information Center (see entry)

EMF Resource Directory
PO Box 1799, Grand Central Station, New
York 10763 Tel: 212 517 2800.

Energy Answers
PO Box 24, Lake Bluff, IL 60044
Tel: 800 776 6761

Home Energy Magazine
2124 Kittredge, Suite 95, Berkeley,
CA 94704

Home Power Journal
PO Box 520, Ashland, OR 97520
Tel: 916 475 3179

Integral Energy News
Sierra Solar Systems, 109 Argall Way,
Nevada City, CA 95959
Tel: 800 517 6527 Fax: 916 265 6151

Solar Living Sourcebook,
Real Goods (see p. 96)

The Smart Kitchen, David Goldbeck, 1989,
Ceres Press, Woodstock, NY

Thermal Delight in Architecture, Lisa
Heschong,1980, M.I.T. Press

Rodney Girdlestone and David Cowan, *Safe
as Houses? Ill-health and Electro-stress in the Home*,
Gateway Books, 1994

*Reinventing the Wheels; The Energy-Efficient Home;
The community Energy Workbook*; all from Rocky
Mountain Institute publications (see entry)

Reducing Radon Risks, booklet free from EPA
Public Information Center (see entry)

Now turn to Part Two, The Directory, for more organizations, suppliers and publications

People are affected by the intensity of light which changes during the day and by the season. Sunlight and artificial light not only vary in strength, they also can be direct, reflected, or diffused. Sunlight is direct when it shines through a window – when it can scorch plants, fade fabrics and cause glare – and reflected when it bounces off indoor or outdoor surfaces; it is diffused when it passes through net drapes, frosted glass, or screens. Bear this in mind when planning the use of artificial lighting.

Changes in light intensity are important to our human rhythms, and have specific effects on our health and well being. For example, the hormone melatonin, secreted by the pineal gland in the brain during darkness or dim light, causes sleepiness; when it is overproduced through excessive exposure to dim lighting, it can indicate the clinical condition called Seasonal Affective Disorder (SAD syndrome).

Any healthy home should use direct sunlight as much as possible, and add artificial lighting in ways which complement the use of each room and add to the overall design. Vary the intensity and quality of light according to the needs of each type of space in the house. Direct lighting is best used for kitchens, offices, workrooms, stairs, and places where bright light is needed for safety. In rooms where a more relaxed and comfortable atmosphere is required, such as living rooms, reflected and diffused lighting is more appropriate. Visible light is made up of a spectrum of lights of different colors; artificial lighting varies in its ability to provide

Jack Wimpenis Stained Glass

light on the same color ranges (wavelengths). An incandescent or tungsten-filament lamp is deficient in blue wavelengths, but rich in red and yellow. Under lighting of this sort, cool colors like blues will lose their brilliance and purity but warm colors will become richer and seem more intense. Fluorescent lighting, however, is deficient in the warmer end of the spectrum and casts a cooler, more blue-green light, although you can offset this by using warm-white tubes. Look for daylight or full spectrum fluorescent tubes which were first developed for workplaces but are now widely available for home use. It is particularly important to use full spectrum lighting if you work at home (see p. 152) or spend long hours indoors.

You can create specific moods in areas of your house through your choice of lighting. Consider the effects of different types of light on the colors you choose for each room, noting the direction and intensity of daylight. Be aware of the effect color has on human behavior and mood, and reflect on the possible effects of different color schemes on members of the family (see p. 106). Vary lighting effects through careful positioning, and via devices such as stained glass shades.

This chapter provides advice about making the most of daylight, and the best choices for artificial lighting throughout your house. Whatever your lighting needs, there are always low-energy options (p. 104) so choose energy-efficient lighting every time, and save money and global resources.

This bathroom, designed by Paul Bierman-Lytle, shows how light can be used to maximize the effect of space. Clever use of mirrors ensures that all available light coming through the windows from outside is reflected back indoors, and carefully positioned lighting complements the direct and reflected light. Subtle fittings enhance the organic shapes and materials in this beautiful, elegant, and truly natural room.

NATURAL LIGHTING

atural outdoor light varies in intensity and quality, both on a daily basis from day to night, and from season to season. Weather patterns and the location of your home also make a difference.

Direct sunlight shining straight through a window is intense, casting shadows and causing glare. Reflected light is softer light bouncing off surfaces outside and inside a room. Diffused light has passed through a filter such as blinds, colored glass, or screens. It is very soft and almost shadowless.

Use direct lighting for kitchens, offices, workrooms and sunspaces, particularly where bright light is essential for safety. Direct light is needed for growing conditions for many plants, but there are limitations: intense sunlight is too hot for many plants, so ensure adequate shady protection; other plants only flourish in shade or softer light.

Use reflected and diffused lighting in living rooms and bed and bathrooms, with focal points of direct lighting where required. Never light a large room with a central overhead light, but use spotlights and uplights of differing intensity.

▲ **Position windows carefully to make the most of available daylight**

▶ **Homes in areas of intense sunlight should rely largely on reflected light**

Designing for light

Daylight is a crucial feature of any natural home (see p. 101) and you can adapt yours to rely only minimally on artificial light. Homes in temperate areas may be daylight-deficient, while those in hotter tropical areas may suffer from too much intense light. Either way, you can ease the situation. There are some simple ways to maximize light without major building work. Increase penetration of natural light by using light-colored surfaces outside windows so more available light is reflected indoors - paint garden walls in light colors, install a pond, lay light paving. Prune any shrubs or trees that block out light, and, indoors, use light colors for walls and floors, and furnishings. Mirrors are useful devices to increase the background level of light in a room.

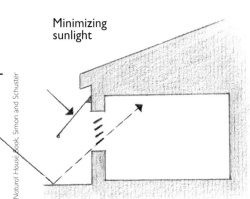

Minimizing sunlight

Minimizing glare

If you are building or retrofitting, consider adapting your existing windows or installing new ones to admit more daylight. Windows high in the walls, or rooflights, admit sunlight to the back of rooms. Or add a sunspace (see p. 61). If you do add new windows, make sure they add light where you want it — for example, morning sun is a welcome addition to any kitchen or bedroom, and late afternoon sun ideal for a living area.

If you live in an area of intense sunlight, you may need to add shading and anti-glare devices around the edge of your home (see p. 64). Awnings and shutters are useful, and plant shade-giving trees or climbers. You could also minimize the window area on the sunny side of the house, and avoid direct light but shade the windows with gauzy drapes or blinds to increase the diffused and reflected light in the house.

Color Rendering Index

The measure of brightness in light is the lumen; the effect of a light source on the color appearance of an object is indicated by the Color Rendering Index (C.R.I.), ranging from 0 to 100. Sunlight is rated 100 on the C.R.I., and any value above 90 is considered full spectrum lighting. Much indoor lighting is bright, but has unbalanced spectral energy distribution. For example, cool white and warm white standard fluorescent lights have lower proportions of violet and blue wavelengths than full spectrum lights, and substantially less red wavelengths, while peaking in yellow. This type of lighting distorts colors, enhances glare and often leads to eyestrain.

Light Source	C.R.I.
Natural daylight	100
Cool white Fluorescent	62
Warm white Fluorescent	56

Lack of sunlight

People who spend a great deal of time in artificial lighting, which does not emit the same balance of colors as sunlight, are depriving themselves of nourishment. Although they can see sufficiently well they may soon start to suffer from a deficiency of natural light. This can lead to a condition known as Seasonal Affective Disorder (SAD syndrome) brought on by lack of sunlight during winter. Poor quality lighting can have serious health consequences. In children, symptoms of inadequate lighting can be similar to those of malnutrition — including poor growth and low learning ability, plus a high level of dental cavities. The UV in both sunlight and full spectrum lighting promotes production of vitamin D, which aids calcium absorption, vital to children and important for women during pregnancy and at menopause.

L ight is electromagnetic radiation of the visible spectrum. The visible spectrum contains different wavelength bands, and our eyes perceive each of these wavelengths as different colors. The energy of sunlight produces all the wavelengths of color, from ultraviolet through the visible spectrum (violet, blue, green, yellow, orange, red) to infrared, in a roughly equal distribution. Once most people worked outdoors in natural light; now many of us work inside, under artificial lighting, and that light needs to reproduce real daylight as faithfully as possible, in order for us to avoid a host of problems.

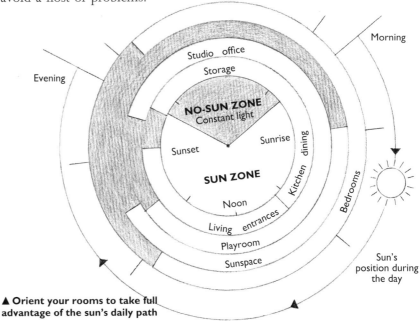

▲ Orient your rooms to take full advantage of the sun's daily path

Natural House Book, Simon and Schuster

Full spectrum lighting

Full spectrum lighting contains the same balance of colors as natural sunlight, and can lift winter depression and improve general health; where it has been installed in factories and other workplaces it has typically reduced sick leave by one-third. Where it is used in schools, pupils suffer less from lethargy and tiredness, and seem able to concentrate for longer periods. In plants it promotes growth and the production of flowers and fruit; in animals it boosts health and fertility.

Full spectrum lamps are more expensive than standard lighting, but they quickly pay for themselves through better health in the home and at work. Most available lighting products use neodymium oxide to filter the yellow light which is excessive in standard fluorescents. Full spectrum lighting is available in standard incandescent bulbs, reflector/flood bulbs for recessed and track lighting, and fluorescent tubes. Some suppliers have desk lamps, light boxes, and other full spectrum products, choose energy-saving versions every time.

Electronic lights

Save energy with these efficient lights from Lights of America (CA). Microchip technology provides amazing light output and energy savings, with safe, cool-operating lights lasting around 16 times longer than conventional incandescent bulbs, Also, they are flicker-free, silent and suitable for any climate as they will even start fine in sub-zero temperatures.

Full spectrum bulbs

TruSpectrum™ bulbs from Full Spectrum Lighting (VT) are low-energy long life fittings that also provide healthy lighting. Each bulb should last between 2500-4000 hours, up to 4 times longer than conventional incandescent or flood bulbs. The company also produce compact low-energy full spectrum fluorescents.

Fingertip control

A light touch is all you need to turn on this battery operated light. Available via Brookstone Hard to Find Tools catalog (NH), this cordless light is perfect to brighten any place that just needs a little light for safety or convenience.

Olive oil lamps

Originally popular in Mediterranean countries in Roman times, olive oil lamps have a timeless simplicity, and burn safely and smoke-free. These lamps are made in the traditional cottage industry handcraft tradition, and are available from Earth Care catalog (CA).

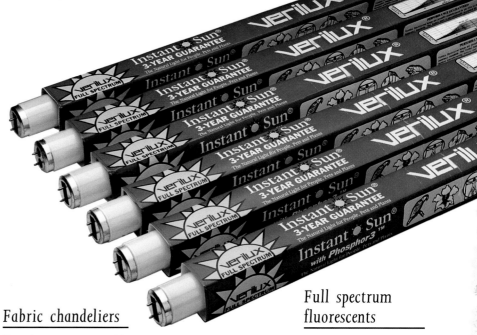

Fabric chandeliers

Transform any room with these extraordinary pendant light shades. Fun and elegant, shades are made from natural fabrics in 6 styles and 20 colors. They are fire-retardant and fit standard pendant light fittings. Made by a young design team in England, these glorious shades and ranges of other lighting features are now available throughout North America. Call Extraordinary Design (UK) for stockists.

Full spectrum fluorescents

Verilux (CA) make a wide range of daylight lamps, including full spectrum fluorescents with built-in UV filtration. Their full spectrum lamps are ideal for home and workplaces, and are often used by keen gardeners as plant house lights.

Healthy light box

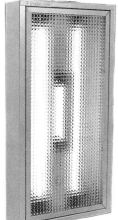

Ott-Lite[R] fitments, available from stockists nationwide, can actually improve your indoor environment! This fixture provides full spectrum light, and is radiation shielded, grounded, and blocks radio frequency waves. Easily portable, it provides all day sunlight quality wherever you need it.

Low-voltage outdoor lights

Save energy outside as well as in! This three-shaded tier walklight from Intermatic (IL) has an attractive verdigris finish to complement any garden design, while retaining low-energy features to make the lamp highly resource-efficient .

LOW-ENERGY LIGHTING

Over 20% of the electricity generated in North America is used for lighting, and approximately half this is wasted in lighting empty rooms, or as heat produced via inefficient lamps. When most people think of lighting they think of the incandescent bulb, a glass envelope surrounding a tungsten filament. Resistance to the flow of electricity through the filament causes it to heat up and glow. But 95% of the energy used by a common incandescent lamp is given off as heat. A conventional 100 watt incandescent bulb produces 1200 lumens (visible light) or 12 lumens of light per watt, while a 20 watt warm-white fluorescent tube produces 60 lumens per watt.

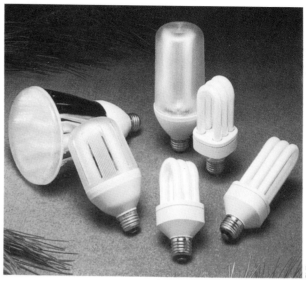

▲ **Indoor, outdoor, bright or gentle – always opt for low-energy bulbs**

Compact fluorescent lights

These bulbs cost more than incandescent bulbs, but they pay for themselves several times over. One standard bulb can last for 10,000 hours (3 years at 12 hours a day) which is ten times the life of an ordinary incandescent bulb. They use about one-fourth of the electricity of the traditional sort, while giving off the same amount of light. In addition, nitrogen oxide and sulfur dioxide emissions are also reduced — both these gases are contributors to smog and acid rain.

Fluorescents

Avoid cool white and daylight types (see p. 101), but choose warm-white or full spectrum high intensity fluorescents. Older fluorescent fittings typically have starting devices containing toxic poly-chlorinated biphenyls (PCBs). These devices may leak and cause toxic air problems, so check the age of your fittings, and if in doubt replace them. Older fittings may also flicker and hum, causing headaches, eyestrain, and general irritability. The best new fittings are low-energy compact fluorescent bulbs.

Alternatives

Compact tungsten-halogen lamps give a bright white light close to full spectrum quality. The most energy-efficient are longlasting low voltage halogen bulbs, ideal for lighting specific areas rather than whole rooms.

Metal-halide lamps produce a similar quality light to high intensity halogen lamps, and are as efficient as fluorescents. Most low-energy lights are now available for all normal light fittings, including table lamps and downlights. Low-energy bulbs are available for 12V and standard 120V power supplies.

Outdoor lighting

Most low-energy lighting is available for outdoor as well as indoor use. The lowest energy fixtures are the solar-powered lights which use PV to make electricity during the daylight which then powers the light at night. There are security models as well as those for accent lighting in your backyard.

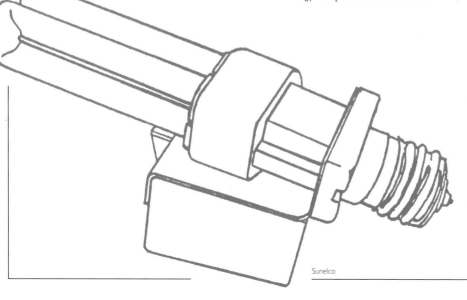

Sunelco

▲ Make your own beeswax candles, or choose classical or fanciful shapes

The light from candles and oil lamps has a very special quality. Soft, gently flickering candlelight or a warmly glowing oil lamp will immediately transform the mood of any interior to create an intimate and relaxed space. Often used for celebrations, dinner parties, and at Christmas, candles and oil lamps are also ideal to light the bathroom if you want to take a relaxing bath or to create a harmonious background for massage, meditation, or making love.

Be careful

Never leave candles or oil lamps burning when you are out of the room, and keep them out of reach of children. Avoid candles on Christmas trees or in paper lanterns. For extra safety place a candle inside a glass and metal lantern.

Also, some hypersensitive individuals should avoid candles as they do increase indoor air pollution through the smoke as they burn.

Types of candles and lamps

Most candles today are made from paraffin wax (a nonrenewable source) but traditional natural beeswax brings a special glow and sweet honey aroma. Choose from handmade solid or honeycomb varieties and small votive candles. A bowl of water with floating candles will enhance any setting.

You can increase the power of candlelight via reflection by placing it next to a mirror or light-toned wall. For an elegant and simple solution, use a recycled metal wall sconce indoors or out. There are many beautiful options for candleholders. Options include reuse of old metal, pottery, or ceramic candlesticks, or buying those made from 100% recycled materials such glass and recycled steel. A chandelier filled with candles makes a spectacular feature.

Candle in the Window

Founded in 1991, "A Candle in the Window" is a place of refuge for homeless people of New York City. But it is more than this, it offers training programs in various skills, such as woodworking, to enable individuals to earn an income. In one creative program, natural honeycomb beeswax candles are hand-rolled, then packed in crates from a woodworking business started by two homeless people trained in the shelter.

Employment continues until an individual can re-establish their life, then the job goes to another homeless person. So, give a helping hand instead of a handout. Buy these candles to help the homeless help themselves (see Earth Care in Resources p. 109).

▲ Traditional oil-lamp shapes make attractive functional candleholders

When choosing scented candles, look for those that use essential oils rather than artificially-produced scents (see p.114). These can be relaxing or stimulating, and be aware of their effects when deciding which scents to use for different occasions and times of day. Oil lamps come in many shapes and sizes, from basic outdoor hurricane lamps to highly ornamented Victorian models.

At the simplest level, you can just float a piece of wick in a small cup of vegetable oil, and light it! Ancient lamps, such as small Greek and Roman clay lamps, sometimes sold as replicas by museum stores, make attractive little lights. You can burn olive oil or vegetable oil in them. With all lamps, keep the oil topped up, and the wick trimmed and set low to avoid smell and smoking, and keep the glass clean.

Natural Choice Catalog

Earth Care Catalog

COLOR

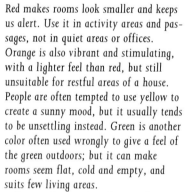

Light and shade affect color in many ways. In pale-colored rooms natural light and reflections will cause the colors on walls and ceiling to vary subtly, and as the natural spectrum of sunlight changes during the day, so the colors in a room seem to alter. You should take account of these qualities of natural light when you plan your decorations and furnishings – for example, light at dawn may make colors appear rosy, then neutral at noon, and bluer in the evening.

Artificial lights can have more drastic effects on color. Ordinary tungsten bulbs tend to add a yellowy-red appearance to a room's colors, and cool white fluorescent lighting gives a predominantly blue effect.

Decorative lighting

Lighting can make a room seem functional, calm, or opulent. Look around for special features such as stained glass lampshades made from recycled glass, recyled metal candlesticks and lampstands, and old oil lamps that can be used as is or converted to take low-energy electric lighting. You can make characterful lamp bases from virtually any found object, but make sure any base is stable, and lampshades must be fireproofed to approved standards.

Using color

Different colors have different effects on individuals, so consider these effects when planning lighting and decoration. One of the easiest ways to create a specific mood in a room is through using colored lighting in prescribed areas, either using candles, colored bulbs or, more often, colored shades which diffuse the light. Light reflected from colored walls can create a very particular feel.

Red makes rooms look smaller and keeps us alert. Use it in activity areas and passages, not in quiet areas or offices. Orange is also vibrant and stimulating, with a lighter feel than red, but still unsuitable for restful areas of a house. People are often tempted to use yellow to create a sunny mood, but it usually tends to be unsettling instead. Green is another color often used wrongly to give a feel of the green outdoors; but it can make rooms seem flat, cold and empty, and suits few living areas.

A room decorated predominantly in blue, on the other hand, can be calming and relaxing, although it may benefit from illumination with areas of warmer lighting. A white-painted room can seem stark and cold in the neutral midday light, but can seem warm and relaxed if you light it with spots of warm color combined with warm or earthy-colored furnishings, rugs, and throws.

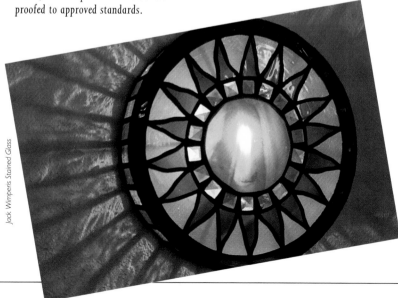

◀ **Lamps made from recycled glass produce interesting color effects**

▲ Light, color and form combine in
this modern eco decor in a San
Francisco hotel foyer, designed by
Michael Moore.

Amory Lovins

*Amory Lovins of the Rocky
Mountain Institute has been
described as the leading global
spokesman in energy efficiency,
and is a hero to many, but he is
as likely to describe himself as
the holder of the world altitude
record for passive-solar bananas!
Whatever description, he has
been an energetic driving force
in energy efficiency for more
than two decades.*

▶ **Amory Lovins, the best-known and
most effective efficient-energy
crusader in North America**

Amory and his family live in a self-designed office/home/greenhouse high in the snowy Colorado Rockies. This Rocky Mountain Institute has 40 employees, yet has no furnace and only uses about $60 worth of electricity per month — less than $10 for domestic use! The Institute is a non-profit research and educational foundation which aims toward fostering the most efficient usage of sustainable resources, leading toward global security. The work concentrates on energy conservation at home, in the workplace, and on a global level.

Energy revolution

Back in 1992 Amory Lovins stated: "The energy revolution has already happened; sorry if you missed it...savings have already cut $150 billion a year off the nation's energy bill. However, there's a way to go." Although we may be saving $150 billion, the energy we're still wasting — using inefficiently — costs

around $300 billion per year. If we fully use all the best technologies, Lovins stated we could save about three-fourths of the electricity currently used in North America, while obtaining services at least as good or better than present.

Lighting

One easy and immediate way to save power is via lighting. The Rocky Mountain Institute has several tips to put us all on the right road: the first step must be to replace incandescent bulbs with compact fluorescents. Then Lovins suggests we use the lighting power of fluorescent lamps more efficiently. One way is to place a shiny piece of metal called an imaging specular reflector above the lamps; then you take out half the lamps and move them elsewhere. Yet the room seems as light because of the effect of the "mirrors". Always use full spectrum bulbs, and control the current to fluorescents with an electronic ballast — the

device which starts and regulates fluorescents. In a typical retrofit this can save between 70-80% of the electricity used per unit of light. Also paint rooms in lighter colors, and use light floor coverings; top-silvered blinds and glass-topped partitions cause light to bounce back through the building; only put lighting where it is needed. If we all use sensible measures in our homes and workplaces Amory Lovins believes we can save about 92% of the lighting energy in the country — and end up with better light, and better general health.

Amory Lovins argues that the global energy problem will be solved by individuals working together with efficiency as their top priority. Some choices involve major lifestyle changes, but resource-efficient lighting is an easy place to start.

*Rocky Mountain Institute, 1379 Snowmass
Creek road, Snowmass, CO 81654-9199.
Tel: 303 970 3851 fax: 303 970 4178*

General organizations

State energy offices:

Alabama	800 392 8098
Alaska	800 478 4636
Arizona	800 352 5499
Arkansas	501 682 1370
California	800 772 3300
Colorado	800 632 6662
Connecticut	203 566 2800
Delaware	800 282 8616
District of Columbia	202 727 1800
Florida	904 488 6764
Georgia	404 656 5176
Hawaii	808 548 4150
Idaho	800 334 7283
Illinois	217 785 2800
Indiana	800 382 4631
Iowa	515 281 5145
Kansas	800 662 0027
Kentucky	502 781 7653
Louisiana	504 342 4594
Maine	207 289 6000
Maryland	301 974 3751
Massachusetts	617 727 4732
Michigan	800 292 9555
Minnesota	800 652 9747
Mississippi	800 222 8311
Montana	406 444 6697
Nebraska	402 471 2867
Nevada	702 687 4990
New Hampshire	800 852 3466
New Jersey	800 492 4242
New Mexico	505 827 5950
New York	800 342 3722
North Carolina	800 662 7131
North Dakota	800 247 1493
Ohio	800 282 0880
Oklahoma	405 521 3173
Oregon	800 221 8035
Pennsylvania	800 692 7312
Rhode Island	800 828 5477
South Carolina	800 851 8899
South Dakota	605 773 3603
Tennessee	800 342 1340
Texas	800 643 7283
Utah	800 662 3633
Vermont	800 642 3281
Virginia	800 552 3831
Washington	800 926 9731
West Virginia	800 642 9012
Wisconsin	608 266 8234
Wyoming	307 777 6079

American Council for an Energy Efficient Economy, (Head Office)
1001 Connecticut Avenue, NW Suite 535, Washington DC 20036
Tel: 202 429 8873

Con Edison Conservation Center (*Enlightened Energy GuideLine*)
Chrysler Bldg, 42nd Street & Lexington Avenue, New York
Tel: 800 343 4646

Electric Power Research Institute
3412 Hillview Avenue, PO Box 10412
Paolo Alto, CA 94303
Tel: 415 855 2411
Lighting information office: 800 525 8555

Illumination Engineering Society
120 Wall St. 17th Floor, NY 10005

National Centre for Appropriate Technology, Assistance Service (NATAS)
US DOE, PO Box 2525, Butte, MT 59702
Tel: 800 428 2525/406 494 4572

Pacific Gas & Electric Energy Center
851 Howard Street, San Francisco
CA 94103
Tel: 415 972 5341 Fax: 415 896 1290

Rocky Mountain Institute
1739 Snowmass Creek Road
Snowmass, CO 81654-9199
Tel: 303 970 3851 Fax: 303 970 4178

EPA Green Lights Program
Green Lights, 6202J, 401 M Street SW
Washington, DC 20460
Tel: 202 775 6650
Current information about energy-efficient lighting

Publications:

Primer on Sustainable Building; Practical Home Energy Savings; Resource-Efficient Housing; The Consumer Guide to Energy Savings, all from Rocky Mountain Institute (see p. 108)

Earthcare catalog
Ukiah, CA 95482-8507
Tel: 800 347 0070

Consumer Guide to Home Energy Savings
from American Council for an Energy-Efficient Economy, California
Tel: 510 549 9914

Electrical Independence Guidebook and Catalog
Integral Energy Systems, 1065 Argall Way, Nevada City, CA 95959
Tel: 800 735 6790

Energy-efficient lighting; Daylighting;
various booklets available from
Illumination Engineering Society
120 Wall Street, 17th Floor
New York, NY 10005

Lighting Equipment and Accessories Guide
and many other useful publications,
EPRI Distribution Center,
207 Coggins Drive, PO Box 23205,
Pleasant Hill, CA 94523
Tel: 510 934 4212 Fax: 510 944 0510

Healing with Color and Light, Theo Gimbel, Fireside, Simon & Schuster, N.Y 1994.

Home Energy Magazine
2124 Kittredge Street, Suite 95
Berkeley, CA 94704
Tel: 510 524 5405

Home Power Magazine
Home Power Inc. PO Box 520,
Ashland, OR 97520
Tel: 916 475 3179/800 707 6585

Light, Medicine of the Future
Santa Fe, Bear and Company, 1991

Real Goods Solar Living Sourcebook
966 Mazzoni St. Ukiah, CA 95482-3471
Tel: 800 762 7325

The Lighting Pattern Book for Homes
Lighting Research Center
Rensselaer Polytechnic Institute, Troy, New York 12180-3590
Tel: 518 276 8716

Now turn to Part Two, The Directory, for more organizations, suppliers and publications

The air that we breathe is contaminated from many sources, through transport, industry, toxic wastes, and chemical preparations. The air indoors can be just as filthy as that outdoors, or may be even more polluted. Many of us now live in super-insulated homes; increased energy-efficiency has meant that the exchange of gases that used to occur around doors and windows, and through building materials and roofs, no longer takes place. If ventilation is poor, the air circulating inside these homes can be stale and dangerously full of chemicals from outgassing of various materials, as well as dirty with the wastes of everyday life. Increased presence of radon gas in homes is particularly worrying (see p. 113).

Inadequately ventilated houses with poor air quality have come to represent what is called Sick Building Syndrome (see pp. 24–25). The pollutants which appear to foster these symptoms are a complex mix of formaldehyde, radon, carbon monoxide, sulfur dioxide, ozone, and particulates such as tobacco smoke. But there are ways to ensure that our homes have clean air.

Start with the building: choose natural materials (see Chapter One) to prevent off-gassing, and replace old materials which fail to meet environmental standards. Make sure that all your interior decoration is non-toxic (see Chapters Seven and Eight). Old paint may contain asbestos and lead; as it is removed it can release dangerous particles into the air so don't try to remove it yourself, but seek professional advice. When removing any paint, avoid chemical strippers (see Chapter Seven) with their high levels of volatile organic compounds (VOCs).

Once you have checked the materials in your house, look at the ventilation. Initially test the air quality. Home test kits and professional testing companies exist to detect the presence of dangerous pollutants in your home or place of work (see Resources p. 121). Radon is a serious concern, and you should certainly consider testing, especially if you are contemplating any remodeling that includes excavation.

Tests can also detect carbon monoxide, lead, electromagnetic fields (EMFs) (see p. 89) and UV radiation. If you suffer from airborne allergies, now common from ozone, VOCs, and molds, you may need to seek the advice of a clinical ecologist (see Resources p. 121). But, whether the problem comes from stale dry air or damp humid conditions, most of us can improve air quality quite simply via a filtration system. This chapter explains what to look for, and the most appropriate systems. Or you could opt for a low-tech approach – use only natural materials and fill your home with plants or plant essences to purify the air. This is not only cheap, it can be spiritually uplifting as well as physically healthy.

Whatever your air quality, you can improve it. But never forget our joint responsibility to reverse the trend of air pollution by forming or joining pressure groups to ensure implementation of clean air policies so that clean air is available for all in the future.

David Pearson

In an ideal world, we could all throw our windows wide open and fill our homes with totally clean, fresh air. It is up to us to make this a reality! We must all live in an environmentally responsible way, while continuing to put pressure on local and national government to implement clean air laws. First steps include avoiding synthetic materials, using less energy, and only using an automobile when 100% necessary.

AIR PURIFICATION

Air inside the home may be as polluted as that outside. Airborne pollutants cause malaise, debility, tiredness, lethargy, headaches, and insomnia for some people; for others they can contribute to serious allergies and environmental illness. Most common pollutants include dust, molds, mildew, VOCs, radon, and other toxic and irritant gases. Most pollutants can be removed, or eradicated, quite simply. Some problems can be detected via home testing kits. Kits exist to detect radon gas (p. 113), carbon monoxide, lead, EMFs (p. 93), and UV radiation. But once a problem is identified, you should get professional advice to deal with it most effectively.

Buildings sealed for heat conservation, and those with central heating systems, may harbor toxins which contribute to sick building syndrome (pp. 24,25). When unhealthy indoor air is the result of a modern draft-free super-insulated environment, you should seek expert advice (see Resources p. 121). You may need to add humidity (p. 117), or take measures to improve ventilation (p. 116). For general household use, to maintain a healthy and freely circulating air supply, use an air purifier. These include filtration systems, ionizers, and ozone generators.

▲ **Ceiling mounted air purifiers suit large rooms and shared spaces**

Filters

The simplest air purifiers typically use activated carbon (charcoal) filters. The carbon adsorbs odor-causing gases and VOCs such as formaldehyde and benzene. Any air purifier can only treat the air that passes through it, and for maximum effectiveness the air in a room should be completely filtered once every 5 to 10 minutes. If your purifier does not include a fan, install separate fans to stir up the air and draw it through the filters. Some filtration systems include an ionizer to charge particles to enhance filtration. Be sure to change filters regularly.

Ionizers

Ions are charged particles in the air that are formed when enough energy acts upon a molecule — such as carbon dioxide, oxygen, water, or nitrogen — to eject an electron. The displaced electron attaches itself to a nearby molecule, which then becomes a negative ion. Ionizers emit negative ions (of oxygen) which collide with airborne particles, giving up the negative charge to the particles. These are attracted to positively-charged particles in the air, which accumulate until the bundle is heavy and falls to the floor. Ionizers are silent and convenient, but look out for cheap models that may emit ozone and EMFs.

▼ **Ionizers can remove airborne contaminants as small as 0.1 microns**

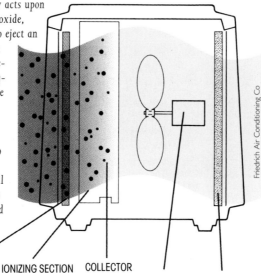

PRE-FILTER | IONIZING SECTION OF ELECTRONIC CELL | COLLECTOR PLATES | 3-SPEED FAN | CARBON FILTER

Ozone generators

Ozone generators may be suitable for eradicating mildew problems in some homes. Ozone (O_3) consists of three oxygen atoms, and is produced by splitting oxygen molecules (O_2). Ozone bonds to (oxidizes) pollutants which can then easily be filtered. Ozone destroys bacteria and viruses, oxidizes contaminants such as iron, and breaks down herbicides and pesticides. But ozone is toxic and dangerous above certain levels, and you shouldn't risk using these systems if anybody in your home is at all chemically sensitive. Always follow manufacturers' instructions very carefully.

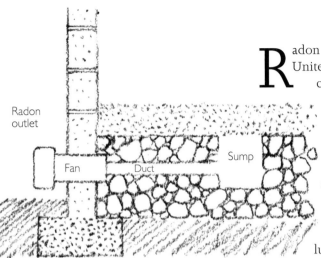

Radon outlet
Fan
Duct
Sump

R adon is the second leading cause of lung cancer in the United States and is estimated to cause around 14,000 lung cancer deaths a year. Although consumer surveys show a high level of awareness that exposure to radon gas can be deadly, the American Lung Association (ALA) states that comparatively few householders have tested their homes for the presence of the gas. Radon problems have been identified throughout North America and the EPA estimates that nearly 1 out of every 15 homes has radon levels above the EPA-recommended action level. If you smoke cigarettes and live in a house with high radon levels, the risk of contracting lung cancer is significantly increased.

Measurement and tests

Radon is an odorless, colorless, radioactive gas produced when radium decays. Radium is itself a decay product of uranium-238. It occurs naturally in certain rocks, groundwater, and soil containing uranium, granite, shale, phosphate, and pitchblend. As radon decays and is inhaled into the lungs, its byproducts release energy that can damage sensitive lung tissue and lead to lung cancer. Radon levels are measured in picocuries per liter of air (pCi/L). No level of radon can be deemed absolutely safe, but an average indoor level is 1.3 picocuries per liter. Both the ALA and the EPA

▲ Sealed floors plus underfloor ventilation can prevent radon seepage

recommend that homeowners take immediate action when indoor levels reach 4 picocuries per liter.

You can test your home using simple, inexpensive radon test kits available from hardware stores and other retail outlets. Short-term or long-term kits (for greater accuracy) can be used. These are then sent for laboratory analysis. The EPA conducts a Radon Measurement Proficiency (RMP) program to evaluate companies that make and analyze test kits. Make sure you any kit you buy is EPA-approved.

What to do

Outside, radon gas is diluted by the air and poses little threat. But indoors radon can accumulate and reach hazardous levels. The most likely source is the soil beneath the home. Radon seeps in via cracks and gaps in the ground-level or basement floors, as well as through pipes, drains, walls, and other openings. In most cases, you can take relatively cheap effective action to mitigate radon's effects. Radon levels will be higher in below-ground areas. Sealing cracks and other openings in basement and ground floor areas will help prevent radon seepage, as will ventilating crawl spaces and the soil under the home foundations.

If you use a contractor to carry out radon tests, choose one who is state certified and/or EPA-listed. Occasionally, radon can also be introduced into the home during repairs or improvements via building materials (such as granite and pumice), bricks, plaster, and concrete made from radon-rich sources. If you buy a newly-built home, find out if it has been built to approved radon-resistant standards.

◄ Be aware of numerous possible sources of radon gas

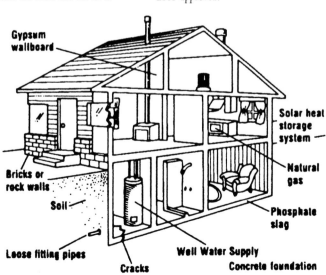

Gypsum wallboard
Solar heat storage system
Natural gas
Bricks or rock walls
Soil
Phosphate slag
Loose fitting pipes
Cracks
Well Water Supply
Concrete foundation

Green Alternatives

FRESH AIR – NATURALLY

Green plants clean the air for us in nature. They take in carbon dioxide and release oxygen. Living plants can help clean and refresh air indoors. They can absorb significant amounts of potentially harmful gases and help clean air inside modern sealed homes. Some common houseplants such as spider plants, philodendron, and golden pothos are fairly efficient at absorbing contaminants even in areas with continuous air changes and people movement. Recent NASA research showed that these plants can remove up to 80% of formaldehyde in a given environment within 24 hours. They may also absorb ozone, fumes from chemical cleaners, radon, and cigarette smoke.

Sounds natural

Noise pollution is a major cause of stress in the modern world. Outdoors, you can reduce noise by screening your house with hedges, earth mounds, and trees. Indoor plants can help absorb noise, and if you have the space, try installing a flowform (see p. 82) indoors, for relaxing sounds and moist air.

◀ **Plants and plant oils freshen and invigorate the air**

Scent

Plants not only give us fresh air, they also produce essential oils or essences in their tissues which can have varied positive effects. No one who has walked through a herb garden on a sunny day, breathing in the heady aromas and brushing the foliage can doubt the effect that essential oils have on the spirit. Aromatherapy is gradually becoming accepted as a treatment for a range of disorders, particularly those where relaxation is needed.

Essential oils of aromatic plants have been used in homes for thousands of years. Minute particles from the oils actually enter the bloodstream through skin or the lungs to invigorate the brain.

Plant oils are widely available in many forms, from herbal pillows to burn treatment cream. A traditional method of diffusing essential oils is by stirring the dried leaves and flowers of aromatic plants in a potpourri. Or they can be diffused through special lamps, or with diffusers placed over candles. Some herbs, such as sage, have been used as purifiers for centuries by Native American Indians. Other cultures traditionally strewed floors with scented herbs.

Cut flowers and aromatic plants grown indoors in pots are obvious ways to freshen the air. Also use aromatic woods such as cedar, sandalwood, juniper, and hickory for storage boxes and for insect deterrence in dresser drawers and cupboards.

▲ **Lavender is one of the most potent scented plant oils**

David Pearson

VENTILATION

We are all conscious of the need to insulate our homes to conserve energy. Many people now live in super-insulated homes which are very energy-efficient, but this may be at some cost to health (see pp. 24, 25). Super-insulation can lead to problems as the air in buildings is polluted with toxic gases, stale breathed air, carbon dioxide, fumes, dusts, and even radon (see pp. 112, 113). The traditional method of airing a room – opening windows – is unacceptable in cool climates because of the loss of heat, and in many areas is a security risk. Good ventilation has become more and more important. Whether you choose active or passive ventilation depends on the climate, the size of your household, and your budget.

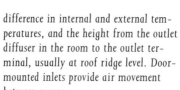

Willan Building Services Ltd

▶ **Healthy homes need adequate ventilation throughout**

Passive ventilation

One way to increase natural ventilation is to use natural, air-porous building materials. Brick, stone, lumber, and plaster will also absorb and release excess moisture, helping to regulate indoor humidity and expel pollutants. Beware of sealants such as paints, varnishes, and plastics, as these may render the materials non-porous.

Passive ventilation which relies on simple vents and differing air pressure on either side of the house, is suitable in warm, temperate climates. Packages are available which operate on the "stack effect" principle. Here the rate of air extraction is governed by the difference in internal and external temperatures, and the height from the outlet diffuser in the room to the outlet terminal, usually at roof ridge level. Door-mounted inlets provide air movement between rooms.

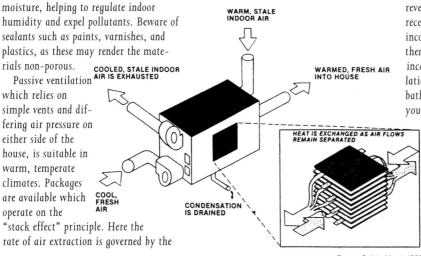

WARM, STALE INDOOR AIR

COOLED, STALE INDOOR AIR IS EXHAUSTED

WARMED, FRESH AIR INTO HOUSE

HEAT IS EXCHANGED AS AIR FLOWS REMAIN SEPARATED

COOL, FRESH AIR

CONDENSATION IS DRAINED

Custom Builder March 1989

Mechanical ventilation

If you live in a hot, humid location, or where it is cold for long periods, you will probably need mechanical ventilation, also called active whole-house ventilation. This uses fans to draw stale, warm air out of the building and draw cool, fresh air in. Systems usually include a heat exchanger, so that heat from stale air is not lost but used to warm incoming outside air. Whole-house active ventilation systems vary, but all incorporate ducting plus a heating system. This warms the air, delivering fresh, filtered and warmed air at floor level to each room and extracting it at a higher level. The system also removes moisture, odors, and pollutants. Kitchens and bathrooms are usually vented separately to prevent high concentrations of smoke, steam, and oil accumulating in the system. A heat exchanger warms incoming air with the heat from outgoing air to maintain energy efficiency.

In homes where cooling is needed in the summer months, some air-to-air heat exchangers are able to go into reverse, so that exhausted, stale air receives heat and humidity from the incoming outdoor air. Cooler, drier air then enters the house. Some systems incorporate a boost option so that ventilation can be increased in kitchens and bathrooms when necessary. Some allow you to double the ventilation to the living room while halving that to bedrooms. Some will even incorporate sensors in each room which measure air quality, temperature and humidity, adjusting the flow of air as programmed.

◀ **Heat exchange and ventilation combine in some systems**

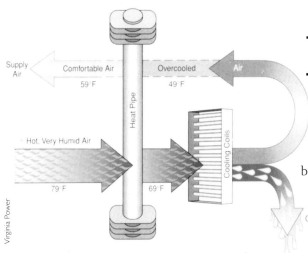

Virginia Power

Supply Air

Comfortable Air 59°F

Overcooled 49°F

Air

Heat Pipe

Cooling Coils

Hot, Very Humid Air 79°F

69°F

Condensate

▲ Heat pipe enhanced air conditioners provide efficient cooling

odern well-insulated homes, particularly those constructed with a vapor barrier, tend to become humid. This may be good for your houseplants, but it is also good for microscopic organisms — algae and molds. If these organisms spread, decay to the building can result as well as allergies for its occupants. In these cases, you may need a dehumidifier

On the other hand, centrally-heated homes may become too dry, which can also cause problems for the inhabitants and their furnishings, plants, and timbers. As with ventilation (p. 112), humidity control depends on your climate, the number of people and animals in the house, and the materials and construction of the house itself. A pleasant internal relative humidity is between 30% and 65% (100% is water-saturated air).

Solutions

In a house with dry air, try to design flowing water into the home in some way to regulate humidity, also increasing the percentage of beneficial ions, and purifying and cooling the air.

Bathrooms and kitchens frequently suffer from excess moisture in the air, which condenses on cold surfaces causing damage to window frames, walls and furnishings. It also leads to problems with molds which are one cause of environmental illness. Make sure you can open windows, and install extractor fans where necessary.

Dehumidification and air conditioning

The cooling coil of a standard air conditioner removes water vapor from the air as it condenses — the colder the cooling coil, the more moisture it removes. But today's energy-efficient air conditioners rarely have very cold coils, so you may need a more sophisticated system.

One solution is a system in which dehumidifier heat pipes are installed, one

David Pearson

section near the return (warm) air, and the other section by the supply (cool) air. The warm return air heats the one and the cool supply air chills the other. Heat is transferred to the cool supply air. The reheat taken from the return air is free. The air going into the cooling coil is precooled, which allows moisture to

▲ The best ventilation of all is natural throughflow of air

condense very early on the cooling coil. More of its thickness is used to condense moisture, and up to two times more water is condensed. Typically 20% to 30% energy savings are possible.

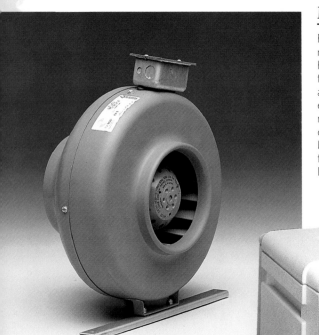

Remote mounted fans

Fantech (FL) fans come in ready-made or kit options. Kits include the appropriate fan, mounting assembly, and accessories. All fans use enclosed external rotor motors which allow opera tion in high moisture, lint- and dust-laden air. Ideal for kitchens, bathrooms, and laundry rooms.

Safety precaution

This easy-to-use kit, available from Environmentally Sound Products catalog (MD), detects dangerous concentrations of carbon monoxide gas long before any harm can occur. If levels of gas increase in the area near the detector, an indicator changes color, and you should take action straight away.

Electronic air cleaner

Lightweight yet heavy duty, this Friedrich Air Contitioning (TX) air cleaner quietly removes indoor air pollutants to leave your air healthy and allergen-free. Safe and effective, tests showed that this air cleaner is able quietly to remove 90% of even the smallest dust particles and toxins from a room in around 10 minutes.

Ionize your air

Electrocorp (CA) ionizers clean and revitalize indoor air. Negative ions not only destroy airborne particulants, they also aid oxygen intake, so you feel the benefit quickly in increased vitality. These small models are useful in homes, offices or vehicles.

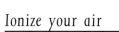

Detect deadly radon

Plug a Radon Alert, from the Real Goods catalog (CA), into a 120 volt outlet in your home, and you have an accurate and continuous monitor. If monitoring shows a hazardous level of radon you must take steps straight off to stop this dangerous gas entering your home.

Freestanding air purifier

This air filtration unit from Allermed (TX) features 360 degree airflow, so it can be placed anywhere in a room, or moved wherever it is needed. Using the latest carbon prefilters and HEPA type filtration unit, this purifier will clean the air throughout an area up to 425 sq ft.

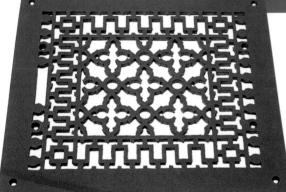

Cast iron grilles

Reggio Registers (MA) manufacture a range of attractive solutions to avoid unsightly heating vents in your homes. The grilles can be mounted in walls, floors, and ceilings to conceal cold air returns and serve as warm air vents. The attractive cast iron and wooden grilles are suitable for most decor styles so you need never compromise efficient air flow.

Cleaning via ozone

Panda ozone generators, from Quantum Electronics (RI) purify your air through the cleansing action of ozone. They eliminate toxins in the air rather than merely filtering them. Effective against VOCs, gases, and other chemical contaminants, they also destroy molds and settle airborne dust.

Healthy Habitats

In 1986 Carl Grimes began to suffer symptoms that he could no longer ignore. They included severe headaches, muscle aches, mental fogginess and incredible fatigue. It took over two years to identify a series of factors that contributed to his ill-health, and to experiment with solutions. Exposure to toxins in the environment were the cause of his illness, and solutions included both medical responses and an indoor environmental cleanup.

◄ **Carl Grimes founded Healthy Habitats to offer whole house testing to improve general indoor air quality**

Even though the current state of knowledge about environmental illness is still primitive, in 1986 it was far worse. Carl was forced to close his previous business, and was unable to work for two years. Fortunately, he found the right people with good suggestions and references, and he has been able to make a good recovery. In addition, one of the doctors he consulted created the idea for Healthy Habitats. This doctor had often observed that many of his patients with allergies responded to medical treatment, then returned before long with renewed sensitivity after unwittingly being exposed to allergens. When he suggested they were being exposed in their homes, their typical responses included denial that such a problem existed; confusion about what that meant or how to deal with it; or recognition and acceptance but uncertainty about how to correct the problem.

So the doctor started referring his patients to Carl Grimes for assistance. He inspected their homes and made informal recommendations about how to proceed. The positive response led to the development of Healthy Habitats, an organization committed to identifying and correcting indoor air quality problems.

Indoor Air Quality (IAQ)

Carl Grimes' activities extend beyond the identification and mitigation of IAQ in homes. He also researches and develops testing methods and is involved with laboratories and medical experts in interpreting and evaluating test results. He has been involved in developing complex systems to suit specific needs in the indoor environment — in homes and institutions — and acts as a consultant representing the specific requirements of his clients to architects, building contractors, and others. He

has also served many times as an expert witness in court hearings. His recommendation concerning mandatory registration for pesticide-sensitive persons has been included in proposed legislation on pesticides, and Carl has worked with the Colorado Department of Agriculture as advisor on pesticide control.

Healthy Habitats provide comprehensive services and testing for the indoor environment, for homes and workplaces. Out of illness, Carl Grimes has carved out a successful enterprise with a significant impact on many people's lives.

Carl Grimes, Healthy Habitats,
1811 S Quebec Way 99, Denver, CO 80231.
Tel: 303 671 9653 Fax: 303 751 0416

General organizations

American Lung Association
1740 Broadway, New York, NY 10019
Tel: 212 315 8700 Fax: 212 265 5642

American Academy of Environmental Medicine (lists clinical ecologists)
PO Box 16106, Denver, CO 80216
Tel: 303 622 9755

Atmosphere Alliance
PO Box 10346
Olympia, WA 98502

Coalition for Clean Air
122 Lincoln Boulevard, Suite 201,
Venice, CA 90291
Tel: 310 450 3190 Fax: 310 399 0769

Citizens for a Better Environment
122 Lincoln Boulevard, Suite 201,
Venice, CA 90291
Tel: 310 450 5192 Fax: 310 399 0769

Electric Auto Association
3210 Lombardy Road
Pasadena, CA 91107
Tel: 818 792 3210

EPA Radon Information (Advisory Services and technical publications)
Tel: 617 565 4502

EPA Indoor Air Quality Information Center
Tel: 800 438 4318/601 688 2457

Environmental Defense Fund
5655 College Avenue
Oakland, CA 94618
Tel: 510 658 8008

Environmental Resource Services
1624 North 11th Avenue,
Phoenix, AZ 85007
Tel: 602 258 6010 Fax: 602 258 6119

Interagency Indoor Air Council
1200 6th Avenue, Seattle, WA 98101
Tel: 206 442 2589

Group Against Smog Pollution (GASP)
875 North College Avenue, Claremont,
CA 91711
Tel: 714 621 8000 Fax: 714 621 8419

International Institute for Bau-Biologie & Ecology
PO Box 387, Clearwater, FL 34615
Tel: 813 461 4371 Fax: 813 441 4373

Natural Resources Defense Council
671 S, Olive Street 1210,
Los Angeles, CA 90014
Tel: 213 892 1500 Fax; 213 629 5389

Plants for Clean Air Council
10210 Bald Hill Road,
Mitchellville, MD 20721
Tel: 301 459 7678 Fax: 301 459 6533

Pollution Probe Foundation
12 Madison Avenue, Toronto, Ontario,
Canada, M5R 2S1
Tel: 416 926 1907

Indoor Air Quality

Air Quality Research (Formaldehyde testing)
901 Grayson Street, Berkeley, CA 94710

Richard Crowther, AIA
401 Madison Street,
Denver, CO 80206
Tel: 303 388 1875

Ecology by Design
(Concepts for a Toxic-free Environment)
1341 Ocean Avenue, Suite 73, Santa
Monica, CA 90401
Tel: 310 394 4146

Environmental Testing and Technology
(testing, research and publications)
PO Box 230369, Encinitas, CA 92023
Tel: 619 436 5990 Fax: 619 436 9448

Healthy Environments
PO Box 426, Snowmass, CO 81654
Tel: 303 925 4400

Healthy Habitats (see p. 120)

Healthy House Institute (see p. 199)

National Electromagnetic Field Testing Association (NEFTA)
628-B Library Place, Evanston, IL 60201
Tel: 708 475 3696

Pace Incorporated
1710 Douglas Drive North,
Minneapolis, MN 55422
Tel: 612 525 3416

Quality Environments
2414 McDuffie Street, Houston,
TX 77019
Tel: 713 520 5900

Publications

Clearing the Air, from Coalition for Clean Air (see entry)

Environmental Regulatory Review, from Pace Incorporated (see entry above)

The Healthy House, John Bower,
(see p. 199) Book and Video

The Natural House Book, David Pearson Simon & Schuster Fireside 1989

Washington State Indoor Air Resource Guide
Interagency Indoor Air Council
1200 6th Avenue, Seattle, WA 98101
Tel: 206 442 2589

Now turn to Part Two, The Directory, for more organizations, suppliers and publications

Positive choices of interior decoration can make your home healthy and earth-friendly. A non-toxic and environment-conscious interior can be just as colorful, varied and stylish as any other. It doesn't have to cramp your personal style — whether you favor colonial, cottage, cabin, or modern. It is just as appropriate for a small city apartment or a spacious suburban or out-of-town house. In fact, incorporating these newer ideals should make your interior more attractive and inviting. Colors, scents, sounds and textures can combine to create an environment that is not only non-toxic but can also rejuvenate and heal you both in body and soul.

Decoration is one of the most popular fields of home improvement and almost everyone gets involved at some time in painting, tiling, or flooring work. Even if you use the services of an interior decorator and contractor, it is just as important how you choose the materials they use. Several architects and interior decorators now specialize in designing "natural" and healthy interiors (see Resources p. 137). Of course, if you do the work yourself, you come into direct contact with the materials and any harmful ingredients they may contain. There is nothing like close contact and personal use of materials to focus the mind on ensuring they are non-toxic! Although too many of the regular decoration materials on sale are still toxic and environmentally damaging, there are a growing number of benign alternatives. This chapter shows you the range available and suggests how to choose, use and source them.

Auro Paints

So, if you are about to decorate a room, avoid solvent-based synthetic products which have harmful VOC emissions, and look for paints, varnishes, and stains that are organic and plant-based or, at least, water-based. If you feel in an experimental mood, try mixing your own paints from natural pigments and oils and apply your own designs and decorative finishes. Also ask whether you need to cover all surfaces with paint or wallpaper — maybe some of the new plaster or raw wood looks so good in its natural state you could leave it as it is. Always look for salvaged materials, such as tiles and wood paneling or boards, which can make excellent and interesting finishes for walls and floors. Don't forget the new high recycled-content decorative materials, such as tiles made from crushed ceramics, recycled glass or recycled tires, and carpets from used PET bottles.

When choosing floor coverings, keep away from synthetic foam-backed wall-to-wall carpets, and consider rugs from beautiful hardwearing natural alternatives such as wool, wool/cotton mixes, and plant fibers ranging from seagrass to maize. Traditional natural linoleum is making a comeback — try this for its vibrant or subtle colors and pleasant aroma. If you're laying a floor, make sure you use properly-managed timber (see p. 31) or use salvaged boards.

Adhesives have traditionally posed health problems but new ranges of water-based, non- or low-toxic alternatives now exist. Or see if you could completely avoid stick-down solutions. Another method of fixing will probably be simpler and less expensive, and will make reuse, repair, and recycling easier.

The outside of this house was painted using natural products that are toxic neither to the painter, nor to the environment. Traditional paints contained many hazardous chemicals, posing problems during application, their lifetime, and disposal. You can now obtain natural non-toxic paints for every type of interior and exterior fiinish. These are not only healthy to use, but come in a wide range of earthy or vibrant colors.

PAINTS AND VARNISHES

W̶e are surrounded by paints, stains, and varnishes. The USA alone sells approximately 1.1 billion gallons of paint annually. Although today's consumer paints are gradually becoming less toxic, many are still made from petrochemicals, particularly those for special exterior uses.

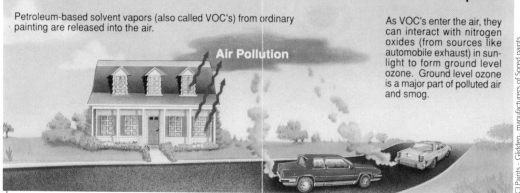

Vapors from Petroleum-based Solvents Can Be Harmful to the Earth's Atmosphere.

Petroleum-based solvent vapors (also called VOC's) from ordinary painting are released into the air.

Air Pollution

As VOC's enter the air, they can interact with nitrogen oxides (from sources like automobile exhaust) in sunlight to form ground level ozone. Ground level ozone is a major part of polluted air and smog.

ICI Paints - Glidden, manufacturers of Spred paints

Oil-based paints

The chief pollutants in petrochemical paints are heavy metals, such as lead, mercury, and cadmium. Although lead has long been banned as a paint constituent, and mercury more recently, they still remain in decorations throughout our homes. These heavy metals found in paint pigments and additives can damage the nervous system and kidneys and may cause cancer. Paint solvents release dangerous volatile organic compounds (VOCs), and contain toxic chemicals. These can cause cancer, nervous system damage, and other serious health problems during application, the life of the product, its removal and disposal. "Low-odor" products contain reduced solvents, but these can be highly volatile and cause rapid outgassing of the VOCs during and soon after application. VOCs contribute to the formation of smog, with its accompanying respiratory damage, and may destroy ozone in the upper atmosphere, allowing devastating ultraviolet light to reach the earth.

▲ **Buy paint carefully to reduce or eliminate its impact on air pollution**

Most stains, varnishes, and sealers contain acetone, lead, methanol, and pentachlorophenol. The distinctive smell of paint is actually dibutyl and diethyl phthalate, and a host of other compounds. Adverse health affects associated with products containing these toxic chemicals include:

• Eye and respiratory irritation
• Headaches and chronic fatigue
• Dizziness and heart irregularities
• Impaired judgment, perception and coordination
• Irritability and mood swings
• Nausea
• Unexplained joint and muscle pain.

Many of these chemicals are probable human carcinogens; others are narcotics which affect the central nervous system and could lead to liver, kidney, and brain damage. About 250,000 new chemical substances are created each year, and no agency can keep pace in documenting the harmful effects of all these.

What is paint?

Most types of paint have four basic components: a resin which hardens and forms the durable coating; a solvent to keep the paint liquid until it is applied, which then evaporates; pigments, and additives to enhance components.

These additives alone can be quite toxic although they comprise a small proportion of the volume of the paint. For example, until 1991, mercury was widely used as a fungicide in latex paints.

Oil-based paints use an oil as the solvent, while water-based paints use mainly water. Latex paint uses water as the principal solvent. Casein-based paint is an old-fashioned paint using milk protein in a whitewash-type base. It is coming back into fashion, particularly for "authentic" old-fashioned furniture finishes. Before you purchase paint, check the ingredients carefully (see p. 126).

Because of the risks they pose to health and the environment, paints have become the focus of public concern and legal and regulatory scrutiny. Over the past decade a number of paint companies have led the way forward, marketing natural paint products. These companies also emphasize sustainable sourcing, non-polluting processing, and environmentally friendly marketing. Following their example, some of the major companies are beginning to introduce new, safer paint products.

Safe paint

Water-based paint uses water as the principal solvent, greatly reducing the hazards of using the paint. In addition, hazardous thinners are not needed for clean-up. Traditional decorating materials are derived from plant and mineral sources and are produced without the ecologically damaging chemical processes, high in energy consumption and equally high in toxic by-products, of petrochemical paints.

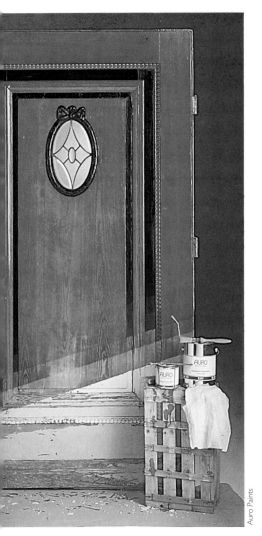

Auro Paints

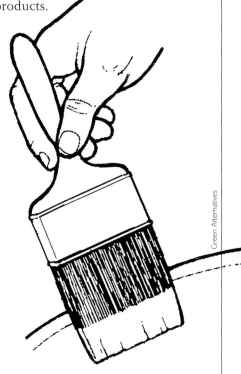

Green Alternatives

◀ **Paints, varnishes and stains can all be made from natural ingredients**

Natural products

Natural paint pigments are largely plant-based, while their thinners, either plant or mineral in origin, include linseed oil, turpentine derived from pine resin, starches, and waxes. Natural varnishes combine resins with scented turpentine oil and various pigments. Unlike synthetic varnishes, they allow the underlying wood to breathe.

The popular ranges of natural paints, varnishes and stains may be supplied ready-mixed in tins, or as base products with optional powdered pigments for the customer to mix. Paints are available for

walls, floors, and metals, and in gloss, semi-gloss, and flat finishes. There are even enamel finish paints, and products for both internal and external use. Look for the Green Seal mark on paint; their standard sets strict limits on emissions of VOCs and other problem ingredients, while maintaining levels of performance. Be prepared to search a little farther than the local hardware store, and don't be fooled by fancy packaging. Check the list of ingredients.

Even if the ingredients sound "natural", it is also important to know about the processing of the product. Linseed oil is a good example: a traditional wood

finisher and varnish made from flax seed, a renewable agricultural crop, it has been used for centuries and smells good too. But until recently standard "boiled" linseed oil sold as a wood finish contained heavy metal additives to aid drying: lead acetate and cobalt manganese. You can now buy linseed oil in which the oil has been heat-treated to give it the drying and performance properties of finishes used a century ago — one preparation mixes the varnish oil with pure beeswax. These products have zero VOCs, contain no petroleum or petroleum derivatives, and are 100% biodegradable. Always try to check before you buy!

PAINTS

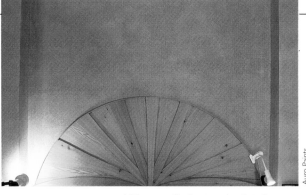

▲ **You can find natural paints in a range of earthy colors**

Removal and disposal of paints presents particular problems. Waste paint can pose a problem for community household hazardous waste (HHW) facilities, not only because of lead and mercury content, but also because of pentachlorophenol (penta), a pesticide formerly used in paint with high longevity and wide dispersion in the environment. This reacts with other airborne compounds, both natural and artificial, adding to the atmospheric VOCs, which are causing concern in many states.

Most of us have cans of old paint in our basement or garage, and we probably can't even remember what they were used for or even what color they are. Never ever put paint waste, stripped paint, old cans, or paint removers, into the garbage. Old paint is often hazardous waste and requires special handling. Newer safer paint left-overs can often be recycled (see p. 185).

Disposal and recycling

British Columbia, Canada, has led the way by requiring all paint manufacturers to collect, at no charge, all unused paint. The law also requires regular reports on the manufacturers' progress in recycling the collected paint. Operational from 1995, it is hoped that other provinces and states will follow this program.

Some manufacturers or stores organize their own collection and recycling systems to recycle discarded paints and varnishes. In a paint-recycling program, unwanted but useable paint is collected, mixed together in large drums, and sent to a paint company where it will be remanufactured. Check if there is a service near you, or if there is a community recycling program. For more information on disposal, contact your local health department or the local EPA office.

When you dispose of small quantities of unused paint, even latex or water-based paint, first make them solid by adding sawdust, or even cat litter, to the tins. Of course, the best idea is to buy only what you need, or you may find some local institution that could benefit from your left-overs. Or you could organize a "drop and swap" when residents can bring useable lead-free paint to a central location, and people can take home what they want, free of charge.

Removing paint and varnish

Until fairly recently most paint strippers were strong volatile solvents. But you can now use water-based strippers which remove both latex and oil-based paints; they take longer to operate but are far safer. Remember that other methods of removing paint — sanding, scraping, or burning — also cause problems in the form of dust, fumes, or burns, and that the paint you are removing may be toxic.

A small job such as stripping a small area of woodwork can be handled with individual protection, such as wetting the surface to prevent dust, and proper disposal. But if you are involved in any major renovation, such as stripping whole walls or tearing out old fixtures covered with old paint and plaster, then your family should move away during the process — particularly children and pregnant women — and make sure you wear protective clothing.

LOOK FOR THESE SAFE INGREDIENTS:

BORAX – natural mineral; mild alkali used in casein paints

BEESWAX – a natural moistener

BORIC SALT – natural mineral; non-volatile medium for wood preservation

CHALK – natural calcium carbonate , finely ground, and therefore fine grained and a brilliant whitening agent. Used as pigment and filler.

CITRUS TERPENE – etheric oil from orange juice production — 'terpene bases' are solvents for resins/waxes.

GLIMMER – natural mineral used as a filler in paints.

KAOLIN – natural clay mineral used as filler in paints.

METHYL CELLULOSE – a thickener from decomposition of wood cellulose; an adhesive and emulsifying agent.

MILK CASEIN – protein from cow's milk; binding agent and emulsifying agent in casein paints.

TITANIUM DIOXIDE – pure white opaque pigment from natural minerals used in paints and white varnishes.

WALL FINISHES

The ways you decorate your home can demonstrate your own uniquely personal taste. Rather than simply following current trends and fashions (which may not suit you at all), be confident about what you like, don't be afraid to express your individuality. This is central to making your home a healthy and harmonious place.

Natural House Book, Simon and Schuster

◀ **Special corners are enhanced with natural wallcoverings**

Personal space

To make the most personal statement, create your own designs, decorative finishes, and motifs. Mix non-toxic, water-based paints to achieve precisely the colors you want, and use simple decorating techniques such as glazing, marbling, scrumble, stippling, rag-rolling, sponging, stencilling, and lime-washing. British interior designer Jocasta Innes, an expert in this field, has written a number of excellent step-by-step books. Her company (with US outlets) also supplies all the paints and materials you will need (see Resources p. 137). You can also try hand-printing wallpapers and fabrics, and use them with other hangings (rugs, patchwork quilts, flags, for example) to decorate walls. You can give a room an especially warm and luxurious feel by stretching thick fabric over a wooden frame, fixed to the wall. This helps thermal insulation and softens acoustics.

Unfinished finishes

Don't be in too great a hurry to cover a wall surface with something else. A newly well-plastered wall or partition looks good without any additional finish, so can plain stone, brick, wood, and earth-built walls.

Many people are attracted toward living in more natural-looking, older, comfortable, lived-in and "weathered" homes. You can achieve this effect quite easily through techniques such as lime-washing floor boards or wooden wall boards or panels; stripping wall paper from older walls and leaving the plaster bare; building up subtle transparent color glazes on walls, and trying "verdigris" (green copper oxide) finishes.

Reused finishes

Visit your local salvage and reclamation centers before you start any work. You may come across interesting wooden wall paneling or boarding, or colorful ceramic, brick or stone tiles. You could even try your hand at making mosaics from broken tiles, chinaware and glass.

Color

Color has powerful healing qualities. Color therapy, an ancient art stretching back to the Egyptians, is very much alive today. When planning interior color schemes, check out books on the subject or consult a trained color therapist. If you are not certain where to begin, start small and try some experiments. Don't make hasty decisions in the building supply store, but make them at home in the room you plan to decorate. Take home samples of different materials — tiles, wallpapers, wallfabrics, paints — and try them out on each wall.

The size, proportion, ceiling heights and window positions of a room will dramatically affect the way textures, tones and colors appear. Borrow swatch books of wallpapers and fabrics from suppliers for a day or two and assess what different combinations look like in the room on different walls, and against your furnishings. Always ask for non-toxic, water-based paints, and wallpapers manufactured from recycled paper or from pulp from managed forests.

▼ **Look out for textured wall finishes made from recycled papers**

Crown Berger

▲ **Wooden floors such as parquet tiles are ideal for allergy sufferers**

David Pearson

Healthy flooring

The type of flooring you choose can significantly affect your health. Although rugs and carpets may be comfortable and look attractive, they can harbor dust and house mites. Vacuuming has its own health problems too. Unless you use a specially-designed vacuum cleaner, most machines (especially older models) will only extract larger dust particles while expelling finer particles into the indoor air you breathe. There can also be problems from outgassing of chemicals used in carpets (see p. 141) and the build-up of electrical static charges from synthetic fibers, such as nylon and polypropylene, as you walk across them. It is best to avoid cheaper synthetic wall-to-wall carpet, instead try a smaller non-fitted carpet or rugs of good quality 100% wool or cotton. Loose lay them so they can be moved, rolled back, and even taken out-of-doors to shampoo and spring clean. If you are prone to asthma and other respiratory diseases, or are chemically-sensitive or allergic, keep to barer harder surfaces which are easier to keep dust, chemical, and mite free and don't need vacuum cleaning. If the floor seems too bare, try a few non-pile, woven mats or rag rugs, preferably of organic cotton, which can be taken up frequently and washed. Stone, brick, and concrete floors can be dusty, and are best sealed with an organic sealant.

Flooring is a very prominent feature of any room – the background or setting for everything else. Your floor covering can set the mood of any room, ranging from practical with hard bare surfaces such as floorboards or tiles, to intimate and luxurious with coverings of deep pile rugs or carpet. Choice will depend to some extent on climate – rugs and carpets are best for areas with cold winter weather, while colder surfaces such as stone, marble, or tiles are preferable in warmer areas. If you have an underfloor heating system, it is a pleasure to leave large areas of the warm floor bare all year round even in cool climates. If you live in an area with seasonal extremes, follow the Greek custom of putting down rugs in the winter but rolling them up in summer to walk barefoot on cool tiled or marble floors! Acoustically, bare hard floors will reflect room sounds while softer, thicker flooring will absorb and soften them.

▶ **Tatami mats are made from rice straw, rushes and cloth covering**

Environmentally sound flooring

Check out the "green" credentials of any materials you use. Make sure any timber products come from a properly managed sustainable source (see p. 31) or try to find reclaimed stocks. Always see if you can find salvaged clay or ceramic tiles, stone, slate, or marble before buying new. If you buy new, look for locally-produced products; this not only reduces transport, energy, and pollution but may also introduce specifically local character. If you use natural cork, always buy "ready to seal" rolls or tiles and use an organic sealer and varnish rather than polyurethane or acrylic polymers.

Colored linoleum is an excellent choice for floors (see p. 141). Or you could use covering made from annually renewable fibers such as seagrass, sisal, jute, coir or maize. Traditional Japanese "tatami" mats are made from rushes and rice straw with a fabric backing.

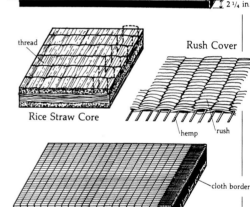

Attractive, hardwearing, and resource-efficient alternatives exist for many floor coverings. For a hard finish on a concrete floor, try terrazzo or "Venetian Mosaic", where small irregular-shaped pieces of waste hard stone and marble are set in cement mortar and ground and polished to give a smooth, easy-to-clean surface. There are tiles made from recycled glass and porcelain, and from recycled tires, plus carpets made from recycled plastics such as PET bottles.

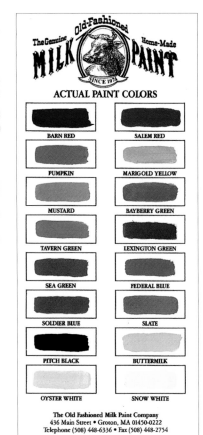

The Genuine Old-Fashioned Home-Made

MILK PAINT

SINCE 1974

ACTUAL PAINT COLORS

BARN RED	SALEM RED
PUMPKIN	MARIGOLD YELLOW
MUSTARD	BAYBERRY GREEN
TAVERN GREEN	LEXINGTON GREEN
SEA GREEN	FEDERAL BLUE
SOLDIER BLUE	SLATE
PITCH BLACK	BUTTERMILK
OYSTER WHITE	SNOW WHITE

The Old Fashioned Milk Paint Company
436 Main Street • Groton, MA 01450-0222
Telephone (508) 448-6336 • Fax (508) 448-2754

Milk paint lives again

Known for centuries, or millennia, milk paint is enjoying a revival. It is lon-glasting and durable, made from milk protein, clay, earth pigments, and lime. Available in a range of earthy and rich colors, this natural paint is manufac-tured by the Old-Fashioned Milk Paint Company (MS), and is particularly suitable where you want an antique-effect finish.

Healthy adhesives

Water-based, non-flammable and solvent-free – choose environmentally-sound carpet adhesives from Envirotec (CA). These offer a sound alternative to the huge numbers of toxic fixatives on the market, and are suitable for those with environmental-sensitivity or allergies.

Organic paints

Auro plant-based natural organic paints are safe and easy to use; they are 100% environmentally clean, pleasantly scented and provide a durable finish. Colors reflect the paints' origins, from earthy and muted colors through to the vibrant shades found in the natural plant world.

Handprinted wall coverings

Pattern People (NH) produce handpainted and handprinted wall coverings on clay-covered recycled papers. Elegant and longlasting, they offer an attractive solution for those who want colorful, individual yet entirely healthy decoration.

Water-based paints

Low-odor water-based paints from AFM (CA) are suitable for even the most chemically-sensitive individuals. Safecoat paint is formaldehyde-free with low VOC content. Varied products are suitable for all household applications.

Solvent-free paints

Consumer pressure and environmental awareness lead even the major chemical companies toward the pollution-free message! Spred 2000 comes from Glidden Paints (OH), a division of ICI; It is solvent-free so doesn't add to air pollution and health problems, yet handles as easily as regular latex paints and provides excellent coverage that dries to a smooth finish.

Hypo-allergenic decorating

Murco (TX) produce quality decorating products specifically for the chemically-sensitive. From interior paints, through filler and joint cement, their products are organic or low-odor latex based. Pleasant to use, even after a full day's decoration, you only need soap and water to clean up.

ADHESIVES

You've probably entered a newly-finished house or office and immediately been invaded by a barrage of unpleasant acrid smells that make your nose itch, your eyes water and your throat hurt! Well, apart from the new paint (and possibly the new synthetic carpet), this is likely to come from the adhesives used all over the building to stick down floor tiles, wood plank or parquet flooring, wall tiles, and the wall-to-wall carpet. Adhesive emissions are literally one of the major headaches of modern building. But, at last a new generation of environmentally-friendly adhesives are becoming widely available at competitive costs and with proven product performance.

▶ **Avoid products which add to the effects of ozone damage**

New adhesives

It is difficult to come up with alternatives to using adhesives to apply small items such as wall and floor tiles. But ranges of healthy adhesives are now appearing. Always read labels carefully and check contents: one manufacturer, for example, states that its new water-based latex products emit no toxic fumes; contain no mineral solvents; are non-flammable; are zero or low in *VOCs*; contain no chlorine, toluene, ammonia, ethylene, or glycol and, are odor-free or very low-odor. This makes them safe for the installer, the householder, and the environment. What is more, their adhesion performance meets, and even exceeds, recommended industry standards.

Non-toxic adhesives are available for the whole range of decorating jobs, from installing carpets, to tiles or parquet flooring. The same manufacturers also produce non-toxic floor underlayment preparations and primers, plus grouts, mastics, mortars, and sealants.

Non-stick methods

Before you reach for adhesives, first think whether there is another way to apply the item. What about using another material or a different finish that can be applied via pegs, screws, bolts, tacks, or nails? Adhesives make removal, reuse, and recycling of materials at least difficult if not impossible. So, for example, rather than choosing wall-to-wall carpet, you could decide on a large rug that needs no fastening at all (see p. 129). If you do need wall-to-wall, choose a carpet with a backing, such as jute, that can be gripped by tack strips next to the baseboards. This also means the carpet can be taken up and reused without the damage that glued foam-backed varieties suffer. If you are laying a new plank floor, rather than gluing to the concrete sub-floor, first space cross battens, then nail to these. Instead of tiles, can you use board, sheet, or slab finishes that can be screwed, nailed, or edge-fixed into position?

Pollution Probe, Ontario

Environmental by Design

David Rousseau is an environmental consultant and experienced healthy buildings expert. In 1990 he teamed up with Kim Leclair, a commercial interior designer. They publish Environmental by Design *to raise general awareness of materials choices, and to encourage people to put health and environmental concerns at the top of the list in everyday decision-making and product specification.*

▶ **Clear graphic symbols illustrate different criteria, and make the product evaluations easily accessible**

Interior materials and finishes listed in Environmental by Design all have environmental and health merits, and their production and use mean less energy depletion and pollution.

Before inclusion, each product is assessed with the help of a survey completed by the manufacturer, interviews, product literature, and Material Safety Data Sheets. A set of specific criteria are evaluated, covering each stage of a product's life: the material acquisition; transportation; installation and use; disposal (or recovery). Company practices and policies are also considered. Although it isn't possible to gain an absolute, numerical evaluation from this assessment, a clear understanding of the issues and impact surrounding each product builds up. The guide uses a set of clear graphic symbols to make the book user-friendly.

Categories

Categories of materials include thermal insulation; interior construction panels; carpeting; flooring (wood, stone, ceramic, and resilient); installation materials (caulking, mortar, grout, and adhesives); wall coverings and finishes (paints, stains,

varnishes, sealers, and treatments); and furniture and accessories.

As products and information are continually changing, Environmental by Design is available on a subscription basis, with twice yearly updates and bulletins. It comes in a loose-leaf binder format, and includes general text and information bulletins discussing the issues surrounding the materials and the industries, as well as concise summaries of general properties for quick reference. Product report sheets are updated in each issue, reviewing each product against the criteria, and indicating its merits. A supplier and manufacturer index follows each section and lists the support/supply network for all products listed, arranged by regions of Canada and the United States.

Indispensable for anyone working within the construction industry, the guide is also highly relevant to owner-builders, and anyone wanting to maintain a healthy home.

Environmental by Design, PO Box 95016 South Van CSC, Vancouver, BC, Canada V6P 6V4. Tel: 604 266 7721

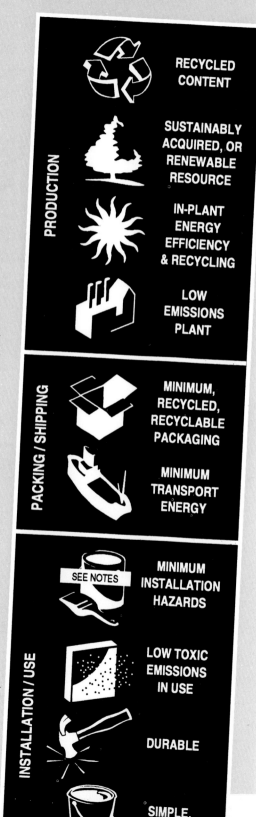

PRODUCTION

RECYCLED CONTENT

SUSTAINABLY ACQUIRED, OR RENEWABLE RESOURCE

IN-PLANT ENERGY EFFICIENCY & RECYCLING

LOW EMISSIONS PLANT

PACKING / SHIPPING

MINIMUM, RECYCLED, RECYCLABLE PACKAGING

MINIMUM TRANSPORT ENERGY

INSTALLATION / USE

SEE NOTES

MINIMUM INSTALLATION HAZARDS

LOW TOXIC EMISSIONS IN USE

DURABLE

SIMPLE,

Natural wood waxes

Os color wood waxes are natural oil-based and micro-porous. They will not flake, crack, peel or blister. If you ever need to renovate a surface finished with Os wax, you merely add another coat on top. Made in Germany, these products are sold in stores throughout North America.

Healthy flooring

Eco-Timber CA) supply tropical hardwoods from managed forests. All their products are certified environmentally-sound from sources with positive employment practices. They provide a wide range of flooring in woods otherwise unavailable in North America.

Water-based wood stain

Environment-friendly stains, colors, and top coats are all available from General Finishes (WI). They provide results every bit as good as those you have come to expect with traditional petrochemical products, with none of the unpleasant side-effects for you or your home.

Hair underfelt

Instead of petrochemical-based underlayments and foams, choose 100% hair underfelt from Colin Campbell (Vancouver). Suitable for any surface, and for domestic and industrial applications, hair underfelt is thermally efficient and flame-retardant.

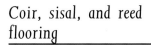

Recycled rubber mats

Sometimes you need heavy-duty mats, in areas that take the hardest wear and tear in your home. Ruff n'Tuff mats from Royal Floormats (CA) are made entirely from recycled rubber. Great for back doors and patios as well as garages.

Recycled biocomposite

There is a revolutionary new material that looks like granite yet works like wood! It is made from recycled wood products and replenishable natural resources. Manufactured by Phenix Biocomposites (MN), make a choice in favor of the environment and ask your local supplier for products made from this material instead of choosing wood, It can be used in any project where you would formerly have opted for wood.

Coir, sisal, and reed flooring

Natural fibers have their own unique textures and beauty. The Natural Design collection from Colin Campbell (Vancouver) provides a range of floorcoverings that maximize the beauty of nature's resources, while technology gives a helping hand to blend the fibers into extremely durable floorcoverings.

Pattern People

Choosing natural products doesn't mean you have to miss out on current art and design trends. Michael and Janice Copeland produce a unique range of beautiful and environmentally sensitive wallcoverings.

▶ **All the Copelands' wallcoverings are printed by hand, using natural colorings on non-toxic paper**

In 1988, disenchanted after a combined twenty-five years' experience of working for commercial wallcovering specialists, Janice and Michael joined forces to create Pattern People, specializing in handpainted and handprinted wallpapers. Although they still supply design and color services to major wallpaper manufacturers, the greater part of their business involves production of their own wallpapers.

The Copelands' previous involvement in largescale production led them to worry about the environmental effects of mass production. So they decided to keep it small and fill a gap in the market by providing healthy and beautiful handmade products. Their custom line of handmade wallpaper is environmentally sound in all aspects, and provides truly individual decoration. All the patterns are hand created and colored with water-based paints on clay-coated recycled papers. The papers are not only fresh and distinctive, they are also washable and strippable without the need for any chemical products.

Pattern People's designs echo their naturalistic approach. Painted by Janice and Michael, these range from elegant luminous striations and sweeping impressionistic themes to star, sun, and floral motifs. The papers' wet brush strokes, smooth and textured metallics, and deep rich color makes them into works of art in their own right. All these non-toxic papers are created specifically to fill customers' orders. So you really can have what you want — and know you're never going to walk into someone else's house to find your paper on the walls!

As demand has grown, the Copelands have branched out to include hand-printed designs on natural fibers — linen and raw silk. They only work with natural raw materials, and customers can choose from a range of prints to match hand-embellished wallpaper borders, or can opt for custom-designed fabrics.

Michael and Janice Copeland, Pattern People, 10 Floyd Road, Derry, NH 03038-4724. Tel: 603 432 7180

General organizations

Environmental Defense Fund
257 Park Avenue South,
New York, NY 10010
Tel: 212 505 2100

INFORM (Environmental research and publications)
120 Wall Street, 16th Floor,
New York, NY 10005-4001
Tel: 212 361 2400

Household Hazardous Waste Project
PO Box 108, Springfield, MO 65804
Tel: 417 836 5777

National Toxics Campaign
37 Temple Place, 4th Floor,
Boston, MA 02111
Tel: 617 482 1477

Pollution Probe Foundation,
12 Madison Avenue, Toronto, Ontario,
Canada, M5R 2S1
Tel: 416 926 1907

EPA Public Information Center,
820 Quincy Street Northwest,
Washington, DC 20011
Tel: 202 829 3535

Certification programs

Green Seal (see p. 153)

Scientific Certification Systems
(see p. 198)

Environmental by Design (see p. 133)

Healthy interior consultants

Bio-Building
PO Box 1561, Sebastopol, CA 95473
Tel: 707 823 2569

Ecologic Homes
Nancy Simpson, PO Box 94, Willits,
CA 95490
Tel & Fax: 707 459 2595

Ecology by Design (Audrey Hoodkiss),
1341 Ocean Avenue, Suite 73, Santa
Monica, CA 90401
Tel: 310 394 4146

The Epsten group
303 Ferguson Street, Atlanta, GA 30307
Tel: 404 577 0370

Gaia Homes
PO Box 223, Horsefly, BC,
Canada, V0L 1LO
Tel: 604 620 3664 Fax: 604 620 3454

Healthy Buildings Associates
7190 Fiske Road, Clinton,
WA 98236
Tel: 206 579 2962

The Healthy House Institute
430 N Sewell Road, Bloomington,
IN 47408
Tel: 812 332 5073 Fax: 812 332 5073

International Institute for Bau-biologie
& Ecology
PO Box 387, Clearwater, FL 34615
Tel: 813 461 4371 Fax: 813 441 4373

Ideal Environments
401 West Adams, Fairfield, IA 52556
Tel: 515 472 6547

Natural Habitat (Valerie Dow)
PO Box 21, Haysville, KS 67060.
Tel: 316 788 1793

Shelter Ecology (Cindy Meehan)
39 Pineridge Road, Asheville NC 28804
Tel: 704 251 5888

SRW Environmental Building Consultancy
Lic 433290, 1075 Montgomery Road,
Sebastopol, CA 95472
Tel: 707 829 8296

Carol Venolia (Architect) (see p. 191)

Sustainable materials

Rain Forest Action Network
450 Sansome Street, San Francisco,
CA 94111
Tel: 415 398 4404

Rainforest Alliance
65 Bleeker Street, New York, NY 10012
Tel: 212 677 1900
Runs the Smart Wood certification programme.

Woodworkers Alliance for Rainforest
Protection (WARP)
1 Cottage St, Easthampton, MA 01027
Tel: 413 586 8156

Eco-Timber International
350 Treat Avenue, San Francisco,
CA 94110-1326
Tel: 415 864 4900 Fax: 415 864 1011

Hendricksen Natürlich (see p. 154)

Publications

Building with Nature Newsletter
PO Box 4417, Santa Rosa, CA 95402
Tel 707 579 2201

Eco-Renovation (The Ecological Home
Improvement Guide), John Harland, Real
Goods Independent Living Books, 966
Mazzoni Street, Ukiah CA 95482

Interior Concerns Magazine and Resource Guide
Victoria Schomer
PO Box 2386, Mill Valley, CA 94942
Tel: 415 389 8049

New Paint Magic, Jocasta Innes, available
from Paint Magic, 2426 Fillmore Street,
San Francisco, CA 94115
Tel: 415 292 7780 Fax: 415 292 7782

Toxics A to Z, A Guide to Everyday Pollution
Hazards, John Harte et al, University of
California Press, 1991

Now turn to Part Two, The Directory, for more organizations, suppliers and publications

Style is vital to any home interior, and style should embrace a broad agenda that includes personal and planetary health. These criteria engender a genuinely "natural style" – one that is harmonious and personal, and healing to body and mind.

Women's Environmental Network

Wood is still one of the most popular materials for home furniture. But is it from endangered tropical rainforests or old-growth North American forests? More furniture manufacturers are beginning to provide information on the sources of the wood they use. This has been helped by the pressure from various forest protection organizations (see p. 31). Two groups – Scientific Certification Systems (SCS) and the Rainforest Alliance – now certify lumber suppliers and furniture manufacturers to help consumers find sustainably grown woods. SCS follows the wood along a "chain of custody" from harvesting through to the finished product. They also examine the producer's forest management practices to ensure that they meet environmental standards. The Rainforest Alliance's "Smart Wood" program helps identify wood and wood products "whose harvesting does not contribute to the destruction of rainforests". There are also companies that make furniture from reclaimed wood and wood waste (see Resources p. 156).

It may be difficult to find out if companies enact fair employment and trading practices; you may have to call a consumer group (see Resources p. 156). Co-op America is one group that produces excellent information via their "National Green Pages" and "Boycott Action News", and everything in their mail-order catalog is carefully selected to meet strict criteria. If you are buying imported products, especially ethnic goods, try to buy from non-profit Alternative Trading Organizations (ATOs) who obtain their goods from community co-operatives. These coops can verify that their goods come from sustainable sources with fair social and economic trading practices. Remember ethnic goods from cultures close at hand, such as Native American Indian crafts of North and South America.

Furniture and furnishings often contain particle board, plastic foam, synthetic fabrics, and stain-retardant sprays. All of these may contain harmful chemicals that can outgas into the indoor air. Plastic foam may also pose a fire risk. Until 1990 foam was also made of ozone-depleting CFCs or toxic methylene chloride. Avoid or minimize this type of furniture, particularly in nurseries or young children's rooms, and in homes whose occupants are chemically sensitive or prone to allergic reactions. Instead, choose products made from non-toxic alternatives, particularly wood or reclaimed lumber furniture finished with organic and water-based sealers, stains, paints, plant/tree oils, or beeswax (see Chapter Seven); upholstery and cushions from cotton and wool fibers, kapok, ramie, or down and feather fillings, and fabrics of renewable fibers such as organic cotton, linen, 100% wool, or wool/cotton mixes. There are also wide ranges of comfortable furniture made from plant materials such as wicker, cane, bamboo, and rattan.

As always, before buying new, try to find and reuse older furniture and furnishings. Look around secondhand stores, and go to auctions and garage sales. There may even be a recycled furniture depot nearby. But make absolutely sure, when reusing old materials, that you don't introduce any potentially harmful chemical finishes into your home.

David Pearson

Look to the past for inspiration for the future! Created long before the advent of any petrochemical based furnishings, this nineteenth century Hungarian farmhouse bedroom combines function with delightful local-style decoration – all from natural fabrics and materials. Truckle beds under the fourposters served as young children's beds, but avoid these nowadays in the interests of improved air circulation.

FURNITURE

Vast quantities of waste material are produced by the lumber industry. Although a considerable amount is now reused for products such as blockboard, bark chippings, and particleboard, much more could be done. Innovative companies now create furniture from wastewood from old pallets and shipping dunnage, from recycled plastics, fiberglass, and even old film sets! Rather than buying virgin furniture, look around for recycled alternatives. All these processes help to minimize landfill, and often create skilled jobs as well.

Coppicewood

Coppicing is a traditional European system of sustainable forest and woodland management. After falling out of favor, it is being revived in some areas. Growing coppicewood is simple and effective. The stump of a felled tree (hazel, willow, ash or beech, for example) is left to shoot. The shoots, according to species, grow to usable sized straightish branches in seven to twenty years. Coppices (areas of woodland with branching tree stumps) are then cut in rotation, ensuring an indefinite supply of timber. Coppiced, small-diameter lumber is an ideal material for some building applications (see p. 32) and for furniture making.

Forest thinnings

Attractive furniture can be produced from sustainable local sources such as forest thinnings. Domestic hardwood thinnings, such as beech and ash, can be used "green" and "in the round".

▲ **This chair is made from coppiced small-diameter poles**

Chair making

To make a surprisingly strong, yet light-weight, comfortable upright chair from hazelwood, choose some cut branches and remove the bark but leave their irregular natural roundwood shape. Make simple woodworking joints in the pieces and assemble them to form the basic framework of the chair. To make the seat and back of the chair, use options, such as thick canvas, interwoven upholstery webbing, wicker, or cane. Finish the wood with a plant-based oil or beeswax.

Plant sources

Another resource for sustainable furniture is renewable material such as wicker, cane, bamboo, and rattan. Wickerwork, using the shoots of pollarded willows (also coppicing), is well known for baskets, lampshades, screens, chairs, and tables. When buying cane, bamboo, and rattan, try to source products from responsible and ethical sources such as ATOs (see p. 138), that support fair employment conditons and sustainable forest management.

▲ **Jute carpeting on stairs combines well with natural floorboards**

David Pearson

Wall-to-wall carpeting

Ideally, you won't have any! But many people still prefer it, and there are ways to make sure it's healthy as well as comfortable. Primarily, choose wool, and remember that a woven carpet does not contain the adhesive needed by tufted carpets. The best wool comes from New Zealand as it is free from most pesticide residues, certainly from organochlorines (OCs) and pentachlorophenol (PCP). Carpet wools from other sources, e.g. Europe and the Middle East, cannot be guaranteed pesticide-free.

Dyes should preferably be vegetable-based, or at least should not be fixed with heavy metal mordants. Watch out for carpets treated against moths, or for longer wear; they may well contain toxic chemicals. And even if your carpet is made from the most natural materials, wall-to-wall can pose particular dirt or mold problems. Try to keep carpets as clean as possible, and always keep them dry. Damp carpets are perfect breeding grounds for microscopic pests and molds. If your carpet does get wet, dry it right away; if it can't be moved, you may have to rent an industrial fan.

Also watch out for underlayments and carpet adhesives which may emit formaldehyde. For carpet padding, use CFC-free foam pads or recycled pads, jute, felted wool, and other natural materials with low-toxic binders and backings. Synthetic jute may be best because PCPs are often applied to jute in its source country to prevent mildew.

Before the advent of the petrochemical industry, which brought synthetic carpets, floor coverings were made of materials gathered from plants and animals. Carpets of man-made fibers, along with their synthetic foam backing, are causing concern to the federal Consumer Product Safety Commission. Presently, two-thirds of the 2.7 billion pounds of carpet yarns sold in the USA are nylon; only $1/2$% are wool. Often the glue used to hold synthetic carpet fibers together causes the problem. 4-phenylcyclohexine (4-PC) in carpet glue has been blamed for eye, nose, throat, and respiratory problems, nausea, fatigue, and memory loss. Formaldehyde and phenols are also often found in synthetics, with resulting health problems from outgassing.

An obvious alternative to a synthetic floorcovering is to leave floors uncovered or partially covered (see p. 129). If a hard covering is needed, consider natural linoleum which is made from linseed oil, cork, tree resin, wood flour, clay pigments, and a jute backing. Rougher, thicker floorcoverings are made from plant fibers such as jute, hemp, sisal, and coir. If you opt for rugs, look for ethnic products which are ofen made from locally-produced cotton or wool, and the work handcrafted by small producers. Find a non-profit outlet distibuting goods that have been hand-made by co-operatives.

▼ **Natural fibers provide attractive durable floorcoverings**

Colin Campbell & Sons

Compact and recycle

Even though you limit your purchases of canned drinks, empty cans seem to pile up horribly quickly. Reduce the problem with this simple can crusher from Real Goods catalog (CA). Your kids will love feeding up to six cans at a time into the machine and pulling the lever!

100% cotton shower curtain

Made of a tightly-woven cotton duck, this curtain is great to use and washes well. You never need experience that clammy plastic feeling in the shower ever again! Keep clean by throwing the curtain in the washing machine, then hang it up and wrinkles will disappear with your first shower. If mildew does occur, remove spots with a paste of water and baking soda rubbed on with the cut side of half a lemon.

Time-tested milling

If you want to grind your flour like the professionals do, try this mill from Walnut Acres Organic Farms catalog (PA). A corundrum-ceramic millstone is electrically powered to grind up to 15 pounds of flour per hour. Ideal for home or community, the mill is housed in an attractive surround, operates quietly, smoothly, at low temperature and with minumum power.

Ceramic sinks

Probably the most attractive sinks around are made by Norstad Pottery (CA). Handmade and colored from a blend of natural, non-toxic clays and minerals, every sink is unique, pairs are similar but never identical. These fine quality sinks add a truly individual touch to any home.

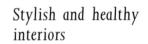

Stylish and healthy interiors

Browse through the Hendricksen Natürlich catalog or visit their store (CA) and your senses truly come alive when presented with stunning ranges of beautiful floor and wall coverings, from entirely natural fibers and fabrics. The colors of their True Linoleum could grace any home, as could their tiles, rugs, and carpets. A full range of non-toxic decorating materials complete the picture.

Lightweight shelving

Easy to assemble, flexible, attractive and economical - what more could you ask for? Made from sustainable timber, these strong shelves come from Pueblo to People (TX), a non-profit organization whose mailorder business benefits artisan and agricultural cooperatives in Latin America.

FABRICS & FIBERS

Over the past decades the textile industry has spent a great deal of time, money and effort developing new and "improved" fibers for furnishings and clothes. But these have typically been "noncellulosic" (derived from minerals and petrochemical sources), such as nylon, polyester, polypropylene, and acrylic. Most of these come from nonrenewable, high-energy, and polluting sources.

Even traditional natural fibers, such as cotton or linen, suffer from being produced with high levels of chemical fertilizer, pesticides, and defoliants. Moreover, toxic chemicals, such as formaldehyde, are used in various fabric finishes while other chemicals are employed to make them stain-resistant and fire-retardant. Not only is the production of these fibers and finishes damaging to the environment, the fabrics themselves add, yet again, to the chemical load imposed on us in our modern homes.

Consumer reaction against chemicals has been growing and is gaining increasing momentum, and more manufacturers are now responding to provide cleaner, "greener", and healthier materials.

Dyes and naturally colored fibers

Low-impact and vegetable dyes are usually used on organic fibers. Low-impact dyes use less water to disperse the dye, so less dye is used and waste water is carefully filtered to remove as many of the dye particles as possible. Vegetable dyestuffs are gathered from natural sources and can be used without heavy metal mordants (fixatives). Although not every color in the petrochemical palette can be produced, a wide and pleasing range of vegetable dyes exist. They also have their own subtle muted shades and earthy colors.

"Naturally colored" fibers also exist. Natural cotton, for example, is usually an oatmeal or brown color, but thanks largely to Sally Fox of Foxfibre, innovations have been made. Interbreeding of short staple, naturally pest-resistant brown cotton with longer-staple white cotton has created a small group of colors — two browns and a green colored cotton, with blue and pink on the way. Wool is naturally available in browns, creamy-whites, grays, and blacks. Hemp, woven with cotton in twill fabric (similar to denim), has a natural green/brown color. Hemp also comes low-impact dyed or whitened with hydrogen peroxide. Linen naturally has a sandy-brown color, but is often dyed.

◄ **Look for wools and plant fibers in many different guises**

Natural House Book Simon and Schuster

Organic alternatives

Choose carefully to find organically produced fibers and fabrics, including cotton, linen, and hemp produced with no pesticides, chemical fertilizers, or defoliants, and untreated with toxic and chemical surface finishes. Organic wool and silk are also available.

Cellulosics

"Cellulosics" are synthetic fibers made from the cellulose in trees and plants - the major fibers being rayon, acetate, and more recently, tencel. As they come from renewable plant sources they should *offer much better possibilities for future synthetics that are environmentally sustainable. However, there are still some problems with the use of chemicals and pollution generated in the production processes, so natural fibers remain the most positive choice.*

Jantz Design, Natural Bedroom Catalog

▲ The right pillow is vital to support both neck and back for healthy sleep

If every room in the house has a different character, the bedroom would normally be described as a tranquil place, inviting, relaxing and peaceful. It is a place where we unwind in restful sleep from the stresses of the day, and greet the new day in very personal routine ways. It may be where we make love, where we pray or meditate. It is often the only private space in the house, and for teenagers especially, the one room where individual taste and character can be displayed.

The choice of room for sleeping is important; it should be as quiet as possible, away from the street and noisier rooms, and a window which receives the early morning sun is ideal. The position of the bed may be important if there are geopathic stress lines or exterior electromagnetic fields to consider (see p. 20). A north-south alignment of the bed will place you in line with the Earth's magnetic field.

Try to invest in high-quality, natural, untreated furnishings in your bedroom. Make sure that carpets, wall hangings, fabrics, furniture, and bedding are made from healthy materials. A sleeper disturbed by airborne toxins will certainly be storing up problems for the future, and outgassing from synthetic furnishings can cause insomnia, headaches, irritability, or exhaustion, and may lead to severe depression.

Beds, futons and mattresses

Humans spend about a third of their lives in bed, and restful, deep sleep is a vital healing process which rejuvenates and removes the stresses of the day. Since we spend so much time there, try to invest in a good quality bed. A bed should be a place of refuge and peace, not a source of backache, neckache, chills, and irritation.

Metal-framed beds are liable to attract magnetism, so choose a solid wooden bed, avoiding particle board and other composites which will contain synthetic glues. A slatted bed will support the mattress or futon while allowing air to circulate. Look for mattresses made from allergy-free, untreated cotton. Despite safety legislation, they can be supplied without fire-retardants by prescription.

Organic cotton futons and mattresses make a sound, firm base. Mattress toppers, or pads, in wool, down, or cotton make an additionally cozy and comfortable sleeping surface. One company has developed the use of recycled plastic drink bottles into a fiber which compares favorably with cotton in futons (see p. 155). It has less environmental impact than commercially-grown cotton.

▶ **Design children's rooms to permit flexibility for growth and change**

Bedding

Sheets, blankets, duvets, comforters, and pillows are widely available in natural materials. Look for bedlinens in naturally colored cotton yarns which need no dyes. Use wool as an insulating material for a comforter; it is light, has better thermal qualities than most synthetics, and responds quickly to the body's temperature.

Bulky pillows may force unnatural neck curvature which is bad for the spine. So choose a specially shaped neck roll, contour pillow, or neck support which allows the neck to rest supported during sleep rather than under stress.

David Pearson

Children's bedrooms

A child's bedroom is one place where they can show their individuality. Opt for flexible arrangements of furnishing, rather than fitted units, and allow older children to plan and choose their own decorations and fittings — with guidance!

Recycled paper shelving

Strong, sturdy, and serviceable, this SlotShelf is made entirely from recycled paper. Look out for these shelves in your local stores or contact the manufacturers, Design Ideas (IL).

Plastic futons?

Every time you put a plastic bottle for recycling you may be helping to provide Rising Star (OR) with the material for their futons! Yet the fiber is as comfortable and more durable than cotton, and the futons are suitable for chemically sensitive and allergy-prone individuals – as well as for anyone who likes their comfort!

Driftwood style and comfort

Handcrafted in New Mexico, this Sundance (UT) easy chair is made from desert driftwood bleached by the sun and polished smooth by wind, sand and water. Comfortable cushioning is covered in cotton tapestry, woven in the mellow colors and ancient patterns of tribal kilims.

Recycling tradition

Adapted from original designs of the early 1800s, this huntboard from Sundance (UT) is made from recycled wood, and recycled windows form the doors in the two compartments.

Traditional cradle

Berea College Crafts (KY) produce fine furniture from selected sustainably-harvested local hardwoods. This Jenny Lind style cradle comes from their collection of early American furniture. Berea College students largely come from the southern Appalachian region, and many have limited financial means, so students work 10 to 20 hours per week producing fine furniture in lieu of fees. Buying from Berea means you are supporting the College, allowing continued traditional craft education to the highest standards.

Button bed

Another example of fine craftsmanship from Berea (see Traditional cradle, left). Up to forty students and full-time craftspeople may work on a single piece of furniture, which is made to exacting standards. Beds can be ordered in wild cherry, Appalachian black walnut, oak, or maple.

Natural bedding

Snuggle up in bedding made entirely from natural fibers – cotton or wool – from Jantz Design (CA). The bedding – from cotton mattresses to woolen comforters – is simple, healthy and comfortable, and uses wool and natural fibers from local sustainable agriculture.

Wool mattress topper

Also from the Natural Bedroom (Jantz Designs), this wool mattress topper adds a soft cushion of comfort to your mattress. Wool is the ideal natural stuffing for bedding, soft, yet supportive and springy enough to retain its resilience night after night for years. It is also naturally mildew- and flame-retardant.

· BATHROOMS

Gone are the clinically austere, purely functional rooms of the past; bathrooms today can be both practical and beautiful. Depending on your choice, the room can be a private, family, or social space. If you are starting from scratch, look for fuel-efficient bathroom heating systems, ceramic fittings, and non-synthetic furnishings.

Never lay carpet in a bathroom (see p. 141), as damp carpet attracts bacteria, molds, and accompanying pollution problems. Good ventilation is vital, so make sure you have an efficient fan system (see Chapter Six), or that you can open doors and windows for throughflow of air. It is an ideal place to grow moisture-loving plants; these will freshen the air, make use of the humidity and condensation, and add to a feeling of well-being.

Natural House Book Simon and Schuster

▲ **Japanese bathrooms are designed to be sociable spaces**

Bathroom decoration

Attractive wall and floor tiles are available made from recycled glass and reused ceramics, or even from recycled tires. If you want a natural wood floor, seal it well with several coats of natural sealant (see p. 126). Walls should be simply painted or tiled so they can be easily wiped down to avoid build-up of condensation and molds.

▼ **Create a comfortable old-fashioned feel with reclaimed fixtures**

David Pearson

Bathroom fittings

Make sure you use water wisely (see Chapter Three), and implement conservation strategies to reuse your bathroom graywater (see p. 80). Water-saving provisions under the Energy Policy Act of 1993 limit the water-flow rates of showerheads and faucets to a maximum of 2.5 gallons per minute. Older fixtures may have flow rates as high as 8 gpm, so replacing existing showerheads can save the average household about 11 gallons a day for fixtures installed after 1980 and about 21 gallons a day for those installed before 1980. Manufacturers offer a full range of shower types among the 2.5 gpm (and lower) showerheads — misty sprinkle, pins-and-needles spray, downpour, pulsating jet, and hard blast.

Where possible, support dealers who supply toilet sinks and other conservation products, and look for old bathtubs and sinks in salvage and reclamation yards.

Cleaning and cleansing

Far too many cleaning materials are still produced from harmful petrochemicals, with their long-term impact on our watercourses and soils. Always choose non-chlorine and non-phosphate bathroom cleansers, and bio-degradeable cosmetics and pharmaceuticals (see p. 150). Plant and mineral products are the best choice for body preparations, or, if you have time, you can make many very efficient cleansing products at home from simple ingredients and herbs. Brushes made from plant fibers rather than plastics, natural sponges, cotton washcloths, and mitts are all pleasant to use as well as naturally healthy.

Lighting

Whatever your power source (see Chapters Two, Four, and Five), take particular care with bathroom lighting. For safety, enclose all lighting fixtures, and operate them via cord-pull switches rather than wall switches. Make or purchase unusual lightpulls from wood or found objects.

Natural products

Cotton shower curtains can be washed time and time again in a washing machine, unlike vinyl curtains. Use unbleached cotton towels and bathrobes, refillable cosmetic bottles, and uncolored recycled, or cotton-based, toilet paper.

The kitchen is the hub of the household. Health begins here, in what we eat and the way it is prepared. The kitchen should be the natural link between people and the food chain. It supports local, sustainable, organic farming and gardening, and is a place where food that is healthy and nourishing to both body and spirit is stored, prepared, and cooked.

Healthy produce

Wherever possible, use local produce, either from your own land or neighboring farm stands, health food stores, or co-ops. Base your meals around produce in season; not only will naturally-ripened fruits taste better than those ripened in storage during transit from overseas, they will not be irradiated, and cost the Earth less to transport. Create demand for organic produce, not only with local organic producers but also in outlets such as supermarkets.

Keep a pantry well stocked with whole grains, beans, dry goods, and condiments. Then, with the addition of very fresh vegetables and fruits, salad greens, and other perishables, you can create a great variety of meals at short notice. Save time and energy by cooking items such as rice, potatoes, millet, even pasta, in bulk for the week, keeping batches in the refrigerator or freezer. Waste nothing: uncooked vegetable scraps should go to make soup stock; everything else can be composted. Get to know your local producers, and preserve (freeze, bottle, can, dehydrate) abundant produce in season.

Equipment

Today's kitchens combine the wisdom of the past with the technology of today. The most energy-efficient stove is the solar cooker, followed by induction cooktops (see p. 90). Or refit old-fashioned stoves for combined cooking and space heating (see p. 57). Energy-efficient refrigerators and freezers are also widely available. And dishwashers can save energy: if used wisely they can use up to 6 gallons of water per load less than washing by hand, according to an Ohio State University study. Controversial evidence links aluminum to Alzheimer's disease, so be safe and avoid all aluminum cookware. Be aware, too, that many foods contain aluminum — including pickles, bleached flour, baking powder, and processed cheese.

Cleaning

A kitchen must be clean but can still be natural. Use common ingredients for cleaning such as baking soda, vinegar, borax, and tea tree oil, combined with vegetable-based soaps and detergents.

Kitchen waste

Kitchen garbage is composed largely of packaging and organic waste. Before buying packaged goods, think about how you will re-use the packaging — some types are more useful than others. Organic waste is tomorrow's food before nature recycles it; compost it in a normal outdoor bin (see p. 169) or an indoor/outdoor vermicomposter, or wormery. Avoid using garbage disposal units as they waste water, and organic waste is best composted.

Choose reusable packaging for school, picnics and trips. Some lunch boxes have handy compartments which do away with the need for extra wrappings. Use reusable products wherever possible, such as cloth coffee filters and shopping bags, and try (for example) cooking in compostable brown paper bags rather than aluminum foil.

NURSERY

Every parent wants to bring up their new baby in as safe and nurturing an environment as possible. Whether or not your natural house has a separate room for the baby, the living space needs careful scrutiny to avoid pollutants and toxins. As it was before the birth, the baby's entire environment now needs to be comforting, secure, peaceful and warm. As the baby grows, those surroundings will also need to be stimulating and responsive.

▶ **Create effective storage space simply from boxes and baskets**

Natural Childhood Simon & Schuster 1994

Furnishing

In the nursery, above all, choose entirely natural furniture, fabrics, and fittings — and opt for wooden toys. A baby's skin is not only softer than adult skin, it's thinner too, and absorbs chemicals much more quickly. Buy a good wooden bed, but effective storage can be made from cardboard boxes and wicker baskets. The preferred fabric for baby's covers and curtains is cotton. Make handmade mobiles from nature's products to decorate the room, seal wood or cork floors with natural sealant, and paint the walls with water-based paints in calming colors (see pp. 124-6). An infant's room should have a good source of reflected or diffused light (see Chapter Five), and should ideally be situated in a quieter part of the house but near to the parent's bedroom.

Never ever use foam-filled furniture in a nursery. It can outgas and may be a fire hazard. A child's mattress must be made of cotton or natural fibers, and should be untreated with any chemical finishes. Then you, too, will be able to sleep in peace knowing your child is safe in a healthy environment.

Bedding and clothing

Toxins that an adult body can deal with are a far greater threat to a baby with a proportionally larger surface area and less internal tissue to absorb pollutants. A baby's detoxifying liver system is small and immature. For this reason, avoid clothing or bedding treated to be "permanent-press", "wrinkle-resistant", or "shrink-proof". These finishes are liable to contain formaldehyde resins, chlorine bleach, dye, and other allergy-forming ingredients. Never buy fabrics that require dry cleaning.

Synthetic fabrics and padding are based on petroleum or cellulose, and are largely unsuitable for babies despite their claims to be durable and washable. Synthetics do not breathe or absorb air or fluids; they are hot and clammy in summer and cold in winter. Always choose natural fabrics such as cotton, linen (flax), and wool.

Cleansing

While you should generally avoid "disposable" products on ecological grounds, the water and detergents used to wash cloth diapers should also be considered. If you buy disposables, avoid cheap generic products, because the perfumes they contain often irritate the baby's skin. Ranges of "green" diapers are now available which are dye-free, fragrance-free and biodegradeable.

If choosing cloth diapers, use 100% cotton material, and avoid plastic or rubber diaper covers which promote skin infections. Use a cotton diaper cover with a waterproof lining. Wash diapers with a fragrance-free, dye-free laundry detergent and avoid fabric softeners and antistatic products. Borax is a safe product for diaper laundry.

Never use adult bath products or skin-care products on a baby, and treat with caution even those marketed as safe, gentle, and pure. In general, lukewarm water and a soft facecloth are all that are needed for cleanliness and comfort.

Christopher Day

▲ This Steiner kindergarten uses soft
colors and natural materials for
equipment and playthings

HOME OFFICES

Millions of people in North America go out to work in offices. Many of these workplaces can make workers ill – through environmental illness caused by VOCs from unhealthy decorations, polluted air and EMFs from VDTs and other office equipment, and general stress caused by transportation problems. The enormous advances in Information Technology mean that working from a home office has become an attractive option for many.

The choice of workspace at home is vital. It should ideally be a quiet space where you can be undisturbed, separate from the rest of the home. You need to concentrate, but you don't want to make the rest of the family uncomfortable.

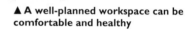

Natural House Book, Simon and Schuster

▲ **A well-planned workspace can be comfortable and healthy**

Low-energy equipment

When purchasing a computer, look for models that have earned the EPA's Energy Star label. Now made by most manufacturers, they use significantly less energy and cost little more than conventional models. Solar-powered computers are also becoming available, and you can purchase solar chargers for portable computers (see Resources p. 157).

When you work at a VDT, sit as far away from the screen as practicable, and use a low frequency (ELF) anti-radiation and anti-glare screen to deflect electromagnetic charges (see p. 93).

▼ **Install a magnetic radiation shield if you habitually use a VDT**

NoRad Corporation, CA

Office materials

Assess everything you use with the dictum: reduce, reuse, recycle. Avoid materials that are toxic, heavily packaged, not recycled, or not recyclable. Use paper made from 100% post-consumer waste or from plant materials such as hemp or recycled cotton denim.

Help in recycling by using gummed paper strips for fastening rather than sticky tape. Never use aerosols, and choose adhesives carefully. If you use a photocopier, keep it in a separate and well-ventilated area.

Business travel

If you go on business trips, go by bike if it's local, go by public transportation wherever possible – you'll find more new customers than in your car! Don't just print your address on your business card, say how to reach the office by public transportation. Spread the message: fewer cars, more planet.

Healthy space

Place your desk in a prominent position, preferably near a large window so that you can benefit from maximum natural light, and good ventilation plus a pleasant view. Any required artificial light should be full spectrum (see p. 100). Choose a comfortable chair that gives you back support, or invest in a chair specifically designed for posture and support (see diagram above). As ever, use only natural furnishings.

Air quality is very important when you are sitting in one room for long periods. If you can't open windows, make sure you have a good ventilation system (see Chapter Six), and include house plants such as spider plants (see p. 114) which help to clean the air. An ionizer will boost the negative ions depleted by electrical equipment. Try to keep the room at an even temperature.

Green Seal

Green Seal is the nonprofit environmental organization in the United States dedicated to promoting the environment by identifying and promoting products and services that are environmentally sound. It awards a "Green Seal of Approval" to products found to cause significantly less harm to the environment than comparable goods.

▶ **Look for the distinctive blue globe with the green check**

Green Seal develops environmental standards for consumer products through a public review process involving manufacturers, environmental organizations, consumer groups, and government agencies. Products are certified by Green Seal only after rigorous testing and evaluation; the Green Seal Certification Mark — the blue globe with the green check — identifies those products which are environmentally preferable, empowering consumers to choose products based on their environmental impacts. Green Seal believes that consumers, individual and institutional, have the power to change the world. Every time a product is purchased, a vote is cast for or against the Earth. What we buy determines how many trees are cut, how much pollution is released into the air and water, and how quickly our limited landfill space is exhausted. By choosing well, consumers send a strong message, using their purchasing power to tell manufacturers that they care about the environmental impact of the products they buy. Manufacturers do listen and sooner or later respond by making "green" products more available.

Environmental standards

To date, Green Seal has awarded its seal of approval to 276 products, certifying products in over 50 categories, including paints, water-efficient fixtures, personal products, re-refined engine oil, paper, energy-efficient lighting, household cleaners, energy-efficient windows, and major household appliances. Over 100 members are registered in Green Seal's new Environmental Partners green procurement plan for institutions. Together, these Environmental Partners wield over $5 billion in purchasing power, including retailers, government agencies, nonprofit groups, associations, utilities, educational institutions, foundations, and other companies. As part of the Environmental Partners Program, Green Seal publishes a series of industry-specific Green Buying Guides, listing environmentally-preferable products and "how-to's" for developing and implementing an environmentally sound purchasing policy.

President of Green Seal is Norman L Dean, a long-time environmental researcher, manager and attorney who recently served as Director of Environmental Quality at National Wildlife Federation. Denis Hayes is Chair of the Board of Directors, he is best known as International Chair of Earth Day 1990.

Green Seal, 1250 23rd Street NW, Suite 275, Washington DC 20013 1101. Tel: 202 331 7337

CASE STUDY

Hendricksen Natürlich

In 1989 Rob Hendricksen discovered some beautiful natural flooring materials that were only available in Europe, not in North America. Soon after, Susan developed environmental illness as a result of new carpeting in their home. These two factors pushed the Hendricksens toward sourcing truly natural materials, and led them to start Hendricksen Natürlich.

▶ **Rob and Susan Hendricksen provide beautiful interiors, naturally**

The Hendricksens' business embraces the vision that we can live in harmony with Mother Earth by using natural products for our interiors. Rob had been laying flooring for 15 years, when he was asked to install a marbelized resilient floor for a Victorian remodel. He discovered that it was produced in Europe from entirely natural materials. Susan had been a decorator for 12 years, and wondered why this material was unavailable in the US. She discovered it had been phased out after World War Two owing to marketing strategies.

Soon after, Susan developed a reaction to new carpeting in their home, and realized she was among the growing numbers of chemically-sensitive individuals. At this point Rob and Susan asked: "If True Linoleum exists, what related products are available to satisfy the need tor purity and safety in homes and working environments?" They co-founded the Natural Building Network, and began a business · specializing in low-toxic flooring, selling a variety of healthy, imported materials.

Misleading labels

The need to offer healthy flooring was also sparked by their concern that the Green Label was misleading consumers. This label, which is claimed to represent safe carpets, was introduced by the carpet industry without the involvement of any outside regulatory agency. It was therefore often found on synthetic carpets. Following hundreds of complaints and inquiries each year about the adverse health effects associated with carpet materials, twenty-six attorney generals signed a petition requesting mandatory health warning labels on carpets. This has resulted in a consumer information label.

Old World answers

"To create healthier indoor environments", explain the Hendricksens, "we reached back to the Old World for our answers. We found that natural fibers remain the primary demand in Europe because of serviceability and beauty. Perhaps consumers moved too quickly into their choices over here these past forty years.

We chose wool carpeting because of its fine qualities. Wool does not need a stain resistant finish and lasts two to three times longer than synthetic carpeting. True Linoleum is made without petrochemicals; therefore it suits our clients needs for healthful products."

Mail order and store service

Now, via their store and their well-produced catalog, Natürlich offer a wide range of thoroughly researched products. These include all wool carpets, True Linoleum in 50 vibrant marbelized colors, natural cork tiles, sustainable pre-finished hardwood floors; seagrass; jute; sisal flooring and area rugs; hand-crafted and glazed tiles, plus accessories such as felt padding, non toxic adhesives, carpet shampoos, and floor wax. The company also does custom installations.

Hendricksen Natürlich, 380F Morris Street, Sebhastopol, CA 95472. Tel: 707 824 0914 fax: 707 824 4069

Rising Star Futons

According to Leslie Blok, at Rising Star Futons, Americans consume 2.5 million plastic bottles every single hour, and that means a lot of futons to her! When you sleep on a comfortable Rising Star futon you are sleeping on several hundred recycled PET bottles.

▶ **Leslie Blok exploring the properties of her Wellspring fiber!**

Rising Star began selling futons, frames and covers in 1986. Leslie based the business on a set of personal beliefs: "My personal goals are to maintain a profitable, thriving, interesting business that is ecologically and socially responsible. These goals are very close to our business goals. Everything we do is oriented in tht direction." In 1989 Leslie started researching the use of recycled fiber and started building prototypes that would make the ultimate recycled futon. She needed to make sure the futons combined the springiness found in a couch with good support. And she wanted to make the futons entirely from post-consumer waste. So Rising Star found Wellmann, a NJ company that melts plastic bottles into pellets to make fiber. Leslie worked with Wellman to develop the fiber for futon use, and they trademarked the fiber as Wellspring. Unselfishly, Leslie decided the fiber was just too good to keep it for herself, so it is also retails separately while Rising Star keep exclusive rights to use it in futons.

Wellspring

Wellspring fiber is made from mountains of recycled clear PET bottles. Aluminum caps and hard polyethylene base cups are removed, then the stripped material is shredded, melted and forced through molds to form thin spaghetti-like fibers. The end product resembles white cotton. But, unlike cotton, Wellspring fibers are lighter and more resilient, and hold their shape and strength well over time. Leslie has created another recycled fiber, called Cloverfill, from green plastic drink bottles. In a different form, this fiber is used to line landfills and roadbeds! A third fiber EcoCore, is made from yet more plastic by-products.

Rising Star Futons obviously attract environmentally-aware homemakers, but comfort is never sacrificed for beliefs — the futons are extremely comfortable, and many people regard them as far superior to the old cotton-style futons. The recycled fiber is hypoallergenic and dust-free. It is also hydrophobic — doesn't retain moisture — and naturally fire-retardant.

Ideology

Leslie has successfully merged personal ideology with sound business practice; she has created the demand for a superior product, her company is socially responsible, and she actively supports local, state, and national environmental groups. The environmental ethic is embodied in the daily operation of the business, run by Lesluie and her mother: recycling and buying recycled (closing the loop) are priorities. Rising Star takes in vast quantities of waste to make their products, but produces minimal waste itself, partly through getting people interested in their by-products, partly through aggressively recycling wherever possible. The company also operates a retail store in Bend, OR, that sells other ecologically sound products as well as Rising Star's own lines.

Leslie Blok, Rising Star Futons, Bend, OR.
Tel: 503 382 4221 fax: 503 383 5925

Colin Campbell Carpets

This family business in Vancouver, British Columbia, demonstrates that big business need not mean that principles get sacrificed as a company grows. Colin Campbell have been supplying high quality and environmentally friendly carpets to the interior design community in Canada for over fifty years.

▶ **Traditional values combine with environmental consciousness at the family business in Vancouver**

A family business, now in its third generation, Colin Campbell is committed to distributing natural wool carpets and environmentally friendly floorcoverings in sisal, reed, and sisal/wool blends. They are always on the lookout for quality products to excite professional designers and homeowners, and source products from across the globe, including imports from mills in Australia, New Zealand, Denmark, the United Kingdom and Greece. They also commission hand-tufted rugs from Thailand and other Eastern countries, ensuring reasonable employment practices are followed.

Anti-chemical
Colin Campbell have come to view manufacturing from natural and renewable source materials as an essential component of the fight to preserve the world in which we live and work, and as a necessary corollary to recycling and reuse. Their constant search for new and better products has resulted in the distribution of products from a handful of companies who are pioneering the development of 100% natural floorcoverings. These are made from wool scoured without chemicals, free from chemical anti-moth treatments, employ no chemical dyes and use natural jute — fixed with natural latex — as backing. So the whole floorcovering is almost 100% biodegradeable. Wherever possible, Colin Campbell source organic wool that has not been treated with pesticides in its country of origin.

Chemical sensitivity
As part of their commitment to healthy homes, many of Colin Campbell's natural floorcoverings are tested in situ by chemically-sensitive individuals, who have reported no problems, but instead typically experience increased comfort and a greater sense of well being. Concern doesn't end with the carpet itself, but extends to installation and care. Chemical adhesives and synthetic seaming tapes are rejected in favor of traditional hand-sewn seams, and a range of natural underlayments — from jute to hair — are available.

Vancouver
Colin Campbell declare that the glorious natural setting of their home town has been a major inspiration to encourage the company to become closer and closer to the environmental movement. But they are now more and more concerned with spreading the message far and wide. They are convinced that consumers would choose chemically-free interiors of they were given the choice, so the company is building a distribution network right across North America to make sure their products are available to environmentally concerned individuals and companies throughout the continent.

Colin Campbell & Son Carpets, 1717 W 5th Avenue, Vancouver, BC, Canada, V6J 1P1. Tel: 604 734 2758 fax: 604 734 1512 Call toll free 1 800 667 5001 for information about distribution network.

General Organizations

The American Council for an Energy-
Efficient Economy (ACEEE)
2140 Shattuck Avenue, Suite 202, Berkeley,
CA 94704
Tel: 510/549-9914

American Furniture Manufacturers
Association
P O Box HP-7, High Point, NC 27261
Tel: 910 884 5000 Fax: 910 884 5303

Co-op America
2100 M Street, NW, Suite. 310,
Washington DC 20063
Tel: 800 424 2667

Anderson Laboratories (carpet testing)
30 River Street, Dedham, MA 02026
Tel: 617 364 7357

The Carpet and Rug Institute
PO Box 2048, Dalton, GA 30722
Tel: 800 882 8846

Carpet Policy Dialogue Group (health hazards)
151 6th Street, O'Keefe Building,
Atlanta, GA 30332
Tel: 404 894 3806 Fax: 404 894 2184

Council for Textile Recycling
Suite 1212,7910 Woodmount Avenue
Bethesda, MD 20814
Tel: 301 718 0671

EPA Public Information
TS799, 401 M Street SW,
Washington, DC 20460
Tel: 202 554 1404

National Recycling Coalition
1101 30th Street NW,Suite 305
Washington, DC 20007
Tel: 202 625 6406

National Center for Environmental
Health Strategies
1100 Rural Avenue, Voorhees, NJ 08043
Tel: 609 429 5358

National Toxics Campaign
37 Temple Place, 4th floor,
Boston, MA0211
Tel: 617 482 1477

National Center for Environmental
Health Strategies
1100 Rural Avernue, Voorhees, NJ 08043
Tel: 609 429 5358

National Resources Defense Council
40 W 20th Street, New York, NY 10011
Tel: 212 727 4474

The New Council on Food Safety
Community Nutrition Institute,
2001 S Street NW, Suite 530
Washington DC 20009

Organic Foods Production Association
of North America
PO Box 31, Belchertown, MA 01007
Tel: 413 332 6821

Public Voice for Food and Health Policy
1001 Connecticut Avenue NW, Suite 522,
Washington DC 20036

FoxFibre Natural Cotton Colors
PO Box 66, Wickenburg, AZ 85358
Tel: 520 684 7199

Texas Organic Cotton Growers Association
201 West Broadway, Brownfield,
TX 79316
Tel: 806 637 4547

Publications

The Wood User's Guide from Rainforest Action
Network, 450 Sansome St, San Francisco,
CA 94111 Tel: 415 398 4404

Clean and Green, The Complete Guide to Nontoxic
and Environmentally Safe Housekeeping, Annie
Berthold-Bond,1990 Ceres Press , PO Box
87, Woodstock, NY 12498.
Tel: 914 679 5573,

The Green PC, Steven Anzonin, Blue Ridge
Summit, PA: Windcrest/McGraw Hill 1993
The Nontoxic Home and Office, Debra Lynn-Dadd
(see page 188)

Healing Environments, Carol Venolia, (see
page 191)

Interior Concerns Resource Guide
PO Box 2386, Mill Valley, CA 94942
Tel: 415 3898049

Nontoxic, Natural & Earthwise, Sustaining the Earth
Debra Dadd-Redalia (see p.188)

Tackling Toxics in Everyday Products, from
INFORM, 381 Park Avenue South, New
York, NY 10016
Tel: 212 689 4040

The Smart Kitchen, guide to energy-efficiency,
recycling, ergonomics, design, non-toxic materials, fixtures and appliances, David Goldbeck, Ceres
Press, PO Box 87, Woodstock, NY 12498.
Tel: 914 679 5573

May All Be Fed: Diet for a New World, John
WilliamRobbins, Morrow & Co, New York,
1992

The Most Energy-Efficient Appliances 1992-93 ,
The American Council for an Energy-
Efficient Economy, Berkeley, CA

National Directory of Organic Wholesalers
Community Alliance with Family Farmers
(CAFF), PO Box 464, Davis, CA 95617
Tel: 916 756-8518

Healthy Homes, Healthy Kids, Joyce Schoemaker
and Charity Vitale, Island Press, PO Box 7,
Covele, CA 95428
Tel: 800 828 1302

Building with Junk and Other Good Stuff, Jim
Broadstreet, Loompanics Unlimited, PO
Box 1197, Port Townsend, WA 98368

Plastic Waste Primer, A Handbook for Citizens,
League of Women Voters, Lyons &
Burford, New York, 1993

Now turn to Part Two, The Directory, for more organizations, suppliers and publications

This century has been marked by an explosive growth of technology which has led us to believe that anything is possible. Along with the numerous positive developments has come the unhealthy attitude that we can control our environment by any means we choose, however energy-consumptive or polluting. This trend probably peaked in the 1970s and 1980s when advertisers pushed people to consume more and more products based on the petrochemical industry in every area of life – from synthetic food through clothing, from building materials to pesticides.

Persistent consumer pressure over the past decade means that healthy options are increasingly available. It is up to every one of us to choose wisely, equipped with current knowledge. The dangers of chemical use are well-documented; Debra Lynn Dadd (Dadd-Redalia), in *Nontoxic, Natural & Earthwise*, stated the position clearly: "In 1987, the United States produced almost 400 billion pounds of synthetic chemicals, over four pounds of manmade substances for every person in this country every day. Worldwide, about 70,000 synthetic chemicals are in use, with nearly 1,000 added every year. Some of these are considered safe for human use, but the vast majority have not been tested fully. Next to nothing is known about the human toxic effects of almost 80% of more than 48,000 chemicals listed by the EPA. Fewer than 1,000 have been tested for immediate acute effects, and only about 500 have been tested for their ability to cause long-term health effects ... complete health-hazard evaluations were available for only 10% of pesticides and 18% of drugs used in this country."

David Pearson

No-one knows how most of the chemicals currently in use will behave when combined or in longterm use. Most of our homes and workplaces are still filled with products made from these synthetic substances. Low-level but niggling symptoms such as headaches and depression are common in even mildly-toxic environments, and while they may not be life-threatening, they indicate something is wrong.

Throughout this book we recommend using materials for building and furnishing houses that avoid the kind of problems associated with synthetic materials and products. As consumers and taxpayers we can (and must) exert influence not only through our impact on the environment that we create for ourselves and our children, but also through raising issues in parents' groups, in the workplace, and in government. As well as acting to help ourselves, we must also foster a climate where preventive health measures are taken, even if corporate profits are decreased.

Look at this book as a guide to help you t o make the transition to a natural, nontoxic, way of living. Few of us follow every one of the recommendations, and compromises are often necessary, if only for the short term. Most of us, for example, still drive cars and live in homes that contain some less-than-natural features. But we can all work toward genuinely natural living. Work at your own pace, but try all the time to improve the environment for yourself and others.

Many new products in the marketplace misleadingly claim to be healthy. Become a fastidious label reader, and consider all the implications of everything you buy. Base your decisions on information, not prejudice.

This kitchen in Penngrove, CA, was remodeled by Carol Venolia, author of Healing Environments. She added arches, a bay window, skylight, and fireplace. Plaster on walls is naturally tinted, the floor is tiled, solid wood cabinets are sealed naturally, and lamps are of alabaster and metal. The California cooler (pantry) saves electricity and keeps grains and produce fresh. The room is airy, attractive, and naturally healthy.

CLEANING PRODUCTS

The Hazardless Home, Oregon Dept of Environmental Quality

Unfortunately, however "natural" your home, it won't clean itself! We need to remove the everyday grime and dirt that humans create, without overloading the natural cleansing systems of the Earth, notably our water courses.

As a first rule, rather than buying a range of different "specialty" products for separate cleaning jobs, choose only one or two general non-toxic cleaning products.

▶ **You need only one or two general cleaners - not an array of chemicals**

Organic cleaners

In a free economic market, the best way to change the way cleansers are made is to buy those which use environmentally-sound ingredients, produced with as little processing as possible, and sold in minimal and reusable packaging. Otherwise follow the "Granny knew best" philosophy, and use cleaners based on vinegar and bicarbonate of soda. You can even use common weeds such as horsetail which contains silica and is an excellent traditional pot scrubber.

Most stores stock ranges of natural cleaners. Become an avid label reader and look for cleaners made from feldspar and glycerine, for vegetable oil-based soaps, and for citrus- or vinegar-based cleansers.

While being careful to examine a product for details of ingredients and manufacture, also take into account the packaging, the advertising, and transportation involved in its marketing. Always think before you buy, buy less, throw away less, and minimize the environmental impact of every product you buy.

General hygiene

Numerous bath and shower gels contain synthetic surfactants such as ammonium lauryl sulfate which produces a thick lather but may irritate the skin. Ethylene glycol is a humectant used in bath products, but is known elsewhere as antifreeze. Although non-irritating, it can cause severe stomach pains if ingested, and respiratory problems if inhaled. Synthetic surfactants, dyes, preservatives and other chemicals commonly found in bathroom products are very slow to biodegrade.

Minimally processed plant and mineral products, are the best choice for all cleaning preparations, if you haven't the time to make your own from simple plant-based ingredients.

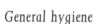

Equipment

Be careful in your choice of cleaner. Most homes use a vacuum, but conventional vacuums tend to release tiny dust particles as they clean, and can cause severe problems for allergy sufferers. Look for one of the many HEPA models or those advertised for allergy-sufferers. Or go for bare floors that can be damp-cleaned, plus washable rugs.

The problem with detergents

Phosphates, chemical compounds containing phosphorus, are found in most detergents. Manufacturers use them because they soften water and loosen dirt particles from surfaces. Unfortunately, there are severe ecological side-effects. As phosphates enter streams and lakes, they fertilize algae to such as extent that it can grow out of control. When the algae die, decomposing bacteria use up more than their share of the precious oxygen in the water needed by other plants and marine life to survive. The result is that streams, rivers, lakes, and seas are dying.

illustration by Karen Hart, courtesy of Metro, Portland, OR

Hazardous household products

Many everyday household and garden products contain hazardous chemicals. Finish what you have, then dispose of the containers carefully (see pp. 184-5), and in the future choose safe alternatives.

If you do ever use or come into contact with hazardous products:

- Wear protective clothing including goggles and a dust mask when working with old paints, old furnishings and dusty areas, and use proper safety equipment
- Work in a well-ventilated area, preferably outdoors
- Store products safely, locked away, in their original containers
- Don't wear soft contact lenses when using hazardous products
- Keep a set of workclothes and wash them thoroughly after exposure
- Change your clothes and wash thoroughly before eating
- Buy only what you need, so that disposal is not a problem

Recommendations

The most important starting point is to be aware of hazards and act responsibly. Watch out for the most common toxins in our homes. Formaldehyde is present in pressed wood, veneers, particle board, synthetic and sheet floors, siding, vinyl wall coverings, fiberboard, furniture, perma-press fabrics, draperies, and carpets. Paradichlorobenzene is found in air fresheners, and in mothballs. Tetrachloroethylene in dry-cleaned clothing. Paint and wood solvents, finishes, and adhesives, pesticides, and herbicides, all contribute toxins to the air that we breathe at home.

Follow the advice in this book about natural materials and positive techniques and you shouldn't go far wrong! Some recommendations are easier to implement than others, for example we should all be able to follow environmental decorating and furnishing advice (opt for wood, cane, and natural materials, choose close-weave natural fiber carpets, avoid synthetics, use water-based decorating products, etc). We can all ensure clean indoor air, and clean water, but our homes may be built to unhealthy designs which store or trap toxins. It may take a while to refit to ecological standards, eradicating any unhealthy building materials, and the transition to healthy energy sources can't be made overnight. "If in doubt, leave it out", is a good dictum when considering new products or materials, but, armed with the knowledge from this book and other sources, you can aim toward a completely healthy and hazard-free home.

Safety

In addition to avoiding hazardous products and toxins in the home, take general safety precautions. Install suitable fire extinguishers on each level of the house and keep an escape ladder near upstairs windows in case of fire. Install smoke alarms in halls, landings, and passages, and check them regularly.

Keep any potentially hazardous products well out of the reach of children, and lock medicines away.

▲ How safe is your home?

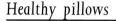

Laundry disks

Perfect for chemically-sensitive people, these ceramic laundry disks from Japan mean that you can wash your clothes without using detergent. Simply drop these three 2¹/₂ inch ceramic disks into your washing machine with your clothes! Metallic elements in the activated ceramics release electrons which then produce ionized oxygen which is a totally natural cleanser which breaks up dirt and organic compounds. If the disks are not available in a store near you, order them from Real Goods catalog (CA).

Healthy pillows

All cotton handmade pillows from KB (TX) make sleeping a dream. From the stuffing to the ticking, even the thread is 100% cotton. Before use, the ticking is pre-washed and rinsed in a solution of baking soda. KB also produce undyed, untreated, unbleached and unbelievably soft sheets and pillow cases.

Vegetable-based cleaners

Life Tree natural cleaning products are made from vegetable-based cleaning agents with essential oil fragrances. They are entirely, and rapidly, biodegradable, and packaged in recycled plastic containers. Available from Environmentally Sound Products catalog (MD), none of these products are tested on animals, and contain no animal ingredients.

Keeping healthy pets

Just because someone is hypersensitive doesn't mean pets are a no-no. Keep animals clean and healthy with a range of products from Natural Animal (FL). All goods are chemical free, cruelty free and earth safe. The same company also market environmentally safe products for your garden.

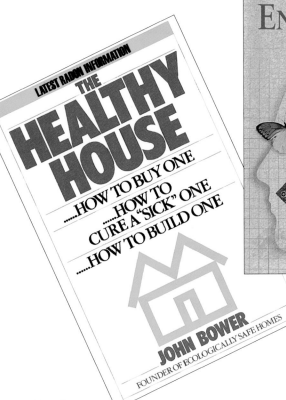

Your Guide to Indoor Well-Being
— UPDATED —

HEALING ENVIRONMENTS

Carol Venolia

LATEST RADON INFORMATION

THE HEALTHY HOUSE

...HOW TO BUY ONE
......HOW TO CURE A "SICK" ONE
......HOW TO BUILD ONE

JOHN BOWER
FOUNDER OF ECOLOGICALLY SAFE HOMES

SUSTAINING THE EARTH

Choosing Consumer Products That Are Safe for You, Your Family, and the Earth

DEBRA DADD-REDALIA
Author of NONTOXIC, NATURAL & EARTHWISE

Read all about it!

Many books exist to help you travel through the maze of advice proffered to chemically-sensitive homeowners. These are three of the best, providing sane, accessible and practical advice to help you to create and maintain a healthy home.

Essential oils for the air

Opt for natural air purification via Air Therapy products from Mia Rose (CA). These non-aerosol sprays of essential oils from citrus fruit must be one of the safest and most effective methods of cleansing the air in your own personal environment. Every droplet of oil contains electrical charges (ions) that attract and neutralize offensive odors. The oils also energize your air to recharge your energy.

Citrus cleaners

Mia Rose also produce concentrated cleaners from citrus oils and plant and vegetable extracts. These are safe for the most sensitive tasks – in baby's nursery, for washing children's clothes, or for the most sensitive individuals. And they smell great too!

ALLERGIES

About 15 % of the population is allergic in the conventional sense to irritants such as pollens, microscopic molds, and dust, and to certain foods, to the point of significant health effects. Symptoms include blocked or runny nose, eye irritation, sore throat, headaches and fever. A further 10% suffer nonconventional allergies, and experience symptoms which are less easy to ascribe to one known cause. A growing subgroup of these people have extreme sensitivities to agents in the air, food, and water, mostly contaminants introduced by industry and other human activity. These people are said to be environmentally or chemically hypersensitive.

Reducing the risks

Throughout this book, products and practices are recommended which reduce the risk of exposure to chemical toxins. Unfortunately you cannot assume that a healthy, active person is immune from developing chemical hypersensitivity. On the contrary, it often seems to be those who have had very active lifestyles who, particularly after illness such as a viral infection, fall prey to sensitization after major exposure to toxins. Women are at greatest risk after pregnancy, during menopause, and before menstruation.

Seeking further help

The branch of medicine which deals with chemical or environmental hypersensitivity is called clinical ecology; if you suspect you have environmental allergies, seek referral to a clinical ecologist (see Resources p. 165).

Sufferers of allergies and environmental sensitivity need to check contents of all home furnishings and household products before use. Several accessible and practical reference books offer good advice, and specialty catalogs can provide information about suitable products (see Resources p. 165).

Pollution Probe, Ontario

Allergy and environmental hypersensitivity

Environmentally hypersensitive individuals suffer intense allergic reactions to very low levels of common air pollutants (see Chapter Six). Symptoms include extreme fatigue, weakness, and confusion; difficulty concentrating, gastrointestinal problems, depression and anxiety, joint and muscle pain, asthma, bronchitis, and headaches.

It appears that a single incidence of overexposure to a chemical can cause oversensitivity, after which a much lower level of exposure can trigger the onset of symptoms. The chemicals which cause initial sensitivity include pesticides, chlorinated compounds, and formaldehyde. Certain molds can also sensitize, allowing new allergies to develop. The most common problems in a workplace are poorly ventilated rooms, when the chemicals in synthetic furnishings and equipment have no means of escape and build up in the dry, hot, carbon dioxide-filled atmosphere. Working during renovations, when dust, microscopic molds and other irritants are released, and when gases from new, toxic building materials are introduced, is another major problem.

Other major air pollutants are the chemicals used in fumigation, pesticides, and standard timber treatment. If you live near roads you will also have car exhaust fumes to deal with. In both workplaces and at home, tobacco smoke is a major irritant and pollutant.

The way to treat an environmental allergy is to isolate any offending chemical(s), and avoid it/them. This may mean significant changes in both lifestyle and living space.

General organizations

Allergy Research Group
PO Box 489, Dept NNE, San Leandro,
CA 94577-0489
Tel: 800 782 4274

American Academy of Environmental
Medicine (*lists clinical ecologists*)
PO Box 1606, Denver, CO 80216
Tel: 303 622 9755

Society for Clinical Ecology
109 West Olive Street,
Fort Collings, CO 80524

Citizens Clearing House for
Hazardous Waste
PO Box 6806, Falls Church, VA 22040
Tel: 703 237 2249

Household Hazardous Waste Project
PO Box 108, Springfield, MO65804
Tel: 417 836 5777

INFORM (*Environmental research and publications*)
120 Wall Street, 16th Floor, New York,
NY 1005-4001
Tel: 212 361 2400 Fax: 212 361 2412

Scientific Certification Systems (SCS)
(see p. 198)

Healthy building

EOS Institute
580 Broadway, Suite 200, Laguna Beach,
CA 92651
Tel: 714 497 1896

Housing Resource Center
1820 West 48th Street,
Cleveland, OH 44102
Tel: 216 281 4663

The Healthy House Institute
430 N Sewell Road, Bloomington,
IN 7408
Tel: 812 332 5073

International Institute for Bau-biologie
& Ecology
PO Box 387, Clearwater, FL 34615
Tel: 813 461 4371 Fax: 813 441 4373

Natural Building Network
PO Box 1110, Sebastopol, CA 95473

Natural House Building Center
RR 1, Box 115F, Fairfield, IA 52556
Tel: 515 472 777,5

Debra Dadd-Redalia (see p. 188)

Carol Venolia (see p. 191)

Catalogs

Allergy Resources
PO Box 888, Palmer Lake,
CO 80133
Tel:719 488 3630 Fax: 719 481 3737

Earthcare
Ukiah, CA 95482-8507
Tel: 800 347 0070

Eco-Design Company – Natural Choice
1365 Rufina Circle, Santa Fe, NM 87501
Tel 505 438 3448

The Cotton Place
Box 59721, Dallas, TX 75229
Tel: 800 451 8866/214 243 4149

Nontoxic Environments
9392 S Gribble Road, Box G
Canby, OR 97013
Tel: 503 266 5244

Nontoxic Environments
PO Box 384, Newmarket, NH 03857
Tel: 603 659 5919 Fax: 603 659 5933

Non-Toxic Hot Line (*products for the
chemically-sensitive*)
830 Meadow Road, Aptos, CA 95003
Tel: 408 684 0199

Bau-biologie Hardware
PO Box 3217, Prescott, AZ 86302
Tel: 602 445 8225

Environmentally Sound Products
8845 Orchard Tree Lane,
Towson, MD 21286
Tel: 800 886 5432/410 825 7200

The Living Source
PO Box 20155, Waco, TX 76702
Tel: 817 776 4878/800 662 8727

Real Goods
966 Mazzoni Street, Ukiah, CA 95482
Tel: 707 468 9214/800 762 7325

Seventh Generation
49 Hercules Drive, Colchester,
Vt 05446-1672
Tel: 800 456 1177 Fax: 800 456 1139

Heart of Vermont
Box 183, Sharon, VT 05065
Tel: 802 763 2720/800 639 4123

Publications

Building with Nature, (Newsletter)
PO Box 4417, Santa Rosa, CA 95402
Tel: 707 579 2201

*Clean & Green, The Complete Guide to Nontoxic
and Environmentally Safe Housekeeping*, Annie
Berthold-Bond, Ceres Press, Woodstock,
New York.

Environmental by Design
PO Box 95016, South Van CSC, Vancouver,
BC V6P 6V4, Canada
Tel & Fax: 604 266 7721
Guide to healthy interior materials

Healing Environments, Carol Venolia (see p.
191)
*Nontoxic, Natural & Earthwise; Sustaining the
Earth*, Debra Dadd-Redalia (Debra Lynn-
Dadd) (see p. 188))

Interior Concerns (Resource Guide)
Victoria Schomer
PO Box 2386, Mill Valley, CA 94942
Tel: 415 389 8049

Safe Home Resource Guide
24 East Avenue, Suite 1300, New Canaan,
CT 06840
Tel: 203 966 2099

Now turn to Part Two, The Directory, for more organizations, suppliers and publications

The backyard is one place where we can all have a positive impact – both locally and globally. By caring for the soil, and planting with thought, we can put energy back into the earth, provide a haven for wildlife, help restore threatened species, and feed and heal ourselves.

Each of us can learn to take care of our own pieces of land – whatever the size – to make them even more healthy for future generations. A healthy garden celebrates the myriad interactions of life, where different life forms interact in order to stimulate and support one another.

When planning your garden, ask yourself some fundamental questions. Decide whether your garden can help you to reduce your energy consumption, or alter your demands on natural resources. Whatever your climate and conditions you may be able to grow enough food to wholly or partly feed yourself and your family. Food healthier than anything you can buy, and at less cost, is only one benefit. Growing your food provides healthy free exercise, brings the family together in a common activity, and brings you back in touch with the earth. It also reduces your demands on a food and transportation system that has heavy environmental costs. You may be able to recycle waste products as productive compost or vital irrigation (see p. 80).

Reflect on the way modern living has destroyed so many natural habitats and wildlife. Ask yourself whether you can do something to repair some of these losses. You should also consider the healing qualities of a garden. On an obvious level you can grow plants that heal you, or that heal the soil. Add to this the soothing sounds of wind blowing through foliage, the healing perfumes of herbaceous plants brushed in passing, and the delightful colors of flowering plants grown in harmony. Your garden can also be an extension and celebration of your spiritual nature (p. 173).

Whatever you plan to make of your backyard, remember that it has its own identity, much bound up with its unique position. First make sure you are familiar with the relevant facts about the piece of land under your stewardship. Build up a profile of your local climate and habitat (see p. 22). In the past, when families stayed put, people grew up with all such knowledge, but in today's migratory society we have to learn about a place when we make it our home. You will want to put a lot of yourself into a garden, but remember, to succeed in harmonious gardening you have to take full account of the natural inclinations of the garden too.

David Pearson

This chapter provides information and inspiration to help you make the most of your backyard. Here you will find advice on growing food and decorative plants without artificial pesticides or fertilizers (p. 171). There is information on encouraging wildlife (p. 172), and on preserving biodiversity by growing heirloom varieties (p. 170). You may not be able to restore your garden to its original habitat, but you can cultivate native species to encourage and maintain local distinctiveness.

This pergola is built at the edge of a stunning garden near Occidental, California. Displays include arrays of traditional and heirloom species, wild plants, and edible varieties. The garden shows the benefits of conservation gardening and making the most of natural resources, while integrating tranquil corners for peace and quiet. Although few of us can aspire to such a scale, such gardens are truly inspirational.

EDIBLE GARDENING

B y "growing your own" you can put something back into the earth while at the same time taking something out! You can improve the soil, conserve species, and have delicious vegetables, herbs, and fruit for the table. Moreover, you gain healthy productive exercise combined with the pleasure of satisfying some of the needs of your family, and probably friends and neighbors too. If your plot is large enough you may even have surplus food to sell.

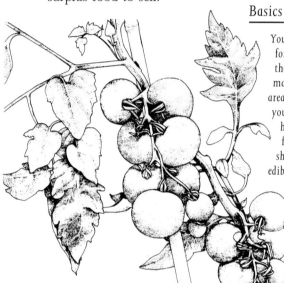

Basics

You may opt for permaculture or forest gardening (see p. 22); if these are not for you, you can still maximize the potential of a small area to grow food. Make the most of your site. Use the walls of your home to protect tender fruits and for climbing plants. If you are short of space, you can even grow edibles in windowboxes, or a window greenhouse!

Even if your soil is well-balanced (see p. 23) demands of cultivation will place a burden on it. So prepare carefully. First dig the ground to clear it and to aerate the soil. While you dig, add valuable compost (p. 113), manure or organic refuse. Once cultivation is underway you will only need to mulch and hoe to keep your soil in good condition.

David Pearson

▲ **If your plot is large enough you can grow food for profit**

Drought gardening

Don't be put off if you are gardening in a comparatively arid area. Some plants will not grow but there are still plenty that will! Plant trees to provide valuable shade for crops and retain moisture in the garden. Make sure you collect rainwater and conserve water (see pp. 72, 73), and use graywater (p. 80) to irrigate all but leafy vegetable crops. In arid climates dryness is due as much to rapid evaporation of soil moisture as to lack of rain, so make sure that your crops are well mulched, preferably growing in raised beds. These offer efficient distribution of water and drainage, deep topsoil and the potential to sustain densely planted crops, which also means good moisture retention. Also choose your plants carefully and avoid those which aren't comparatively drought-tolerant.

What to plant

Planning is all important so begin in the middle of winter, curled up with a few good seed catalogs. Don't stick to standard varieties from garden centers but seek out traditional local varieties which score best on taste, health, and genetic importance. Native varieties are a botanical ark, a treasure for the future in an era of monocropping and pesticides. So sow those seeds!

Consult a local seed savers group about locally distinctive varieties (see Resources p. 181) and learn to save your own seeds too! Don't stick to conventional vegetables, try flowers and even "weeds".

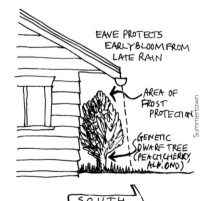

EAVE PROTECTS EARLY BLOOM FROM LATE RAIN

AREA OF FROST PROTECTION

GENETIC DWARF TREE (PEACH, CHERRY, ALMOND)

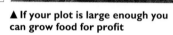
SOUTH

Summertown

◄ **Eaves can provide protection to shelter tender edibles**

By composting all your organic household waste to make nutrient-filled, soil-enhancing compost you take part in nature's cycle, instead of disrupting it. Composting is based on the principle that everything that lives eventually dies and decomposes; dead matter is broken down to its simple constituents which become available to other organisms for their growth. Making compost is simply an accelerated process of natural decomposition and decay, assisting certain bacteria to work rather than leaving the process to chance.

Compost bins

In order to encourage aerobic decay and efficient compost, any heap of decaying matter should be aerated. You can build your own compost bins with lumber, use old plastic drums, or buy bins in wood or plastics. Traditional compost heaps or mounds should be turned with a fork regularly, but some bins make the task of turning the compost easy through an integral central pivot. Many have slatted sides allowing easy access to the compost once made. To decide which kind and size of bin is suitable for you, consider the type and quantity of materials you will be composting, how much space you have, and whether or not you have access to a shredder for woody waste.

Soil biodynamics

Originally conceived by Rudolf Steiner, the Austrian philosopher and educationalist, biodynamic gardening builds on traditional organic husbandry, using crop rotations and leguminous soil enrichers. It also encompasses the belief that cosmic forces affect the ways our plants grow and develop.

Biodynamic gardeners or farmers use special preparations made from minerals which act on the soil in the way that homeopathic remedies act on the body. The main preparations are made according to strict practices and used in tiny quantities. Two of these sprays are used on the soil on specific occasions, while others are used to speed up activity in the compost heap.

▶ **Make sure air can circulate, and that compost can be removed easily**

Worm bins

If most of your compostable garbage comes from the kitchen, consider a worm bin or wormery. These contain manure or brandling worms, Eisenia foetida, which eat nitrogen-rich food such as kitchen waste. They don't smell, you don't have to handle the worms, and they make rich compost in a few months. Some worm bins produce liquid fertilizer which is drained through a special tap. Others produce rich crumbly compost.

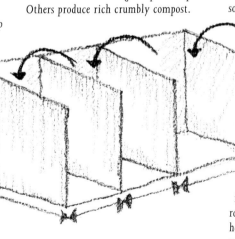

▲ **These systems store composting matter at three stages of maturity**

Dynamic accumulation

Many leguminous plants – clovers, peas, lupins – are known as accumulators. They have nodules sheltering bacteria which can fix nitrogen from the air into a form usable by plants. They can thrive in poor soils, and add nitrogen to any soil when they are dug in. Many common weeds and other plants accumulate additional elements, and can be used in the same way, as green manures. If an accumulator is allowed to grow in an area rich in minerals and then plowed into a mineral-deficient one, usable minerals are also transferred.

The most important accumulator is seaweed, widely obtainable in powdered, liquid, or calcified form. Seaweed provides a wide range of trace elements and minerals, hormones and amino acids, which promote growth and increase resistance to pests and diseases.

SEEDS AND HERBS

Diversity is nature's protection against calamity. If a huge field of plants is genetically identical, one virus or pest can kill the lot. Monoculture therefore relies on artificial fertilizers and poisonous pesticides, devastating land and water and putting farmers in poorer countries out of business. About 97% of food plant varieties available only fifty years ago no longer exist.

Nowadays, as humans have wiped out nearly all the genetic diversity of food plants in many areas throughout the globe, half the world subsists on corn, rice, and wheat. Nature has evolved hundreds of thousands of these three staples, adapted to all the habitat niches in which they grow, but agribusiness has whittled these down to a handful.

◀ **Native wildflowers are beautiful, traditional, and attract wildlife**

Vermont Wildflowers

Seed Saving

First drained through selective breeding, the gene pool now suffers through genetic engineering. Selected plant species have been promoted for our use and bred to withstand pesticides and to store and travel well, at the expense of genetic robustness, fertility, or taste. We lose 27,000 plant species a year with all their reliant animal and insect species.

We should all try to preserve plants no longer grown commercially. This will avoid further loss to the gene pool, and protect against continuous potentially disastrous consequences of monocropping. By planting original species we can regain the specific identity of local areas, their ecological and cultural diversity.

Heirloom varieties

Try to find varieties of seeds which have historically flourished in your area or type of climate. Go for seeds or seedlings untreated with chemical preservatives or pesticides, open-pollinated, and regionally specific. Such seeds are often naturally resistant to many pests and diseases, and can provide tasty food. If your local garden store can't help, join one of the many Seed Saving groups in North America (see Resources p. 180).

Create a flourishing herb garden using heirloom species — check out the wild plants which flourish locally as well as well known varieties. If space allows, plant traditional varieties of fruit trees, and sow native wildflowers.

Companion plants

Most plants thrive in mixed planting, and increased benefits come through companion planting. Some plants protect others against pests and diseases, improve soil fertility, provide shelter from sun and wind, and attract pollinators. French marigolds, for example, deter whitefly away from your tomatoes, and summer savory deters onion root fly. Yarrow helps in pest control and aiding growth of nearby plants — numerous examples can be found in gardening manuals (see Resources p. 181).

▼ **Save your seeds! They are nature's treasures for the future**

Seed Savers Catalog

Barriers and traps

Barriers don't kill pests, but they do prevent them reaching places where you don't want them. Various light covers and nets can protect plants from birds and insects. Gravel around plants or bands of copper around raised beds can keep slugs away. Greased or sticky tapes can stop insects walking up tree trunks or large shrubs. Pheromone traps are widely available and are highly effective for some pests. Sticky barriers can also act as traps.

▲ **Know your pests and learn to control them without chemicals**

You need never have a pest problem in your garden. The best way to avoid it is to build healthy soil, concentrate on growing native plants, plant in raised beds, plus practice crop rotation and garden diversity. However, if unwanted pests do infiltrate your garden you can control them without harmful chemical strategies. Chemical residues from pesticides in soils destroy the natural ecology of an area, enter our drinking water, and contaminate soil and the food chain, so steer clear.

When selecting organic pest control, always remember the interdependence of life; if you disrupt one aspect of any ecosystem, however small, you affect other parts as well. You must first identify any pest or disease. The choice of pest control depends on the problem. Options are generally hand weeding, barriers, traps, biological control, and least-toxic chemical control as a last resort. You need to know your garden well, and a knowledge of garden entomology is important.

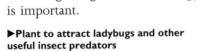

▶ **Plant to attract ladybugs and other useful insect predators**

Botanical pesticides

All pesticides are, by definition, toxic to some living things. They also often have direct or indirect effects on other living things. Botanicals are derived directly from plants or animals. Their toxicity varies but they break down rapidly in the environment rather than accumulating like chemicals. Although no pesticide is "safe" some are safer to use than others. Some botanicals lose their strength in time, others increase in power. Most are effective in use for a short time only.

Botanicals include rotenone, sabadilla, pyrethrin, azadirachtin, ryania, and quassia. Some are toxic to beneficial as well as harmful insects; rotenone is toxic to humans, birds,, and fish, and fish and

other cold-blooded animals are harmed by pyrethrins. Sabadilla will harm bees so only use when bees are hived. Read the labels of any pesticides carefully. Timing can be crucial, as many botanicals will be effective on insects only at certain stages in their development.

Salt, copper, soap, sulfur, oil, and wood ash have all been used as pesticides at different times. They are most successful against soft-bodied insects and eggs. Common "horticultural oil" is a mixture of water and refined petroleum or vegetable oils. This helps control many soft-bodied insects such as aphids, spider mites, webworms, and various other caterpillars. Some oils can harm whiteflies, scales, and psyllids, as well as some beneficial insects.

Biological controls

Beneficial insects include hover flies, lacewings and ladybugs. These efficient predators feed on other insects particularly aphids and ants. Small animals such as hedgehogs and voles are also great friends to your garden, as are many birds and squirrels.

Chronic pest infection may be treated by microbial controls, which cause disease in pests. Those which spread bacterial infection, such as Bacillus thuringiensis, or Bt, are termed bacterial insecticides. Other biological controls include caterpillar-killing viruses, fungi for controlling soil-dwelling insects and protozoa for reducing pests such as corn borers and tent caterpillars.

Common Sense Gardening

WILDLIFE

The growing human population is daily using up more land for housing, for leisure and recreation, for growing food, and for mineral extraction. Moreover, individuals constantly want more – increased goods and services, more choices. Each human activity has an impact on the natural world and leads to habitat destruction. Giving back a little space to wildlife in our own backyards is the least we can do.

Animals need the scruffy tracts of wilderness which planners shun. These spaces need as much diversity in species as possible, from decomposers and insects right up to hawks and foxes. Wild land is not derelict land, already despoiled by humans and bearing the scars of previous human use. Derelict land will eventually become wilderness, but it takes a long time. Nor are manicured, vacuumed, tidy backyards sanctuaries for wild creatures. In your own place, allow untidiness. Animals are shy and timid. Leave them alone whenever possible.

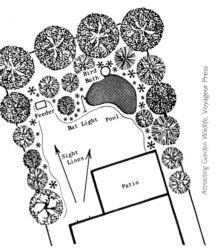

▲ **Design your garden with special features to encourage wildlife**

Gardening for wildlife

In planning or adapting your garden, think about the basic needs of birds and animals.

For shelter, animals need protection from severe weather, safe roosting and hiding areas, and space to rear young. Ground-dwelling animals also need pathways of safe cover. For food, despite seasonal changes of location, many creatures welcome additions to their staple diet, either from food plants yielding fruit or insects, or from feeding stations. And don't forget water, the third requirement. If you have a natural water source, make a pond or slow-moving stream available to wildlife. If not, try to provide a pool, or bath which will become a focal point for wildlife.

Unless you have a huge backyard, it will not meet all the needs of wildlife for shelter, food, and water, so creatures will come and go. Find out what species it is possible to attract in your area, and aim to supply their needs. Also, talk to neighbors about any interest they may have in encouraging wildlife. Encourage them to shun pesticides too. The larger the area planned as a refuge, the better.

Planting to encourage wildlife

Decide which of the possible species you would most like to attract — amphibians, bats, birds, mammals — and plant accordingly. Remember, you are not just providing shelter and food for some animals, but also shelter and food for their prey. Many good sources of information exist on which plants to grow in order to encourage certain animal species (see Resources p. 181). As a general rule, common native species provide the best food sources for indigenous wildlife.

Shelter for birds and animals

You can provide cheaply made boxes to encourage bird and bat visitors. If you have a pond or wet area, devise a dark, damp place (a deep hole in a stone wall, for example) as a natural refuge for toads. A heap of stones in a hot area will shelter lizards; piles of dry grass attract snakes. Spend a little time and your effort will be well rewarded.

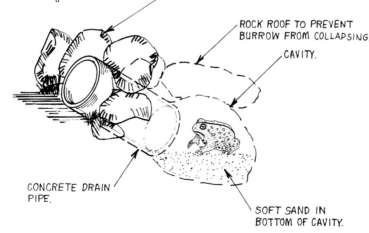

ROCKERY OR ROCK WALL.

ROCK ROOF TO PREVENT BURROW FROM COLLAPSING

CAVITY.

CONCRETE DRAIN PIPE.

SOFT SAND IN BOTTOM OF CAVITY.

◀ **Provide toads with daytime retreats and hiding places**

Attracting Garden Wildlife, Voyageur Press

Natural House Book, Simon and Schuster

▲ A Japanese-style path curves to slow hurrying footsteps

▼ Whatever the scale of garden, water adds a contemplative quality

David Pearson

Enjoying even a small amount of gardening, handling soil, watering plants, sweeping leaves, or just pottering about the greenhouse can often be enough to relax you, make you feel grounded, balanced, and at peace with yourself. If you live in a crowded city it may be the one place that helps you cope with the pace and stress of society around you. Peter Harper, author and organic landscape designer for the Centre for Alternative Technology, Wales, gives an excellent overview of the many garden traditions which recognize this healing power.

"Gardens crop up in the tradition of many ancient religions. The biblical Garden of Eden represented static primal innocence and perfection, that yet contained the seeds of innovation and creative risk. Muslims and Christians inherited the myth of Eden and also a Persian invention: paradise. In the form of a walled garden with lakes, fountains, and fruit trees, paradise became a place for healing the human spirit and, very naturally, the model of what the righteous could expect after death. It is no accident that monotheistic religions emphasised the model of a perfectly designed and regulated garden rather than raw nature. Those that believed in an Earth Mother, and in a pantheon of nature spirits who inhabited rocks, trees, rivers, and so on, were ruthlessly persecuted. Yet in the East, pantheism reached an ineffable sophistication in the philosophy of Lao Tzu, while in the West the Druids embraced it. In fact, indigenous peoples the world over remain pantheistic in their beliefs. And it is no surprise that, at a time of environmental concern, the sacredness of nature is taken seriously once more.

Back in the East, Buddhism has generally been one of the contemplative religions that emphasized detachment from the world. Zen, however, developed practices that used everyday events, tasks, and crafts as tools for spiritual development. Zen gardens are famous for a sense of peace, order, and simplicity, in which all extraneous and distracting elements have been removed. Single rocks and pools with slow-moving fish serve as aids to meditation. The same spirit is found in the fastidiousness and restraint of traditional Japanese gardens. ... There are places, ... where nature's spirits are consciously invoked. But you do not have to be a practising pagan or pantheist for your garden to become a place for spiritual growth and healing. Set aside a quiet spot where you feel right and are least likely to be disturbed. This is your sanctuary." (from *The Natural Garden Book*, Simon & Schuster, 1994).

Natural bat homes

Encourage bats with this sturdy and attractive bat box from Real Goods catalog (CA). Constructed of sustainably-forested timber, it provides an ideal habitat for bat visitors and gives you the chance to observe these fascinating creatures.

Native wildflowers for every State or Province

Wherever you live in North America, Vermont Wildflower Farm can send you the mixture of favorite wild annuals and perennials for your region. Wherever you live, you can support conservation and local distinctiveness by purchasing these seeds.

Roll your own compost

The Bio-Sphere from The Gardener's Supply Company (VT) composts large volumes of leaves, grass, and organic matter. You simply roll it over to your leaf piles, load it up and roll it away! A quick push every few days is all it takes to mix and aerate and provide crumbly compost in 3 to 6 weeks.

Cut clean with a reel mower

Light, economical, low-maintenance, and environmentally-responsible, the American Lawn Mower Company (IN) produce a range of reel mowers. They cut cleanly, perform well, and maintenance merely means sharpening the blades every other season.

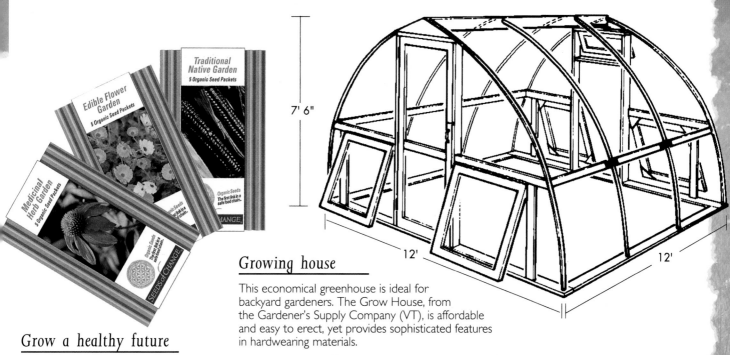

Grow a healthy future

Seeds of Change (NM) gift sets feature organically-grown, open-pollinated seeds, selected for flavor, nutrition, hardiness, and significance for diversity. Support this organization and support our genetic future while pre-serving the best of the past.

Growing house

This economical greenhouse is ideal for backyard gardeners. The Grow House, from the Gardener's Supply Company (VT), is affordable and easy to erect, yet provides sophisticated features in hardwearing materials.

7' 6"

12'

12'

Recline in style

Practical, functional, stylish, and eco-friendly, this recliner from Barlow Tyrie (NJ) is made from teak from managed populations in Java. The company has the Good Wood Seal of Approval, and is listed in the Good Wood Guide, so you can recline in comfort with a clear conscience.

Garden helpers

Sometimes your garden needs a little extra help. Concern Garden Products from Necessary Organics (VA) offer gardeners gently effective and affordable solutions to encourage the healthiest gardens.

SUSTAINABLE STRUCTURES

The natural garden borrows from nature the idea of integration. Virtually everything in the backyard can have several functions; the more the better. Moreover, many garden structures can be created with reused and recycled products.

When planning or making additions to your garden, think of as many uses as possible for each item. For instance, a new fence may be necessary to mark territory, but it can also keep out animals, preserve privacy, define a view, provide a growing frame for climbing plants, provide backing for seats, reduce noise, provide shade and shelter, be beautiful, store heat, and be a habitat for birds. If you have water in your garden, take a look at the flowforms described on page 82. Flowforms combine artistic and spiritual aspects found in the best of gardens, and are practical on many levels for the immediate environment and for human use and pleasure.

Master Garden Products, Inc

Building and landscaping

A huge range of recycled content products is available from specialty merchants for drainage structures, paving, fences, retaining walls, and furniture. Recycled rubber pavers or bricks made from oil-containing soils or recycled glass tiles (see p. 132) are available for exterior walkways. Recycled plastic lumber or plastic/wood composite lumber provides durable alternatives to solid wood for exterior uses such as fences, benches, decking, docks, retaining walls, picnic tables and landscape borders. Some plastic lumber makers use commingled plastic waste which may include paper and metal. Some mix plastic with recycled tire rubber. Some plastic lumber contains wood fiber.

◀ Greenhouse, shed, or playhouse? Structures need not be permanent

▼ Look out for hosepipe made from recycled rubber tires

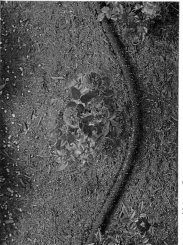

Aquapore Moisture Systems

Growing spaces

Whereas greenhouses are often dedicated to plant growing, sunspaces, sunsheds, or conservatories combine this function with living space. Whatever form your extra growing space takes, avoid wasting heat from it or heating it artificially. If your sunspace adjoins the house, make sure extra heat is diverted by a fan system into the house when additional heat is needed (see p. 61).

In addition to polytunnels or green-

houses, cloches made from PVC or glass prolong the growing season in cool zones; they give seeds and plants a head start by warming the soil and protecting from late frosts. The most basic cloches of all are simply made from cut-off plastic drink bottles, or construct larger structures from recycled window frames. You can water your garden, preferably with household graywater (see p. 80), using soaker hoses made from recycled rubber.

In some areas, yard debris is collected and composted for backyard use, saving

landfill and making valuable mulch and compost. Inquire about local programs. If none exist, how about setting one up among your neighbors? Don't forget to use recycled lumber or recycled plastic compost bins for the job!

Robert Kourik

Robert Kourik is a sustainable gardener par excellence. In 1970 he stitched together the ecology flag which flew above his high school on Earth Day, and he has been involved with the green movement ever since. Organic gardening, sustainable landscape design, water conservation and the complexities of drip-irrigation and graywater-irrigation systems are his specialities.

◀ **Robert Kourik is a hands-on expert and enthusiast about gardening and water conservation**

Kourik, who describes himself as proudly having a degree from "the School of Hard Knocks", started a one-person landscape maintenance business in 1974, and began developing his own techniques for the organic care of lawns, flowers, shrubs, and trees, eventually branching out into the design and installation of ornamental landscapes. One of his most successful food-garden installations was blended into an ornamental garden with permanent stone paths and brick-walled terracing, visible from the owners' kitchen window. Observing how well this worked, Robert originated a new gardening trend he called "edible landscaping " the integration of the best of ornamental-landscape design with the practical pleasures of a food garden.

Water conservation

During the California drought of 1977-78, Robert resourcefully installed plumbing to help his clients irrigate their gardens with used shower-bath- and laundry-water. From these first primitive graywater systems, he has continued to refine his technology. In 1988 he published the definitive Gray Water Use in the Landscape and in 1990 this publication was used as a model for the first legal graywater ordinance in the US, in Santa Barbara (California).

In 1979, Robert became a resident of the Farallones Institute Rural Center (Occidental, CA), a premier force of the 1970s and 1980s in the development of integrated systems utilizing solar technology, organic gardening techniques, water conservation/recycling and all aspects of resource management. For two years, as Director of the Institute's Edible Landscape Program, he offered a variety of hands-on workshops, seminars, and lectures. In 1986, he self-published Designing and Maintaining your Edible Landscape – Naturally (Metamorphic Press), an invaluable 400-page guide which continues to outclass and outsell all other books on the subject.

Robert is still involved in refining drip-irrigation methods, as described in Drip Irrigation for Every Landscape and All Climates (Metamorphic Press 1992). He also contributes to numerous gardening publications and proffers practical hands-on advice wherever possible. He produces a quarterly newsheet, Bob's Honest to Goodness Newsletter, to update fellow gardeners on his most recent experiences with (and opinions on) edible landscaping, drip irrigation, graywater use, water conservation, and general environmental issues. Knowledgeable, practical and fun, Robert Kourik is always eager to share his enthusiasm about conservation in general and your backyard in particular.

Robert Kourik, Landscape consultant and designer, also journalist, publisher/author 17200 Fitzpatrick Lane, Occidental, CA 95465. Tel: 707 874 2606

Recyled tire hoses

Reuse, recycle, and conserve water as your garden flourishes! Moisture Master soaker hoses from Aquapore (AZ) are made from 65% recycled tire rubber, and weep water gently into the ground, nourishing plant roots directly while using up to 70% less water than conventional hoses.

Heavy duty gloves

Suede pigskin gloves from Womanswork (ME) are perfect jobs requiring hand dexterity as well as protection (and men are allowed to wear them too!). Womenswork will even replace single glove if one gets destroyed, lost, or eat by animals!

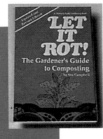

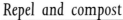

Repel and compost

Citronella-scented lotions and ecosprays from Environmentally Sound Products (MD) help deter biting bugs from feasting on you while you prepare your perfect compost!

Healthy hammocks

Every Twin Oaks (MO) organic cotton rope hammock is handwoven in a crafts community in the Missouri Ozarks. The cotton is grown organically and processed without bleaches, dyes ,or harmful chemicals. And the hammocks are ultra-comfortable and big enough for the largest bodies!

Mulching mower

Ryobi (SC) take hassles out of lawn care with this mulching mower. Battery-operated, cordless, gasless, and bagless, the mower makes grass cutting easier on you and the environment.

Weathervane

This unconventional sun and moon banner weathervane, hand-crafted from copper, is available from Wind & Weather (CA), along with a wide range of traditional and modern sundials.

RESOURCES

General organizations

American Community Gardening
Association
325 Walnut Street, Philadelphia,
PA 19106
Tel: 215 625 8280

American Horticultural Therapy
Association
362A Christopher Avenue,
Gaithersburg, MD 20879
Tel: 301 948 3010

Bio-dynamic Farming and Gardening
Association
PO Box 550, Kimberton, PA 19442
Tel: 215 935 7797

Brooklyn Botanic Garden
1000 Washington Avenue,
Brooklyn, NY 11225
Tel: 718 941 4044

Business for Social Responsibility
Group promoting sustainable development
1010-1030 15th Street NW,
Washington DC 20005
Tel: 202 842 5400 Fax: 202 842 3135

Canadian Biodiversity Institute (education,
information dissemination, and research)
3551 Blanchfield Road, Osgoode,
ON, Canada, K0A 2W0
Tel: 613 826 2190 Fax: 613 241 2292

Committee for Sustainable Agriculture
PO Box 1300, Colfax, CA 95713
Tel: 916 346 2777

Canadian Nature Federation
1 Nicholas Street, Suite 520, Ottawa,
Ontario, Canada, K1N 7B7
Tel: 613 562 3447 Fax: 613 562 3371

Natural Gardening Research Center
Box 149, Sunman, IN 47041

Common Ground Garden Program
2615 S Grand Avenue, Suite 400,
Los Angeles, CA 90007
Tel: 213 744 4349 Fax: 213 745 7513

Community-supported Agriculture of
North America (CSA)
c/o WTIG, 818 Connecticut Ave NW,
#800, Washington, DC 20006
Tel: 202 785 5135.

National Gardening Association
180 Flynn Avenue. Burlington, VT 05401
Tel: 802 863 1308

Edible Garden

Ecology Action of the Mid-Peninsula
5798 Ridgewood Road, Willits, CA 95490
Tel: 707 459 0150

Robert Kourik (see p. 177)

Natural Organic Farmers Association
140 Chestnut Street, West Hatfield,
MA 01088

Northeast Organic Farming Association of
New Jersey
31 Titus Mill Road, Pennington, NJ 08534
Tel: 609 737 6848

Organic Foods Production Association of
North America
PO Box 1078, Greenfield, MA 01301
Tel: 413 774 7511

Permaculture Publications Services
PO Box 672 Dahlognega, GA 30533

Rodale Institute Research Ccenter
611 Siegfriedale Road, Kutztown, PA
19530
Tel: 215 683 1400

Soil improvement

Solid Waste Composting Council
114 South Pitt Street, Alexandria, VA
22314
Tel: 703 739 2401

Conservation/Heirloom Plants

Center for Plant Conservation
Missouri Botanical Gardens
PO Box 299, St Louis, MO 63166
Tel: 314 577 9450

Gardens North
5984 Third Line Road North RR3, North
Gower, Ontario K0A 2T0, Canada
Tel: 613 489 0065

Native Plant Society
1722 J Street, Sacramento, CA 98514
Tel: 916 447 2677

New England Wildflower Society
Garden in the Woods
Framlingham MA 01701
Tel: 617 877 7630

National Wildflower Research Center,
2600 FM 973 North Austin
TX 78725-4201
Tel: 752 929 3600

Seeds of Change
PO Box 15700
Santa Fe, NM 87506-5700
Tel: 505 438 8080

Seed Savers Exchange
3076 North Winn Road
Decorah, IA 52101
Tel: 319 382 5872

Native Seed Foundation
Star Route
Dept W, Moyie Springs, !D 83845
Tel: 208 267 7938

Nature Conservancy
1815 North Lynn Street, Arlington, VA
22209
Tel: 703 841 5300

Vermont Wildflower Farm
Route 7, Charlotte, VT 05445
Tel: 802 425 3500

Biological pest control

Bio-Integral Resource Center (BIRC)
PO Box 7414, Berkeley, CA 94707
Tel: 510 524 1758

Environmental Protection Agency (EPA)
Public Information Center,
820 Quincy Street Northwest, Washington,
DC 20011
EPA Pesticide Hotline: 800 858 7378

EPA Dept of Pesticide Regulation
1020 N Street, Room 161,
Sacramento, CA 95814
Tel: 916 324 4100

Gardens Alive (supplies and information)
5100 Schenley Place
Lawrenceburg, IN 47025
Tel: 812 537 8650

Wildlife

Bat Conservation International
PO Box 162603, Austin TX 78716
Tel: 512 327 9721

National Wildlife Federation
1400 16th Street NW,
Washington, DC 20036
Tel 202 797 6850

New York Turtle and Tortoise Council
63 Amsterdam Avenus, Suite 365
New York, NY 10023
Tel 212 459 4803

Publications

Common-Sense Pest Control, Daar and Olkowski,
1991, The Taunton Press, Box 5506,
Newtown, CT 06470-5506
Tel: 800 283 7252

The Complete Book of Edible Landscaping, Rosalind
Creasy, Sierra Club Books, 730 Polk Street,
San Francisco CA 94109
Tel 800 935 1056

Designing and Maintaining Your Edible Landscape
Naturally, Robert Kourik, Metamorphic
Press, PO Box 1841, Santa Rosa, CA 95402

Rodale's Book of Composting, 1992, Rodale
Press, PA

Rodale's Successful Organic Gardening, Vegetables,
Herbs, Patricia Michalak,1993, Rodale Press,
Emmaus PA

Rodale's Illustrated Encyclopedia of Gardening and
Landscaping Techniques, 1990, Rodale Press

Endangered and Threatened Wildlife and Plants, from
U.S. Fish and Wildlife Service, Publications,
4401 North Fairfax Drive, Mail Stop 130
Webb, Arlington, VA 22203
Tel: 703 358 1711.

Energy-Efficient and Environmental Landscaping
BackHome Books, PO Box 70,
Hendersonville, NC 28793
Tel: 800 992 2546

Forest Gardening, Robert A J de Hart, 1990,
Green Books

Green Schools Biodiversity Booklet
Ocean Voice International, 2883 Otterson
Drive, Ottawa, ON K1V 7B2
Tel/Fax: 613 521 4205

Let it Rot!: The Gardener's Guide to Composting,
available from: Environmentally Sound
Products, 8845 Orchard Tree Lane,
Towson, MD 21286.
Tel: 800 886 5432/410 825 7200

The Meaning of Gardens, Mark Francis and
Randolph Hester, 1992, MIT Press, 55
Hayward Street, Cambridge, MA 02142.
Tel 800 356 0343

The Natural Garden Book, Peter Harper, 1994,
Simon & Schuster, NY

Nature Canada, (bi-monthly)
1 Nicholas Street, Suite 520, Ottawa,
Ontario, Canada, K1N 7B7
Tel: 613 562 3447 Fax: 613 562 3371

Organic Gardening, (9 issues per year)
PO Box 7320, Red Oak IA 51591
Tel: 800 666 2206

Plants for Play - A plant selection for children's
outdoor environments, Robin Moore 1993, MIG
communications

Plant Conservation Directory, annually issued
from Plant Conservation Center (see entry)

Seeds of Change, Harper San Francisco, 1160
Battery Street, San Francisco, CA 94111
Tel: 800 328 5125

Start with the Soil, Grace Gershuny, 1993,
Rodale Press, PA

The Backyard Landscaper, Ireland-Gannon
Associates, Inc, Home Planners Inc, 3275
West Ina Road, Suite 110, Tucson,
AZ 85741

The Chemical-Free Lawn, Warren Schultz,
1989, Rodale Press, PA

Suppliers of Beneficial Organisms in North America,
Charles D Hunter, free from EPA Dept of
Pesticide Regulation (see entry)

Worms Eat my Garbage, Mary Appelhof,
Flower Press, 10332 Shaver Road,
Kalamazoo, MI 49002
Tel 616 327 0108

Xeriscape Gardening (Water Conservation for the
American Landscape), Connie Ellesson, Tom
Stephens and Doug Welsh, 1992,
Macmillan Publishing, NY
Tel: 800 257 5755

BackHome magazine (see p. 190)
PO Box 70
Hendersonville, NC 28793
Tel: 704 696 3838 Fax: 704 696 0700

Garbage (bi-monthly)
2 Main Street, Gloucester MA 01930

Horticulture (monthly)
PO Box 53880, Bouilder, CO 880322

Hortideas (monthly)
460 Black Lick Road, Gravel Switch,
KY 40328

Organic Gardening (nine issues per year)
33 East Minor Street, Emmaus, PA 18098

Now turn to Part Two, The Directory, for more organizations, suppliers and publications

David Pearson

Every product eventually becomes garbage, and-may pollute our land and our seas. We must learn to consume less, throw away less, and consciously choose energy-efficient products at every level of consumption. Throughout North America states and provinces have begun to implement effective recycling progams over recent years. Many states have passed reduce and recycle statutes to jump-start the market for recycled products. "Rates and dates" legislation makes manufacturers responsible for using a certain percentage of recycled materials (the rate) in all their products or packaging by a certain year (the date). Other legislation ensures that all products achieve a threshold of reusability and recyclability.

California led the way down one path to aggressive recycling following the Integrated Waste Management Act of 1989 (AB 939): this required that 25% of waste was diverted from landfills by 1995, aiming for 50% by 2000. Recycling Market Development Zones (RMDZ) provide direct loans to recycling businesses and local governments in their areas. The province of Ontario implemented a significant "Green Workplace" initiative in 1992 which has led to recycling and resource-efficient practices becoming the norm throughout businesses. Many states now prohibit disposal in landfills for non-hazardous solid waste with the consequence that companies have discovered that a little additional effort and environmental zeal can mean a significant reduction in the amount of solid waste requiring disposal.

Solid waste disposal is gradually, through government policies and individuals' and companies' practices, being transformed from a problem into a resource-building industry. The rate of recycling has grown from 9% in 1989 to approximately 21% in 1995. Landfilling has declined significantly over the past six years. Curbside recycling programs have increased, and composting facilities for municipal solid waste (MSW) are continuing to grow — up to 30% of MSW is currently being recycled or composted, and the amount is growing. An increasing number of states have implemented enforced composting for yard materials.

But there is no point in lobbying governments to implement recycling policies if we don't all make a concerted effort in our home practices. Throughout this book, we advocate the choice of recycled goods wherever possible — from building materials to personal products. Recycling is more than simply putting separate newspapers, cans and bottles out for curbside pickup, it is about making conscious choices about what we consume and what we waste. Increasing public awareness of the need to reuse and recycle is only one part of the story.

Critics of recycling point to the stockpiles of recyclable materials which eventually end up in landfill, incineration, or are shipped long distances for disposal. For recycling programs to be efficient, manufacturers need to create demand for products which contain recycled material. Consumers have to close the loop — we must not only reuse or put out our garbage for recycling, we must buy recycled products in preference to others.

We must make the conscious decision to throw away less, and make sure everything we do discard gets recycled (see following pages). We must always demand recycled goods over others, and if necessary pay a little more. If you are fully aware of what it means to reuse, repair, and recycle, you'll find ways to do so.

Reduce your waste and recycle everything you can — facilities exist for most materials, from paper to paint, from metals through batteries. Even if you can't recycle, make sure you dispose of your waste safely. Use local recycling centers and curbside pickups, lobby for increased facilities to dispose of hazardous waste, but above all, choose products carefully and end up with less garbage and a cleaner environment.

RECYCLING

Recycling facilities exist for most of the things we throw away. Make sure you use them, or, if there are none in your area, lobby to get services provided. The following list provides guidelines to safe disposal for recycling, as suggested by Debra Dadd-Redalia in *Sustaining the Earth* (see p. 188). Never throw any of the following items in your garbage can. Call your local recycling center to check on curbside collections or drop-off places and times. Some recycling companies provide recycling bins free of charge to customers. Find out about hazardous waste disposal facilities and other specialized recycling options from your local environmental-health department or branch of the EPA. If your local authorities don't provide satisfactory local recycling facilities, make them aware of the need.

Aluminum

Send all aluminum cans and foil products to the recycling center. Every ton of recycled aluminum over new reduces energy use by 95% (enough to power an average home for $3\frac{1}{2}$ years), and reduces air and water pollutants by the same percentage.

Batteries

Use rechargeable batteries, and take old ones to a hazardous-waste collection. Never throw batteries in the dump as they are filled with heavy metals. Improperly disposed-of household batteries release mercury into the environment. Return all car batteries to gas stations where they will be recycled – each battery contains a highly toxic mix of lead and sulfuric acid.

Fabrics

Compost natural fibers or recycle old clothes and fabrics. Never send synthetic fibers to the municipal dump – they do not biodegrade.

Food waste

Compost, or use for animal feed. You can even make your own wormery using recycled tires. Also, support local food-exchange programs that pick up leftover food from businesses and deliver it to free-food programs.

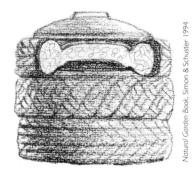

Natural Garden Book, Simon & Schuster 1994

Glass

All glass bottles and jars can be recycled, as long as they are clean and free of metal. Recycling centers cannot accept light bulbs, dishes, or plate glass, but there may be a program in your area that recycles these materials. Ask your local public or environmental health department, or contact the Citizens Clearing House for Hazardous Waste for your local group (see Resources, p. 165).

Household and building materials

Take lumber, doors, windows, plumbing fixtures, and other reusable building materials to your local reclamation center/salvage yard. They may even pay you for your waste.

Some paint companies will collect your old paint to remanufacture it, or you may have a local paint exchange program (see p. 126).

Drawings by Karen Hart, courtesy of Metro, Portland, OR

Metals

All metals should be recycled — larger items can go for scrap; cans should be rinsed and taken to the recycling center. Recycled metals currently provide approximately 50% of all lead, 40% of all copper, 35% of all gold, and 25% of all silver used in North America. Recycling lead reduces energy use by 60%, recycling copper by 87%.

Motor oil

Recycle used motor oil at a gas station or at a dump that will accept it. Never ever dispose of it down a household drain: it contains toxins such as lead, chromium, naphthalene, chlorinated hydrocarbons, and other dangerous chemicals.

Paper and paperboard

All types of paper can be recycled, but some magazines use coated paper and hot-melt glues for binding, with mailing labels that are not water soluble. Check with your recycling center where to send these for recycling.

Plastics

Avoid purchasing them in the first place. They do not biodegrade in dumps. The best long-term solution for most plastics is to eliminate their use entirely. For now, if you do buy products made from or packaged in plastic, make sure they are recycled and recyclable.

Tires

There may be a rubber-recycling plant in your area; if not, lobby for one. Used tires are a useful material for products from building materials through truck-bed liners through irrigation piping to carpet underlayment and mats.

Hazardous household waste

Some communities have specific days when they collect household hazardous wastes and take them to a reprocessing center. Find out from your local public or environmental health department. Dispose of all existing toxic wastes carefully, and find safe alternatives in the future. Anything that is hazardous to dispose of must be hazardous to use, so avoid these products.

Never dispose of the following hazardous household products in your ordinary garbage:

Cleaning materials: Ammonia cleaners, chlorine bleach; all petrochemical cleansers; disinfectants; drain openers; furniture and floor polish; lye; metal polish; oven cleaner; carpet cleaners; mothballs; drycleaning solvent.

Cosmetics: Nail polish and remover; depilatory cream; hair-permanent solutions; hair dye.

Medicines: Chemotherapy drugs; liquid medicine; thermometers or mercury from broken thermometers; prescription medicine; rubbing alcohol; lice shampoo.

Building supplies: Asbestos; fluorescent lamp fittings; glues and cements; wood preservatives.

Hobby supplies: Artist's mediums, thinners, fixatives; acrylic paint; chemistry sets; oil paint; photogaphic chemicals; resins, fiberglass and epoxy; adhesives.

Painting supplies: Latex-based paint, oil-based paint; paint stripper; paint thinner, turpentine, mineral spirits.

Garden supplies: Fungicides; herbicides; insecticides; rat poison; snail and slug poison; soil fumigants; weed killer.

Automotive supplies: Aluminum cleaner; auto-body filler; automatic transmission fluid; brake fluid; carburetor cleaner; fuel; kerosene; car wax; lubricating oil; used motor oil.

Other products: Aerosol cans containing any pressure or fluid; butane lighters; flea powder; pet shampoo; shoe dye and polish.

green experts

The field of "green", healthy, and spiritual design is a rich and varied one with many exciting developments taking place all the time. To find your way in this changing field, you may need expert advice. In this chapter, we feature individuals and organizations with specialist knowledge in various fields who can inspire and help you when planning your natural home. The consultants who helped put the *Catalog* together are also featured. These case studies represent examples of some of the pioneers who are working at the frontier, but, if space allowed, many more would be included. All are experienced and committed, in their own area, to showing practical ways in which we can all live more responsible and sustainable lifestyles. If you have direct practical knowledge of one particular topic, your experience is also valuable. So why not write about it, or teach it, and pass on your knowledge?

Most of these "green" experts have presented their work in newsletters, publications, and videos. Some run seminars, tours, and hands-on workshops. Many offer advice and professional services. Information on others can be found in the Resources pages at the end of chapters in Part One and in the Subject Listings in Part Two.

Debra Dadd-Redalia

She's been called "the queen of green," "the guru of nontoxic living," and "the godmother of natural living," and has written consumer guidebooks many refer to as their bibles. Always one step ahead, her well-researched books have been a leading influence on the green market – to consumers, marketers, and manufacturers – for more than a decade.

Back in 1980, when a "green" product was one the color of grass and hazardous waste was something you only found in a factory, Debra Dadd-Redalia was diagnosed with an immune system disorder commonly known now as environmental illness or chemical sensitivity. Her widely varied symptoms were disabling, but she was told there was no cure –other than removing all toxic chemicals from her home. As no books on household toxics or nontoxic alternative products were then available, she set out to write one, and in the process healed herself and countless others.

After self-publishing her first consumer manual for those with chemical sensitivities, the makers of nontoxic Bon Ami Polishing Cleanser sent her on a media tour to promote the concept of nontoxic cleaning products. By then it had become clear that the issue of chemicals in products was much larger than the effect on a few sensitive individuals; as she researched toxic chemicals in products Debra found that many products contained chemicals that are harmful to the general public, and that illness caused by these household toxics could be

prevented. *Nontoxic & Natural* was published in 1984, followed by *The Nontoxic Home* in 1986. Both books not only alerted consumers to toxic dangers, but offered alternatives.

By 1987, Debra was living in a completely nontoxic home in an idyllic Northern California forest. Realizing that our consumer choices affected the larger environment as well as our own health, she began to research the environmental effects of consumer products. In 1990 she produced a guidebook of "earthwise" products that had environmental benefits, such as being recycled, energy efficient, biodegradable, or organically grown.

As products with environmental claims flooded the market, Debra became concerned that many of the products that made the claims were nothing more than green hype. Because there were no standards or guidelines for evaluating green products, Debra set out to discover what it means to truly live in a way that is responsible to the earth. Her most recent book, *Sustaining the Earth*, calls for sustainability to be used as the standard for evaluating consumer products, and shows consumers how to evaluate products for themselves.

"While green products are definitely a step in the right direction," says Debra, "the next leap is going to be for us to question consumerism itself. We can provide for our needs in a sustainable way only if we look at what we need, and how we obtain it, in a different manner than we're accustomed to."

Where will she lead us next?

Debra Dadd-Redalia is the author of Sustaining the Earth *(William Morrow, 1994);* The Nontoxic Home & Office *(Jeremy P. Tarcher, 1992); and* Nontoxic, Natural & Earthwise *(Jeremy P. Tarcher, 1990). She also acts as a consultant; write to her at PO Box 279, Forest Knolls CA 94933*

Guy Dauncey

Faced with a 60-acre derelict cement plant in the middle of a forest, few of us could envisage the site transformed into a thriving sustainable community. But Guy Dauncey did! Between 1990–1994 he was environmental and community development consultant for a major project to transform just such a site into a new town for 12,000 people.

If you drive 30 minutes north of Victoria, on Vancouver Island, you reach the abandoned site of a former cement plant. Surrounded by 1,500 acres of forest, and with its own water source, this is Bamberton. This will be home for 12,000 people, in a community to be built by the South Island Development Corporation over 20 years, with investment from four labor union pension funds.

The planning for the new town took place from 1990–1992, and the final approvals are expected to be complete by 1998. The town is designed as a traditional neighborhood development with narrow interconnecting streets, village greens, front porches, and a pedestrian emphasis, harking back to the way towns were designed when the automobile was less dominant. The town will house people of all ages and incomes, with its own local economy, and a detailed commitment to ecological sustainability.

Some areas of the site have special ecological significance. These are being fully protected. There will be native plant species comprising 25% of each lot in public spaces; an emphasis on natural drainage, maximizing the flow of rain water back to the land instead of channeling it away through storm drains; a tertiary sewage treatment system; a community composting plant, and a community recycling program. The housing goal has been to aim to maximize overall sustainability while allowing builders comparative freedom. The whole site is a "registered building scheme", enabling the developer to lay down development standards both for outline design and for energy efficiency. Every house must achieve a level of energy efficiency equivalent to the Canadian R2000 standard, and undesirable building materials such as formaldehydes and oil based paints have been banned. The

weekly recycling of construction materials is mandatory. To encourage builders to move further toward sustainability, a voluntary "E3" program (Energy, Environment, Efficiency) program has been drafted, based on the Green Builder Program from Austin, Texas. The program is based on recycled content, recyclability, non-toxicity, embodied energy, and local production, giving a house an overall rating varying from 1 to 4 stars. So consumers can choose to order a 4-star house, allowing builders to market their skill at building the most resource-efficient houses for green home buyers. The Bamberton Builders Forum provides builders with the latest information on sustainable techniques and materials, and an "approved builder" scheme operates.

One of Guy Dauncey's new projects is the development of a solar ecovillage for 5,000 people outside Tucson, Arizona. This is to be a model for water, energy, and transportation efficiency, and a new role model for development. All that is missing at the moment is $10 million of investment capital! Guy is also working on various smaller projects, and writing.

Guy Dauncey, Sustainable Communities Consultancy, 2069 Kings Rd, Victoria, British Columbia V8R 2P6, Canada. Tel & fax: 604 592 4473

Richard Freudenberger *and* BackHome *magazine*

Two decades ago, as a fledgling New York City automotive journalist, Richard took a leap of faith into the mountains of Western North Carolina when he was hired by *Mother Earth News* founder John Shuttleworth to oversee a renewable-energy research facility and help develop an Eco-Village where new ideas could be conceived, tested, and shared with the magazine's readership.

At the time, recycling was a subject untouched by press or populace; energy conservation seen as the government's job; indigenous or alternative construction methods were too counterculture to be taken seriously; organic food production was too much trouble.

Yet the findings reported by the publication's small appropriate-engineering and intensive-gardening staff were eagerly anticipated with each new issue. The magazine's folksy style encouraged rather than alienated would-be do-it-yourselfers, who in turn contributed their own experiences in print. The 624-acre Eco-Village became a mecca for "doers" of all types – a place where people ready to take responsibility for their own lives could attend intensive seminars taught by experts in every field, and return home with the practical experience needed to build, grow and nurture.

Political and cultural change gradually took their toll on that original publication, which failed at the end of a twenty-year reign after its sale to a New York entrepreneur. Determined to keep its spirit alive, a number of the original editorial, gardening, and research staff pooled their resources to launch *BackHome* magazine in the spring of 1990. Richard and his partners launched BackHome on a grand total of $2,800 scraped together from unused vacation checks!

Getting back to their roots involved more than simply reviving tradition. Changes in economies, technology, and attitudes called for a different approach to a saner lifestyle. With the new decade, an emphasis was placed on careful planning, with social networking contributing to the success of each endeavor. Accordingly, the pages of *BackHome* combine a hands-on, down-to-earth approach with the practical application of modern technology to present working guidelines for those preparing to tread a softer path.

BackHome has been described as a "toolbox with covers"...a "how-to magazine with heart". It's a personal, generation-spanning family magazine, to be saved and used year in. It is largely written by staff and readers who are living the life portrayed, so it covers matters as diverse as renewable-energy sources, making a living in a decentralized work environment, raising safe fresh garden produce, and organizing community actions. And it delivers the goods without preaching, and with no political agenda.

BackHome *magazine is published in Hendersonville, North Carolina. The magazine also sponsors selected workshops and runs a mail-order book outlet. Tel: 704 696 3838*

Carol Venolia

Carol Venolia is an architect, writer and lecturer. Her work has always had two components: design and information; both are rooted in her passion to understand the nature of life and to create human habitats that celebrate life.

Long ago it struck her that buildings have been one of the ways in which we pretend that humans are separate from the rest of nature, so she determined to create buildings that are just the opposite: environments that help us to understand and express the continuity of all life. Carol's architectural practice has been largely residential, and she has worked with a variety of materials, including rammed earth and straw bale, chosen for their vitality, as well as with standard materials.

Conventional architects might list light, space, form, and function among the most important considerations when planning a building for a client; Carol also tries to respond to the client's lifestyles and dreams, as well as to the site, healthy materials, resource efficiency, solar heating and daylighting, natural cooling, indoor-outdoor connections, and pure pleasure.

Realizing that clients can't ask for something they can't imagine, and that architects can't offer perspectives they haven't explored, Carol has been highly involved in the informational and theoretical basis for a livelier architecture. Underlying her work is the belief that this culture must learn to value life more if we are to continue to survive and thrive.

In *Healing Environments*, Carol takes a positive holistic approach to human-environment relations, looking at how light, color, sound, symbolism, plants, and other factors can influence our physical and mental well-being. She looks at ways in which we can change our perceptions and surroundings to increase our vitality and sense of connectedness with life. *Building with Nature Newsletter* continues the flow of information and inspiration, and attempts to look at topics from many perspectives at once. For example, rather than looking at energy-efficiency, or recycled materials, on their own, she encourages debate that includes health issues, wider environmental issues, and so on. Carol is committed to a holistic view, in which no one topic should be seen in isolation from its wider context.

Networking and sharing information is also vital to Carol's work. She is co-founder of the Natural Building Network, a group which meets monthly in Northern California to hear speakers and share experiences. Her whole outlook is guided by a sense of delight, fun, and a higher purpose in our human endeavors.

Carol Venolia, PO Box 4417, Santa Rosa CA 95402

Helmut Ziehe

Helmut Ziehe is President of the International Institute for Bau-biologie and Ecology (IBE). The Institute deals with the impact that buildings have on people's health and on the environment. Bau-biologie evolved in Germany in the early 60s and has since spread from the German-speaking countries in Europe to the rest of the world. It translates as "the study of the holistic interaction between life and the living environment."

The IBE is a non-profit organization in Clearwater, Florida, which aims to educate people (professionals and the general public) about the health hazards that may exist in their homes and workplaces. It trains people to detect such hazards and proposes appropriate ways to eliminate them. The Institute also proposes new building design concepts and encourages the development of non-toxic or low-toxic building materials and building systems. And it offers two correspondence courses, numerous seminars, books and instruments, and consultations.

Following architectural studies at the Technical University in Berlin, Helmut Ziehe took a post-graduate degree in Tropical Architecture at the AA School of Architecture in London. He worked and lived in Sweden, Denmark, Greece, and Great Britain, as well as in North Africa, before making his home in Clearwater. As well as this international perspective he has signifi-cant professional experience. This includes planning hospitals, hotels, and housing units for small communities, as well as small-scale industrial developments and homes.

He founded the IBE in England in 1984, and in the USA in 1986.

Over 700 English-speaking students around the world have studied IBE's correspondence courses, and environmental inspectors certified by IBE can carry out home inspections throughout North America. The Institute is also involved with architects and builders' associations, and hopes that links with universities and colleges will one day lead to their offering courses in Bau-biologie.

Helmut Ziehe hopes that the IBE's education programs will inspire people to make changes needed to create sustainable living and building habits. If we make these changes, he believes we can look forward to a more positive future.

Institute for Bau-biologie and Ecology, PO Box 387, Clearwater, FL 34615. Tel : 813 461 4371; fax: 813 441 4373

Seed Savers Exchange

Eight thousand backyard gardeners are searching the countryside for endangered vegetables, fruits, and grains. They are members of the Seed Savers Exchange (SSE), a non-profit organization that is saving old-time food crops from extinction. Kent and Diane Whealy founded SSE in 1975 after an elderly relative bestowed three kinds of garden seeds brought from Bavaria four generations earlier. The Whealys began searching for other "heirloom varieties" and soon discovered a vast, little-known genetic resource.

Since the Mayflower first landed, gardeners from every corner of the world have brought along favorite seeds when their families immigrated. Many of these varieties are still being maintained by gardeners and farmers in isolated rural areas and ethnic enclaves. When elderly seed savers pass away, unless their seeds are replanted by other gardeners, the strains become extinct. This is a disaster for genetic diversity, and future generations will never enjoy the delicious colors, scents, and/or flavors.

SSE's members are maintaining thousands of heirloom varieties, traditional Indian crops, garden varieties of the Mennonite and Amish, vegetables long since disappeared from seed catalogs. Members distribute these seeds to ensure their survival – SSE has no financial interest in any of these varieties, they want only to save them for future generations to enjoy.

One of SSE's projects is Seed Savers International, designed to collect and maintain endangered garden species from the former Soviet Union and Eastern Europe. Many Eastern countries are dazzlingly rich in traditional varieties, but those fragile resources are quickly being lost as Western agricultural technology floods in, along with American, Dutch, and Japanese seeds. SSI has developed a network of plant collectors in Eastern countries, and has sponsored collecting expeditions in Russia, Azerbaijan, Romania, and Poland.

In 1986 SSE purchased Heritage Farm, in Decorah, Iowa. This 140 acre farm includes a conference center and camp, and 1,500 heirloom varieties are grown annually for seed in large organic gardens, Visitors and helpers are very welcome!

SSE books include the *Seed Savers Yearbook, Garden Seed Inventory* and the invaluable *Seed to Seed*, documenting seed saving techniques across the board. These publications provide masses of horticultural information, and access to thousands of heirloom varieties that are not available elsewhere. But, most important of all, by supporting SSE you will help save what remains of our vanishing plant heritage, protecting vital diversity for future generations.

Seed Savers Exchange, 3076 North Winn Rd. Decorah, Iowa 52101. Tel: 319 382 5872

Haiku Houses

"**N**ature, strength, and flexibility are the secrets of the tree, the pole, and Haiku Houses." These houses are based on the timber framed country houses of 16th century Japan. Available as self-assembly kits, they combine ancient Japanese architectural sensitivity with state-of-the-art engineering, and will survive earthquakes, hurricanes, fires, and floods.

These houses combine western refinements with basic design reminiscent of ancient Japanese country houses. Every timber is custom-crafted to give the feeling of a completely handmade structure. The poles and beams are wire-brushed, notched, shaped, rounded, pre-drilled, and numbered and delivered anywhere in the world with easy-to-understand assembly drawings so that the main frame can be erected in just a few days.

Haiku houses are logical for any site, blending with their environment and using natural protective forces. They are significantly different from traditional Japanese wood-framed construction in one important respect: traditionally posts and beams were notched together without any reinforcing connections. During an earthquake, the post-and-beam joints could suddenly separate, causing collapse of the entire structure. Haiku Houses, on the other hand, use steel plates and bolts to connect structural beams with large diameter vertical poles. This provides a positive connection which can stretch and bend without collapsing during an earthquake. During construction, for additional

strength and horizontal stability, the poles are embedded deeply in the ground sunk in concrete. These houses really can survive whatever nature throws at them, and they have been called "disaster-proof houses".

Nature's remarkable cooling system is put to good use though the age-old "Venturi" principle. Rising warm air is pulled up and out of the house through vents in the roof, and incoming cooling air through vents at floor level.

All wood in Haiku Houses comes from managed forests. Poles, paneling, and timbers are douglas fir, redwood, or cedar; ceilings are combed spruce, doors from cherry wood, and floors are oak or maple. The classic roof tiles come from Japan. A Haiku house is truly natural and elegant – an "oasis of peace and serenity".

For color catalog send $15.00 to: Haiku Houses, 250 Newport Center Drive, Suite 200, Newport Beach, CA 92660

Cal-Earth

Spurning concrete and modern high rises in favor of traditional adobe and domes, architect Nader Khalili chose the Mojave Desert as the location for his earth-architecture institute – Cal-Earth.

In 1975, Khalili gave up a lucrative architectural practice to spend five years touring his native Iran, studying age-old methods and esthetics of adobe architecture. Founded on the principles of the arch, vault, and dome, this ancient method of building with earth is simple, environmentally harmonious, energy-efficient, and affordable. Khalili believes these timeless principles hold the key to structures of the future.

"Everywhere I went I found roadside kilns, some of them fifty or a hundred years old, undamaged, hard as rock. I thought to myself, those people should be moved into kilns! And then I started thinking how to make a kiln into a house, and then a house into a kiln." He developed this into his "ceramic houses" where the interiors of the clay-domed house were sprayed with glazes, and the whole structure fired from within, like a huge pot, making it sturdy enough to withstand earthquakes common in Iran.

Rather than using conventional wood and minerals, Nader experimented with solar power, and soon found that the sun's energy, sufficiently concentrated, would fuse bricks together and glaze their surfaces. In the 1980s NASA also became interested in its possible applications for fusing lunar rocks and soil for buildings and roads on the moon. But Khalili's urgent mission is to help the poor and homeless, particularly in underdeveloped countries. He is also passionate in wanting to change the attitude of policymakers, architects, and builders everywhere to take earth building seriously and make it a priority.

Always searching for ways to make earth building simpler and easier, Nader has used earth-filled jute sandbags or recycled rice bags and, more recently, has developed what he calls Superadobe. Here, woven polyprolylene tube – commonly used for flood control – is filled with site earth and laid in an almost continuous coil to form the circular walls and domed roof of the buildings. Barbed wire "stitches" the coils together and adds earthquake stabilization. Finally, adobe is applied inside and out to complete this strong yet simple, earth building.

Over the years, through regular workshops and student programs, people from all over the world have experienced first hand the excitment and practical joys of earth building.

"The timeless essence of the elements [earth, water, air and fire], the timeless natural forms of arches, vaults, and domes, the principle of gravity and the spirit of quest will give you the ability to build anywhere in the world with only what is around you. I believe that the architecture of utopia begins with the unity of these elements."

(Nader Khalili)

For further information, contact: Cal-Earth, California Institute of Earth Building & Architecture, 10225 Baldy Lane, Hesperia, CA 92345. Tel: 619 244 0614; fax 619 956 7533

The Center for Resourceful Building Technology

In 1990 the Center for Resourceful Building Technology (CRBT) was founded by builder Steve Loken. He was concerned about environmental degradation from resource extraction, and at the same time frustrated by the declining quality of materials supplied to construction sites. Loken founded CRBT to gather information on, and inform the public about, environmentally-responsible resource-efficient building materials and technologies. CRBT's approach includes research, education, and demonstration.

CRBT has become a recognized source on resource-efficient building. Researchers collect and evaluate information about new and existing building materials. Their criteria are based on efficient use of limited natural resources, recyclability or renewability, and lower energy use.

Manufactures whose products fulfil the criteria are listed in CRBT's *Guide to Resource Efficient Building Elements*. This directory is updated and expanded each year.

Steve Loken and his colleagues pass the word on via talks to audiences ranging from the general public to building industry and environmental professionals. They have lectured all over the United States and Canada, and also in Australia.

In 1992 CRBT completed ReCRAFT 90, a demonstration home building project using resource-efficient and recycled building materials. This project led to CRBT's work as a consulting body to other organizations across the United States. In spring 1995, CRBT began construction on its second demonstration house in Missoula, Montana. This Timber-Tech House highlights advances in the efficient use of wood fiber in an affordable, easy to replicate, urban infill home.

Steve and the team aim to expand the CRBT's publishing activities, and develop educational outreach programs for schools. They also plan to sponsor building material salvage and reuse in building retrofit applications.

Center for Resourceful Building Technology, PO Box 3838, Butte, MT 59702. Tel: 406 549 7678

Ken Ceder and Ott Biolights

Twenty-five years ago Dr John Ott realized the potentially harmful effects of unnatural lighting. He pioneered full-spectrum lighting, and a new science – photobiology. But at the time Ott's ideas were largely rejected by a world still suspicious of new ideas.

Natural light is health-giving and restorative, and for eons this light was taken for granted, unquestioned. Then people started tinkering with it, creating artificial light to alter the natural balance of day and night, indoors and outdoors. Unfortunately, over the past decades light has too often come to mean sickly yellowish, distorted-spectrum fluorescent light. This unhealthy indoor light has come to be universally widespread in homes and workplaces, with negative consequences for health and creativity.

Today the evidence supporting Ott's earlier work has become indisputable. Research from many different sources has come to show conclusively that indoor radiation-shielded full spectrum lighting is the next best thing to the sun's rays, and can be just as nourishing as natural sunlight. Full spectrum light hastens the human healing process – mentally and physically – and has a positive impact on people suffering from immune deficiency diseases such as Chronic Fatigue Immune Deficiency (CFIDS), Seasonal Affective Disorder (SAD), and even cancers.

In 1987, Ken Ceder was looking for an ecologically-positive product to develop, manufacture, and market. He was looking for something that he could really believe in, that would contribute to general health and welfare. When he came across Dr Ott's experiments he couldn't believe that this work had been so ignored or undervalued. Ignoring earlier prejudices, he determined to use Ott's work as the basis for manufacturing healthy lighting products. Under his leadership, Ott Biolight Systems began as a small Santa Barbara lighting firm, producing a range of domestic full spectrum lights, and the company has now grown into a high-tech firm with special expertise in phototherapy. It researches and produces biologically beneficial lighting for domestic and industrial markets throughout North America and abroad, and offers consultation and information services.

Ken Ceder modestly says that he just happened to be in the right place at the right time. Increasing green awareness through media and education over the last ten years has led people to realize the positive impact of full spectrum lights. It also means people are beginning to understand the harm they may be inflicting on themselves by living indoors under common fluorescents, and to recognize that full spectrum lights are not a luxury but a necessity. Even the FDA recommends some Ottlights as therapeutic devices.

Ken Ceder, Ott Biolight Systems, 28 Parker Way, Santa Barbara, CA 93101. Tel: 805 564 3467; fax 805 564 2147

Scientific Certification Systems

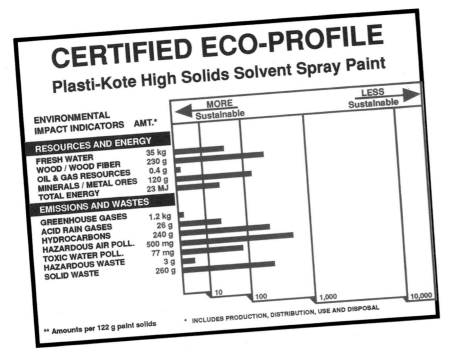

CERTIFIED ECO-PROFILE

Plasti-Kote High Solids Solvent Spray Paint

ENVIRONMENTAL IMPACT INDICATORS	AMT.*
RESOURCES AND ENERGY	
FRESH WATER	35 kg
WOOD / WOOD FIBER	230 g
OIL & GAS RESOURCES	0.4 g
MINERALS / METAL ORES	120 g
TOTAL ENERGY	23 MJ
EMISSIONS AND WASTES	
GREENHOUSE GASES	1.2 kg
ACID RAIN GASES	26 g
HYDROCARBONS	240 g
HAZARDOUS AIR POLL.	500 mg
TOXIC WATER POLL.	77 mg
HAZARDOUS WASTE	3 g
SOLID WASTE	260 g

MORE Sustainable ← → LESS Sustainable

10   100   1,000   10,000

* INCLUDES PRODUCTION, DISTRIBUTION, USE AND DISPOSAL

** Amounts per 122 g paint solids

Scientific Certification Systems, 1611 Telegraph Avenue, Suite 111, Oakland, CA 94612. Tel: 510 832 1415

SCS is an independent labeling and testing organization based in Oakland, California. Founded in 1984, it aims to spur the private and public sectors toward more environmentally sustainable policy planning, product design, management, and production. SCS conducts independent evaluations of environmental and food safety claims, and conducts life-cycle assessments (LCAs) in a wide range of industries.

Introduced in 1990, the Environmental Claim Certification Program is the nation's first scientific system for independently verifying the accuracy of environmental claims on products. The program highlights manufacturers' efforts to improve the environmental performance of their products and production systems. SCS also works with leading retailers to help them monitor the environmental claims made by their vendors, and to make sure these claims meet green marketing guidelines.

Based on the findings of detailed industrial and consumer LCAs, SCS helps companies and institutions to determine the environmental profiles of existing operations, and to evaluate the environmental advantages associated with various products and material choices. They also assess improvement strategies, and document environmental achievements in the marketplace.

The stream of supposedly green products now flooding the marketplace means an ever-growing need for rigorous testing and labeling. SCS has pioneered an approach called Certified Eco-Profile Labeling. Instead of a traditional "seal of approval", Eco-profiles provide critical information about the impact on the environment of any product. SCS results appear directly on product labels. These labels, offered to any product that undergoes an LCA, provide consumers, manufacturers, policy makers, and the general public with information necessary to make informed environmental choices.

SCS launched a Forest Conservation Program (FCP) in 1991, to identify forest management practices which sustain timber resources, maintain the ecological viability of the forest, and benefit the larger community. They also operate a third-party certification system for testing pesticide residues in fresh produce, showcasing farmers who produce food that meets exceptionally high standards, and providing retailers with critical information relating to pesticide use.

The Healthy House Institute

Lynn and John Bower know personally the importance of living in a healthy house. After a six year home restoration project during the 1970s, Lynn became seriously ill. In common with most other people at the time, the couple used typical building and decorating products such as particleboard, plywood, synthetic carpeting, and so on. And, they carried out all the work themselves while living in the house. Unfortunately several years passed before they realized Lynn had become chronically sick as a direct result of her exposure to the toxic chemicals that were outgassing from the very materials they had used to "improve" their home.

So they decided to move to a rural location and construct a "healthy house". Although John had a wealth of environmental engineering experience, building a truly healthy house proved challenging. Few books were available on the subject in the mid-1980s, so he spent a great deal of time researching in libraries, reading any relevant material he could find, and talking with technical representatives from major companies.

The result of this research was John's first book, *The Healthy House*, 1989, and the start of their business, Ecologically Safe Homes. John was soon asked to speak at conferences in the US and Canada sponsored by building associations, home inspectors, governmental agencies, colleges, and universities. In 1993, in order to stress the informational thrust of their business, Ecologically Safe Homes

became The Healthy House Institute, a private resource company whose main aim is to improve indoor air quality by promoting healthier house construction and lifestyle. John and Lynn felt that, despite increasing interest in health and ecology, the potentially negative effects of common building materials and household items remained either largely unknown or ignored by most architects, designers, builders, and homeowners. The Institute aims to provide up-to-date information via books, videos, lectures, and consultations. It supplies accessible information about healthy alternatives and where to obtain them, explanations of the correct use of products, and emphasize the importance of adequate ventilation.

The Institute's first hands-on project was the construction, in 1993, of a model Healthy House. A book and accompanying video documented the actual building materials and techniques used to create this attractive, energy-efficient, and healthy home. Lynn and John are currently involved in building a new healthy house for themselves, and they have recently released two more books, *Understanding Ventilation* by John and *The Healthy Household* by Lynn. Lynn's health is much better, having lived in a healthy home now for nearly ten years, although she does still suffer some hypersensitivities. Time will tell what future projects are in store for them, as they continue their commitment to making every house a healthy house.

John and Lynn Bower, The Healthy House Institute, 430 N Sewell Road, Bloomington, IN 7408. Tel: 812 332 5073; fax: 812 332 5073

part two

DIRECTORY OF
PRODUCTS AND
SERVICES

The Directory provides you with further sources of advice, guidance and information on all the topics covered in Part One. Use it to access all the products, services and information that you need to make your natural home a reality. Listings include products, organizations, catalogs, retailers, magazines and publications.

Entries are organized to echo the structure of Part One. In addition to listings arranged according to the topics covered in Part One chapters, further sections list useful books and publications.

To find, for example, a supplier of photovoltaic cells, use the Contents pages and Index to look up the page numbers where the topic is featured in Part One and in the Directory. Suppliers will be listed in the Directory under the Soft Energy heading, subheading Photovoltaics, page 52. If you don't find what you need, refer back to the Resources at the end of the relevant chapter in Part One, and find an organization that may be able to help you.

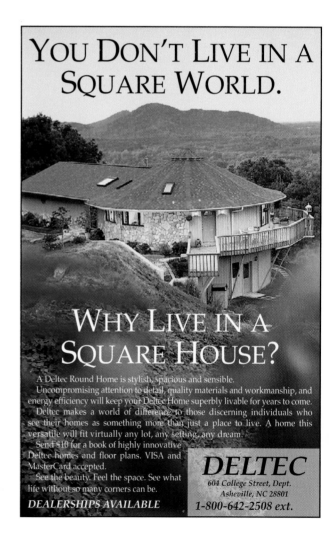

CONTENTS

All the information contained in the Directory is, to the best of Gaia Books' knowledge, correct at the time of going to print. However, companies move, and people change direction, so we apologize for any errors occurring now or in the future. Also, although we have done our best to include a representative sample of individuals, companies, organizations and products, there may be some others that you would like to see included, or even those that you think should be omitted from future editions. Please contact the publishers with any updates and additional information - this is your Directory so your suggestions will be gratefully received.

Feng Shui ~ page 20

MAUREEN L BELLE • Biarch, Systems Earth, PO Box 495, Langley, WA 98260 • Tel: 206 579 1535 Fax: 206 579 1545 • *Feng Shui practitioner. Safe Environmental Designer, 20 years design and construction experience. Consultation. Lectures.*

MARY CORDARO • 12439 Magnolia Boulevard, no 263, Valley Village, CA 91607 • Tel: 310 838 2892 / 818 981 7245 Fax: 810 766 5882 • *Feng Shui and Bau-biology classes worldwide.*

FOURTH DIMENSION HOUSING • PO Box 44, Rainier, WA 98576 • Tel: 360 446 7715 Fax: 360 446 1163 • *Architectural designs using sacred geometry, Feng Shui, and Universal principles.*

MELANIE LEWANDOWSKI • PO Box 536, New Hope, PA 18938 • Tel: 215 862 5788

NATURAL HABITAT • Valerie Dow, PO Box 21, Haysville, KS 67060 • Tel: 316 788 1793 • Creating natural, harmonious living spaces. Certified Bau-biologie consultant and inspector. Feng Shui practitioner.

Permaculture ~ page 22

THE ALTER PROJECT • Slippery Rock University, Slippery Rock, PA 16057-1326 • Tel: 412 738 2068 • *Alternative Living Technologies and Energy Research.*

BAY AREA PERMACULTURE GROUP • 1850 Union Street, #1138, San Francisco, CA 94123 • Tel: 415 761 8220

CENTRAL ROCKY MOUNTAIN PERMACULTURE INSTITUTE • PO Box 631, Basalt, CO 81621 • Tel: 303 927 4158

ECOVILLAGE TRAINING CENTER • Box 90, Summertown, TN 38483 • *Natural systems, Buildings, Gardens, Permaculture, Waste treatment, Energy. Workshops and Consultations.*

ELFIN PERMACULTURE • PO Box 672, Dahlonega, GA 30533-0672

GAP MOUNTAIN PERMACULTURE • 9 Old County Road, Jaffrey, NH 03452 • Tel: 603 532 6877

HIDDEN SPRINGS NURSERY • 170 Hidden Springs Lane, Cookeville, TN 38501 • Tel: 615 268 2592

HIGH ALTITUDE PERMACULTURE INSTITUTE • Box 238, Ward, CO 80481 • Tel: 303 459 3494

KOOTENAY PERMACULTURE • Box 43, Winlaw, BC, Canada, V0G 2J0 • Tel: 604 226 7302 • *Design, consultation, and education.*

LIVING SYSTEMS DESIGNS • Route 1, Box 28, Leicester, NC 28748 Tel: 704 683 4946

LOST VALLEY CENTER • 81868 Lost Valley Lane, Dexter, OR 97431 • *Permaculture education.*

PERMACULTURE COMMUNICATIONS • PO Box 101, Davis, CA 95618

PERMACULTURE DRYLANDS • PO Box 133, Pearce, AZ 85625 • Tel: 602 824 3456 Fax: 602 824 3542 • *Education and research institute. Publish "Permaculture Drylands Journal".*

PERMACULTURE INSTITUTE OF NORTHERN CALIFORNIA • PO Box 341, Point Reyes Station, CA 94956 • Tel: 415 663 9090

PERMACULTURE INSTITUTE OF SOUTHERN CALIFORNIA • 1027 Summit Way, Laguna Beach, CA 92651 • Tel: 714 494 5843

PERMACULTURE RESOURCES • 56 Farmersville, Califon, NJ 07830 • Tel: 800 832 6285 and PO Box 1173, Cedar Crest, NM 87008 • Tel: 800 874 1641 • *Wholesale book and video sales.*

Home and environment ~ page 23

See also listings for Healthy Building pages 207-11

GREGORY ACKER • 720 Northwest 23rd Avenue, Portland, OR 97210-3211 • Tel: 503 222 2890 Fax: 503 222 4143 • *Architect, consultant, contractor, solar and environmental design.*

MAUREEN L BELLE • see entry for page 20

PAUL BIERMAN-LYTLE • The Masters Corporation, PO Box 514, 289 Mill Road, New Canaan, CT 06840 • Tel: 203 966 3541 Fax: 203 966 2807 • *Founder of The Masters Corporation. Leading architect with excellent experience of healthy, non-toxic, and sustainable buildings.*

BIOSPHERE II • Space Biosphere Adventures, Box 689, Oracle, AZ 85623 • *Enclosed ecosystems in glass and steel structure in Arizona desert.*

CCD ARCHITECTURE • 6839 Tulip Hill Terrace, Bethesda, MD 20816 • Tel: 301 320 3887 Fax: 703 893 0400 • *Natural, healthy, practical, Frank Lloyd Wright-inspired.*

CENTER FOR MAXIMUM POTENTIAL BUILDING SYSTEMS • Pliny Fisk, 8604 FM 969 Austin, TX 78724 • Tel: 512 928 4786 Fax: 512 926 4418 • *Publish "Energy Aware Planning Guide".*

COLUMBIA DESIGN GROUP • PO Box 16554, Portland, OR 97216-0554 • Tel: 503 761 1586 • *Thirty exciting architectural designs in a range of styles and sizes - each specifying safer, less toxic building materials and construction techniques. Construction drawings available.*

CROXTON COLLABORATIVE • 1122 Madison Avenue, New York, NY 10028 • Tel: 212 794 2285 Fax: 212 517 2221

M.B. CUSHMAN DESIGN INC • PO Box 655, 82 Park Street, Stowe, VT 05672 • Tel: 802 253 2169 Fax: 802 253 2160 • *We are a full service architectural firm working in an integrative and collaborative environment to design client and site specific buildings in all climates. We specialize in rural planning and housing, historic renovation and outdoor experiential educational facilities. Our commitment is to incorporate natural materials, environmental consciousness, and response to personal detail through all levels of the design and construction phases.*

DEBRA DADD-REDALIA • PO Box 279, Forest Knolls, CA 94933 Tel: 415 488 4612 Fax: 415 488 0915 • *An expert on environmentally safe and responsible products, Debra Dadd-Redalia works to promote healthy living through consulting, lecturing, and writing. See p. 188.*

ECODESIGN RESOURCE SOCIETY (EDRS) • PO Box 3981, Main Post Office, Vancouver, BC, Canada, V6B 3Z4 • Tel: 604 738 9334 Fax: 604 689 7016 • *Publish "Eco-Design Quarterly". Aims to provide the public, design, building, and manufacturing industries the means to make informed, healthy, and environmentally sensitive choices via a resource center (see below), publications, and activities.*

ECODESIGN RESOURCE CENTER • 201-1102 Homer Street, Vancouver, BC, Canada, V6B 2X6 • Tel: 604 689 7086 • *The Center offers a comprehensive resource of general and technical information on ecological design, planning, and development. Library, catalogue, and product database are free of charge.*

ECO-HOME NETWORK • 4344 Russell Avenue, Los Angeles, CA 90027 • Tel: 213 662 5207 • *Eco-home network improves human health and planetary well-being through demonstration, education, and building a constituency for sustainable urban living. Tours.*

DAVE FOWLER/JIM WINSLOW • Pacific Housing Systems, 696 San Ramon Valley Boulevard, Danville, CA 94303 • Tel: 510 569 0935

CLINT GOOD ARCHITECTS • PO Box 143, Lincoln, VA 22078 • *Architect specializing in healthy building. Co-author of "Healthful Houses".*

HABITAT FOR HUMANITY INTERNATIONAL • 121 Habitat Street, Americus, GA 31709-3498 • Tel: 912 924 6935 • *Rehabbed inner city homes. Neighborhood Empowerment Program.*

ED LOWANS • Lowans and Stephen, RR 8, Orangeville, Ontario, Canada L9W 3T5 • Tel & Fax: 519 940 0964 • *Environmental Consultant. Advanced Design, Healthy Buildings, and Natural Regeneration Systems.*

GEORGE MINARDOS BUILDER • 1537 Wellesley Avenue, Los Angeles, CA 90025 • Tel: 310 207 3640 • *Our design and construction "green team" specializes in sustainable building techniques for new and existing projects.*

NETWORK FOR SUSTAINABLE NEW YORK CITY • 150 West 28th Street, Suite 1501, New York, NY 10001-6103 • Tel: 212 645 2213 Fax: 212 645 2214

NORTHWEST ECOBUILDING GUILD • 217 9th Avenue North, Seattle, WA 98109 • Tel: 206 622 8350 • *Publishes "Eco-Building Times".*

PENINSULAR CONSERVATION CENTER FOUNDATION • 2448 Watson Court, Palo Alto, CA 94303 • Tel: 415 494 9301 • *Specialized collection of environmental and conservation information.*

PLANETARY SOLUTIONS • PO Box 1049, Boulder, CO 80306 • Tel: 303 442 6228 Fax: 303 442 6474 • *Less-toxic and resource-efficient materials for architects, builders, dealers, and whole house projects. Ecobuilding consulting services. Showroom. Library.*

ROCKY MOUNTAIN INSTITUTE • 1739 Snowmass Creek Road, Snowmass, CO 81654-9199 • Tel: 303 927 3851 Fax: 303 927 3240 • *A leader in energy resource-efficiency research and policy. Publish "The Resource-Efficient Housing Guide" and many other books and newsletters. See page 108.*

SHARED LIVING RESOURCE CENTER • 2375 Shattuck Avenue, Berkeley, CA 94704 • Tel: 510 548 6608 • *Information on shared living ideas, co-housing, and community planning.*

STEVEN J. SHELDON & ASSOCIATES • 313 N Main Street, Suite C, Sebastopol, CA 95472 • Tel: 707 823 6331

PAOLO SOLERI • Arcosanti, 6433 Doubletree Road, Scottsdale, AZ 85253 • *Pioneer architect of Arcosanti and Cosanti, Arizona. Author of "Arcology: The City in the Image of Man".*

SRW ENVIRONMENTAL BUILDING CONSULTANT AND CONSTRUCTION • Lic 433290, 1075 Montgomery Road, Sebastopol, CA 95472 • Tel: 707 829 8296 • *Offering a professional evaluation of your building materials, systems, and finishes to ensure a healthful, non-toxic indoor environment.*

SUSTAINABLE ARCHITECTURE™ • Lawrence Schechter, Architect, 208 Oak Street, Suite 202, Ashland, OR 97520 • Tel: 503 482 6332 • *Timeless architecture of innovative design and alternative construction for health/regeneration, energy-efficiency, mental/spiritual upliftment, a sustainable future.*

SUSTAINABLE BUILDING COLLABORATIVE • 815 Southeast Clatsop, Portland, OR 97202 • Tel: 503 235 0137

SYMBIOS: ECO-DESIGN & CONSTRUCTION • 865 Florida Street Studios, Dept # 1, San Francisco, CA 94141-0664 • Tel: 415 285 6454 Fax: 415 821 1755 • *A holistic design/build company specializing in ecological building, sustainable development, and landscape restoration. Projects range from residential to commercial in urban and rural areas. Services include architecture, engineering, landscaping, and construction.*

SYSTEMIC ECOLOGICAL ARCHITECTURE • Walter Scott Perry, 8834 Hollywood Hills Road, Los Angeles, CA • Tel: 213 650 2827 Fax: 310 297 0908 • *A consulting design practice that specializes in an architecture that promotes personal and planetary sustainability and well being.*

URBAN ECOLOGY • 405 14th Street, Suite 701, Oakland, CA 94612 • Tel: 510 251 6330 • *City planning, newsletter, urban projects, conferences.*

SIM VAN DER RYN • Suite 185, 10 Libertyship Way, Sausalito, CA 94965 • Tel: 415 332 5806 Fax: 415 331 5526 • *Leading eco-architect founder member of Ecological Design Society.*

GREG VANMECHELEN • 1634, Hearst Avenue, Berkeley, CA • Tel: 510 549 9581 Fax: 510 841 9060 • *Architect. Designs to create your unique environment. Designs to benefit the world's environment.*

CAROL VENOLIA • PO Box 4417, Santa Rosa, CA 95402-4417 • Tel: 707 579 2201 Fax: 707 884 1235 • *Architect. Author of "Healing Environments". Editor of "Building with Nature". See p. 191.*

DAVID WANN • 600 East Asbury Street, Denver, CO 80210 • Tel: 303 722 2782 • *Author of "Biologic Architecture"*

MALCOLM WELLS • PO Box 1149, Brewster, MA 02631 • Tel: 508 896 6850 Fax: 508 896 5116 • *Leading architect of underground buildings. Author of "Gentle Architecture" and "Infra Structures".*

JONATHAN YARDLEY • PO Box 960, Ganges, BC, Canada, V0S 1E0 • *Environmental architect. Member of Vancouver Eco Design Resource Society.*

Healthy building ~ pages 24-25

See also listings for Home and environment pages 205-7 and Earth building materials pages 211-12

MARK ABRAHAM • 265 North Front Street, Sarnia, Ontario, Canada, N7T 7K4 • Tel: 519 542 7751 • *Educational workshops on breathing walls, Bau-biologie.*

A.C.E. (Alternative & Conservation Energies, Inc.) • Varsity Execucenter, 1700 Varsity Estates Drive NW, Calgary, Alberta, Canada, T3B 2W9 • Tel: 403 286 1407 Fax: 403 286 1407 • *Architecture, earth buildings, straw bale, rammed earth, healthy buildings.*

ALCYONE ARCHITECTURE INTERNSHIPS • 1965 Hilt Road, Hornbrook, CA 96044 • Tel: 916 475 3310

AMERICAN INSTITUTE OF ARCHITECTS COMMITTEE ON THE ENVIRONMENT • 1735 New York Avenue NW, Washington, DC 20006-5292 • Tel: 202 626 7300 / 800 635 2724 Fax: 202 626 7518 • *AIA Environmental Resource Guide.*

ARCHITECTS, DESIGNERS & PLANNERS FOR SOCIAL RESPONSIBILITY (ADPSR) • National Office: 1807 West Sunnyside, Suite 300, Chicago, IL 60640 • Tel: 312 275 2498 • *ADSPR update, bimonthly bulletin, Architectural Resource Guide e.g. "Sourcebook for Sustainable Design" by San Francisco chapter. Chapters in Boston, and other major cities.*

TOM BENDER • Nehalem, OR 97131 • Tel: 503 368 6294 • *Builder of exemplary healthy house on Oregon coast. Consultant and architect.*

BUILD GREEN PROGRAM • Ortech, 2395 Speakman Drive, Mississauga, Ontario, Canada, L5K 1B3 • Tel: 416 8222 4111

BUILDING EDUCATION CENTER • 812 Page Street, Berkeley, CA 94710 • Tel: 510 525 7610 Fax: 510 525 0855

BUILDING WITH NATURE • PO Box 4417, Santa Rosa, CA 95402 • Tel: 707 579 2201 Fax: 707 884 1235 • *Newsletter.*

CANADIAN HOUSING INFORMATION CENTER (LIBRARY) • 682 Montreal Road, Ottawa, Ontario, Canada, K1A 0P7 • Tel: 613 748 2367 Fax: 613 748 6192 • *Publications on sustainable construction, indoor air quality, energy efficiency, healthy building.*

CENTER FOR RESOURCEFUL BUILDING TECHNOLOGY (CRBT) • Box 3413, Missoula, MT 59806 • Tel: 406 549 7678 • *Publishes "Guide to Resource-Efficient Building Elements" (GREBE). See p. 196.*

CLODAGH ARCHITECTURAL DESIGN • 365 1st Avenue, New York, NY 10010 • Tel: 212 673 9202 Fax: 212 614 9125 • *Interior design.*

MARY CORDARO • 12439 Magnolia Boulevard, no 263, Valley Village, CA 91607 • Tel: 310 838 2892 / 818 981 7245 Fax: 810 766 5882 • *Healthy Bedrooms by Certified Bau-Biologists. Comprehensive EMF bio-electric testing: magnetic/electric fields, body voltage. Feng Shui and Bau-biology classes worldwide.*

ROBERT CORNELL & ASSOCIATES • 8780 National Boulevard, # 222, Culver City, CA 90232 • Tel: 310 842 8015 • *Landscape Design.*

RICHARD L CROWTHER • 401 Madison Street, Unit A, Denver, CO 80206 • Tel: 303 338 1875 • *Architecture, passive solar design and engineering, publishing, writing, invention, newsletter.*

DEBOER ARCHITECTS • Darrel DeBoer, 1835 Pacific Avenue, Alameda, CA 94501 • Tel: 510 865 3669 • *Specializing in providing a service to those who have not used an architect before. Uses reclaimed lumber and non-toxic finishes.*

EARTHWISE SEATTLE HOME • PO Box 21331, Seattle, WA 98111 • Tel: 206 682 6897 • *Resource center for energy-efficient building, healthy materials, sustainable construction.*

ECOLOGICAL DESIGN ASSOCIATION (EDA) • British School, Slad Road, Stroud, Glos GL5 1QW, UK • Tel: (+44) 1453 765575 Fax: (+44) 1453 759211 • *Founded by the author, David Pearson.*

ECOLOGICAL DESIGN INSTITUTE (EDI) • Suite 185, Ten Libertyship Way, Sangalito, CA 94965 • Tel: 415 332 5806 • *Network of architects, designers, and others to facilitate eco-projects and education programs.*

ECOLOGIC HOMES • Nancy Simpson, PO Box 94, Willits, CA 95490 • Tel & Fax: 707 459 2595 • *Certified Bau-biologist. Residential Designer. MCS consultant since 1984. Sick Buildings solutions. Energy-efficient planning.*

ECOLOGICALLY SAFE HOMES • 430 N Sewell Road, Bloomington, IN 47408 • Tel: 812 332 5073 Fax: 812 332 5073 • *John Bower, specialist in non-toxic materials research.*

ECOLOGY BY DESIGN (CONCEPTS FOR A TOXIC-FREE ENVIRONMENT) • Audrey Hoodkiss, 1341 Ocean Avenue, Suite 73, Santa Monica, CA 90401 • Tel: 310 394 4146 • *Full-service environmental consulting and design firm. Specialists in IAQ, air and water purification. Distributor of environmental products.*

ECOLOGY HOUSES • Examples of specially designed and built eco-logically sound homes can be found at:
4289 State Street, Santa Barbara, CA 93110 • Tel: 805 967 9200
1441 Pearl Street, Boulder, CO 80302 • Tel: 303 939 0204
1512 Larimer Street, Denver, CO 80202 • Tel: 303 534 7975
341 SW Morrison, Portland, OR 97204 • Tel: 503 223 4883
Maine Mall, South Portland, ME 04106 • Tel: 207 775 7441

ENVIRONMENTAL BUILDING SUPPLIES • 1314 Northwest Northrup Street, Portland, OR 97209 • Tel: 503 222 3881 Fax: 503 222 3756 • *Supplier, showroom, and resource for environmentally sound building products.*

ENVIRONMENTAL BY DESIGN • PO Box 95016, South Van CSC, Vancouver, BC, Canada, V6P 6V4 • Tel & Fax: 604 266 7721 • *A Guide for Designers, Architects, and Builders making environmentally aware material choices.*

ENVIRONMENTAL CONSTRUCTION NETWORK • c/o Ed Lowans, RR 8, Orangeville, Ontario, Canada, L9W 3T5 • Tel & Fax: 519 940 0964 • *Listings of Environmental Design and Construction goods and Services in North America, and International Associations.*

ENVIRONMENTAL CONSTRUCTION OUTFITTERS (ECO) • 44 Crosby Street, NY 10012 • Tel: 800 238 5008 / 212 334 9659 Fax: 212 226 8084 • See p. 45.

ENVIRONMENTAL TESTING & TECHNOLOGY • PO Box 230369, Encinitas, CA 92023-0369 • Tel: 619 436 5990 Fax: 619 436 9448 • *Investigations for building-related health problems.*

EOS INSTITUTE • 580 Broadway, Suite 200, Laguna Beach, CA 92651 • Tel: 714 497 1896 Fax: 714 494 7861 • *Resource Center for sustainable living. Publish "Earthword" quarterly. Library and workshops.*

ENVIRONMENTAL HEALTH NETWORK • PO Box 575, Corte Madera, CA 94935 • Tel: 415 331 2148

ENVIRONMENTAL HEALTH WATCH • 4115 Bridge Avenue, Cleveland, OH 44113 • *Healthy House Catalog.*

THE EPSTEN GROUP • 303 Ferguson Street, Atlanta, GA 30307 • Tel: 404 577 0370 • *Environmentally sound, healthful architectural design/consulting. Residential/Commercial. Healthful Homes. Energy/Water/Material conservation. Passive solar. Non-polluting/recycled building materials.*

FOURTH DIMENSION HOUSING • Healthy Home Designs, Jocelyn Eastland, PO Box 44, Rainier, WA 98576 • Tel: 360 446 7715 Fax: 360 446 1163 • *Architectural designs using sacred geometry, Feng Shui, and Universal principles.*

GAIA HOMES (MARCO HAESSIG) • PO Box 223, Horsefly, BC, Canada, V0L 1L0 • Tel: 604 620 3664 Fax: 604 620 3454 • *Consulting for Bau-Biologie. We design and construct your healthy home and work place.*

GLOBAL NETWORK OF ORGANIZATIONS FOR ENVIRONMENTALLY CONSCIOUS AND HEALTHY BUILDINGS (ECOHB) • c/o IBO, Landstr, Haupstr 67, 1030 Vienna, Austria

GREENSOURCE • 12 Alfred Street, Suite 300, Woburn, MA 01801 • Tel: 617 933 2772 Fax: 617 944 7839 • *Michael A. Pais. Providing residential construction with sustainability, healthy indoor air quality, energy efficiency, resource conservation and environmental responsibility. We protect your health in the home and minimize the impact of the construction and operation of your home on the environment.*

HAIKU HOUSES (GORDON STEEN) • Design Plaza, 250 Newport Beach, CA 92660 • Tel: 714 720 7417 • *Made of all natural materials following a 500 year-old Japanese tradition, the Haiku House is an oasis of peace and tranquillity, designed to withstand fire, earthquakes and hurricanes .* See p. 194.

HEALTHY BUILDINGS ASSOCIATES • 7190 Fiske Road, Clinton, WA 98236 • Tel: 206 579 2962 • *Publish "Healthy Buildings Resource Guide". Environmental inspections, indoor air quality design and consulting. Home plans.*

THE HEALTHY HOUSE INSTITUTE • 430 N Sewell Road, Bloomington, IN 47408 • Tel: 812 332 5073 Fax: 812 332 5073 • *Promotes healthier house construction and lifestyle. Provides books, videos, and other information on known negative effects of common building materials to architects, designers, builders, and home owners.* See p. 199.

SARAH JONES HOLLAND • RR 1 Box 4011C, Camden, Maine 04843 • Tel: 207 236 6112 • *Architect.*

HOUSING RESOURCE CENTER • 1820 West 48th Street, Cleveland, OH 44102 • Tel: 216 671 4082 • *Healthy building conference and catalog.*

JAMES T HUBBELL • 930 Orchard Lane, Santa Ysabel, CA 92070 • Tel: 619 765 0171

IDEAL ENVIRONMENTS • 401 West Adams, Fairfield, IA 52556 • Tel: 515 472 6547 • *Bau-biology, consultation, environmental building inspections, healthy building workshops.*

INSTITUTE FOR BIODYNAMIC SHELTER • 86 Washington Road, Waldboro, ME 04572 • Tel: 207 832 5157 Fax: 207 832 7314 • *A non-profit organization that designs and demonstrates biodynamic structures to help forge a vital reunion between earth and spirit.*

INTERNATIONAL INSTITUTE FOR BAU-BIOLOGIE & ECOLOGY INC (IBE) • PO Box 387, Clearwater, FL 34615 • Tel: 813 461 4371 Fax: 813 441 4373 • *Bau-biologie (building biology) is the study of the impact of building environment upon the health of people and the application of this knowledge to the construction of healthy homes and workplaces. Correspondence courses.* See p. 192.

INTERNATIONAL ECOLOGICAL DESIGN SOCIETY • PO Box 11645, Berkeley, CA 94712 • Tel: 510 869 5051 Fax: 415 332 5808

RICHARD KADULSKI • no. 208-1280 Seymour Street, Vancouver, BC, Canada, V6B 6N9 • Tel & Fax: 604 689 1841 • *Architect.*

DAVID KIBBEY • 1618 Parker Street, Berkeley, CA 94703 • Tel & Fax: 510 841 1039 • *Environmental Building Inspections, Healthy Design and Materials Consultation. Member of ADPSR.*

MARY KRAUS • 67 N Pleasant Street, Amherst, MA 01002 • Tel: 413 253 4090 • *Architect. Healthful, ecologically sound design, co-housing, and sustainable community design.*

TIM MALONEY, ONE DESIGN INC • 724 Mountain Falls Road, Winchester, VA 22602 • Tel: 703 877 2172

WILLIAM MCDONOUGH • William McDonough Architects • 410 East Water Street, Charlottesville, VA 22902 • Tel: 804 979 1111 Fax: 804 979 1112 • *Leading environmental architect with many projects including Wal-Mart's "Eco-Mart", Kansas. Dean of School of Architecture, University of Virginia.*

NACUL CENTER • 592 Main Street, Amherst, MA 01002 • Tel: 413 253 8025 • *Healthy building construction, architectural design.*

NATURAL ASSOCIATION OF HOME BUILDERS • NAHB Research Center • 400 Prince George's Boulevard, Upper Marlboro, MD 20772-8731 • Tel: 301 249 4000 Fax: 301 249 0305 • *Programs include innovative home building methods and resource-conserving products.*

NATURAL BUILDING NETWORK • PO Box 1110, Sebastopol, CA 95473 • *Group of designers, builders, suppliers, and educators dedicated to creating healthful, spirited, and ecologically sensitive buildings.*

THE NATURAL HOUSE BUILDING CENTER • RR1, Box 115 F, Fairfield, IA 52556 • Tel: 515 472 7775

SHELTER ECOLOGY • Cindy Meehan, 39 Pineridge Road, Asheville NC 28804 • Tel: 704 251 5888 • *Specializing in consultations to help identify alternative resources and design methods for healthy (working and living) interior spaces.*

SHELTER INSTITUTE • 38 Center Street, Bath, ME 04530 • Tel: 207 442 7938 Fax: 207 442 7938 • *Teaches classes year round in cost and energy-efficient house design, renovation, and construction. Free brochure.*

SOLAR SURVIVAL ARCHITECTURE • PO Box 1041, Taos, NM 87571 • *Founded by Mike Reynolds, designer and builder of "Earthships Vol. 1 & 2". Videos and Courses.*

SUNRISE DESIGN CENTER • Deborah Warner, South 29175 Highway 3, St. Maries, ID 83861 • Tel: 208 689 3820 • *For a more energy-efficient home: architectural design and drafting, technical assistance, graphics and logos, renderings.*

SUSTAINABLE HOME DESIGNS • Christopher Leininger, 206 Maple Drive, Industry, PA 15052-8719 • Tel: 412 643 8719 • *M.S. Sustainable systems. Certified Bau-Biologist.*

SWANSON ASSOCIATES • 601 23rd Street, Fairfield, Iowa 52556 • Tel: 515 472 8217 Fax: 515 472 1678 • *Environmental Design and Construction. Very low toxic buildings. Certified Bau-biologist.*

SRW ENVIRONMENTAL BUILDING CONSULTANT AND CONSTRUCTION • Lic 433290, 1075 Montgomery Road, Sebastopol, CA 95472 • Tel: 707 829 8296 • *Offering a professional evaluation of your building materials, systems, and finishes to ensure a healthful, non-toxic indoor environment.*

TAYLOR DESIGN ASSOCIATES • Box 39, Newfane Road, S Wardsboro, VT 05355 • Tel: 802 896 6891

Bau-biologie (bau rhymes with how and means building)

■ The science of the holistic interactions between life and living environment
■ the study of the impact which the manmade environment has upon the health of people
■ the application of this information with the intention of producing healthy built environments

Building ecology

■ the relation of the building to the environment

TURTLE HOUSE INSTITUTE • PO Box 2335, Sebastopol, CA 95473-2335 • Tel: 707 573 6020 • *Classes, seminars, referrals, information, consultation.*

UNDERSET BUILDING DESIGNS • Dennis Road, Angola, NY 14006 • Tel: 716 549 1554 • *Earth-sheltered monolith concrete, steel reinforced, passive solar building. Design and consulting.*

YESTERMORROW DESIGN/BUILD SCHOOL • RRI Box 97-5, Warren, VT 05674 • Tel: 802 496 5545 Fax: 802 496 5540

Organic and Steiner design ~ *page 26*

CCD ARCHITECTURE • 6839 Tulip Hill Terrace, Bethesda, MD 20816 • Tel: 301 320 3887 Fax: 703 893 0400 • *Natural, healthy, practical, Frank Lloyd Wright-inspired architecture.*

ARTHUR DYSON AIA • 754 P Street, Suite C, Fresno, CA 93721 Tel: 209 486 3582

JAMES T HUBBELL • 930 Orchard Lane, Santa Ysabel, CA 92070 • Tel: 619 765 0171

BART PRINCE • 501 Monte Vista NE, Albuquerque, NM 87106 • Tel: 505 256 1961 Fax: 505 268 9045

RUDOLF STEINER CENTRE • 9100 Bathurst, Toronto, Ontario, Canada L3T 3N3 • *Contact for information on Steiner-based design.*

RUDOLF STEINER INSTITUTE • PO Box 0990, Planetarium Street, New York, NY 10024 • *Contact for information on Steiner-based design.*

STEVEN J. SHELDON & ASSOCIATES • 313 N Main Street, Suite C, Sebastopol, CA 95472 • Tel: 707 823 6331

MALCOLM WELLS • PO Box 1149, Brewster, MA 02631 • Tel: 508 896 6850 Fax: 508 896 5116

Spiritual design ~ *page 27*

FOURTH DIMENSION HOUSING • PO Box 44, Rainier, WA 98576 • Tel: 360 446 7715 Fax: 360 446 1163 • *Architectural designs using sacred geometry, Feng Shui, and Universal principles.*

INSTITUTE FOR BIODYNAMIC SHELTER • 86 Washington Road, Waldboro, ME 04572 • Tel: 207 832 5157 Fax: 207 832 7314 • *A non-profit organization that designs and demonstrates biodynamic structures to help forge a vital reunion between earth and spirit.*

NATURAL BUILDING NETWORK • PO Box 1110, Sebastopol, CA 95473 • *Group of designers, builders, suppliers, and educators dedicated to creating healthful, spirited, and ecologically sensitive buildings.*

Earth building materials ~ *page 28*

See also listings for Straw-bale construction page 218

A.C.E. (Alternative & Conservation Energies, Inc.) • Varsity Execucenter, 1700 Varsity Estates Drive NW, Calgary, Alberta, Canada, T3B 2W9 • Tel: 403 286 1407 Fax: 403 286 1407 • *Architecture, earth buildings, straw bale, rammed earth, healthy buildings.*

ADOBE BUILDING SUPPLY • 5609 Alameda Place, NE Albuquerque, NM 87111 • Tel: 505 828 9800 Fax: 505 828 0204 • *Hand peeled vigas and latillas, rough sawn beams and corbels, pine and juniper planking, slate and satillo tile, quality custom carving.*

ADOBE FARMS • Route 1, Box 113-E, Burnet, TX 78611 • *Pressed adobe bricks.*

ADOBE MASTERS • 1594-A San Mateo Lane, Santa Fe, NM 87501 • Tel: 505 988 5851 / 7176 Fax: 505 986 8559 • *Forty years experience building with adobe.*

ADOBE/SOLAR ASSOCIATES • 2907 Agua Fria, Santa Fe, NM 87505 • Tel: 505 984 0077 • *Workshops.*

ADOBE TILE AND STONE INC • 8917 4th NW, Albuquerque, NM 87114 • Tel: 505 898 0848 Fax: 505 890 0858 • *Saltillo, Terra Cotta, Mexican Bricks, Blocks, Flagstone, Mexican Stone.*

CALIFORNIA INSTITUTE OF EARTH ART AND ARCHITECTURE • (Cal-Earth), 10376 Shangri La Avenue, Hesperia, CA 92345 • Tel: 619 244 0614 Fax: 619 244 2201 • *The Apprenticeship Retreat with Architect Nader Khalili, at Cal Earth (California Institute of Earth Art and Architecture) in Earth Architecture, Adobe, Rammed Earth, Straw Bale, Ceramic Houses, and Superadobe (stabilized sandbag coils). If you have a vision for building a community or your home, your school or career, or even to help others to build theirs, give us just one week of your time and we will empower you to realize that dream — without cutting a single tree, by using the earth under your feet and utilizing the elements of sun, wind, water, and fire. Fee $2,000. Write for more information.* See p. 195.

CARTEM PRODUCTS LTD • Billesdon, Leicester LE7 9AE, United Kingdom • Tel: (+44) 153 755 733 Fax: (+44) 153 755 744 • *Makers of the Cartem 'Elephant' blockmaker for high-quality stabilized soil blocks. Contact UK address for distributors in the US and Canada.*

COB COTTAGE COMPANY • Box 123, Cottage Grove, OR 97424 • Tel: 503 942 3021

CONSTRUCTION PROFESSIONALS INC • Tel: 505 344 1776 • *Specialists in Adobe.*

CULHANE CONTRACTING • HC 29, Box 645, Prescott, AZ 86301 • Tel & Fax: 602 778 3496 • *All types of adobe masonry and plaster.*

FOUNTAINHEAD NATURAL HOMES • 11965 Monclova Road, Swanton, OH 43558 • Tel: 419 825 3031 • *Rammed Earth. Alternative enclosures. Plastered Bale wall panels. Free brochures.*

FRIENDS OF ADOBE • PO Box 7725, Albuquerque, NM 87194 • Tel: 505 243 7801

MCM MARKETING INC • PO Box 12123, Mill Creek, WA 98012 • Tel: 206 487 1453 Fax: 206 487 3793 • *Representing ecologically sound building products.*

NATURAL HOUSE BUILDING CENTER • RR 1 Box 115F, Fairfield, IA 52556 • Tel: 515 472 7775 • *Learn about timber framing and straw-clay construction, as well as roofs, earth plastering and earth floors, from MoosePrints, a 35-page booklet available for $7 ppd.*

NATURE HOMES • Abi Allen, Box 10506, Bernalillo, NM 87004 • Tel: 505 867 3893 • *Designer of low-toxic, energy-efficient earth homes.*

PACIFIC ADOBE • 13207 Herrick, Sylmar, CA 91342 • Tel: 818 362 0235 Fax: 818 362 6123 • *Interlocking block machines.*

H PARNEGG REALITY INC • 6301 Uptown Boulevard, NE, Albuquerque, NM 87110 • Tel: 505 883 6161 • *Adobe and Passive Solar specialists.*

DAVID C PETERSON CONSTRUCTION • 4215 Roma NE, Albuquerque, NM 87108 • Tel: 505 266 2751 • *Adobe design and craftsmanship.*

PUEBLO BUILDERS • 1917 North Santa Fe Avenue, Pueblo, CO 81003 • Tel: 719 544 1381 • *Contractors, managers, consultants.*

RAMMED EARTH INSTITUTE • 2319 21st Avenue, Greeley, CO 80631

RAMMED EARTH SOLAR HOMES INC • 265 West 18th Street, No. 3, Tucson, AZ 85701 • Tel: 602 623 2784 Fax: 602 623 1219 • *Cement stabilized adobe and rammed earth.*

RAMMED EARTHWORKS • Blue Mountain Road, Wilseyville, CA 95257 • Tel: 209 293 4924 • *Builders using the rammed earth process.*

RELIANCE CONSTRUCTION CO • 925 Coal Avenue SW, Albuquerque, NM 87102 • Tel: 505 843 9575 • *Design, Construction, Consulting. Specializing in south-west styles.*

RIO ABAJO ADOBE • 07 Industrial Park Lane, Belen, NM 87002 • Tel: 505 864 6191 • *Sold-Delivered-Laid.*

SAN TAN ADOBE INC • 5391 Quail Trail Queen Creek, AZ 85242 • Tel: 602 895 0087 • *Manufacturing quality stabilized adobe.*

BOB AND DEE SMITH • PO Box 913, Hotchkiss, CO 81419 • Tel: 303 872 2142 • *Compressed adobe blocks. Laid direct from the machine by contractors and owners.*

SOLAR ENERGY INTERNATIONAL • PO Box 715, Carbondale, CO 81623 • Tel: 303 963 8855 • *Workshops on solar design, straw-bale, adobe, and rammed earth construction.*

SOUTHWEST SOLARADOBE SCHOOL • PO Box 153, Bosque, NM 87006 • Tel: 505 861 1255 • *Classes in Adobe, rammed earth, and passive solar. Now available: Adobe Codes, listing the major codes for adobe building from Arizona, New Mexico, Texas, with California details.*

WM STODDARD CONSTRUCTION INC • Tel: 505 898 6733 • *Twenty years in the earth-building industry.*

TERRA BLOCK • 1302 S Shields, A2-1, Fort Collins, CO 80521 • Tel: 303 484 4233 Fax: 303 493 3045 • *An ultra-compressed earth block made possible by applying space-age technology to the time-honored art of adobe.*

TERRA GROUP LTD • 1058 Second Avenue, Napa, CA 94558 • Tel: 707 224 2532 Fax: 707 258 1878 • *Classes, publications, earth building.*

WESTERN ADOBE • 7800 Tower Road SW, Albuquerque, NM 87105 • Tel: 505 836 1839

Bricks and tiles ~ page 29

ADOBE BUILDING SUPPLY • 5609 Alameda Place, NE Albuquerque, NM 87111 • Tel: 505 828 9800 Fax: 505 828 0204 • *Hand peeled vigas and latillas, rough sawn beams and corbels, pine and juniper planking, slate and satillo tile, quality custom carving.*

ADOBE FARMS • Route 1, Box 113-E, Burnet, TX 78611 • *Pressed adobe bricks.*

BRICK INSTITUTE OF AMERICA • 11490 Commerce Park Drive, Reston, VA 22091-1525 • Tel: 703 620 0010 Fax: 703 620 3928

BUCHTAL ARCHITECTURAL CERAMICS • 1325 Northmeadow Parkway, Suite 114, Roswell, GA 30076 • Tel: 404 442 5500 Fax: 404 442 5502

ENDICOTT CLAY PRODUCTS COMPANY • PO Box 17, Fairbury, Nebraska 68352 • Tel: 402 729 3315

ENDICOTT TILE LTD • PO Box 645, Fairbury, Nebraska 68352 • Tel: 402 729 3323

FLUID-TECH STERN INC • 2310 Davis Street, San Leandro, CA, 94577 • Tel: 510 638 4421 • *Sodium Silicate.*

GLEN-GERY CORPORATION • 1166 Spring Street, PO Box 7001, Wyomissing, PA 19610-6001 • Tel: 610 374 4011 Fax: 610 374 1622 • *Manufactures face and paving brick for both residential and architectural applications. Product catalogs available upon request.*

GTE CORPORATION • Wellsboro, PA 16901 • Tel: 717 724 8200 • *Recycled glass tiles.*

MCA CLAY ROOF TILE • 1985 Sampson Avenue, Corona CA 91719 • Tel: 909 736 9590 Fax: 909 736 6052

PHOENIX SCIENTIFIC INDUSTRIES • Suite B9, 3620 N High Street, Columbus, OH 43214 • Tel: 614 267 0100 • *Phoenix Brick makes a range of pavers, bricks etc., from reclaimed fly ash.*

SUMMITVILLE TILES • PO Box 73, Summitville, OH 43962 • Tel: 216 236 6614 Fax: 216 236 6615 • *Summitville Tiles produce a complete line of eco-friendly porcelair pavers, made from recycled post-industrial waste products - superior durability under extreme conditions.*

TILES DE SANTA FE INC • PO Box 3767, Santa Fe, NM 87501-0767 • Tel: 505 455 7466 • *Hand made tile floors. Free brochure.*

Stone ~ page 30

3-10 INSULATED FORMS, LP • PO Box 46790, Omaha, NE 68128 • Tel: 402 592 7077

ADOBE TILE AND STONE INC • 8917 4th NW, Albuquerque, NM 87114 • Tel: 505 898 0848 Fax: 505 890 0858 • *Saltillo, Terra Cotta, Mexican Bricks, Blocks, Flagstone, Mexican Stone.*

ADVANCED CONCRETE TECHNOLOGY • 67 South Bedford Street, Burlington, MA 01803 • Tel: 617 272 0588 • *Dry stacked wood fiber forms filled with reinforced concrete.*

AIR KRETE • Nordic Builders, 162 North Sierra Court, Gilbert, AZ 85234 • Tel: 602 892 0603 • *Air Krete is a completely non-toxic cementitious based foam insulation used in new or existing frame or block, walls or ceilings.*

AMERICAN CONFORM INDUSTRIES INC • 1820 Santa Fe Street, Santa Ana, CA 92705 • Tel: 714 662 1100 • *SmartBlock™ expanded polystyrene permanent modular framework.*

BEDROCK INDUSTRIES • 620 N 85th Street, Seattle, WA 98103 • Tel: 206 781 8200 • *Stone flooring/post consumer waste.*

BELL CONCRETE INDUSTRIES INC • 327 N 19th Street, PO Box 1561, Middlesboro, KY 40965 • Tel: 606 248 3236 Fax: 606 248 5222

BUECHEL STONE CORPORATION • W 3639 Highway H, Chilton, WI 53014-9643 • Tel: 414 849 9631

ENERGCORP INC • 4203 W Adams, Phoenix, AZ 85009 • Tel: 602 470 0223 • *EnerGBlock Wall System.*

FASWALL CONCRETE SYSTEMS • 1676 Nixon Road, Augusta, GA 30906 • Tel: 706 793 8880 • *Mineralized wood/concrete blocks.*

FIBERSTONE QUARRIES, INC • PO. Box 1026, 1112 King Street, Quincy, FL 323551 • Tel: 904 627 1083 Fax: 904 627 2640 • *'Molded stone' product simulates quarried and carved stone. Wall veneer and trim system and custom decorative elements from non-toxic, recycled cellulose and post-industrial waste.*

IN-FORM CANADA INDUSTRIES LTD • 1199 West Hastings, 10th Floor, Vancouver, BC, Canada, V6E 3T5 • Tel: 604 682 6200 • *Insulated concrete.*

INSULATED MASONRY SYSTEMS INC • 7234 East Shoeman Lane, Suite 1, Scottsdale, AZ 85251 • Tel: 602 970 0711

MAXITO INDUSTRIES LTD • 1817 Ocean Surf Place, South Surrey, BC, Canada V4A 9P1 • Tel & Fax: 604 535 7160 • *Pre-manufactured foundation forms are attached to floor panels on the job site, thereby eliminating all site labour. The system automatically adjusts to uneven ground conditions, and includes all insulation and waterproofing.*

MEARL CORPORATION • 220 W Westfield Avenue, Roselle Park, NJ 07204 • Tel: 908 245 9500 • *Foamed concrete.*

NAILITE INTERNATIONAL • 1251 NW 165th Street, Miami, FL 33169-5871 • Tel: 305 620 6200 • *Eco-conscious alternatives to shakes, shingles, and stone cladding.*

NEW ENGLAND HEARTH AND STONE • 127 North Street, Goshen, CT 06756 • Tel: 203 491 3091

NORTH AMERICAN CELLULAR CONCRETE • 3 Regency Plaza, Suite 6, Providence, RI 02903 • Tel: 401 621 8108

PACIFIC STRATEGIES • 1101 Connecticut Avenue NW, no 100, Washington DC 200036 • Tel: 202 828 2435 • *Simulated marble/recycled stone content.*

PHENIX™ BIOCOMPOSITES • PO Box 609, Mankato, MN 56002-0609 • Tel: 507 931 5573 Fax: 507 931 5573 • *Environ™ biocomposite made from recycled and replenishable resources looks like granite yet works like wood.*

PUMICE-CRETE BUILDING SYSTEMS • PO Box 539, El Prado, NM 87529 • *Appropriate building technologies including low density, cast on site, insulating concrete; passive solar designs and systems; water collection and conservation; reduced use of wood; traditional and modern styling.*

RASTRA BUILDING SYSTEMS INC • 6421 Box Spring Boulevard, Riverside, CA 92507 • Tel: 909 653 3346 • *Rastra system beams consist of recycled post-consumer styrene pellets and steel and portland cement.*

STONEWARE TILE COMPANY • 1650 Progress Drive, Richmond, IN 47374 • Tel: 3137 935 4760

STRUCTURAL SLATE CO • 222 E Main Street, Pen Argyl, Pennsylvania, PA 18072 • Tel: 215 863 4141 Fax: 215 863 7016 • *Since 1918 we have supplied Pennsylvania Natural Slate products. Some residential products are flooring, countertops, fireplace facings.*

SUPERLITE BLOCK • 4150 W Turney, Phoenix, AZ 85019 • Tel: 602 352 3500 / 800 366 7877

THERMALOCK PRODUCTS INC • 162 Sweeney Street, N Tonawanda, NY 14120 • Tel: 716 695 6000 • *Thermalock concrete masonry blocks utilize expanded polystyrene to form connective webs between two concrete faces.*

Sustainable timber ~ page 31

A & M WOOD SPECIALITY • Cambridge, Ontario, Canada • Tel: 519 653 9322

ALBANY WOODWORKS • PO Box 729, Albany, LA 70711-0729 • Tel: 504 567 1155 • *Reclaimed Heartwoods, newly milled antique Heart Pine and Virgin Tidewater Cypress.*

ALMQUIST LUMBER • 100 Taylor Way, Blue Lake, CA 95521 • Tel: 707 668 5454 • *Wood from Plan Piloto in Mexico, salvaged California hardwoods. Endorsed by RAN.*

ALPINE STRUCTURES INC • PO Box 1006, Providence Road, Oxford, NC 27565 • Tel: 800 672 2326 / 919 693 6667

A.W.A.R.E. • Box 1031, Redway CA 95560 • *Association. of Woodworkers Advocating Respect for the Environment.*

BEAR CREEK LUMBER INC • PO Box 669, Winthrop, WA 98862 • Tel: 509 997 3110 Fax: 509 997 2040 • *Natural wood products.*

BERRY SAWMILLS • Box 191, Redway, CA 95060 • Tel: 707 923 2979 • *Second growth Redwood and Douglas Fir.*

BOISE CASCADE CORPORATION • One Jefferson Square, PO Box 50, Boise, ID 83728-0001 • Tel: 800 232 0788 / 208 384 7151 • BCI™ joist consisting of a plywood web between laminated veneer lumber flanges. VERSA-LAM™ laminated lumber veneer.

CALIFORNIA HARDWOOD PRODUCERS • 1980 Grass Valley Highway, Auburn, CA • Tel: 916 888 8191 • California Red Oak.

CHAMPION INTERNATIONAL CORPORATION • PO Box 1593, Tacoma, WA 98401 • Tel: 206 572 8300 • Finger-jointed lumber.

CHAMPION RIDGE LUMBER COMPANY • PO Box 272, Whitehaven, CA 95489 • Sells the Redwood and Douglas Fir that the big timber companies leave behind.

COLLINS PINE • 1618 SW 1st Avenue, Suite 300, Portland, OR 97201 • Tel: 503 227 1219 • SCS Certified program.

CONKLIN'S AUTHENTIC BARNWOOD AND HAND HEWN BEAMS • RR 1, Box 70, Susquehanna, PA 18847-9751 • Tel: 717 465 3832 Fax: 717 465 3832

CONSTANTINE • 2050 Eastchester Road, Bronx, NY 10461 • Tel: 718 792 1600

CONTACT LUMBER • 1881 SW Front Avenue, Portland, OR 97201 • Tel: 800 547 1038 • Oak over moldings, oak veneer over fingerjoint soft-wood, uses 11 times less oak and small pieces of pine for resource efficiency.

CRAFTSMANS GALLERY • RR 1, Chatsworth, Ontario, Canada • Tel: 519 794 3865 Fax 519 794 4449 • Cabinets, trim and doors for the home. Built-in longevity reduces landfill demand. Canadian craftsmanship at its best.

CULTURAL SURVIVAL • 215 First Street, Cambridge, MA 02142 • Tel: 617 621 3818 • Has a program to market sustainably harvested rain-forest products as part of their work advocating the rights of indigenous peoples and ethnic minorities worldwide. Many commercial products obtain their raw rain-forest products through Cultural Survival programs. They also sell plain Brazil nuts, cashews and cashew fruit.

CUT & DRIED HARDWOODS • 241 S Cedros Avenue, Solana Beach, CA 92075 • Tel: 619 481 0442 Fax: 619 481 2949 • Rick Jackson. Wood from Pilato in Mexico. RAN endorsed.

DULUTH TIMBER COMPANY • PO Box 16717, Duluth, MN 55816 • Tel: 218 727 2145 Fax: 218 722 0393 • Flooring, beams, etc. resawn from salvaged industrial timbers. Doug Fir, Antique Pine, Redwood, White Pine. Call for prices and availability.

ECOFORESTRY INSTITUTE • PO Box 12543, Portland, OR 97212 • Tel: 503 231 0576

ECOTIMBER INTERNATIONAL • 350 Treat Avenue, San Francisco, CA 94110-1326 • Tel: 415 864 4900 Fax: 415 864 1011 • Smart Wood supplier. Distributes hardwood lumber, flooring, millwork, and architectural quality veneered panels from certified "well-managed" tropical and domestic forestry operations.

EDENSAW WOODS • Port Townsend, WA • Tel: 800 745 336 • Hardwoods from managed plantations.

ENVIRESOURCE INC • 110 Madison Avenue North, Bainbridge Island, WA 98110 • Tel: 206 842 9785 • Sustainable yield hardwoods.

ETEX LTD • PO Box 80807, Las Vegas, NV 89180 • Tel: 800 543 5631 • Electro-gun for use against drywood termites.

FLORIDA RIDGE WOOD PRODUCTS • 4114 Bridges Road, Groveland, FL 34736 • Tel: 904 787 4251 • Recycled lumber.

FOREST STEWARDSHIP COUNCIL • PO Box 849, Richmond VT 05477 • Tel: 802 434 3101 • Developing program to accredit wood certification programs worldwide.

FOREST TRUST WOOD • PO Box 519, Santa Fe, NM 87504 • Tel: 505 983 8992 Fax: 505 986 0798 • Michael Grant. Hand-peeled logs and poles for building and fence materials (RAN endorsed).

WARREN FULLER • 11750 Hillcrest Road, Medford, OR 97404 • Tel: 503 772 8577 • Second growth Redwood and Douglas Fir from naturally downed trees. (RAN endorsed).

GEORGIA PACIFIC • 133 Peachtree Street, NE, Atlanta, GA 30303 • Tel: 404 652 4000 / 800 447 2882 • Laminated veneer lumber beams and headers. Wood I Beam joists consist of CDX plywood webs and machine stress-rated 2'x4' lumber.

GILMER WOOD CO • 2211 NW Saint Helen's Road, Portland, OR 97210 • Tel: 503 274 1271 • Hardwoods from managed plantations.

GOODWIN HEART PINE CO • Route 2 Box 119-A, Micanopy, FL 32667 • Tel: 800 336 3118 / 904 373 9663 • Sawn woods and antique pine.

GREENHEART-DURAWOOD INC • PO Box 757, South Amboy, NJ 08879 • Tel: 800 783 7220 • Inherently rot-resistant wood.

GRIDCORE SYSTEMS INTERNATIONAL • 5963 La Place Court, Suite 207, Carlsbad, CA 92008 • Tel: 619 431 8494 Fax: 619 431 2834 • Alternative lumber products.

GROFF LUMBER COMPANY INC • 7902 4th Street NW, Albuquerque, NM 87114 • Specialists in "Santa Fe" style. Vigas, Latillas, Rough sawn lumber, Corbels etc.

HANDLOGGERS HARDWOOD • 135 E Francis Drake Boulevard, Larkspur, CA 94939 • Tel: 415 461 1180 • Hardwoods from managed plantations.

HARMONY EXCHANGE • Route 2, Box 843, Big Hill Road, Boone NC 28607 • Tel: 800 756 9663 / 704 264 2314 Fax: 704 264 4770 • Reclaimed and resawn Douglas Fir ,and Heartpine timbers and flooring. Water based floor finishes. Call for catalog.

SHAW HAZEN • PO Box 230, Orinda, CA 94563 • Tel: 510 254 1720 • A woodworker who cuts down backyard trees for a living. Tremendous slabs of figured walnut and local oak, with the occasional madrone, camphor etc!

INSTITUTE FOR SUSTAINABLE FORESTRY • PO Box 1580, Redway, CA 95560 • Tel: 707 923 4719 • Administers Pacific Certified Ecological Forest Products certification program.

INTO THE WOODS • 300 N Water Street, Petulama, CA 94952 • Tel: 707 763 0159 • Sawn wood and recycled woods.

J & J CONSTRUCTION • 410 Broadway, Suite B, Santa Monica, CA 90401 • Tel: 310 395 753, 478 2800 • Wood from Belize. RAN endorsed.

JAGER INDUSTRIES INC • 8835 Macleod Trail SW, Calgary, AB, Canada, T2H OM3 • Tel: 403 259 0700

JEFFERSON LUMBER COMPANY • PO Box 696, McCloud, CA 96057 • Tel: 916 235 0609 Fax: 916 235 0434 • Recycled lumber.

THE JOINERY CO • PO Box 518, Tarboro, NC 27886 • Tel: 800 726 7463 / 919 823 3306 • Recycled lumber.

LARSON WOOD PRODUCTS INC • 31421 Coburg Bottom Loop, Eugene, OR 97401 • Tel: 503 343 5229 • Smart Wood supplier.

NATURAL Wood Products For the Home

BEAR CREEK LUMBER

For Information: **(509) 997-3110**   FAX (509) 997-2040
or write to BCL P.O. Box 669, Winthrop, WA 98862 USA

LIVE OAK STRUCTURAL INC • 801 Camellia Street, Suite B, Berkeley, CA 94710 • Tel: 510 524 7101 Fax: 510 524 7240 • *Pioneers of the termi-barrier; a non-toxic method of subterranean termite control in existing homes and new constructions.*

LIVERMORE • The Wood Mill, PO Box 146, East Livermore, ME 04228 • Tel: 207 897 5211 • *Wood floors and homes.*

LOUISIANA-PACIFIC • 2706 Highway 421, North Willington, NC 28401 • Tel: 910 762 9878 / 800 999 9105 • *Innovative building products using alternative resources.*

THE LUTHIER'S MERCANTILE • 412 Moore Lane, Healdsburg, CA 95448 • Tel: 707 433 1823 • *Hardwoods from managed plantations.*

MACMILLAN-BLOEDEL • Athens, GA Tel: 800 667 7828 or • British Columbia, Canada • Tel: 604 526 3624 • *Parallam boards and beams.*

MEDITE CORPORATION • Box 4040, Medford, OR 97501 • Tel: 503 779 9595 / 800 676 3339 • *Alternative lumber products.*

MENOMINEE TRIBAL ENTERPRISES • Box 10, Neopit, WI 54135 • Tel: 715 756 4943 • *SCS Certified program.*

MOUNTAIN LUMBER • PO Box 289 D, Ruckersville, VA 22968 • Tel: 800 445 2671 • *Recycled lumber.*

MOUNT STORM • 7890 Bell Road, Windsor, CA 95492 • Tel: 707 838 3177 • *Hardwoods from managed plantations.*

NASCOR INCORPORATED • 1212 34th Avenue SE, Calgary, AB, Canada, T2G 1V7 • Tel: 403 243 8919

NATURAL RESOURCES • Michael Evenson, PO Box 191, Redway, CA 95560 • Tel: 707 923 2979 Fax: 707 629 3663 • *Reclaimed lumber (Redwood, Douglas Fir, Port Orford Cedar). Certified ecologically harvested forest management plans and products.*

NORTHERN HARDWOOD LUMBER • 520 Matthew Street, Santa Clara, CA • Tel: 408 727 2211 • *Smart Wood supplier.*

PAGLIACCO TURNING & MILLING • PO Box 225, Woodacre, CA 94973 • Tel: 415 488 4333 Fax: 415 488 9372 • *Offers a complete line of standard and custom-manufactured products for restorations, new construction, and remodelling. For exterior work California Redwood offers superior decay and termite resistance. Interior turnings are available in Redwood, Douglas Fir, Mahogany, and oak.*

PERMA-CHINK SYSTEMS INC • 1605 Prosser Road, Knoxville, TN 37914 • Tel: 800 548 3554 • *Non-toxic boron wood preservative.*

PITTSFORD LUMBER • 500 State Street, Pittsford NY 14534 • Tel: 716 381 3489 • *Hardwoods from managed plantations.*

PORTICO SA, ROYAL MAHOGANY PRODUCTS INC • 6190 Regency Parkway, Suite 314, Atlanta, GA 30071 • Tel: 404 729 1600 • *SCS Certified program.*

RAINFOREST ACTION NETWORK • 450 Sansome Street, San Francisco, CA 94111 • Tel: 415 398 4404 • *Publish "The Wood Users Guide" by Pamela Wellner and Eugene Dickey which discusses the problems with rain-forest woods and gives a comprehensive overview of domestic wood and non wood alternatives. Lists tree species and descriptions, and suppliers of ecologically sensitive woods. Catalog of books on rain-forest issues as well as a few products that contain rain-forest ingredients.*

RAINFOREST ALLIANCE, • 65 Bleecker Street, New York NY 10012-2420 • Tel: 212 677 1900 • *Administers Smart Wood™ certification program for rain forest woods.*

ROGUE INSTITUTE FOR ECOLOGY AND ECONOMY • Ashland, Oregon • Tel: 503 482 6031

ROSBORO LUMBER CO • PO Box 20, Springfield, OR 97477 • Tel: 503 746 8411 Fax: 503 726 8919

SCIENTIFIC CERTIFICATION SYSTEMS • 1611 Telegraph Avenue, Suite 1111, Oakland, CA 94612 • Tel: 510 832 1415 • *Certifies sustainable sources of lumber.*

SEA STAR TRADING COMPANY • PO Box 513, Newport, OR 97365 • Tel: 503 265 9616 / 800 359 7571 Fax: 503 265 3228 • *Smart Wood supplier. Sea Star's new tropical hardwood program, Perpetua Hardwoods™, is based on stewardship of resources, involvement of local communities, and protection of the environment.*

SEVEN ISLANDS LAND MANAGEMENT CO • 304 Hancock Street, Suite 2A, PO Box 1168, Bangor, ME 04402-1168 • Tel: 207 947 0541 • *The largest SCS Certified well-managed forest in North America. Spruce framing lumber, cedar shingles, hardwood lumber, and hardwood flooring.*

SMART WOOD™ • Rainforest Alliance, 65 Bleecker Street, New York NY 10012-2420 • Tel: 212 677 1900 • *Certification program for wood.*

STANDARD STRUCTURES INC • PO Box K, Santa Rosa, CA 95402 • Tel: 707 544 2982 • *Engineered wood products.*

SUPERIOR WOOD SYSTEMS • PO Box 1208, Superior, WI 54880 • Tel: 715 392 1822 Fax: 715 392 3484

TECTON LAMINATES • 2700 Pinegrove Avenue, Suite 43, Port Huron, MI 48060 • Tel: 800 825 8720 / 313 385 8809

TROPICAL FOREST FOUNDATION • Keister Evans, 1421 Prince Street, Suite 230, Alexandria, VA 22314 • Tel: 703 838 5546

TRUITT & WHITE LUMBER CO INC • 642 Hearst Avenue, Berkeley, CA 94710 • Tel: 510 841 0511 • *Lumber, ACQ Preserve™, Building Materials.*

TRUS JOIST MACMILLAN (TJM) • 200 East Mallard Drive, Boise, Idaho 83706 • Tel: 208 364 1200 / 800 338 0515 Fax: 208 364 1300 • *Structural engineered lumber uses less wood fiber and an expanded timber resource base to produce high-performance building materials.*

TRUSWAL • 1101 N Great Southwest Parkway, Arlington, TX 76011 • Tel: 800 521 9790 Fax: 817 652 3079

TUCKAWAY TIMBER CO • Pinnacle Hill, Lyme, NH 03768 • Tel: 603 795 4534

UNADILLA LAMINATED PRODUCTS • 32 Clifton Street, Unadilla, NY 13849 • Tel: 607 369 9341

UNICORE • Fiber Converters Inc, 125 East Broadway, Three Rivers, MI 49093 • Tel: 616 279 5171 • *Alternative lumber products.*

WOODWORKERS ALLIANCE FOR RAINFOREST PROTECTION (WARP) • 1 Cottage Street, Easthampton, MA 01027 • Tel: 413 586 8156 • *Guidance in selecting hardwoods. A grass-roots association of wood-workers and wood users that supports sustainable development of forest resources and provides information about responsible timber management and wood use.*

WATERSHED SALES CORPORATION • PO Box 31588, New Braunfels, TX 78131 • Tel: 512 629 4246

WILD IRIS FORESTRY • PO Box 1423, Redway, CA 95560 • Tel: 707 923 2344 • *Recycled lumber.*

WILLAMETTE INDUSTRIES ENGINEERED WOOD PRODUCTS • PO Box 277, Saginaw, OR 97472 • Tel: 503 744 4664

WILSON WOODWORKS • 108 Hydeville Road, Stafford, CT • Tel: 203 684 9112

WOODWORKERS SUPPLY • 5402 South 40th Street, Phoenix, AZ • Tel: 602 437 4415 • *Hardwoods from managed plantations.*

Shakes and shingles ~ page 32

AMERICAN CHEM-WOOD PRODUCTS • PO Box C, Albany, OR 97321 • Tel: 503 928 6397

B.C. SHAKE & SHINGLE ASSOCIATION • 9414A - 288 Street, Maple Ridge, BC, Canada, V2X 8Y6 • Tel: 604 462 8961 Fax: 604 462 9386 • *Western Red Cedar shakes and shingles are aesthetically pleasing and offer lasting value. They are produced from a renewable resource which helps protect our environment.*

CEDAR SHAKE & SHINGLE BUREAU • 515-116th Avenue NE, Suite 275, Bellevue, WA 98004 • Tel: 206 453 1323 Fax: 206 455 1314 *Quality and grading standards. "Certi" labels certify products made by its membership.*

CERTAINTEED CORPORATION ROOFING GROUP • PO Box 860, Valley Forge, PA 19482 • Tel: 800 274 8530

CLASSIC PRODUCTS • 8510 Industry Park Drive, PO Box 701, Piqua, OH 45356 • Tel: 513 773 9840 / 800 543 8938 Fax: 513 773 9261 • *Rustic Shingle offers the look of wood shakes with the durability of recycled aluminum. Energy efficiency, fire safety, and a lifetime of mainte-nance-free beauty.*

CROWE INDUSTRIES LTD • 116 Burris Street, Hamilton, Ontario, Canada, L8M 2J5 • Tel: 905 529 6818

EIGER BUILDING PRODUCTS • 4770 Biscayne Boulevard, Suite 1020, Miami, FL 33137 • Tel: 305 573 7778

ENVIROTECH INDUSTRIES • 12221 Merit Drive, Suite 1390, Dallas, TX 75251 • Tel: 214 991 4499

ETERNIT • PO Box 679, Blandon, PA 19510-0679 • Tel: 215 926 0100 Fax: 215 926 9232

FIBERCEM CORPORATION • PO Box 411368, Charlotte, NC 28241 • Tel: 704 588 6693 / 800 346 6147

GEORGIA-PACIFIC • 133 Peachtree Street NE, Atlanta, GA 30303 • Tel: 404 652 4000 / 800 447 2882

GERARD ROOFING TECHNOLOGIES • 955 Columbia Street, Brea, CA 92621-2927 • Tel: 714 529 0407 / 800 841 3213

JAMES HARDIE BUILDING PRODUCTS INC • 10901 Elm Avenue, Fontana, CA 92335 • Tel: 909 356 6300 Fax: 909 355 4907 • *Manufactures environment-friendly fiber-cement roofing and siding products. These products give homeowners the look of wood without wood's heavy maintenance requirements.*

LOUISIANA-PACIFIC • 2706 Highway 421, North Willington, NC 28401 • Tel: 910 762 9878 / 800 999 9105 • *Innovative building prod-ucts using alternative resources.*

MASONITE CORPORATION • 1 South Wacker Drive, Chicago, IL 60606 • Tel: 800 255 0785

MAXITILE INC • 17141 S Kingsview Avenue, Carson, CA 90746 • Tel: 800 338 8453

METAL SALES MANUFACTURING CORPORATION • 6260 Downing, Denver, CO 80216 • Tel: 800 289 7663

NAILITE INTERNATIONAL • 1251 NW 165th Street, Miami, FL 33169-5871 • Tel: 305 620 6200 • *Eco-conscious alternatives to shakes, shingles, and stone cladding.*

NATIONAL INSTITUTE OF BUILDING SCIENCES • 1201 S Street NW, Suite 400, Washington DC 20005 • Tel: 202 289 7800

OUTWATER PLASTIC LUMBER • 4 Passaic Street, Woodridge, NJ 07075 • *Recycled plastic material for building.*

PHENIX™ BIOCOMPOSITES • PO Box 609, Mankato, MN 56002-0609 • Tel: 507 931 5573 Fax: 507 931 5573 • *Environ™ biocomposite made from recycled and replenishable resources looks like granite yet works like wood.*

RTS COMPANY • 1805 Newton Avenue, San Diego, CA 92113 • Tel: 619 696 0102

SEVEN ISLANDS LAND MANAGEMENT CO • 304 Hancock Street, Suite 2A, PO Box 1168, Bangor, ME 04402-1168 • Tel: 207 947 0541 • *The largest SCS Certified well-managed forest in North America. Spruce framing lumber, cedar shingles, hardwood lumber and hardwood flooring.*

SUPRADUR • PO Box 908, Rye, NY 10580 • Tel: 914 967 8230 / 800 223 1948

TERRA ROOFING PRODUCTS • PO Box 1960, Fontana, CA 92335 • Tel: 800 576 8372 • *TERRA Shake: the Earth Renewable Resource Alternative made from lightweight fiber cement.*

TRUS JOIST CORPORATION • PO Box 60 Boise, Idaho 83707 • Tel: 208 322 4931

ZAPPONE™ MANUFACTURING • N 2928 Pittsburg, Spokane, WA 99207 • Tel: 509 483 6408 / 800 285 2677

Boards and sheets ~ page 33

ABT BUILDING PRODUCTS • PO Box 98, Highway 268, Roaring River, NC 28669 • Tel: 800 334 3551

AFM CORPORATION • 24000 West Highway 7, Box 246, Excelsior, MN 5331-0246 • Tel: 612 474 0809 / 800 255 0176 • *The R-control structural building panel is a strong, super-insulated component.*

AGRIBOARD INDUSTRIES • Box 645, Fairfield, IA 52556 • Tel: 515 472 0363

BARRIER SYSTEM • PO Box 346, Canasota, NY 13032 • Tel: 315 697 7224

BELLCOMB TECHNOLOGIES • 70 N 22nd Avenue, Minneapolis, MN 55411 • Tel: 617 521 2425

CAN-FIBRE GROUP LTD • Suite 100-1500 W Georgia Street, Vancouver, BC, Canada, V6G 2Z6

DOMTAR • Box 543, 24 Frank Lloyd Wright Drive, Ann Arbor, MI 48106 • Tel: 313 930 4700

DOMTAR GYPSUM • 122 Old Dover Road, Newington, NH 03801 • Tel: 800 366 8274

EAGLE PANEL SYSTEMS • PO Box 748, Florissant, MO 63032 • Tel: 314 653 0205 / 800 643 3786

ENERCEPT INC • 3100 9th Avenue SE, Watertown, SD 57201 • Tel: 605 882 2222

ETERNIT • Box 679, Blandon, PA 19510-0679 • Tel: 215 926 0100

EVANITE FIBER CORPORATION • Box E, Corvalis, OR 97339 • Tel: 503 655 3383

FIBRECEM CORPORATION • 11000-1 S Commerce Boulevard, PO Box 411368, Charlotte, NC 28241 • Tel: 704 588 6693 / 800 346 6147

FIBRELAM • Box 2002, Doswell, VA 23047 • Tel: 804 876 3135

FURMAN LUMBER INC • Box 130, Nutting Lake, MA 01865 • Tel: 800 843 9663

GEORGIA-PACIFIC • 133 Peachtree Street NE, Atlanta, GA 30303 • Tel: 404 652 4000 / 800 447 2882

GRIDCORE SYSTEMS • 1400 Canal Avenue, Long Beach, CA 90813 • Tel: 310 901 1492 Fax: 310 901 1499

HARMONY EXCHANGE • Route 2, Box 843, Boone, NC 28607 • Tel: 704 264 2314

HOMASOTE COMPANY • Box 7240, West Trenton, NJ 08628-0240 • Tel: 800 257 9491 • *Manufacturers of building products made from recycled newsprint including various fiberboard materials.*

JAMES HARDIE BUILDING PRODUCTS INC • 10901 Elm Avenue, Fontana, CA 92337 • Tel: 909 356 6300 / 800 426 4051

J-DECK INC BUILDING SYSTEMS • 2587 Harrison Road, Columbus, OH 43204 • Tel: 614 274 7755

LOUISIANA-PACIFIC • 2706 Highway 421, North Willington, NC 28401 • Tel: 910 762 9878 / 800 999 9105 • *Innovative building products using alternative resources.*

MANSION INDUSTRIES • Box 2220, City of Industry, CA 91746-2220 • Tel: 818 968 9501

MEADOWOOD INDUSTRIES • 33242 Red Bridge Road, Albany, OR 97321 • Tel: 503 259 1303

MEDITE CORPORATION • Box 4040, Medford, OR 97501 • Tel: 503 779 9595 / 800 676 3339 Fax: 503 779 9921 • *Formaldehyde-free particle and fiber boards.*

NASCOR INCORPORATED • 2820 Centre Avenue NE, Calgary, AB, Canada, T2A 7P5 • Tel: 403 248 9890 Fax: 403 248 2405

NIAGARA FIBERBOARD INC • 10 Stevens Street, Lockport, NY 14095 • Tel: 716 434 8881

OREGON STRAND BOARD CO • 34363 Lake Creek Drive, Brownsville, OR 97327 • Tel: 503 466 5177 / 800 533 3374 Fax: 503 466 5559 • *Comply - composite plywood. Solid core structural APA rated panels made from fir veneers and recycled wood waste, bonded with phenolic resin.*

PANTERRE AMERICA • 2700 Wilson Boulevard, Arlington, VA 22201 • Tel: 703 247 3140

RODMAN INDUSTRIES • PO Box 76, Marinette, WI 54143 • Tel: 715 735 9500 Fax: 715 735 6148

SHELTER ENTERPRISES • PO Box 618 Saratoga Street, Cohoes, NY 12047 • Tel: 518 237 4101

SILVA FOREST FOUNDATION • PO Box 9, Slocan Park, BC, Canada, B0G 2EO • Tel: 604 226 7222 Fax: 604 226 7446

SIMPLEX PRODUCTS • Box 10, Adrian, MI 49221 • Tel: 517 263 8881

TEMPLE PRODUCTS • PO Box N, Diboll, TX 75941 • Tel: 409 829 5511 / 800 676 3339

TRI-CELL CORPORATION • 3841 Swanson Court, Gurnee, IL 60031 • Tel: 708 336 1321 / 800 352 3300

US BUILDING PANELS INC • 10901 Lakeview Avenue SW, Tacoma, WA 98499 • Tel: 206 581 0288

WEYERHAEUSER • 4111 East Four Mile Road, Grayling, MI 49738 • Tel: 517 348 2881

WILLAMETTE INDUSTRIES • Box 907, Albany, OR 97321 • Tel: 503 926 7771

WINTER PANEL CENTRAL • 16745 W Blue Mound Road, Brookfield, WI 53005-5938 • Tel: 414 784 9097 / 800 527 3895

Breathing walls ~ *page 36*

See also following listings for Straw-bale construction

ALSITE SUPPLY • Sacramento, CA • Tel: 916 922 9327 • *Distributor of "Denny Foil".*

MARK ABRAHAM • 265 North Front Street, Sarnia, Ontario, Canada, N7T 7K4 • Tel: 519 542 7751 • *Educational workshops on breathing walls.*

EXCEL INDUSTRIES LIMITED • 13 Rassau Industrial Estate, Ebbw Vale, Gwent, NP3 5SD, United Kingdom • Tel: (+44) 1495 350655 Fax: (+44) 1495 350146 • *Manufacturers of 'Warmcel' cellulose insulation. Leading British company that has been involved in tests and certification. Contact UK headquarters for US and Canadian distributors.*

FOUNTAINHEAD NATURAL HOMES • 11965 Monclova Road, Swanton, OH 43558 • Tel: 419 825 3031 • *Plastered Bale wall panels.*

INTERNATIONAL CELLULOSE CORPORATION • 12315 Robin Boulevard, Houston, TX 77045-0006 • Tel: 800 444 1252 Fax: 713 433 2029 • *Celbar is 'The natural choice' for home insulation. Composed of natural fibers recycled from paper, Celbar provides a high R-value and minimizes air and sound infiltration.*

ROCKY MOUNTAIN SUPPLY • 1901 Broadway, Alameda, CA 94501 • Tel: 510 522 3544 • *Distributor of "Denny Foil".*

BUILDING

SPARFIL INTERNATIONAL INC • 376 Watline Avenue, Mississuaga, Ontario, Canada, L4Z 1X2 • Tel: 416 507 1163 • *Sparfil wall system, insulated cellular concrete blocks.*

UNIQUE BUILDING SUPPLY • Santa Ana, CA • Tel: 714 558 0677 • *Distributor of "Denny Foil".*

WEST MATERIALS INC • 101 West Burnsville Parkway, Burnsville, MN 55337 • Tel: 612 890 3152 • *EnerBlock molded polystyrene inserts insulate the cores of concrete masonry units.*

WORLD FIBER TECHNOLOGIES • 155 Capitol Mall, Suite 525, Sacramento, CA 07210 • Tel: 916 446 2563

Straw-bale construction ~ page 37

A.C.E. (Alternative & Conservation Energies Inc) • Varsity Exececenter, 1700 Varsity Estates Drive NW, Calgary, Alberta, Canada, T3B 2W9 • Tel: 403 286 1407 Fax: 403 286 1407 • *Architecture, earth buildings, straw bale, rammed earth, healthy buildings.*

BALE BUILDERS • 798 South Spring Street, Ukiah, CA 95482 • Tel: 707 462 2368 • *Straw bale building workshops.*

CALIFORNIA INSTITUTE OF EARTH ART AND ARCHITECTURE • Geltaftan Foundation, 10376 Shangri La Avenue, Hesperia, CA 92345 • Tel: 619 244 0614 Fax: 619 244 2201 • *Founded by Architect, Nader Khalili. Superadobe, Straw Bale, Sandbag, Ceramic Architecture. If you have a vision for building a community or your home, your school or career, or even to help others to build theirs, give us just one week of your time and we will empower you to realize that dream – without cutting a single tree, by using the earth under your feet and utilizing the elements of sun, wind, water, and fire. Fee $2,000. Write for more information • See p. 195.*

THE CANELO PROJECT • HC1 Box 324, Canelo/Elgin, AZ 85611 • Tel: 520 455 5548 Fax: 520 455 9360 • *Comprehensive Straw Bale Workshops: wall systems, carpentry, foundations, plasters, and floors. Techniques emphasize combining straw with earthen/clay materials and bamboo. House tours, work-tours in Mexico and consulting.*

DEVELOPMENT CENTER FOR APPROPRIATE TECHNOLOGY • David Eisenberg, 2702 E Seneca Street, Tucson, AZ 85716 • Tel: 520 326 1418

EOS INSTITUTE • 580 Broadway, no 200, Laguna Beach, CA 92651 • Tel: 714 497 1896 Fax: 714 494 7861 • *Resource Center for sustainable living. Publications, library, workshops.*

GREENFIRE INSTITUTE • 1509 Queen Anne Avenue N, # 606, Seattle, WA 98109 • Tel: 206 284 7470 • *Straw bale and other sustainable construction workshops.*

NATIONAL CENTER FOR APPROPRIATE TECHNOLOGY • PO Box 3838, Butte, MT 59702-2525 • Tel: 406 494 4572 / 800 428 2525 Fax: 406 494 2905

NATURAL HOUSE BUILDING CENTER • RR 1, Box 115F, Fairfield, IA 52556 • Tel: 515 472 7775 • *Holistic home-building workshops including light clay, earth plastering, and stabilized earth floor constructions. Publications.*

OUT ON BALE (UN) LTD • 1037 E Linden Street, Tuscon, AZ 85719 • Tel: 602 624 1673 • *Information and resource clearing house for straw-bale construction.*

RESEARCH ADVISORY NETWORK • Bob Theis, c/o DSA Architecture, 1107 Virginia Street, Berkeley, CA 94702

SKILLFUL MEANS BUILDERS • PO Box 207, Junction City, CA 96048 • *Workshops*

SOLAR ENERGY INTERNATIONAL • PO Box 715, Carbondale, CO 81623 • Tel: 303 963 8855 Fax: 303 963 8866 • *Workshops on solar design, straw-bale, adobe, and rammed earth construction.*

SWANSON ASSOCIATES • 601 23rd Street, Fairfield, Iowa 52556 • Tel: 515 472 8217 Fax: 515 472 1678 • *Environmental Design and Construction. Straw/clay, straw bale designs and construction. Fascuall 'Natural Breathing' wall designs and construction. Certified Bau-biologist.*

STRAW BALE CONSTRUCTION ASSOCIATION • 31 Old Arroyo Chamiso, Santa Fe, NM 87505 • Tel: 505 989 4400

STRAWBALE RESEARCH FUND and COMMUNITY RESEARCH CENTER (CIRC) • PO Box 42663, Tucson, AZ 85733

STRAWCRAFTERS • 3785 Moorhead, Boulder, CO 80303 • *Workshops.*

SOUTHWEST SOLARADOBE SCHOOL • PO Box 153, Bosque, NM 87006 • Tel: 503 252 1382

Windows ~ page 38

See also following listings for Glass and glazing, and for Sunspace and Solar windows on p. 228.

ALSIDE • PO BOX 2010, Akron, OH 44309 • Tel: 216 922 2202

BERKELEY ARCHITECTURAL SALVAGE • 722 Folger Avenue, Berkeley, CA 94710 • Tel: 510 849 2025 • *Salvaged building materials include: hardware, interior trim, doors, windows, plumbing fixtures.*

BETTER CALIFORNIA WINDOWS AND DOORS • 9 Ryan Lane, Cotati, CA 94931 • Tel: 707 795 9409 • *Energy-efficient windows.*

EAGLE WINDOW AND DOOR • 375 East 9th Street, Dubuque, IO 52004 • Tel: 319 556 2270

FOUR SEASONS SUN ROOMS • 5005 Veterans Memorial Highway, Holbrook, NY 11741 • Tel: 516 563 4000 Fax: 516 563 4010

G & A NATURAL LIGHTING • 586 Weddell Drive, Suite 2, Sunnyvale, CA 94089 • Tel 408 541 8930 Fax: 408 541 8949 • *SOLATUBE™ - The high performance natural alternative to the skylight.*

MILGARD • 3800-136th Street NE, Marysville, WA 98271 • Tel: 800 562 8444 / 206 659 0836

NATIONAL WOOD WINDOW AND DOOR ASSOCIATION • 1400 East Touhy Avenue, Des Plaines, IL 60018 • Tel: 312 299 5200

SOLAR COMPONENTS CORPORATION • 121 Valley Street, Manchester, NH 03103-6211 • Tel: 603 668 8186 • *Distributors of Sun-Lite solar glazing.*

SOLATUBE™ • 5825 Avenida Encinas, Suite 101, Carlsbad, CA 92008 • Tel: 619 929 6060 • *Using a unique roof-mounted reflector and mirrored transfer tubing, it delivers more light, more economically, than much larger traditional skylights.*

SOUTHWALL TECHNOLOGIES • 1029 Corporation Way, Palo Alto, CA • Tel: 800 365 8794 / 415 962 9111

SUNTEK • 6817A Academy Parkway, East Albuquerque, NM 87109 • Tel: 505 345 4115

VINYL WINDOW AND DOOR INSTITUTE • 355 Lexington Avenue, New York, NY 10017 • Tel: 212 351 5400.

WENCO WINDOWS • PO Box 1248, Mount Vernon, OH 43050-8248 • Tel: 800 458 9128 / 614 397 1144

WINTER SEAL VINYL • 1300 Dussel, Maumee, OH 43537 • Tel: 419 897 9500

Glass and glazing ~ page 39

ACCURATE DORWIN CO • 660 Nairn Avenue, Winnipeg, MB, Canada, R2L 0X5 • Tel: 204 667 4640 Fax: 204 663 0020

AMERICAN ARCHITECTURAL MANUFACTURERS ASSOCIATION • 1540 East Dundee Road, Suite 310, Palatine, IL 60067 • Tel: 708 202 1350

ARCTIC GLASS & WINDOW OUTLET • 565 County T, Hammond, WI 54015 • Tel: 715 796 2291 / 800 428 9276

CANADIAN INSTITUTE FOR RESEARCH AND CONSTRUCTION • Building Materials Center M-20, Ottawa, Ontario, Canada, K1A 0R6 • Tel: 613 993 2463 Fax: 613 952 7673 • *Canadian Construction Materials Center. Information and advice on latest resource-efficient materials for all your construction needs.*

CANADIAN WINDOW AND DOOR MANUFACTURERS ASSOCIATION • 27 Goulburn Avenue, Ottawa, Ontario, Canada, K1N 8C7

GLASSTECH • 3825 Willat Avenue, Culver City, CA 90232 • Tel: 310 202 6001 • *Created from broken pieces of glass laminated to a new piece of tempered glass, secondary use is derived from consumer waste.*

NATIONAL ENERGY CONSERVATION ASSOCIATION • PO Box 3214, Winnipeg, Manitoba, R3C 4E7 • Tel: 204 783 1273 Fax: 204 774 6702

NATIONAL FENESTRATION RATINGS COUNCIL (NFRC) • 1300 Spring Street, Suite 120, Silver Spring, MD 20910 • Tel: 301 589 6372

SUNDANCE SUPPLY • 1678 Shattuck Avenue, Suite 173, Berkeley, CA 94709 • Tel: 510 845 0525 Fax: 510 845 9450 • *Components for site-built greenhouses, sunrooms, skylights, and pool enclosures.*

Doors ~ page 40

BERKELEY ARCHITECTURAL SALVAGE • 722 Folger Avenue, Berkeley, CA 94710 • Tel: 510 849 2025 • *Salvaged building materials include: hardware, interior trim, doors, windows, plumbing fixtures.*

BETTER CALIFORNIA WINDOWS AND DOORS • 9 Ryan Lane, Cotati, CA 94931 • Tel: 707 795 9409 • *Energy-efficient doors.*

CANADIAN WINDOW AND DOOR MANUFACTURERS ASSOCIATION • 27 Goulburn Avenue, Ottawa, Ontario, Canada, K1N 8C7

CASTLEGATE ENTRY SYSTEMS • 911 East Jefferson Street, PO Box 76, Pittsburg, KS 66762 • Tel: 800 835 0364

EAGLE WINDOW AND DOOR • 375 East 9th Street, Dubuque, IO 52004 • Tel: 319 556 2270

GRAND RIVER DOOR INC • PO Box 15360, Rio Rancho, NM 87174 • Tel: 505 867 4110 Fax: 505 867 9711

JELD-WEN • PO Box 1329, Klamath Falls, OR 97601-0268 • Tel: 800 877 9842

MADAWASKA DOORS INC • PO Box 850, Bolton, Ontario, Canada, L7E 5T5 • Tel: 800 263 2358

MASONITE CORPORATION • 1 South Wacker Drive, Chicago, IL 60606 • Tel: 800 446 1649

NATIONAL WOOD WINDOW AND DOOR ASSOCIATION • 1400 East Touhy Avenue, Des Plaines, IL 60018 • Tel: 312 299 5200

PACIFIC MATERIALS EXCHANGE • 1522 N Washington Street, Suite 202, Spokane, WA 99201 • Tel: 509 325 0551 • *On-line network of 40 Exchange centers.*

PEACHTREE DOORS • Box 5700, Norcross, GA 30091-5700 • Tel: 800 447 4700

PEASE INDUSTRIES INC • 7100 Dixie Highway, Fairfield, OH 45014 • Tel: 800 883 6677

PERMA-DOOR • 9017 Blue Ash Road, Cincinnati, OH 45242 • Tel: 513 745 6400

ROYAL MAHOGANY PRODUCTS • Division of Portico, S.A., 6190 Regency Parkway, Suite 314, Atlanta, GA 30071 • Tel: 404 446 8849 Fax: 404 446 8884 • *Mahogany doors from well-managed forests.*

THERMACORE • 3200 Reach Road, Williamsport, PA 17701 • Tel: 800 233 8992 • *CFC- and HCFC-free insulated doors.*

THERMA-TRU CORPORATION • PO Box 8780, Maumee, OH 43537 • Tel: 419 882 5625

Reduce, reuse, recycle ~ page 41

For recycled wood see Sustainable timber listings pages 213-16

AGED WOOD, 2331 E Market Street, York, PA 17402 • Tel: 800 233 9307 / 717 840 0330

ALBANY WOODWORKS • PO Box 729, Albany, LA 70711-0729 • Tel: 504 567 1155

BATHCREST INC • 2425 S Progress Drive, Salt Lake City, Utah 84119 • Tel: 800 826 6790 • *Save your money and the environment. Bathcrest refinishes existing tubs saving you up to 80% over replacement.*

BERKELEY ARCHITECTURAL SALVAGE • 722 Folger Avenue, Berkeley, CA 94710 • Tel: 510 849 2025 • *Salvaged building materials include: hardware, interior trim, doors, windows, plumbing fixtures.*

CALDWELL BUILDING WRECKING • 195 Bayshore Boulevard, San Francisco, CCA 94124 • Tel: 415 550 6777 • *Recycled lumber and various building materials.*

CAPITOL LUMBER COMPANY • PO Box 967, Chino, CA 92710 • Tel: 909 591 4861 • *Supplier of TREX wood-polymer composite decking, made from reclaimed plastic and waste-wood.*

CENTER MILLS ANTIQUE WOOD • PO Box 16, Aspers, PA 17304 • Tel: 717 334 0249

CERTAINTEED CORPORATION INSULATION GROUP • PO Box 860, Valley Forge, PA 19482 • Tel: 215 341 700 • *Fiberglass batts made with 5% pre-consumer and 20% post-consumer recycled glass.*

COASTAL MILLWORKS • 1335 Marietta Boulevard, NW, Atlanta, GA 30318 • Tel: 404 351 8400

DULUTH TIMBER COMPANY • PO Box 16717, Duluth, MN 55816 • Tel: 218 727 2145 Fax: 218 722 0393 • *Flooring, beams, etc. resawn from salvaged industrial timbers. Doug Fir, Antique Pine, Redwood, White Pine. Call for prices and availability.*

THE EPSTEN GROUP • 303 Ferguson Street, Atlanta, GA 30307 • Tel: 404 577 0370 • *Environmentally sound architectural design/consulting. Residential/Commercial. Non-polluting/recycled building materials.*

HAMMER'S PLASTIC RECYCLING • RR 3 Box 182, Highway 20 & 65 North, Iowa Falls, IA 50126 • Tel: 515 648 5073 Fax: 515 648 5074

INTO THE WOODS • 300 N Water Street, Petaluma, CA 94952 • Tel: 707 763 0159 • *Recycled woods.*

STEVE MACK • Chasehill Farms, Ashaway, RI 02804 • *Salvaged houses.*

MAXWELL PACIFIC • PO Box 4127, Malibu, CA 90264 • Tel: 310 457 4533 Fax: 310 457 8308 • *Reclaimed and antique timbers, barnwood, flooring. Fir, pine, redwood, cedar.*

OHMEGA SALVAGE • 2407 San Pablo Avenue, Berkeley, CA 94702 • Tel: 510 843 7368 • *Salvaged building materials include doors, windows, tile, stone, plumbing fixtures.*

P & N RECYCLING • 140 Mariposa Terrace, Medford, OR 97504 • Tel: 503 772 4132

PACIFIC MATERIALS EXCHANGE • 1522 N Washington Street, Suite 202, Spokane, WA 99201 • Tel: 509 325 0551 • *On-line network of 40 exchange centers.*

PHOENIX RECYCLED PLASTICS • 225 Washington Street, Conshohocken, PA 19428 • Tel: 610 940 1590 • *Plastic lumber for all your outdoor needs!*

PIONEER MILLWORKS • 1755 Pioneer Road, Shortsville, NY 14548 • Tel: 716 289 3090

PLANETARY SOLUTIONS • PO Box 1049, Boulder, CO 80306 • Tel: 303 442 6228 • *Less-toxic and resource-efficient materials for architects, builders, dealers and whole house projects. Ecobuilding consulting services. Showroom. Library.*

G R PLUME CO • Suite B-11 & 12, 1301 Meador Avenue, Bellingham, Washington 98226 • Tel: 206 676 5658 • *Architectural timber millwork from reclaimed Douglas Fir timbers.*

RECYCLED LUMBER WORKS • 596 Park Boulevard, Ukiah, CA 95482 • Tel: 707 462 2567

SOLID CEDAR STRUCTURES • 295 Fifth Street West, Sonoma, CA 95476 • Tel: 707 935 3826 Fax: 707 935 1743

STAFFORD HARRIS INC • 1916 Pike Place 705, Seattle, WA 98101-1056 • Tel: 206 682 4042 Fax: 206 447 1670 • *Publishes the Harris Directory of recycled content building materials. Available on recycled MAC or DOS disks.*

TIRESIAS INC • PO Box 1864, Orangeburg, SC 29116-1864 • Tel: 803 534 8478

URBAN ORE • 1333 6th Street, Berkeley, CA 94710 • Tel: 510 559 4460 • *Salvaged building materials include doors, windows, tile, stone, and plumbing fixtures.*

WHAT ITS WORTH • PO Box 162135, Austin, TX 78716 • Tel: 512 328 8837 • *Reclaimed timber for flooring, posts, and beams.*

THE WOOD CELLAR • 1206 Laskin Road, Suite 202, Virginia Beach, VA 23451 • Tel: 800 795 9114

WOODHOUSE • PO Box 7336, Rocky Mount, NC 27804 • Tel: 919 977 7336

Owner-building and Retrofit ~ page 42

AUGUSTA HERITAGE ART CENTER • Davis & Elkins College, 100 Campus Drive, Elkins, WV 26241 • Tel: 304 636 1903

BUILDING EDUCATION CENTER • 812 Page Street, Berkeley, CA 94710 • Tel: 510 525 7610

CO-OP AMERICA • 2100 M Street, NW, no. 310, Washington DC 20063 • Tel: 800 424 2667

EARTHWOOD BUILDING SCHOOL • 366 Murtagh Hill Road, W Chazy, NY 12992 • Tel: 518 493 7744

ECOCITY BUILDERS • 5427 Telegraph Avenue, W2, Oakland CA 94609

ECO VILLAGE COHOUSING PROJECT • Anabel Taylor Hall, Cornell University, Ithaca, NY 14853 • Tel: 607 255 8276

INNOVATIVE HOUSING • 2169 East San Francisco Boulevard, San Rafael, CA 94901 • Tel: 415 457 4593

LOS ANGELES ECO VILLAGE PROJECT • 3551 White House Place, Los Angeles, CA 90004 • Tel: 213 738 1254

NATIONAL ASSOCIATION OF HOUSING COOPERATIVES • 1614 King Street, Alexandria, VA 22314 • Tel: 703 549 5201

OWNER-BUILDER CENTER • 1516 Fifth Street, Berkeley, CA 94710 • Tel: 415 848 5950

SHELTER INSTITUTE • 38 Center Street, Bath, ME 04530 • Tel: 207 442 7938 Fax: 207 442 7938 • *Teaches classes year round in cost and energy-efficient house design, renovation, and construction. Free brochure.*

SOLAR COMPONENTS CORPORATION • 121 Valley Street, Manchester, NH 03103 • Tel: 603 668 8186

URBAN ECOLOGY • 405 14th Street, Suite 701, Oakland, CA 94612 • Tel: 510 251 6330

YESTERMORROW DESIGN/BUILD SCHOOL • RR 1, Box 97-5, Warren, VT 05674 • Tel: 802 496 5545 Fax: 802 496 5540

Kit homes ~ page 43

ADVANCE CANVAS • Box 28, Ridgeway, CO 81432 • *Yurts.*

AMERICAN INGENUITY • 3500 Harlock Road, Melbourne, FL 32934 • Tel: 407 254 4220 Fax: 407 254 9283 • *Dome kits.*

BOREALIS YURTS • PO Box 362, Dover-Foxcroft, ME 04426 • Tel: 207 564 2159

DELTEC • 604 College Street, Asheville, NC 28801 • Tel: 704 253 0483 / 800 642 2508 Fax: 704 254 1880 • *Deltec makes round houses. Well they're not exactly round; exterior walls are panelized in flat, eight-foot sections, complete with siding and windows. The finished houses consist of anywhere from 10 to 20 flat 'facets'. Plan book $10; with video $19.95.*

DESIGN WORKS INC • 11 Hitching Post Road, Amherst, MA 01002 Tel: 413 549 4763 Fax: 413 549 7375 • *Home improvement: Raise the roof, add a porch, renovate the kitchen, or build an addition or new home - all with the 3-D Home Kit. Call for sample kit, brochure or information.*

FOURTH DIMENSION HOUSING • PO Box 44, Rainier, WA 98576 • Tel: 360 446 7715 Fax 360 446 1163 • *Arched Domes™ resonating Nature's harmonics. Design/build or kits.*

LIVING SHELTER CRAFTS TIPIS AND YURTS • PO Box 4069, West Sedona, AZ 86340 • Tel: 602 230 4283 • *Beautiful nomadic dwellings at affordable prices. High quality materials. Brochures and workshops.*

NOMADIC ARTS • 458 Hines Hill Road, Hudson, OH 44236 • *Yurts.*

PACIFIC YURTS INC • 77456 Highway 99 South, Cottage Grove, OR 97424 • Tel: 503 942 9435

WILDERNESS LOG HOMES • PO Box 902, Plymouth, WI 53073-0902 • Tel: 414 893 8416 Fax: 414 892 2414

THE YURT FOUNDATION • Bucks Harbor, Machiasport, ME 04655

Timber frames ~ page 44

JIM BARNA LOG SYSTEMS • PO Box 4529, Oneida, TN 37841 • Tel: 800 962 4734

BEHM DESIGN AND CONSTRUCTION • PO Box 0-18, Bowan Island, BC, Canada, V0N 1G0 • Tel: 604 947 0057

DAVIS FRAME CO • PO Box 1079L, Claremont, NH 03743 • Tel: 603 543 0993 • *Handcrafted timber frame homes of distinctive quality.*

FOUNTAINHEAD NATURAL HOMES • 11965 Monclova Road, Swanton, OH 43558 • Tel: 419 825 3031 • *Hand-crafted timber frames. Free brochures.*

FOUNTAINHEAD TIMBER HOMES • 5048 Trellis Way, Sylvania, OH 43560 • Tel: 419 885 1464 • *Construction and design of timber homes.*

GASTINEAU LOG HOMES • Box 248, New Bloomfield, MO 65063 • Tel: 314 896 5122

HEARTWOOD LOG HOMES LIMITED • RR 1, Margaretville, NS, Canada, B0S 1N0

LINWOOD HOMES • 8250 River Road, Delta, BC, Canada, V4G 1B5 • Tel: 800 663 2558 • *Kit or frame.*

FREDERICK J MILLER • Custom Woodworks, RR 1, Chatsworth, Ontario, Canada, N0H 1G0

NATURAL HOUSE BUILDING CENTER • RR 1 Box 115F, Fairfield, IA 52556 • Tel: 515 472 7775 • *Learn about timber framing and straw-clay construction, as well as roofs, earth plastering and earth floors, from MoosePrints, a 35-page booklet available for $7 ppd.*

ORIGINAL LOG HOMES • PO Box 1301, 100 Mile House, BC, Canada, V0K 2E0

PACIFIC POST & BEAM • PO Box 17308, San Luis Obispo, CA 93406 • Tel: 805 543 7565 • *Pacific Post & Beam is a full service timber framing and timber truss company in California using new or recycled wood and non-toxic materials.*

PACIFIC TIMBER FRAME • RR 2 Comp 9A, P.V. Crossroad, Armstrong, BC, Canada, V0E 1B0 • Tel: 604 546 9926

REAL LOG HOMES • PO Box 202, Hartland, VT 05048 • Tel: 800 732 5564

SOLID CEDAR STRUCTURES • 295 Fifth Street West, Sonoma, CA 95476 • Tel: 707 935 3826 Fax: 707 935 1743

SUN PINE HOMES • 915 E Gurley Street, Prescott, AZ 86301 • Tel: 602 778 6600

THISTLEWOOD TIMBER FRAME HOMES • RR 2, Markdale, Ontario, Canada, N0C 1H0 • Tel: 519 986 3280 Fax 519 986 4461 • *Specializes in handcrafted timber frame buildings using traditional wooden joinery. Salvaged and recycled wood is available for all Thistlewood projects.*

TIMBER FRAMERS GUILD OF NORTH AMERICA • PO Box 1046, Keene, NH 03431 • Tel: 603 357 1706

TIMBERCRAFT HOMES • 85 Martin Road, Port Townsend, WA 98368 • Tel: 206 385 3051 Fax: 206 385 7745

WILDERNESS LOG HOMES • PO Box 902, Plymouth, WI 53073 • Tel: 800 237 8564

YESTERMORROW DESIGN/BUILD SCHOOL • RR 1, Box 97-5, Warren, VT 05674 • Tel: 802 496 5545 Fax: 802 496 5540

Photovoltaics and solar collector panels ~ *page 52*

ABRAHAM SOLAR EQUIPMENT • 124 Creekside Pl, Pagosa Springs, CO 81147 • Tel: 800 222 7242

ADVANCE SOLAR • PO Box 23, Capella, CA 95418 • Tel: 707 485 0588 Fax: 707 485 0831

ALTERNATIVE ENERGY ENGINEERING • Box 339, Redway, CA 95560 • Tel: 707 923 2277 • *Catalog sales of solar, wind, and other alternative energy products.*

ALTERNATIVE SOLAR PRODUCTS • 27420 Jefferson, Suite 104B, Temecula, CA 92590 • Fax: 909 308 2388 • *Solar and wind power.*

AMERICAN COUNCIL FOR AN ENERGY-EFFICIENT ECONOMY • 1001 Connecticut Avenue, NW 535, Washington DC 20036 • Tel: 202 429 8873 • and at 2140 Shattuck Avenue, no 202, Berkeley, CA 94704 • Tel: 510 549 9914

AMERICAN SOLAR ENERGY SOCIETY • 2400 Central Avenue, Suite G1, Boulder • CO 80301 • Tel: 303 443 3130

AMERICAN SOLAR NETWORK • 12811 Bexhill Court, Herndon, VA 22071 • Tel: 904 284 2997

APPLIED PHOTOVOLTAICS • Box 2773, Stauntan, VA 24401 • Tel: 301 963 0141

ARRAY TECHNOLOGIES • PO Box 751 Albuquerque, NM 87103 • Tel: 505 242 8024 Fax: 505 242 2863 • *Wattsun freon-free solar tracker.*

ASCENSION TECHNOLOGY • PO Box 314, Lincoln Center, MA 01773 • Tel: 617 890 8894

ASTRODYNE CORPORATION • 412 High Plain Street, Walpole, MA 02081 • Tel: 508 668 2311 Fax: 508 668 9942 • *Range of products includes portable solar generators.*

BACKWOODS SOLAR ELECTRIC SYSTEMS • 8530 Rapid Lightning Creek Road, Sandpoint, ID 83864 • Tel: 208 263 4290 • *Solar electric power for remote homes. Send for catalog.*

B.C. SOLAR • PO Box 1117, Laytonville, CA 95454 • Tel: 707 984 8203 • *Sunflower™ Solar Tracker – For 12, 24, 36 volt systems - uses less than 2 watt hours per day per axis at 12 volts. Controls on the pole. Sizes up to 24 panels.*

BLACKHAWK SOLAR • PO Box 1468, Quincy, CA 95971 • Tel: 916 283 1396

BOBIER ELECTRONICS INC • 37 Murdoch Avenue, Parkersburg, WV 26101 • Tel: 304 485 7150

CARRIZO SOLAR CORPORATION • Tel: 800 776 6718 • *Available through dealers. Call for your nearest dealer.*

CEDAR VALLEY WORKSHOPS • 215 E Muskegon Street, Cedar Springs, MI 49319 • Tel: 616 696 0603

CENTER FOR THE BIOLOGY OF NATURAL SYSTEMS • Queens College, Flushing, NY 10003 • Tel: 718 420 1133

CITIZENS FOR CLEAN ENERGY • PO Box 17147, Boulder, CO 80308 • Tel: 303 443 6181

DANKOFF SOLAR PRODUCTS INC • 100 Ricardo Road, Santa Fe, NM 87501 • Tel & Fax: 505 820 6611 • *Energy-efficient water pumps for well pumping, water lift and pressurizing, specifically designed for off-grid photovoltaic power.*

EARTHLAB ENERGY SYSTEMS • 358 South Main Street, Willits, CA 95490 • Tel: 707 459 6272 • *Quality independent residential and commercial power systems.*

EARTHSTAR ENERGY SYSTEMS • Route 220 at US Route 1, PO Box 626, Waldboro, ME 04572 • Tel: 207 832 6861 Fax: 207 832 7314 • *Radiant heating technologies, whole house ventilation, thermal solar systems, and graywater heat recovery since 1980.*

ECOLOGY SYSTEMS • 3863 Short Street, Dubuque, IA 52002 • Tel: 319 556 4765 • *Photovoltaic systems and equipment.*

ENERGY ANSWERS • PO Box 24, Lake Bluff, IL 60044 • Tel: 800 776 6761 / 708 234 2515 • *Catalog of energy-saving products and solar equipment.*

ENERGY EFFICIENCY AND RENEWABLE ENERGY CLEARING HOUSE (EREC) • PO Box 3048, Merrifield, VA 22116 • Tel: 800 363 3732

ENERGY EFFICIENT ENVIRONMENTS • Tel: 800 336 3749 • *Catalog of environmentally friendly and energy saving products for your home.*

ENERGY SYSTEMS SPECIALISTS • 250 Main Street, Placerville, CA 95667 • Tel: 800 500 ENERGY • *Engineering, design, consulting, sales.*

ENVIRONMENTAL SOLAR DESIGN INC • 11237 Magnolia Boulevard, North Hollywood, CA 91601 • Tel: 818 762 6624 Fax: 818 762 2513 • *Suppliers of photovoltaic equipment.*

FLEETFOOT FUELS • Renewable Energy Department, 323 Royston, Eaton Rapids, MI 48827 • *Alcohol, solar, wind, methane, hydropower and others. Latest information, many contacts and plans available. Send $10.00.*

FLORIDA SOLAR ENERGY CENTER • 300 State Road, no. 401, Cape Canaveral, FL 32920 • Tel: 407 783 0300

FOWLER SOLAR ELECTRIC • PO Box 435, Worthington, MA 01098 • Tel: 413 238 5974 • *Mail-order pricing with quality service and support.*

FUSION INFORMATION CENTER • Institute for New Energy, Utah Research Park, PO Box 58639, Salt Lake City, UT 84109 • Tel: 801 583 6232 • *The world's best source of information on enhanced energy systems.*

GREAT LAKES RENEWABLE ENERGY ASSOCIATION • c/o NMEAC PO Box 1166, Traverse City, MI 49685-1166 • Tel: 616 228 7159

HEINZ SOLAR • 19345 N Indian Avenue, no. H, PO Box 1009, N Palm Springs, CA 92258 • Tel: 619 251 6886 Fax: 619 251 6886 • *Solar-powered lighting systems. Publisher of "Homestead Enterprises".*

HITNEY SOLAR PRODUCTS, INC • 2655 North Highway 89, Chino Valley, AZ 86323 • Tel: 602 636 1001 • *Stockist of Siemens solar electric power systems.*

INDEPENDENT POWER CO • PO Box 649, North San Juan, CA 95960

KANSAS WIND POWER • (Dept NHC) 13569 214th Road, Holton, KS 66436 • Tel: 913 364 4407 • *WIND/SOLAR ELECTRIC SYSTEMS. See main entry on page 225.*

KEEP IT SIMPLE SYSTEMS (KISS) • 32 S Ewing, Suite 330, Helena, MT 59601 • Tel: 406 442 3559 • *Solar Power for portable computers! Unique flexible and durable solar panels designed to run or recharge many popular portable computers.*

MASSACHUSETTS AUDUBON SOCIETY • South Great Road, Lincoln, MA 01773 • Tel: 617 259 9500 • *Offers eight booklets that describe energy solutions clearly and simply, including weatherization, solar, insulation, financing tips, and more.*

MIDWAY LABS INC • 1818 East 71st Street, Chicago, IL 60649 • Tel: 312 667 7863 Fax: 312 667 6577 • *Produces low cost concentrator photovoltaic systems. Uses innovative optical and solar cell designs to provide reliable electrical energy at the lowest cost per watt.*

MIDWEST RENEWABLE ENERGY ASSOCIATION • PO Box 249, Amherst, WI 54406 • Tel: 715 824 5166

NATURAL RESOURCES DEFENSE COUNCIL • 40 West 20th Street, New York, NY 10011 • Tel: 212 727 2700

NCI INFORMATION SYSTEMS INC • 8260 Greensboro Drive, Suite 400, McLean, VA 22102 • Tel: 703 903 0325 Fax: 703 903 9750 • *Renewable and energy-efficient technologies.*

NORTHERN CALIFORNIA SOLAR ENERGY ASSOCIATION • PO Box 3008, Berkeley, CA 94703 • Tel: 510 869 2759

NORTHEAST SUSTAINABLE ENERGY ASSOCIATION • 23 Ames Street, Greenfield, MA 01301 • Tel: 413 774 6051

NUCLEAR FREE AMERICA • 325 E 25th Street, Baltimore MD 21218 • Tel: 301 235 3575

OFF-LINE • PO Box 231, North Fork, CA 93643 • Tel: 209 877 7080 • *All major brands for residential power, water systems, phones, wind power, photovoltaic and hydro. Design, installation and mail order.*

PACIFIC GAS & ELECTRIC ENERGY CENTER • 851 Howard Street, San Francisco, CA 94103 • Tel: 415 973 7268 Fax: 415 896 1290 • Smarter Energy Line: 800 933 9555 • *Assists designers in maximizing energy efficiency and occupant comfort for buildings in PG&E's territory.*

PHOTOCOMM INC • PO Box 14230, Scottsdale, AZ 85267-4230 • Tel: 602 951 6330 / 800 544 6466 • *Suppliers of solar electric systems including ANANDA Power Technologies Inc and TRACE Engineering.*

PUBLIC CITIZEN • 215 Pennsylvania Avenue SE, Washington, DC 20003 • Tel: 202 546 4996 • *Founded in 1971 by Ralph Nader, it publishes the "National Directory of US Energy Periodicals" (includes more than 700 publications on all kinds of energy) and the "National Directory of Safe Energy Organizations" (more than 1000 citizen and other non-profit groups actively promoting energy efficiency and renewable technologies, or opposing nuclear energy).*

PUMICE-CRETE BUILDING SYSTEMS • PO Box 539, El Prado, NM 87529 • *Appropriate building technologies including: passive solar designs, solar electric systems.*

REAL GOODS • 555 Leslie Street, Ukiah, CA 95482 • Tel: 800 762 7325 • *Real Goods is your complete resource for ENERGY EFFICIENT LIVING. Compact fluorescent lighting; solar, wind, and hydro power, rechargeable batteries and chargers; water conservation products; home safety products; natural pest control; recycled products; solar toys; maps, books and gifts. Free catalog. See p. 96.*

RENEWABLE ENERGY DEVELOPMENT INSTITUTE (REDI) • 733 South Main Street # 234, Willits, CA 95490 • Tel: 707 459 1256 Fax: 707 459 0366 • *REDI Net renewable energy data resource.*

REVCO SOLAR ENGINEERING INC • 26631 Cabot Road, no B, Laguna Hills, CA 92653 • Tel: 714 367 0740

ROBBINS ENGINEERING INC • 1641 McCullock Boulevard 25-294, Lake Havasu City, AZ 86403 • Tel: 602 855 3670 • *Sun-tracking equipment for utility-size solar arrays.*

ROCKY MOUNTAIN INSTITUTE • 1739 Snowmass Creek Road, Snowmass, CO 81654-9199 • Tel: 303 927 3851 Fax: 303 927 3240 • *A leader in energy resource-efficiency research and policy. Publications include "The Resource-Efficient Housing Guide" and a newsletter.*

SEMCO • 2021 Zearing Avenue NW, Albuquerque, NM 87104 • Tel: 800 245 0311

SIEMENS SOLAR INDUSTRIES • 4650 Adehr Lane, Camarillo, CA 93011 • Tel: 805 482 6800 • *Call for your local dealer.*

SIERRA SOLAR SYSTEMS • 109 Argall Way, Nevada City, CA 95959 • Tel: 800 517 6527 Fax: 916 265 8441 • *Since 1980, specialists in residential solar electric systems, solar pumping and energy conservation. Complete power systems. Photovoltaic power for teleworking. Energy-efficient appliances.*

SMALL POWER SYSTEMS • 74550 Dobie Lane, Covelo, CA 95428 • Tel: 800 972 7179 • *Solar Trackers. Solar absorption refrigeration.*

SOBEL SOLAR • 1911 Euclid Street, Santa Monica, CA 90404 • Tel: 310 395 2200

THE SOLAR CENTER • 1115 Indiana Street, San Francisco, CA 94107

SOLAR COMPONENTS CORPORATION • 121 Valley Street, Manchester, NH 03103-6211 • Tel: 603 668 8186 • *"Energy Saver's Catalog" of components and systems for solar heating.*

SOLAR COOKERS INTERNATIONAL • 1724 11th Street, Sacramento, CA 95814 • Tel: 916 444 6616 • *Solar cookers.*

SOLAR DEPOT INC • 61 Paul Drive, San Rafael, CA 94903 • Tel: 415 499 1333 Fax: 415 499 0316 • *Photovoltaic systems and components.*

SOLAR DESIGN ASSOCIATES • PO Box 242, Harvard, MA 01451-0242 • Tel: 508 456 6855

SOLAR ELECTRIC SPECIALITIES • PO Box 537, Willits, CA 95490 • Tel: 707 459 9496/800 344 2003 Fax: 707 459 5132 • *Distribute photovoltaic power systems.*

SOLAR ENERGY INDUSTRY ASSOCIATION • 1730 North Lynn Street, Suite 610, Arlington, VA 22209-2009 • Tel: 703 524 6100

SOLAR ENERGY INTERNATIONAL • PO Box 715, Carbondale, CO 81623 • Tel: 303 963 8855 Fax: 303 963 8866 • *Workshops on solar design, straw-bale, adobe, and rammed earth construction.*

SOLAR ENERGY SOCIETY OF CANADA • 72 Robertson Road, Nepean, Canada, K2H 9R6 • Tel: 613 523 0974

SOLAREX CORPORATION • 630 Solarex Court, Frederick, MD 21701 • Tel: 301 698 4200 Fax: 301 698 4201

SOLAR HOME DESIGN HOMESTEAD ENTERPRISE • 30151 Navarro Ridge Road, Albion, CA 95410

SOLAR QUEST/BECKER ELECTRIC • 11743 Maltman Drive, Grass Valley, CA 95945 • Tel: 800 959 6354 • *New products include: See-thru thin photovoltaic skylights. Catalog $3.95*

SOLAR PATHFINDER • 25720 465th Avenue, Hartford, SD 57033 • Tel: 605 528 6473 • *Instrument used to quickly and accurately site solar homes, photovoltaic panels and solar collectors.*

SOLAR RESEARCH • 525 N 5th Street, PO Box 869, Brighton, MI 48116 • Tel: 313 227 1151 Fax: 313 227 3700 • *Components for solar energy systems.*

SOLAR SPECTRUM • W4622 Kyes Road, Tomahawk, WI 54487 • Tel: 715 453 2803 • *Specializes in sales and installation of photovoltaic, wind, and hydro-electric systems; solar hot air and hot water systems.*

SOLAR SURVIVAL • Box 250, Cherry Hill Road, Harrisville, NH 03450 • Tel: 603 827 3811 • *Designs and information for total solar living.*

SOLAR TECHNOLOGY INSTITUTE • PO Box 1115, Carbondale, CO 81623-1115 • Tel: 303 963 0715

SOLAR WORKS • 64 Main Street, Montpelier, VT 05602 • Tel: 802 223 7804 Fax: 802 223 8980

SOLEC INTERNATIONAL INC • 12533 Chadron Avenue, Hawthorne, CA 90250 • Tel: 310 970 0065 • *Manufacturer of solar electric power equipment.*

SOLO POWER • 1011A Sawmill Road, NW Albuquerque, NM 87125 • Tel: 800 279 7656 Fax: 505 242 8340

SPECIALTY CONCEPTS INC • 8954 Mason Avenue, Chatsworth, CA 91311 • Tel: 818 998 5253 Fax: 818 998 5253 • *Control systems for photovoltaic installations.*

SUNELCO • PO Box 1499, Hamilton, MT 59840 • Tel: 800 338 6844/406 363 6924 Fax: 406 363 6046 • *Solar electric systems – complete power systems for your home. Whether you are far from the utility grid or just not interested in "hooking-up" - Sunelco can be of help. Our 120 page Planning Guide and Catalog answers your questions. $4.95.*

SUNLIGHT ENERGY CORPORATION • 4411 Echo Lane, Glendale, AZ 85302 • Tel: 800 338 1781 Fax: 602 939 8706

SUNNYSIDE SOLAR INC • RD4 Box 808, Green River Road, Brattleboro VT 05301 • Tel: 802 257 1482 Fax: 802 254 4670 • *Supplies small, medium, and large sized photovoltaic systems for both remote and non-remote locations.*

SUNTRAK • 2350 E 91st Street, Indianapolis, IN 46240 • Tel: 317 846 2150 • *Determine the sun's path across the sky for any day and place in the world.*

SUN UTILITY NETWORK • 626 Wilshire Boulevard, Suite 711, Los Angeles, CA 90017 • Tel: 800 822 7652/213 614 8667

SUNWATT • RFD Box 751, Addison, ME 04606 • Tel: 207 497 2204 • *Solar electric products including hybrid modules for both electricity and hot water and solar battery rechargers.*

TRACE ENGINEERING • 5916-195th Northeast, Arlington, WA 98223 • Tel: 360 435 8826 Fax: 360 435 2229 • *We provide 120/240 volt electricity anywhere. Prime power or backup power for most electrical appliances.*

UNION OF CONCERNED SCIENTISTS • 26 Church Street, Cambridge, MA 02238 • Tel: 617 547 5552

UNITED SOLAR SYSTEMS CORPORATION • 5278 Eastgate Mall, San Diego, CA 92121 • Tel: 619 625 2080 • *Uni-Solar®: the leader in thin-film photovoltaic technology.*

US BATTERY MANUFACTURING COMPANY • 1675 Sampson Avenue, Corona, CA 91719 • Tel: 909 371 8090 Fax: 909 371 4671 • *Batteries for photovoltaic systems.*

UTILITY FREE™ INC • 402 Park Avenue, Suite C, Basalt, CO 81621 • Tel : 970 927 1331 Fax: 970 927 1325/800 766 5550 • *"UtilityFree" Newsletter.*

WILLIAM LAMB CORP • 10615 Chandler Boulevard, North Hollywood, CA 91601 • Tel: 818 980 6248 • *Distributor of solar power systems.*

WORLD POWER TECHNOLOGIES • 19 Lake Avenue North, Duluth MN 55802 • Tel: 218 722 1492 Fax 218 722 0791 • *Our literature explains wind and wind-solar electric systems you can install yourself. Send for it today! See main entry on page 225.*

ZOMEWORKS CORPORATION • PO Box 25805, 1011A Sawmill Road, NW, Albuquerque, NM 87125 • Tel: 800 279 6342 Fax: 505 243 5187 • *TRACK RACK Passive Solar Tracker for Photovoltaic Modules.*

Wind power ~ *page 53*

ALTERNATIVE ENERGY ENGINEERING • Box 339, Redway, CA 95560 • Tel: 707 923 2277 • *Catalog sales of wind energy products.*
ALTERNATIVE SOLAR PRODUCTS • 27420 Jefferson, Suite 104B, Temecula, CA 92590 • Fax: 909 308 2388 • *Solar and wind power.*

AMERICAN WIND ENERGY ASSOCIATION • 122 C Street, NW, Fourth Floor, Washington DC 20001 • Tel: 202 383 2500 Fax: 202 383 2505

BATTELLE • Pacific Northwest Labs, Battelle Boulevard, PO Box 999, Richland, WA 99352 • Tel: 509 375 2981 Fax: 509 375 2592

BERGEY WINDPOWER INC • 2001 Priestley Avenue, Norman, OK 73069 • Tel: 405 364 4212 Fax: 405 304 2078 • *Firm specializing in smallscale (0.85 to 10kW) wind turbines since 1977.*

CANADIAN WIND ENERGY ASSOCIATION (CanWEA) • 2415 Holly Lane, Suite 250, Ottawa, Ontario, Canada, K1V 7P2 • Tel: 613 736 9077

CELESTIAL WIND CARILLONS • Route 1, Box 494, Eureka Springs, AZ 72632 • Tel: 800 822 1562

ECOLOGY SYSTEMS • 3863 Short Street, Dubuque, IA 52002 • Tel: 319 556 4765 • *Wind generators.*

ENDLESS ENERGY CORPORATION • RR 2, Box 2370, New Gloucester, MI 04260 • Tel: 207 926 4698 • *Wind farms.*

EVERFAIR ENTERPRISES • 2520 Northwest 16th Lane, No 5, Pompano, FL 33064 • Tel: 305 968 7358

FLEETFOOT FUELS • Renewable Energy Department, 323 Royston, Eaton Rapids, MI 48827 • *Alcohol, solar, wind, methane, hydropower, and others. Latest information, many contacts and plans available. Send $10.00.*

KANSAS WIND POWER • (dept NHC) 13569 214th Road, Holton, KS 66436 • Tel: 913 364 4407 • *WIND/SOLAR ELECTRIC SYSTEMS. Make your own electricity. Be more self-reliant. Save energy. We have many items including: Propane refrigerators, lights, heaters. Solar charge controllers. Mounts, trackers. Meters, battery chargers, fuses, efficient Sun Frost refrigerators, DC & AC lights, inverters, circuit breakers, pumps, low cost DC motors, hydraulic ram pumps, fans, evaporative coolers, grain mills, bed warmers, wood fired water heating, tankless instant water heaters, efficient clothes washer, composting toilets, low flush toilets, solar fence chargers, handy pocket tools, solar cookers, solar water stills, books, shortwave radios, foods. General catalog: $4.00. We also have Windmill water pumper/Hand pump catalog for $5.00. DC powered garden tractors information packet for $6.00. Foreign shipping: add $5.00 each catalog/packet. Discount prices. Our 20th year!*

LAKE MICHIGAN WIND & SUN • 3971 East Bluebird Road, Forestville, WI 54213 • Tel: 414 837 2267 Fax: 414 837 7523

NORTHERN POWER SYSTEMS • 1 North Wind Road, Moretown, VT 05660 • Tel: 802 658 0075 Fax: 802 496 2953

OFF-LINE • PO Box 231, North Fork, CA 93643 • Tel: 209 877 7080 • *All major brands for residential power, water systems, phones, wind power, photovoltaic and hydro. Design, installation and mail order.*

REAL GOODS • **555 Leslie Street, Ukiah, CA 95482 • Tel: 800 762 7325** • *Real Goods is your complete resource for ENERGY EFFICIENT LIVING. Compact fluorescent lighting; solar, wind, and hydro power, rechargeable batteries and chargers; water conservation products; home safety products; natural pest control; recycled products; solar toys; maps, books and gifts. Free catalog. See p. 96.*

SOLAR SPECTRUM • W4622 Kyes Road, Tomahawk, WI 54487 • Tel: 715 453 2803 • *Specializes in sales and installation of photovoltaic, wind and hydro-electric systems.*

SOLTEK SOLAR ENERGY LTD • 2-745 Vanalam Avenue, Victoria, BC, Canada, V8Z 3B6 • Tel: 604 727 7720

SOUTHWEST WINDPOWER • 1855 West Kaibab Lane, Flagstaff, AZ 86001 • Tel: 520 779 9643

TRILLIUM WINDMILLS INC • Campbell Road, RR # 3, Orillia, Ontario, Canada, L3V 6H3 • Tel: 705 326 6513 Fax: 705 326 2778 • *Rutland windchargers – 18W, 72W and 250W @ 22mph battery charging wind turbines ideal for remote homes, RVs, boats, telecoms.*

WIND BARON CORPORATION • PO Box 3777, Flagstaff, AZ 86003 • Tel: 520 526 6400 Fax: 520 526 5498

WINDSTREAM POWER SYSTEMS INC • 1 Mill Street, Burlington, VT 05402 • Tel: 802 658 0075 Fax: 802 658 1098

WIND TURBINE INDUSTRIES • 16801 Industrial Circle, SE, Prior Lake, MN 55372 • Tel: 612 447 6064 Fax: 612 447 6050

WINDBUGGER • 48 SW Fourth Street, Homestead, FL 33030 • Tel: 305 247 2868 • *Wind generators.*

WORLD POWER TECHNOLOGIES • 19 Lake Avenue North, Duluth MN 55802 • Tel: 218 722 1492 Fax 218 722 0791 • *Whisper wind generators from World Power embody over 20 years experience manufacturing small, quiet and ultra-reliable wind generators for home and farm use. We have the widest select of models for total independence or for interconnection with the grid or your engine generator. Our literature explains wind and wind-solar electric systems you can install yourself. Send for it today!*

Water generators ~ *page 54*

FLEETFOOT FUELS • Renewable Energy Department, 323 Royston, Eaton Rapids, MI 48827 • Tel: 517 663 3382 • *Alcohol, solar, wind, methane, hydropower and others. Latest information, many contacts and plans available. Send $10.00.*

HARRIS HYDROELECTRIC • 632 Swanton Road, Davenport, CA 95017 • Tel: 408 425 7652 • *Hydro-power for home use.*

JACK RABBIT MARINE INC • 425 Fairfield Avenue, Stamford, CT • Tel: 203 961 8133

JADE MOUNTAIN • PO Box 4616, Boulder, CO 80306 • Tel: 303 449 6601 Fax: 303 449 8266

LIL OTTO HYDROWORKS! • PO Box 203, Hornbrook, CA 96044 • Tel: 916 475 3401

OFF-LINE • PO Box 231, North Fork, CA 93643 • Tel: 209 877 7080 • *All major brands for residential power, water systems, phones, wind power, photovoltaic and hydro. Design, installation and mail order.*

REDWOOD ALLIANCE • PO Box 293, Arcata, CA 95521 • Tel: 707 822 7884 Fax: 707 822 8640

SOLAR SPECTRUM • W 4622 Kyes Road, Tomahawk, WI 54487 • Tel: 715 453 2803 • *Sales and installation of hydro-electric systems.*

SUNSTREAM RENEWABLE POWER SYSTEMS • Route 2 Box 1250, Burnsville, NC 28714 • Tel: 704 675 5753

WATER POWER MACHINERY COMPANY • PO Box 9723, Midland 08, TX 79708 • Tel: 915 697 6955 • *Complete systems or individual components for all size and head sites.*

NATIONAL TECHNICAL INFORMATION SERVICE • US Dept of Commerce, 5285 Port Royal Road Springfield, VA 22161 • Tel: 703 487 4600

RUTAN RESEARCH • PO Box 50, Liberty Center, IA 50145 • Tel: 515 288 7862

SNOW-BELT ENERGY CENTER • 286 Wilson Street, Highway-B, Amherst, WI 54406 • Tel: 715 824 3982 • *Wood, pellet and gas burning products; also chimneys, hot tubs, solar energy products.*

SOUTHEAST REGIONAL BIOMASS ENERGY PROGRAM • c/o Tennessee Valley Authority, CEB 5C, Muscle Shoals, AL 35660 • Tel: 205 386 3086

US DEPARTMENT OF ENERGY • Biofuels Systems Division EE-331, 1000 Independence Avenue, SW, Washington DC 20585 • Tel: 202 586 8072

WATER & ENERGY MANAGEMENT • 79 Hillmont Place, Danville, CA 94526 • Tel: 510 820 6603 • *Consulting engineers specializing in co-generation, bio-mass, feasibility studies.*

WESTERN REGIONAL BIOMASS ENERGY PROGRAM • c/o Western Regional Power Area Administration, A7100, PO Box 3402, Golden, CO 80401 • Tel: 303 275 1706

Biomass ~ *page 55*

BIOFUELS FEEDSTOCK DEVELOPMENT PROGRAM • Oak Ridge National Laboratory, PO Box 2008, Oak Ridge, TN 37831-6352 • Tel: 615 576 5132

BIOFUELS AMERICA! • 26 Lorin Dee Drive, Westerlo, NY 12193 • Tel: 518 797 3377 • *Promotes renewable energy and reduced dependence on oil through community development, waste reduction, environmentally sustainable economics.*

BIOFUELS INFORMATION CENTER • National Renewable Energy Laboratory, 1617 Cole Boulevard, Golden, CO 80401 • Tel: 303 275 3000

CHIPTEC WOOD ENERGY SYSTEMS • 48 Helen Avenue, South Burlington, VT 05403 • Tel: 802 658 0956 Fax: 802 660 8904 • *Biomass gasifiers for space and process heat.*

DAHL WOOD STOVES • Highway 11 West, Baudette, MN 56623 • Tel: 218 634 1100

ECOLOGY ACTION • 5798 Ridgewood Road, Willits, CA 95490-9730 • Tel: 707 459 0150 Fax: 707 459 5409 • *For over two decades Ecology Action has been researching sustainable soil fertility and the miniaturization of agriculture.*

ELECTRIC POWER RESEARCH INSTITUTE • Storage and Renewables Division, 3412 Hillview Avenue, Palo Alto, CA 94304 • Tel: 415 855 2000

GREAT LAKES REGIONAL BIOMASS ENERGY PROGRAM • c/o Council of Great Lakes Governors, 35 East Wacker Drive, Suite 1850, Chicago, IL 60601 • Tel: 312 407 0177

HEATMOR • Highway 11 East, Box 787, Warroad, MN 56763 • Tel: 218 386 2769

LEINEN CORN HOME HEATERS • 1143 Highway J, Tigerton, WI 54486 • Tel: 715 535 2653

Co-generation ~ *page 56*

BUDERUS HYDRONIC SYSTEMS INC • 50B Northwestern Drive, Salem, NH 03079 • Tel: 603 898 0505 Fax: 603 898 1055

COMMUNITY ENERGY SERVICES CORPORATION • 1013 Pardee Street, Berkeley, CA 94710 • Tel: 510 644 8546 • *Helps businesses to identify energy resources and conservation opportunities.*

FUTURE RESOURCES INC • 2000 Center Street, Suite 418, Berkeley, CA 94704 • Tel: 510 644 2700 • *Engineering and environmental permit support.*

NEXT STEP ENERGY SYSTEMS • 30497 Chippewa Trail, New Auburn, WI 54757 • Tel: 715 967 2730

PARSONS BRINCKERHOFF ENERGY GROUP SYSTEMS • 303 2nd Street, Suite 805 N, San Francisco, CA 94107 • Tel: 415 281 8700 • *Co-generation system design.*

STANDFORD ENERGY SYSTEMS • 1901 Old Middlefield Way, # 18, Mountain View, CA 94043 • Tel: 415 967 2007 • *Designs, installs, and services co-generation and other alternative energy systems.*

TECOGEN INC • 4968-17th Street, San Francisco, CA 94117 • Tel: 415 564 6781 • *Manufactures, sells, and services small packaged co-generation systems.*

WATER & ENERGY MANAGEMENT • 79 Hillmont Place, Danville, CA 94526 • Tel: 510 820 6603 • *Consulting engineers specializing in co-generation, bio-mass, and feasibility studies.*

Back-up heating ~ *page 57*

AGA CORPORATION • PO Box 246, Amasa, MI 49903 • Tel: 906 822 7311

AQUA-THERM • Route 1, Box 1, Brooten, MN 56316 • Tel: 800 325 2760 • *Manufacturers of outside wood burning furnaces for home heating and water heating.*

AUSTROFLAMM • 2210 Alexander Street, Salt Lake City, UT 84119 • Tel: 801 972 9400 • *Makers of WEGA Austrian pellet stoves.*

BIOFIRE INC • 3220 Melbourne, Salt Lake City, UT 84106 • Tel: 801 486 0266 Fax: 801 486 8100 • *For centuries Europeans enjoyed wonderful radiant heat produced by Tilestoves.*

CHIPTEC WOOD ENERGY SYSTEMS • 48 Helen Avenue, South Burlington, VT 05403 • Tel: 802 658 0956 Fax: 802 660 8904

CRD PRECISION FABRICATORS INC • Route 5, Box 190, Highway 178, Chippewa Falls, WI 54729 • Tel: 715 723 9667 Fax: 715 726 1080 • *Manufacturers of Energy King Legacy wood stoves and fireplaces.*

DAHL WOOD STOVES • Highway 11 West, Baudette, MN 56623 • Tel: 218 634 1100

DIETMEYER, WARD & STROUD INC (DWS) • PO Box 323, Vashon Island, WA 98070 • Tel: 800 325 3629 Fax: 206 463 6335 • *Manufacture many models of masonry heaters.*

ENVIROTECH RADIANT FIREPLACES • Division of Dietmeyer, Ward and Stroud Inc (see above) • Tel: 800 325 3629 Fax: 206 463 6335 • *Modularized Masonry Heater Kits. Heat with clean, renewable energy. The look of a traditional fireplace that is good for the environment.*

EUROPEAN MASONRY • 706 California Boulevard, Napa, CA 94559 • Tel: 707 259 0208 • *Stockists of the Tulikivi soapstone heater.*

FOUNTAINHEAD NATURAL HOMES • 11965 Monclova Road, Swanton, OH 43558 • Tel: 419 825 3031 • *Masonry heaters. Free brochure.*

GLOWCORE® • Corporate Headquarters, PO Box 360591, Cleveland, OH 44136-0010 and 97 Kent Avenue, Kitchener, Ontario, Canada, N2G 4J1 • *Manufacturers of the UniCore™ high-efficiency boiler which heats both your home and your water.*

ISLAND HOT TUB CO • 3545 E Quade Road, Clinton, WA 98236 • Tel: 360 579 8578 • *'Chofu water heater' – a high-efficiency wood-fired water heater that circulates water by thermosyphon, no pump needed. Stainless steel water jacket with interior baffle system. Used for heating hot tubs, thermal mass, or domestic hot water. Has a 32,000 BTU output. Can be used with a propane burner. Stainless steel hot tub – Japanese-style flat bottom, 5 ft diam x 2 ft deep. Allows outstretched legs. Stainless steel for easy cleaning and durability, insulated with cedar outside. Made for use with the Chofu heater. Chofu water heater $540, Stainless steel hot tub $995.*

ISLAND OFURO INC (USA East) • R2 Box 210B, Centerpoint, IN 47840 • Tel: 812 835 2697 • *Distributors of Chofu wood-fired hot bath heater.*

KACHELOFEN GROUP INC • PO Box 157, Geyserville, CA 95441-0157 • Tel: 503 482 5356

KACHELOFEN INSTITUTE • PO Box 3339, Ashland, OR 97520 • Tel: 503 535 2955

MASONRY FIREPLACE AND CHIMNEY ASSOCIATION • 1600 Spring Hill Road, Suite 305, Vienna, VA 22182 • Tel: 703 749 6229 Fax: 703 749 6227

MASONRY HEATER ASSOCIATION OF NORTH AMERICA • 11490 Commerce Park Drive, Suite 300, Reston, Virginia 22091 • Tel: 703 620 3171

NATIONAL CENTER FOR APPROPRIATE TECHNOLOGY • National Appropriate Technology Assistance Service, PO Box 2525, Butte, MT 59702-2525 • Tel: 800 428 2525 / 406 494 5472 Fax: 406 494 2905 • *Toll-free service answers technical questions on wood stoves and renewable energy economics.*

NATIONAL STEELCRAFTERS OF OREGON INC • PO Box 24910, Eugene, OR 97402 • Tel: 503 683 3210 • *Manufacturers of Breckwell pellet stoves.*

NEW ENGLAND HEARTH & STONE • 127 North Street, Goshen, CT 06756 • Tel: 203 491 3091 • *Rod Zander, Stove Mason specializes in masonry heaters of soapstone, brick and tile; soapstone countertops, sinks, tile. Meticulous craftsmanship.*

SNORKEL STOVE CO • 102 Eliot Avenue W, Seattle, WA 98119 • Tel: 206 340 0981

SNOW-BELT ENERGY CENTER • 286 Wilson Street, Highway-B, Amherst, WI 54406 • Tel: 715 824 3982 • *Specializes in wood, pellet, and gas burning products; also chimneys, hot tubs, solar energy products.*

SOLAR RATING AND CERTIFICATION CORPORATION • Suite 800, 1001 Connecticut Avenue NW, Washington DC 20036

TULIKIVI US INC • 255 Ridge McIntyre Road, Charlottesville, VA 22902 • Tel: 804 977 5500 Fax: 804 977 5164 • *Soapstone stoves to traditional Finnish designs - quality with warmth.*

VERMONT CASTINGS® • Prince Street, Randolph, VT 05060 • Tel: 802 728 3181/800 227 8683 • *Clean-burning, wood, pellet and gas stoves and fireplaces in several colors. Call for a free Fireside Advisor magazine. A video tape is $9.95.*

WOODSTOCK SOAPSTONE CO • 66 Airpark Road, Dept 356, West Lebanon, NH 03784 • Tel: 800 866 4344

Solar water heating ~ *page 60*

See also Listings for Sunspaces and solar windows page 228

AMERICAN SOCIETY OF HEATING, REFRIGERATION AND AIR-CONDITIONING ENGINEERS INC (ASHRAE) • 1791 Tullie Circle NE Atlanta, GA 30325-2305 • Tel: 404 636 8400

BIO-ENERGY SYSTEMS INC • PO Box 191, Ellenville, New York 12428-0191 • Tel: 914 647 6700 Fax: 914 647 6828

CONTROLLED ENERGY CORP • Fiddlers Green, Waitfield, VT 05673 • Tel: 802 496 4436 • *Makers of Aqua Star tankless gas water heaters.*

HELIOCOL™ • United Marketing Associates, Inc, 13620 49th Street North, Clearwater, FL 34622 • Tel: 813 572 6655 Fax: 813 572 7922 • *Heliocol solar pool heating systems.*

HYDRONIC ENERGY INC • 3307 104th Street, PO Box 3779, Des Moines, IA 50322 • Tel: 515 276 4935

NEXT STEP ENERGY SYSTEMS AND BUILDERS • 30497 Chippewa Trail, New Auburn, WI 54757-8128 • Tel: 715 967 2730

RADCO PRODUCTS INC • 2877 Industrial Parkway, Santa Maria, CA 93455 • Tel: 805 928 1881 Fax: 805 928 5587 • *High performance solar collectors.*

ROCKY MOUNTAIN INSTITUTE • 1739 Snowmass Creek Road, Snowmass, CO 81654-9199 • Tel: 303 927 3851 Fax: 303 927 3240 • *A leader in energy resource-efficiency research and policy. Publications include "The Resource-Efficient Housing Guide" and a newsletter.*

SCHOLFIELD SOLAR • 2450 Channel Drive, Suite A, Ventura, CA 93993 • Tel: 805 653 0797/800 232 8009 • *Solar pool and domestic water heating. Radiant Floor heating.*

SENNERGETICS • 8751 Shirley Avenue, Northridge, CA 91324 • Tel: 818 885 0323 • *Solar water heating.*

SOLAR COMPONENTS CORPORATION • 121 Valley Street, Manchester, NH 03103-6211 • *Produce "The Energy Saver's Catalog". Stockists of E-Z HEAT by Hi-Temp solar heating system for above-ground pools.*

SOLAR DEPOT • 61 Paul Drive, San Rafael, CA 94903 • Tel: 415 499 1333 • *Wholesale supplier of Solectrogen Solar Electric Generators and Solar Water Heaters.*

SOLAR INDUSTRIES • 1985 Rutgers University Boulevard, Lakewood, NJ 08701 • Tel: 908 905 0440 Fax: 908 905 9899 • *Aquatherm solar pool heaters. The simple, economical, natural way to let the sun heat your pool. Works in all climates around the world.*

SOLAR QUEST/BECKER ELECTRIC • 11743 Maltman Drive, Grass Valley, CA 95945 • Tel: 800 959 6354 • *Freeze-proof SOL-Perpetua™ self-pumping solar hot water system - uses no electricity. Catalog: $3.95.*

SOLAR SPECTRUM • W4622 Kyes Road, Tomahawk, WI 54487 • Tel: 715 453 2803 • *Solar hot air and hot water systems.*

SUNQUEST • 1555 Rankin Avenue, Newton, NC, 28658 • Tel: 704 465 6805 Fax: 704 465 7370 • *Solar water heating.*

THERMO DYNAMICS LTD • 81 Thornhill Drive, Dartmouth, Nova Scotia, Canada, B3B 1R9 • Tel: 902 468 1001 Fax: 902 468 1002 • *Makers of solar hot water heating systems.*

Sunspaces and solar windows ~ page 61

See also listings for Windows pages 218-9

CREATIVE STRUCTURES • 1765 Walnut Lane, Quakertown, PA 18951 • Tel: 215 538 2426 Fax: 215 538 7308 • *Manufacturers of Solid Wood Sunrooms.*

ENERTIA BUILDING SYSTEMS • Route 1, Wake Forest, NC 27587 • Tel: 919 556 7876 Fax: 919 556 7414

FOUR SEASONS SUNROOMS • 5005 Veterans Memorial Highway, Holbrook, NY 11741 • Tel: 800 368 7732

LINDAL CEDAR SUNROOMS • PO Box 24426, Seattle, WA 98124 • Tel: 206 725 7111

SOLAR SURVIVAL • Box 250, Cherry Hill Road, Harrisville, NH 03450 • Tel: 603 827 3811 • *Designs and information for Total Solar Living.*

SOLAR WORKS • 64 Main Street, Montpelier, VT 05602 • Tel: 802 223 7804

SUNDANCE SUPPLY • 1678 Shattuck Avenue, Suite 173, Berkeley, CA 94709 • Tel: 510 845 0525 Fax: 510 845 9450 • *Components for site-built greenhouses, sunrooms, skylights, and pool enclosures.*

UNDER GLASS MANUFACTURING CORPORATION • PO Box 323, Wappingers Falls, NY 12590 • Tel: 914 298 0645

VEGETABLE FACTORY INC • PO Box 1353, Stamford, CT 06904 • Tel: 203 324 0010

Thermal walls and floors ~ page 62

BRIGHTWATER ENTERPRISES • 1734 Brevard Road, Suite 111, Hendersonville, NC 28739 • Tel: 704 891 5570

COMMAND AIRE • Geothermal Heating Systems, Box 2015, Lower Borough, PA 15068 • Tel: 412 335 3303

EARTH SYSTEMS • 258 McBrine Drive, Kitchener, Ontario, Canada, N2R 1H8 • Tel: 800 GO EARTH

EARTHSTAR ENERGY SYSTEMS • RT 220 at US Route 1, Waldoboro, ME 04572 • Tel: 207 832 6861 Fax : 207 832 7314 • *Design, supply, and manufacture of radiant heating technologies, whole house ventilation, thermal solar systems, and graywater heat recovery since 1980.*

NEXT STEP ENERGY SYSTEMS AND BUILDERS • 30497 Chippewa Trail, New Auburn, WI 54757-8128 • Tel: 715 967 2730 • *Radiant underfloor heating systems.*

PASSIVE SOLAR INDUSTRIES COUNCIL • 1511 K Street, NW, Suite 600, Washington DC 20005

RADIANT ENERGY SYSTEMS • 1818 Harmon Street, Berkeley, CA 94703 • Tel: 510 654 1586 • *Provides contracting, design, and installation of in-floor radiant heating systems.*

ROCKY MOUNTAIN RESEARCH CENTER • PO Box 4694, Missoula MT 59806 • *Output includes: videos, books, information sheets and consultation services on all aspects of Passive Annual Heat Storage.*

SCHOLFIELD SOLAR • 2450 Channel Drive, Suite A, Ventura, CA 93993 • Tel: 805 653 0797/800 232 8009 • *Radiant Floor heating.*

THERMAL ENERGY STORAGE SYSTEMS • RR 1, Box 3, Beanville Road, Randolph, VT 05060

WARM FLOORS • 211 Gateway Road West, Suite 208, Napa, CA 94558 • Tel: 707 257 0880 Fax: 707 257 0119

Heat exchangers ~ page 63

AIRXCHANGE INC • 401 VFW Drive, Rockland MA 02370 • Tel: 617 871 4816

AIR CHANGER HRVs • Preston Brock Manufacturing Company, Box 3367, 1297 Industrial Road, Cambridge, Ontario, Canada, N3H 4T8

ALTECH ENERGY • 7009 Raywood Road, Madison, WI 53713 • Tel: 608 221 4499 Fax: 608 221 2824 • *Makers of Newaire™ air-to-air heat exchange ventilators.*

AMERICAN ALDES VENTILATION CORP • 4537 Northgate Court, Sarasota, FL 34234-2124 • Tel: 813 351 3441

CONSERVATION ENERGY SYSTEMS INC • 2525 Wentz Avenue, Saskatoon, Saskatchewan, Canada, S7K 2K9 • Tel: 306 242 3663 / 800 667 3717 Fax: 306 242 3484

CSRI, PURE AIR SYSTEMS INC • Box 418, Plainfield, IN 46168 • Tel: 317 839 9135

ENVIRONMENTAL AIR LTD • Box 10, Cocagne, NB, Canada, E0A 1K0 • Tel: 506 576 6672

HEAT-PIPE TECHNOLOGY INC • PO Box 999, Alachua, FL 32615 • Tel: 904 462 3464 Fax: 904 462 2041 • *Passive whole house dehumidification.*

MOUNTAIN ENERGY & RESOURCES INC • 15800 West Sixth Avenue, Golden, CO 80401 • Tel: 303 279 4971

SOLARATTIC INC • 15548 95th Circle NE, Elk River, MN 55330 • Tel: 612 441 3440 Fax: 612 441 7174 • *Attic-based heat exchangers which eliminate the need for roof mounted panels.*

SOLAR RESEARCH • Refrigeration Research Inc, 525 North Fifth Street, PO Box 869, Brighton, MI 48116 • Tel: 313 227 1151

THERMA-STOR PRODUCTS GROUP • DEC International Inc, PO Box 8050, Madison, WI 53708 • Tel: 800 533 7533 / 608 222 3484 Fax: 608 222 1447 • *Heat recovery ventilators, fans, home ventilating systems and supplies.*

VENMAR VENTILATION • 1715 Haggerty Street, Drummondville, Quebec, Canada, J2C 5P7 • Tel: 819 477 6226

Shading, cooling and venting ~ *page 64*

See also listings for Ventilation pages 244-5

ALTERNATIVE RESEARCH CENTER INC • PO Box 383, Vail, AZ 85641-0383 • Tel: 602 647 7220

AMERICAN FORESTS • PO Box 2000, Washington, DC 20013-2000 • Tel: 202 667 3300 • *Cool Communities program.*

APPROPRIATE TECHNOLOGY • Box 975, 7 Technology Drive, Brattleboro, VT 05302-0975 • Tel: 802 257 4500/4501 • *Quilted insulation fabric, window, air conditioner cover, vent covers.*

COOL TOWER SYSTEMS • 8611 N Black Canyon, no 216, Phoenix AZ 85021 • Tel: 602 995 2101

CUSTOM COOL TOWER & SOLAR DESIGN • 5085 S Melpomene Way, Tuscon, AZ 85747 • Tel: 602 885 7925

ENERGY CRAFTED HOMES • 441 Stuart Street, Boston, MA 01230 • Tel: 617 236 1500 • *Manual on energy-efficient home construction, ventilation, safe indoor air.*

ENVIRONMENTAL RESEARCH LABORATORY • 2601 E Airport Drive, Tucson, AZ 85706 • Tel: 520 741 1990

PLANETARY DESIGN CORPORATION • 2 Arizona Center, Suite 1555, Phoenix, AZ 85004 • Tel: 602 252 4396 Fax: 602 252 4355

ROCKY CREEK HYDRO • 2173 Rocky Creek Road, Colville, WA 99114 • *Ceiling fans.*

THERMA-STOR PRODUCTS GROUP • DEC International Inc, PO Box 8050, Madison, WI 53708 • Tel: 800 533 7533/608 222 3484 Fax: 608 222 1447 • *Fresh air ventilators, heat recovery ventilators, fans, home ventilating systems, and supplies.*

URBAN CONSORTIUM ENERGY TASK FORCE • Public Technology Inc, 1301 Pennsylvania Avenue, NW, Washington, DC 20004 • Tel: 202 626 2400

VENMAR VENTILATION • 1715 Haggerty, Drummondville, Quebec, Canada, J2C 5P7 • Tel: 819 477 6226 Fax: 819 474 3066

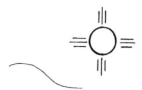
ZOMEWORKS • PO Box 25805, 1011A Sawmill Road Northwest, Albuquerque, NM 87125 • Tel: 505 242 5354 Fax: 505 243 5187 • *Seasonally adjustable sunshades, insulating louvres, diurnally automatic shade devices.*

Insulation ~ *page 65*

See also listings for Breathing Walls pages 217-18

AFM CORPORATION • 24000 West Highway 7, Box 246, Excelsior, MN 5331-0246 • Tel: 612 474 0809/800 255 0176 • *Perform Guard® environmentally sound insect resistant EPS insulation.*

AIR KRETE • 162 North Sierra Court, Gilbert, AZ 85234 • Tel: 602 892 0603 • *Air Krete non-toxic cementitious foam insulation.*

ALL-SEAL INSULATION • PO Box 13048 Fort Wayne, IN 46866 • Tel: 219 432 7591 • *Cellulose insulation*

ALL-WEATHER INSULATION CO INC • Springfield, KY 40069 • Tel: 606 336 3931 • *Cellulose insulation.*

AMERICAN CELLULOSE MANUFACTURING INC • Route 1, Box 162, Minonk, IL 61760 • Tel: 309 432 2507 • *Manufacturer of IN-CIDE insulation.*

AMERICAN ENVIRONMENTAL PRODUCTS • PO Box 38, Elkwood, VA 22718 • Tel: 800 488 5565/703 825 8000 • *Cellulose insulation.*
AMERICAN INSULATION CO • PO Box 91, Bloomer, WI 54724 • Tel: 715 568 3898 • *Cellulose insulation.*

CAN-CELL INDUSTRIES INC • 16355-130 Avenue, NW, Edmonton, Alberta, Canada, T5V 1K5 • Tel: 403 447 1255 • *Cellulose insulation.*

CELL-PAK INC • PO Box 1023, Decatur, AL 35602 • Tel: 205 350 3311 • *Cellulose insulation.*

CELLULOSE INDUSTRY STANDARDS REINFORCEMENT PROGRAM • 1315 Talbott Tower, Dayton, OH 45402 • Tel: 513 222 1024

THE CELLULOSE INSULATION MANUFACTURERS ASSOCIATION • 136 South Keowee Street, Dayton, OH 45402 • Tel: 513 222 2462

CELOTEX BUILDING PRODUCTS DIVISION • PO Box 31602, Tampa, FL 33631 • Tel: 813 873 1700 • *Tuff-R insulating sheathing.*

CENTRAL FIBER CORPORATION • 4814 Fiber Lane, Wellsville, KS 66092-0749 • Tel: 913 883 4600 • *Cellulose insulation.*

CERTAINTEED CORPORATION INSULATION GROUP • PO Box 860, Valley Forge, PA 19482 • Tel: 215 341 700 • *Fiberglass batts made with 5% pre-consumer and 20% post-consumer recycled glass.*

CHAMPION INSULATION • Lomira, WI R • Tel: 414 269 4311 • *Cellulose insulation.*

CLAYVILLE INSULATION • Burley, ID • Tel: 208 678 9791 • *Cellulose insulation.*

EARTH SOURCE INSULATION • PO Box 835, Lone Pine, CA 93545 • Tel: 619 876 4266/5242 • *Distributors/installers of Air Krete non-toxic foam insulation.*

ECOLOGY HOUSE • 12 Madison Avenue, Toronto, Ontario, Canada, M5R 2S1 • *Published a pamphlet: "Energy Conservation in the home".*

ECO-RIGHT PRODUCTS • 44 Crosby Street, New York, NY 10012 • Tel: 212 334 9659/800 238 5008 Fax: 212 226 8084 • *InsulCot cotton insulation for residential, commercial, and metal buildings.*

ENERGY KING • 14235 Southeast 98th Court, Clackamas, OR 97015 • Tel: 503 653 5000 • *Cellulose insulation.*

ENERGY ZONE MANUFACTURING INC • Buffalo, MN • Tel: 612 682 5755 • *Cellulose insulation.*

EXCEL INDUSTRIES LIMITED • 13 Rassau Industrial Estate, Ebbw Vale, Gwent, NP3 5SD, United Kingdom • Tel: (+44) 1495 350655 Fax: (+44) 1495 350146 • *Manufacturers of 'Warmcel' cellulose insulation. Leading British company that has been involved in tests and certification. Contact UK headquarters for US and Canadian distributors.*

GREENWOOD COTTON INSULATION PRODUCTS INC • PO Box 1017, Greenwood, SC 29648 • Tel: 800 546 1332 Fax: 800 942 4814 • *Greenwood cotton insulation is made from recycled textile fabrics. It is soft and completely non-toxic.*

HAMILTON MANUFACTURING • 118 Market Avenue, Twin Falls, ID 83304 • Tel: 208 733 9689/800 777 9689 • *Cellulose insulation.*

IN-CIDE TECHNOLOGIES INC • 50 North 41st Avenue, Phoenix, AZ 85009 • Tel: 602 233 0756 / 800 777 4569 • *In-Cide (R) PC cellulose insulation. IN-CIDE is the only EPA-recognized pest control insulation. This insulation is manufactured at a number of licensed distributors.*

INSUL SHUTTER • PO Box 888, 69 Island Street, Keene, NH 03431 • Tel: 603 352 2727 • *Insulating fabrics for windows.*

INTERNATIONAL CELLULOSE CORPORATION • 12315 Robin Boulevard, Houston, TX 77045 • Tel: 800 444 1252 Fax: 713 433 2029 • *Celbar is the "natural choice" for home insulation. Composed of natural fiber recycled from paper, Celbar provides a high R-value and minimizes sound and air infiltration.*

LOUISIANA-PACIFIC • Fenton, MO • Tel: 314 343 9103/800 299 0028 • *Nature Guard cellulose insulation.*

MANVILLE BUILDING INSULATION • PO Box 5108, Denver, CO 80217-5108 • Tel: 303 978 2785 • *Fiberglass insulation batts with 20% recycled glass content.*

MASSACHUSETTS AUDUBON SOCIETY • South Great Road, Lincoln, MA 01773 • Tel: 617 259 9500 • *Offers eight booklets that describe energy solutions clearly and simply, including insulation, financing tips, and more.*

MIDWEST FASWALL INC • 404 N Forrest Avenue, Ottumwa, IA 52501 • Tel: 515 682 1212 Fax: 515 683 1212 • *Faswall insulating wall forms for reinforced concrete structures.*

NORDIC BUILDERS • 162 N Sierra Court, Gilbert, AZ 85234 • Tel: 602 892 0603 • *Air Krete non-toxic cementitious foam insulation.*

OTTAWA FIBRE INC • Box 415, RR 4, Ottawa, Ontario, Canada, K1G 3N2 • Tel: 613 736 1215 • *Fiberglass insulation products utilizing recycled glass.*

PALMER INDUSTRIES INC • 10611 Old Annapolis Road, Frederick, MD 21701-3347 • Tel: 301 898 7848 Fax: 301 898 3312 • *Air Krete non-toxic cementitious foam insulation.*

PETIT INDUSTRIES INC • PO Box 1156, Saco, ME 04072-1156 • Tel: 207 283 1900 Fax: 207 283 1905

REFLECTIX INC • PO Box 108, Markleville, IN 46056 • Tel: 317 533 4332/800 879 3645 Fax: 317 533 2327 • *Remember Reflectix for all your reflective insulation needs!*

SCHULLER INTERNATIONAL • 717 17th Street, PO Box 5108, Denver, CO 80217 • Tel: 800 654 3103 Fax: 303 978 3661

SOUTHERN CELLULOSE • 6057 Boat Rock Boulevard, Atlanta, GA 30336 • Tel: 800 666 3590 • *IN-CIDE cellulose insulation.*

SPARFIL INTERNATIONAL INC • 376 Watline Avenue, Mississuaga, Ontario, Canada, L4Z 1X2 • Tel: 416 507 1163 • *Sparfil wall system, insulated cellular concrete blocks.*

THERMOGUARD INSULATION CO • 451 Charles Street, Billings, MT 59101 • Tel: 800 821 5310/406 252 1938 and Spokane, WA 99212 • Tel: 800 541 0579/509 535 4600 • *Isolite cellulose insulation and Fiber Mulch.*

VINEYARD COMFORTS • RFD 40, Vineyard Haven, MA 02568 • Tel: 508 693 1583 Fax: 508 693 2933 • *Insulated window coverings.*

WEST MATERIALS INC • 101 West Burnsville Parkway, Burnsville, MN 55337 • Tel: 612 890 3152 • *EnerBlock molded polystyrene inserts insulate the cores of concrete masonry units.*

WINDOW QUILT • Northern Cross Industries, 7 Technology Drive, Brattleboro, VT 05301 • Tel: 800 257 4501 Fax: 800 257 9246 • *Decorative insulating window shade that rolls out of the way when not in use. Reduces air infiltration, considerably enhances insulation even on double-paned windows, reduces condensation, reduces solar gain and noise level.*

Water management ~ *pages 72-3*

ALTERNATIVE ENERGY ENGINEERING INC • 445-B Conger Street, Garberville, CA 95440 • Tel: 707 923 2277 Fax: 707 923 3009 • *By harnessing the energy from a head of water, the High Lifter Pump drives a portion of this water uphill. Efficient and economical.*

CLAYTON EXPRESS • Fishergreen, Ripon, North Yorkshire, HG4 1NL, United Kingdom • Tel: (+44) 1765 690906 • *Water pumps. Contact UK address for US and Canadian distributors.*

CONTROLLED ENERGY SYSTEMS • Fiddler's Green, Waitsfield, VT 05603 • Tel: 802 496 4436 / 800 642 3111 Fax: 802 496 6924 • *'Aqua Bank' system diverts fresh water from waste system to toilet bank or to holding tank for landscape use.*

DEPARTMENT OF WATER RESOURCES • State of California, PO Box 942836, Sacramento, CA 94236 • Tel: 916 653 5791

DRIPWORKS - EVERLINER • 380 Maple Street, Willits, CA 95490 • Tel: 800 522 3747 • *Pond and water tank liners. Low-cost, custom, one-piece - any size - wooden, steel, or cement tank.*

IRRIGRO • LPO 360, 1555 Third Avenue, Niagara Falls, NY 14304 and PO Box 1133, St Catherine's, Ontario, Canada, L2R 7A3 • *Drip irrigation products including sample kits.*

PUMICE-CRETE BUILDING SYSTEMS • PO Box 539, El Prado, NM 87529 • *Appropriate building technologies including: water collection and conservation.*

ZELLERBACH, A MEAD CO • 1010 West 19th Street, National City, CA 92050 • *Makers of Waterwick Systems.*

Water saving ~ *page 74*

ACTECH INC • 8032 Cedar Row Boulevard, Westerville, OH 43081-5547 • Tel: 800 243 3599 • *Water and energy-saving products including shower heads, toilet kits, faucet aerators, and water meters. Free catalog.*

CONTROL FLUIDICS INC • 124 West Putnam Avenue, Greenwich, CT 06830 • Tel: 203 661 5599

ECO-STORE INC • 2421 Edgewater Drive, Orlando, FL 32804 • Tel: 407 426 9949 • *An environmental action company selling water savers, cleaners, pet supplies, gifts etc. Woman-owned.*

ENERGY ANSWERS • PO Box 24, Lake Bluff, IL 60044 • Tel: 800 776 6761 • *Water saving products.*

THE EPSTEN GROUP • 303 Ferguson Street, Atlanta, GA 30307 • Tel: 404 577 0370 • *Environmentally sound, healthful architectural design/consulting. Residential/Commercial. Healthful Homes. Energy/Water/Material conservation. Passive solar. Non-polluting/recycled building materials.*

ENVIRONMENTAL DESIGNWORKS • PO Box 26A88, Los Angeles, CA 90026 • Tel: 213 386 5812 FAX: 213 386 5828 • *Inventors of Zippy Fingerinse Fountain line of products.*

ENVIRONMENTALLY SOUND PRODUCTS • 8845 Orchard Tree Lane, Towson, MD 21286 • Tel: 800 886 5432 • *Household products for green and healthy living.*

ENVIRESOURCE INC • 110 Madison Avenue North, Bainbridge Island, WA 98110 • Tel: 206 842 9785 • *Water-saving devices.*

FOR YOUR HEALTH PRODUCTS • 6623 Hillandale Road, Chevy Chase, MD 20815 • Tel: 301 654 1127 Fax: 301 654 2125

INTERNATIONAL ENVIRONMENTAL SOLUTIONS INC • PO Box 8111, Clearwater, FL 34618 • Tel: 813 367 4660 • *Manufactures Automatic Faucet Control (AFC) which eliminates wasted water at kitchen and bathroom faucets and stops dripping without changing stems.*

MAGNETIZER GROUP INC • BOOS 1000, Point Pleasant Pike, Gardenville, PA 18926 • Tel: 215 766 8660 • *Magnetizer Patented Water Systems: stop hard, corrosive water naturally; no chemicals. Lifetime warranty. Easy installation. Dealers welcome.*

PROGRESSIVE PLANET DISTRIBUTING COMPANY • 96 Arapahoe Suite B, Boulder, CO 80302 • Tel: 303 444 3109 / 800 604 3109 Fax: 303 449 7540 • *Wide range of ecologically sound mail-order products for the whole house including water-saving shower heads and sink aerators.*

REAL GOODS • 555 Leslie Street, Ukiah, CA 95482 • Tel: 800 762 7325 • *Real Goods is your complete resource for ENERGY EFFICIENT LIVING. Compact fluorescent lighting; solar, wind, and hydro power, rechargeable batteries and chargers; water conservation products; home safety products; natural pest control; recycled products; solar toys; maps, books and gifts. Free catalog. See p. 96.*

RESOURCES CONSERVATION INC • PO Box 71, Greenwich, CT 06836 • Tel: 203 964 0600 Fax: 203 324 9352 • *Produces a range of water-saving devices including faucet aerators and toilet tank water savers.*

SUNSTAR ENTERPRISES • 127 North Las Posas, San Marcos, CA 92069 • Tel: 800 438 8677 • *Thermal Insulating Spa and Hot tub cover conserves heat and water and reduces the need for chemical cleaners.*

TELEDYNE ISOTOPES • 50 Van Buren Avenue, PO Box 1235, Westwood, NJ 06775-1235 Tel: 201 664 5586 • *Water Pik Super Saver and Original Shower Massage showerheads are Green-Seal certified.*

TRADEMARK SALES AND MARKETING • PO Box 4026, Appleton, WI 54915 • Tel: 800 622 1818 • *Water conservation products.*

WATER CONSERVATION SYSTEMS INC • Damonmill Square, Concord, MA 01742 • Tel: 508 369 3951 / 800 462 3341 • *Water conserving bath fixtures, appliances, and irrigation systems.*

Toilets ~ *page 75*

AMERICAN STANDARD • 1 Centennial Plaza, Piscataway, NJ 08855 • Tel: 800 223 0068 • *'New Cadet' water-saving toilet.*

ARTESIAN PLUMBING PRODUCTS • 201 E 5th Street, Mansfield, OH 44901 • Tel: 419 522 4211

BIOLET • Damonmill Square, Concord, MA 01742 • Tel: 800-5-BIO-LET Fax: 508 369 2484 • *A self-contained, biological toilet system that requires no plumbing. Hygienic, odor-free.*

BIO-SUN SYSTEMS INC • Box 134A-RD2, Millerton, PA 16936 • Tel: 717 537 2200 • *Suppliers of Toiletronic compost toilets, and Envirolet waterless toilet systems, which include battery-operated models.*

BRIGGS • 4350 W Cypress Street, Suite 800, Tampa, FL 33607 • Tel: 800 627 4447 / 813 878 0178

CLIVUS MULTRUM INC • 104 Mount Auburn Street, Cambridge, MA 02138 • Tel: 617 491 0051 Fax: 617 491 0053 • *Composting toilets.*

COMPOSTING TOILET SYSTEMS • PO Box 1928, Newport, WA 99156-1928 • Tel: 509 447 3708 • *Odorless, waterless, non-polluting. For home, cabin, shop, or public facilities. In use throughout North America.*

CRANE PLUMBING • 1235 Hartrey Street, Evanston, IL 60202 • 'Crane-Miser' water-saving toilet.

ELJER PLUMBING WARE • 17120 Dallas Parkway, Dallas, TX 75248 • Tel: 800 435 5372 • 'Preserver 2' and Ultra-One/G' water-saving toilets.

ENVIRONMENTAL ENGINEERING CONSULTANTS INC • 7 Marble Street, 4th Floor, PO Box 65, Whitman, MA 02382 • Tel: 617 447 2610 Fax: 617 447 6515

FOR YOUR HEALTH PRODUCTS • 6623 Hillandale Road, Chevy Chase, MD 20815 • Tel: 301 654 1127 Fax: 301 654 2125 • Manufacturers' representative for POP Flush™ toilet water savers.

GERBER PLUMBING FIXTURES CORP • 4656 W Touhy Avenue, Chicago, IL 60646 • Tel: 312 675 6570

GLOBAL HYGIENE SYSTEMS • 9101 Melrose Avenue, # 201 Los Angeles, CA 90046-7026 • Tel: 213 782 3885 • Distributor of Lubidet a unique water-saving personal hygiene system.

KOHLER COMPANY • Kohler, WI 53044 • Tel: 800 456 4537 • 'Wellworth Lite' water-saving toilet.

MANSFIELD PLUMBING PRODUCTS • 150 First Street, Perrysville, OH 44864 • Tel: 419 938 5211 • Water-saving toilets.

MICROPHOR INC • PO Box 1460, Willits, CA 95490-1460 • Tel: 800 358 8280 • 'LF 16R' water-saving toilet.

POP FLUSH • 1309 Hampton Road, San Marcos, CA 92060 • Tel: 619 598 6544

SANITATION EQUIPMENT LIMITED • 35 Citron Court, Concord, Ontario, Canada, L4K 2S7 • Tel: 905 738 0055 / 800 366 7317 Fax: 905 738 2483 • Save water. Save money. Prevent pollution. Ultra-Flush® low water toilet. Flushes with just 1 quart. Call for free information. Manufacturers of Liquid Gold rapid dissolving toilet tissue.

SUN-MAR CORP • 900 Hertel Avenue, Buffalo, NY 14216 • Tel: 905 332 1314 and 5035 North Service Road, C9-10 Burlington, Ontario, Canada, L7L 5V2 • Makers of both electrical and non-electrical composing toilets, including self-contained 'cottage toilets'.

TOTO KIKI USA INC • 415 W Taft Avenue, Unit A, Orange, CA 92665 • Tel: 714 282 8686

TURBOFLUSH • Box 31622, Tampa, FL 33631-3662 • Tel: 800 627 4443

UNIVERSAL RUNDLE CORPORATION • 217 North Mill Street, Newcastle, PA 16103 • Tel: 800 955 0316 • 'Atlas' water-saving toilet.

WATER WISE • 2131 East Middle Drive, Freeland, WA 98249 • Tel: 206 730 7992 • Composting toilets, low water flush toilets.

Water standards ~ *page 76*

ADOPT-A-STREAM • PO Box 435, Pittsford, NY 14534-0435 • Tel: 716 392 6450 • Assists volunteers in starting stream monitoring programs.

AMERICAN ENVIRONMENTAL LABORATORIES INC • 60 Elm Hill Avenue, Leominster, MA 01453 • Tel: 800 522 0094

AMERICAN RIVERS • 801 Pennsylvania Avenue SE, Suite 400, Washington, DC 20003-2167 • Tel: 202 547 6900 • Promotes the protection and restoration of river systems.

CLEAN-FLO LABORATORIES INC • 2525 Xenum Lane North, Plymouth, MN 55343 • Tel: 612 557 6723 Fax: 612 557 6773 • Lake and pond restoration using mechanical, biological, and non-toxic methods.

CLEAN WATER NETWORK • 1350 New York Avenue NW, Washington DC 20005

ENVIRONMENTAL DEFENSE FUND • 257 Park Avenue South, New York, NY 10010 • Tel: 212 505 2100 • A national non-profit organization which links science, economics, and law to create innovative, economically viable solutions to today's environmental problems.

ENVIRONMENTAL PROTECTION AGENCY (EPA) • Public Information Center, 820 Quincy Street, Northwest, Washington DC 2001 • Tel: 202 260 7751

HACH COMPANY • Box 389, 5600 Lindberg Drive, Loveland, CO 80539 • Tel: 800 227 4224 303 669 3050 • Catalog of test kits, pH testing, chlorine testing.

HEALTHY ENVIRONMENTS • PO Box 423, Snowmass, CO 81654 • Tel: 303 925 4400 • Water testing. Catalog.

HYDRO-ANALYSIS ASSOCIATES INC • RD1 Noble Street Extension, Kutztown, PA 19530 • Tel: 215 683 7474

INFORM INC • 120 Wall Street, 16th Floor, New York, NY 10005-4001 • Tel: 212 361 2400 Fax: 212 361 2412 • National non-profit environmental research organization currently focussing on strategies to reduce industrial and municpal waste and preserve air and water quality.

IZAAK WALTON LEAGUE OF AMERICA • 1401 Wilson Boulevard, Level B, Arlington, VA 22209-2138 • Tel: 703 528 1818 • Provides assistance to individuals wishing to monitor and improve water quality.

NATIONAL TESTING LABORATORIES • 6151 Wilson Mills Road, Cleveland, Ohio 44143 • Tel: 216 449 2524 • Drinking water specialists. Affordable, convenient, fast. Guaranteed analysis for bacteria, metals, and chemicals in your drinking water.

NORTHWEST ENVIRONMENTAL ADVOCATES • 133 SW Second Avenue, Portland, OR 97204 • Tel: 503295 0490

PACE INCORPORATED • 1710 Douglas Drive North, Minneapolis, MN 55422 • Tel: 612 544 5543 • *Publishes "Environmental Regulatory Review".*

POLLUTION PROBE FOUNDATION • 12 Madison Avenue, Toronto, Ontario, Canada, M5R 2S1 • Tel: 416 926 1907 • *Organization dedicated to creating positive environmental change through action, education, and the use of research. With increasing public support and awareness, Pollution Probe Foundation works with government and industry toward building a sustainable society. Write for information packages on a wide range of issues.*

PROGRESSIVE PLANET DISTRIBUTING COMPANY • 96 Arapahoe Suite B, Boulder, CO 80302 • Tel: 303 444 3109 / 800 604 3109 Fax: 303 449 7540 • *Wide range of ecologically sound mail-order products for the whole house including a home water audit kit.*

RADON, SOILS, WATER TESTING LABORATORY • 7080 Price-Hilliard Road, Plain City, OH 43064 • Tel: 614 873 8821

SPECTRUM LABS INC • 301 West County Road E-2, New Brighton, MN 55112 • Tel: 800 447 5221

SUBURBAN WATER TESTING LABORATORY • 4600 Kutztown Road, Temple, PA 19560 • Tel: 800 433 6595 • *Water testing.*

THE WATER FOUNDATION • Box H2O, Brainerd, MN 56401 • Tel: 218 829 3616 • *Aims to improve and maintain high-quality water supplies.*

WATER TEST CORPORATION • 28 Daniel Plummer Road, Goffstown, NH 03045 • Tel: 800 426 8378 • *Testing.*

WATER TEST CORPORATION OF AMERICA • 33 South Commercial Street, Manchester, NH 03101

Water purification ~ page 77

CITIZENS CLEARING HOUSE FOR HAZARDOUS WASTE • PO Box 926, Arlington, VA 22216 • Tel: 202 276 7070 • *Information on water filters.*

CLEAR POOL USA LTD • Manchester, NH and Daytona, FL • Tel & Fax: 603 647 8208 / 800 892 5327 • *Clear Pool clarifies pool water and reduces eye and skin irritation.*

DEL INDUSTRIES • 3428 Bullock Lane, San Luis Obispo, CA 93401 • Tel: 800 676 1335 • *Manufactures ozone systems for environmentally safe air and water purification. Whole house and portable units.*

ECOLOGY BY DESIGN (CONCEPTS FOR A TOXIC-FREE ENVIRONMENT) • Audrey Hoodkiss, 1341 Ocean Avenue, Suite 73, Santa Monica, CA 90401 • **Tel:** 310 394 4146 • **Full-service environmental consulting and design firm. Specialists in IAQ, air and water purification. Distributor of environmental products.**

ECOSOFT ENGINEERING • 426 E North Street, # 28, Waukesha, WI 53188 • Tel: 800 275 7070 • *Softens hard water electronically, removes limescale from plumbing.*

ECO SOURCE CATALOG • PO Box 1656, Sebastopol, CA 95473-1656 • Tel: 707 829 3506 Fax: 707 829 7811 • *AFM water and air purification equipment.*

ENVIRONMENTAL PURIFICATION SYSTEMS • 3548 O'Connor Drive, Lafayette, CA 94549 • Tel: 510 284 2129

ENVIRONMENTALLY SOUND PRODUCTS • 8845 Orchard Tree Lane, Towson, MD 21286 • Tel: 800 886 5432 • *Household products for green and healthy living including water filters.*

FOR YOUR HEALTH PRODUCTS • 6623 Hillandale Road, Chevy Chase, MD 20815 • Tel: 301 654 1127 • *Manufacturers' representative for Sprite Shower Dechlorinators.*

GLOBAL ENVIRONMENTAL TECHNOLOGIES (GET) • PO Box 8839, Allentown, PA 18105 • Tel:800 800 8377 • *Manufactures TerraFlo® water treatment and home conservation products.*

IDEAL ENVIRONMENTS INC • Roger Maurice, 401 W Adams, Fairfield, IA 52556 • Tel: 515 472 6547

ION & LIGHT • 2263 Sacramento Street, San Francisco, CA 94115 • Tel: 415 346 1682 Fax: 415 346 0529

LAKOTA SCIENTIFIC INC • 1643 Dunlap Street North, Apartment 7, St Paul, MN 55108 • Tel: 612 489 5782 / 800 945 5782 • *Residential water filters using a five-stage filtration process.*

LIFESOURCE WATER SYSTEMS • 523 S Fair Oaks Avenue, Pasadena, CA 91105 • Tel: 818 792 9996 Fax: 818 792 4214 • *Non-chemical water treatment products for home, business, industrial, and agricultural purposes. Maintenance-free and environmentally friendly.*

MULTIPRO ENVIRONMENTAL • 1021 Lake Lane, Pennsburg, PA 18073 • Tel: 800 900-FIRST • *Water treatment products. Testing and free consultation.*

MULTI-PURE • 21339 Nordhoff Street, Chatsworth, CA 91311 • Tel: 818 341 7577 Fax: 818 341 5275 • *Manufacturer of high-quality, affordably-priced water treatment devices that reduce a wide range of contaminants from drinking water.*

NATIONAL ECOLOGICAL AND ENVIRONMENTAL DELIVERY SYSTEM (NEEDS) • 527 Charles Avenue 12-A, Syracuse, NY 13209 • Tel: 800 634 1380 / 315 446 1122 • *Water purifiers.*

NIGRA ENTERPRISES • 5699 Kanan Road (BR), Agoura, CA 91301-3328 • Tel: 818 889 6877 • *Water purification systems.*

PURA-TECH • PO Box 298, Groveport, OH 43125 • Tel: 614 836 9422

QUALITY ENVIRONMENTS • 2414 McDuffie Street, Houston, TX 77019 • Tel: 713 520 5900 • *Water filters.*

SOLAR DETOXIFICATION PROGRAM • National Renewable Energy Laboratory, 1617 Cole Boulevard, Golden, Colorado 80401-3393 • Tel: 303 231 1258

ULTRA-HYD • 361 Easton Road, Horsham, PA 19044 • Tel: 215 674 1625

Activated Carbon Filters

ABSOLUTE ENVIRONMENTAL'S ALLERGY PRODUCTS AND SERVICES STORE • 2615 S University Drive, Davie, FL 33328 • Tel: 305 472 3773 800 329 3773 • *Activated carbon filters with KDF (sink and shower filters). Catalog.*

H2O PURIFICATION INC • General Ecology of New England, 456 Tunxis Hill Road, Fairfield, CT 06430 • Tel: 203 384 9335

AQUATHIN • 2800 West Cypress Creek Road, Fort Lauderdale, FL 33309 • Tel: 305 784 9100

AUTHENTIC MARKETING • 40 (NH) Waterside Plaza, New York, NY 10010 • Tel: 212 779 -INFO • *Fountain of Health home countertop pour thru water purifier by Hallmark.*

CLEAN-FLO LABORATORIES INC • 2525 Xenum Lane North, Plymouth, MN 55343 • Tel: 612 557 6723 Fax: 612 557 6773 • *Lake and pond restoration using mechanical, biological, and non-toxic methods.*

ENVIRONMENTAL PURIFICATION SYSTEMS • 3548 O'Connor Drive, Lafayette, CA 94549, USA • Tel: 510 284 2129 • *Stainless steel water filters.*

THE FILTER STORE • PO Box 425, Rush, NY 14543 • Tel: 800 828 1494 Fax: 716 624 1205 • *Filter products catalog.*

FLOWRIGHT • 1495 NW Gilman Boulevard, Issaquah, WA 98027 • Tel: 206 392 8357

E L FOUST CO INC • PO Box 105, Elmhurst, IL 60126 • Tel: 708 834 5104 Fax: 708 834 5341 • *Water purification.*

GENERAL ECOLOGY INC • 151 Sheree Boulevard, Lionville, PA 19353 • Tel: 215 363 7900

GLOBAL ENVIRONMENTAL TECHNOLOGIES • Box 8839, Allentown, PA 18105 • Tel: 215 821 4901 • *KDF water filtration system.*

HALLMARK PRODUCTS DIVISION • SLP Technology Corporation, 4191 Bulldog Road, Cedar City, Utah 84720 • *'Fountain of Health' home countertop pour thru water purifier.*

NONTOXIC ENVIRONMENTS • Box 384, Newmarket, NH 03857 • Tel: 603 659 5919 Fax: 603 659 5933

OZARK ANALYTICAL WATER LAB • 114 Spring Street, Sulphur Springs, AR 72768 • Tel: 501 298 3483

PACIFIC ENVIRONMENTAL • 931 Metro Drive, Monterey Park, CA 91754 • Tel: 800 243 8775

RECOVERY ENGINEERING • 2229 Edgewood Avenue South, Minneapolis, MN 55426-2822 • Tel: 612 541 1313

RESTORE THE EARTH • 2204 Hennepin Avenue South, Minneapolis, MN 55405 • Tel: 612 374 3738 • *Reverse osmosis and carbon block water systems.*

R H OF TEXAS • PO Box 780392, Dallas, Texas 75378 • Tel: 214 351 6681 Fax: 214 902 8859 • *Aqua Clear SS water filtration system.*

WATER TECHNOLOGIES CORPORATION • 14405 21st Avenue North, Plymouth, MN 55447 • Tel: 612 473 1625 • *Travelling personal filter.*

Distillers

DURASTILL OF NEW YORK INC • PO Box 2023, 375 Great Neck Road, Great Neck, NY 11021 • Tel: 516 829 6034

SCIENTIFIC GLASS COMPANY • PO Box 25125, 113 Phoenix NW, Albuquerque, NM 87125 • Tel: 505 345 7321 • *Rain-Crystal™ water distiller.*

SUNWATER™ SOLAR CO • 8762 West Tripp Canyon Road, Pima, AZ 85543 • Tel: 520 485 0023 • *Solar water stills for residential, commercial, and community use.*

WATERWISE • PO Box 45963, Center Hill, FL 33514-0459 • Tel: 904 787 5008 Fax: 904 787 8123 • *Purest drinking water. Homemade distilled is best! Simple countertop appliance. Free information.*

Graywater ~ page 80

ADVANCED ENVIRONMENTAL SOLUTIONS INC • PO Box 399, Hagan, GA 30429 • Tel: 912 739 8809 • *Uses natural bacteria to digest organic waste. Can be used in septic tanks, ponds, grease traps, wastewater treatment systems.*

AGWA SYSTEMS • 801 South Flower Street, Burbank, CA 91502 • Tel:800 473 9426 • *Manufacturer of graywater irrigation system.*

CONTROLLED ENERGY SYSTEMS • Fiddler's Green, Waitsfield, VT 05603 • Tel: 802 496 4436 / 800 642 3111 Fax: 802 496 6924 • *'Aqua Bank' system diverts fresh water from waste system to toilet bank or to holding tank for landscape use.*

EARTHSTAR ENERGY SYSTEMS • Route 220 at US Route 1, PO Box 626, Waldboro, ME 04572 • Tel: 207 832 6861 Fax: 207 832 7314 • *Graywater heat recovery systems.*

IRRIGRO • LPO 360, 1555 Third Avenue, Niagara Falls, NY 14304 and PO BOX 1133, St Catherine's, Ontario, Canada, L2R 7A3 • *Drip irrigation products including sample kits.*

OASIS BIOCOMPATIBLE PRODUCTS • 5 San Marcos Trout Club, Santa Barbara, CA 93105-9726 • Tel: 805 967 3222 Fax: 805 967 3229 • *Oasis Biocompatible Cleaners biodegrade into plant nutrients! The only cleaners proven safe for reusing graywater for irrigation - the ecologically superior option.*

REWATER SYSTEMS • 438 Addison Avenue, Palo Alto, CA 94301 • Tel: 415 324 1307 • *Manufacturer of graywater irrigation system.*

WATER WISE • PO Box 45963, Center Hill, FL 33514-0459 • Tel: 904 787 5008 Fax: 904 787 8123 • *Graywater treatment systems.*

ZELLERBACH, A MEAD CO • 1010 West 19th Street, National City, CA 92050 • *Makers of Waterwick Systems.*

Wholewater systems and flowforms ~ pages 81-82

CLEAN-FLO LABORATORIES INC • 2525 Xenum Lane North, Plymouth, MN 55441 • Tel: 612 557 6723 Fax: 612 557 6773

EBB & FLOW • Simon Charter, Ruskin Mill, Millbottom, Nailsworth, Glos, United Kingdom • Tel: (+44) 1453 836060 • *Wholewater systems and flowforms. Contact the UK office for North American distributors.*

IRIS WATER & DESIGN • Langburn Bank, Castleton, Whitby, North Yorkshire, YO21 2EU, United Kingdom • Tel: (+44) 1287 660002 Fax: (+44) 1287 660004 • *A unique range of sculptured water features. Contact the UK address for US and Canadian distributors.*

WATERFORMS INC • Route 177, PO Box 930, Blue Hill, ME 04614 • Tel: 207 374 2384 Fax: 207 374 2383 • *Design, manufacture, and install flowing water environments for all types of interior and exterior settings as well as for pond reclamation and surface water run-off systems.*

WATER RESEARCH INSTITUTE OF BLUE HILL • Route 177, PO Box 930, Blue Hill, ME 04614 • Tel: 207 374 2384 Fax: 207 374 2383 • *Educational and outreach programs for children and adults to explore the beauty of water's rhythms and the relationship of these to rhythms and forms in the organic world.*

Control systems ~ pages 88-89

See also listings for Soft Energy pages 222-30

ABBEON CAL INC • 123 Gray Avenue, Santa Barbara, CA 93101 • Tel: 805 966 0810 / 800 922 0977 Fax: 805 966 7659 • *Catalog of Hygrometers, thermometers etc.*

AMERICAN COUNCIL FOR AN ENERGY-EFFICIENT ECONOMY • 1001 Connecticut Avenue NW, no 535, Washington DC 20036 • Tel: 202 429 8873 and 2140 Shattuck Avenue, no 202, Berkeley, CA 94704 • Tel: 510 549 9914

AMERICAN SOLAR ENERGY SOCIETY • 2400 Central Avenue, Suite G1, Boulder CO 80301 • Tel: 303 443 3130

BAYVIEW TECHNOLOGY GROUP • 35 Bayview Drive, Sac Carlos, CA 94070 • Tel: 415 592 9664 Fax: 415 593 0156 • *LaserMiser saves power by automatically switching laser printers on and off based on usage.*

B.C. SOLAR • PO Box 1117, Laytonville, CA 95454 • Tel: 707 984 8203. • *SUNFLOWER™ SOLAR TRACKER – For 12, 24, 36 volt systems – uses less than 2 watt hours per day per axis at 12 volts. Controls on the pole. Sizes up to 24 panels.*

BIOLOGA • D-88662 Uberlingen-Goldbach, Germany • Tel: (+49) 7551 5498 Fax: (+49) 7551 65965 • *The latest designs complementing Building-biology techniques: Demand Switches, Radio Controls, Shielding etc. Call or fax for US distributors.*

ELECTRON CONNECTION • PO Box 442, Medford, OR 97501 • Tel: 916 475 3401

ENDOTRONIC GMBH • 7989 Argenbuhl, Germany • Tel: (+49) 75 66465 • *Manufacture an electrical Demand Switch.*

ENER-G-POLARI-T • PO Box 2449, Prescott, AZ 86302-2449 • Tel: 520 778 5039 / 800 593 6374 Fax: 520 771 0611 • *Products for calmer, less-stressful living including Cook's Elemental Diodes to hold your electrical system in balance. Free catalog.*

ENERGY EFFICIENCY AND RENEWABLE ENERGY CLEARING HOUSE (EREC)• PO Box 3048, Merrifield, VA 22116 • Tel: 800 363 3732

THE ENERGY GROUP • PO Box 337, Little Falls, NJ 07424 • Fax: 201 956 2940 • *Reducing operating cost: our speciality.*

ENVIRONMENTAL PROTECTION AGENCY (EPA) • Public Information Center, 820 Quincy Street NW, Washington DC 20036 • Tel: 202 452 1999

E SOURCE • 1033 Walnut, Boulder, CO 80302 • Tel: 303 440 8500 Fax: 303 440 8502 • *Techniques for energy efficiency.*

FANTECH • 1712 Northgate Boulevard, Sarasota, FL 34235 • Tel: 941 357 2947 Fax: 941 355 0377

FOWLER SOLAR ELECTRIC INC • PO Box 435, Worthington, MA 01098 • Tel: 413 238 5974 • *Mail-order pricing with quality service and support. Catalog includes information and lists of specific products including controls.*

GENERAL ELECTRIC (CANADA) • 1130 Boulevard Charec West, Quebec, Canada, G1N 2E2 • Tel: 418 682 8500 • *Meters.*

IDEAL ENVIRONMENTS INC • Roger Maurice, 401 W Adams, Fairfield, IA 52556 • Tel: 515 472 6547 • *Radio-controlled switch to shut off electricity in the bedroom.*

IOWA STATE UNIVERSITY OF SCIENCE AND TECHNOLOGY ELECTRIC POWER RESEARCH CENTER, 111 Coover Hall, Ames, IO 50011-1045 • Tel: 515 294 8057 Fax: 515 294 8432

KEEP IT SIMPLE SYSTEMS (KISS) • 32 S Ewing, Suite 330, Helena, MT 59601 • Tel: 406 442 3559 • *Solar Power for portable computers! Unique flexible and durable solar panels designed to run or recharge many popular portable computers.*

NUSUN INC • 842 South Jefferson Avenue, West Jefferson, NC 28694 • Tel: 919 246 5143 • *Small EV controllers and EV charging stations.*

THE ROCKY MOUNTAIN INSTITUTE • 1739 Snowmass Creek Road, Old Snowmass, CO 81654-9199 • Tel: 303 927 3851 Fax: 303 927 3420 • *See p. 108.*

SMALL POWER SYSTEMS • 74550 Dobie Lane, Covelo, CA 95428 • Tel: 800 972 7179

SOLAR PATHFINDER • 25720 465th Avenue, Hartford, SD 57033 • Tel: 605 528 6473 • *Instrument used to site solar homes, photovoltaic panels, and solar collectors quickly and accurately.*

SOLAR TECHNOLOGY INSTITUTE • PO Box 1115, Carbondale, CO 81623-1115 • Tel: 303 963 0715

SOLARWEST ELECTRIC INC • 232 Anacapa Street, Santa Barbara, CA 93101 • Tel: 805 963 9667 Fax: 805 963 9929

SPECIALTY CONCEPTS INC • 8954 Mason Avenue, Chatsworth, CA 91311 • Tel: 818 998 5238 Fax: 818 998 5253 • *Photovoltaic battery charge regulators, monitors, and system controls.*

SUNRISE DESIGN CENTER • Deborah Warner, South 29175 Highway 3, St. Maries, ID 83861 • Tel: 208 689 3820 • *For a more energy-efficient home: architectural design and drafting, technical assistance, graphics and logos, renderings.*

SUN SELECTOR • PO Box 1545, Parkersburg, WV 26101 • Tel: 304 485 7150 • *Omnimeter is a specialized computer control system for DC monitoring.*

Stoves ~ page 90

APPLIED ENGINEERING • 218 Dartmouth SE, Albuquerque, NM 87106 • Tel: 505 256 1261 • *Solar cookers.*

BURNS-MILWAUKEE INC • 4010 West Douglas Avenue, Milwaukee, WI 53209 • Tel: 414 438 1234 Fax: 414 438 1604 • *Villager Sun Oven.*

GENERAL ELECTRIC (CANADA) • 1130 Boulevard Charec West, Quebec, Canada, G1N 2E2 • Tel: 418 682 8500 Fax: 418 682 8550 • *Induction cooktops.*

KANSAS WIND POWER • (dept NHC) 13569 214th Road, Holton, KS 66436 • Tel: 913 364 4407 • *Solar cookers.*

SOLAR CHEF • 2412 Robinson Road, Grants Pass, OR 97527 • Tel: 503 471 4371 • *Solar cookers.*

SOLAR COOKERS INTERNATIONAL • 1724 11th Street, Sacramento, CA 95814 • Tel: 916 444 6616 • *Solar cookers including designs to make your own.*

SUN OVEN • Ethel and Ken Farnsworth, 138 Willoway Drive, Boise, ID 83705 • Tel: 208 336 4883 • *Manufacturers of Sun Oven™ solar power cookers.*

ZOMEWORKS • PO Box 25805, 1011A Sawmill Road Northwest, Albuquerque, NM 87125 • Tel: 505 242 5354 Fax: 505 243 5187 • *Solar cookers.*

Refrigerators ~ *page 91*

AMERICAN SOCIETY OF HEATING, REFRIGERATION AND AIR-CONDITIONING ENGINEERS INC (ASHRAE) • 1791 Tullie Circle NE Atlanta, GA 30325-2305 • Tel: 404 636 8400

THE CONSERVE GROUP • Box 1560, Bethlehem, PA 18016 • Tel: 610 691 8024 • *Any refrigerator can be super-efficient with CHILLshield – the refrigerator vapor barrier.*

LOW KEEP REFRIGERATION • 2465 Second Avenue, Otsego, MI 49078-9406 • Tel: 616 692 3015

NORCOLD • 600 Kuther Road, Sidney, OH 45365 • *Manufacture a range of energy-efficient refrigerators including RV refrigerators.*

PHOTOCOMM INC • PO Box 14230, Scottsdale, AZ 85267 • Tel: 800 544 6466 / 602 951 6330 • *Vestfrost low-energy freezer. Makers of Vestfrost low-energy CFC-free refrigerators and freezers, solar electric power systems, solar and gas powered refrigerators/freezers.*

SMALL POWER SYSTEMS • 74550 Dobie Lane, Covelo, CA 95428 • Tel: 800 972 7179 • *Solar absorption refrigeration.*

SUN FROST REFRIGERATORS • PO Box 1101, 824 L Street, Arcata, CA 95521 • Tel: 707 822 9095 Fax: 707 822 6213 • *The world's most energy efficient, using 60-90% less energy than standard models. DC models for alternative energy/AC models for cutting utility bills. Free literature.*

Low-voltage equipment ~ *page 92*

ENVIRESOURCE INC • 110 Madison Avenue North, Bainbridge Island, WA 98110 • Tel: 206 842 9785 • *Energy-saving devices.*

EXCELTECH • 2225 East Loop 820 North, Fort Worth, TX 76118-7101 • Tel: 817 595 4969 / 800 886 4683 Fax: 817 595 1290 • *Range of affordable sine wave inverters.*

GREEN TECHNOLOGIES INC • 5490 Spine Road, Boulder, CO 80301 • Tel: 303 581 9600 • *Green Plug electricity saver for household appliances.*

NORTHWEST ENERGY STORAGE • 10418 Highway 95 North, Sandpoint, ID 83864 • Tel: 208 263 6142 • *Lineage 2000 lead acid battery ideal for alternative energy users.*

POWER STAR PRODUCTS • 10011 N Foothill Boulevard, Cupertino, CA 95014 • Tel: 408 973 8502 Fax: 408 973 8573 • *Range of power inverters for all types of appliances.*

REAL GOODS • 555 Leslie Street, Ukiah, CA 95482 • Tel: 800 762 7325 • *Real Goods is your complete resource for ENERGY EFFICIENT LIVING. Compact fluorescent lighting; solar, wind, and hydro power, rechargeable batteries and chargers; home safety products; solar toys. Free catalog. See p. 96*

SCIENTIFIC CERTIFICATION SYSTEMS • 1611 Telegraph Avenue, Suite 1111, Oakland, CA 94612-2118 • Tel: 510 832 1415 • *Grants independent certification of environmental claims. See p. 198.*

SUN FROST

Energy Efficient REFRIGERATOR FREEZER

Quiet — Uses 60-90% Less Energy
•AC Models for Cutting Utility Bills
•DC Models for Alternative Energy

P.O. Box 1101, Arcata, CA 95518
(707) 822-9095

SIERRA SOLAR SYSTEMS • 109 Argall Way, Nevada City, CA 95959 • Tel: 800 517 6527 Fax: 916 265 8441 • *Energy-efficient appliances.*

SUNBELT BATTERY COMPANY • 525 South McClintock Drive no 103, Tempe, AZ 85281 • Tel: 602 968 8068 Fax: 602 968 9838 • *Batteries, chargers, test equipment and much more.*

STATPOWER TECHNOLOGIES CORPORATION • 7725 Lougheed Highway, Burnaby, BC, Canada, V5A 4V8 • Tel: 604 420 1585 Fax: 604 420 1519 • *Prowatt power inverters.*

TRACE ENGINEERING • 5916-195th Northeast, Arlington, WA 98223 • Tel: 360 435 8826 Fax: 360 435 2229 • *We provide 120/240 volt electricity anywhere. Prime power or backup power for most electrical appliances. Power inverters.*

TUMBLER TECHNOLOGIES • 1340 Fulton Place, Fremont, CA 95439 • Tel: 510 226 2780 • *Power inverters.*

VANNER WELDON INC • 4282 Reynolds Drive, Hilliard, OH 43026 • Tel: 614 771 2718 Fax: 614 771 4904 • *Vanner Power products. Power conversion and control systems for mobile, remote, and alternative energy applications.*

Electromagnetic field testing ~ *page 93*

BIO-PHYSICS MERSMANN INC • 122 Belmont Street, Watertown, MA 02172 • Tel: 617 926 7671 Fax: 617 926 5154 • *EMF testing. Instrument design and manufacture.*

M SPARK BURMASTER • Home Environmental Options, RR 1 Box 77A, Chaseburg, WI 54621 • *Testing services.*

MARY CORDARO • 12439 Magnolia Boulevard, no 263, Valley Village, CA 91607 • Tel: 310 838 2892 / 818 981 7245 Fax: 810 766 5882 • *Comprehensive EMF bio-electric testing: magnetic/electric fields, body voltage.*

VALERIE DOW • Box 21, Haysville, KS 67060 • Tel: 316 788 1793 • *Testing services.*

LAWRENCE GUST • 262 Victor-Egypt Road, Victor, NY 14564 • Tel: 716 924 9073 • *Testing services.*

ELECTRIC FIELD MEASUREMENTS (EFM Company) • Route 183, RR 2, W Stockbridge, MA 01266 • Tel: 413 637 1929 Fax: 413 637 2826 • *Multimeters for single axis electric and magnetic field measurements.*

ELECTRO-POLLUTION SUPPLY • PO Box 3217, Prescott, AZ 86302 • Tel: 602 445 8225 Fax: 602 445 5413 • *EMF shielding systems and testing.*

ENVIRONMENTAL ELECTRICS • PO Box 10284, San Rafael, CA 94912 • Tel: 415 721 1515 • *EMF surveys, electrical contracting.*

ENVIRONMENTAL RISK TESTING, THREE PHASE ELECTRIC • 1155 North Slate Street, no 420, Bellingham, WA 98225 • Tel: 206 734 6777 • *EMF testing, environmental home inspections.*

ENVIRONMENTAL TESTING AND TECHNOLOGY • PO Box 230369, Encinitas, CA 92023 • Tel: 619 436 5990 Fax: 619 436 9448 • *Investigations for building-related health problems. Electro-magnetic field testing and mitigation, low EMF wiring systems.*

HEALTHFUL HARDWARE • PO Box 3217, Prescott, Arizona, AZ 86303 • Tel: 602 445 8225 • *Video "Current Switch, How to Identify and Reduce or Eliminate Electromagnetic Fields".*

HEALTHY ENVIRONMENTS • PO Box 423, Snowmass, CO 81654 • Tel: 303 925 4400 • *EMF testing. Catalog.*

IDEAL ENVIRONMENTS INC • 401 W Adams, Fairfield, IA 52556 • Tel: 515 472 6547 • *Testing services, lectures, products.*

INTERNATIONAL INSTITUTE FOR BAU-BIOLOGIE & ECOLOGY INC • PO Box 387, Clearwater, FL 34615 • Tel: 813 461 4371 Fax: 813 441 4373 • *Advice and testing of products. See p. 193.*

ION & LIGHT • 2263 Sacramento Street, San Francisco, CA 94115 • Tel: 415 346 1682 Fax: 415 346 0529 • *Electric field meters.*

LAND & SEA ELECTRIC • Alternative Building Consultants Company, 444 Brickell Avenue Plaza, 51-273, Miami, FL 33131 • Tel: 305 674 9716 • *EMF testing, environmental home inspections.*

MAGNETIC SCIENCES INTERNATIONAL • Box 850-295, HCR-2, Tucson, AZ 85735 • Tel: 602 822 2355 Fax: 602 822 1640 • *Manufacturer of Gaussmeter and other instruments for measuring magnetic fields from power lines, transformers, computers, house wiring, and appliances.*

SUSAN McCRONE • Safe Home Detective, W294 N 5260 Merton Avenue, Hartland, WI 53029 • Tel: 414 367 7308 • *Testing services.*

NATIONAL ECOLOGICAL AND ENVIRONMENTAL DELIVERY SYSTEM (NEEDS) • 527 Charles Avenue 12A, Syracuse, NY 13209 • Tel: 800 634 1380 • *The Clarus system uses a new algorithm-based technology to 'organize', 'align', and 'entrain' the random, chaotic or 'non-binary' photons existing in high and low frequency magnetic fields. Clarus systems are available for home, auto, workplace, computer, and video applications.*

NATIONAL ELECTROMAGNETIC FIELD TESTING ASSOCIATION (NEFTA) • 628-B Library Place, Evanston, IL 60201 • Tel: 708 475 3696 • *NEFTA is the only international Registry of independent companies and individuals involved professionally in electromagnetic field (EMF) testing, consulting, mitigation, and research. NEFTA is a public service organization with members across the US including Alaska and Hawaii, and in Canada.*

NATIONAL INSTITUTE OF ELECTROMEDICAL INFORMATION INC • PO Box 4633, Bay Terrace, NY 11360-4633 • Tel: 212 410 8083 • *Networking, legal expert witness testimony on EMF.*

NONTOXIC ENVIRONMENTS • 9392 Gribble Road, Canby, OR 97013 • Tel: 503 266 5244 Fax: 503 266 5242 • *Mail-order company specializing in products for aware and chemically sensitive individuals.*

NORAD CORPORATION • 1160 East Sandhill Avenue, Carson, CA 90746 • Tel: 310 605 0808 / 800 262 3260 Fax: 310 605 5051 • *NoRad™ Radiation Shield will fit virtually all computer displays.*

OSM ENGINEERING • 1143 Fir Avenue, Inglewood, CA 90301 • Tel: 213 671 4082 • *EMF testing.*

QUALITY ENVIRONMENTS • 2414 McDuffie Street, Houston, TX 77019 • Tel: 713 520 5900

RADIATION PROTECTION SERVICES INC • PO Box 2395, Darlen, CT 06820 • Tel: 203 324 7967

SAFE ENVIRONMENTS • 2625 Acatraz Avenue, Suite 342, Berkeley, CA 94705 • Tel: 510 549 9693 Fax: 510 849 4465 • *EMF inspections.*

WILL SPATES • 1848 Oak Lake Drive, Clearwater, FL 34624 • Tel: 813 448 0915 • *Testing services.*

TESLATRONICS INC • 4303 Vineland Road, Suite F-8, Orlando, FL 32811 • Tel: 407 481 0160 Fax: 407 481 0164 • *Worldwide marketer of single- and three-axis Gaussmeters, provides cost-effective, accurate instruments to measure ELF/VLF magnetic fields.*

VITALITY CONCEPTS INC • 1406 W Summerdale Avenue, Chicago, IL 60640-2116 • Tel: 800 252 0200 Fax: 312 275 7997 • *Field testing in the area of 60Hz invisible light spectrum.*

WALKER SCIENTIFIC INC • Rockdale Street, Worcester, MA 01606 • Tel: 508 852 3674 / 800 962 4638 • *Determine electromagnetic hot spots in your home with a Walker Scientific ELF Monitor (Gaussmeter).*

ZERO PROFILE • 6984 McKinley Street, Sebastopol, CA 95472 • Tel: 707 823 6931 • *EMF field surveys and research, design etc.*

The liveability of a house is enhanced by mechanical systems which work transparently to provide a healthy environment, improving the comforts of home with noiseless, efficient operation.

EARTH★STAR
energy systems

Earthstar Energy Systems is an innovative company dedicated to the development, design, and supply of affordable mechanical systems to build with. From our begining in 1980, we set out to reenvision the house and its systems in an integrative, wholistic way, assembling a complement of equipment, expertise and design methodology which together would support and expand our ability to build environmentally sound, solar heated homes which are healthy, comfortable, and efficient in the use of materials and energy.

At that time we spoke of striving for self sufficiency, now we call it sustainability. We're not there yet, but we've made progress and attained many of our early goals. We have a comprehensive array of high quality systems and innovative design methods backed by experience hard to find anywhere. Whether you are building an efficient home using more conventional construction methods, or an alternative home of organic design with natural materials, we have appropriate equipment. Wherever you are building or remodeling, let us help you with integrated design, material supply, technical knowhow, and enthusiasm!

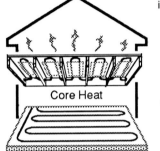

Radiant Heat Distribution

Core Heat

+

Skin Effect

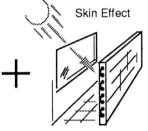

Active Mass Walls

+

Autonomous Regulation

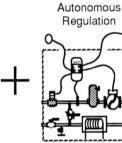

Control Module

+

Energy Source

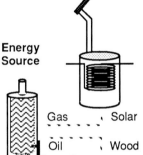

Gas · Solar
Oil · Wood

Construction techniques suitable for use with Earthstar radiant heating.

☑ wood
cement
sand
clay/straw
rammed earth
adobe block
syndecrete

The above pictures represent some of the elements we work with for heating. Radiant heating the floor using proven Pex pipe technology, we design for lowest temperature operation in conjunction with all flooring types. New as well as existing floors which are accessible can be fitted. Our control methods provide continous circulation with weather responsive feedback. By monitoring outdoor and indoor temperatures and precise adjustment of supply temperature, overheating & underheating effects are eliminated. More mass becomes advantageous, as internal circulation adds to the available surface area to charge and discharge thermal energy. It is common to heat a house in subzero weather with 80°F water. Sunlight reaching a floor or wall with radiant heat can be absorbed, moderating temperature swings and spreading passive gains throughout the house. The control module is the system brains which regulates this like your body regulates its temperature- varing temperature and circulation between skin and core and metabolic input. Any source of heat can be used, and we have experience in integrating many combinations. Send us your plans or sketches, and we'll workup your ideas and fleshout the details.

Other Things We Offer:

Earthstar Solar Thermal Tanks for hot water and space heat feature sizes from 20 to 2000 gallons.
Ventilation Equipment from passive humidity regulation to energy recovery systems.
Pex Manifolded Plumbing Systems for safe water and easy installation.
The original award winning Graywater Heat Reclaimer by Earthstar
Composting Toilets, gravity feed Cistern Tanks and much more!
Many years of practical experience as builders, engineers, and humans, we offer a common sense integrated design approach for the real world, knowledgeable in the building arts and sciences.

Technical ! Support

before, during, and after the sale

plumbing & control tie in diagrams

wiring diagrams

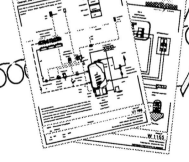

layout blueprints

Technical Support

for installation, service, and maintenance

10% OF OUR PROFIT SUPPORTS ONGOING RESEARCH AND DEMONSTRATION OF ALTERNATIVE CONSTRUCTION THROUGH DONATIONS TO THE INSTITUTE FOR BIODYNAMIC SHELTER AND OTHER MEMBER BASED NONPROFIT ENVIRONMENTAL EDUCATIONAL ORGANIZATIONS. IF YOU KNOW OF A WORTHY ORGANIZATION BUILDING AN EDUCATIONAL CENTER, SCHOOL, OR DEMONSTRATION PROJECT, HAVE THEM CONTACT US. THANK YOU!

For information, ideas, free estimates, technical support, or sales, contact us at: **Earthstar Energy Systems**

phone (207) 832- 6861
Fax (207) 832- 7314

USA 800- 323- 6749
Maine 800- 660- 6749

PO Box 626 Rt 220 at US Rt 1
Waldoboro, ME, USA 04572

Natural lighting ~ *page 100*

G & A NATURAL LIGHTING • 586 Weddell Drive, Suite 2, Sunnyvale, CA 94089 • Tel 408 541 8930 Fax: 408 541 8949 • *SOLATUBE™ – The high performance natural alternative to the skylight.*

MITSUBISHI INTERNATIONAL CORPORATION • 520 Madison Avenue, New York, NY 10022 • Tel: 212 605 2390 Fax: 212 605 1746 • *'Himawari' system transmits sunlight indoors through optical fibers.*

SOLA*TUBE • 586 Weddell Drive, Suite 2, Sunnyvale, CA 94089 • Tel: 408 541 8930 / 800 699 7652 Fax 408 541 8949 • *The Sola*Tube is the latest in high-technology skylights. Please call to learn more about the energy-efficient lighting.*

THE SUN-PIPE CO INC • PO Box 2223, Northbrook, IL 60065 • Tel: 800 844 4786 / 708 272 6977 Fax: 708 272 6972 • *The Sun-pipe lets in natural light.*

Healthy lighting ~ *page 101*

See also listings for Natural Lighting, above

ANGELO BROTHERS COMPANY • 12401 McNulty Road, Philadelphia, PA 19154 • Tel: 215 671 9015

BOMMARITO LIGHTING • 16001 Larch Way, Lynnwood, WA 98037 • Tel: 206 782 7883 • *Full-spectrum, incandescent, and fluorescent color-corrected long-life bulbs.*

FULL SPECTRUM LIGHTING • 27 Clover Lane, Burlington, VT 05401 • Tel: 800 261 3100 / 802 863 3100 Fax: 802 658 2808 • *TruSpectrum™ bulbs provide a healthier, more natural light for people, pets, and plants. A whiter and brighter light allowing you to see colors more accurately while reducing eyestrain and fatigue.*

HEALTHY LIGHTS • Dan Kassell, Network 25 West Fairview Avenue, Dover, NJ 07801 • Tel: 800 777 4636 • *Full Spectrum Vitalities and Neo-White bulbs for home and office.*

HEINZ SOLAR • 19345 N Indian Avenue, no. H, PO Box 1009, N Palm Springs, CA 92258 • Tel: 619 251 6886 Fax: 619 251 6886 • *Solar-powered lighting systems. Publisher of "Homestead Enterprises".*

ION & LIGHT • 2263 Sacramento Street, San Francisco, CA 94115 • Tel: 415 346 1682 Fax: 415 346 0529 • *Full-spectrum lights.*

LIFE LONG LIGHTS • 2124 Kittredge Street, # 168, Berkeley, CA 94703 • Tel: 510 649 5754 • *Vita-Lite full spectrum fluorescents.*

THE LIGHT SOURCE • 1136 Darrow Avenue, Evanston, IL 60202 • Tel: 708 328 5950 • *Full spectrum, natural daylight fluorescents, super-efficient compact fluorescents, and halogen floodlights.*

LUMIRAM CORPORATION • PO Box 297, Mamaroneck, NY 10543 • Tel: 914 698 1205

NETWORK • 25 West Fairview Avenue, Dover, NJ 07801 • Tel: 800 777 4636 • *Vita Lite – Full spectrum natural light. Healthy lights. Excellent for use in your home or office.*

NONTOXIC ENVIRONMENTS • 9392 Gribble Road, Canby, OR 97013 • Tel: 503 266 5244 Fax: 503 266 5242

OTT BIOLIGHT SYSTEMS INC • 28 Parker Way, Santa Barbara, CA 93101 • Tel: 805 564 3467 / 800 234 3724 Fax: 805 564 2147 *OTT bioLIGHTSYSTEMS is the leader in biologically beneficial, full-spectrum, ergonomic lighting. Call for information and free brochure. See p. 197.*

PANASONIC LIGHTING PRODUCTS • 1 Panasonic Way, Secaucus, NJ 07094 • Tel: 201 348 5380

PROGRESSIVE PLANET DISTRIBUTING COMPANY • 96 Arapahoe Suite B, Boulder, CO 80302 • Tel: 303 444 3109 / 800 604 3109 Fax: 303 449 7540 • *Wide range of ecologically sound mail-order products for the whole house including full spectrum lighting.*

QUALITY ENVIRONMENTS • 2414 McDuffie Street, Houston, TX 77019 • Tel: 713 520 5900 • *Full spectrum lighting.*

SIMMONS COMPANY • 54 Shallowford Road, PO Box 3193, Chattanooga, TN 37404-0193 • Tel: 800 533 6779 • *Natural spectrum lighting. Discount prices. Vita-Lite. Chromalux. OttLite. Sun Box.*

SUNELCO • PO Box 1499, 100 Skeels, Hamilton, MT 59840 • Tel: 406 363 6924 Fax: 406 363 6046 • *Catalog of healthy and energy-efficient lighting products.*

VERILUX CORPORATION • 626 York Street, Vallejo, CA 94590 Tel: 800 786 6850 Fax 707 554 8370 • *Verilux Instant Sun - The natural light for people, pets, and plants.*

VITALITY CONCEPTS INC • 1406 W Summerdale Avenue, Chicago, IL 60640-2116 • Tel: 800 252 0200 / 312 275 1443 Fax: 312 275 7997 • *Full spectrum lighting for the light of day, indoors. Full spectrum lighting duplicates the spectral energy distribution of outdoor lighting at midday.*

Low-energy lighting ~ *page 104*

See also listings for Healthy lighting, above

ACTECH INC • 8032 Cedar Row Boulevard, Westerville, OH 43081-5547 • Tel: 800 243 3599 • *Compact energy-saving fluorescents.*

BROOKSTONE HARD TO FIND TOOLS CATALOG • 17 Riverside Street, Nashua, NH 03062 • Tel: 800 846 3000 • *Products include energy-saving bulbs.*

CON EDISON CONSERVATION CENTER • Chrysler Building, 42nd Street and Lexington Avenue, New York, NY • Tel: 800 343 4646

ECOLOGY SYSTEMS • 3863 Short Street, Dubuque, IA 52002 • Tel: 319 556 4765 • *Compact fluorescent lights.*

ECO SOURCE CATALOG • PO Box 1656, Sebastopol, CA 95473-1656 • Tel: 707 829 3506 Fax: 707 829 7811 • *Energy-efficient lighting.*

EDCO ELECTRONIC INC • 2209 American Avenue, Hayward, CA 94545 • Tel: 800 424 LAMP (CA) / 800 544 LAMP (outside CA)

ELECTRIC POWER RESEARCH INSTITUTE • 3412 Hillview Avenue, PO Box 10412, Palo Alto, CA 94303 • Tel: 415 855 2411 / 800 525 8555 • *Research, development, and delivery of high-value technological advances through networking and partnership with the electricity industry.*

ENERGY ANSWERS • PO Box 24, Lake Bluff, IL 60044 • Tel: 800 776 6761 • *Energy-saving products including compact fluorescent lights.*

ENERGY FEDERATION INC (EFI) • 14 Tech Circle, Natick, ME 01760 1086 • Tel: 508 653 4299

ENERTRON TECHNOLOGIES • 1215 C Park Center Drive, Vista, CA 92083 • Tel: 800 537 7649 Fax: 619 548 5332

ENVIRONMENTALLY SOUND PRODUCTS • 8845 Orchard Tree Lane, Towson, MD 21286 • Tel: 800 886 5432 • *Household products for green and healthy living. Range includes low-energy lighting.*

EPA GREEN LIGHTS PROGRAM • Green Lights, 6202J, 401 M Street SW, Washington DC 20460 • Tel: 202 775 6650 • *Current information about energy-efficient lighting.*

FEIT ELECTRIC COMPANY • 2042 Vernon Avenue, Los Angeles, CA 90058 • Tel: 213 235 3348 Fax: 213 235 1315

FRED DAVIS CORPORATION-ENERGY LIGHTING SPECIALISTS • 93 West Street, Medford, MA 02052 • Tel: 508 359 3610 Fax: 508 359 3644 • *Compact fluorescents of all kinds.*

ENTERPRISER LIGHTING INC • 12509 Patterson Avenue, Richmond, VA 23233 • Tel: 804 784 0330 / 800 394 2852 Fax: 804 784 0334 • *Light bulb guaranteed to last 100 years with normal use.*

G E LIGHTING • 16257 Laguna Canyon Road, # 100, Irvine, CA 92710 • Tel: 714 450 4700 Fax: 714 450 4712

ILLUMINATION ENGINEERING SOCIETY • 120 Wall Street, 17th Floor, New York, NY 10005 • *Many booklets on energy-efficient lighting and daylighting.*

INTERMATIC • Intermatic Plaza, Spring Grove, IL 60081 • *Verde Finish duplicates look of antiquity on low voltage outdoor lights. Low voltage fluorescent lamp fixtures are UL listed and operate at low temperatures.*

LIFE LONG LIGHTS • 2124 Kittredge Street, # 168, Berkeley, CA 94703 • Tel: 510 649 5754 • *Energy-saving fluorescent tubes and halogen floodlights.*

LIGHT BULBS UNLIMITED • 1712 East Chapman, Orange, CA 92667 • Tel: 714 532 1410 Fax: 714 532 6254

LIGHTS OF AMERICA • 611 Reyes Drive, Walnut, CA 91789 • Tel: 909594 7883 Fax: 909 594 6758 • *Large range of energy-saving lights.*

LIGHT SOURCE • 1136 Darrow Avenue, Evanston, IL 60202 • Tel: 708 328 5950 • *Full-spectrum, natural daylight fluorescents, super-efficient compact fluorescents, and halogen floodlights.*

LIGHT SOLUTIONS • 934 MacArthur Boulevard, Oakland, CA 94610 • Tel: 510 893 0134

MITOR INDUSTRIES INC • PO Box 4339, Mankato MN 56002-4339 • Tel: 507 387 1599 • *A truly compact fluorescent lamp, thermally protected, quiet and reliable, long life and high color rendering.*

NEWTON ELECTRICAL SUPPLY • 48 Mechanic Street, Newton, MA 02164 • Tel: 617 527 2040 Fax: 617 527 4534

PACIFIC GAS & ELECTRIC ENERGY CENTER • 851 Howard Street, San Francisco, CA 94103 • Tel: 415 972 5341 • *A hands-on energy education center where designers as well as the public can learn about the impact of their technology choices on a building's energy usage.*

PANASONIC LIGHTING PRODUCTS • 1 Panasonic Way, Secaucus, NJ 07094 • Tel: 201 348 5380

PHILIPS LIGHTING • 200 Franklin Square Drive, PO Box 6800, Somerset, NJ 08875-6800 and 601 Milner Avenue, Scarborough, Ontario, Canada, M1B 1M8 • Tel: 416 292 3000 Fax: 416 754 6265 • *Full range of energy-efficient lamps including the SLS family of Earth Light lamps which offers the ultimate in high efficiency and compactness. The new I.Q. Lighting™ series is a new family of 'intelligent' bulbs including the Auto-Off™, Dimmer™ and Back-up™ which offer energy savings convenience and safety.*

PHOTOCOMM INC • PO Box 14230, Scottsdale, AZ 85267 • Tel: 800 544 6466 / 602 951 6330 • *Area lighting systems provided by solar electric modules. Full range of energy-efficient lamps.*

REAL GOODS • 555 Leslie Street, Ukiah, CA 95482 • Tel: 800 762 7325 • Real Goods is your complete resource for **ENERGY EFFICIENT LIVING** including compact fluorescent lighting. Free catalog. See p. 96.

RISING SUN ENTERPRISES • Box 1728, Basalt, CO 81621 • Tel: 303 927 8051 • *Energy-efficient lighting. Catalog and information.*

SIEMENS • PO Box 6032, Camarillo, CA 93011-6032 • Tel: 800 233 1106 • *Solar-powered outdoor lighting.*

SIERRA SOLAR SYSTEMS • 105 Argall Way, Nevada City, CA 95959 • Tel: 800 735 6790 • *Low-energy lighting. Catalog.*

SOLAR OUTDOOR LIGHTING • 3131 SE Waaler Street, Stuart, FL 34997 • Tel: 407 286 9461 • *Solar-powered outdoor lighting.*

TERON LIGHTING CORP • 124 W 66th Street, Cincinnati, OH 45216 • Tel: 513 242 7004 • *Manufacturers of decorative energy-saving fluorescent and HPS lighting fixtures.*

WHITE LIGHT ELECTRIC CO INC • The Light Bulb Place, 1821 University Avenue, Berkeley, CA 94704 • Tel: 510 845 8535 • *Energy-saving light fixtures and conversions plus bulbs of all kinds.*

ZOMEWORKS • 1011 Sawmill Road Northwest, PO Box 25805, Albuquerque, NM 87125 • Tel: 505 242 5354 Fax: 505 243 5187 • *Stand-alone solar-powered outdoor lighting system.*

STATE ENERGY OFFICES • See Resources p. 109 for details.

Candles and lamps ~ *page 105*

EARTH CARE CATALOG • Ukiah, CA 95482-8507 • Tel: 800 347 0070 Fax: 707 468 9486 • *Candles and candleholders for all occasions. Olive oil lamps too.*

EARTHWOOD • PO Box 193, Cedar Crest, NM 87008 • Tel: 505 281 1509 • *Terracotta and Buff sconces of high fired stoneware.*

ELAZAR'S OLIVE OIL LAMPS • PO Box 1384, Longview, WA 98632-7815 • Tel: 800 600 LAMP Fax: 206 425 9867 • *No soot, no smell, the most environmentally correct flame you can have. Cotton swab wicks. Catalog available upon request.*

EXTRAORDINARY DESIGN • 77 Conway Road, Southgate, London N14 7BD, United Kingdom • Tel & Fax: (+44) 181 808 3969 • *Elegant, fun knitted pendant light shades. Contact UK office for US and Canadian distributors.*

LOTUS LIGHT ENTERPRISES INC • Lotus Drive, Silver Lake, WI 53170 • Tel: 800 548 3824 • *Hand-dipped taper candles.*

Color ~ *page 106*

BARBARA BRENNAN SCHOOL OF HEALING • PO Box 2005, East Hampton, NY 11937 • Tel: 516 324 9745

INTERNATIONAL ASSOCIATION FOR COLOR THERAPY • 73 Elm Bank Gardens, London SW13 0NX, United Kingdom • Tel: (+44) 1453 832150

MANIFESTING INNER LIGHT • Sausolito, CA • Tel: 415 332 4663

JACK WIMPERIS STAINED GLASS • Piccadilly Mill, Stroud, Glos, United Kingdom • Tel: (+44) 1453 764151 • *Contact UK office for North American distributors.*

Air purification ~ page 112

ABSOLUTE ENVIRONMENTAL'S ALLERGY PRODUCTS AND SERVICES STORE • 2615 S University Drive, Davie, FL 33328 • Tel: 305 472 3773 / 800 329 3773

AERO HYGIENICS™ INC • 5247 San Fernando Road West, Los Angeles, CA 90039 • Tel: 800 346 4642 Fax: 213 245 3028 • *Feel the difference clean air makes. For cleaner, healthier indoor air start using HYGI-FLO® activated carbon filters today.*

AIRGUARD INDUSTRIES • PO Box 32578, Louisville, KY 40232 • Tel: 502 969 2304 Fax: 502 969 2759 • *Filters.*

AIR PURIFICATION PRODUCTS • PO Box 454, Royce City, TX 75089 • Tel: 214 635 9565 Fax: 214 635 2713

AIR QUALITY CONTROL • 16808 Chagrin Boulevard, Box 1090, Shaker Heights, OH 44120 • Tel: 216 561 7981

AIR QUALITY ENGINEERS • 23340 Winpark Drive, Minneapolis, MN 55427 • Tel: 800 328 0787

AIR QUALITY RESEARCH INC • 901 Grayson Street, Berkeley, CA 94710 • *Formaldehyde testing.*

AIR QUALITY SCIENCE INC • 1331 Capital Crescent, Atlanta, GA 30067 • Tel: 404 933 0638 • *Environmental chamber testing.*

ALLERGEN AIR FILTER CORPORATION • 5205, Ashbrook, Houston, TX 77081 • Tel: 909 668 2371 Fax: 713 668 6815 • *Filters.*

ALLERMED CORPORATION • 31 Steel Road, Wylie, TX 75098 • Tel: 214 442 4898 Fax: 214 442 4897 • *AllerMed High Efficiency Air Purifiers specially designed for anyone with allergies, asthma, respiratory problems, and chemical sensitivities. HEPA, Carbon, Ionizers.*

ALPINE AIR OF MASSACHUSETTS • 220 Reservoir Street, Needham Heights, MA 02194 • Tel: 800 628 2209 Fax: 617 449 8099

ALPINE AIR PURIFIERS • 844 10th Street, # A Santa Monica, CA 90403-1606 • Tel: 310 452 1293

AMERICAN ACADEMY OF ENVIRONMENTAL MEDICINE • PO Box 16106, Denver, CO 80216 • Tel: 303 622 9755 • *Contact for information about clinical ecologists.*

APPLIED TECHNICAL SERVICES INC • 1190 Atlanta Industrial Drive, Marietta, GA 30066 • *Formaldehyde testing.*

ASSAY TECHNOLOGY • 1070 East Meadow Circle, Palo Alto, CA 94303 • Tel: 415 424 9947 / 800 833 1258 Fax: 415 424 0336 • *The technology leader in personal monitoring for chemicals in the workplace. A full line of monitors includes: Formaldehyde monitor, Organic vapor monitor.*

ATMOSPHERE ALLIANCE • PO Box 10346, Olympia, WA 98502

AUSTIN AIR SIERRA • 701 Seneca Street, Buffalo, NY 14210 • Tel: 800 724 8403 • *HEPA type portable filters.*

BAUBIOLOGY HARDWARE • Box 3217, Prescott, AZ 86302 • Tel: 602 445 8225 • *Air filters, in-home testing kits. Catalog.*

BRK ELECTRONICS INC • 780 McClure Road, Aurora, IL 60504-2495 • Tel: 708 851 7330 • *Carbon dioxide detector.*

BRYANT • Box 70, Indianapolis, IN 46206 • Tel: 417 243 0851

CENTERCORE • 1355 West Front Street, Plainfield, NJ 07063 • Tel: 800 220 5640 • *Air filtration system.*

CITIZENS FOR A BETTER ENVIRONMENT • 122 Lincoln Boulevard, Suite 201, Venice, CA 90291 • Tel: 310 450 5192 Fax: 310 399 0769

COALITION FOR CLEAN AIR • 901 Wilshire Boulevard, Suite 350, Santa Monica, CA 90401 • Tel: 310 260 4770 Fax: 310 260 4774

MARY CORDARO • 12439 Magnolia Boulevard, no 263, Valley Village, CA 91607 • Tel: 310 838 2892 / 818 981 7245 Fax: 810 766 5882

CRSI • Pure Air Systems, Inc, Box 418, Plainfield, IN 46168 • Tel: 317 839 9135 • *HEPA air filtration systems, portable and whole house.*

THE DASUN COMPANY • PO Box 668, Escondido, CA 92033 • Tel: 800 433 8929 Fax: 619 746 8865 • *All natural Zeolite – Nature's natural air cleanser utilizing a natural negative electrostatic charge.*

DEL INDUSTRIES • 3428 Bullock Lane, San Luis Obispo, CA 93401 • Tel: 800 676 1335 • *Manufactures ozone systems for environmentally safe air and water purification. Whole house and portable units.*

DUST FREE • Box 519, Royse City, TN 75189 • Tel: 800 441 1107

ECOLOGY BY DESIGN (CONCEPTS FOR A TOXIC-FREE ENVIRONMENT) • Audrey Hoodkiss, 1341 Ocean Avenue, Suite 73, Santa Monica, CA 90401 • Tel: 310 394 4146 • *Full-service environmental consulting and design firm. Specialists in IAQ, air, and water purification. Distributor of environmental products.*

ECO SOURCE CATALOG • PO Box 1656, Sebastopol, CA 95473-1656 • Tel: 707 829 3506 Fax: 707 829 7811 • *Air purification equipment.*

EFM COMPANY • 86 Interlaken Road, West Stockbridge, MA 01266 • Tel: 413 637 1929 Fax: 413 637 2826

ELECTROCORP • 1435 North Dutton Avenue, Santa Rosa, CA 95401 • Tel: 707 525 0711 • *Ionizers.*

ENVIROCLEAN PRODUCTS • Tel: 800 866 0037 • *'Living Air' purification units. Free information.*

ENVIRONMENTAL DEFENSE FUND • 5655 College Avenue, Oakland, CA 94618 • Tel: 510 658 8008

ENVIRONMENTALLY SOUND PRODUCTS • Sims Company, Inc, 8845 Orchard Tree Lane, Towson, MD 21286 • Tel: 800 886 5432 • *Household products for green and healthy living.*

ENVIRONMENTAL PURIFICATION SYSTEMS • PO Box 191, Concord, CA 64522 • Tel: 510 284 2129 / 800 829 2129 • *Air filtration systems.*

ENVIRONMENTAL SYSTEMS • 1052 170th Street, Plainfield, IO 50666-9786 • Tel: 319 276 3049 Fax: 319 276 4882

ENVIRONMENTAL TESTING & TECHNOLOGY • PO Box 230369, Encinitas, CA 92023 • Tel: 619 436 5990 Fax: 619 436 9448 • *Indoor air quality testing. Environmental building inspections.*

FILTRX • 11 Hansen Avenue, New City, NY 10956 • Tel: 914 638 9708 • *High-efficiency control of fine dusts, pollens etc.*

FOR YOUR HEALTH PRODUCTS • 6623 Hillandale Road, Chevy Chase, MD 20815 • Tel: 301 654 1127 Fax: 301 654 2125 • *Many home health products including air filters.*

E L FOUST CO INC • PO Box 105, Elmhurst, IL 60126 • Tel: 708 834 5104 / 800 225 9549 Fax: 708 834 5341 • *Since 1974 we have manufactured a high quality line of air purifiers for home, office, and automobiles. Independently tested to achieve results to control indoor air pollution including smoke, allergens, and chemicals. Products are also available to improve your home's environment. Free catalogs and brochures.*

GROUP AGAINST SMOG POLLUTION (GASP) • 875 North College Avenue, Claremont,CA 91711 • Tel: 714 621 8000 Fax: 714 621 8419

W W GRAINGER • 5959 W Howard Street, Chicago, IL 60648 • Tel: 708 982 9000 • *Catalog includes filters.*

HEALTHY ENVIRONMENTS • PO Box 423, Snowmass, CO 81654 • Tel: 303 925 4400 • *Air and EMF testing. Catalog.*

HEALTHY HABITATS • Carl Grimes, 1811 S Quebec Way 99, Denver, CO 80231 • Tel: 303 671 9653 Fax: 303 751 0416 • *Indoor air quality mitigator. See p. 120.*

HONEYWELL INC • 1985 Douglas Drive N, Golden Valley MN 55422 • Tel: 800 543 9149 / 612 542 3357 • *Electrostatic filters.*

HONEYWELL ENVIRACARE FILTERS • Environmental Air Control, 747 Bowman Avenue, Hagerstown, MD 21740 • Tel: 800 332 1110

HURST ENGINEERING RESEARCH & TESTING LABORATORIES • Route 4, Box 59, Highway 211, Winder, GA 30680 • Tel: 404 867 3187 • *Indoor air quality information.*

IDEAL ENVIRONMENTS • Roger Maurice, 401 W Adams, Fairfield, IO 52256 • Tel: 515 472 6547

INTERNATIONAL INSTITUTE FOR BAU-BIOLOGIE & ECOLOGY INC • PO Box 387, Clearwater, FL 34615 • Tel: 813 461 4371 Fax: 813 441 4373 • *See p. 192*

ION & LIGHT • 2263 Sacramento Street, San Francisco, CA 94115 • Tel: 415 346 1682 Fax: 415 346 0529 • *Ozonators, ionizers.*

LAWRENCE GUST • 4091 Echo Woods Drive, Atlanta, GA 30021 • Tel: 404 292 9784

LAWRENCE BERKELEY LABORATORY, ENERGY & ENVIRON-MENT DIVISION • University of California, Berkeley, CA 94720 • Tel: 510 486 5001 • *Indoor Environment Program involves testing and measuring indoor air quality.*

HAL LEVIN & ASSOCIATES • 2548 Empire Grade, Santa Cruz, CA 95060 • Tel: 408 425 3946 • *Environmental consultation, publishes "Indoor Air Bulletin".*

DOUGLAS LICHTER • 202 12th Avenue, Indian Rocks Beach, FL 34635 • Tel: 813 596 7786.

SUSAN McCRONE • Safe Home Detective, W294 N 5260 Merton Avenue, Hartland, WI 53029 • Tel: 414 367 7308

MULTIPRO ENVIRONMENTAL • 1021 Lake Lane, Pennsburg, PA 18073 • Tel: 800 900-FIRST • *Air treatment products. Testing and free consultation.*

NATIONAL RESOURCES DEFENSE COUNCIL • 40 W 20th Street, New York, NY 10011 • Tel: 212 727 4474

NEWTRON PRODUCTS • 3874 Virginia Avenue, Cincinnati, OH 45227 • Tel: 800 543 9149 • *Electrostatic filters.*

NIGRA ENTERPRISES • 5699 Kanan Road, Agoura, CA 91301 • Tel: 818 889 6877 • *Environmental systems broker: Air systems.*

NONTOXIC ENVIRONMENTS • 9392 Gribble Road, Canby, OR 97013 • Tel: 503 266 5244 Fax: 503 266 5242 • *Mail-order company specializing in products for aware and chemically sensitive individuals.*

O3 LLC • PO Box 40061, Overland Park, KS 66204 • Tel: 913 642 3516 Fax: 913 642 3516 • *Ozone Indicator.*

PACE INCORPORATED • 1710 Douglas Drive North, Minneapolis, MN 55422 • Tel: 612 544 5543 • *Publishes "Environmental Regulatory Review".*

POLLUTION PROBE FOUNDATION • 12 Madison Avenue, Toronto, Ontario, Canada, M5R 2S1 • Tel: 416 926 1907 • *Organization dedicated to creating positive environmental change through action, education, and the use of research. With increasing public support and awareness, Pollution Probe Foundation works with government and industry toward building a sustainable society. Write for information packages on a wide range of issues.*

PURE AIR SYSTEMS INC • PO Box 418, Plainfield, IN 46168 • Tel: 317 839 9135 • *Air filtration system to combat indoor air pollution.*

QUALITY ENVIRONMENTS • 2414 McDuffie Street, Houston, TX 77019 • Tel: 713 520 5900 • *Air cleaners.*

QUANTUM ELECTRONICS CORPORATION • 31 Graystone Street, Warwick, RI 02886 • Tel: 401 732 6770 Fax: 401 732 6772 • *Manufacture ozone generators/air purifiers.*

QUANTUM GROUP INC • 11211 Sorrento Valley Road, No D, San Diego, CA 92121 • *Carbon monoxide testing.*

SAFE ENVIRONMENTS • 2625 Acatraz Avenue, Suite 342, Berkeley, CA 94705 • Tel: 510 549 9693 Fax: 510 849 4465 • *EMF and indoor air quality inspections.*

SAFE HAVEN ENVIRONMENTAL PRODUCTS AND CONSULTING • 5858 North Magnolia, Chicago, IL 60660 • Tel: 800 996-PURE • *Living Air Purification Systems utilize the principles of nature to create activated fresh air indoors.*

SHELTER ECOLOGY • 39 Pine Ridge Road, Asheville, NC 28804 • Tel: 704 251 5888

SIMS COMPANY INC • 8845 Orchard Tree Lane, Towson, MD 21286 • Tel: 800 886 5432 • *Carbon monoxide test kit.*

THERMA-STOR PRODUCTS GROUP • DEC International Inc, PO Box 8050, Madison, WI 53708 • Tel: 800 533 7533 / 608 222 3484 Fax: 608 222 1447 • *Air purifying ventilator.*

THURMOND AIR QUALITY SYSTEMS • Box 940001, Plano, TX 75094-0001 • Tel: 214 422 4000 / 800 AIRPURE • *Whole-house system.*

UNIVERSAL AIR PRECIPITATOR • 1500 McCully, Monroeville, PA 15146 • Fax: 412 372 0803 • *Electronic air cleaners remove airborne particulates to .01 micron at 96% efficiency.*

Radon ~ page 113

AIR CHECK INC • 570 Butler Bridge Road, Fletcher, NC 28732 • Tel: 704 684 0893 / 800 247 2435 Fax: 704 684 8498 • *Charcoal packet test. Alpha Track 30 day minimum – maximum 1 year test.*

AMERICAN LUNG ASSOCIATION (ALA) • 1740 Broadway, New York, NY 10019-4374 • Tel: 800 586 4872 / 212 315 8700 Fax: 212 265 5642 • *Call for information about Radon testing, mitigation, and lung health. Also for qualified Radon testing firms. ALA also publish "Indoor Air Pollution Fact Sheet - Radon".*

ECODEX CORPORATION • 594 Marrett Road, Suite 18, Lexington, MA 02173 • Tel: 617 862 4300 • *EPA approved Radon testing. Publishes "Indoor Health".*

ENVIRONMENTAL PROTECTION AGENCY (EPA) • Public Information Center, 820 Quincy Street Northwest, Washington DC 20011 • Indoor Air Hotline: 800 438 4318 / 601 688 2457 Radon information: 617 565 4502 • *Information and resource on indoor air pollution. Call for advisory services and technical publications on Radon.*

ENVIRONMENTAL RESOURCE SERVICES INC • 1624 North 11th Avenue, Phoenix, AZ 85007 • Tel: 602 258 6010 Fax: 602 258 6119 • *Advises on and tests, ventilation systems and testing procedures.*

INFORM INC • 120 Wall Street, 16th Floor, New York, NY 10005-4001 • Tel: 212 361 2400 Fax: 212 361 2412 e-mail: Inform@igc.apc.org • *National non-profit environmental research organization currently focusing on strategies to reduce industrial and municipal waste and preserve air and water quality. Publishes a number of books on toxic substances including* Tackling Toxics in Everyday Products, *a directory of organizations concerned about toxics in consumer and building products.*

RADON DETECTION SERVICES • 1011 Brookside Road, Suite 270, Allentown, PA 18106 • Tel: 215 481 9555

RADON ENVIRONMENTAL MONITORING INC • 3334 Commercial Avenue, Northbrook, IL 60662 • Tel: 312 256 9494

RADON LTD • 411 North Weinback Avenue, Evansville, IN 47711 • Tel: 812 479 3110

THE RADON PROJECT • PO Box 90069, Pittsburgh, PA 15224

RADON, SOILS, WATER TESTING LABORATORY • 7080 Price-Hilliard Road, Plain City, OH 43064 • Tel: 614 873 8821

RADON TESTING CORP OF AMERICA • Trent Building, Box 258, Irviongton, NY 10533 • Tel: 800 457 2366 • *Main-in radon test kits.*

REAL GOODS • 555 Leslie Street, Ukiah, CA 95482 • Tel: 800 762 7325 • *Real Goods is your complete resource for ENERGY EFFICIENT LIVING. Products include Radon detector and Radon Alert test kits. Free catalog. See p. 96.*

REEP INC • 300 Corporate Court, So Plainfield, NJ 07080 • Tel: 800 REEP-INC. E PERM • *System, mail-in testing kit.*

SAFER HOME TEST KIT • 325 Oakhurst, Beverley Hills, CA 90210 • Tel: 310 550 7600 Fax: 310 552 0011

TELEDYNE ISOTOPES • 50 Van Buren Avenue, PO Box 1235, Westwood, NJ 06775-1235 • Tel: 800 666 0222 Fax: 201 664 5586 • *Charcoal canister, radon home/commercial test kit.*

U.S. TOXIC SUBSTANCE TESTING • 804 Second Street Pike, Southampton, PA 18966 • Tel: 215 953 9200 Fax: 215 953 8837

Fresh air – naturally ~ page 114-15

AUROMA INTERNATIONAL INC • PO Box 1008, Silver Lake, WI 53170 • Tel: 414 889 8569 • *Incense sticks and burners.*

CLEAR LIGHT • The Cedar Company, Box 551, State Road 165 Placitas, NM 87043 • Tel: 505 867 2381 Fax: 505 867 2925 • *Cedar spray air scents.*

THE DASUN COMPANY • PO Box 668, Escondido, CA 92033 • Tel: 619 480 8929 / 800 433 8929 Fax: 619 746 8865 • *All natural Zeolite - nature's natural air cleanser utilizing negative electrostatic charge.*

MIA ROSE AIR THERAPY • 3555 B Harbor Gateway S, Cost Mesa, CA 92626 • Tel: 800 292 6339 / 714 662 5465 • *Pet Air® contains natural citrus scents to eliminate odors and clean the air naturally.*

NATURAL CHEMISTRY • 244 Elm Street, New Canaan, CT 06840 • Tel: 203 966 8761 • *Natural enzyme odor control formula.*

NATURE'S MIST • James M McLaughlin, New Products Inc, 1444 Old Louisquisset Park, Lincoln, RI 02865 • *Air freshener.*

NON-SCENTS • Patricia Anderson, Van Cleave and Associates, 133 North Huffman Street, Naperville, IL 60540-4816 • Tel: 800 822 9499 • *Distributor natural compound (zeolites) for odor elimination, cat litter compound.*

PLANTS FOR CLEAN AIR COUNCIL • 10210 Bald Hill Road, Mitchellville, MD 20721 • Tel: 301 459 7678 Fax: 301 459 6533 • *Different plants absorb different pollutants and help to clean the air. Call or write for more information.*

Ventilation ~ page 116

AIR CHANGER HRVs • Preston Brock Manufacturing Co, Box 3367, 1297 Industrial Road, Cambridge, Ontario, Canada, N3H 4T8

AIRXCHANGE INC • 401 VFW Drive, Rockland, MA 02370 • Tel: 617 871 4816

ALTECH ENERGY • 7009 Raywood Road, Madison, WI 53713 • Tel: 608 221 4499 Fax: 608 221 2824 • *Manufacturer of NEWAIRE™ air-to-air heat exchange ventilators.*

AMERICAN ALDES VENTILATION CORP • 4537 Northgate Court, Sarasota, FL 34234 • Tel: 813 351 3441

CAN-AERECO VENTILATION • 5 Sandhill Court, Unit C, Brampton, Canada, L6T 5J5 • Tel: 905 790 8667 Fax: 905 790 1133

CONSERVATION ENERGY SYSTEMS • Box 582416, Minneapolis, MN 55458-2416 • Tel: 800 667 3717 and Canada 306 242 3663

RICHARD L CROWTHER • Architect, 401 Madison Street, Unit A, Denver, CO 80206 • Tel: 303 338 1875 • *Architecture, passive solar design and engineering, publishing, invention, newsletter. Author of several books on air quality.*

CRSI Pure Air Systems Inc • Box 418, Plainfield, IN 46168 • Tel: 317 839 9135

ENERGY CRAFTED HOMES • 441 Stuart Street, Boston, MA 01230 • Tel: 617 236 1500 • *Manual on energy-efficient home construction, ventilation, safe indoor air.*

ENVIRONMENTAL AIR LTD • Box 10, Cocagne, New Brunswick, Canada, EOA 1KO • Tel: 506 576 6672

ENVIRONMENTAL RESOURCE SERVICES INC • 1624 North 11th Avenue, Phoenix, AZ 85007 • Tel: 602 258 6010 Fax: 602 258 6119 • *Advises on and tests, ventilation systems and testing procedures.*

FANTECH INC • 1712 Northgate Boulevard, Sarasota, FL 34234 • Tel: 813 351 2947 / 800 747 1762 Fax: 813 355 0377 • *Manufacturer of innovative ventilation fans - phone for your local distributor.*

THE HEALTHY HOUSE INSTITUTE • 430 N Sewell Road, Bloomington, IN 47408 • Tel: 812 332 5073 Fax: 812 332 5073 • *Provides information on known negative effects of common building materials to architects, designers, builders, and home owners. See p. 199.*

HONEYWELL INC • 1985 Douglas Drive North, Golden Valley, MN 55422 • Tel: 800 543 9149 / 612 542 3357

INDOOR AIR QUALITY INFORMATION CLEARINGHOUSE • Tel: 800 438 4318 / 301 585 9020

INTERAGENCY INDOOR AIR COUNCIL • 1200 6th Avenue, Seattle, WA 98101 • Tel: 206 442 2589 • *Publishes the 'Washington State Indoor Air Resource Guide'.*

MOUNTAIN ENERGY & RESOURCES INC • 15800 W Sixth Avenue, Golden, CO 80401 • Tel: 303 279 4971

REGGIO REGISTER COMPANY • PO Box 571, Ayer, MA 01432-0511 • Tel: 508 772 3493 Fax: 508 772 5513 • *Decorative cast-iron or wooden grilles for cold air return outlets.*

ROCKY CREEK HYDRO • 2173 Rocky Creek Road, Colville, WA 99114 • Fax: 509 684 3973 • *Manufacturer of retrofitted ceiling fans which work on DC power.*

R & S ENVIRO PRODUCTS LIMITED • 1 Church Street, Unit 0, Keswick, Ontario, Canada, L4O 3E9 • Tel: 905 476 5336 Fax: 905 476 0475 • *Air vents.*

THERMA-STOR PRODUCTS GROUP • DEC International Inc, PO Box 8050, Madison, WI 53708 • Tel: 800 533 7533 / 608 222 3484 Fax: 608 222 1447 • *Air purifying ventilators, heat recovery ventilators, fans, home ventilating systems and supplies.*

VENMAR VENTILATION • 1715 Haggerty Street, Drummondville, Quebec, Canada, J2C 5P7 • Tel: 819 477 6226

VENT-AIRE • 4850 Northpark Drive, Colorado Springs, CO 80918 • Tel: 719 599 9080

Humidity ~ *page* 117

AMERICAN SOCIETY OF HEATING, REFRIGERATION AND AIR-CONDITIONING ENGINEERS INC (ASHRAE) • 1791 Tullie Circle NE Atlanta, GA 30325-2305 • Tel: 404 636 8400

APPROPRIATE TECHNOLOGY • Box 975, 7 Technology Drive, Brattleboro, VT 05302-0975 • Tel: 802 257 4500/4501 • *Quilted insulation fabric, window, air conditioner cover, vent covers.*

ASSAY TECHNOLOGY • 1070 East Meadow Circle, Palo Alto, CA 94303 • Tel: 415 424 9947 / 800 833 1258 Fax: 415 424 0336 • *The technology leader in personal monitoring for chemicals in the workplace. A full line of monitors includes: Formaldehyde monitor, Organic vapor monitor.*

FRIEDRICH AIR CONDITIONING CO • 4200 North PanAm Expressway, PO Box 1540, San Antonio, TX 78295-1540 • Tel: 210 225 2000 Fax: 210 228 1709 • *Electronic air cleaners.*

HEAT PIPE TECHNOLOGY INC • 803 NE 1st Street, PO Box 999, Alachua, FL 32615 • Tel: 904 462 3464 Fax: 904 462 2041 • *Dehumidifier heat pipes for whole house dehumidification. Energy saving technology.*

P & K MICROBIOLOGY SERVICES INC • 1879 Old Cuthbert Road, Unit 5, Cherry Hill, NJ 08034 • Tel: 609 427 4044 Fax: 609 427 0232 • *Microbiological laboratory analysis for bioaerosol mold and bacteria.*

SANYO FISHER AIR CONDITIONING • 21350 Lassen Street, Chatsworth, CA 91311 • Tel: 818 998 7322

Paints and varnishes ~ *pages* 124-6

AMERICAN FORMULATING & MANUFACTURING (AFM) • 350 West Ash Street, Suite 700, San Diego, CA 92101 • Tel: 800 239 0321 / 619 239 0321 Fax 619 239 0565 • *Coatings, cleaners, sealers formulated without toxic chemicals. SafeChoice products prevent indoor air pollution, and are safe for the chemically sensitive.*

ALLSAFE • 5364 Pan American NE • Albuquerque, NM 87109 • Tel: 505 881 2103 • *Fewer additives in paints.*

AQUAZAR • Stan Schwartz, 5162 Homer Lane, Placntia, CA 92670 • Tel: 714 528 4598 • *Water-based polyurethane.*

AURO GmbH • Postfach 1238, D-38002, Braumschweig, Germany *See below for North American suppliers.*

AURO/TEEKAH INC • 5015 Yonge Street, North York, Ontario, Canada, M2N 5P1 • Tel: 416 229 4199 • *Auro European natural paints, adhesives, sealers etc.*

W M BARR & CO • PO Box 1879, Memphis, TN 38101 • Tel: 901 775 0100 • *Easy Off Paint Stripper.*

BAUBIOLOGIE HARDWARE • Box 3217, Prescott, AZ 86302 • Tel: 602 445 8225 • *AFM paints and sealers.*

BEST PAINT CO • PO Box 3922, Seattle, WA 98124 • Tel: 206 783 9938 • *Low VOC, low odor paints.*

BIO-BUILDING • PO Box 1561, Sebastopol, CA 95473 • Tel: 707 823 2569

BIOFA, BAU INC • PO Box 190, Alton NH 03809 • Tel: 603 226 3868 • *Natural paints and varnishes.*

BIX MANUFACTURING COMPANY • PO Box 69, Ashland City, TN 37015 • Tel: 615 792 3260 • *Bix Hydro.*

BONAKEMI USA INC • 14805 East Moncrieff Place, Aurora, CO 80011-1207 • Tel: 800 872 5515 / 303 371 1411 • *Our fillers, stains, sealers, finishes, and maintenance products are the most durable and environmentally safe products available worldwide.*

CARVER TRIPP • Parks Corporation, One West Street, Fall River, MA 02720 • Tel: 1 800 225 8543 Fax: 508 674 8404 • *Safe & Simple™ products free of toxic vapors and harsh solvent odors.*

CON-LUX COATINGS • Edison, NJ 08818-0847 • Tel: 908 287 4000 • *Con-Lux color dynamics are free of lead and mercury compounds. Low VOC content.*

CREATIVE TECHNOLOGIES GROUP INC • 14 Whitsett Street, Greenville, SC 29601 • Tel: 803 271 9194 • *Woodfinishers Pride.*

TAMARA DIAMOND • Tel: 310 827 1080 • *Product Consultant. Eco-Safe Building Products.*

EARTH STUDIO • Tel: 707 823 2569 • *Retails AURO natural paints and finishes. We also offer several journals dealing with issues of building ecology.*

ECO-DESIGN COMPANY • 1365 Rufina Circle, Santa Fe, NM 87501 • Tel: 505 438 3448 Fax: 505 438 6315 • *'Bio-shield' and 'Livos' paints from Germany. Healthy home products. Publish "The Natural Choice Catalog".*

ECO HOUSE (1988) INC • Livos Plant Chemistry Canada, PO Box 220, Stn A Fredericton, NB, Canada, E3B 4Y9 • Tel: 506 366 3529 Fax: 506 366 3577 • *Low toxicity paint and home products.*

ECOLOGY BOX • 425 East Washington, Ann Arbor, MI 48101 • Tel: 313 662 9131 • *Filters, sealers, paints, adhesives etc.*

ECOS PAINT • PO Box 375, Saint Johnsbury, VT 05819 • Tel: 802 748 9144 • *VOC-free paints.*

ENVIRESOURCE INC • 110 Madison Avenue North, Bainbridge Island, WA 98110 • 206 842 9785 • *Non-toxic paints and finishes.*

ENVIRONMENTAL BY DESIGN • PO Box 95016, South Van CSC, Vancouver, BC, Canada, V6P 6V4 • Tel & Fax: 604 266 7721 • *Guide to healthy interior materials. See p. 133.*

ENVIRONMENTAL DEFENSE FUND • 257 Park Avenue South, New York, NY 10010 • Tel: 212 505 2100 • *A national non-profit organization which links science, economics, and law to create innovative, economically viable solutions to today's environmental problems.*

ENVIRESOURCE INC • 110 Madison Avenue North, Bainbridge Island, WA 98110 • Tel: 206 842 9785 • *Non-toxic paints and finishes.*

ENVIRO SPRAY • South Bay Depot Road, Fields Landing, CA 95537-0365 • Tel: 707 443 9323 • *Water-based, CFC free, acrylic enamel spray paint.*

EPA PUBLIC INFORMATION CENTER • 820 Quincy Street Northwest, Washington, DC 20011 • Tel: 202 829 3535

FRAZEE PAINT AND WALLCOVERINGS • 6625 Miramar Road, San Diego, CA 92121 • Tel: 619 276 9500 Fax: 619 552 3203 • *Frazee Paint manufactures a variety of high quality paints incorporating the latest technology to create environmentally friendly, low odor, low VOC coatings.*

GARRETT WADE CO • 161 Avenue of the Americas, New York, NY 10013 • Tel: 800 221 2942 / 212 807 1155 • *Tried & True Varnish Oil and Original Wood Finish. Heat treated Linseed oil.*

GENERAL FINISHES • PO Box 51567, New Berlin, WI 53151 • Tel: 414 786 6050 Fax: 414 786 6509 • *Environmentally friendly, water-based staining system, country colors, and clear finishes.*

GLIDDEN SPRED 2000 • 925 Euclid Avenue, Cleveland, OH 44115 • Tel: 800 221 4100 • *The Clean Air Choice™- no VOCs.*

GREEN SEAL • 1250 23rd Street NW, Suite 275, Washington, DC 2003 1101 • Tel: 202 331 7337 • *Grants environmental seal of approval and sets standards for choosing products. Standards are available to consumers. See p. 153.*

HARMONY EXCHANGE • Route 2, Box 843, Big Hill Road, Boone NC 28607 • Tel: 800 756 9663 • *Water-based floor finishes.*

THE HEALTHY HOUSE INSTITUTE • 430 N Sewell Road, Bloomington, IN 47408 • Tel & Fax: 812 332 5073 • *Promotes healthier house construction and lifestyle. Provides books, videos and other information on known negative effects of common building materials to architects, designers, builders, and home owners. See p. 199.*

HOUSEHOLD HAZARDOUS WASTE PROJECT • PO Box 108, Springfield, MO 65804 • Tel: 417 836 5777 • *A community health and environment education program sponsored by the Missouri Department of Natural Resources. Publishes the informative and comprehensive "Guide to Hazardous Products Around the Home", which discusses in detail everything from labeling to hazardous ingredients and homemade alternatives.*

INFORM INC • 120 Wall Street, 16th Floor, New York, NY 10005-4001 • Tel: 212 361 2400 Fax: 212 361 2412 • *National non-profit environmental research organization currently focusing on strategies to reduce industrial and municipal waste and preserve air and water quality. Publishes a number of books on toxic substances including "Tackling Toxics in Everyday Products", a directory of organizations concerned about toxics in consumer and building products.*

INTERNATIONAL INSTITUTE FOR BAU-BIOLOGIE & ECOLOGY INC • PO Box 387, Clearwater, FL 34615 • Tel: 813 461 4371 Fax: 813 441 4373 • *Contact for advice on organic paints, stains, strippers, and varnishes. See p. 192.*

KAUPERT CHEMICAL & CONSULTING INC • 39119 Deerhorn Road, Springfield, OR 97478 • Tel: 503 747 2509 • *All-purpose wood and masonry sealants, Protect-n-Seal, and Seal-n-Oil.*

MILE HIGH CROWN INC • DBA Crown Corporation, NA, 1801 Wynkop Street, Suite 235, Denver, CO 80202 • Tel: 303 292 1313 Fax: 303 292 1933

MILLER PAINT COMPANY • 317 SE Grand Avenue, Portland, OR 97214 • Tel: 503 233 4021 • *Low biocide, no fungicide paints. Large selection of interior and exterior primers/finishes available.*

MURCO • 300 NE 21st Street, Fort Worth, TX 76106 • Tel: 817 626 1987 • *Low-toxic paints and drywall filler.*

NATIONAL FOUNDATION FOR THE CHEMICALLY HYPERSENSITIVE • PO Box, Wrightsville Beach, NC 28480 • Tel: 919 256 5391

NATIONAL INSTITUTE OF HEALTH AND SAFETY • 9000 Rockville Pike, Bethesda, MD 20814 • Tel: 301 496 4000

NATIONAL TOXICS CAMPAIGN • 37 Temple Place, 4th Floor, Boston, MA 02111 • Tel: 617 482 1477

THE NATURAL CHOICE, LIVOS • Livos Plant Chemistry, 1365 Rufina Circle, Santa Fe, NM 87501 • Tel: 505 438 3448 Fax: 505 438 0199 • *Non-toxic home products, natural paints, adhesives, wood finishes, cleansers. Catalog.*

NEGLEY PAINT CO • PO Box 47848, San Antonio, TX 78265-8848 • Tel: 512 651 6996 • *Low toxic paint.*

NIGRA ENTERPRISES • 5699 Kanan Road, Agoura, CA 91301 • Tel: 818 889 6877 • *Environmental systems broker: paints, sealers etc.*

OLD FASHIONED MILK PAINT CO • Box 222, Groton, MA 01450 • Tel: 508 448 6336 Fax: 508 448 2754 • *Natural casein paints made from a milk base.*

OSTERMAN & SCHEIWE, USA • OS Color, PO Box 669, Spanaway, WA 98387 • Tel: 800 344 9663 • *Natural oil based OS Color, Wood Waxes, and Paints.*

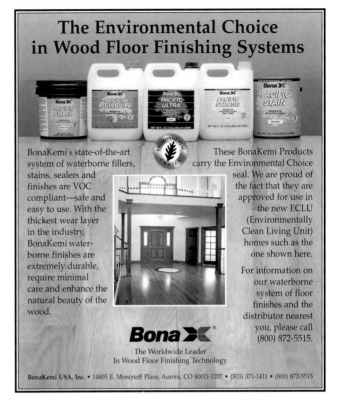

The Environmental Choice in Wood Floor Finishing Systems

BonaKemi's state-of-the-art system of waterborne fillers, stains, sealers and finishes are VOC compliant—safe and easy to use. With the thickest wear layer in the industry, BonaKemi waterborne finishes are extremely durable, require minimal care and enhance the natural beauty of the wood.

These BonaKemi Products carry the Environmental Choice seal. We are proud of the fact that they are approved for use in the new ECLU (Environmentally Clean Living Unit) homes such as the one shown here.

For information on our waterborne system of floor finishes and the distributor nearest you, please call (800) 872-5515.

Bona X
The Worldwide Leader
In Wood Floor Finishing Technology

BonaKemi USA, Inc. • 14805 E. Moncrieff Place, Aurora, CO 80011-1207 • (303) 371-1411 • (800) 872-5515

PACE CHEMICAL INDUSTRIES INC • 3681 Sagunto Street, Unit 104, PO Box 1946, Santa Ynez, CA 93460 • Tel & Fax: 805 686 0745 • *Right-On Crystal Aire, a hard clear finish, low-toxic paints, sealers, varnishes.*

PAINT MAGIC • 2426 Fillmore Street, San Francisco, CA 94115 • Tel: 415 292 7780 Fax: 415 292 7782 • *Jocasta Innes products.*

PALMER INDUSTRIES INC • 10611 Old Annapolis Road, Frederick, MD 21701-3347 • Tel: 301 898 7848 Fax: 301 898 3312 • *Palmer Industries manufacters specialty Coating and Insulation for the commercial and residential markets. Our research and development of environmentally safe products for the chemically sensitive has bee ongoing for 18 years. Solvent-free wood and masonry coatings.*

POLLUTION PROBE FOUNDATION • 12 Madison Avenue, Toronto, Ontario, Canada, M5R 2S1 • Tel: 416 926 1907

PRATT & LAMBERT PAINTS • 75 Tonawanda Street, PO Box 22, Buffalo, NY 14207 • Tel: 716 873 6000 Fax: 716 873 9920

RAINFOREST HARVEST ECO-WOOD FINISHES • 53A Church Street, Cambridge, MA 02138 • *Beeswax polish from the rainforest.*

REPUBLIC PAINTS • 1128 N Highland Avenue, Hollywood, CA 90038 • Tel: 213 957 3060 • *Pristine latex is the Clean Air Paint. It is virtually odorless and doesn't contain any petroleum solvents (VOCs) that cause air pollution. It has greater hiding power than most latex paints and can be used on plaster, drywall, wood masonry, and primed metal surfaces.*

SCIENTIFIC CERTIFICATION SYSTEMS (SCS) • 1611 Telegraph Avenue, Suite 1111, Oakland, CA 94612-2118 • Tel: 510 832 1415 • *Grants independent certification of environmental claims. See p. 198.*

SEA STAR TRADING COMPANY • PO Box 513, Newport, OR 97365 • Tel: 503 265 9616 / 800 359 7571 Fax: 503 265 3228 • *Hydrocote wood finishes.*

SHAKER SHOPS WEST • PO Box 487, Inverness, CA 94937 • Tel: 415 669 7256 Fax: 415 669 7327 • *Classic Shaker design authentically reproduced furniture, accessories, and milk paint. Many kits allow assembly and finishing without toxins. Catalog $2.50.*

SINAN CO • PO Box 857, Davis, CA 95617-0857 • Tel: 916 753 3104 • *AURO natural paints and sealers imported from Germany.*

THE SOFTNESS GROUP • 250 Park Avenue, SO, 9th Floor, New York, NY 10003 • Tel: 212 674 7600 • *Woodfinisher's Pride.*

SPECIALTY ENVIRONMENTAL TECH INC • 4520 Glenmeade Lane, Auburn Hills, MI 49326 • Tel: 313 340 0400

SPECTRA-TONE PAINT COMPANY • 9535 Klingerman Street, South El Monte, CA 91733-1775 • Tel: 800 272 4687

WEATHER BOS • 1774 Rainier Avenue S, Suite 130, Seattle, WA 98144 • Tel: 206 329 3663

WOODWORKER'S STORE CATALOG • 21801 Industrial Boulevard, Rogers, MN 55374 • Tel: 612 428 2199 • *Woodfinishers Pride wood finish, non-solvent, non-toxic.*

WOODWORKERS SUPPLY • 1108 N Glenn Road, Casper, WY 82601 • Tel: 800 645 9292 • *The only paint remover to strip aggressively without dangerous odor, according to "Fine Woodworking" (November 1994 p. 121)*

WM ZINSSER & CO INC • 173 Belmont Drive, Somerset, NJ 08875 • Tel & Fax: 602 460 5343 • *Manufacturers of shellac, shellac-base, B-I-N primer-sealer, and other decorating specialities.*

Wall finishes ~ page 128

See also listings for Paints, above

COVERAGE INC • Box 8498, Warwick, RI 02888 • Tel: 401 738 1197 • *Wallpaper made of recycled paper. Covers flaws in wall with prior caulking.*

CROWN CORPORATION NA • 1801 Wynkoop Street, Denver, CO 80202 • Tel: 800 422 2099 / 303 292 1313 • *Anaglypta supadurable wall covering made of 90% recycled cotton and 10% forest managed trees from Finland. No chemical treatments, no backing, no glues.*

DESIGN MATERIALS INC • 241 South 55th Street, Kansas City, KS 66106 • Tel: 800 654 6451 Fax: 913 342 9826 • *Sisal wall covering.*

EUROTAP • 12228 Venice Boulevard, # 146 Los Angeles, CA 90066 • Tel: 800 388 9255 • *Wallpaper made of recycled paper, textured, covers flaws in wall without prior caulking, no additives.*

FIBERSTONE QUARRIES INC • PO. Box 1026, 1112 King Street, Quincy, FL 323551 • Tel: 904 627 1083 Fax: 904 627 2640 • *'Molded stone' product simulates quarried and carved stone. Wall veneer and trim system and custom decorative elements from non-toxic, recycled cellulose and post-industrial waste.*

FLEXI WALL SYSTEMS • Box 88, Liberty, SC 29657 • Tel: 800 843 5394 • *"Faster Plaster" Gypsum coated, low toxicity wall fabric.*

GUILFORD OF MAINE • 5300 Corporate Grove Drive, Southeast 200, Grand Rapids, MO 49512 • Tel: 616 554 2250 • *Ecodeme is a wall fabric product. using 44% post-consumer recycled waste.*

MAYA ROMANOFF CORPORATION • 1730 W Greenleaf, Chicago, IL 60626 • Tel: 312 465 6909. Fax: 312 465 7089 • *Environmentally healthier wallpaper.*

OHIO HEMPERY • 7002 SR 329, Caysville, OH 45735 • Tel: 800 BUY HE • *Hemp fabrics by the roll or by the meter. Hemp seed, oil, paper, twine, body care, and other products.*

PALLAS TEXTILES • 8687 Melrose Avenue, Pacific Design Center, Los Angeles, CA 90069 • Tel: 310 659 2133 • *"Earth Paper" is a unique combination of natural materials: it comprises 65% pulp, 25% stone powder, and 8% straw.*

PATTERN PEOPLE INC • 10 Floyd Street, Derry, NH 03038 • Tel: 603 432 7180 • *Environmentally friendly hand painted paper panels for walls. See p. 136.*

STONEWARE TILE CO • 1650 Progress Drive, Richmond, IN 47374 • Tel: 317 935 4760 Fax: 317 935 3971 • *Division of Terra-Green Technologies. Manufacturer of Traffic Tile - a single-fired glass-bonded tile manufactured with over 70% recycled glass. Can be used safely on floors and walls in interior and exterior applications.*

SWEDE-TECH • 3081 E Commercial Boulevard, Suite 103, Ft Lauderdale, FL 33308 • Tel: 305 771 0204 • *Also available at Environmental Construction Outfitters, Tel: 800 238 5008 • Glass fiber wallcovering - white, may be painted, non-irritating fibers.*

Floor finishes ~ page 129

See also listings for Sustainable timber pages 213-16; Bricks and tiles pages 212-13; Stone page 213

ADOBE TILE AND STONE INC • 8917 4th NW, Albuquerque, NM 87114 • Tel: 505 898 0848 Fax: 505 890 0858 • *Saltillo, Terra Cotta, Mexican Bricks, Blocks, Flagstone, Mexican Stone.*

ALBANY WOODWORKS • PO Box 729, Albany, LA 70711-0729 • Tel: 504 567 1155 Fax: 504 567 2417 • *Natural furniture, flooring, doors, and stairs.*

BANGOR CORK • William and D Street, Box 125, Pen Argyl, PA 18072 • Tel: 215 863 9041 • *Untreated cork flooring.*

BEDROCK INDUSTRIES • 620 N 85th Street, Seattle, WA 98103 • Tel: 206 781 7025 • *Stone flooring/post consumer waste.*

BIG CITY FOREST • 1809 Carter Avenue, Bronx, NY 10457 • Tel: 718 731 3931 • *Builds furniture and flooring from wooden shipping pallets and other reclaimed lumber.*

BONAKEMI USA INC • 14805 East Moncrieff Place, Aurora, CO 80011-1207 • Tel: 800 872 5515 / 303 371 1411 • *BonaKemi is the 'environmental choice' for waterborne floor finishing systems. Our fillers, stains, sealers, finishes and maintenance products are the most durable and environmentally safe products available worldwide.*

CASA MEXICANA • PO Box 87, Mesilla Park, NM 88047 • Tel: 505 523 2777

CASA TALAVERA LTD • 621 Rio Grande Boulevard NW, Albuquerque, NM 87104 • Tel: 505 243 2413 Fax: 505 242 2282 • *Mexican Talavera tiles and washbasins.*

COASTAL MILLWORKS • 1335 Marietta Boulevard, NW Atlanta, GA 30318 • Tel: 404 351 8400 • *Recycled flooring (pine).*

CREATIVE TECHNOLOGIES GROUP INC • 14 Whitsett Street, Greenville, SC 29601 • Tel: 803 271 9194 • *Woodfinishers Pride.*

DODGE-REGUPOL INC • Box 989, Lancaster, PA 17603 • Tel: 717 295 3400 • *Untreated cork flooring, 6300 series.*

DULUTH TIMBER COMPANY • PO Box 16717, Duluth, MN 55816 • Tel: 218 727 2145 Fax: 218 722 0393 • *Flooring, beams, etc. resawn from salvaged industrial timbers. Doug Fir, Antique Pine, Redwood, White Pine. Call for prices and availability.*

DURABLE CORP • 75 N Pleasant Street, Norwalk, OH 44857 • Tel: 800 537 6287 • *Rubber tiles/post consumer waste. Wood link mats.*

ECOTIMBER INTERNATIONAL INC • 350 Treat Avenue, San Francisco, CA 94110-1326 • Tel: 415 864 4900 Fax: 415 864 1011 • *Offers woods from envionmentally sound sources. Distributes flooring.*

EL DORADO VELVET TILE • 2876 South Vail Avenue, City of Commerce, CA 90040 • Tel: 213 727 1935 • *Recycled rubber flooring tile made of nylon cord from tires vulcanized to rubber, fabric reinforced backing.*

ENVIRESOURCE INC • 110 Madison Avenue North, Bainbridge Island, WA 98110 • Tel: 206 842 9785 • *Flooring, sustainable yield hardwoods.*

FIRED EARTH PLC • Twyford Mill, Oxford Road, Adderbury, Oxon OX17 3HP, U K • Tel: (+44) 1295 812088 Fax: (+44) 1295 810832 • *Contact UK headquarters for export information.*

FLEXCO CO • PO Box 553, Tuscumbia, AL 35674 • Tel: 800 633 3151 / 205 383 7474 • *Flex-Tuft™ rubber floor tile made from reclaimed commercial tire components reinforced by nylon scrim, then bonded to vulcanized rubber backing.*

GERBERT LIMITED • PO Box 4944, Lancaster, PA 17604 • Tel: 717 299 5035/5083 Fax: 717 394 1937 • *DLW linoleum. Composed of natural materials from sustainable farm crops.*

GOODWIN HEART PINE CO • Route 2 Box 119-A, Micanopy, FL 32667 • Tel: 800 336 3118 / 904 373 9663

G R PLUME COMPANY • 1301 Meador Avenue, Suite B11 and 12, Bellingham, WA 98226 • Tel: 206 676 5658 Fax: 360 738 1909 • *Resawn timbers, old growth wood.*

GTE CORPORATION • Wellsboro, PA 16901 • Tel: 717 724 8200 • *Recycled glass tiles.*

HARMONY EXCHANGE • Route 2, Box 843, Big Hill Road, Boone NC 28607 • Tel: 800 756 9663 / 704 264 2314 Fax: 704 264 4770 • *Reclaimed and resawn Douglas Fir and Heartpine timbers and flooring. Water based floor finishes. Call for catalog.*

HENDRICKSEN NATÜRLICH • 7120 Keating Avenue, Sebastopol, CA 95472 (store address) • Tel: 707 829 3959 • or for a catalog: PO Box 1677, Sebastopol, CA 95473-1677 • Tel: 707 824 0914 Fax: 800 329 9398 • *Highest quality natural floor covering products for home and office, Wool carpeting, natural linoleum, cork, grasses and area rugs. See p. 154.*

INNOVATIVE WASTE TECHNOLOGIES INC • 100-1 Grosvenor Square, Annacis Island, New Westminster, BC, Canada, V3M 5S1 • Tel: 604 524 5263 Fax: 504 524 1241 • *Durable Rubberloc™ pavers made from recycled scrap automobile tires provide a unique paved surface for commercial, consumer, and recreational applications.*

IPOCORK LTD • 1280 Roberts Boulevard, Suite 403, Kennesaw, GA 30144

JEFFERSON LUMBER COMPANY • PO Box 696, McCloud, CA 96057 • Tel: 916 235 0609 Fax: 916 235 0434

LANCASTER COLONY COMMERCIAL PRODUCTS • PO Box 630, Columbus, OH 43216 • Tel: 800 292 7260 • *Rubber and PVC tiles and matting, made from recycled materials.*

LIVERMORE • The Wood Mill, PO Box 146, East Livermore, ME 04228 • Tel: 207 897 5211 • *Wood floors.*

MATS INC • PO Box 916, Braintree, MA 02184 • Tel: 617 848 6313 • *A variety of flooring products made with recycled rubber or recycled PVC.*

MAT-MAN INC • 5312 E Desmet, Spokane, Washington 99212 • Tel: 509 536 8169 • *Custom-sized mats for entry, walkway, or artefacts for shops manufactured from recycled tires.*

MAXITO INDUSTRIES LTD • 1817 Ocean Surf Place, South Surrey, BC, Canada V4A 9P1 • Tel & Fax: 604 535 7160 • *Pre-manufactured foundation forms are attached to floor panels on the job site, thereby eliminating all site labour. The system automatically adjusts to uneven ground conditions, and includes all insulation and waterproofing.*

MAXWELL PACIFIC • PO Box 4127, Malibu, CA 90264 • Tel: 310 457 4533 Fax: 310 457 8308 • *Reclaimed and antique timbers, barnwood, flooring. Fir, pine, redwood, cedar.*

MENOMINEE TRIBAL ENTERPRISES • Box 10, Neopit, WI 54135 • Tel: 715 756 4943 • *SCS Certified program.*

METROPOLITAN CERAMICS • PO Box 9240, Canton, OH 44711 9240 • Tel: 216 484 4887 • *Quarry tiles made from recycled in-house materials that would normally be waste.*

NAIRN FLOORS INTERNATIONAL • 560 Weber Street North, Waterloo, Ontario, Canada, N2L 5C6 • Tel: 519 884 2602 • *Natural linoleum and wooden flooring.*

NON-TOXIC ENVIRONMENTS • 6135 NW Mountain View Drive, Corvallis, OR 97330 • Tel: 503 745 7838 • *Natural linoleum. Catalog.*

NORTHERN HARDWOOD LUMBER • 520 Matthew Street, Santa Clara, CA • Tel: 408 727 2211 • *Smart Wood supplier.*

PACIFIC STRATEGIES • 1101 Connecticut Avenue, NW # 1000, Washington DC 200036 • Tel: 202 828 2435 • *Simulated marble/ recycled stone content.*

RAINFOREST ACTION NETWORK • 450 Sansome Street, San Francisco, CA 94111 • Tel: 415 398 4404 • *Publish "The Wood Users Guide" by Pamela Wellner and Eugene Dickey which discusses the problems with rain-forest woods and gives a comprehensive overview of domestic wood and non wood alternatives. Lists tree species and descriptions, and suppliers of ecologically sensitive woods. They also have a small catalog of books on rain-forest issues as well as a few products that contain rain-forest ingredients.*

RAINFOREST ALLIANCE • 65 Bleeker Street, New York, NY 10012-2420 • Tel: 212 677 1900 • *Runs the Smart Wood™ certification program.*

RB RUBBER PRODUCTS • 904E 10th Avenue, McMinnville, OR 97128 • Tel: 503 472 4691 / 800 525 5530 • *Rubber matting made from 100% recycled waste tire rubber.*

RCM INTERNATIONAL • PO Box 327, Elk River, MN 55330 • Tel: 800 328 9203 / 612 421 4501 • *Interlocking floor tiles manufactured from recycled polyvinyl chloride (PVC).*

RESOURCE INTERNATIONAL • 1325 Imola Avenue W, no 109, Napa, CA 94559 • Tel: 707 226 9582 • *Flooring manufactured from recycled, reclaimed, sustainably managed or lesser-known species. Formaldehyde-free adhesives with non-toxic finishes.*

ROYAL FLOORMATS • 5951 East Firestone Boulevard, South Gate, CA 90280-3795 • Tel: 800 237 8628 / 310 928 3381 Fax: 310 928 7080 • *Floor mats made from 80% recycled post-consumer tire rubber.*

SEVEN ISLANDS LAND MANAGEMENT CO • 304 Hancock Street, Suite 2A, PO Box 1168, Bangor, ME 04402-1168 • Tel: 207 947 0541 • *Hardwood flooring. SCS Certified program.*

STONEWARE TILE CO • 1650 Progress Drive, Richmond, IN 47374 • Tel: 317 935 4760 Fax: 317 935 3971 • *Division of Terra-Green Technologies. Manufacturer of Traffic Tile - a single-fired glass-bonded tile manufactured with over 70% recycled glass. Can be used safely on floors and walls in interior and exterior applications.*

STRUCTURAL SLATE CO • 222 E Main Street, Pen Argyl, Pennsylvania, PA 18072 • Tel: 215 863 4141 Fax: 215 863 7016 • *Since 1918 we have supplied Pennsylvania Natural Slate products including flooring.*

SUMMITVILLE TILES INC • PO Box 73, Summitville, OH 43962 • Tel: 216 223 1511 • Fax: 216 233 1414 and 2050 S State College Boulevard, Anaheim, CA 92806 • Tel: 714 978 1847 Fax: 714 978 6091

SYNDESIS • 2908 Colorado Avenue, Santa Monica, CA 90404-3616 • Tel: 310 829 9932 Fax: 310 829 5641 • *A natural cement-based, precast terrazzo product with 41% recycled content.*

TERRA-GREEN TECHNOLOGIES • 405 Headquarters, Millersville, MD 21108 • Tel: 410 987 3407 • *Manufacturer of Tierra Classic glazed tiles (bathroom) produced from recycled glass and traditional ceramic materials.*

TILES DE SANTA FE INC • PO Box 3767, Santa Fe, NM 87501-0767 • Tel: 505 455 7466 • *Hand made tile floors. Call or write for free brochure.*

TURTLE PLASTICS • 2366 Woodhill Road, Cleveland, OH 44106 • Tel: 216 791 2100 • *Turtle Tiles and Grit Top Tiles, interlocking grid-surface tiles made of 100% recycled PVC. Grit Top uses recycled carbide grit.*

VALLEY WESTERN • Box 8007, El Monte, CA 91734 • *Distributor of cork flooring.*

WHAT IT'S WORTH • PO Box 162135, Austin, TX 78716 • Tel: 512 328 8837 • *Reclaimed timber flooring.*

WOODWORKERS ALLIANCE FOR RAINFOREST PROTECTION (WARP) • 1 Cottage Street, Easthampton, MA 01027 • Tel: 413 586 8156 • *Maintains a list of suppliers that use wood from well-managed or recycled sources.*

Adhesives ~ page 132

AMERICAN FORMULATING AND MANUFACTURING (AFM) • 350 West Ash Street, Suite 700, San Diego, CA 92101 • Tel: 800 239 0321 / 619 239 0321 Fax 619 239 0565 • *Wallpaper paste.*

AURO/TEEKAH INC • 5015 Yonge Street, North York, Ontario, Canada, M2N 5P1 • Tel: 416 229 4199 • *Auro European adhesives and sealers.*

BIOFA, BAU INC • Box 190, Alton, NH 03809 • Tel: 603 364 2400

DEVOE AND REYNOLDS • 4000 DuPont Circle, Louisville, KY 40207 • Tel: 502 897 9861 • *Natural wallpaper glue.*

ECOLOGY BOX • 425 East Washington, Ann Arbor, MI 48101 • Tel: 313 662 9131 • *Adhesives.*

ENVIRESOURCE INC • 110 Madison Avenue North, Bainbridge Island, WA 98110 • 206 842 9785 • *Non-toxic adhesives.*

GARLAND-WHITE & CO • PO Box 365, Union City, CA 94587 • Tel: 510 471 5666 • *Mortar and tile grouts.*

LATICRETE INTERNATIONAL INC • 1 Laticrete Park North, Bethnay, CT 06525-3498 • Tel: 203 393 0010 / 800 243 4788 Fax: 203 393 1684 • *Mortar and tile grouts.*

THE NATURAL CHOICE, LIVOS • Livos Plant Chemistry, 1365 Rufina Circle, Santa Fe, NM 87501 • Tel: 505 438 3448 Fax: 505 438 0199 • *Wallpaper paste, no biocides, no fungicides, natural ingredients. BIOSHIELD LINE, the Natural Choice, carries a cellulose-based glue suitable for paper hanging.*

RESOURCE INTERNATIONAL • 1325 Imola Avenue W, no 109, Napa, CA 94559 • Tel: 707 226 9582 • *Formaldehyde-free adhesives with non-toxic finishes.*

ROMAN ADHESIVES • Calumet City, IL 60409 • Tel: 708 891 0188 • *Natural wallpaper adhesive.*

SINAN CO • Box 857, Davis, CA 95617-0857 • Tel: 916 753 3104 • *AURO adhesives imported from Germany.*

W F TAYLOR CO INC • 11545 Pacific Avenue, Fontana, CA 92335 • Tel: 909 360 6677 Fax: 909 360 1177 and 2110 Powers Ferry Road, Suite 230, Atlanta, GA 30339 • Tel: 404 850 9144 Fax: 404 850 9152 • *Timberline Envirotec Wood Flooring Adhesive, non-flammable, solvent- and odor-free, VOC compliant. Contains no ozone depleting chlorinated solvents. Envirobond: environmentally safe ceramic adhesive.*

Interior decoration consultants~ *page 137*

See also listings for Home and environment pages 205-7 and Healthy building pages 207-11

MARK ABRAHAM • 265 North Front Street, Sarnia, Ontario, Canada, N7T 7K4 • Tel: 519 542 7751

MAUREEN L BELLE • Biarch, Systems Earth, PO Box 495, Langley, WA 98260 • Tel: 206 579 1535 Fax: 206 579 1545

TOM BENDER • Nehalem, OR 97131 • Tel: 503 368 6294

BARBARA BRENNAN SCHOOL OF HEALING • PO Box 2005, East Hampton, NY 11937 • Tel: 516 324 9745

MARY CORDARO • 12439 Magnolia Boulevard, no 263, Valley Village, CA 91607 • Tel: 310 838 2892 / 818 981 7245 Fax: 810 766 5882

COUNTRY COMFORT INTERIORS • 623 NW Hill Street, Bend, OR 97701 • Tel: 503 385 1147

DEBRA DADD-REDALIA • PO Box 279, Forest Knolls, CA 94933 • Tel: 415 488 4612. See p. 188.

DARREL DEBOER • DeBoer Architects, 1835 Pacific Avenue, Alameda, CA 94501 • Tel: 510 865 3669

ECOLOGIC HOMES • Nancy Simpson, PO Box 94, Willits, CA 95490 • Tel & Fax: 707 459 2595

ECOLOGY BY DESIGN (CONCEPTS FOR A TOXIC-FREE ENVIRONMENT) • Audrey Hoodkiss, 1341 Ocean Avenue, Suite 73, Santa Monica, CA 90401 • Tel: 310 394 4146

THE EPSTEN GROUP • 303 Ferguson Street, Atlanta, GA 30307 • Tel: 404 577 0370

GAIA HOMES • PO Box 223, Horsefly, BC, Canada, V0L 1L0 • Tel: 604 620 3664 Fax: 604 620 3454 • Consulting for Bau Biologie. We design and construct your healthy home and work place.

MARCO HAESSIG • PO Box 223, Horsefly, British Columbia, Canada V0L 1L0 • Tel: 604 620 3664 Fax 604 620 3454

HEALTHY BUILDINGS ASSOCIATES • 7190 Fiske Road, Clinton, WA 98236 • Tel: 206 579 2962 • Publish "Healthy Buildings Resource Guide". Design and consultiation.

IDEAL ENVIRONMENTS • 401 West Adams, Fairfield, IA 52556 • Tel: 515 472 6547

INTERNATIONAL ASSOCIATION FOR COLOR THERAPY • 73 Elm Bank Gardens, London SW13 0NX, United Kingdom • Tel: (+44) 1453 832150

DAVID KIBBEY • 1618 Parker Street, Berkeley, CA 94703 • Tel & Fax: 510 841 1039 • Environmental Building Inspections, Healthy Design and Materials Consultation.

ANGELA MARASCO INTERIOR DESIGN • 529 Sausalito Boulevard, Sausalito, CA 94965 • Tel: 415 331 6905 Fax: 415 331 5264 • Environmentally conscious design, Education, Research, Consulting.

NATURAL HABITAT • PO Box 21, Haysville, KS 67060. Valerie Dow • Tel: 316 788 1793

SRW ENVIRONMENTAL BUILDING CONSULTANT AND CON-STRUCTION • Lic 433290, 1075 Montgomery Road, Sebastopol, CA 95472 • Tel: 707 829 8296 • Offering a professional evaluation of your building materials, systems, and finishes to ensure a healthful, non-toxic indoor environment.

SHELTER ECOLOGY • Cindy Meehan, 39 Pineridge Road, Asheville NC 28804 • Tel: 704 251 5888 • Specializing in consultations to help identify alternative resources and design methods for healthy (working and living) interior spaces.

SOCIETY FOR CLINICAL ECOLOGY • 109 West Olive Street, Fort Collings, CO 80524

SRW ENVIRONMENTAL BUILDING CONSULTANT AND CON-STRUCTION • Lic 433290, 1075 Montgomery Road, Sebastopol, CA 95472 • Tel: 707 829 8296 • Offering a professional evaluation of your building materials, systems, and finishes to ensure a healthful, non-toxic indoor environment.

CAROL VENOLIA • PO Box 4417, Santa Rosa, CA 95402-4417 • Tel: 707 579 2201 Fax: 707 884 1235 • Architect. Author of "Healing Environments". Editor of "Building with Nature". See p. 191.

Furniture ~ page 140

A DESERT FORM, LTD • 2173 West Running Deer Drive, Apache Junction, AZ 85219 • Tel: 602 463 2490 • Handcrafted products made from cactus wood; high environmental awareness reflected in all activities.

ALBANY WOODWORKS • PO Box 729, Albany, LA 70711 • Tel: 504 567 1155 Fax: 504 567 2417 • Natural furniture.

AMERICAN FURNITURE MANUFACTURERS ASSOCIATION • PO Box HP-7, High Point, NC 27261 • Tel: 910 884 5000 Fax: 910 884 5303 • The nation's largest non-profit, voluntary trade organization for furniture manufacturers.

AMERICAN SOCIETY OF FURNITURE DESIGNERS • PO Box 2688, 521 South Hamilton Street, High Point, NC 27261 • Tel: 919 884 4074

BEAR CREEK LUMBER INC • PO Box 669, Winthrop, WA 98862 • Tel: 509 997 3110 Fax: 509 997 2040 • Natural wood products.

BEREA COLLEGE CRAFTS • CPO 2316, Berea, KY 40404 • Tel: 606 986 9341 • Handmade, hardwood furniture from the hands of Berea College students and master crafts people.

BIG CITY FOREST • 1809 Carter Avenue, Bronx, NY 10457 • Tel: 718 731 3931 • Builds furniture from wooden shipping pallets and other reclaimed lumber.

BRIGHT FUTURES • 3120 Central Avenue, SE Albuquerque, NM 87106 • Handmade futons and accessories with organic cotton coverings encased in FoxFiber™ for the chemically sensitive.

CD WOODWORKS • 474 Lois Lane, Sedro-Woolley, WA 98284 • Tel: 206 856 4947 • Furniture from reclaimed lumber and mill ends.

CO-OP AMERICA • 2100 M Street, NW, no 310, Washington DC 20063 • Tel: 800 424 2667 • Products and services guaranteed to come from groups which are socially and environmentally responsible and which practice a spirit of co-operation in the workplace.

CRAFTSMANS GALLERY • RR 1, Chatsworth, Ontario, Canada • Tel: 519 794 3865 Fax: 519 794 4449 • Cabinets, trims and doors for the home. Built-in longevity reduces landfill demand. Canadian craftsmanship at its best.

DEERFIELD WOODWORKING • PO Box 275, Deerfield, MA 01342 • Tel: 413 532 2377 • Bookcases, tables etc.

DESIGN BY META MORF INC • 2706 North Mississippi Street, Portland, OR 97227 • Tel: 503 282 9922 • Seating and tables from post-consumer recycled plastic.

DESIGN IDEAS™ • PO Box 2967, Springfield, IL 62708 • Tel: 217 753 3081 / 800 426 6394 Fax: 217 753 3080 • Catalog of bright and interesting products for the home.

THE EARTH SHOP • Latham Circle Mall, Latham, NY 1210 • Tel: 518 783 3163 Fax: 518 783 3164 • Offers a complete line of earth-friendly and socially conscious goods and gifts which focus on an appreciation of nature and the diversity of people around the world.

EARTHLYGOODS LTD • 372 Danforth Avenue, Toronto, Ontario, Canada, M4K 1N8 • Tel: 416 466 2841 Fax: 416 466 2841 • Retailers of a full range of environmental products. We only carry the best. Worldwide mail order.

ENVIRONMENTALLY SOUND PRODUCTS • 8845 Orchard Tree Lane, Towson, MD 21286 • Tel: 800 886 5432 Fax: 410 825 7202 • Research. Wholesale distributor. Mail order service.

FAIRHAVEN WOOD WORKS • 72 Blatchley Avenue, New Haven, CT 06513 • Tel: 203 776 3099 Fax: 203 772 4153 • *Fine wooden furniture in Shaker, Mission, and Contemporary styles.*

HAND IN HAND CATALOG • Route 26, RR 1, Box 1425, Oxford, ME 04270 • Tel: 800 872 9745 Fax: 207 539 4415

HEART OF VERMONT • The Old Schoolhouse, Route 132, Box 183, Sharon, VT 05065 • Tel: 800 639 4123 / 802 763 2720 Fax: 802 763 2075 • *Furniture and healthy bedding. Catalog.*

HULL COVE JOB SHOP • PO Box 281, Jamestown, RI 02835 • Tel: 401 423 0433 • *Wind and solar powered workshop making antique reproduction beds and other furniture.*

THE HUMMER CRAFT WORKS • HCR 32, Box 122, Ulvalde, TX 78801 • Tel: 512 232 6167 • *Offers handmade objects from dead wood.*

JANTZ DESIGN • Box 3071, Santa Rosa, CA 95402 • Tel: 800 365 6563 / 707 823 8834 • *Furniture and organic wood. Catalog.*

KINGSLEY-BATE LTD • 5587-B Guinea Road, Fairfax, VA 22032 • Tel: 703 978 7200 • *Outdoor teak and mahogany furniture made from sustainably harvested plantations in Indonesia.*

LARSON WOOD PRODUCTS INC • 31421 Coburg Bottom Loop, Eugene, OR 97401 • Tel: 503 343 5229

LIVING PLANET CATALOG • 340 East 4th Street, Long Beach, CA 90802 • Tel: 310 495 0276 • *A special collection of gifts that celebrate personal and planetary growth.*

LIVING SHELTER CRAFTS • PO Box 4069, West Sedona, AZ 86340 • Tel: 520 230 4283 / 800 899 1924

THE MART STORE • 153 West Ohio Street, Chicago, IL • Tel: 312 670 8155 • *Exotic hardwoods from old African Railroad ties are used to make attractive furniture.*

NAPA VALLEY BOX CO • 11995 El Camino Real, San Diego, CA 92130 • Tel: 619 259 3000 • *Solid wood CD and cassette storage.*

NATIONAL TOXICS CAMPAIGN • 37 Temple Place, 4th floor, Boston, MA 0211 • Tel: 617 482 1477

N E INDUSTRY • 1322 Grand Avenue, Phoenix, AZ 85007 • Tel: 602 256 6476 • *Custom furniture and accessories from recycled materials.*

NEW WORLD FURNITURE • PO Box 20957, San Jose, CA 95160 • Tel: 408 268 1670 Fax: 408 268 7451 • *Manufacturer of indoor and patio furniture from recycled redwood.*

NONTOXIC ENVIRONMENTS • 9392 Gribble Road, Canby, OR 97013 • Tel: 503 266 5244 Fax: 503 266 5242 • *Mail-order company specializing in products for aware and chemically sensitive individuals.*

NORTHWEST FUTONS • PO Box 14952, Portland, OR 97214 • Tel: 503 224 3199 Fax: 503 231 9489

PLOW & HEARTH • PO Box 5000, Route 230W Madison, VA 22727 • Tel: 800 627 1712 • *A mail-order retailer of outdoor teak furniture made from sustainably harvested wood.*

PORTICO SA, ROYAL MAHOGANY PRODUCTS INC • 6190 Regency Parkway, Suite 314, Atlanta, GA 30071 • Tel: 404 729 1600 • *SCS Certified program.*

PURE LIVING STORE • Village Faire Shoppes, 1100 South Coast Highway, # 221, Laguna Beach, CA 92651 • Tel: 714 376 8867 • *Home furnishings and accessories.*

RAINFOREST ACTION NETWORK • 450 Sansome Street, San Francisco, CA 94111 • Tel: 415 398 4404 • *Publish "The Wood Users Guide" by Pamela Wellner and Eugene Dickey which discusses the problems with rainforest woods and gives an overview of domestic wood and non wood alternatives. Lists tree species and descriptions, and suppliers of ecologically sensitive woods. They also have a catalog of books on rainforest issues as well as a few products that contain rainforest ingredients.*

RAINFOREST ALLIANCE • 65 Bleeker Street, New York, NY 10012 • Tel: 212 677 1900 • *Runs the Smart Wood certification program.*

RESOURCE INTERNATIONAL • 1325 Imola Avenue W, no 109, Napa, CA 94559 • Tel: 707 226 9582 • *Furniture, Furnishings and Flooring. Manufactured from recycled, reclaimed, sustainably managed or lesser-known species. Formaldehyde-free adhesives with non-toxic finishes.*

RESOURCE REVIVAL • 2342 NW Marshall, Portland, OR 97210 • Tel: 800 866 8823 / 503 266 6001 Fax: 503 226 6397 • *Furniture, belts, collars, picture frames, straps, and more made from reused material.*

SCIENTIFIC CERTIFICATION SYSTEMS • 1611 Telegraph Avenue, Suite 1111, Oakland, CA 94612 • Tel: 510 832 1415 • *Certifies sustainable sources of lumber.*

SEVENTH GENERATION STORE • Colchester, VT 05446-1672 • Tel: 800 456 1177 Fax: 800 456 1139 and 176 Battery Street, Burlington, VT 05401 • Tel: 802 658 7770

SHAKER SHOPS WEST • PO Box 487, Inverness, CA 94937 • Tel: 415 669 7256 Fax: 415 669 7327 • *Classic Shaker design authentically reproduced furniture, accessories, and milk paint. Many kits allow assembly and finishing without toxics. Catalog $2.50.*

SHAKER WORKSHOPS • PO Box 1028, Concord, MA 01742 • Tel: 617 646 8985

SMITH & HAWKEN • 117 E Strawberry Drive, Mill Valley, CA 94941 • Tel: 415 383 4415 • *Cedar furniture from sustainably harvested wood.*

SOFA U LOVE • 11948 San Vicente, Brentwood, CA • Tel: 310 207 2540 • *Down-filled sofas with natural cotton slipcover and cushion pillows.*

SPIN-OFFS • 1860 West 220th Street, # 410, Torrance, CA 90501 • Tel: 310 318 0566 / 310 320 7523 • *Fine furniture built from recycled entertainment industry sets.*

J W STANNARD CO • 611 Commerce Drive, Largo, FL 34640 • Tel: 813 587 0900 • *Wind chimes.*

STRUCTURAL SLATE COMPANY • 222 E Main Street, Pen Argyl PA 18072 • Tel: 215 863 4141 Fax: 610 863 7016 • *Since 1918, The Structural Slate Company has supplied Pennsylvania Natural Slate products. Some residential products are flooring, countertops, and fireplace facings.*

SUNDANCE • 1909 South 4250 West, Salt Lake City, UT 84104 • Tel: 800 422 2770 Fax: 800 834 9445 • *Mail-order catalog.*

TERRA VERDE • 120 Wooster Street, New York, NY 10012 • Tel: 212 925 4355 Fax: 212 925 4540 • *The ecological department store.*

TWIN OAKS HAMMOCKS • Box N, Tecumseh, MO 65760 • Tel: 417 679 4682 Fax: 417 679 4684 • *Earth-friendly comfort! Luxurious hammocks, handwoven from Organic Cotton and Recycled Polyester rope. Call or write for free information.*

WOODWORKERS ALLIANCE FOR RAINFOREST PROTECTION (WARP) • 1 Cottage Street, Easthampton, MA 01027 • Tel: 413 586 8156 • *Maintains a list of suppliers that use wood from well managed or recycled sources.*

Rugs & carpets ~ page 141

See also listings for Floor finishes pages 248-9

ABSOLUTE ENVIRONMENTAL'S ALLERGY PRODUCTS AND SERVICES STORE • 2615 S University Drive, Davie, FL 33328 • Tel: 305 472 3773 • *Formaldehyde-free carpeting.*

AMERICAN FORMULATING & MANUFACTURING (AFM) • 350 West Ash Street, Suite 700, San Diego, CA 92101 • Tel: 800 239 0321 / 619 239 0321 Fax 619 239 0565 • *Carpet Guard non-toxic spray – locks in odors and creates a non-flammable air drying/air curing water-soluble siliconate, designed to impart water repellence to carpet.*

ANDERSON LABORATORIES • 30 River Street, Dedham, MA 02026 • Tel: 617 364 7357 • *Tests carpets.*

BENTLEY MILLS • 14641 E Don Julian Road, City of Industry, CA 91746 • Tel: 800 423 4709 Fax: 818 333 3103 • *Manufactures high-performance commercial carpets utilizing leading-edge technology.*

BREMWORTH CARPETS • 1940 Olivera Road, Suite C, Concord, CA 94520 • Tel: 800 227 3408 • *Woven wool with jute backing or polypropylene backing.*

THE CARPET AND RUG INSTITUTE • PO Box 2048, Dalton, GA 30722 • Tel: 800 882 8846 • *Publishes free brochures "Carpet, The Choice for Every Walk of Life", which provides helpful information about carpet selection, and "Carpet Care and Maintenance for Maximum Performance", a full color guide for preserving your carpet investment. Send SAE.*

CARPET POLICY DIALOGUE GROUP • 151 6th Street, O'Keefe Building, Atlanta, GA 30332 • Tel: 404 894 3806 Fax: 404 894 2184 • *Concerned with the health hazards contained in some carpeting materials.*

CAROUSEL CARPETS • 1 Carousel Lane, Ukiah, CA 95482 • Tel: 707 485 0333 Fax: 707 485 5911 • *Natural fiber carpet manufacturer with natural latex backings.*

COLIN CAMPBELL & SONS • 1717 W 5th Avenue, Vancouver, BC, Canada, V6J 1P1 • Tel: 604 734 2758 Fax: 604 734 1512 • *Proud to provide the public and industry with a source for environmentally sensitive carpets. Products include: Gaskell Textiles 100% Hair carpet underfelt for long-term resilience. Also Coir, sisal, and reed floorcoverings. See p. 156.*

COLLINS AND AIKMAN • Floor Coverings Division, 311 Smith Industrial Boulevard, PO Box 1447, Dalton, GA 30722-1447 • Tel: 404 259 9711 • *Powerbond RS low emission carpet.*

COUNTRY COMFORT INTERIORS • 623 Northwest Hill Street, Bend, OR 97701 • Tel: 503 385 1147 • *Country Comfort sells and installs low-toxic floor and window coverings.*

DELLINGER INC • 1943 North Broad, Rome, GA 30161 • Tel: 706 291 7402 • *Custom-made, loomed carpets to your design, natural fibers.*

DESIGN MATERIALS INC • 241 S 55th Street, Kansas City, KS 66106 • Tel: 913 342 9796 Fax 913 342 9826 • *Natural fiber floorcoverings, rugs, and wallcoverings.*

DESSO CARPET • Box 1351, Wayne, PA 19087 • Tel: 800 368 1515 • *Woven wool carpet with jute backing.*

DURA UNDERCUSHION LTD • 8525 Delmeade Road, Montreal, QBE, Canada, H4T 1M1 • Tel: 514 737 6561 Fax: 514 342 7940 • *Heavy duty carpet pad made from 100% post-consumer tire rubber.*

DW INTERIORS/ECO CARPET ASSOCIATES • 6205 Van Nuys Boulevard, Van Nuys, CA 91401 • Tel: 818 786 0681 Fax: 818 786 6217 • *Furnishes and installs carpeting and padding from post-consumer materials for both residential and commercial customers.*

ECOLOGY BY DESIGN • 1341 Ocean Avenue, Suite 73, Santa Monica, CA 90401 • Tel: 213 394 4146 • *Safeguard, low toxic fifth generation nylon carpeting.*

EL DORADO VELVET TILE • 2876 South Vail Avenue, City of Commerce, CA 90040 • Tel: 213 727 1935 • *Recycled rubber flooring tile made of nylon cord from tires vulcanized to rubber, fabric reinforced backing.*

ENVIRONMENTAL PROTECTION AGENCY (EPA) • TS799, 401 M Street SW, Washington DC 20460 • Tel: 202 554 1404 • *Publish "Indoor Air Quality and New Carpet: What you Should Know".*

ENVIRORITE • 306 Snelling Avenue S, Suite 8, St. Paul, MN 55105 • Tel: 612 690 4799 • *Carpet cleaning for the environmentally sensitive.*

ETI ENVIRONMENTAL TECHNOLOGY INC • South Bay Depot Road, Fields Landing, CA 95537 • Tel: 707 443 9323 Fax: 707 443 7962 • *Fiber-Lok rug backing prevents sliding and skidding. Safe and simple to apply; cleans up with soap and water.*

EX: INC • 400 East 56th Street, New York, NY 10022 • Tel: 212 758 2593 • *A variety of cork products.*

FIBREWORKS • 1729 Research Drive, Louisville KY 40299 • Tel: 800 843 0063 / 502 499 9944 • *Fibreworks offers Jute, Sisal and Coir floorcovering. Made entirely of renewable natural fibers, these rugs are in tune with the environmental concerns of the 90s.*

FORBO NORTH AMERICA • PO Box 667, Hazelton, PA 18201 • Tel: 800 233 0475 / 717 459 0771 • *Linoleum flooring.*

FOREIGN ACCENTS • 2825 E Broadbent Parkway, NE, Albuquerque, NM 87107 • Tel: 800 880 0413 or 505 344 4833 • *Offers a wide variety of natural fiber handwoven rugs in colorful contemporary and ethnic patterns.*

GERBERT LIMITED • PO Box 4944, Lancaster, PA 17604 • Tel: 717 299 5035/5083 Fax: 717 394 1937 • *DLW linoleum. Composed of natural materials from sustainable farm crops.*

GLOBAL RECYCLED PRODUCTS • PO Box 301, Kittery, ME 03904-0301 • Tel: 217 439 5080

HENDRICKSEN NATÜRLICH • 7120 Keating Avenue, Sebastopol, CA 95472 (store address) • Tel: 707 829 3959 • Catalog from: • PO Box 1677, Sebastopol, CA 95473-1677 • Tel: 707 824 0914 Fax: 800 329 9398 • *Highest quality natural floor covering products for home and office, Wool carpeting, natural linoleum, cork, grasses, and area rugs.*

HELIOS CARPET • Box 1938, Calhoun, GA 30703 • Tel: 800 843 5138 • *Natural fibers, no topical treatments, jute backing.*

HOMASOTE COMPANY • Box 7240, West Trenton, NJ 08628-0240 • Tel: 609 883 3300 • *440 CarpetBoard and Comfort Base™ carpet underlayments made from 100% recycled newsprint cellulose.*

IMAGE CARPETS • Highway 140, PO Box 5555, Armuchee, GA 30105 • Tel: 404 235 8444 / 800 722 2504 Fax: 706 234 3463 • *Wearlon® carpets with 100% recycled PET plastic fibers (soft drink and ketchup bottles) as carpet face fibers. Duratron® carpets made from combination of PET fibers and nylon. Also produce Enviro-Tech® carpets.*

LANCASTER COLONY COMMERCIAL PRODUCTS • PO Box 630, Columbus, OH 43216 • Tel: 800 292 7260 • *Rubber and PVC tiles and matting, made from recycled materials.*

JACK LENOR LARSON • 41 East 11th Street, New York, NY 10003 • Tel: 212 674 3993 • *Natural fiber carpeting.*

MATS INC • PO Box 916, Braintree, MA 02184 • Tel: 617 848 6313 • *A variety of flooring products made with recycled rubber or recycled PVC.*

MAT-MAN INC • 5312 E Desmet, Spokane, Washington 99212 • Tel: 509 536 8169 • *Custom-sized mats for entry, walkway, or artefacts for shops manufactured from recycled tires.*

METROPOLITAN CERAMICS • PO Box 9240, Canton, OH 44711 9240 • Tel: 216 484 4887 • *Quarry tile made from recycled in-house materials that would normally be waste.*

NATIONAL CENTER FOR ENVIRONMENTAL HEALTH STRATEGIES • 1100 Rural Avenue, Voorhees, NJ 08043 • Tel: 609 429 5358

NO FAULT INDUSTRIES INC • 11325 Pennywood Avenue, Baton Rouge, LA 70809 • Tel: 800 232-7766 / 504 293-7760 • *Saf Dek™ poured rubber decking surface. Seamless, porous, resilient, slip resistant.*

NECESSARY TRADING COMPANY • One Nature's Way, New Castle, VA 24127 • Tel: 540 864 5103

OSCODA PLASTICS INC • 731 Morley Drive, Saginaw, MI 48601 • Tel: 800 544 9538 • *PROTECT-ALL FLOORING, 100% recycled vinyl. Available in sheet - good sizes - an interlocking tile, six colors and two thicknesses.*

PACIFIC STRATEGIES • 1101 Connecticut Avenue NW, no 100, Washington DC 200036 • Tel: 202 828 2435 • *Simulated marble and recycled stone content flooring.*

PRESTIGE MILLS • 83 Harbor Road, Port Washington, NY 11050 • Tel: 516 767 1110 • *100% sisal carpeting/latex backing.*

PURE PODUNK • RR 1, Box 69, Thetford Center, VT 05075 • *Area rugs on linen backing from organic domestic wool.*

RB RUBBER PRODUCTS • 904E 10th Avenue, McMinnville, OR 97128 • Tel: 503 472 4691 / 800 525 5530 • *Rubber matting made from 100% recycled waste tire rubber.*

RCM INTERNATIONAL • PO Box 327, Elk River, MN 55330 • Tel: 800 328 9203 / 612 421 4501 • *Interlocking floor tiles manufactured from recycled polyvinyl chloride (PVC).*

RETURN TO TRADITION • 3319 Sacramento Street, San Francisco, CA 94118 • Tel: 415 921 4180 • *Natural hand-dyed wool Turkish carpet.*

ROYAL FLOORMATS • 5951 East Firestone Boulevard, South Gate, CA 90280-3795 • Tel: 800 237 8628 / 310 928 3381 Fax: 310 928 7080 • *Floor mats made from 80% recycled post-consumer tire rubber.*

ALISON T SEYMOUR • 5423 W Marginal Way, SW Seattle, WA 98106 • Tel: 206 935 5471 • *100% sisal carpeting, and other natural carpeting with latex backing.*

SUPERIOR FLOORING • 803 Jefferson Street, Wausau, WI 54401 • Tel: 800 247 4705 • *Pesticide free flooring. Random lengths available.*

SUSTAINABLE LIFESTYLES • PO Box 313, Excelsior, MN 55331 • Tel: 800 287 3144 • *Sisal floor covering (office) non-toxic, from sustainable forestry.*

TACFAST SYSTEMS • 15 Wertheim Court, Suite 710, Richmond Hill, Ontario, Canada, L4B 3H7 • Tel: 905 886 0785 Fax: 905 886 5765 • *The TacFast system is healthier and cleaner than conventional carpet. No need for liquid adhesives; simple to remove and reuse Tacfast carpets.*

TALISMAN MILLS INC • 6000 Executive Drive, Mequon, WI 53092 • Tel: 800 482 5466 • *Envirelon™ carpets made from 100% post-consumer recycled PET plastic.*

TURTLE PLASTICS • 2366 Woodhill Road, Cleveland, OH 44106 • Tel: 216 791 2100 • *Turtle Tiles and Grit Top Tiles, interlocking grid-surface tiles made of 100% recycled PVC. Grit Top uses recycled carbide grit.*

WESTERN SOLUTIONS • 3100 South Susan Street, Santa Ana, CA 92704 • Tel: 714 546 6630 Fax: 714 546 2028 • *The first mill in the United States to dedicate itself to manufacturing carpet made solely from recyclable nylon fibers and yarns.*

Fabrics & fibers ~ *page 144*

ATLANTIC RECYCLED PAPER COMPANY (ARP/NOPE) • Box 39179, Baltimore, MD 21212 • Tel: 301 323 2811 • *100% cotton shower curtain. Replaces vinyl liners. Keeps water in the tub, machine washable. White or Natural.*

THE COTTON PLACE • Box 59721, Dallas, TX 75229 • Tel: 800 451 8866 / 214 243 4149 • *Natural fibers. Catalog.*

COTTON PLUS LIMITED • Route One, Box 120, O'Donnell, TX 79351 • Tel: 806 439 6646 Fax: 806 439 6647 • *From field to finished product, Cotton Plus links producers, mills, manufacturers, and consumers. Specializing in organically grown products. Promoting and encouraging responsible use of resources.*

COTTON THREADS CLOTHING • Route 2, Box 90, Halletsville, TX 77964 • Tel: 409 562 2153 • *Mail-order organic clothing.*

COUNCIL FOR TEXTILE RECYCLING • Suite 1212, 7910 Woodmount Avenue Bethesda, MD 20814 • Tel: 301 718 0671

COUNTRY COMFORT INTERIORS • 623 Northwest Hill Street, Bend, OR 97701 • Tel: 503 385 1147 • *Country comfort sells and installs low-toxic floor and window coverings.*

CROCODILE TIERS • 402 North 99th Street, Mesa, AZ 85207 • Tel: 602 373 9823 • *Formaldehyde testing of fabrics, chemical-free fabrics.*

DEEPA TEXTILES • 333 Bryant Street, Suite 160, San Francisco, CA 94107 • Tel: 800 8-DEEPTX / 415 621 4171 • *Upholstery fabrics, no topical treatments.*

DESIGN MATERIALS INC • 241 S 55th Street, Kansas City, KS 66106 • Tel: 913 342 9796 Fax 913 342 9826 • *Natural fiber wallcoverings.*

DORAN TEXTILES INC • PO Box 9000, Shelby, NC 28151-9000 • Tel: 800 888 2484 Fax: 704 487 2064

DYERSBURG FABRICS INC • 1460 Broadway, 16th Floor, New York, NY 10036 • Tel: 212 869 6600 Fax: 212 869 5759 • *Dyersburg has led the way in developing environmentally correct fleece products. Dyersburg's ECO Collection includes 89% ECO, 100% ECO Wool.*

GRATEFUL THREADS • 1301 Spruce Street, Boulder, CO 80302 • Tel: 800 317 8122 • *Decorative throws and rugs. Grateful Threads is dedicated to and pioneering the use of organic cotton in quality home fashion.*

GREENSLEEVES • Green Market, 710 Route 202, New Salem, MA 01355 • Tel: 508 544 7911 • *Clothing and accessories from organically grown textiles. Retail and wholesale. Mail order.*

FIBER NATURALS • Green Market, 710 Route 202, New Salem, MA 01355 • Tel: 508 544 7911 • *Organic, naturally colored, naturally dyed and other low-chemically treated textiles for manufacturers and the home sewer. Mail order and retail store.*

FOXFIBRE • Natural Colors Inc, Sally Vreseis Fox, Wickenburg, AZ • Tel: 520 684 7199 • *Naturally colored fabrics, 100% cotton, undyed, untreated.*

GARNET HILL • 262 Main Street, Franconia, NH 03580 • Tel: 800 622 6216 / 603 823 5545 Fax: 603 823 7034 • *Catalog offers an array of exclusive all-natural linens, furnishing, and accessories for the home, and clothing for the family. All are created with the finest quality material, craftsmanship, and fabrics which ensures they will endure from one generation to the next.*

HOMESPUN • Box 3223-NHC, Ventura, CA Energy Depot, CA 95916 / 3821-02325 • Tel: 805 642 8111 Fax: 805 642 0759 • *Interestingly textured, neutral, 10' wide cotton fabrics, no chemical finishes. For seamless draperies, walls, upholstery, slipcovers, bedspreads, tablecloths. Catalog/swatches $2.*

HOUSE OF HEMP • Box 14603, 2111 E Burnside Street, Portland, OR 97204 Tel: 503 232 1128 • *Hemp fabrics.*

IDA GRAE • 424 LaVerne Avenue, Mill Valley, CA 94941 • Tel: 415 388 6101 • *Custom yardage, natural dyes, natural fibers.*

THE INSTITUTE FOR HEMP • Tel: 612 222 2628 • *Hemp products and information. Free catalog.*

INSUL SHUTTER • PO Box 888, 69 Island Street, Keene, NH 03431 • Tel: 603 352 2726 • *Insulating fabrics for windows.*

JACK LENOR LARSEN • 41 East 11th Street, New York, NY 10003 • Tel: 212 674 3993 • *Drapery fabrics, untreated surfaces.*

JANTZ DESIGN • Box 3071, Santa Rosa, CA 95402 • Tel: 800 365 6563 / 707 823 8834 • *Wool mattress pads, natural comforters, and cotton bedding. Catalog,*

JOINT VENTURE HEMPERY • Box 2006, Main Station, Vancouver, BC, Canada, V6B 3P8 • Tel: 604 737 8539

JUST HEMP • 216 Calle Los Molinos, San Clemente, CA 92672 • Tel: 818 449 4573 Fax: 818 578 3493

KENAF INTERNATIONAL LTD • 120 E Jay Avenue, McAllen, TX 78504 • Tel: 210 687 2619 Fax: 210 687 2045

MALDEN MILLS • 46 Strafford Street, Lawrence, MA 08141 • Tel: 508 685 6341

MOTHER HART'S • 3300 S Congress Avenue, Unit 21, Boynton Beach, FL 33424-4229 Tel: 407 738 5866 • *Catalog, 100% all natural, undyed, unbleached, no-formaldehyde cotton sheets, and untreated bath towels.*

NATURAL COTTON COLOURS INC • 67 N Tegner Street, PO Box 66, Wickenburg, AZ 85358 • Tel: 602 684 7199

OCARINA TEXTILES • 16 Cliff Street, New London, CT 06320 • Tel: 203 437 8189 • *Fabrics.*

OHIO HEMPERY • 7002 SR 329, Caysville, OH 45735 • Tel: 800 BUY HE • *Hemp fabrics by the roll or by the meter. Hemp seed, oil, paper, twine, body care and other products.*

ORGANIC COTTONS • 103 Hoffecker Road, Phoenixville, PA 19460 • Tel: 610 495 9986 • *Mail-order clothing, pillows etc.*

ORGANIC INTERIORS • 8 College Avenue, Nanuet, NY 10954 • Tel: 914 623 2114 • *Organic cotton fabric, fill, wool fill, drapes etc.*

PUEBLO TO PEOPLE • 2105 Silber Road, Suite 101, Houston, TX 77055 • Tel: 800 843 5257 / 713 956 1172 Fax: 713 956 8443 • *Handwoven rugs, blankets, tablecloths, tapestries, baskets, pottery and bookshelves from indigenous artisans in ten Latin American countries. Handwoven clothing and organic foods, too. Free Catalog.*

SAJAMA ALPACA AND DESIGNS • PO Box 1209, Ashland, OR 97520 • Tel: 800 736 0949 Fax: 503 488 3949 • *Specialize in fibers that are free of toxic mordants, dyes, and mothproofing. A full line of Alpaca products for hand spinners, knitters and weavers.*

SUREWAY TRADING • 826 Pine Avenue, Suite 6 & 5, Niagara Falls, NY 14301 • Tel: 416 596 1887 Fax: 716 282 8211 • *Silks, dyes, and scarves.*

TEST FABRICS • Box 420, Middlesex, NJ 08846 • Tel: 908 469 6446 • *Catalog.*

TEXAS ORGANIC COTTON GROWERS ASSOCIATION • 201 West Broadway, Brownfield, TX 79316 • Tel: 806 637 4547

TWIN OAKS HAMMOCKS • Box N, Tecumseh, MO 65760 • Tel: 417 679 4682 Fax: 417 679 4684 • *Earth-friendly comfort! Luxurious hammocks, handwoven from Organic Cotton and Recycled Polyester rope. Call or write for free information.*

Bedrooms ~ *page 145*

ALLERGY CONTROL PRODUCTS • 96 Danbury Road, Box 793, Ridgefield, CT 06877 • Tel: 800 422-DUST • *Barrier cloths for bedding.*

ALLERGY RELIEF SHOP • 2932 Middlebrook Park, Knoxville, TN 37921 • Tel: 615 522 2795 • *Bedding, mattress sets, barrier cloths, and sheets. Catalog,*

BIO CLINIC • Sunrise Medical, 4083 E Airport Drive, Ontario, CA 91761 • Tel: 800 347 7780 • *100% cotton covers and some poly products certified by Green Cross.*

BRIGHT FUTURES • 3120 Central Avenue, SE Albuquerque, NM 87106 • *Handmade futons and accessories with organic cotton coverings encased in FoxFiber™ for the chemically sensitive.*

MARY CORDARO • 12439 Magnolia Boulevard, no 263, Valley Village, CA 91607 • Tel: 310 838 2892 / 818 981 7245 Fax: 810 766 5882 • *Healthy Bedrooms by Certified Bau-Biologists.*

COTTLAND BEDDING COMPANY, INC • 641 South Cooper Street, Memphis, TN 38104 • Tel: 901 278 4994 • *American made futon frames, mattresses and covers.*

CROWN CITY MATTRESS • 250 South San Gabriel Boulevard, San Gabriel, CA 91776 • Tel: 213 681 6356 Fax: 818 796 9101 • *Manufacture mattresses, box springs, and futons with natural, renewable materials. Organically grown cotton is used and wool processed without chlorine.*

DONA DESIGNS • 1611 Bent Tree Street, Seagoville, TX 75159 • Tel: 214 287 7834 • *Organic cotton pillows and bedding.*

GARNET HILL • The Original Natural Fibers Catalog, 262 Main Street, Franconia, NH 03580 • Tel: 800 622 6216 • *Natural fiber bedding and clothing. Catalog.*

HEART OF VERMONT • The Old Schoolhouse, Route 132, Box 183, Sharon, VT 05065 • Tel: 802 763 2720 / 800 639 4123 • *Healthy bedding and furniture. Catalog.*

HULL COVE JOB SHOP • PO Box 281, Jamestown, RI 02835 • Tel: 401 423 0433 • *Wind and solar powered workshop making antique reproduction beds.*

IDEAL ENVIRONMENTS INC • Roger Maurice, 401 W Adams, Fairfield, IA 52556 • Tel: 515 472 6547 • *Radio-controlled switch to shut off electricity in the bedroom.*

THE JANICE CORP • 198 Route 46, Budd Lake, NJ 07828 • Tel: 201 691 2979 • *Bedding, mattress sets, padding, and barrier cloths.*

JANTZ DESIGN • Box 3071, Santa Rosa, CA 95402 • Tel: 800 365 6563 / 707 823 8834 • *Wool mattress pads, natural comforters, furniture, organic wood and cotton bedding. Catalog.*

KAREN'S NON-TOXIC PRODUCTS • 1839 Dr. Jack Road, Conowingo, MD 21918 • Tel: 800 KARENS-4 • *Pillows. Catalog.*

THIS MAY BE THE ONLY BED MORE NATURAL THAN OURS.

At Royal-Pedic we handcraft designer quality mattresses with the kinds of materials Mother Nature would approve of. 100% cotton, pure lambswool and natural latex foam. Natural fibers breathe easier, conform better to your body and last longer than synthetics. Most important, they don't contain petrochemical synthetics which emit toxic fumes. **For a free brochure, call 1-800-487-6925.**

SINCE 1946

Royal-Pedic ®
THE HEALTHY BED.

ORGANIC COTTON AVAILABLE

Featuring the Royal-Pedic Pillowtop Mattress • Royal-Pedic All Cotton Mattress Royal Latex Mattress • Royal Latex Quilt-top Mattress • Adjustable Electric Beds • Iron beds

Royal-Pedic Showroom, 119 N. Fairfax Avenue, Los Angeles, CA 90036 (213) 932-6155
1-800-487-6925 M-F 10A-6P, Sat. 10A-5P PST.

KB COTTON PILLOWS INC • PO Box 57, De Soto, TX 75123 • Tel: 214 223 7193 / 800 544 3752 • *Pure 100% cotton pillows - staple cotton, air tested to be chemically free. Ticking pre-washed in baking soda solution. Received the 'non-toxic' rating by Debra Lynn Dadd. Sizes: Standard, K, Q, Travel/Youth, Baby, Continental in white, ticking stripe, or natural unbleached ecru fabric. Please call and leave name, address, and phone number for information and order forms.*

MOTHER HART'S • 3300 S Congress Avenue, Unit 21, Boynton Beach, FL 33424-4229 Tel: 407 738 5866 • *Catalog, 100% all natural, undyed, unbleached, no-formaldehyde cotton sheets.*

NATURAL BEDROOM • 175 North Main Street, Sebastopol, CA 95472 • Tel: 707 823 8834 Fax: 707 823 0106 • *100% natural fiber sleep pillows, wool comforters and baby bedding. Call or write for a free catalog.*

NATURAL RESOURCES • 745 Powderhorn, Monument, CO 80132 • Tel: 719 488 3630 / 800 USE-FLAX • *Natural bedding, pillows, barrier cloth, and mattress sets.*

NATIONAL ECOLOGICAL AND ENVIRONMENTAL DELIVERY SYSTEM (NEEDS) • 527 Charles Avenue 12A, Syracuse, NY 13209 • Tel: 800 634 1380 / 315 446 1122 • *Catalog, Barrier cloths.*

NORTHWEST FUTONS • PO Box 14952, Portland, OR 97214 • Tel: 503 224 3199 Fax: 503 231 9489

OGALLALA DOWN COMFORTER CO • Box 830, Searle Field, Ogallala, NE 69153 • Tel: 308 284 8404 • *Natural down comforters.*

ORGANIC COTTONS • 103 Hoffecker Road, Phoenixville, PA 19460 • Tel: 610 495 9986 • *Mail-order clothing, pillows etc.*

ORGANIC INTERIORS • 8 College Avenue, Nanuel, NY 10954 • Tel: 914 623 21114 • *Organic bedroom drapes and bedding.*

RICHMOND COTTON CO • 529 5th Street, Santa Rosa, CA 95401 • Tel: 800 992 8924 • *Natural blankets and children's products.*

RISING STAR FUTONS • 35 North West Bond Street, Bend, OR 97701 • Tel: 800 828 6711 / 503 382 4221 Fax: 503 3835925 • *Non-allergenic, chemical-free premium-quality futons, all sizes; shipped UPS. Call for your free catalog.* See p. 155.

ROYAL-PEDIC • 119 no Fairfax Avenue, Los Angeles, CA 90036 • Tel: 213 932 6155 Fax: 213 932 6158 • *The Mattress made healthier so you sleep better, and feel better.*

SDH ENTERPRISES • 1717 Solano Way, # 23 Concord, CA 94520 • Tel: 415 685 7035 • *Untreated bedding.*

SEVENTH GENERATION • 49 Hercules Drive, Colchester, VT 05446-1672 • Tel: 800 444 7336 • *Chemical-free, undyed bedding, linens, towels, and undergarments. Household products. Catalog.*

TERRA VERDE • 120 Wooster Street, New York, NY 10012 • Tel: 212 925 4355 Fax: 212 925 4540 • *Retail store and mail order for non-treated bedding.*

VINEYARD COMFORTS • RFD 40, Vineyard Haven, MA 02568 • Tel: 508 693 1583 Fax: 508 693 2933 • *Comforters filled with wool from sheep on Martha's Vineyard. Also wool batting for mattress covers, pillows, and insulated window coverings.*

Bathrooms ~ page 148

ALEXANDRA AVERY • 4717 SE Belmont Street, Portland, OR 97215 • Tel: 800 669 1863 • *Alexandra Avery, Purely Natural. Aromatherapy, Skin Care, Custom Facials, Bath and Body Botanical Perfumes. Garden formulas provide active help to those desiring a 100% natural, effective and affordable approach to skin care.*

ATLANTIC RECYCLED PAPER COMPANY (ARP/NOPE) • Box 39179, Baltimore, MD 21212 • Tel: 301 323 2811 • *100% cotton shower curtain. Replaces vinyl liners. Keeps water in the tub, machine washable. White or Natural.*

AUBREY ORGANICS • 4419 N Manhattan Avenue, Tampa, FL 33614 • Tel: 800 282 7394 • *Natural cosmetics.*

AVEDA • 4000 Pheasant Ridge Drive, Minneapolis, MN 55449 • Tel: 800 328 0849 • *Natural cosmetics.*

BATHCREST INC • 2425 S Progress Drive, Salt Lake City, UT 84119 • Tel: 800 826 6790 Fax: 801 977 0328 • *Save your money and the environment. Bathcrest refinishes existing tubs saving you up to 80% over replacement.*

C'EST NATURAL • c/o For Your Health Products, 6623 Hillandale Road, Chevy Chase, MD 20815 • Tel: 301 654 1127 Fax: 301 654 2125 • *Body Crystal deodorant stone.*

CLEAR LIGHT • The Cedar Company, Box 551 – State Road 165 Placitas, NM 87043 • Tel: 505 867 2381 • *The cedar-based body-care products manufacturer.*

DRY CREEK HERB FARM • 13935 Dry Creek Road, Auburn, CA 95602 • Tel: 916 878 2441 • *Earth-borne collection of skin care products.*

EARTH TOOLS • 9754 Johanna Place, Shadow Hills, CA 91040 • Tel: 800 825 6460 / 818 353 5883 • *Products for the Natural Home, all at great prices. Call for free catalog.*

EARTH PRESERV • PO Box 142286, Irving, TX 75014 • Tel: 214 717 0399 Fax: 214 541 1514 • *Natural bathroom products and other lovely things for the home.*

ENVISION FORT HOWARD CORPORATION • Green Bay, WI 54307 • Tel: 414 435 8821 • *Recycled tissues, toilet paper etc.*

DON JOHNSON KITCHENS & BATHS • Suite 1375 Merchandise Mart, Chicago, IL 60654 • Fax: 312 644 8139 • *Designers, consultants, suppliers and installers of 'chemically reduced environment' products for the bathroom.*

KISS MY FACE • 144 Main Street, Box 224, Gardiner, NY 12525-0224 • Tel: 800 262 5477 • *Natural cosmetics.*

LOGONA • 580-B Dutch Valley Road, Atlanta, GA 30324 • Tel: 800 648 6654 • *Natural cosmetics.*

NADINA'S CREMES • 3600 Clipper Mill Road, Suite 140, Baltimore, MD 21211 • Tel: 800 722 4292 Fax: 410 235 3011 • *Scented body cremes in beautiful handmade ceramic jars for moisturizer, massage, bath oil, and aromatherapy.*

THE NATURAL BATH • PO Box 97, Haddonfield, NJ 08033 • Tel: 609 427 0115

NATURE LINE • Alan Stuart Inc, New York, NY 10018 • *Bath accessories and brushes.*

NORSTAD POTTERY • 253 South 25th Street, Richmond, CA 94804 • Tel: 510 620 0200 Fax: 510 620 0303 • *Hand-thrown bathroom sinks.*

PAUL PENDERS • 1340 Commerce Street, Petaluma, CA 94954 • Tel: 800 473 6337 • *Natural cosmetics.*

PROGRESSIVE PLANET DISTRIBUTING COMPANY • 96 Arapahoe Suite B, Boulder, CO 80302 • Tel: 303 444 3109 / 800 604 3109 Fax: 303 449 7540 • *Wide range of ecologically sound mail-order products for the whole house. Bathroom products include Ecco Bella Botanicals and Kingsley bath accessories.*

RACHEL PERRY • 9111 Mason Avenue, Chatsworth, CA 91311 • Tel: 800 966 8888 • *Natural cosmetics.*

SDH ENTERPRISES • 1717 Solano Way, # 23 Concord, CA 94520 • Tel: 415 685 7035 • *Bath accessories.*

SHIVANI • PO Box 377, Lancaster, MA 01523 • Tel: 800 237 8221 • *Natural cosmetics.*

SIMPLERS BOTANICAL CO • Box 39, Forestville, CA 95436 • *Fine Botanical Body Care since 1981.*

SMITH'S HEALTHY CHOICES • 3463 Yonge Street, Toronto, Canada, M4N 2N3 • Tel: 416 488 2600 Fax: 416 484 8855 • *Store and Catalog for non-toxic products, Natural and Speciality Pharmaceuticals, Health Care, Body Care, Building and Maintenance Products.*

SYNDESIS INC • 2908 Colorado Avenue, Santa Monica, CA 90404 • Tel: 310 829 9932 Fax: 310 829 5641 • *SYNDECRETE is an innovative solid architectural surfacing material for sinks, bathtubs, and showers.*

TOBLER, TONNEAU & CANVAS • PO Box 214, Eldred, PA 16731 • Tel: 800 814 5110 • *Manufacturers of 'The Shower Curtain'. Made of 100% natural cotton canvas, environmentally smart, allergy free.*

TRADITIONAL PRODUCTS COMPANY • PO Box 564, Creswell, OR 97426 • Tel: 503 895 2957 • *Mail-order products including wooden-handled plant bristle brushes, sisal mitts, and wooden combs.*

VITAE BODY CARE • 576 Searls Avenue, Nevada City, CA 95959 • Tel: 800 643 3011 • *Products include aromatic sprays, lotions, bath gels, massage oils and candles. Free catalog.*

WELEDA PHARMACY • 841 South Main Street, PO Box 769, Spring Valley, NY 10977 • Tel: 914 352 6145

Kitchens ~ page 149

AEG • Andi-Co, Appliances Inc, 65 Campus Plaza, Edison, NJ 08837 • Tel: 800 344 0043 • *Energy-saving dishwasher, stainless steel interior.*

APPLIED ENGINEERING • 218 Dartmouth SE, Albuquerque, NM 87106 • Tel: 505 256 1261 • *Solar cookers.*

AMERICOLD • Ken Taulbee • Tel: 205 734 9160 • *Energy-efficient refrigerators and low CFC refrigerators.*

THE BAKER'S CATALOG • PO Box 876, Norwich Vermont 05055-0876 • *Mail-order catalog of baking trays, flours and kitchen utensils, and much more!*

BOSCH CORP • 2800 South 25th Avenue, Broadview, IL 60153 • Tel: 708 865 5200 / 800 866 2022 • *Distributor information. Water-saving dishwashers, noise reduction, energy saving.*

BURNS-MILWAUKEE INC • 4010 West Douglas Avenue, Milwaukee, WI 53209 • Tel: 414 438 1234 Fax: 414 438 1604 • *Villager Sun Oven.*

THE CONSERVE GROUP • Box 1560, Bethlehem, PA 18016 • Tel: 610 691 8024 • *Any refrigerator can be super-efficient with CHILLshield - the refrigerator vapor barrier.*

DESIGN CONCEPTS INC • Henry Jacoby, 314 Aspetuck Village, Huntington, CT 06484 • Tel: 203 926 0115 • *Healthy kitchen concepts, certified designer.*

ECOLOGY BY DESIGN • (CONCEPTS FOR A TOXIC-FREE ENVIRONMENT) • Audrey Hoodkiss, 1341 Ocean Avenue, Suite 73, Santa Monica, CA 90401 • Tel: 310 394 4146 • Kitchen consultant, Woodcabinets, healthy finishes.

ECOTECH RECYCLED PRODUCTS • 14241, 60th Street North, Clearwater, FL 34620-2706 • Tel: 800 780 5353 Fax: 813 538 8550 • *Lidded recycling container.*

ELECTRON CONNECTION • Box 442, Medford, OR 97501 • Tel: 916 475 3401 • *Appliances and miscellaneous products.*

ENERGY CONCEPTS CO • 627 Ridgely Avenue, Annapolis, MD 21401 • Tel: 301 266 6521 • *Solar thermal refrigerator and icemaker.*

FORBO INDUSTRIES • 17711 Valley View, Cerritos, CA 90701 • Tel: 800 526 1627 • *Manufacturer of Marmoleum Fresco sheet linoleum – non-toxic and natural.*

GENERAL ELECTRIC (CANADA) • 1130 Boulevard Charec West, Quebec, Canada, G1N 2E2 • Tel: 418 682 8500 Fax: 418 682 8550 • *Induction cooktops.*

GREEN TECHNOLOGIES INC • 5490 Spine Road, Boulder, CO 80301 • *Green Plug electricity saver for household appliances.*

HEALTHY HARVEST INC • PO Box 861, Madison, CT 06443-0861 • Tel: 203 245 2033 Fax: 203 245 7539 • *Healthy Harvest Fruit and Vegetable Rinse dissolves 95% of the wax and lifts residues to the surface where water can wash them away.*

HEARTLAND APPLIANCES, INC • 5 Hoffman Street, Kitchener, Ontario, Canada, N2M 3M5 • Tel: 519 743 8111 Fax: 519 743 1665 • *Wood-fired kitchen stoves.*

HOME CANNING SUPPLY AND SPECIALITIES • PO Box 1158, 2117 Main Street, Ramona, CA 92065 • Tel: 619 788 0520 Fax: 619 789 4745 • *Catalog of all you need to make your own preserves.*

DON JOHNSON KITCHENS & BATHS • Suite 1375 Merchandise Mart, Chicago, IL 60654 • Fax: 312 644 8139 • *Designers, consultants, suppliers, and installers of 'chemically reduced environment' products for the kitchen.*

KANSAS WIND POWER • (dept NHC) 13569 214th Road, Holton, KS 66436 • Tel: 913 364 4407 • *Solar cookers.*

LOW KEEP REFRIGERATION • 2465 Second Avenue, Otsego, MI 49078-9406 • Tel: 616 692 3015 • *Makers of high-efficiency refrigerators for home and business, 12 and 24v DC, 115v AC.*

MIELE APPLIANCES INC • 22 D Worlds Fair Drive, Somerset, NJ 08873 • Tel: 908 560 0899 800 289 MIELE • *German-made appliances, stainless steel interior, energy saving and water saving.*

NEFF KITCHENS • Tel: 800 268 4527 • *98% formaldehyde-free kitchen design.*

THE NEW COUNCIL ON FOOD SAFETY • Community Nutrition Institute, 2001 S Street NW, Suite 530 • Washington DC 20009

NEW ENGLAND HEARTH & STONE • 127 North Street, Goshen, CT 06756 • Tel: 203 491 3091 • *Rod Zander, Stove Mason specializes in soapstone countertops, sinks, tiles. Meticulous craftsmanship.*

NORCOLD • 600 Kuther Road, Sidney, OH 45365 • *Manufacture a range of energy-efficient refrigerators including RV refrigerators.*

NORSTAD POTTERY • 253 South 25th Street, Richmond, CA 94804 • Tel: 510 620 0200 Fax: 510 620 0303 • *Hand-thrown kitchen sinks.*

ORGANIC FOODS PRODUCTION ASSOCIATION OF NORTH AMERICA • PO Box 1078, Greenfield, MA 01301 • Tel: 413 774 7511

P/F CONSUMER PRODUCTS • 1500 South Hellman, Ontario, CA 91761 • Tel: 909 947 6711 • *Aluminum can crusher.*

PHILIPS • address to come • address to come • *Makers of Whirlpool high-efficiency refrigerators.*

PHOTOCOMM INC • PO Box 14230, Scottsdale, AZ 85267-4230 • Tel: 800 544 6466 / 602 951 6330 • *Vestfrost low-energy freezer. Makers of Vestfrost low-energy CFC-free refrigerators and freezers, solar electric power systems, solar and gas-powered fridges and freezers.*

PROGRESSIVE PLANET DISTRIBUTING COMPANY • 96 Arapahoe Suite B, Boulder, CO 80302 • Tel: 303 444 3109 / 800 604 3109 Fax: 303 449 7540 • *Ecologically sound mail-order products for the house. Kitchen products include muslin coffee socks, net bags, and keep saks.*

PUBLIC VOICE FOR FOOD AND HEALTH POLICY • 1001 Connecticut Avenue NW, Suite 522, Washington DC 20036

REAL GOODS TRADING CORPORATION • 555 Leslie Street, Ukiah, CA 95482 • Tel: 800 762 7325 • Your complete resource for energy efficient living. See p. 96.

SMALL POWER SYSTEMS • 74550 Dobie Lane, Covelo, CA 95428 • Tel: 800 972 7179 • *Solar absorption refrigeration.*

SOLAR CHEF • 2412 Robinson Road, Grants Pass, OR 97527 • Tel: 503471 • *Solar cookers.*

SOLAR COOKERS INTERNATIONAL • 1724 11th Street, Sacramento, CA 95814 • Tel: 916 444 6616 • *Solar cookers including designs to make your own.*

STABER INDUSTRIES INC • 4411 Marketing Place, Groveport, OH 43125 • Tel: 800 848 6200 • *System 2000 clothes washer designed to use less water, less energy, and less detergent.*

SUNELCO • Box 1499, Hamilton, MT 59840 • Tel: 406 363 6924 • *Appliances available. Catalog,*

SUN FROST REFRIGERATORS • PO BOX 1011, 824 L Street, Arcata, CA 95521 • Tel: 707 822 9095 Fax: 707 822 6213 • *Energy-efficient refrigerators and freezers.*

SUN OVEN • Ethel and Ken Farnsworth, 138 Willoway Drive, Boise, ID 83705 • Tel: 208 336 4883 • *Manufacturers of Sun Oven™ solar power cookers.*

SYNDESIS INC • 2908 Colorado Avenue, Santa Monica, CA 90404 • Tel: 310 829 9932 Fax: 310 829 5641 • *SYNDECRETE is an innovative solid architectural surfacing material for counter tops, tiles, and sinks.*

TREE SAVER • PO Box 22745, Denver, CO 80222 • Tel: 303 695 6163 • *Reusable trash liner made of water resistant yet washable oxford nylon cloth.*

TRILLIUM PRODUCTS INC • PO Box 157, Cannon Falls, MN 55009-0157 • *Makers of Lunch Locks, wrapper-free lunch boxes.*

ZOMEWORKS • PO Box 25805, 1011A Sawmill Road Northwest, Albuquerque, NM 87125 • Tel: 505 242 5354 Fax: 505 243 5187 • *Solar cookers.*

Nursery ~ page 150

ALL-ONE-GOD-FAITH INC • PO Box 28 Escondido, CA 92033 • Tel: 619 743 2211 / 619 745 7069 • *Baby care products, hair care, essential oils/fragrances, soy products, no-salt products.*

AWARE DIAPERS INC • PO Box 2591, Greeley, CO • Tel: 303 352 6822 / 800 748 1606 • *100% cotton form fitting diapers.*

BABY BUNZ & CO • Box 1717, Sebastopol, CA 94953 • Tel: 707 829 5347 • *Natural fiber diapers and baby products.*

BIOBOTTOMS • Box 6009, Petaluma, CA 94953 • Tel: 707 778 7945 • *Diapers and diaper covers.*

THE BLUE EARTH • 2899 Agoura Road, Suite 625, Westlake Village, CA 91361 • Tel: 800 825 4540 / 818 707 2187 • *Baby personal care items. Catalog.*

BUMKINS • 7720 E Redfield Road, Suite 4, Scottsdale, AZ 85260 • Tel: 606 483 7070 • *One-piece diaper w/nylon cover.*

COTTONTAILS INTERNATIONAL • 3300 Bee Caves Road, # 650, Austin, TX 78746 • Tel: 800 873 2686 / 512 329 2920 • *Diapers.*

THE R DUCK COMPANY INC • 650 Ward Drive, Suite H, Santa Barbara, CA 93111 • Tel: 800 422-DUCK • *Diaper covers/print & colors.*

ENVIRO-TOTE INC • 4 Cote Lane, Bedford, NH 03110-5805 • Tel: 800 233 7254 / 603 647 7171 Fax: 603 647 0116

HANNA ANDERSON • 1010 NW Flanders, Portland, OR 97209 • Tel: 800 222 0544

HEART OF VERMONT • Environmental Home Furnishings, The Old Schoolhouse, Route 132, Box 183, Sharon, VT 05065 • Tel: 802 763 2720 / 800 639 4123 • *Catalog.*

INKANYEZI RAINBOW PROJECT • PO Box 1123, Blue Hill, ME 04614 • Tel: 207 374 2405 Fax: 207 374 2383 • *Exquisite ethnic dolls from South Africa as well as other African crafts.*

KOOSHIES DIAPERS INT • 132 West High Street, Wills Point, TX 75169 • Tel: 903 873 2581 • *100% cotton diapers and covers.*

THE NATURAL BABY CO • RD 1 Box 160S, Titusville, NJ 08560 • Tel: 609 737 2895

NATURAL BEDROOM • 175 North Main Street, Sebastopol, CA 95472 • Tel: 707 823 8834 Fax: 707 823 0106 • *100% natural fiber sleep pillows, wool comforters and baby bedding. Call or write for a free catalog.*

ORGANIC BABY/DIAPERAPS • 9760 Owensmouth Avenue, Chatsworth, CA 91311 • Tel: 818 886 7471 Fax: 818 886 4033 • *Manufacturer of quality infant wear from organic cotton also manufacture and distribute fine natural diapering products, training pants, and a new swimsuit diaper.*

PURE PODUNK • RR 1 Box 69, Thetford Center, VT 05075 • Tel: 800 333 4505 • *Toys, bedding, clothing, and diapers.*

RICHMAN COTTON CO • 529 5th Street, Santa Rosa, CA 95401 • Tel: 800 992 8924 • *Natural blankets and children's products.*

SEVENTH GENERATION • 10 Farrell Street, So Burlington, VT 05403 • Tel: 800 456 1177 • *Catalog. Toys and diapers.*

SNUGGLEBUNDLE ENTERPRISES • 6325-9 Falls of Neuse Road no 321, Raleigh, NC 27615 • Tel: 919 990 2353 • *Green cotton products for babies include diapers, layette, bath products and much more.*

WILD THINGS • Box 445, Newtown, PA 18940 • *Catalog of rainsticks, wooden snakes, critters, etc.*

Home offices ~ page 152

A TO Z PRINTING • 815 M Street, Lincoln, NE 68508 • Tel: 402 477 0815 • *Offers services to consumers with smaller orders.*

ALTE SCHULE USA • 704 E Palace Avenue, # 4 Sante Fe, NM 87501 • Tel: 505 983 2593 Fax: 505 438 6240 • *Recycled paper products from Germany, wooden writing utensils, artist-quality colored pencils in raw cedar and more.*

ATLANTIC RECYCLED PAPER COMPANY (ARP/NOPE) • Box 11021, Baltimore, MD 21212 • Tel: 301 323 2811

BANDELIER ENVIRONMENTAL PAPERS • Sante Fe, NM 87505 • Tel: 800 366 4071

BAYVIEW TECHNOLOGY GROUP • 35 Bayview Drive, San Carlos, CA 94070 • Tel: 415 592 9664 Fax: 415 593 0156 • *LaserMiser saves electrical power by automatically switching laser printers on and off based on usage.*

BRUSH DANCE • 100 Ebbtide Avenue, Building No 1, Sausalito, CA 94965 • Tel: 800 531 7445 / 415 331 9030 Fax: 415 331 9059 • *Brush Dance helps people express their deepest feelings with recycled paper bookmarks, cards, journals, posters and T-shirts, nightshirts and magnets.*

CHRISTIAN COMPUTER AND COMMUNICATIONS MINISTRY • PO Box 101914, Denver, CO 80250 • Tel: 303 620 7121 • *Provides "green" PCs and monitors to non-profit organizations at wholesale prices.*

CONSERVATREE PAPER COMPANY • 10 Lombard Street, Suite 250, San Francisco, CA 94111 • Tel: 415 433 1000 • *Leader in the recycled paper industry.*

EARTH CARE PAPER INC • Box 7070, Madison, WI 53707 • Tel: 608 277 2900 • *Caters to small and quantity buyers. Catalog.*

ECO SOURCE CATALOG • PO Box 1656, Sebastopol, CA 95473-1656 • Tel: 707 829 3506 Fax: 707 829 7811 • *Energy-efficient lighting, recycled paper products, health products etc.*

EVERGREEN COMPUTER SYSTEMS • 661 G Street, Arcata, CA 95521 • Tel: 800 775 7476 • *Healthy, energy-efficient computer systems at mail order prices. All systems come with a low-radiation color monitor and energy saving features.*

FOREST SAVER INC • 1860 Pond Road, Ronkonkoma, NY 11779 • Tel: 800 777 9886 Fax: 516 585 6962 • *100% post-consumer stationery items made from old maps.*

GRC • 20650 Prairie Street, Chatsworth, CA 91311 • Tel: 818 709 1234 • *Quality remanufactured laser and ink jet cartridges. Call for your nearest dealer.*

GREENDISK INC • 15530 Woodinville-Redmond Road, Woodinville, WA 98072 • Tel: 206 489 2550 • *Recycled obsolete software and diskettes.*

GREEN EARTH OFFICE SUPPLY • PO Box 719, Redwood Estates, CA 95044 • Tel: 800 327 8449 Fax: 408 353 1346 • *Environmentally friendly office and school supplies. Recycled products, tree-free paper and more! Free catalog.*

THE GREEN OFFICE • 3412 Bloomfield Shore Drive, West Bloomfield, MI 48323 • Tel: 810 737 0971 • *Mail order supplier of non-toxic or recycled business supplies.*

INKJET RENEW • 1534 East Edinger, Santa Ana, CA 92705 • Tel: 714 972 8142 • *Inkjet cartridges for printers, plotters, and faxes are recycled. Postal recycling service.*

THE JOHN ROSSI COMPANY INC • 180 South Highland Avenue, Ossining, NY 10562 • Tel: 914 941 1752 Fax: 914 941 1810 • *Retreads – Journals and planner made from recycled tires and newspaper.*

KEEP IT SIMPLE SYSTEMS (KISS) • 32 S Ewing, Suite 330, Helena, MT 59601 • Tel: 406 442 3559 • *Solar Power for portable computers! Unique flexible and durable solar panels designed to run or recharge many popular portable computers.*

NOESTING INC • Bronx, NY 10454 • Tel: 914 664 2252 • *Recycled paper clips.*

NORAD CORPORATION • 1160 East Sandhill Avenue, Carson, CA 90746 • Tel: 310 605 0808 / 800 262 3260 Fax: 310 605 5051 • *NoRad™ Radiation Shield will fit virtually all computer displays.*

PATRIOT PAPER • 892 River Street, Hyde Park, MAS 02136 • Tel: 800 447 3111 • *100% recycled. Minimum order 10,000 lbs.*

PHOENIX DESIGNS • 10875 Chicago Drive, Zeeland, MI 49464 • Tel: 616 654 5323 / 800 253 2733 • *Recyclable office chairs.*

PROGRESSIVE PLANET DISTRIBUTING COMPANY • 96 Arapahoe Suite B, Boulder, CO 80302 • Tel: 303 444 3109 / 800 604 3109 Fax: 303 449 7540 • *Ecologically sound mail-order products including hemp and cereal straw paper and writing instruments made from fallen twigs.*

RECYCLED PAPER COMPANY INC • 185 Corey Road, Boston, MA 02146 • Tel: 617 277 9901 / 212 675 8198 (NY) • *Recycled paper.*

RECYCLED WORLDS CONSULTING • The Grayson Building, 4414 Regent Street, Suite 200, Madison, WI 53705-4961 • Tel: 603 231 1100 • *WasteSort computer software.*

SOPHISTICATED CIRCUITS INC • 19017 120th Avenue, no 106, Bothell, WA 98011 • Tel: 206 485 7979 • *Innovative Macintosh hardware accessories and memory modules with lifetime warranty. System's energy consumption is managed by PowerKey™.*

SUN REMANUFACTURING CORPORATION • 40 West Hoover Avenue, Mesa, AZ 85210 • Tel: 800 828 8617 / 602 833 5600 • *Remanufacture nylon fabric printer ribbons for dot matrix printers.*

TREE FREE ECOPAPER • One World Trade Center, 121 SW Salmon, Suite 1100, Portland, OR 97204 • Tel: 800 775 0225 / 503 690 4052 • *Hemp paper.*

Cleaning products ~ *page 160*

4 THE PLANET INC • RD 1 Box 20-1A, S Kortright, NY 13842 • Tel: 800 253 4836 • *Cleaning products.*

AMERICAN FORMULATING AND MANUFACTURING (AFM ENTERPRISES INC) • PO Box 124698, San Diego, CA 92101-4698 • *Coatings, cleaners, sealers formulated without toxic chemicals. SafeChoice products prevent indoor air pollution, and are safe for the chemically sensitive.*

ALLENS NATURALLY • PO Box 514, Farmington, MI 48332 • Tel: 313 453 5410 • *Cruelty-free biodegradable laundry and dish washing detergent and other household cleaners.*

AUBREY ORGANICS • 4419 N Manhattan Avenue, Tampa, FL 33614 • *Soap-based cleaning products, no synthetics, organic hair, skin and body care products.*

BAU-BIOLOGIE HARDWARE • PO Box 3217, Prescott, AZ 86302 • Tel: 602 445 8225

BISSELL INC • Grand Rapids, MI 49504 • Tel: 616 453 4451 • *Carpet sweepers.*

BI-O-KLEEN INDUSTRIES INC • PO Box 82066, Portland, OR 97282-0066 • Tel: 503 557 0216 Fax: 503 557 7818 • *Manufacture a line of premium natural cleaners and pet care products made from the highest quality ingredients to exacting standards. Non-biotoxic, highly concentrated, and versatile.*

BON AMI COMPANY/FAULTLESS STARCH • 1025 W 8th Street, Kansas City, MO 64101 • Tel: 816 842 1230 Fax: 816 842 3417 • *Bon Ami is different from most cleaning products, and has no chlorine, phosphates, or dyes.*

CHANDLER-SLACK & CO • PO Box 417, Boylston, MA 01505 • Tel: 508 869 2477 • *Cloth mops and dusters.*

CHEMPOINT PRODUCTS INC • 188 Shadow Lake Road, Ridgefield, CT 06877-1032 • Tel: 203 778 0881 Fax: 203 778 0911 • *CITRA-SOLV a biodegradable super-concentrated, all-purpose cleaner.*

CLARK BUSSEY DISTRIBUTING • Independent Greenway Dist., 9017 Pioneer Lane, Loomis, CA 95650 • Tel: 916 652 4234 • *Environmentally friendly laundry, cleaning products and personal care products.*

CITIZENS CLEARING HOUSE FOR HAZARDOUS WASTE • PO Box 6806, Falls Church, VA 22040 • Tel: 703 237 2249

COASTLINE PRODUCTS • PO Box 6397, Santa Ana, CA 92706 • Tel: 800 554 4111 / 800 554 4112 Fax: 714 554 6861 • *Free catalog.*

COUNTRY SAVE DETERGENT • 3410 Smith Avenue, Everett, WA 98201 • Tel: 206 258 1171 • *Phosphate-free detergent, biodegradable.*

DESERT ESSENCE • Box 588, Topanga, CA 90290 • *Non-synthetic soaps and detergents; Australian tea tree oils used as disinfectants.*

EARTHCARE • Ukiah, CA 95482-8507 • Tel: 800 347 0070 *Catalog includes environmentally responsible cleaning products.*

EARTH FRIENDLY PRODUCTS • PO Box 607, Wood Dale, IL 60191

EARTHLY MATTERS • 2719 Phillips Highway, Jacksonville, FL 32207 • Tel: 904 771 8544 • *Biodegradable products for household and commercial use.*

EARTHRITE • 23700 Mercantile Road, Beachwood, OH 44122 • Tel: 800 328 4408 • *Cleaners.*

EARTH WISE INC • 1790 30th Street, Boulder, CO 80301 • Tel: 303 447 0119

EARTH TOOLS • 9754 Johanna Place, Shadow Hills, CA 91040 • Tel: 800 825 6460 / 818 353 5883 • *Cleaning and conservation products for the Natural Home, all at great prices. Call for free catalog.*

ECO CLEAN • 4017 North 69th Street, Scottsdale, AZ 85251 • Tel: 602 947 5286 • *Environmentally friendly cleaning products for allergy sufferers and the chemically sensitive.*

ECO-DESIGN COMPANY • 1365 Rufina Circle, Santa Fe, NM 87501 • Tel: 505 438 3448 Fax: 505 438 6315 • *Healthy home products. Publish "The Natural Choice Catalog".*

ECO HOUSE (1988) INC • Livos Plant Chemistry Canada, PO Canada E3B 4Y9 • Tel: 506 366 3529 Fax: 506 366 3577 • *Home products.*

ECOLO INTERNATIONAL LTD • Naturally Yours, Lancaster, CA • Tel: 417 865 6260 • *Concentrated cleaning products.*

ECO-SEARCH • PO Box 13424, RTP, NC 27709-3424 • Tel: 919 467 1452 • *Research, consultation, and information on food and chemical sensitivities.*

ECO SOURCE CATALOG • PO Box 1656, Sebastopol, CA 95473-1656 • Tel: 707 829 3506 Fax: 707 829 7811

ECO-STORE INC • 2421 Edgewater Drive, Orlando, FL 32804 • Tel: 407 426 9949 • *An environmental action company selling water savers, cleaners, pet supplies, gifts etc. Woman-owned.*

ECOVER • Mercantile Food Company, Georgetown, CT 06829 • *Each product is specially formulated to meet a specific cleaning need. Biodegradable and not harmful to septic tanks. Products include: dishwashing liquid, fabric conditioner, floor soap, toilet cleaner, tub & tile cleanser, wool washing liquid.*

ENVIRESOURCE INC • 110 Madison Avenue North, Bainbridge Island, WA 98110 • 206 842 9785 • *Non-toxic cleaning products.*

ENVIRONMENTAL BY DESIGN • PO Box 95016, South Van CSC, Vancouver, BC, Canada, V6P 6V4 • Tel & Fax: 604 266 7721 • *Guide to healthy interior materials. See p. 133.*

ENVIRONMENTALLY SOUND PRODUCTS • 8845 Orchard Tree Lane, Towson, MD 21286 • Tel: 800 886 5432 / 410 825 7200 • *Household products for green and healthy living.*

ENVIRORITE • 306 Snelling Avenue S, Suite 8, St. Paul, MN 55105 • Tel: 612 690 4799 • *Carpet cleaning for the environmentally sensitive.*

ENVIROWISE • 1566 Randolph Avenue, St. Paul, MN 55105 • Tel: 612 690 4799 / 800 798 6332 orders only • *Safe, non-toxic carpet cleaning for the chemically sensitive.*

EOS INSTITUTE • 580 Broadway, Suite 200, Laguna Beach, CA 92651 • Tel: 714 497 1896

EUREKA VACUUM • 1201 E Bell Street, Bloomington, IL 61701 • *Central vacuum, new filter similar to Swedish model.*

EUROCLEAN • 905 West Irving Park Road, Itasca, IL 60143 • Tel: 800 545 4372 / 312 773 2111 • *HEPA vacuum.*

FOR YOUR HEALTH PRODUCTS • 6623 Hillandale Road, Chevy Chase, MD 20815 • Tel: 301 654 1127 Fax: 301 654 2125 • *Manufacturers' representative. Retail mail-order catalog of quality environmental and health-related products designed to help the allergic, chemically sensitive and environmentally aware individual, including, allergy vacuum cleaners, and less-toxic home care materials.*

FUTURE BEST INC • 392 Holly Drive, Southampton, PA 18966 • Tel: 800 626 5889 • *Environmentally responsible and health safe cleaning products.*

HEALTHFUL HARDWARE • PO Box 3217, Prescott, AZ 86302 • Tel: 602 445 8225 • *Bau-biologie Hardware. Catalog of healthy building materials and devices.*

HEALTHY KLEANER • The GreenSpan™ PO Box 4656, Boulder CO 80306 • Tel: 1-800-EARTH29 • *Healthy Kleaner is a waterless hand cleaner that is non-toxic and biodegradable. It is designed for use on other surfaces full strength or diluted in water. Mail order.*

HEART OF VERMONT • Box 183, Sharon, VT 05065 • Tel: 802 763 2720/800 639 4123

HOKY AMERICA CORP • PO Box 966, Lakeville, MN 55044 • Fax: 612 469 5435 • *Carpet sweepers.*

HOME HEALTH • 949 Seahawk Circle, Virginia Beach, VA 23452 • Tel: 800 278 7092 • *Mail-order catalog including cleaning products.*

HOME TRENDS • 1450 Lyell Avenue, Rochester, NY 14606-2184 • Tel: 716 254 6520 • *Complete range of home care products. Catalog.*

HOUSEHOLD HAZARDOUS WASTE PROJECT • PO Box 108, Springfield, MO 65804 • Tel: 417 836 5777 • *A community health and environment education program sponsored by the Missouri Department of Natural Resources. Publishes the informative and comprehensive "Guide to Hazardous Products Around the Home", which discusses in detail everything from labeling to hazardous ingredients and homemade alternatives.*

INFORM INC • 120 Wall Street, 16th Floor, New York, NY 10005-4001 • Tel: 212 361 2400 Fax: 212 361 2412 • *National non-profit environmental research organization currently focussing on strategies to reduce industrial and municipal waste and preserve air and water quality. Publishes a number of books on toxic substances including "Tackling Toxics in Everyday Products", a directory of organizations concerned about toxics in consumer and building products.*

KAREN'S NON-TOXIC PRODUCTS • 1839 Dr Jack Road, Conowingo, MD 21918 • Tel: 800 KARENS 4 • *No animal testing, unscented products. Catalog.*

THE LIVING SOURCE • PO Box 20155, Waco, TX 76702 • Tel: 817 776 4878 / 800 662 8727 • *Catalog of products for the environmentally aware and chemically sensitive.*

MIA ROSE PRODUCTS INC • 177-F Riverside Avenue, Newport Beach, CA 92626 • Tel: 800 292 6339 • *Citri-Glow™ total home cleaner. Air Therapy – a chemical free method of cleansing the air.*

NATURAL ANIMAL • 7000 US 1 North, St. Augustine, FL 32095 • Tel: 904 824 5884 / 800 274 7387 Fax: 904 824 5100 • *Since 1979 Natural Animal has provided the most complete line of earth-safe products for pets, homes, and people.*

NATURAL CHEMISTRY • 244 Elm Street, New Canaan, CT 06840 • Tel: 203 966 8761 • *Window cleaner, bio-clean, natural enzymes.*

THE NATURAL CHOICE, LIVOS • Livos Plant Chemistry, 1365 Rufina Circle, Santa Fe, NM 87501 • Tel: 505 438 3448 Fax: 505 438 0199 • *Non-toxic home products, and cleansers. Catalog.*

NILFISK • 300 Technology Drive, Malvern, PA 19355 • Tel: 215 647 6420 / 800 NILFISK • *GS-90 allergy-vac, wet-dry HEPA.*

NONTOXIC ALTERNATIVES • 178 Zander Drive, Orinda, CA 94563 • Tel: 510 254 9093

NONTOXIC ENVIRONMENTS INC • PO Box 384, Newmarket, NH 03857 • Tel: 603 659 5919 Fax: 603 659 5933 • *Building and household products for the chemically sensitive. Mail-order catalog.*

NON-TOXIC HOT LINE • 830 Meadow Road, Aptos, CA 95003 • Tel: 408 684 0199 • *Catalog and retail sales of products for the chemically sensitive.*

OASIS BIOCOMPATIBLE PRODUCTS • 5 San Marcos Trout Club, Santa Barbara, CA 93105-9726 • Tel: 805 967 3222 Fax: 805 967 3229 • *Oasis biocompatible cleaners are designed and tested from the ground for gray water reuse. Oasis Laundry Detergent and Oasis Dishwash/All Purpose Cleaner biodegrade entirely into plant nutrients and contain no sodium, chlorine, or boron. Available from Real Goods Trading Company (see below) and in Western health food stores.*

OKO-CLEAN • Tel: 800 243 3665 • *Micro-fibers eliminate household cleaners using untreated PET fibers that break the surface tension of water. Free information.*

ORANGE GLO NORTHWEST • PO Box 70171, Eugene, OR 97401 • Tel: 800 672 6456 • *Concentrated household cleaning products made from the peels of oranges.*

PACE INCORPORATED • 1710 Douglas Drive North, Minneapolis, MN 55422 • Tel: 612 544 5543 • *Publishes "Environmental Regulatory Review".*

RAINMAN INTERNATIONAL • 1154 Werth Avenue, Menlo Park, CA 94025 • Tel: 800 892-RAIN • *Ambio-clean Super Concentrate cleaners are storm drain compatible.*

REAL GOODS • 555 Leslie Street, Ukiah, CA 95482 • Tel: 800 762 7325 • *Real Goods is your complete resource for* **ENERGY EFFICIENT LIVING.** *Compact fluorescent lighting; solar, wind, and hydro power, rechargeable batteries and chargers; water conservation products; home safety products; natural pest control; recycled products; solar toys; maps, books and gifts. Free catalog.* See p. 96.

R E K A INTERNATIONAL • 2530 Mercantile Drive, # 1, Rancho Cordova, CA 95742 • Tel: 916 852 5150 Fax: 916 852 5152 • *You can clean your home without polluting your environment with REKA cloth and water only. Pure and simple.*

RESTORE THE EARTH • 2204 Hennepin Avenue South, Minneapolis, MN 55405 • Tel: 612 374 3738 • *Vegetable based, biodegradable, nontoxic household cleaning products.*

R H OF TEXAS • PO Box 780392, Dallas, Texas 75378 • Tel: 214 351 6681 Fax: 214 902 8859

SCHWEITZER ENTERPRISES LTD • 100 Howe Street, Suite 606, New Haven, CT 06511 • Tel: 203 773 3942 • *Importers of Tri-Clean Laundry Discs which clean clothes without the use of detergent!*

SCIENTIFIC CERTIFICATION SYSTEMS (SCS) • 1611 Telegraph Avenue, Suite 1111, Oakland, CA 94612-2118 • Tel: 510 832 1415 • *Grants independent certification of environmental claims.* See p. 198.

SINAN CO • Box 857, Davis, CA 95617-0857 • *Vegetable-based, unscented cleaning products.*

SMITH'S HEALTHY CHOICES • 3463 Yonge Street, Toronto, Canada, M4N 2N3 • Tel: 416 488 2600 Fax: 416 484 8855 • *Store and Catalog for non-toxic products.*

SUNRISE LANE • 780 Greenwich Street, New York, NY 10014 • Tel: 212 242 7014 • *Life Tree, Lotus line of cleaners.*

UNICLEAN • Edward & Sons Trading Co, Carpinteria, CA 93014 • *Natural cleaner, coconut and soy oil.*

Hazard-free home ~ page 161

AMERICAN ACADEMY OF ENVIRONMENTAL MEDICINE • PO Box 16106, Denver, CO 80216 • Tel: 303 622 9755 • *Contact for information about clinical ecologists.*

AMERICAN LUNG ASSOCIATION (ALA) • 1740 Broadway, New York, NY 10019-4374 • Tel: 800 586 4872

BIO-INTEGRAL RESOURCE CENTER • PO Box 7414, Berkeley, CA 94707 • Tel: 510 524 2567 Fax: 510 524 1758 • *BIRC publications provide information on environmentally safe and effective methods of managing pests in the home, garden, and in agriculture. Memberships also.*

BUG-OFF INC • Route 2, Box 248C, Lexington, VA 24450 • Tel: 703 463 1760 • *Herbal insect repellents for people, pets and home. Catalog.*

CONSUMERS FEDERATION OF AMERICA • 1424 16th Street, Northwest, Washington, DC 20036

CONSUMER PRODUCT SAFETY COMMISSION • 1111 18th Street Northwest, Washington, DC 20207 • Tel: 800 638 8326

GREEN BAN • Box 146, Norway, IA 52318 • Tel: 319 446 7495 • *Natural pest control for people and pets.*

GREEN SEAL • 1250 23rd Street NW, Suite 275, Washington, DC 2003 1101 • Tel: 202 331 7337 • *Grants environmental seal of approval and sets standards for choosing products. Standards are available to consumers. See p. 153.*

INSECT ASIDE • PO Box 7, 102 W Adams Street, Farmington, WA 99128 • Tel: 509 287 2200 Fax: 509 287 2400 • *The Bug Catcher Vacuum reaches and remove all kinds of living bugs and seals them in a patented disposable cartridge. Lightweight, cordless, rechargeable.*

INSECTO PRODUCTS INC • 630 North Eckhoff Street, Orange, CA 92668 • Tel: 714 939 9192 • *Manufacturers of INSECTO which kills bugs by dehydration.*

INVISIBLE GARDENERS OF AMERICA • 29169 Heathercliff Road 216-408, Malibu, CA 90265 • Tel: 310 457 4438 / 800 354 9296 • *Natural pest control for home and garden.*

THE MEMRY CORPORATION • Memry Plumbing Products Corp, 83 Keeler Avenue, Norwalk, CT 06854 • Tel: 800 782 7840 / 203 853 9777 • *Anti-scald device for water faucets.*

MIA ROSE AIR THERAPY • 3555 B Harbor Gateway S, Cost Mesa, CA 92626 • Tel: 800 292 6339 / 714 662 5465 • *Pet Air® contains natural citrus scents to eliminate odors and clean the air naturally.*

NATIONAL INSTITUTE OF HEALTH AND SAFETY • 9000 Rockville Pike, Bethesda, MD 20814 • Tel: 301 496 4000

NATURAL ANIMAL INC • PO Box 1177, St Augustine, FL 32085 • Tel: 800 274 7387 • *Products for the health and safety of pets, people and the planet.*

THE SAFETY ZONE • Aegis Retail Corporation, 701 Westchester Avenue, Suite 312W, White Plains, NY 10604 • Tel: 914 997 1935 / 800 999 3030 • *Retail stores, safety catalog.*

SEABRIGHT LABORATORIES • 4067 Watts Street, Emeryville, CA 94710 • Tel: 800284 7363 • *Non toxic pest control products.*

SEVENTH GENERATION • 49 Hercules Drive, Colchester, VT 05446-1672 • Tel: 800 456 1177 Fax: 800 456 1139

SOCIETY FOR CLINICAL ECOLOGY • 109 West Olive Street, Fort Collins, CO 80524

ART SLATER • UC Berkeley, Department of Entomology, Berkeley, CA • *Control of ants, carpenter ants, termites and other pests.*

TALLON TERMITE & PEST CONTROL • 1949 East Market Street, Long Beach, CA 90805 • Tel: 310 422 1131 Fax: 310 423 6146 • *Non-petrochemical integrated pest management.*

Allergies ~ page 164

See also listings for Air purification pages 242-3

ABSOLUTE ENVIROMENTAL'S ALLERGY PRODUCTS AND SERVICES STORE • 2615 S University Drive, Davie, FL 33328 • Tel: 305 472 3773 / 800 329 3773 • *Mattress and pillow case protectors, barrier cloths, and chemical free sheets.*

AERO HYGIENICS INC • 5247 San Fernando Road West, Los Angeles, CA 90039 • Tel: 800 346 4642 Fax: 213 245 3028 • *Feel the difference clean air makes. For cleaner, healthier indoor air start using HYGI-FLO® activated carbon filters today.*

AMERICAN FORMULATING AND MANUFACTURING (AFM) • 1140 Stacy Court, Riverside, CA 92507 • Tel: 714 781 6860 • *Sealants and other products for allergic consumers.*

ALK AMERICA INC • 132 Research Drive, Milford, CT 06460 • Tel: 800 325 7354. 203 877 4782 • *Dust collection test kit - indoor allergen analysis.*

ALLERGY CONTROL PRODUCTS • 96 Danbury Road, Box 793, Ridgefield, CT 06877 • Tel: 800 422-DUST • *Barrier cloths for bedding, filters, books for allergy sufferers, ACS dust mite control.*

ALLERGY RELIEF SHOP • 2932 Middlebrook Park, Knoxville, TN 37921 • Tel: 615 522 2795 • *Bedding, mattress sets, barrier cloths, and sheets. Catalog.*

ALLERGY RESEARCH GROUP • PO Box 489, Dept NNE, San Leandro, CA 94577-0489 • Tel: 800 782 4274

ALLERGY RESOURCES • PO Box 888, Palmer Lake, CO 80133 • Tel: 800-USE-FLAX / 719 488 3630 Fax: 719 481 3737 • *Allergy Resources offers the most comprehensive selection of quality holistic alternatives including organic foods, nutritional supplements, natural cosmetics and more. Call for a free catalog.*

ALLERGY STORE • 7345 Healdsburg, Sebastopol, CA 95472 • Tel: 800 950 6202. *Catalog.*

ALLERMED CORPORATION • 31 Steel Road, Wylie, TX 75098 • Tel: 214 442 4898 • *AllerMed High-Efficiency Air Purifiers specially designed for anyone with allergies, asthma, respiratory problems and chemical sensitivities. Hepa, Carbon, Ionizers.*

BRIGHT FUTURES • 3120 Central Avenue, SE Albuquerque, NM 87106 • *Handmade futons and accessories with organic cotton coverings encased in FoxFiber™ for the chemically sensitive.*

THE COTTON PLACE • Box 59721, Dallas, TX 75229 • Tel: 800 451 8866 / 214 243 4149 • *Natural fibers. Catalog.*

CROWN CITY MATTRESS • 250 South San Gabriel Boulevard, San Gabriel, CA 91776 • Tel: 213 681 6356 Fax: 818 796 9101 • *Manufactures mattresses, box springs and futons with natural, renewable materials. Organically grown cotton is used and wool processed without chlorine.*

DONA DESIGNS • 1611 Bent Tree Street, Seagoville, TX 75159 • Tel: 214 287 7834 • *Organic cotton pillows and bedding.*

DUST FREE INC • Box 519, Royse City, TX 75189 • Tel: 800 441 1107 / 214 635 9565 • *Electrostatic air filters. Air testing equipment.*

HEART OF VERMONT • The Old Schoolhouse, Route 132, Box 183, Sharon, VT 05065 • Tel: 800 639 4123 / 802 763 2720 Fax: 802 763 2075 • *A full range of products for the chemically sensitive. Catalog.*

THE JANICE CORP • 198 Route 46, Budd Lake, NJ 07828 • Tel: 201 691 2979 • *Bedding, mattress sets, padding, and barrier cloths.*

JANTZ DESIGN • Box 3071, Santa Rosa, CA 95402 • Tel: 800 365 6563 707 823 8834 • *Wool mattress pads, natural comforters, furniture, organic wood, and cotton bedding. Catalog.*

KB COTTON PILLOWS INC • PO Box 57, De Soto, TX 75123 • Tel: 214 223 7193 / 800 544 3752 • Pure 100% cotton pillows - staple cotton, air tested to be chemically free. Ticking pre-washed in baking soda solution. Received the 'non-toxic' rating by Debra Lynn Dadd. Sizes: Standard, K, Q, Travel/Youth, Baby, Continental. Please call and leave name, address, and phone number for information and order forms.

MIELE APPLIANCES INC • 22D World's Fair Drive, Somerset, NJ 08873 • Tel: 908 560 0899 / 800 843 7231 Fax: 908 560 9649 • *HEPA filtered vacuums. Call for your nearest dealer.*

MOTHER HART'S • 3300 S Congress Avenue, Unit 21, Boynton Beach, FL 33424-4229 Tel: 407 738 5866 • *100% all natural, undyed, unbleached, no-formaldehyde cotton sheets, and untreated bath towels. Catalog.*

NATURAL RESOURCES • 745 Powderhorn, Monument, CO 80132 • Tel: 719 488 3630 / 800 USE-FLAX • *Natural bedding, pillows, barrier clothes, mattress sets.*

NATIONAL ECOLOGICAL AND ENVIRONMENTAL DELIVERY SYSTEM (NEEDS) • 527 Charles Avenue 12A, Syracuse, NY 13209 • Tel: 800 634 1380 / 315 446 1122 • *Products for the allergic and chemically sensitive. Catalog.*

NILFISK • 300 Technology Drive, Malvern, PA 19355 • Tel: 215 647 6420 / 800 NILFISK • *GS-90 allergy-vac, wet-dry HEPA.*

PURE AIR SYSTEMS • 701 Sundown Circle, PLAINFIELD, IN 46168 • *HEPA filtered vacuum cleaner.*

RISING STAR FUTONS • 35 North West Bond Street, Bend, OR 97701 • Tel: 800 828 6711 / 503 382 4221 Fax: 503 3835925 • *Non-allergenic, chemical-free premium quality futons, all sizes; shipped UPS. Call for your free catalog. See p. 155.*

Edible gardening ~ page 168

See also listings for Seeds and herbs page 268-70

ABUNDANT LIFE SEED FOUNDATION • PO Box 772, Port Townsend, WA 98368 • *Non-profit foundation dedicated to preserving open-pollinated untreated seed. Vegetables, medicinal and culinary herbs, wildflowers, trees. Over 600 varieties. Heirloom and old-fashioned seeds. Send $2.00 for catalog.*

APPLESEED WOOL CORPORATION • PO Box 101, 55 Bell Street, Plymouth, OH 44865 • Tel: 419 687 9665 • *Wool-based horticultural products such as mulch and basket liners.*

BIO-DYNAMIC FARMING AND GARDENING ASSOCIATION • PO Box 550, Kimberton, PA 19442 • Tel: 215 935 7797 • *Founded in 1938 this is the oldest group advocating an ecological, sustainable approach to agriculture. Publishes a newsletter and has books, advisory service, training programs, and conferences on biodynamic growing.*

BUSINESS FOR SOCIAL RESPONSIBILITY • 1010-1030 15th Street NW, Washington DC 20005 • Tel: 202 842 5400 Fax: 202 842 3135 • *Group promoting sustainable development, publishes "Earth Enterprise Exchange" newsletter.*

CANADIAN BIODIVERSITY INSTITUTE • 3551 Blanchfield Road, Osgoode, Ontario, Canada, K0A 2W0 • Tel: 613 826 2190 Fax: 613 241 2292 • *Focuses on biodiversity education, information dissemination and research.*

CANADIAN NATURE FEDERATION • 1 Nicholas Street, Suite 520, Ottawa, Ontario, Canada, K1N 7B7 • Tel: 613 562 3447 Fax: 613 562 3371 • *Conservation, education, and publishing programs. Publish "Nature Canada".*

COMMITTEE FOR SUSTAINABLE AGRICULTURE • PO Box 1300, Colfax, CA 95713 • Tel: 916 346 2777 • *An educational organization to provide information on ecological farming to farmers to help them make the change. Publications are also relevant to the general public.*

COMMUNITY SUPPORTED AGRICULTURE OF NORTH AMERICA • c/o WTIG, 818 Connecticut Avenue NW, # 800, Washington, DC 20006 • Tel: 202 785 5135 • *Has an annotated directory of CSAs across the country, and a book on how to start a CSA.*

COOK'S GARDEN • PO Box 65, Londonderry, VT 05148 • Tel: 802 824 3400 • *The complete kitchen garden catalog: extensive list for salad greens, plus cutting flowers; all seeds untreated. Good practical advice.*

ROBERT CORNELL & ASSOCIATES • 8780 National Boulevard, # 222, Culver City, CA 90232 • Tel: 310 842 8015 • *Landscape Design.*

DEER VALLEY FARM • RD 1, PO Box 173, Guilford, NY 13780 • Tel: 607 764 8556 • *Organically grown food. Catalog 75c.*

ECOLOGY ACTION OF THE MID-PENINSULA • 5798 Ridgewood Road, Willits, CA 95490 • Tel: 707 459 0150 • *A non-profit organization dedicated to finding practical solutions to environmentally based urban and rural food, clothing, shelter, and energy issues through research, development, educational, and outreach programs.*

EDIBLE LANDSCAPING • PO Box 77, Afton, VA 22920 • *Containerized fruit plants that look good, including gooseberries, pawpaws, and pine nuts, as well as more conventional "less care" fare. Catalog free.*

EVERGREEN Y H ENTERPRISES • PO Box 17538, Anaheim, CA 92817 • *Oriental vegetable seeds, cookbooks, garden books.*

EVERYTHING UNDER THE SUN • PO Box 663, Winters, CA 95694 • Tel: 916 795 5256 • *Organic solar dried fruits and nuts from California.*

FARM VERIFIED ORGANIC INC • RR 1, Box 40A, Medina, ND 58467 • Tel: 701 486 3578 • *International certification program assuring the authenticity of organic food and fiber.*

FEDCO SEEDS INC • PO Box 520, Waterville, ME 04903 • Tel: 207 873 7333 • *This worker and consumer-owned co-operative supplies untreated garden seeds, trees, bulbs, perennials, seed potatoes, organic farm and garden supplies all at low prices.*

FINCH BLUEBERRY NURSERY • PO Box 699, Bailey, NC 27807 • Tel: 919 235 4664 • *Specialists in blueberry plants: Northern Highbush, Southern Highbush, Southern Rabbiteye. Free catalog.*

GARDENS ALIVE! • 5100 Schenley Place, Lawrenceburg, IN 47025 • Tel: 812 537 8650 Fax: 812 537 5108 • *America's number one source for organic garden products.*

HIDDEN SPRINGS NURSERY • 170 Hidden Springs Lane, Cookeville, TN 38501 • Tel: 615 268 2592 • *Unusual edible landscape plants. Organic methods.*

ROBERT KOURIK • Box 1841, Santa Rosa, CA 95402 • Tel: 707 874 2606 Fax: 707 874 2606 • *Landscape designer, author, publisher, consultant, and freelance writer. See p. 177.*

MUSHROOM PEOPLE • Box 220, Summertown TN 38483 • Tel: 615 964 2200 • *Grow mushrooms – many fast-fruiting, edible strains. How-to book. Free 300-item catalog.*

NATURAL ORGANIC FARMERS ASSOCIATION • 140 Chestnut Street, West Hatfield, MA 01088

NORTHEAST ORGANIC FARMING ASSOCIATION OF NEW JERSEY • 31 Titus Mill Road, Pennington, NJ 08534 • Tel: 609 737 6848 • *Non-profit organization that promotes organic farming and gardening in New Jersey through certification, education, marketing and legislation.*

OHIO EARTH FOOD • 5488R Swamp, Hartville, OH 44632 • Tel: 216 877 9356 Fax: 216 877 4237 • *Organic fertilizers, insect controls. Testing for lawn, garden, farm. Free catalog.*

ORGANIC FOODS PRODUCTION ASSOCIATION OF NORTH AMERICA • PO Box 1078, Greenfield, MA 01301 • Tel: 413 774 7511

PACIFIC GREEN • PO Box 3588, Portland, OR 97208 • Tel: 503 285 8279 Fax: 503 289 4179 • *Supplier of "Wild about Organic" T-shirts.*

RAINTREE NURSERY • 391 Butts Road, Morton, WA 98356 • Tel: 206 496 6400 • *"Complete Book of Edible Landscaping".*

RODALE INSTITUTE RESEARCH CENTER • 611 Siegfriedale Road, Kutztown, PA 19530 • Tel: 215 683 1400 • *Large organic farm carrying out research into organic agriculture. Public tours and workshops.*

ROOTS AND LEGENDS • 38 Miller Avenue, Mill Valley, CA 94941 • Tel: 415 381 5631 • *Chinese herbs and herbal remedies by mail order.*

THE TOMATO SEED COMPANY • PO Box 323, Metuchen, NJ 08840 • Tel: 503 895 2957 • *Organically grown and open-pollinated tomato seeds. Free catalog.*

SHEPHERD'S GARDEN SEEDS • 6116, Highway 9, Felton, CA 95018 • Tel: 203 482 3638 • *Gourmet-quality herbs, vegetables, and salads from all over the world as well as flowers for fragrance and cutting.*

WALNUT ACRES • Penns Creek, PA 17862 • Tel: 800 433 3998 / 717 837 0601• *Organic whole foods direct from the farm.*

Soil improvement ~ *page 169*

ALBERMARLE DISTRIBUTORS • PO Box 9038-396, Charlottesville, VA 22906 • Tel: 804 293 4534 • *Distributors of EcoPot™ – made from recycled newspapers.*

ALTERNATIVE GARDEN SUPPLY, INC • (DBA) Chicago Indoor Garden Supply, 297 North Barrington Road, Streamwood, IL 60107 • Tel: 800 444 2837 • *Complete line of organic fertilizers and pesticide-free garden products for both indoors and out.*

AMERICAN LAWNMOWER COMPANY • PO Box 369, Shelbyville, IN 46176 • Tel: 317 631 0260 Fax: 317 392 4118 • *Manufactures a compact push mower. Clippings are scattered and act as a natural fertilizer as they decompose.*

BEAVER RIVER ASSOCIATES INC • Box 94, West Kingston RI 02892 • Tel: 401 782 8747 • *Worm World worm castings, a natural organic plant food and fertilizer.*

BIOBIN • 8407 Lightmoor Court, Bainbridge, WA 98110 • Tel: 206 842 6641 • *Composting bins/recycling bins.*

BOUNTIFUL GARDENS/ECOLOGY ACTION • 18001 Shafer Ranch Road, Willits, CA 95490 • Tel: 707 459 6410 • *Sustainable Biointensive Food-growing – organic, improves soil, highly productive. Free catalog (classes, publications – in 7 languages – seeds, and tools) send name and address.*

COMPOST HAPPENS • 9355 Sisson Highway, Eden, NY 14057 • Tel: 716 992 2260

COMPOSTING TOILET SYSTEMS • PO Box 1928, Newport, WA 99156-1928 • Tel: 509 447 3708 • *Tumbling organic composter.*

DeMENNO-KERDOON • 2000 N Alameda Street, Compton, CA 90222 • Tel: 310 537 7100 Fax: 310 639 2946

ENVIRO-CYCLE SYSTEMS INC • 100 Ronson Drive, Rexdale, Ontario, Canada, M9W 1B6 • Tel: 416 246 0562 Fax: 416 246 9651 • *The only two-in-one recycling system that produces both liquid and solid fertilizer.*

ENVIRESOURCE INC • 110 Madison Avenue North, Bainbridge Island, WA 98110 • Tel: 206 842 9785 • *Composting and garden supplies.*

EVERGREEN BINS • Box 70307, Seattle, WA 98107 • Tel: 206 783 7095

FLOWERFIELD ENTERPRISES • 10332 Shaver Road, Kalamazoo, MI 49002 • Tel: 616 327 0108 • *Use red worms to convert organic waste into nutrient-rich humus in your own garden.*

GARDEN CITY SEEDS • 1324 Red Crow Road, Victor, MT 59875 • Tel: 406 961 4837 • *Organic fertilizers. Part of the non-profit Down Home Project.*

GARDENER'S SUPPLY COMPANY • 128 Intervale Road, Burlington, Vermont 05401 • Tel: 802 660 3500 / 800 955 3370 Fax: 802 660 3501 • In Canada call: 905 940 5586 • *The widest selection of gardening products for flower, vegetable, and landscape growing. Organic solutions, home composters including the Bio-Sphere, the Grow House, and many other environmentally friendly products. Free catalog.*

GARDEN-VILLE OF AUSTIN • 8648 Old Bee Cave Road, Austin, TX 78735 • Tel: 512 288 6115 • *Supplier of bulk composts, organic fertilizers, and tools.*

GEDYE COMPOST BINS • Waste Master, Box 2501, Palm Springs, CA 92263.

LANE INC • (SEA-BORN) Box 204, Charles City, IA 50616 • Tel: 515 228 2000 Fax: 515 228 4417 • *The best garden fertilizers, plant food, fish, seaweed, kelp. New customers – 10% discount.*

MARTINSON-NICHOLLS INC • 7243-A Industrial Park Boulevard, PO Box 296, Mentor, OH 44061-0296 • Tel: 216 951 1312 Fax: 216 951 1315 • *DC1050 Yard waste composting container. Waste is reduced naturally before pick-up.*

NATURAL EXPERIENCE ORGANIC LAWN CARE • Walter Zilnicki, Jr, PO Box 215, Aquebogue, NY 11931 • Tel: 516 722 3947 • *Using only natural products, plants and grasses are encouraged to grow from the healthy nutrients in the soil.*

NATURAL GARDENING COMPANY • 217 San Anselmo Avenue, San Anselmo, CA 94960 • Tel: 707 766 9303 Fax: 707 766 9747 • *Gardening supplies.*

NATURAL GARDENING RESEARCH CENTER • Box 149, Sunman, IN 47041

NATURE'S BACKYARD INC • 126 Duchaine Boulevard, New Bedford, MA 02745 • Tel: 508 995 7008 • *Environmentally beneficial products made from 100% post-consumer recycled plastic including the Brave New Composter.*

NECESSARY ORGANICS • One Nature's Way, PO Box 305, New Castle, VA 24127 • Tel: 703 864 5103 Fax: 703 864 5186 • *Providing natural plant care and pest control choices for farmers and gardeners. Now also introduces' Concern™' garden products with three pest controls, two plant foods, and a composter, composed of naturally derived ingredients.*

NITRON INDUSTRIES • PO Box 1447, Fayetteville, AR 72702 • Tel: 800 835 0123 • *Manufacturer of organic fertilizers, enzymes, and soil conditioners.*

N-VIRO INTERNATIONAL • 3450 W Central Avenue, no. 328, Toledo, OH 43606 • Tel: 419 535 6374 • *N-Viro's patented technology transforms organic sludge and manure into an environmentally safe, nearly odor-free organic ag-lime product that looks and performs like natural soil.*

OASIS MAUI INC • PO Box 330094, Kahuluhi, HI 96733 • Tel: 808 877 2518 • *Natural lawn and garden supply company. The Oasis Group runs a children's organic gardening project in conjunction with local schools.*

OHIO EARTH FOOD • 5488R Swamp, Hartville, OH 44632 • Tel: 216 877 9356 Fax: 216 877 4237 • *Organic fertilizers. Testing for lawn, garden, farm. Free catalog.*

PEAK MINERALS-AZOMITE INC • 205 Eagle Point Drive, Branson, MO 65616 • *Azomite – Natural source of minerals and trace elements for plant nutrition and growth.*

PLASTOPAN NORTH AMERICA INC • 812 East 59th Street, Los Angeles, CA 90001 • Tel: 213 231 2225 Fax: 213 231 2068 • *Producer of the Bio-Actor – a composter made from 100% top-quality post-consumer plastic resin.*

PLOW & HEARTH • PO Box 5000, Madison, VA 22727-1500 • Tel: 1-800-627 1712 • *Mail-order catalog of products for country living includes composters.*

RINGER CORPORATION • 9959 Valley View Road, Eden Prairie, MN 55344 • Tel: 612 941 4180 Fax: 612 941 5031 • *Fertilizers.*

SMITH & HAWKEN • 25 Corte Madera, Mill Valley, CA 94941 • Tel: 415 459 7859 Fax: 415 383 7030 • *Catalog includes earthwise garden products, snail guards, and new reel mowers.*

SOLID WASTE COMPOSTING COUNCIL • 114 South Pitt Street, Alexandria, VA 22314 • Tel: 703 739 2401 • *The only association devoted to promoting composting. Developing national standards for municipal and home compost.*

SPRING GREEN ENTERPRISES • 709 South Front Street, Mankato, MN 56001 • Tel: 507 388 2261 Fax: 507 388 2458 • *Natural soybean based fertilizer.*

VERMONT NATURAL AG PRODUCTS (VNAP) • Middlebury, VT • 802 388 1137 • *An anaerobic digester handles large quantities of farm manure to produce compost and compost-based bag goods including germinating mix, perennial and nursery mixes and bulk soil amendments.*

WOOD RECYCLING INC • PO Box 6087, Peabody, MA 01961 • Tel: 508 535 4144 / 800 982 8732 Fax: 508 535 4252 • *100% recycled wood fiber and newsprint mixed with grass seed to prevent soil erosion on hillsides.*

THE WORM FACTORY • Route 3, Box 200, Dover, AR 72837 • *Plans for worm-composting bin.*

Seeds and herbs ~ *page 170*

ABUNDANT LIFE SEED FOUNDATION • PO Box 772, Port Townsend, WA 98368 • Tel: 360 385 5660 Fax: 206 385 7455 • *Non-profit foundation dedicated to preserving open-pollinated untreated seed. Vegetables, medicinal and culinary herbs, wildflowers, trees. Over 600 varieties. Heirloom and old-fashioned seeds.*

ACRES USA • PO Box 9547, Kansas City, MO 64133 • Tel: 816 737 0064 • *Books on organic gardening and farming Free catalog.*

agACCESS • PO Box 2008, Davis, CA 95617 • Tel: 916 756 7177 • *Books on organic gardening and farming. Free catalog.*

BOUNTIFUL GARDENS/ECOLOGY ACTION • 18001 Shafer Ranch Road, Willits, CA 95490 • Tel: 707 459 6410 • *Seeds and tools. Send name and address.*

BUTTERBROOKE FARM • 78 Barry Road, Oxford, CT 06483 • Tel: 203 888 2000 • *Old-time tried and true untreated vegetable seeds from a co-op network of organic growers and seed savers. Send large SAE for list.*

CENTER FOR PLANT CONSERVATION • Missouri Botanical Garden, PO Box 299, St. Louis, MO 63166 • *Publishes "The Plant Conservation Directory", which includes state and federal regulations, and lists of people and organizations involved in conserving rare and endangered plants.*

COASTAL GARDENS AND NURSERY • 4611 Socastee Boulevard, Myrtle Beach, SC 29575 • Tel: 803 293 2000 • *Hostas, shade plants, natives for wetlands and pond sites, perennials and daylilies.*

COLDSTREAM FARM • 2030 "S" Free Soil Road, Free Soil, MI 49411-9752 • *Trees and shrubs for reforestation, woodlots, and wildlife habitat. Free catalog.*

COMPANION PLANTS • 7247 N Coolville Ridge, Athens, Ohio 45701 • Tel: 614 592 4643 • *Herbs, plants, and seeds. 600+ varieties of culinary, medicinal, dye, shamanistic etc. plants from around the world. Send $3.00 for our descriptive mail-order catalog.*

CORNS • Carl and Karen Barnes, Route 1, PO Box 32, Turpin, OK 73950 • Tel: 405 778 3615 • *Organization dedicated to the production and preservation of the genetic diversity of open-pollinated corn varieties. Seeds for sale.*

CUMMINS GARDEN • 22 Robertsville Road, Marlboro, NJ 07746 • *Dwarf rhododendrons and conifers, deciduous and evergreen azaleas, and companion plants.*

DEEP DIVERSITY • PO Box 190, Gila, NM 88038 • *Organically grown and wild crafted open-pollinated seeds. Free catalog.*

DRY CREEK HERB FARM & LEARNING CENTER • 13935 Dry Creek Road, Auburn, CA 95602 • Tel: 916 878 2441 Fax: 916 878 6772 • *Large range of organic or wildcrafted herbs plus commercially grown Chinese herbs.*

EARTHLY GOODS • PO Box 614, New Albany, IN 47151 • Tel: 812 944 3283 • *Over 100 varieties of wildflower seeds.*

ECOGENESIS INC • 16 Jedburgh Road, Toronto, Ontario, Canada, M5M 3J6 • Tel: 416 489 7333 • *Environmentally friendly untreated seeds. Open-pollinated insect and disease resistant varieties for organic gardens. Hardy plants, great taste. Easy growing. $2.00 Catalog.*

ED HUME SEEDS • PO Box 1450, Kent, WA 98035 • *Untreated vegetable, herb, and flower seeds for cool-climate or short-season growing.*

EVERGREEN Y H ENTERPRISES • PO Box 17538, Anaheim, CA 92817 • *Oriental vegetable seeds, cookbooks, garden books.*

FAR NORTH GARDENS • 16785 Harrison, Livonia, MI 48154 • Tel: 810 486 4203 • *Rare flower seeds with special emphasis on Barnhaven primroses.*

FEDCO SEEDS INC • PO Box 520, Waterville, ME 04903 • Tel: 207 873 7333 • *This worker and consumer-owned co-operative supplies untreated garden seeds, trees, bulbs, perennials, seed potatoes, organic farm and garden supplies all at low prices.*

FORESTFARM • 990 Tetherhouse Road, Williams, OR 97544 • *Amazing Selection: Plants for wildlife, xeriscape, American natives, more. Descriptive catalog.*

FROSTY HOLLOW • Box 53, Langley, WA 98260 • *Pacific Northwest natives from trees to grasses, all gathered in a sustainable manner. Send large SAE for seed list.*

GARDEN CITY SEEDS • 1324 Red Crow Road, Victor, MT 59875 • Tel: 406 961 4837 • *Untreated vegetable, flower, and herb seeds, acclimatized for Northern conditions. Part of the non-profit Down Home Project.*

GARDENS NORTH • 5984 Third Line Road North, RR 3, North Gower, Ontario, Canada, K0A 2T0 • Tel & Fax: 613 489 0065 • *Hardy perennial seed for the Canadian garden.*

GARDENS OF THE BLUE RIDGE • PO Box 10, Pineola, NC 28662 • Tel: 704 733 2417 • *Nursery-grown native wildflowers, trees, and shrubs. In wildflower business for 100 years.*

GARDEN-VILLE OF AUSTIN • 8648 Old Bee Cave Road, Austin, TX 78735 • Tel: 512 288 6115 • *Supplier of native plants, seeds, and tools.*

GOODWIN CREEK GARDENS • PO Box 83, Williams, OR 97544 • Tel: 503 846 7357 • *Organically grown seeds for native American herbs. Free catalog.*

GOSSLER FARMS NURSERY • 1200 Weaver Road, Springfield, OR 97478-9691 • Tel: 503 746 6611 • *Specializing in magnolias, along with Hamamelis, Stewartia, and many other companion plants.*

GREER GARDENS • 1280 Goodpasture Island Road, Eugene, OR 97401 • Tel: 503 686 8266 • *Rare and unusual trees and shrubs, rhododendrons, conifers, Japanese maples, bonsai material, and rock garden plants.*

GREEN BEANS • Green Market, 710 Route 202, New Salem, MA 01355 • Tel: 508 544 7911 • *Retail store sells organic herbs and plants and organic gardening supplies.*

HALCYON GARDENS • PO Box 75, Wexford, PA 15090 • Tel: 412 935 2233 • *Organically grown herb seeds. Free catalog.*

HEIRLOOM GARDENS • PO Box 138, Guerneville, CA 95446 • *A source for seeds of old and almost-forgotten flowers and herbs. One of the most interesting and informative catalogs.*

HOLBROOK FARM AND NURSERY • Route 2, Box 223, Fletcher, NC 28732 • Tel: 704 891 7790 • *Unusual perennials and wildflowers, along with ferns and woody plants. Free catalog.*

HORTICULTURAL ENTERPRISES • PO Box 810082, Dallas, TX 75381 • *A display poster offers a tongue-searing selection of chilies.*

ISON'S NURSERY • Route 1, PO Box 190, Brooks, GA 30205 • Tel: 404 599 6970 • *Muscadine and scuppernong grapes and other small fruits. Free catalog.*

JERRY HORNE • 10195 SW 70th Street, Miami, FL 33173 • *Tropical ferns, bromeliads, and unusual and rare plants for the collector. Send large SAE for list.*

JOHNNY'S SELECTED SEEDS • 310 Foss Hill Road, Albion, ME 04910 • Tel: 207 437 9294 Fax: 207 437 2165 • *Johnny's offers over 600 hardy seed varieties for vegetables, flowers and herbs, plus tools, garden equipment, and books. Catalog gives very useful cultural information. Free catalog.*

LAUREL HILL PRESS • Box 16516, Chapel Hill, NC 27516 • Tel: 800 942 6516 • *One hundred species of wild flowers. Mail order available.*

LEDDEN'S • PO Box 7, Sewell, NJ 08080 • Tel: 609 468 1000 • *Vegetable and flower seeds, plus lawn and garden supplies. Free catalog.*

LE JARDIN DU GOURMET • PO Box 75B, St. Johnsbury Center, VT 05863 • *Catalog includes recipes and 5 sample packets of herb seed. Herb and perennial plants, shallots, herb and veggie seeds, gourmet foods.*

MEADOWBROOK HERB GARDEN • Route 138, Wyoming, RI 02898 • Tel: 401 539 7603 • *Bio-dynamically and organically grown herbal products. Send self-addressed, stamped envelope for catalog.*

McCRORY'S SUNNY HILL HERB FARM • 33152 La Place Court, Eustis, FL 32726 • Tel: 904 357 9876 • *Herbs in pots including Gotu-Kola, "a tasty salad plant said to improve memory".*

MOON MOUNTAIN WILDFLOWERS • PO Box 725, Carpinteria, CA 93014 • Tel: 805 684 2565 • *Seeds for wildflowers of the US, featuring California natives, regional and speciality mixes, and ornamental grasses.*

MOUNTAIN ROSE HERBS • PO Box 2000E, Redway, CA 95560 • Tel: 707 923 3941 • *Organically grown herbs and seeds. Catalog.*

MUSSER FORESTS • PO Box 340, Dept 23-B, Indiana, PA 15701-0340 • Tel: 412 465 5685 • *Evergreen and hardwood seedlings and transplants for a wide range of soil types and climates. Ornamental shrubs and ground covers. Substantial discounts for bulk purchases. Free catalog.*

NATIONAL WILDFLOWER RESEARCH CENTER • 2600 FM 973 North, Austin, TX 78725-4201 • Tel: 512 929 3600

NATIVE GARDENS • 5737 Fisher Lane, Greenback, TN 37742 • Tel: 615 856 0220 • *"Helping to keep your corner of the earth in good working order." Natives are featured in this well-produced catalog with a cover that removes to become a garden almanac and calendar.*

NATIVE SEEDS/SEARCH • 2509 N Campbell Avenue, no 325, Tucson, AZ 85719 • Tel: 520 327 9123 • *Non-profit seed conservation organization focusing on the traditional native crops of the US south west and north west Mexico. Demonstration garden open daily at Tucson Botanical Gardens, 2150 N Alvernon, Tucson.*

NATURE CONSERVANCY • 1815 North Lynn Street, Arlington, VA 22209 • Tel: 703 841 5300 • *Natural Heritage Program lists endangered plants. Call for the Program office in your area.*

NICHE GARDENS • 1111 Dawson Hill Road, Chapel Hill Road, NC 27516 • Tel: 919 967 0078 • *Nursery-propagated North American natives; selected perennials, grasses, and under-used shrubs and trees.*

NICHOLS GARDEN NURSERY INC • 1190 Old Salem Road NE, Albany, OR 97321 • Tel: 503 928 9280 • *Seed and nursery business specializing in hard to find varieties.*

ORNAMENTAL EDIBLES • 3622 Weedin Court, San Jose, CA 95132 • Tel: 408 946 7333 • *Vegetables, herbs, and edible flowers pretty enough for the front yard. Bulk seed list for speciality market growers.*

PEACE SEEDS • PO Box 190, Gila, NM 88038 • *A planetary gene pool of organically raised plants and trees from huge firs to garbanzo beans. More than just a catalog, this book is an education in nutrition and plant diversity.*

PEACEFUL VALLEY FARM SUPPLY • PO Box 2209, Grass Valley, CA 95945 • Tel: 916 272 4769 • *Very large selection of seeds for cover crops, vegetables, wildflowers, and grasses; natural pest controls, tools, animal health products, and more. Free catalog.*

PERENNIAL PLEASURES NURSERY • PO Box 128, Brick House Road, East Hardwick, VT 05836 • Tel: 802 472 5104 • *Established in 1979, to supply authentic plants for 17th, 18th, and 19th century restoration gardens.*

W H PERRON CO LTD • 515 Boul Labelle, Chomedey, Laval, PQ, Canada, H7V 2T3 • *Specializes in vegetables and flowers suitable for eastern Canada. Largest French mail-order seed company in North America. Catalog $3.00.*

PINETREE GARDEN SEEDS • Box 300, New Gloucester, ME 04260 • Tel: 207 926 3400 • *Hundreds of small, economical seed packets for food and flowers along with books, good gadgets, and tools. Free catalog.*

PLANTS OF THE SOUTHWEST • Route 6, Box 11A, Santa Fe, NM 87501 • *Native (and introduced) vegetables, herbs, cover crops, and wildflowers for dry regions. Catalog $3.50.*

RICHTERS • Goodwood, ON, Canada, L0C 1A0 • Tel: 905 640 6677 Fax: 905 640 6641 • *Canada's Herb Specialists.*

JOHN ROGERS • 115 E Avenue C, Melbourne, FL 32901 • Tel: 407 725 1923 • *Paradise gardening, permaculture options, enchanted, reforested human habitat and livelihood.*

RONNIGER'S SEED POTATOES • Star Route 104, Moyie Springs, ID 83845 • *155 kinds of organic potatoes (in six colors), along with lots of spud lore. Also cover crops, sunchokes, and garlic. Catalog $1.00.*

ROOTS AND LEGENDS • 38 Miller Avenue, Mill Valley, CA 94941 • Tel: 415 381 5631 • *Chinese herbs and herbal remedies by mail order.*

SANDY MUSH NURSERY • 316 Surrett Cove Road, BHM Leicester, NC 28746-9622 • *Over 1100 herb and garden plants, as well as seeds.*

SEEDS BLUM • Idaho City Stage, Boise, ID 83706 • *A nice collection of heirloom seeds, including Moon and Stars watermelon.*

J L HUDSON, SEEDSMAN • PO Box 1058, Redwood City, CA 94064 • *An impressive collection of open-pollinated seeds from around the world. Free catalog.*

SEED SAVERS EXCHANGE (SSE) • 3076 North Winn Road, Decorah, IA 52101 • Tel: 319 382 5990 • *See p. 193*

SEEDS OF CHANGE • PO Box 15700, Santa Fe, NM 87506 • Tel: 505 438 8080 Fax: 505 438 7052 • *Beautiful catalog of unusual seeds from a group committed to preserving the diverse gene pool which modern farming is tending to homogenize.*

SELECT SEEDS – ANTIQUE FLOWERS • 180 Stickney Hill Road, Union, CT 06076 • *Old-fashioned and heirloom flower seeds. Emphasis on those good for cutting and fragrance. Send SAE for list.*

SHEPHERD'S GARDEN SEEDS • 6116, Highway 9, Felton, CA 95018 • Tel: 203 482 3638 • *Gourmet-quality herbs, vegetables, and salads from all over the world as well as flowers for fragrance and cutting.*

R H SHUMWAY'S • PO Box 1, Graniteville, SC 29829 • *Open-pollinated vegetable seeds, along with flowers, fruit trees, and more. Free catalog.*

SOUTHERN EXPOSURE SEED EXCHANGE • PO Box 158, North Garden, VA 22959 • *Over 450 varieties of nonhybrid, heirloom, and rare vegetable seeds including perennial onions and garlic. Seed-saving supplies.*

STARK BROTHERS' NURSERY • PO Box 10, Louisiana, MO 63353 • Tel: 314 754 5511 • *Fruit trees, bushes, and vines; ornamental, shade, and nut trees; roses and shrubs. Free catalog.*

WILLIAM SWIRIN • 3 Henderson Court, Greensboro, NC 27410 • *Catalog free. Heritage seeds of vegetables, flowers, herbs.*

TALAVAYA SEEDS • PO Box 707, Santa Cruz Station, Santa Cruz, NM 87507 • Tel: 505 753 5801 • *Catalog of a seed bank with more than 1300 strains of open-pollinated seeds. Free catalog.*

TERRA CEIA FARMS • RR 2, Box 167, Pantego, NC 27860 • Tel: 919 943 2865 • *A wide selection of bulbs and tubers, as well as perennials at low prices. 50 years in the mail-order business. Free catalog.*

THOMPSON & MORGAN • Box 1308, Jackson, NJ 08527-0308 • Tel: 908 363 2225 • *Over 2000 varieties, including the rare and unusual. Free 200-page color catalog.*

TWILLEY SEEDS • PO Box 65, Dept 675, Trevoss, PA 19053 • Tel: 215 639 8800 • *Vegetable and flower seeds "for fresh market, roadside and U-pick growers."*

THE VERMONT WILDFLOWER FARM • Route 7, Charlotte, VT • Tel: 802 425 3500 Fax: 802 425 3504 • *America's Wildflower Seed Specialists. Seed catalog available.*

WATERFORD GARDENS • 74 E Allendale Road, Saddle River, NJ 07458 • Tel: 201 327 0721 • *Everything for the water garden.*

WE-DU NURSERY • Route 5, Box 724, Marion, NC 28752 • Tel: 704 738 8300 • *US, Chinese, Japanese, and Korean wild-flowers, rare plants, rock plants.*

WILLHITE SEED COMPANY • Box 23, Poolville, TX 76487 • Tel: 817 599 8656 • *Over 350 varieties, including watermelon, corn, cantaloupe, cucumber, bean, okra, peas, squash. Free catalog.*

WOODLANDERS INC • 1128 Colleton Avenue, Aiken, SC 29801 • Tel: 803 648 7522 • *Founded to make available to gardeners the flora of the US Southeast. Offerings now include those suited to zones 6-9 worldwide.*

Pest control ~ page 171

ARBICO • PO Box 4247 CRB, Tucson, AZ 85738 • Tel: 602 825 9785 • *Producer and distributor of organic gardening supplies, beneficial insects etc.*

BENEFICIAL INSECT COMPANY • 244 Forrest Street, Fort Mill, SC 29715 • Tel: 803 547 2310 • *Suppliers of high-quality beneficials for the control of pests, insects, and mites in the least toxic ways.*

BIO-INTEGRAL RESOURCE CENTER • PO Box 7414, Berkeley, CA 94707 • Tel: 510 524 2567 Fax: 510 524 1758 • *BIRC publications provide information on environmentally safe and effective methods of managing pests in the home, garden, and in agriculture. Memberships also.*

BIOLOGICAL URBAN GARDENING SERVICES (BUGS) • PO Box 76, Citrus Heights, CA. 95611-0076 • Tel: 916 726 5377 • *The Voice of Ecological Urban Horticulture – an international membership organization devoted to reducing the use of agricultural/horticultural chemicals. Quarterly newsletter.*

BOUNTIFUL GARDENS • 5798 Ridgewood Road, Willits, CA 95490 • Tel: 707 459 6410 • *Pest control. Catalog.*

BOZEMAN BIOTECH • PO Box 3146, Bozeman, MT 59772 • Tel: 800 289 6656 • *Natural products for the control of pests.*

BRICKER'S ORGANIC FARMS INC • 824-HS Sandbar Ferry Road, Augusta GA 30901 • *Pyrethrins, rotenone, sabadilla, soaps.*

BUG SUCKER BILOU INC • Box 7, Farmington, WA 99128 • Tel: 509 287 2000 • *Houdini, bug vacuum.*

CO-OP GARDENING GROUP • PO Box 155, Red Lion, PA 17356 • *Azadirachtin, pyrethrins, rotenone, sabadilla.*

COPPERBRITE • Box 50610, Santa Barbara, CA 93150-0610 • *Snail control.*

EARLEE INC • 2002 Highway 62, Jeffersonville, IN 47130 • *Pyrethrins, rotenone, soaps. Sticky strips, safer insecticides.*

ENVIRONMENTALLY SOUND PRODUCTS • 8845 Orchard Tree Lane, Towson, MD 21286 • Tel: 800 886 5432 / 410 825 7200 • *Garden and household products for green and healthy living. Includes Natrapel insect repellent. Catalog.*

FAIRFIELD-AMERICAN CORP • 201 Route 17 N, Rutherford, NJ 07070 • Tel: 201507 4880 • *Silica gels w/wo pyrethrins.*

GARDEN CITY SEEDS • 1324 Red Crow Road, Victor, MT 59875 • Tel: 406 961 4837 • *Pest controls. Part of the non-profit Down Home Project.*

GARDENS ALIVE! • 5100 Schenley Place, Lawrenceburg, IN 47025 • Tel: 812 537 8650 Fax: 812 537 5108 • *Catalog of organic garden products including: Azadirachtin, oils, pyrethrins, rotenone, ryania, sabadilla, soaps.*

GARDEN-VILLE OF AUSTIN • 8648 Old Bee Cave Road, Austin, TX 78735 • Tel: 512 288 6115 • *Supplier of natural pest controls.*

GARDENER'S SUPPLY COMPANY • 128 Intervale Road, Burlington, VT 05401 • Tel: 802 863 1700

HARMONY FARM SUPPLY & NURSERY • PO Box 460, Graton, CA 95444 • *Azadirachtin, oils, pyrethrins, ryania, sabadilla, soaps.*

INVISIBLE GARDENERS OF AMERICA • 29169 Heathercliff Road 216-408, Malibu, CA 90265 • Tel: 310 457 4438 / 800 354 9296 • *Natural pest control for home and garden.*

LAKON HERBALS • Box 252, Montpelier, VT 05601 • Tel: 802 223 5563 • *Bygone Bugs, herbal repellents.*

LAND STEWART • 434 Lower Road, Box 356, Souderton, PA 18964 • Tel: 800 848 3043 • *Lure box.*

LIVE OAK STRUCTURAL INC • 801-B Camelia Street, Berkeley, CA 94710 • Tel: 510 524 7101 • *Pioneers of the termi-barrier; a non-toxic method of subterranean termite control in existing homes and new construction.*

MELLINGER'S INC • 2310 W South Range Road, North Lima, 44452 9731 • *Natural snail control.*

NATURAL FARM PRODUCTS INC • Route 2, Box 201A, Spencer Road, SE Kalkaska, MI 49646 • Tel: 616 369 2465

NATURAL PEST CONTROL • 8864 Little Creek Drive, Orangeville, CA 95662 • Tel: 916 726 9855

NATURE GARD™ • Sudbury Consumer Products Company, 301 West Osborn, Phoenix, AZ 85013-3928 • Tel: 800 548 2828 • *A user-friendly nematode product that helps destroy soil-dwelling insect larvae and pupae.*

NATURE'S CONTROL • Box 35, Medford, OR 97501 • Tel: 503 899 8318

NECESSARY ORGANICS • One Nature's Way, PO Box 305, New Castle, VA 24127 • Tel: 703 864 5103 Fax: 703 864 5186 • *Providing natural plant care and pest control choices for farmers and gardeners. Now also introduces "Concern™" garden products with three pest controls, two plant foods and a composter, composed of naturally derived ingredients.*

NITRON INDUSTRIES • PO Box 1447, Fayetteville, AR 72702 • Tel: 800 835 0123 • *Manufacturer of enzymes and natural pest controls.*

OHIO EARTH FOOD • 5488R Swamp, Hartville, OH 44632 • Tel: 216 877 9356 Fax: 216 877 4237 • *Insect controls. Testing for lawn, garden, farm. Free catalog.*

ORGANIC CONTROL INC • 5132 Venice Boulevard, Los Angeles, CA 90019 • Tel: 213 937 7444 • *Beneficial insects for pest control.*

PEACEFUL VALLEY FARM SUPPLY • Tel: 916 272 4769 • PO Box 2209, Grass Valley, CA 95945 • *Azadirachtin, oils, pyrethrins, quassia, rotenone, ryadia, sabadilla, soaps.*

REAL GOODS • 555 Leslie Street, Ukiah, CA 95482 • Tel: 800 762 7325 • *Real Goods is your complete resource for ENERGY EFFICIENT LIVING including natural pest control. Free catalog. See p. 96.*

RINCON-VITOVA INSECTARIES • Box 95, Oak View, CA 93022 • Tel: 800 248 2847 / 805 643 5407

RINGER CORPORATION • 9959 Valley View Road, Eden Prairie, MN 55344 • Tel: 612 941 4180 Fax: 612 941 5031 • *Biological pesticides.*

SEABRIGHT LABORATORIES • 4026 Harlan Street, Emeryville, CA 94608 • Tel: 800 284 7363 • *Stickem Green, Roach Free, Yellow Jacket Traps.*

TALLON TERMITE AND PEST CONTROL • 1949 East Market Street, Long Beach, CA 90805 • Tel: 310 422 1131 Fax: 310 423 6146 • *Less-toxic pest controls include: birth regulators for fleas, citrus-based sprays, borate based products, insect traps, electrical barriers, biological controls.*

UNIQUE INSECT CONTROL • 5504 Sperry Drive, Citrus Heights, CA 95621

ENVIRONMENTAL PROTECTION AGENCY (EPA) • Public Information Center, 820 Quincy Street Northwest, Washington DC 20011 • Tel: 202 829 3535 • *EPA Pesticide Hotline: 800 858 7378. A 24-hour database provides information on health effects and ingredients of pesticides.*

Wildlife ~ *page 172*

ABSOLUTELY BATS • PO Box 1393, Rockville, MD 20849 • Tel: 301 309 6610

ALICE'S HERBS • 4950 Femrite Drive, Madison, WI 53716 • Tel: 800 276 4911

BACKYARD WILDLIFE PROGRAM • Saskatchewan Environment and Resource Management – Wildlife Branch, Room 436, 3211 Albert Street, Regina, SK, Canada, S4S 5W6 • Tel: 306 787 2314 Fax: 306 787 9544 • *Promotes habitat enhancement projects to benefit native wildlife species - for urban residents as well as rural, and greenspace managers.*

BRUSHY MOUNTAIN BEE FARM • Route One, Moravian Falls, NC 28654 • *Quality beekeeping equipment and supplies. Free catalog.*

COLDSTREAM FARM • 2030 "S" Free Soil Road, Free Soil, MI 49411-9752 • *Trees and shrubs for reforestation, woodlots, and wildlife habitat. Free catalog.*

CWF BACKYARD HABITAT PROGRAM • 2740 Queensview Avenue, Ottawa, ON, Canada, K2B 1A2 • Tel: 800 563-WILD • *Produces manual with over 100 backyard habitat enhancement projects.*

EARTHLY GOODS • PO Box 614, New Albany, IN 47151 • Tel: 812 944 3283 • *Supplier of birdhouses, feeders, bat boxes etc. made of 100% surplus wood from lumberyards.*

ENVIRONMENTAL EDUCATION FARM FOUNDATION • 25344 County Road, 95 Davis, CA 95616 • Tel: 916 758 1387 Fax: 916 758 1316 • *Bat roosting tubes.*

FORESTFARM • 990 Tetherhouse Road, Williams, OR 97544 • *Amazing Selection: Plants for wildlife, xeriscape, American natives, more. Descriptive catalog.*

GRANTHAMS LANDING WORKSHOP • Box 62, Granthams Landing, BC, Canada, V0N 1X0 • Tel: 604 886 3159 • *The original 'Welcome Bat™' Bat House.*

NATIONAL WILDLIFE FEDERATION • 1400 16th Street Northwest, Washington DC 20036 • Tel: 202 797 6800

NATURAL WORLD INTERACTIONS INC • PO Box 2250, Halesite, NY 11743-0687 • Tel: 800 WINGS 67 • *Natural wild bird food and 'Wings EcoFeeder™'.*

NATURE CONSERVANCY • 1815 North Lynn Street, Arlington, VA 22209 • Tel: 703 841 5300 • *Natural Heritage Program lists endangered plants. Call for the Program office in your area.*

PARADISE WATER GARDENS • 14 May Street, Whitman, MA 02382 • *Mail-order pond suppliers.*

VAN NESS WATER GARDENS • 2460 North Euclid Avenue, Upland, CA 91786 • *Mail-order pond suppliers.*

PALMETTO WATERWORKS • PO Box 2331, Columbia, SC 29202 • *Mail-order pond suppliers.*

LILYPONS WATER GARDENS • PO Box 10, Lilypons, MD 21717 • *Mail-order pond suppliers.*

PLOW & HEARTH • PO Box 5000, Madison, VA 22727-1500 • Tel: 800 627 1712 • *Mail-order catalog includes bird boxes.*

Spiritual garden ~ *page 173*

ROY-FISHER ASSOCIATES • Jupiter, FL 33458 • Tel: 407 747 3462 • *Landscape architects.*

Sustainable structures ~ *page 176*

AQUAPORE MOISTURE SYSTEMS INC • 610 S 80th Avenue, Phoenix, AZ 85043 • Tel: 602 936 8083 Fax: 602 936 9040 • *Moisture Master soaker hose and rubber sprinkler hose are made of 65% recycled tires. They're great for watering your garden.*

BAMBOO-SMITHS • PO Box 1801, Nevada City, CA 95959 • Tel: 916 265 8866 • *Bamboo fences and gates.*

BARLOW TYRIE INC • 1263 Glen Avenue, Suite 230, Moorestown, NJ 08057 • Tel: 609 273 7878 Fax: 609 273 9199 • *Teak recliner from sustainably managed forests. Catalog of garden furniture.*

CASTLE TIRE AND RUBBER CO • PO Box 99, 1415 Ritner Highway, Carlisle, PA 17013 • Tel: 800 233 7165 • *Recycled tires for outdoor paving.*

DRIPWORKS-EVERLINER • 380 Maple Street, Willits, CA 95490 • Tel: 800 522 3747 • *Pond and water tank liners. Low-cost, custom, one-piece – any size – wooden, steel or cement tank.*

EARTHLY GOODS • PO Box 614, New Albany, IN 47151 • Tel: 812 944 3283 • *Supplier of birdhouses, feeders, bat boxes etc. made of 100% surplus wood from lumberyards.*

EARTH TOOLS • 9754 Johanna Place, Shadow Hills, CA 91040 • Tel: 800 825 6460 / 818 353 5883 • *Products for the Natural Home and garden, all at great prices. Call for free catalog.*

ECO-CHAR® • Sub-Continent Inc, Box 4266, San Rafael, CA 94913 • Tel: 800 521 5553 / 415 492 2220 Fax: 415 472 0389 • *Mesquite bean pods for gas and charcoal grilling, charcoal briquets made from nutshells and fire starter made from corn.*

ECO DESIGN CO • 1365 Rufina Circle, Santa Fe, NM 87502 • Tel: 505 438 3448 • *Natural Choice catalog contains many interesting products including composters, seeds, garden tools, and bird boxes.*

ENVIROEDGE • 3433 West Harvard Street, Building A, Santa Ana, CA 92704 • Tel: 800 549 3343 • *Solid Slats™ decorative fencing is made from 97% recycled plastic from at least 25% post-consumer sources.*

ENVIROSAFE PRODUCTS INC • Box 1074, Murray Hill Station, New York, NY 10156-0604 • Tel: 718 968 0199 • *Recycled mailboxes/posts, recycled benches, plastic fencing-recycled products.*

ENVIROTIRE INC • 1904 Third Avenue, Seattle, WA 98101 • Tel: 206 587 6018 Fax: 206 587 6205 • *Rubber-modified asphalt concrete paving material from recycled tires.*

Wood Fired Water Heater

CHOFU WATER HEATER $540

A high-efficiency wood-fired water heater that circulates water by thermosyphon, no pump needed. Used for heating hot tubs, thermal mass, or domestic hot water.

STAINLESS STEEL HOT TUB $995

Japanese-style flat bottom, 5 ft diam x 2 ft deep.
Allows outstretched legs. Made for use with the Chofu heater.

Send for free brochure and catalogue to: ISLAND HOT TUB CO. 3545 E Quade Road, Clinton, WA 98236. Phone: 360 579 8578

FOUNTAINS INCORPORATED • 103 Park Avenue, New York, NY 10017 • Tel: 212 679 5596 Fax: 212 679 5595 • *Innovative ecological fountain design.*

INNOVATIVE WASTE TECHNOLOGIES INC • 100-1 Grosvenor Square, Annacis Island, New Westminster, BC, Canada, V3M 5S1 • Tel: 604 524 5263 Fax: 504 524 1241 • *Durable Rubberloc™ pavers made from recycled scrap automobile tires provide a unique paved surface for commercial, consumer and recreational applications.*

ISLAND HOT TUB CO • 3545 E Quade Road, Clinton, WA 98236 • Tel: 360 579 8578 • *'Chofu water heater' – a high-efficiency wood-fired water heater and hot tub – Japanese-style flat bottom, 5 ft diam x 2 ft deep. Allows outstretched legs. Stainless steel for easy cleaning and durability, insulated with cedar outside.*

IRRIGRO • LPO 360, 1555 Third Avenue, Niagara Falls, NY 14304 • Tel: 905 688 4090 • and PO BOX 1133, St Catherine's, Ontario, Canada, L2R 7A3 • *Drip irrigation products including sample kits.*

KINGSLEY BATE LTD • 5587-B Guinea Road, Fairfax, VA 22032 • Tel: 703 978 7200 • *A collection of hand carved and traditional outdoor furniture in solid teak. Smart Wood certification.*

THE KINSMAN COMPANY • River Road, Point Pleasant, PA 18950 • Tel: 215 297 5613 • *Organic gardening supplies. Free catalog.*

LIVING SYSTEMS • PO Box 98122, Des Moines, WA 98198 • Tel: 800-566-GROW • *Gro-Cart™ starts seeds conveniently, reliably, safely indoors. The cart frame is made from recycled plastic lumber.*

MARTINSON-NICHOLLS, INC • 7243-A Industrial Park Boulevard, PO Box 296, Mentor, OH 44061-0296 • Tel: 216 951 1312 Fax: 216 951 1315 • *DC1050 Yard waste composting container. Waste is reduced naturally before pick-up.*

MAT FACTORY • 760 West 16th Street, Suite E, Costa Mesa, CA 92627 • Tel: 714 645 3122 • *Safety matting; interlocking tiles – suitable for play areas.*

MAXRAY IRRIGATION • Tel: 800 446 2972 / 310 312 3060 • *Unique moisture-activated irrigation system automatically regulates watering, reducing consumption up to 70%. Solar/AC power.*

NATURE'S BACKYARD INC • 126 Duchaine Boulevard, New Bedford, MA 02745 • Tel: 508 995 7008 • *Environmentally beneficial products made from 100% post-consumer recycled plastic including the Brave New Composter.*

THE NATURAL GARDENING COMPANY • 217 San Anselmo Avenue, San Anselmo, CA 94960 • Tel: 415 456 5060 • *Organic gardening supplies. Free catalog.*

NECESSARY TRADING COMPANY • PO Box 305, New Castle, VA 24127 • Tel: 703 864 5103 • *Organic gardening supplies. Free catalog.*

NEW WORLD FURNITURE • PO Box 20957, San Jose, CA 95160 • Tel: 408 268 1670 • *Patio furniture from recycled redwood.*

PHOENIX RECYCLED PLASTICS • 225 Washington Street, Conshohocken, PA 19428 • Tel: 610 940 1590 • *Plastic lumber for all your outdoor needs!*

PLOW & HEARTH • PO Box 5000, Madison, VA 22727-1500 • Tel: 800 627 1712 • *Mail-order catalog – garden furniture, reel mower.*

RANCHO RECYCLED PRODUCTS • 27840 Del Rio Road, Suite C, Temecula, CA 92590-2618 • Tel: 909 676 4813 Fax: 909 676 0108 • *Fencing, decks and rails, tables and benches made from recycled plastic.*

RYOBI AMERICA CORPORATION • 5201 Pearman Dairy Road, Suite 1, Anderson, SC 29625-8950 • Tel: 800 525 2579 • *Power-propelled mulching mower. No emissions, low noise.*

SEARS ROEBUCK & CO • 1630 Cleveland Avenue, Kansas City, MO 64127-2246 • *New reel mowers.*

TOPTROWEL INNOVATIVE SURFACES • 600 East Ocean Boulevard, Suite 400, Long Beach, CA 90802 • Tel: 301 633 3000 • *Recycled rubber poured-in place topping material.*

TREX™ • Mobil Chemical Company, Composites Products Division, 800 Connecticut Avenue, Norwalk, CT 06856 • Tel: 800-BUY TREX • *Trex™ is a wood-polymer composite which can be used for a wide range of uses such as decking and landscaping. Made from reclaimed plastic and waste wood.*

TWIN OAKS HAMMOCKS • Box N, Tecumseh, MO 65760 • Tel: 417 679 4682 Fax: 417 679 4684 • *Earth-friendly comfort! Luxurious hammocks, handwoven from Organic Cotton and Recycled Polyester rope.*

VERMONT COUNTRY STORE • 668 Main Street, Weston, VT 05161 • Tel: 802 824 3184 • *New reel mowers.*

WIND & WEATHER • The Albion Street Water Tower, PO Box 2320, Mendocino, CA 95460 • Tel: 707 964 1284 / 800 922 9463 Fax: 707 964 1278 • *Products include weather vanes and sundials.*

CHARLES WOLF & ASSOCIATES • PO Box 282, Cumming, GA 30130 • *New reel mowers.*

WOMANSWORK • PO Box 543, York, ME 03909-0543 • Tel: 207 363 0805 • *Hardwearing gloves designed specially for women.*

WOOD RECYCLING INC • PO Box 6087, Peabody, MA 01961 • Tel: 508 535 4144 / 800 982 8732 Fax: 508 535 4252 • *100% recycled wood fiber and newsprint mixed with grass seed to prevent soil erosion on hillsides.*

Recycling ~ pages 184-85

The majority of suppliers in this Directory use and promote recycled products.

For specific information on your local recycling centers turn first to your area Green Pages, where available, see page 284

ALAMEDA COUNTY WASTE MANAGEMENT AUTHORITY • 777 Davis Street, Suite 200, San Leandro, CA 94577 • Tel: 510 614 1699 Fax: 510 614 1698 • *Publishes a local directory for the recycling of construction and demolition materials.*

AMERICAN RECYCLER CONTAINERS • 687 County Square Drive, Ventura, CA 93003 • Tel: 805 658 6423

AMERICAN RECYCLING MARKET • PO Box 577, Ogdensburg, NY 13669 • Tel: 800 267 0707• *Produce Recycled Products Guide, listing hundreds of recycled product manufacturers and distributors.*

APICS • The Remanufacturing Specific Industry Group, 500 West Annandale Road, Falls Church, VA 22046 • Tel: 703 237 8344 • *Information on remanufacturing in industry.*

BIOBIN • 8407 Lightmoor Court, Bainbridge, WA 98110 • Tel: 206 842 6641 • *Composting bins/recycling bins.*

CALIFORNIANS AGAINST WASTE FOUNDATION • 926 J Street, Ste 606, Sacramento, CA 95814 • Tel: 916 443 5422 • *pressure group and grassroots organization who also publish Shoppers Guide to Recycled Products.*

CAN-RAM • PO Box 270275, San Diego, CA 92198 • Tel: 619 486 3326

CITIZENS CLEARINGHOUSE FOR HAZARDOUS WASTE • PO Box 6806, Falls Church, VA 22040 • Tel: 703 237 2249 • *Check for your local group as this organization works with over 8,000 local grassroots groups, and is a service center for environmental groups. Helps with community toxics issues such as hazardous waste dumps and other toxic exposures.*

COMMUNITY RECYCLING & RESOURCE RECOVERY INC • 9189 De Garmo Street, Sun Valley, CA 91352 • Tel: 818 767 6000 Fax: 818 768 0541 • *Full service recycling company specializing in mixed solid waste processing and recovery of cardboard, mixed paper, metal and aluminum. Also offering wood and demolition waste recycling as well as mixed organic materials composting.*

COUNCIL FOR TEXTILE RECYCLING • Suite 1212, 7910 Woodmont Avenue, Bethesda, MD 20814 • Tel: 301 718 0671 • *Information on recycling textiles.*

ECO FIBRE CANADA INC • 347 Taylor Road, # 4, RR 4 Niagara-on-the-Lake, Ontario, Canada, LOS 1JO • *Textile recovery and recycling.*

ECOLOGY CENTER • 2530 San Pablo Avenue, Berkeley, CA • Recycling hotline: 510 527 5555 Bookstore: 510 548 2220 • *Recycling curbside pick-up, bookstore, and resource center.*

ECO-POP DESIGNS • PO 269 Pacifica, CA 94044 • Tel: 415 738 8127 • *Waste recycling containers.*

ECOTECH RECYCLED PRODUCTS • 14241, 60th Street North, Clearwater, FL 34620-2706 • Tel: 800 780 5353 Fax: 813 538 8550 • *Comprehensive suppliers of products made from recycled materials, including lidded recycling containers, and produce Eco-Tech Recycled Products Catalog.*

ENVIRO-CYCLE SYSTEMS INC • 100 Ronson Drive, Rexdale, Ontario, Canada, M9W 1B6 • Tel: 416 246 0562 Fax: 416 246 9651 • *A two-in-one recycling system that produces both liquid and solid fertilizer.*

ENVIRONMENTAL ACTION COALITION • 625 Broadway, New York, NY 10012 • Tel: 212 677 1601

ENVIRONMENTAL DEFENSE FUND • 5655 College Avenue, Oakland, CA 94618 • Tel 510 658 8008 • *EDF employ a variety of environmental professionals to find innovative solutions to a broad array of environmental problems. EDF programs include promoting recycling and solid waste reduction, and also play a significant role in reducing the use of toxic chemicals nationally.*

FLOWERFIELD ENTERPRISES • 10332 Shaver Road, Kalamazoo, MI 49002 • Tel: 616 327 0108 • *Promoting worm composting and other backyard composting methods, produce fun educational publications*

GLASS PACKAGING INSTITUTE • 1801 K Street Northwest, Suite 1105-L, Washington, DC 20006 • Tel: 202 887 4850 • *Offers educational materials on recycling glass.*

GREEN GLASS INC • 132 Riverside Road, N Vancouver, BC, Canada, V7H 1T9 • *Recycled glass made into bottles and glasses.*

HAMMER'S PLASTIC RECYCLING • 10252 Highway 65, N Iowa Falls, IA 50126 • Tel: 515 648 5073 • *Manufactures 100% recycled plastic products.*

INFORM, Inc • 381 Park Avenue South, New Tork, NY 1001 • Tel: 212 689 4040 • *Publish Business Recycling Manual, practical advice for private enterprise with a glossary of recycling and marketing terms, equipment directory and lists of commercial waste recycling*

INTEGRATED WASTE MANAGEMENT BOARD • Hotline: 800 553 2962 • *General information on recycling*

INNOVATIVE WASTE TECHNOLOGIES INC • 100-1 Grosvenor Square, Annacis Island, New Westminster, BC, Canada, V3M 5S1 • Tel: 604 524 5263 Fax: 504 524 1241 • *Uses recycled scrap automobile tires to provide a unique paved surface for commercial, consumer and recreational applications.*

THE JOHN ROSSI COMPANY INC • 180 South Highland Avenue, Ossining, NY 10562 • Tel: 914 941 1752 Fax: 914 941 1810 • *Paper products made from recycled tires and newspaper.*

THE LOOP GROUP • 200 Poplar Street, North Aurora, IL 60542 • Tel: 708 897 5883 Fax: 708 897 5898 • and 1280 Iroquois Drive, Naperville, IL 60563 • Tel: 708 897 5883 • *Free information on closing the loop.*

THE MART STORE • 153 West Ohio Street, Chicago, IL • Tel: 312 670 8155 • *Exotic hardwoods from old African Railroad ties are used to make attractive furniture.*

METRO SOLID WASTE MANAGEMENT • 200 Southwest First Avenue, Portland, OR 97201 • Tel: 503 221 1646

NATIONAL RECYCLING COALITION • 1101 20th Street NW, Suite 305, Washington, DC 20007 • Tel: 202 625 6406 • *Offers fact sheets, reports, and directories related to recycling.*

NATIONAL SOLID WASTES MANAGEMENT ASSOCIATION • 1730 Rhode Island Avenue Northwest, Washington, DC 20036 • Tel: 202 861 0708

NEW CONSUMER INSTITUTE • PO Box 51, Wauconda, IL 60084 • Tel: 800 343 9204 • *Clearing House of information on green and socially responsible products and services.*

NORTH CAROLINA RECYCLING ASSOCIATION • 7330 Chapel Hill Road, Suite 207, Raleigh, NC 27607 • Tel: 919 851 8444

OAKLAND RECYCLING ASSOCIATION • 1212 Broadway, Suite 830, Oakland, CA 94612-1826 • Tel: 510 444 1621 • *Construction material recovery site.*

PALLAS TEXTILES • 8687 Melrose Avenue, Pacific Design Center, Los Angeles, CA 90069 • Tel: 310 659 2133 • *'Earth Paper' is a unique combination of natural materials: it comprises 65% pulp, 25% stone powder and 8% straw.*

PHOENIX RECYCLED PLASTICS • 225 Washington Street, Conshohocken, PA 19428 • Tel: 610 940 1590 • *Plastic lumber for all your outdoor needs!*

THE PLACTORY, INC • 986 Tower Plaza, Santa Cruz, CA 95062 • Tel: 800 538 0738 • *Plastic molding recycler and mold maker - low cost ways to recycle "hard to recycle" plastic.*

PLASTOPAN NORTH AMERICA INC • 812 East 59th Street, Los Angeles, CA 90001 • Tel: 213 231 2225 Fax: 213 231 2068 • *Produce the Bio-Actor composter made from 100% top-quality post-consumer plastic resin. Also produce a range of refuse and recycling collection containers.*

RAYMOND COMMUNICATIONS, INC • 6429 Auburn Avenue, Riverdale, MD • Tel: 301 345 4237 • *Publishers of* State Recycling Laws Update, *newsletter giving independent analysis of state legislation and legislation in Canada and Europe; consultants on green packaging, solid waste issues, and commercial waste management.*

RANCHO RECYCLED PRODUCTS • 27840 Del Rio Road, Suite C, Temecula, CA 92590-2618 • Tel: 909 676 4813 Fax: 909 676 0108 • *Fencing, decks and rails, tables and benches made from recycled plastic.*

REAL GOODS • 555 Leslie Street, Ukiah, CA 95482 • Tel: 800 762 7325 • Real Goods is your complete resource for ENERGY EFFICIENT LIVING. Free catalog includes recycled goods. See p. 96.

REAL RECYCLED • 1541 Adrian Road, Burlingame, CA 94010 • Tel: 415 259 3921 Fax: 415 692 4820 • *A wide range of post consumer recycled items: cardboard loose-leaf binders, outdoor furniture, paper and envelopes and futon mattresses. Free catalog.*

RECY-CAL SUPPLY CO • 40880 B County Center Drive, Suite P, Temecula, CA 92591 • Tel: 909 695 5225 Fax: 909 695 5228 • *Recycling containers.*

RECYCLE AMERICA • *Call 213 732 9253 Hotline for recycling numbers for your area.*

RECYCLED MATERIALS NEWSLETTER • 731 D Loma Verde Avenue, Palo Alto, CA 94303 • Tel: 415 856 0634 • *Connects contractors removing building materials with those who might need them.*

RECYCLED PRODUCTS CO • 230 Canton Avenue, Milton, MA 01286 • Tel: 617 698 7236

RECYCLED PRODUCTS INFORMATION CLEARINGHOUSE • 528 Hempstead Way, Springfield, CA 22151 • Tel: 703 941 4452 • *Resource and information center providing recycled product research, information, leaflets, guidance and referrals, also EPA guidelines fact sheets.*

ENVIRONMENTAL NEWSLETTERS, INC •11906 Paradise Lane, Herndon, VA 22071 • Tel: 703 758 8436 • *Publish* Recycled Products Business Letter *to help companies market their recycled products more effectively.*

RECYCLING CONTAINER SALES • PO Box 130, Plainwell, MI 49080 • Tel: 616 685 1654 Fax: 616 685 2345 • *Bins for recycling.*

RESOURCE REVIVAL • 2342 NW Marshall, Portland, OR 97210 • Tel: 503 266 6001/800 866 8823 Fax: 503 226 6397 • *Furniture, belts, collars, picture frames, straps, and more made from reused material.*

RE-TIRING • PO Box 505-EM, Roy, UT 84067 • *Free information on aspects of using recycled authomobile tires.*

ROADRUNNERS RECYCLERS INC • PO Box 1617, El Prado, NM 87529 • Tel: 505 776 3707 • *Community-owned recycling center which accepts glass, cardboard, newspaper, aluminum, paper and tin.*

STAFFORD HARRIS INC • 1916 Pike Place, no 705, Seattle, WA 98101-1056 • Tel: 206 682 4042 Fax: 206 447 1670 • *Resources for waste management, resource planning, database for recycled content of building materials.*

STEEL CAN RECYCLING INSTITUTE • 680 Andersen Drive, Pittsburgh, PA 15220 • Tel: 412 922 2772 / 800 876 SCRI • *Information on recycling steel cans.*

20/20 RECYCLING CENTERS • 1731 Pomona Road, Corona, CA 91720 • Tel: 909 279 2200 Fax: 909 279 1619

SOLID WASTE ALTERNATIVES PROJECT – ENVIRONMENTAL ACTION FOUNDATION • 1525 New Hampshire Avenue NW, Washington, DC 20036 • *Information on recycling.*

SOLID WASTE COMPOSTING COUNCIL • 114 South Pitt Street, Alexandria, VA 22314 • Tel: 703 739 2401 • *The only association devoted to promoting composting. Developing national standards for municipal and home compost.*

SOUND RESOURCE MANAGEMENT GROUP • 119 Pine Street, Suite 203, Seattle, WA 91010 • Tel: 206 622 9454 • *Research and consultations on recycling, composting and waste reduction; the company aims to implement effective economical, accessible, and environmentally sound programs for waste management.*

URBAN ORE INFORMATION SERVICES • 133 Sixth Street, Berkeley, CA 947109 • Tel: 510 559 4454 Fax: 510 528 1540 • *Referral, general information and publications*

USA. RECYCLING SERVICES CO • 499 Lawrence Road, Kings Park, NY 11754 • Tel: 516 368 5533 • *Solid waste management recycling. Distributes 100% post-consumer paper products.*

USED RUBBER USA • 597 Haight, San Francisco, CA 94117 • Tel: 415 626 7855 • *Accessories made with recycled tires.*

VANCE IDS INC • 6239 Edgewater Drive, Orlando, FL 32810 • Tel: 407 292 2809 • *Designs and manufactures systems for disposal of hazardous waste.*

VITAL VISIONS CORPORATION • Route 1, Box 95, Freeport, FL 32439 • Tel: 904 835 2121 Fax: 904 835 4768 • *Recycling bins.*

Building ~ pages 18-49

BACKHOME • PO Box 70, Hendersonville, NC 28793 • Tel: 704 696 3838 • *Practical information on home energy, self-reliant living, recycling, gardening etc. See p. 190.*

BUILDING WITH NATURE • PO Box 4417, Santa Rosa, CA 95402-4417 • Tel: 707 579 2201 / 707 884 4513 Fax: 707 884 1235 • *A bi-monthly newsletter on sustainable architecture. Geared for design professionals, but easy to read and interesting to anyone who is interested in the practicalities of natural building. See p. 191.*

CO-HOUSING • Co-Housing Network, PO Box 2585, Berkeley, CA 94702 • Tel: 303 494 8458 (editorial) 510 526 6124 (business)

COHOUSING NEWSLETTER • c/o Innovative Housing, 2169 East San Francisco Boulevard, Suite E, San Rafael, CA 94901 • Tel: 415 457 4593

COHOUSING QUARTERLY • 155 Pine Street, Amherst, MA 01002

COMMUNITIES MAGAZINE • Journal of Co-operative Living, c/o FIC, 1118 Round Bute Drive, Fort Collins, CO 89524 • Tel: 303 224 9080

CO-OP AMERICA QUARTERLY • 1612 K Street NW, Suite 600, Washington DC 20006 • Tel: 202 872 5307 • *Covers emerging ideas and models for a just and sustainable society.*

E MAGAZINE • PO Box 5098, Westport, CT 06881 • Tel: 203 854 5559 • *A clearing house of information, news, and commentary on environmental issues.*

EARTH ENTERPRISE EXCHANGE NEWSLETTER • Business for Social Responsibility, 1010-1030 15th Street NW, Washington DC 20005 • Tel: 202 842 5400 • Fax: 202 842 3135

EARTH FIRST JOURNAL • PO Box 1415, Eugene, OR 97440 • Tel: 503 741 9191 • *Independent periodical dedicated to the environmental movement.*

EARTH STAR/WHOLE LIFE TIMES • PO Box 390436, Cambridge, MA 02139 • Tel: 617 661 7327 • *Promotes natural and healthy living.*

EARTHWORD JOURNAL • 580 Broadway, Suite 200, Laguna Beach, CA 92651 • Tel: 714 497 1896 • *Educational journal addressing practical solutions for living sustainably.*

ECO-BUILDING TIMES • Northwest EcoBuilding Guild, 217 9th Avenue North, Seattle, WA 98109 • Tel: 206 622 8350

ECODESIGN • The British School, Slad Road, Stroud, Glos GL5 1QW, UK • Tel: (+44) 1453 765575 Fax: (+44) 1453 759211 • *Journal of the Ecological Design Association. Available via membership subscription.*

ECO-DESIGN QUARTERLY • Eco-Design Resource Society, PO Box 3981, Main Post Office, Vancouver, BC, Canada, V6B 3Z4 • Tel: 604 738 9334

ECOLOGY BY DESIGN • 1341 Ocean Avenue, Suite 73, Santa Monica, CA 90401 • Tel: 310 394 4146

ENVIRON Magazine • PO Box 2204, Fort Collins, CO 80522 • Tel: 303 224 0083 • *Ongoing coverage of ecologic architecture & building; water, air and food pollution; geographic relocation assessments, marketplace maneuvers to increase healthy choices. Four 40-page issues for $18.*

ENVIRONMENTAL BUILDING NEWS • RR 1, Box 161, Brattleboro, VT 05301 • Tel: 802 257 7300 • Fax: 802 257 7304 • *A bimonthly newsletter for builders, architects, and owner-builders. The leading publication on environmentally responsible design and construction.*

ENVIRONMENTAL BY DESIGN • PO Box 95016, South Van CSC, Vancouver, BC, Canada, V6P 6V4

ENVIRONMENTAL REGULATORY REVIEW • Pace Incorporated, 1710 Douglas Drive North, Minneapolis, MN 55422 • Tel: 612 544 5543

ENVIRONMENTAL RESOURCE GUIDE • American Institute of Architects, 1735 New York Avenue, NW, Washington DC 20006 • Tel: 800 365 2724

FINE HOMEBUILDING • 63 South Main Street, PO Box 5506, Newtown, CT 06470 • Tel: 203 4268171 Fax: 203 426 3434

GREEN BUILDING NEWS • 21 1/2 Dudley Avenue, Venice, CA 90291 • Tel: 310 399 9318

HEALTHY BUILDINGS RESOURCE GUIDE • Healthy Buildings Associates, 7190 Fiske Road, Clinton, WA 98236 • Tel: 206 579 2962

IN BUSINESS • PO Box 323, Emmaus, PA 18049 • Tel: 215 967 4135 • *A bi-monthly journal oriented to small manufacturers and retailers of environmental products.*

IN CONTEXT • Context Institute, PO Box 11470, Bainbridge Island, WA 98110 • Tel: 206 842 0216 • *"A quarterly of humane sustainable culture", envisions, explores, and clarifies the many ways cultures can be both humane and sustainable — and how we can get there. If you want one publication about our emerging sustainable society, this is it.*

INDOOR HEALTH • Ecodex Corporation, 594 Marrett Road, Suite 18, Lexington, MA 02173 • Tel: 617 862 4300

THE LAST STRAW • Journal of Strawbale Construction • Available from Out-on-Bale, 1037 East Linden Street, Tucson, AZ 85719 • Tel: 602 624 1673

NEW AGE JOURNAL • PO Box 52375, Boulder, CO 80321-3275 • Tel: 800 234 4556 • *Bi-monthly New Age magazine which includes natural living topics.*

THE PERMACULTURE ACTIVIST • PO Box 1209, Black Mountain, NC 28711 • Tel: 704 683 4946

PERMACULTURE DRYLANDS JOURNAL • PO Box 133, Pearce, AZ 85625

PROGRESSIVE ARCHITECTURE • 600 Summer Street, Stamford, CT 06904 • Tel: 203 348 7531

RESOURCE RECYCLING • 1206 NW 21st Avenue, Portland, OR 97209

REUSE NEWS • c/o Sherlock Enterprises, 609 Hobart Road, Hanover, PA 17331 • *Monthly newsletter offers tips on reusing everything from chopsticks to panty hose.*

SAFE HOME RESOURCE GUIDE • 24 East Avenue, Suite 1300, New Canaan, CT 06840 • Tel: 203 966 2099

SOUTHEAST PERMACULTURE NEWS • 160 King Street, Abingdon, VA 24210

STATE RECYCLING LAWS UPDATE • Raymond Communications, Inc, 6429 Auburn Avenue, Riverdale, MD 20737 • Tel: 301 345 4237 Fax: 301 345 4768 • *Quarterly newsletter with independent analysis of state legislation. Contents include: research, consulting on green packaging, solid waste issues, commercial waste management.*

TERRAIN • Ecology Center Bookstore, 2530 San Pablo Avenue, Berkeley, CA 94702 • Tel: 510 548 2220 • *Monthly environmental journal.*

THE URBAN ECOLOGIST • c/o Urban Ecology, 405 14th Street, Suite 701, Oakland, CA 94612 • Tel: 510 251 6330

Soft energy ~ pages 50-69

See also general listings for Building, above

APPROPRIATE TECHNOLOGY NEWS • Jade Mountain, PO Box 4616, Boulder, CO 80306-4616

ENERGY SAVER'S CATALOG • Solar Components Corporation, 121 Valley Street, • Manchester, NH 03103-6211 • Tel: 603 668 8186

HOME ENERGY • 2124 Kittredge Street, # 95, Berkeley, CA 94794 • Tel: 510 524 5405 • *Bi-monthly magazine on residential energy conservation, including new energy-saving technologies and tips for home energy savings.*

HOME POWER JOURNAL • PO Box 520, Ashland, OR 97520 • Tel: 916 475 3179 • *Bi-monthly magazine about residential renewable energy systems. Covers the culture of people making their own electrical power in small-scale systems using renewables: photovoltaics, micro-hydro, and wind. Explores issues and technical details.*

INDEPENDENT ENERGY • 620 Central Avenue, North, Milaca, MN 56353 • Tel: 800 922 3736

INTEGRAL ENERGY NEWS • Sierra Solar Systems, 109 Argall Way, Nevada City, CA 95959 • Tel: 800 517 6527 Fax: 916 265 6151

MOTHER EARTH NEWS • 24 E 23rd Street, New York, NY 10010 • Tel: 800 937 4287 • *"The original country magazine" was one of the early pioneer publications on sustainable living. Geared for people who live in the country, but useful for anyone wanting to live more sustainably.*

NEW ENERGY NEWS • Fusion Information Center, • Institute for New Energy, Utah Research Park, PO Box 58639, Salt Lake City, UT 84109 • Tel: 801 583 6232

NUCLEUS • Magazine of the Union of Concerned Scientists, Cambridge, MA

PUBLIC CITIZEN (National Directory of Safe Energy Organizations) • 215 Pennsylvania Avenue SE, Washington DC 20003 • Tel: 202 546 4996

SOLAR INDUSTRY JOURNAL • 777 North Capitol Street NE, Suite 805, Washington DC 20002 • Tel: 202 408 0660 • *Quarterly overview of national and international trends. Exhaustive summaries of laboratory research, projects, conferences, politics and legislation, tax credits and government programs.*

UTILITY FREE NEWSLETTER • Utility Free, Inc, 0050 Road 110, Glenwood Springs, CO 81601 • Tel: 800 766 550 Fax: 303 928 0847

WISCONSIN RENEWABLE ENERGY QUARTERLY (RENEW) • 222 South Hamilton, Madison WI 53703 • Tel: 608 255 4044

Water ~ pages 70-85

See also general listings for Building pages 276-7

CLEAN WATER ACTION NEWS • 317 Pennsylvania Avenue SE, Washington DC 20003 • Tel: 202 547 1116

EARTHWORD JOURNAL • 580 Broadway, Suite 200, Laguna Beach, CA 92651 • Tel: 714 497 1896 • *Educational and practical journal.*

E-THE ENVIRONMENTAL MAGAZINE • PO Box 6667, Syracuse, NY 13217 • Tel: 800 825 0061 • *A bi-monthly magazine that is a clearing house of news, information, and commentary on environmental issues to inform and inspire individuals to bring about improvements. Not many articles on products or life-style, but has environmental product ads.*

GREEN SCHOOL BIODIVERSITY BOOKLET • Ocean Voice International, 2883 Otterson Drive, Ottawa, Ontario, Canada, K1V 7B2

US WATER NEWS • 230 Main Street, Halstead, KS 67056 • Tel: 316 835 2222

WORLDWATCH MAGAZINE • Worldwatch Institute, 1776 Massachusetts Avenue NW, Washington DC 20036 • Tel: 202 452 1999 • *Monitors environmental trends. Six issues per year.*

Sane electrics ~ pages 86-97

See also listings for Soft energy page 277

MICROWAVE NEWS • Edited and published by Louis Slesin, PO Box 1799, Grand Central Station, New York 10763 • Tel: 212 517 2800

MOTHER JONES • PO Box 469024, Escondido, CA 92046 • Tel: 415 665 6637 • *Award-winning investigative reporting includes features on the environment and health.*

NUCLEAR MONITOR • Nuclear Information and Resource Service, 1424 16th Street NW, Suite 601, Washington, DC 20036 • Tel: 202 328 0002 • *Watchdog and consumer magazine .*

REDUCING RADON RISKS • booklet free from EPA Public Information Center

SOLAR LIVING SOURCEBOOK • Real Goods, 966 Mazzoni Street, Ukiah, CA 95482-3471 • Tel: 800 762 7325

Lighting ~ pages 98-109

See also listings for Soft energy page 277

EARTHCARE CATALOG • Ukiah, CA 95482-8507 • Tel: 800 347 0700

ELECTRICAL INDEPENDENCE GUIDEBOOK AND CATALOG • Integral Energy Systems, 1065 Argall Way, Nevada City, CA 95959 • Tel:800 735 6790

Air ~ pages 110-121

ENVIRON Magazine • PO Box 2204, Fort Collins, CO 80522 • Tel: 303 224 0083 • *Ongoing coverage of ecologic architecture & building; water, air and food pollution; geographic relocation assessments, marketplace maneuvers to increase healthy choices. Four 40-page issues for $18.*

ENVIRONMENTAL REGULATORY REVIEW • Pace Incorporated, 1710 Douglas Drive North, Minneapolis, MN 55422 • Tel: 612 525 3416

INDOOR HEALTH • Ecodex Corporation, 594 Marrett Road, Suite 18, Lexington, MA 02173 • Tel: 617 862 4300 • *Newsletter.*

Decoration ~ pages 122-137

See also general listings for Building pages 276-7

CONSCIOUS CHOICE • 920 West Franklin, no 301, Chicago, IL 60610 • Tel: 312 440 4373 • *Topics covered include the environment, natural foods, holistic health, and spirituality.*

THE CRAFTS REPORT • PO Box 1992, Wilmington, DE 19899 • Tel: 302 656 2209 • *Informs, instructs, and inspires the craftsperson while encouraging social and environmental responsibility.*

INTERIOR CONCERNS • Victoria Schomer • PO Box 2386, Mill Valley, CA 94942 • Tel: 415 389 8049 • *A bi-monthly newsletter providing information for designers, architects, builders, and homeowners on environmental products, issues, and industry changes. They also have an "Interior Concerns Resource Guide" that lists products, manufacturers, consultants, and other resources.*

REUSE NEWS • c/o Sherlock Enterprises, 609 Hobart Road, Hanover, PA 17331 • *Monthly newsletter offers tips on reusing everything from chopsticks to panty hose.*

THE WARY CANARY NEWSLETTER • c/o WC Press, 2013 Orchard Place, Fort Collins, CO 80521 • *Four 16 page newsletters for $20, targeting an audience that's been environmentally impacted and sensitized (like coal mine canaries) by today's "better living through chemistry".*

Furniture and furnishings ~ pages 138-157

See general listings for Building pages 276-7 and Decoration, above.

MOTHERING • PO Box 1690, Santa Fe, NM 87504 • Tel: 505 984 8116 • *A comprehensive, quarterly magazine on natural mothering. Includes articles written by mothers and resources for all types of natural products used by babies, children, and mothers.*

Non-toxic home ~ pages 158-165

See general listings for Building pages 276-7 and Decoration, above.

BUILDING WITH JUNK AND OTHER GOOD STUFF • Jim Broadstreet, Loompanics Unlimited, PO Box 1197, Port Townsend, WA 98368

EARTHWISE CONSUMER • PO Box 279, Forest Knolls, CA 94933 • Tel: 415 488 4614

ESSENTIAL LIVING • Maia Institute, RR 1, Box 1310, Moretown, VT 05660 • Tel: 802 244 1309 • *A thoughtful, small bi-monthly newsletter about "examining our personal lives with an eye towards making changes that will both decrease the stresses we put on our planet and increase the joy and satisfaction in our own lives".*

NATURAL HEALTH • PO Box 57329, Boulder, CO 80322-7320 • Tel: 800 666 8576 • *Bi-monthly guide to wellbeing includes natural living topics.*

NEW AGE JOURNAL • PO Box 52375, Boulder, CO 80321-3275 • Tel: 800 234 4556

PLASTIC WASTE PRIMER, A HANDBOOK FOR CITIZENS • League of Women Voters, Lyons & Burford, New York, 1993

THE WOOD USER'S GUIDE TO TOXICS A TO Z, • from Rainforest Action Network, 450 Sansome Street, San Francisco, CA 94111 • Tel: 415 398 4404

WORLDWATCH MAGAZINE • Worldwatch Institute, 1776 Massachusetts Avenue NW, Washington, DC 20036 • Tel: 202 452 1999 • Monitors environmental trends. Six issues per year.

Backyard ~ pages 166-181

AMERICAN HARVEST • 3 Gold Center, Suite 221, Hoffman Estates, IL 60195 • Tel: 708 934 7655 • A newsletter focused on "celebrating the fresh fruits and vegetables harvested from America's gardens, big and small." For gardeners and cooks, with a "green" philosophy.

BACKWOODS MAGAZINE • 1257 Siskiyou Boulevard, # 213, Ashland, OR 97520 • Tel: 916 459 3300

BACKHOME • PO Box 70, Hendersonville, NC 28793 • Tel: 704 696 3838 • Practical information on home energy, self-reliant living, recycling, gardening etc.

COMMON GROUND • The Conservation Fund, 1880 N Kent Street, Suite 1120, Arlington, VA 22209 • Tel: 703 525 6300 • Six issues per year.

COMPOST PATCH, INC • 306 Coleridge Avenue, Altoona, PA 16602 • Tel: 814 946 9291 • Ideas and visions for a sustainable world.

COUNTRY LIFE • The Creamery, Charlotte, VT 05445 • Tel: 800 344 3350 • Bi-monthly magazine geared to people who live close to the earth in the country. Topics are more focused on gardening and practical house-holding.

THE ECOLOGIST • MIT Press Journals/Circulation Dept, 55 Hayward Street, Cambridge, MA 02142 • Tel: 617 253 2889 • Six issues per year.

EVERYONE'S BACKYARD • membership magazine of Citizens Clearinghouse for Hazardous Wastes, PO Box 6806, Falls Church, VA 22040 • Tel: 703 237 2249

GREEN SCHOOLS BIODIVERSITY BOOKLET • Ocean Voice International, 2883 Otterson Drive, Ottawa, ON K1V 7B2 • Tel & Fax: 613 521 4205

HORTICULTURE • PO Box 53880, Bouilder, CO 880322 • Monthly.

HORTIDEAS • 460 Black Lick Road, Gravel Switch, KY 40328 • Monthly.

MOTHER EARTH NEWS • 24 E 23rd Street, New York, NY 10010 • Tel: 800 937 4287 • "The original country magazine" was one of the early pioneer publications on sustainable living. Geared for people who live in the country, but useful for anyone wanting to live more sustainably.

NATURE CANADA • Canadian Nature Federation, 1 Nicholas Street, Suite 520, Ottawa, Ontario, Canada, K1N 7B7 • Tel: 613 562 3447 Fax: 613 562 3371

NATURE CONSERVANCY MAGAZINE • 1815 North Lynn Street, Arlington VA 22209 • Tel: 703 841 5300

ORGANIC GARDENING • Box 7320, Red Oak, IA 51591 0320 • Tel: 800 666 2206 • The classic bi-monthly organic gardening magazine since 1942.

ORGANIC GARDENING • 33 East Minor Street, Emmaus, PA 18098 • Nine issues per year.

THE PERMACULTURE ACTIVIST • PO Box 1209, Black Mountain, NC 28711 • Tel: 704 683 4946

PERMACULTURE DRYLANDS JOURNAL • PO Box 133, Pearce, AZ 85625 • Tel: 602 824 3456 Fax: 602 824 3542

PLANT CONSERVATION DIRECTORY • Plant Conservation Center, Missouri Botanical Garden, PO Box 299, St. Louis, MO 63166 • Annual issue.

SEED • 27 E 59th Street, New York, NY 10022

SOUTHEAST PERMACULTURE NEWS • 160 King Street, Abingdon, VA 24210

SUPPLIERS OF BENEFICIAL ORGANISMS IN NORTH AMERICA • Charles D Hunter, free from EPA Dept of Pesticide Regulation

TERRAIN • Ecology Center Bookstore, 2530 San Pablo Avenue, Berkeley, CA 94702. • Tel: 510 548 2220 • Monthly environmental journal.

THE URBAN ECOLOGIST, • c/o Urban Ecology, 405 14th Street, Suite 701, Oakland, CA 94612 • Tel: 510 251 6330

WORLDWATCH MAGAZINE • Worldwatch Institute, 1776 Massachussetts Avenue NW, Washington DC 20036-1904 • Tel: 202 452 1999 • Monitors environmental trends. Six issues per year.

Recycling ~ pages 182-185

RECYCLED PRODUCTS BUSINESS LETTER • Environmental Newsletters, 11906 Paradise Lane, Herndon, VA 22071 • Tel: 703 758 8436 • Designed to help companies market their recycled products more effectively.

RESOURCE RECYCLING • 1206 NW 21st Avenue, Portland, OR 97209

REUSE NEWS • c/o Sherlock Enterprises, 609 Hobart Road, Hanover, PA 17331 • Monthly newsletter offers tips on reusing everything from chopsticks to panty hose.

STATE RECYCLING LAWS UPDATE • published by Raymond Communications, Inc, 6429 Auburn Avenue, Riverdale, MD 20737 • Tel: 301 345 4237 Fax: 301 345 4768 • Quarterly newsletter with independent analysis of state legislation. Contents include: research, consulting on green packaging, solid waste issues, commercial waste management.

Building ~ pages 18-49

A Building Revolution: How Ecology and Health Concerns are Transforming Construction, David Malin Roodman and Nicholas Lenssen, Worldwatch Paper 124 • 1776 Massachusetts Avenue NW, Washington DC 20036

Air to Air Heat Exchangers, William Shurcliff, Brick House Publishing, 1980, Andover, MA

Builders Guide to Residential Construction Waste Management and *Resource Conservation Research House* guide and video, National Association of Home Builders • 400 Prince George's Boulevard, Upper Marlboro, MD 20772

Building with Heart, Christopher Day, 1990, Green Books, Devon, UK

Build it with Bales, Stephen O. MacDonald and Matts Myhrman • $18.00 from: Out on Bale, 1037 E Linden Street, Tuscon, AZ 85719

Clearcut, The Tragedy of Industrial Forestry, ed Bill Devall, 1994, Sierra Club Books/Earth Island Press • Sierra Club Store Orders, 730 Polk Street, San Francisco, CA 94109

CoHousing: A Contemporary Approach to Housing Ourselves, Katherine McCamant and Charles Durrett, 1988, Habitat Press/Ten Speed Press

Collaborative Communities: Co-Housing, Central Living and other New Forms of Housing with Shared Facilities, Dorit Fromm, 1991, Van Nostrand Reinhold, NY

Design for the Real World: Human Ecology and Social Change, Victor Papanek, 1984, Thames and Hudson, UK

Directory Of Recycled Building And Construction Products, The Clean Washington Center • Dept of Trade and Economic Development, 2001 6th Avenue, Suite 2700, Seattle, WA 98121

Earth Building Encyclopedia, Jo Tibbets, Southwest Solaradobe • PO Box 153, Bosque, NM

Earth to Spirit: In Search of Natural Architecture, David Pearson, 1995, Chronicle Books, San Francisco, CA

Eco-Renovation, Edward Harland, Real Goods Independent Living Books • 966 Mazzoni Street, Ukiah, CA 95482

Exploring Ancient Native America, David Hurst Thomas, Macmillan, NY • *Excellent appendix with directions to Native American sites in United States.*

Feng Shui Handbook: How to Create a Healthier Living and Working Environment, Master Lam, 1996 Henry Holt, NY

Feng Shui: The Chinese Art of Designing a harmonious Environment, Derek Walters, Fireside, Simon and Schuster, NY

The Forest and The Trees (A Guide to Excellent Forestry), Gordon Robinson, 1988, Island Press • PO Box 7, Corvelo, CA 95428

Forest Journey, the Role of Wood in the Development of Civilization, John Perlin, 1991, Harvard University Press, Cambridge, MA

The Gaia Atlas of Cities: New Directions for Sustainable Urban Living, Herbert Giradet, 1992, Gaia Books, London, UK

Gentle Architecture, Malcolm Wells, 1982, McGraw-Hill, NY

Guide To Resource Efficient Building Elements, Center for Resourceful Building Technology • PO Box 3866, Missoula, MT 59806 • *A reference guide to manufacturers of building products with recycled content, sustainable, or resource-efficient origins. Also looks at job site waste management.*

Healing Environments, Carol Venolia, 1992, Celestial Arts, CA

Healthful Houses: How to Design and Build Your Own, Clint Good with Debra Lynn Dadd, 1988, Guaranty Press

Healthy House Building, John Bower, 1989, John Stuart Lyle, NY

How much is enough? Alan Durning, 1992, Norton, NY

Making a Molehill out of a Mountain, Greater Toronto Homebuilders' Association • 20 Upjohn Road, North York, Ontario, Canada, M3B 2V9

Muir's Original Log Home Guide for Builders and Buyers • Route 2, Box 581, Cosby TN 37722

Native American Architecture, Peter Nobokov and Robert Easton, 1989, Oxford University Press, NY

The Natural House Book, David Pearson, 1989, Fireside, Simon and Schuster, NY

A Pattern Language, Christopher Alexander, 1977, Oxford University Press, NY

Permaculture: A Designers Manual, Bill Mollison, Permaculture Resources • 56 Farmersville, Califon, NJ 07830

Permaculture: A Practical Guide for a Sustainable Future, Bill Mollison, Permaculture Drylands • PO Box 27371, Tucson, AZ 85726-7371

Places for the Soul: Architecture as a Healing Art, Christopher Day, 1990, Collins, Glasgow, UK

Rain Forest In Your Kitchen, Martin Teitel, 1992, Island Press, Washington, DC.

Rebuilding Community in America – Housing for Ecological Living, Personal Empowerment and the New Extended Family, Ken Norwood & Kathleen Smith , Shared Living Resource Center, Berkeley, CA

Safe as Houses? Ill-health and Electro-stress in the Home, Rodney Girdlestone and David Cowan, 1994, Gateway Books, NY.

Straw Bale Building and The Building Codes, David Eisenberg • $9.00 from Out on Bale, 1037 E Linden Street, Tuscon, AZ 85719 • *How to work with your local code officials to obtain a permit to build using straw bale construction.*

Straw Bale House, Steen, Steen, and Bainbridge, Back Home Books • PO Box 70, Hendersonville, NC 28792

Straw Bale Portfolio, Bob Lanning • $15.00 from: Out on Bale, 1037 E Linden Street, Tuscon, AZ 85719 • *Architect's portfolio of designs for straw-bale homes and guest-houses.*

A Straw-Bale Primer, Stephen and Orien MacDonald • PO Box 58, Gila, NM 88038

The Source Book For Sustainable Design: A Guide to Environmentally Responsible Building Materials and Processes, Architects for Social Responsibility • 248 Franklin Street, Cambridge, MA 02139 • *A comprehensive look at every aspect of building design and construction focusing on the use of sustainable components.*

Super Insulated Houses and *Underground Houses,* Rob Roy, 1994, Sterling Publishing, NY

Sustaining the Earth: Choosing Consumer Products That Are Safe for You, Your Family and the Earth, Debra Dadd-Redalia, 1994, Hearst Books, NY

The Temple in the House, Anthony Lawler, 1994, Tarcher Putnam, NY
Thermal Delight in Architecture, Lisa Heschong, 1980, M.I.T. Press

Thermal Shutters and Shades, William Shurcliff, 1980, Brick House Publishing, Andover, MA

The Timeless Way of Building, Christopher Alexander, 1979, Oxford University Press, NY

Underground Houses, Rob Roy, Earthwood Building School • 366 Murtagh Hill Road, West Chazy, NY 12992

Wildwood: A forest for the future, Ruth Loomis and Merv Wilkinson, Reflections Publisher • PO Box 178, Gabriola, BC, Canada, VOR 1XO

The Wood User's Guide, Rainforest Action Network • 450 Sansome Street, San Francisco, CA 94111 • *Contains lists of tropical and temperate wood alternatives, non wood alternatives, and other suppliers.*

Soft energy ~ pages 50-69

The American Farm, Harnessing The Sun To Feed The World, National Technical Information Service, Springfield, VA

Community Energy Workbook, The Rocky Mountain Institute •1379 Snowmass Creek Road, Snowmass, CO 81654 • Tel: 303 927 3851

The Consumer Guide to Energy Savings, The Rocky Mountain Institute •1379 Snowmass Creek Road, Snowmass, CO 81654 • Tel: 303 927 3851

Consumer Guide to Home Energy Savings, Alex Wilson and John Morrill American Council for an Energy-Efficient Economy • 1001 Connecticut Avenue NW, Suite 555, Washington DC 20036

Consumer Information Catalog, United States Government Printing Office • Pueblo Documents Distribution Center, Pueblo, CO 81009 • *Tips for Energy Savers booklet.*

Cooling Our Communities: A Guidebook On Tree Planting And Light-Colored Surfacing, Environmental Protection Agency, 1992 • Superintendent of Documents, PO Box 371954, Pittsburgh, PA 15220-7954

The Efficient House Sourcebook, The Rocky Mountain Institute • 1379 Snowmass Creek Road, Snowmass, CO 81654• Tel: 303 927 3851

Energy Saver's Handbook for Town and City People, Massachussetts Audubon Society, 1992, Rodale Press, PA

Energy Source Directory, Iris Communications • 258 East 10th Avenue, Suite E, Eugene, OR 97401-3284

Energy Unbound, a fable for America's future, Amory Lovins, Hunter Lovins and Seth Zuckerman, 1986, Sierra Club Books, San Francisco, CA

Homemade Money, Rocky Mountain Institute •1379 Snowmass Creek Road, Snowmass, CO 81654-9199 • Tel: 303 927 3851

Hot Water From The Sun A Consumer Guide, US Government Printing Office, • Washington, DC 20402 • #023-00-00620-1

The Independent Home: Living Well With Power From The Sun, Wind and Water, Michael Potts, 1993, Chelsea Green Publishing, VT

Living on 12 Volts with Ample Power, David Smead and Ruth Ishihara, Fowler Solar Electric Inc • PO Box 435, Worthington, MA 01098

Practical Home Energy Savings, The Rocky Mountain Institute, • 1379 Snowmass Creek Road, Snowmass, CO 81654 • Tel: 303 927 3851

Primer on Sustainable Building, Rocky Mountain Institute • 1379 Snowmass Creek Road, Snowmass, CO 81654 • Tel: 303 927 3851

Real Goods Solar Living Sourcebook • 966 Mazzoni Street, Ukiah, CA 95482-3471 • Tel: 800 762 7325

The Solar Electric Independent Home Book, Fowler Solar Electric Inc • PO Box 435, Worthington, MA 01098

State Of The Art Energy-Efficiency: Future Directions, American Council For An Energy-Efficient Economy, Berkeley, CA, 1991

Super Insulated Houses and Air to Air Heat Exchangers, William Shurcliff, Brick House Publishing, 1980, Andover, MA

Thermal Shutters and Shades, William Shurcliff, Brick House Publishing, 1980, Andover, MA.

Your Home Cooling Energy Guide, John Krigger, 1992, Saturn Resources Management, Helena, MT.

Water ~ pages 70-85

Abandoned Seas, Reversing the Decline of the Oceans, Peter Weber, Worldwatch Paper 116 • Worldwatch Institute, 1776 Massachusetts Avenue NW, Washington DC 20036

Clean Water in your Watershed (A Citizen's Guide to Watershed Protection) Terrene Institute • 1717 K Street NW, Washington, DC 20006. Tel: 202 833 8317

Create an Oasis with Greywater, Art Ludwig, Oasis Biocompatible Products • 5 San Marcos Trout Club, Santa Barbara, CA 93105-9726 • *The most comprehensive information source available on greywater reuse.*

Designing Drip Irrigation for Every Landscape and all Climates, Robert Kourik, 1992, Edible Publications • PO Box 1841, Dept W, Santa Rosa, CA 95402

Drinking Water Hazards: How to Know if there are Toxic Chemicals in your Water and What to Do if there are, John Cary Stewart, 1990, Envirographics, Hiram, OH

Entering the Watershed (A new approach to save America's river ecosystems), Bob Doppelt et al, 1993, Island Press • PO Box 7, Covelo, CA 95428

Environmental Testing: Where to look, What to look for, How to do it, and What does it mean? Citizens Clearing House for Hazardous Waste • PO Box 6806, Falls Church, VA 22040

Gray Water Use in the Landscape, Robert Kourik, 1988, Edible Publications • PO Box 1841, Dept W, Santa Rosa, CA 95402

Great Lakes, Great Legacy? Theodora Colbern, Alex Davidson and Sharon Green, 1990, Institute for Research on Public Policy • World Wildlife Fund, PO Box 4866, Hampden Station, Baltimore, MD 21211

Is Your Water Safe to Drink?, Consumer Reports Books • 540 Barnum Avenue, Bridgeport, CT 06608

Lead and your Drinking Water, EPA booklet • Tel: 202 260 2080 for general EPA information.

Planning for an Individual Water System, The American Association for Vocational Instructional Materials

Removal of Radon from Household Water, EPA booklet • Tel: 202 260 2080 for general EPA information.

Statewide Wetlands Strategies (A guide to protecting and managing the resource), World Wildlife Fund, 1992, Island Press • PO Box 7, Covelo, CA 95428

Toxics A to Z: a guide to everyday pollution hazards, John Harte et al, 1991, University of California Press, Berkeley, CA

Upstream Solution to Downstream Pollution (A Citizen's Guide to Protecting Seacoasts and the Great Lakes by Cleaning up Polluted Runoff), Sara Chasis et al, NRDC Publications • 40 W 20th Street, New York, NY 10011

Water in Environmental Planning, Thomas Dunne and Luna Leopold, 1978, W H Freeman & Co • 4419 W 1980 Street, Salt Lake City, UT 84104

Water Books Catalog, AgAccess • PO Box 2008, Davis, CA 95617

Water Treatment Handbook, Rodale Product Testing Guide, Northeast Publishing Inc • PO Box 571, Emmaus, PA 18049

Wetland Creation and Restoration, Jon Kusler and Mary Kentula, 1990, Island Press • PO Box 7, Covelo, CA 95428

Sane electrics ~ pages 86-97

See books for Soft energy page 281

AC Magnetic Field Measurement, Ed Leeper, Monitor Industries, CO

The Body Electric: Electromagnetism and the Foundation of Life, Robert O Becker and Gary Selden, 1985, William Morrow and Co, NY

Cross-Currents: The Promise of Electromedicine, the Perils of Electropollution, Robert O. Becker, Jeremy P. Tarcher, Los Angeles, CA

Currents of Death: Power Lines, Computer Terminals and the Attempt to Cover Up Their Threat to Your Health, Paul Broder, 1989, Simon and Schuster, NY

Electromagnetic Fields in Your Environment: Magnetic Field Measurements of Everyday Electrical Devices • Tel: 202 260 2080 for general EPA information.

EMF Resource Directory • PO Box 1799, Grand Central Station, New York 10763 • Tel: 212 517 2800

Environmental Testing: Where to look, What to Look for, How to do it, and What Does it Mean?, Citizens Clearing House for Hazardous Waste • PO Box 6806, Falls Church, VA 22040

Healthy Buildings Resource Guide, Healthy Buildings Associates • 7190 Fiske Road, Clinton, WA 98236 • Tel: 206 579 2962

The Most Energy-Efficient Appliances, American Council for an Energy-Efficient Economy • 1001 Connecticut Avenue, NW Suite 535, Washington DC 20036

Safe as Houses? Ill-health and Electro-stress in the Home, Rodney Girdlestone and David Cowan, 1994, Gateway Books

Lighting ~ pages 98-109

See general books for Soft energy page 281 and Sane electrics, above

Cooling Our Communities: A Guidebook On Tree Planting And Light-Colored Surfacing, Environmental Protection Agency, 1992 • Superintendent of documents, PO Box 371954, Pittsburgh, PA 15220-7954

Energy-Efficient Lighting; Daylighting, Illumination Engineering Society • 120 Wall Street, 17th Floor, New York, N 10005

Lighting Equipment and Accessories Guide, EPRI Distribution Center • 207 Coggins Drive, PO Box 23205, Pleasant Hill, CA 94523 • Tel: 510 934 4212 • Many other useful publications.

Healing with Color and Light, Theo Gimbel, 1994, Fireside, Simon & Schuster, NY

Light, Medicine of the Future, 1991, Bear and Company, Santa Fe.

The Lighting Pattern Book for Homes, Lighting Research Center • Rensselaer Polytechnic Institute, Troy, NY 12180-3590

Air ~ pages 110-121

Clearing the Air, Coalition for Clean Air • 122 Lincoln Boulevard, Suite 201, Venice, CA 90291

Environmental Testing: Where to look, What to Look for, How to do it, and What Does it Mean?, Citizens Clearing House for Hazardous Waste • PO Box 6806, Falls Church, VA 22040

Removal of Radon from Household Water, EPA booklet • Tel: 202 260 2080 for general EPA information.

Washington State Indoor Air Resource Guide, Interagency Indoor Air Council • 1200 6th Avenue, Seattle, WA 98101

Decoration ~ pages 122-137

See general books for Building pages 280-1

Eco-Renovation (The Ecological Home Improvement Guide) John Harland, Real Goods Independent Living Books • 966 Mazzoni Street, Ukiah, CA 95482

Environmental By Design • PO Box 95016, South Van CSC, Vancouver, BC, Canada, V6P 6V4 • Guide to healthy interior materials.

Feng Shui Handbook: How to Create a Healthier Living and Working Environment, Master Lam, 1996, Henry Holt, NY

Green Pages: The Contract Interior Designer's Guide To Environmentally Responsible Products And Materials, compiled by Andrew Fuston and Kim Plaston • Available from the authors: Tel: 212 779 3365 / 212 964 3332 • A resource guide to environmentally responsible products, manufacturers, consultants, mail order catalogs etc.

New Paint Magic, Jocasta Innes,1992, Pantheon (Random House), NY • *Book of exciting decorative paint techniques.*

Nontoxic, Natural & Earthwise, Debra Lynn-Dadd, 1990, Jeremy P Tarcher, Los Angeles

Toxic Carpet III, Glenn Beebe • PO Box 39344, Cincinnati, OH 45239

Furniture and furnishings ~ pages 138-157

See general books for Building pages 280-1

Clean and Green, The Complete Guide to Nontoxic and Environmentally Safe Housekeeping, Annie Berthold-Bond, 1990, Ceres Press, NY

The Green PC, Steven Anzonin, 1993, Windcrest/McGraw Hill

Interior Concerns Resource Guide • PO Box 2386, Mill Valley, CA 94942 • *Looseleaf folder product guide.*

The NonToxic Home and Office, Debra Lynn-Dadd, 1992, Jeremy P. Tarcher, Los Angeles, CA

Rain Forest In Your Kitchen, Martin Teitel, 1992, Island Press, Washington, DC

Recipes from an Ecological Kitchen, Lorna J Sass, 1992, William Morrow & Co, NY

The Smart Kitchen, David Goldbeck, 1989, Ceres Press, NY

Status Report on the use of Environmental Labels worldwide, EPA document #742-R93-003, 1993 • EPA office of Pollution Prevention and Toxics, Washington, DC 20460

Sustaining the Earth: Choosing Consumer Products That Are Safe for You, Your Family and the Earth, Debra Dadd-Redalia, 1994, Hearst Books, NY

Non-toxic home ~ pages 158-165

Clean and Green, The Complete Guide to Nontoxic and Environmentally Safe Housekeeping, Annie Berthold-Bond, 1990, Ceres Press, NY

Guide To Hazardous Products Around The Home, Household Hazardous Waste Project • PO Box 108, Springfield, MO 65804 • *Discusses in detail everything from labeling to hazardous ingredients and homemade alternatives.*

Healthy Homes, Healthy Kids, Joyce Schoemaker and Charity Vitale, Island Press • PO Box 7, Covelo, CA 95428

National Directory of Organic Wholesalers, Community Alliance with Family Farmers (CAFF) • PO Box 464, Davis, CA 95617 • Tel: 916 756 8518

Nontoxic, Natural & Earthwise, Debra Lynn-Dadd, 1990, Jeremy P Tarcher, Los Angeles, CA

Tackling Toxics In Everyday Products, INFORM, Inc • 120 Wall Street, 16th Floor, New York, NY 10005-4001 • *A directory of organizations concerned about toxics in consumer and building products.*

Toxics A to Z: a guide to everyday pollution hazards, John Harte et al, 1991, University of California Press, Berkeley, CA

The Way we Grow, Anne Witten Garland with Mothers and Others for a Livable Planet, 1993, Berkeley Books, NY

Backyard ~ pages 166-181

America's Neighborhood Bats, Merlin D Tuttle, 1988, University of Texas Press

The Backyard Landscaper, Ireland-Gannon Associates • Home Planners, 3275 West Ina Road, Suite 110, Tucson, AZ 85741 • *Forty professionally designed landscape plans for backyards.*

The Chemical-Free Lawn, Warren Schultz, 1989, Rodale Press, PA

Chicken Little, Tomato Sauce and Agriculture, Joan Dye Gussow, 1991, The Bootstrap Press, NY

Common-Sense Pest Control, Daar and Olkowski, 1991, The Taunton Press • Box 5506, Newtown, CT 06470-5506 Tel: 800 283 7252

The Complete Book of Edible Landscaping, Rosalind Creasy, Sierra Club Books • 730 Polk Street, San Francisco, CA 94109

Comprehensive Information Source On Greywater Reusepermaculture: A Practical Guide For A Sustainable Future, Bill Mollison, Permaculture Drylands • PO Box 27371, Tucson, AZ 85726-7371

Designing and Maintaining Your Edible Landscape Naturally, Robert Kourik, Metamorphic Press • PO Box 1841, Santa Rosa, CA 95402

The Earth and You, Eating for Two, April Moore, 1993, Potomac Valley Press, Washington DC

The Earth Manual, (How to Work on Wild Land without Taming It), Malcolm Margolin, 1985, Heyday Books • PO Box 9145, Berkeley, CA 94709

Economics and Biodiversity, J McNeely, 1988, International Union for the Conservation of Nature

Endangered and Threatened Wildlife and Plants • Free booklet available from US Fish and Wildlife Service, Publications Unit, 4401 North Fairfax Drive, Mail Stop 130 Webb, Arlington, VA 22203

Enduring Seeds (Native American Agriculture and Wild Plant Conservation), Gary Paul Nabhan, 1989, North Point Press • Putnam Publishing, PO Box 506, East Rutherford, NJ 07073

Energy Efficient and Environmental Landscaping, BackHome Books • PO Box 70, Hendersonville, NC 28793

Farming in Nature's Image, Judith Soule and Jon Piper, 1992, Island Press • PO Box 7, Covelo, CA 95482

Flowering Plants of the World, Vernon Heywood, 1993, Oxford University Press, NY

Food for the Future, Consitions and Contradictions of Sustainability, ed Patricia Allen, 1993, John Wiley and Sons, NY

Forest Gardening, Robert A J de Hart, 1990, Green Books, UK

G is for EcoGarden, Nigel Dudley and Sue Stickland, 1991, Simon & Schuster, NY

Garden Pools and Fountains, Edward B Claflin, 1988, Ortho Books, NY

Landscaping for Wildlife, Carol Henderson 1987, Minnesota Bookstore/Documents Division • 117 University Avenue, St Paul, MN 55155

Let it Rot! The Gardener's Guide to Composting • Environmentally Sound Products, 8845 Orchard Tree Lane, Towson, MD 21286

May All Be Fed: Diet for a New World, John William Robbins, 1992, Morrow & Co, NY

The Meaning of Gardens, Mark Francis and Randolph Hester, 1992, MIT Press, Cambridge, MA

National Directory Of Organic Wholesalers, Community Alliance with Family Farmers (CAFF) • PO Box 464, Davis, CA 95617

The Natural Garden Book, Peter Harper, 1994, Simon and Schuster, NY

On the brink of Extinction, Edward Wolf, Worldwatch paper 78, Worldwatch Institute • 1776 Massachusetts Avenue NW, Washington DC 20036

Organic Farming, Nicolas Lampkin, 1990, Farming Press UK • AgAccess, PO Box 2008, Davis, CA 95617

The Plant Conservation Directory, Center for Plant Conservation • Missouri Botanical Garden, PO Box 299, St Louis, MO 63166

Plants for Play — A Plant selection for children's outdoor environments, Robin Monroe, 1993, MIG Communications

Permaculture: A Designers Manual, Bill Mollison, Permaculture Resources • 56 Farmersville, Califon, NJ 07830

Rodale's Book of Composting, 1992, Rodale Press, PA

Rodale's Illustrated Encyclopedia of Gardening and Landscaping Techniques, 1990, Rodale Press, PA

Rodale's Successful Organic Gardening, Vegetables, Herbs, Patricia Michalak, 1993, Rodale Press, PA

Sacred Trees, Nathaniel Altman, 1994, Sierra Club Books, CA

Seeds of Change, Harper San Francisco, CA

Seed to Civilization, The Story of Food, Charles B Heiser, 1990, Harvard University Press, MA

Start with the Soil, Grace Gershuny, 1993, Rodale Press, PA

Sustainable Agricultural Systems, Clive A Edwards, 1990, Soil and Water Conservation Society • 7515 NE Ankeny Road, Ankeny, IA 50021

Water Gardens: A Harrowsmith Gardener's Guide, David Archibald and Mary Patton, 1990, Camden House, VT

Wilderness at the Edge, Utah Wilderness Coalition 1993, PO Box 11446, Salt Lake City, UT 84147

Worms Eat my Garbage, Mary Appelhof, Flower Press • 10332 Shaver Road, Kalamazoo, MI 49002

Xeriscape Gardening (Water conservation for the American Landscape), Connie Ellesson, Tom Stephens and Doug Welsh, 1992, Macmillan Publishing, NY

Recycling ~ *pages 182-185*

See also general listings for Recycling pages 277-8

The Biocycle Guide To Maximum Recycling, Biocycle • 419 State Avenue, Emmaus, PA 18049 • *A comprehensive guidebook on recycling.*

The Harris Directory, Stafford Harris, Inc • 1916 Pike Place 705, Seattle, WA 98101-1056 • *Directory of recycled content building materials.*

Recyclers Handbook: Simple things you can do, The Earthworks Group, 1990, Earthworks Press, Berkeley, CA

Resource Conservation Research House guide and video, National Association of Home Builders • 400 Prince George's Boulevard, Upper Marlboro, MD 20772

Shoppers' Guide to Recycled Products, Californians against Waste Foundation • 909 12th Street, Suite 201, Sacramento, CA 95814

Green pages

Austin Environmental Directory
PO Box 1374, Austin, TX 78767
Tel: 512 447 8712

Bay Area Green Pages
Green Media Group, PO Box 11314, Berkeley, CA 94701
Tel: 510 534 3470

Earth Day: Green Pages Directory To Make Every Day Earth Day
18 E 16th Avenue, Columbus, OH 43201
Tel: 614 888 2196

Greater LA. Green Pages
Green Media Group, PO Box 11314, Berkeley, CA 94701
Tel: 510 534 3470

The Green Guide / Washington DC
523 Constitution Avenue, NE, Washington, DC 20002
Tel: 202 543 1214

Houston Very Green Pages
PO Box 27630, Houston, TX 77227
Tel: 713 524 6077

Minnesota Green Pages
Minnesota Chapter of the International Alliance for Sustainable Agriculture
1701 University Avenue SE, Minneapolis, MN 55414
Tel: 612 331 1099

Natick Green Pages
75 West Street, Natick, MA 01760
Tel: 508 651 7310

Vermont Green Pages
RD 1 Box 85A, Groton, VT 05046
Tel: 802 592 3447

Willamette Green Pages
PO Box 12156, Eugene, OR 97440
Tel: 503 485 0177

PREFACE

THIS is the age of science, of steel—of speed and the cement road. The age of hard faces and hard highways. Science and steel demand the medium of prose. Speed requires only the look—the gesture. What need then, for poetry?

Great need!

There are souls, in these noise-tired times, that turn aside into unfrequented lanes, where the deep woods have harbored the fragrances of many a blossoming season. Here the light, filtering through perfect forms, arranges itself in lovely patterns for those who perceive beauty.

It is the purpose of this little volume to enrich, ennoble, encourage. And for man, who has learned to love convenience, it is hardly larger than his concealing pocket.

ROY J. COOK, *Editor.*

Acknowledgments

The selections by Emerson, Burroughs, Holmes, Lowell, Sill, Whittier, Cary, Larcom, and Longfellow are used by permission of and special arrangement with Houghton-Mifflin Company, authorized publishers of their works.

Grateful acknowledgment is also made to D. Appleton & Company, F. W. Bourdillon, Bobbs-Merrill Company, Charles Scribner's Sons, Doubleday-Page & Company, Little, Brown & Company, George H. Doran Company, Lothrop, Lee & Shepard Company, A. P. Watt & Son. *The Academy,* London, and the Librarian, University of Edinburgh, without whose kind co-operation this collection could not have been made.

Bettmann

The Builders

HENRY WADSWORTH LONGFELLOW
(Born February 27, 1807; died March 24, 1882)

All are architects of Fate,
　Working in these walls of Time;
Some with massive deeds and great,
　Some with ornaments of rhyme.

Nothing useless is, or low;
　Each thing in its place is best;
And what seems but idle show
　Strengthens and supports the rest.

For the structure that we raise,
　Time is with materials filled;
Our todays and yesterdays
　Are the blocks with which we build.

Truly shape and fashion these;
　Leave no yawning gaps between;
Think not, because no man sees,
　Such things will remain unseen.

In the elder days of Art,
　Builders wrought with greatest care
Each minute and unseen part;
　For the gods see everywhere.

Let us do our work as well,
　Both the unseen and the seen;
Make the house where gods may dwell
　Beautiful, entire, and clean.

Else our lives are incomplete,
　Standing in these walls of Time,
Broken stairways, where the feet
　Stumble, as they seek to climb.

1

Build today, then, strong and sure,
  With a firm and ample base;
And ascending and secure
  Shall tomorrow find its place.

Thus alone can we attain
  To those turrets, where the eye
Sees the world as one vast plain,
  And one boundless reach of sky.

Bettmann

Opportunity

EDWARD R. SILL

(Born April 29, 1841; died February 27, 1887)

This I beheld, or dreamed it in a dream:—
There spread a cloud of dust along a plain;
And underneath the cloud, or in it, raged
A furious battle, and men yelled, and swords
Shocked upon swords and shields. A prince's banner
Wavered, then staggered backward, hemmed by foes.

A craven hung along the battle's edge,
And thought, "Had I a sword of keener steel—
That blue blade that the king's son bears—but this
Blunt thing!"—he snapped and flung it from his hand.
And lowering crept away and left the field.

Then came the king's son, wounded, sore bestead,
And weaponless, and saw the broken sword,
Hilt-buried in the dry and trodden sand,
And ran and snatched it, and with battle-shout
Lifted afresh he hewed his enemy down,
And saved a great cause that heroic day.

2

Out to Old Aunt Mary's

JAMES WHITCOMB RILEY

"On an early day in a memorable October, Reuben A. Riley and his wife, Elizabeth Marine Riley, rejoiced over the birth of their second son. They called him James Whitcomb ——————."

From *The Complete Works of James Whitcomb Riley*. Bobbs-Merrill Company (in 6 volumes).

Mr. Riley always replied when asked the direct question as to his age. "I am this side of forty." October 7, 1853, is the generally accepted date of his birth.

(Died July 22, 1916)

Wasn't it pleasant, O brother mine,
In those old days of the lost sunshine
   Of youth—when the Saturday's chores were through,
   And the "Sunday's wood" in the kitchen, too,
   And we went visiting, "me and you,"
      Out to Old Aunt Mary's?

It all comes back so clear today!
Though I am as bald as you are gray—
   Out by the barn-lot, and down the lane,
   We patter along in the dust again,
   As light as the tips of the drops of the rain,
      Out to Old Aunt Mary's!

We cross the pasture, and through the wood
Where the old gray snag of the poplar stood,
   Where the hammering red-heads hopped awry,
   And the buzzard "raised" in the clearing sky,
   And lolled and circled, as we went by,
      Out to Old Aunt Mary's.

And then in the dust of the road again;
And the teams we met, and the countrymen;
   And the long highway, with sunshine spread
   As thick as butter on country bread,
   Our cares behind, and our hearts ahead
      Out to Old Aunt Mary's.

Why, I see her now in the open door,
Where the little gourds grew up the sides, and o'er
   The clapboard roof!—And her face—ah, me!
   Wasn't it good for a boy to see—
   And wasn't it good for a boy to be
      Out to Old Aunt Mary's?

The jelly—the jam and the marmalade,
And the cherry and quince "preserves" she made!
   And the sweet-sour pickles of peach and pear,
   With cinnamon in 'em, and all things rare!—
   And the more we ate was the more to spare,
      Out to Old Aunt Mary's!

And the old spring-house in the cool green gloom
Of the willow-trees, and the cooler room
   Where the swinging-shelves and the crocks were kept—
   Where the cream in a golden languor slept
   While the waters gurgled and laughed and wept—
      Out to Old Aunt Mary's!

And as many a time have you and I—
Barefoot boys in the days gone by—
   Knelt, and in tremulous ecstasies
   Dipped our lips into sweets like these,—
   Memory now is on her knees
      Out to Old Aunt Mary's!

And O, my brother, so far away,
This is to tell you she waits *today*
   To welcome us:—Aunt Mary fell
   Asleep this morning, whispering, "Tell
   The boys to come!" And all is well
      Out to Old Aunt Mary's!

From *Afterwhiles*, by James Whitcomb Riley. Copyright 1898. Used by special permission of the publishers, the Bobbs-Merrill Company.

The complete edition of Riley's poems includes many stanzas which are familiar only to the student of Riley's poems. Most editors omit the next to the last stanza, as the poem stands complete, but it is the opinion of Prof. R. M. Alden of Stanford University that with this omission the continuity of thought is broken.

Bettmann

Each and All

RALPH WALDO EMERSON
(Born May 25, 1803; died April 27, 1882)

Little thinks, in the field, yon red-cloaked clown
Of thee from the hill-top looking down;
The heifer that lows in the upland farm,
Far-heard, lows not thine ear to charm;
The sexton, tolling his bell at noon,
Deems not that great Napoleon
Stops his horse, and lists with delight,
Whilst his files sweep round yon Alpine height;
Nor knowest thou what argument
Thy life to thy neighbor's creed has lent.
All are needed by each one,—
Nothing is fair or good alone.
I thought the sparrow's note from heaven,
Singing at dawn on the alder bough;
I brought him home, in his nest, at even;
He sings the song, but it cheers not now;
For I did not bring home the river and sky;
He sang to my ear,—they sang to my eye.

The delicate shells lay on the shore;
The bubbles of the latest wave
Fresh pearls to their enamel gave,
And the bellowing of the savage sea
Greeted their safe escape to me.
I wiped away the weeds and foam—
I fetched my sea-born treasures home;
But the poor, unsightly, noisome things
Had left their beauty on the shore
With the sun and the sand and the wild uproar.

The lover watched his graceful maid,
As 'mid the virgin train she strayed,
Nor knew her beauty's best attire
Was woven still by the snow-white choir.
At last she came to his hermitage,

Like the bird from the woodlands to the cage;
The gay enchantment was undone—
A gentle wife, but fairy none.

Then I said, "I covet truth;
Beauty is unripe childhood's cheat;
I leave it behind with the games of youth."
As I spoke, beneath my feet
The ground-pine curled its pretty wreath,
Running over the club-moss burrs;
I inhaled the violet's breath;
Around me stood the oaks and firs;
Pine cones and acorns lay on the ground;
Over me soared the eternal sky,
Full of light and of deity;
Again I saw, again I heard,
The rolling river, the morning bird;
Beauty through my senses stole;
I yielded myself to the perfect whole.

The Rhodora

On Being Asked Whence Is the Flower

RALPH WALDO EMERSON

In May, when sea-winds pierced our solitudes,
I found the fresh Rhodora in the woods,
Spreading its leafless blooms in a damp nook,
To please the desert and the sluggish brook.
The purple petals, fallen in the pool,
Made the black water with their beauty gay;
Here might the redbird come his plumes to cool,
And court the flower that cheapens his array.
Rhodora! if the sages ask thee why
This charm is wasted on the earth and sky,
Tell them, dear, that if eyes were made for seeing
Then Beauty is its own excuse for being:
Why thou wert there, O rival of the rose!
I never thought to ask, I never knew:
But, in my simple ignorance, suppose
The self-same Power that brought me there brought you.

Bettmann

Charge of the Light Brigade

ALFRED TENNYSON
(Born August 6, 1809; died October 6, 1892)

Half a league, half a league,
Half a league onward,
All in the valley of Death
  Rode the six hundred.
"Forward, the Light Brigade!
Charge for the guns!" he said:
Into the valley of Death
  Rode the six hundred.

"Forward, the Light Brigade!"
Was there a man dismayed?
Not tho' the soldiers knew
  Someone had blundered:
Theirs not to make reply,
Theirs not to reason why,
Theirs but to do and die:
Into the valley of Death
  Rode the six hundred.

Cannon to right of them,
Cannon to left of them,
Cannon in front of them
  Volleyed and thunder'd;
Storm'd at with shot and shell,
Boldly they rode and well,
Into the jaws of Death,
Into the mouth of Hell,
  Rode the six hundred.

Flashed all their sabres bare,
Flashed as they turned in air,
Sab'ring the gunners there,
Charging an army, while
  All the world wondered:
Plunged in the battery smoke,

Right through the line they broke;
Cossack and Russian
Reeled from the sabre-stroke
   Shattered and sundered.
Then they rode back, but not—
   Not the six hundred.

Cannon to right of them,
Cannon to left of them,
Cannon behind them
   Volleyed and thundered;
Stormed at with shot and shell,
While horse and hero fell,
They that had fought so well
Came thro' the jaws of Death,
Back from the mouth of Hell,
All that was left of them,
   Left of six hundred.

When can their glory fade?
Oh, the wild charge they made!
   All the world wondered.
Honor the charge they made!
Honor the Light Brigade,
   Noble Six Hundred!

The Night Has a Thousand Eyes

FRANCIS WILLIAM BOURDILLON
(Born March 22, 1852; died January 13, 1921)

The night has a thousand eyes,
   And the day but one;
Yet the light of the bright world dies
   With the dying sun.

The mind has a thousand eyes,
   And the heart but one;
Yet the light of a whole life dies
   When love is done.

The House by the Side of the Road

SAM WALTER FOSS

(Born June 19, 1858; died February 26, 1911)

"He was a friend to man, and he lived
In a house by the side of the road."—*Homer*

There are hermit souls that live withdrawn
    In the place of their self-content;
There are souls like stars, that dwell apart,
    In a fellowless firmament;
There are pioneer souls that blaze their paths
    Where highways never ran—
But let me live by the side of the road
    And be a friend to man.

Let me live in a house by the side of the road,
    Where the race of men go by—
The men who are good and the men who are bad,
    As good and as bad as I.
I would not sit in the scorner's seat,
    Or hurl the cynic's ban—
Let me live in a house by the side of the road
    And be a friend to man.

I see from my house by the side of the road,
    By the side of the highway of life,
The men who press with the ardor of hope,
    The men who are faint with the strife.
But I turn not away from their smiles nor their tears,
    Both parts of an infinite plan—
Let me live in a house by the side of the road
    And be a friend to man.

I know there are brook-gladdened meadows ahead
    And mountains of wearisome height;
That the road passes on through the long afternoon
    And stretches away to the night.
But still I rejoice when the travelers rejoice,
    And weep with the strangers that moan,
Nor live in my house by the side of the road
    Like a man who dwells alone.

Let me live in my house by the side of the road—
    It's here the race of men go by.
They are good, they are bad, they are weak, they are
        strong,
    Wise, foolish—so am I;
Then why should I sit in the scorner's seat,
    Or hurl the cynic's ban?
Let me live in my house by the side of the road
    And be a friend to man.

Used by special arrangement with the publishers, Lothrop, Lee & Shepard Co.

I Have a Rendezvous with Death

ALAN SEEGER

(Born June 22, 1888; died July 4, 1916)

I have a rendezvous with Death
    At some disputed barricade
    When Spring comes round with
        rustling shade
    And apple blossoms fill the air.
I have a rendezvous with Death
When Spring brings back blue days and fair.

It may be he shall take my hand
And lead me into his dark land
    And close my eyes and quench my breath;
It may be I shall pass him still.
I have a rendezvous with Death
On some scarred slope of battered hill,
    When Spring comes round again this year
    And the first meadow flowers appear.

God knows 'twere better to be deep
    Pillowed in silk and scented down,
Where love throbs out in blissful sleep,
    Pulse nigh to pulse, and breath to breath,
Where hushed awakenings are dear . . .
    But I've a rendezvous with Death
        At midnight in some flaming town,
When Spring trips north again this year,
    And I to my pledged word am true,
    I shall not fail that rendezvous.

One of the greatest poems written during the First World War.

From *Poems by Alan Seeger*. Copyright 1916, by Charles Scribner's Sons.

Bettmann

In Flanders Fields

LIEUT.-COL. JOHN McCRAE

The author of this poem, a member of the
first Canadian contingent, died in France
on January 28, 1918, after four years of
service on the western front.

In Flanders fields the poppies blow
Between the crosses, row on row,
　　That mark our place; and in the sky
　　The larks, still bravely singing, fly
Scarce heard amid the guns below.

We are the Dead. Short days ago
We lived, felt dawn, saw sunset glow,
　　Loved and were loved, and now we lie
　　　　In Flanders fields.

Take up our quarrel with the foe;
To you from failing hands we throw
　　The torch; be yours to hold it high.
　　If ye break faith with us who die
We shall not sleep, though poppies grow
　　　　In Flanders fields.

By courtesy of Punch.

Moonlight

From "The Merchant of Venice"

WILLIAM SHAKESPEARE

How sweet the moonlight sleeps upon this bank!
Here will we sit, and let the sound of music
Creep in our ears: soft stillness, and the night,
Become the touches of sweet harmony.

Sit, Jessica: look, how the floor of heaven
Is thick inlaid with patines of bright gold:
There's not the smallest orb which thou behold'st,
But in his motion like an angel sings,
Still quiring to the young-ey'd cherubims.

11

Bettmann

O Captain!
My Captain!

WALT WHITMAN
(Born May 31, 1819; died March 26, 1892)

O Captain! my Captain! our fearful trip is done;
The ship has weather'd every rack, the prize we sought is
    won;
The port is near, the bells I hear, the people all exulting,
While follow eyes the steady keel, the vessel grim and
    daring:

But O heart! heart! heart!
  O the bleeding drops of red,
    Where on the deck my Captain lies,
      Fallen cold and dead.

O Captain! my Captain! rise up and hear the bells;
Rise up—for you the flag is flung—for you the bugle'trills;
For you bouquets and ribbon'd wreaths—for you the shores
    a-crowding;
For you they call, the swaying mass, their eager faces
    turning:

Here Captain! dear father!
  This arm beneath your head;
    It is some dream that on the deck
      You've fallen cold and dead.

My Captain does not answer, his lips are pale and still;
My father does not feel my arm, he has no pulse or will;
The ship is anchor'd safe and sound, its voyage closed and
    done;
From fearful trip the victor ship comes in with object won:

Exult, O shores, and ring, O bells!
  But I, with mournful tread,
    Walk the deck my Captain lies,
      Fallen cold and dead.

The Chambered Nautilus

OLIVER WENDELL HOLMES

(Born August 29, 1809; died October 7, 1894)

Bettmann

This is the ship of pearl which, poets feign,
    Sails the unshadowed main,—
    The venturous bark that flings
On the sweet summer wind its purpled wings
In gulfs enchanted, where the Siren sings,
    And coral reefs lie bare,
Where the cold sea-maids rise to sun their streaming hair.

Its webs of living gauze no more unfurl;
    Wrecked is the ship of pearl!
    And every chambered cell,
Where its dim dreaming life was wont to dwell,
As the frail tenant shaped his growing shell,
    Before thee lies revealed,—
Its irised ceiling rent, its sunless crypt unsealed!

Year after year beheld the silent toil
    That spread his lustrous coil;
    Still, as the spiral grew,
He left the past year's dwelling for the new,
Stole with soft step its shining archway through,
    Built up its idle door,
Stretched in his last-found home, and knew the old no more.

Thanks for the heavenly message brought by thee,
    Child of the wandering sea,
    Cast from her lap, forlorn!
From thy dead lips a clearer note is born
Than ever Triton blew from wreathèd horn!
    While on mine ear it rings,
Through the deep caves of thought I hear a voice that
    sings:—

13

Build thee more stately mansions, O my soul,
    As the swift seasons roll!
    Leave thy low-vaulted past!
Let each new temple, nobler than the last,
Shut thee from heaven with a dome more vast,
    Till thou at length art free,
Leaving thine outgrown shell by life's unresting sea!

Bettmann

Christmas Everywhere

PHILLIPS BROOKS
*(Born December 13, 1835; died January
23, 1893)*

Everywhere, everywhere, Christmas tonight!
Christmas in lands of the fir-tree and pine,
Christmas in lands of the palm-tree and vine,
Christmas where snow peaks stand solemn and white,
Christmas where cornfields stand sunny and bright.
Christmas where children are hopeful and gay,
Christmas where old men are patient and gray,
Christmas where peace, like a dove in his flight,
Broods o'er brave men in the thick of the fight;
Everywhere, everywhere, Christmas tonight!

For the Christ-child who comes is the Master of all;
No palace too great, no cottage too small.

Taken from *Christmas Songs and
Easter Carols,* by Phillips Brooks.
Copyright 1903, by E. P. Dutton & Co.

Little Boy Blue

EUGENE FIELD

(Born September 3, 1850; died November 4, 1895)

Bettmann

The little toy dog is covered with dust,
  But sturdy and stanch he stands;
And the little toy soldier is red with rust,
  And his musket moulds in his hands.
Time was when the little toy dog was new,
  And the soldier was passing fair,
And that was the time when our Little Boy Blue
  Kissed them and put them there.

"Now, don't you go till I come," he said,
  "And don't you make any noise!"
So toddling off to his trundle-bed
  He dreamt of the pretty toys.
And as he was dreaming, an angel ·song
  Awakened our Little Boy Blue,—
Oh, the years are many, the years are long,
  But the little toy friends are true!

Ay, faithful to Little Boy Blue they stand,
  Each in the same old place,
Awaiting the touch of a little hand,
  The smile of a little face.
And they wonder, as waiting these long years through,
  In the dust of that little chair,
What has become of our Little Boy Blue
  Since he kissed them and put them there.

Bettmann

The Daffodils

WILLIAM WORDSWORTH
(Born April 7, 1770; died April 23, 1850)

I wandered lonely as a cloud
    That floats on high o'er vales and hills,
When all at once I saw a crowd,
    A host, of golden daffodils,
Beside the lake, beneath the trees,
Fluttering and dancing in the breeze.

Continuous as the stars that shine
    And twinkle on the Milky Way,
They stretched in never-ending line
    Along the margin of a bay:
Ten thousand saw I at a glance,
Tossing their heads in sprightly dance.

The waves beside them danced, but they
    Outdid the sparkling waves in glee;
A poet could not but be gay
    In such a jocund company
I gazed, and gazed, but little thought
What wealth the show to me had brought;

For oft, when on my couch I lie
    In vacant or in pensive mood,
They flash upon that inward eye
    Which is the bliss of solitude;
And then my heart with pleasure fills,
And dances with the daffodils.

Bettmann

June

From "The Vision of
Sir Launfal"

JAMES RUSSELL LOWELL
*(Born February 22, 1819; died August 12,
1891)*

Over his keys the musing organist,
    Beginning doubtfully and far away,
First lets his fingers wander as they list,
    And builds a bridge from Dreamland for his lay:
Then, as the touch of his loved instrument
    Gives hope and fervor, nearer draws his theme,
First guessed by faint auroral flushes sent
    Along the wavering vista of his dream.

    Not only around our infancy
    Doth heaven with all its splendors lie;
    Daily, with souls that cringe and plot,
    We Sinais climb and know it not.

Over our manhood bend the skies;
    Against our fallen and traitor lives
The great winds utter prophecies;
    With our faint hearts the mountain strives;
Its arms outstretched, the druid wood
    Waits with its benedicite;
And to our age's drowsy blood
    Still shouts the inspiring sea.

Earth gets its price for what Earth gives us;
    The beggar is taxed for a corner to die in,
The priest hath his fee who comes and shrives us,
    We bargain for the graves we lie in;
At the devil's booth are all things sold,
Each ounce of dross costs its ounce of gold;
For a cap and bells our lives we pay,
    Bubbles we buy with a whole soul's tasking;
'Tis heaven alone that is given away,
    'Tis only God may be had for the asking;
No price is set on the lavish summer;
June may be had by the poorest comer.

And what is so rare as a day in June?
   Then, if ever, come perfect days;
Then Heaven tries earth if it be in tune,
   And over it softly her warm ear lays;
Whether we look, or whether we listen,
We hear life murmur, or see it glisten;
Every clod feels a stir of might,
   An instinct within it that reaches and towers,
And, groping blindly above it for light,
   Climbs to a soul in grass and flowers;
The flush of life may well be seen
   Thrilling back over hills and valleys;
The cowslip startles in meadows green,
   The buttercup catches the sun in its chalice,
And there's never a leaf nor a blade too mean
   To be some happy creature's palace;
The little bird sits at his door in the sun,
   Atilt like a blossom among the leaves,
And lets his illumined being o'errun
   With the deluge of summer it receives;
His mate feels the eggs beneath her wings,
And the heart in her dumb breast flutters and sings;
He sings to the wide world and she to her nest—
In the nice ear of Nature, which song is the best?

Now is the high-tide of the year,
   And whatever of life hath ebbed away
Comes flooding back with a ripply cheer,
   Into every bare inlet and creek and bay;
Now the heart is so full that a drop overfills it,
We are happy now because God wills it;
No matter how barren the past may have been,
'Tis enough for us now that the leaves are green;
We sit in the warm shade and feel right well
How the sap creeps up and the blossoms swell;
We may shut our eyes, but we cannot help knowing
That skies are clear and grass is growing;
The breeze comes whispering in our ear,
That dandelions are blossoming near,
   That maize has sprouted, that streams are flowing,
That the river is bluer than the sky,
That the robin is plastering his house hard by;
And if the breeze kept the good news back,
For other couriers we should not lack;
   We could guess it all by yon heifer's lowing,—
And hark! how clear bold chanticleer,
Warmed with the new wine of the year,
   Tells all in his lusty crowing!

Bettmann

Ode to the West Wind

PERCY BYSSHE SHELLEY

(Born August 4. 1792; died July 8. 1822)

O wild West Wind, thou breath of Autumn's being,
  Thou, from whose unseen presence the leaves dead
Are driven, like ghosts from an enchanter fleeing,
  Yellow, and black, and pale, and hectic red,
Pestilence-stricken multitudes! O thou
  Who chariotest to their dark wintry bed
The winged seeds, where they lie cold and low,
  Each like a corpse within its grave, until
Thine azure sister of the Spring shall blow
  Her clarion o'er the dreaming earth, and fill
(Driving sweet buds like flocks to feed in air)
  With living hues and odors plain and hill:
Wild Spirit, which art moving everywhere;
Destroyer and preserver; hear, oh hear!

Thou on whose stream, mid the steep sky's commotion,
  Loose clouds like earth's decaying leaves are shed,
Shook from the tangled boughs of heaven and ocean,
  Angels of rain and lightning! there are spread
On the blue surface of thine airy surge,
  Like the bright hair uplifted from the head
Of some fierce Maenad, ev'n from the dim verge
  Of the horizon to the zenith's height,
The locks of the approaching storm. Thou dirge
  Of the dying year, to which this closing night
Will be the dome of a vast sepulchre,
  Vaulted with all thy congregated might
Of vapors, from whose solid atmosphere
Black rain, and fire, and hail, will burst: oh hear!

Thou who didst waken from his summer-dreams
  The blue Mediterranean, where he lay,
Lull'd by the coil of his crystalline streams,
  Beside a pumice isle in Baiae's bay,

19

And saw in sleep old palaces and towers
    Quivering within the wave's intenser day,
All overgrown with azure moss, and flowers
    So sweet, the sense faints picturing them! Thou
For whose path the Atlantic's level powers
    Cleave themselves into chasms, while far below
The sea-blooms and the oozy woods which wear
    The sapless foliage of the ocean, know
Thy voice, and suddenly grow gray with fear
And tremble and despoil themselves: oh hear!

If I were a dead leaf thou mightest bear;
    If I were a swift cloud to fly with thee;
A wave to pant beneath thy power, and share
    The impulse of thy strength, only less free
Than Thou, O uncontrollable! If even
    I were as in my boyhood, and could be
The comrade of they wanderings over heaven,
    As then, when to outstrip thy skyey speed
Scarce seem'd a vision,—I would ne'er have striven
    As thus with thee in prayer in my sore need.
Oh! lift me as a wave, a leaf, a cloud!
    I fall upon the thorns of life! I bleed!
A heavy weight of hours has chain'd and bow'd
One too like thee—tameless, and swift, and proud.

Make me thy lyre, ev'n as the forest is:
    What if my leaves are falling like its own!
The tumult of thy mighty harmonies
    Will take from both a deep autumnal tone,
Sweet though in sadness. Be thou, Spirit fierce,
    My spirit! be thou me, impetuous one!
Drive my dead thoughts over the universe,
    Like wither'd leaves, to quicken a new birth;
And, by the incantation of this verse,
    Scatter, as from an unextinguish'd hearth
Ashes and sparks, my words among mankind!
    Be through my lips to unawaken'd earth
The trumpet of a prophecy! O Wind,
If Winter comes, can Spring be far behind?

Bettmann

The Snowstorm

RALPH WALDO EMERSON
(Born May 25, 1803; died April 27, 1882)

Announced by all the trumpets of the sky,
Arrives the snow, and, driving o'er the fields,
Seems nowhere to alight: the whited air
Hides hills and woods, the river, and the heaven,
And veils the farmhouse at the garden's end.
The sled and traveler stopped, the courier's feet
Delayed, all friends shut out, the housemates sit
Around the radiant fireplace, enclosed
In a tumultuous privacy of storm.

Come, see the north wind's masonry.
Out of an unseen quarry evermore
Furnished with tile, the fierce artificer
Curves his white bastions with projected roof
Round every windward stake or tree or door.
Speeding, the myriad-handed, his wild work
So fanciful, so savage, naught cares he
For number or proportion. Mockingly
On coop or kennel he hangs Parian wreaths;
A swan-like form invests the hidden thorn;
Fills up the farmer's lane from wall to wall,
Maugre the farmer's sighs; and at the gate
A tapering turret overtops the work.
And when his hours are numbered, and the world
Is all his own, retiring, as he were not,
Leaves, when the sun appears, astonished Art
To mimic in slow structures, stone by stone,
Built in an age, the mad wind's night-work,
The frolic architecture of the snow.

Bettmann

To a Skylark

PERCY BYSSHE SHELLEY
(Born August 4, 1792; died July 8, 1822)

Hail to thee, blithe spirit!
  Bird thou never wert,
That from heaven, or near it,
  Pourest thy full heart
In profuse strains of unpremeditated art.

Higher still and higher
  From the earth thou springest,
Like a cloud of fire;
  The blue deep thou wingest,
And singing still dost soar, and soaring ever singest.

In the golden lightning
  Of the sunken sun,
O'er which clouds are brightening,
  Thou dost float and run,
Like an unbodied joy whose race is just begun.

The pale purple even
  Melts around thy flight;
Like a star of heaven,
  In the broad daylight
Thou art unseen, but yet I hear thy shrill delight,

Keen as are the arrows
  Of that silver sphere,
Whose intense lamp narrows
  In the white dawn clear,
Until we hardly see, we feel that it is there.

All the earth and air
  With thy voice is loud,
As, when night is bare,
  From one lonely cloud
The moon rains out her beams, and heaven is overflowed.

What thou art we know not;
      What is most like thee?
From rainbow clouds there flow not
      Drops so bright to see,
As from thy presence showers a rain of melody.

Like a poet hidden
      In the light of thought,
Singing hymns unbidden,
      Till the world is wrought
To sympathy with hopes and fears it heeded not;

Like a high-born maiden
      In a palace tower,
Soothing her love-laden
      Soul in secret hour
With music sweet as love, which overflows her bower;

Like a glow-worm golden
      In a dell of dew,
Scattering unbeholden
      Its aerial hue
Among the flowers and grass, which screen it from the view;

Like a rose embowered
      In its own green leaves,
By winds deflowered,
      Till the scent it gives
Makes faint with too much sweet these heavy-wingèd thieves.

Sound of vernal showers,
      On the twinkling grass,
Rain-awakened flowers,
      All that ever was
Joyous and clear and fresh thy music doth surpass.

Teach us, sprite or bird,
      What sweet thoughts are thine!
I have never heard
      Praise of love or wine
That panted forth a flood of rapture so divine.

Chorus hymeneal
      Or triumphal chant,
Matched with thine, would be all
      But an empty vaunt,—
A thing wherein we feel there is some hidden want.

What objects are the fountains
   Of thy happy strain?
What fields or waves or mountains?
   What shapes of sky or plain?
What love of thine own kind? what ignorance of pain?

With thy clear keen joyance
   Languor cannot be;
Shadow of annoyance
   Never came near thee;
Thou lovest, but ne'er knew love's sad satiety.

Waking or asleep,
   Thou of death must deem
Things more true and deep
   Than we mortals dream,
Oh how could thy notes flow in such a crystal stream?

We look before and after,
   And pine for what is not;
Our sincerest laughter
   With some pain is fraught;
Our sweetest songs are those that tell of saddest thought.

Yet if we could scorn
   Hate and pride and fear;
If we were things born
   Not to shed a tear,
I know not how thy joy we ever should come near.

Better than all measures
   Of delightful sound,
Better than all treasures
   That in books are found,
Thy skill to poet were, thou scorner of the ground!

Teach me half the gladness
   That thy brain must know,
Such harmonious madness
   From my lips would flow,
The world should listen then, as I am listening now.

Bettmann

Hiawatha's Childhood

HENRY WADSWORTH LONGFELLOW
(Born February 27, 1807; died March 24, 1882)

By the shores of Gitche Gumee,
By the shining Big-Sea-Water,
Stood the wigwam of Nokomis,
Daughter of the Moon, Nokomis.
Dark behind it rose the forest,
Rose the black and gloomy pine-trees,
Rose the firs with cones upon them;
Bright before it beat the water,
Beat the clear and sunny water,
Beat the shining Big-Sea-Water.
  There the wrinkled old Nokomis
Nursed the little Hiawatha,
Rocked him in his linden cradle,
Bedded soft in moss and rushes,
Safely bound with reindeer sinews;
Stilled his fretful wail by saying,
"Hush! the Naked Bear will hear thee!"
Lulled him into slumber, singing,
"Ewa-yea! my little owlet!
Who is this, that lights the wigwam?
With his great eyes lights the wigwam?
Ewa-yea! my little owlet!"
  Many things Nokomis taught him
Of the stars that shine in heaven;
Showed him Ishkoodah, the comet,
Ishkoodah, with fiery tresses;
Showed the Death-Dance of the spirits,
Warriors with their plumes and war-clubs,
Flaring far away to northward
In the frosty nights of winter;
Showed the broad white road in heaven,
Pathway of the ghosts, the shadows,
Running straight across the heavens,
Crowded with the ghosts, the shadows.

At the door on summer evenings,
Sat the little Hiawatha;
Heard the whispering of the pine-trees,
Heard the lapping of the waters,
Sounds of music, words of wonder;
"Minne-wawa!" said the pine-trees,
"Mudway-aushka!" said the water.

Saw the fire-fly Wah-wah-taysee,
Flitting through the dusk of evening,
With the twinkle of its candle
Lighting up the brakes and bushes,
And he sang the song of children,
Sang the song Nokomis taught him:
"Wah-wah-taysee, little fire-fly,
Little flitting, white-fire insect,
Little, dancing, white-fire creature,
Light me with your little candle,
Ere upon my bed I lay me,
Ere in sleep I close my eyelids!"

Saw the moon rise from the water,
Rippling, rounding from the water,
Saw the flecks and shadows on it,
Whispered, "What is that, Nokomis?"
And the good Nokomis answered:
"Once a warrior, very angry,
Seized his grandmother, and threw her
Up into the sky at midnight;
Right against the moon he threw her;
'Tis her body that you see there."

Saw the rainbow in the heaven,
In the eastern sky the rainbow,
Whispered, "What is that, Nokomis?"
And the good Nokomis answered:
" 'Tis the heaven of flowers you see there;
All the wild-flowers of the forest,
All the lilies of the prairie,
When on earth they fade and perish,
Blossom in that heaven above us."

When he heard the owls at midnight,
Hooting, laughing in the forest,
"What is that?" he cried in terror;
"What is that," he said, "Nokomis?"
And the good Nokomis answered:
"That is but the owl and owlet,
Talking in their native language,
Talking, scolding at each other."

Then the little Hiawatha
Learned of every bird its language,
Learned their names and all their secrets,

How they built their nests in summer,
Where they hid themselves in winter,
Talked with them whene'er he met them,
Called them "Hiawatha's Chickens."
   Of all beasts he learned the language,
Learned their names and all their secrets,
How the beavers built their lodges,
Where the squirrels hid their acorns,
How the reindeer ran so swiftly,
Why the rabbit was so timid,
Talked with them whene'er he met them,
Called them "Hiawatha's Brothers."

Bettmann

The Happy Warrior

WILLIAM WORDSWORTH
(Born April 7, 1770; died April 23, 1850)

Who is the happy Warrior? Who is he
That every man in arms should wish to be?
   It is the generous Spirit, who, when brought
Among the tasks of real life, hath wrought
Upon the plan that pleased his boyish thought:
Whose high endeavors are an inward light
That makes the path before him always bright:
Who, with a natural instinct to discern
What knowledge can perform, is diligent to learn;
Abides by this resolve, and stops not there,
But makes his moral being his prime care;
Who, doomed to go in company with Pain,
And Fear, and Bloodshed, miserable train!
Turns his necessity to glorious gain;
In face of these doth exercise a power
Which is our human nature's highest dower;
Controls them and subdues, transmutes, bereaves
Of their bad influence, and their good receives:
By objects, which might force the soul to abate
Her feeling, rendered more compassionate;
Is placable—because occasions rise
So often that demand such sacrifice;

27

More skillful in self-knowledge, even more pure,
As tempted more; more able to endure,
As more exposed to suffering and distress;
Thence also, more alive to tenderness.
—'Tis he whose law is reason; who depends
Upon that law as on the best of friends;
Whence, in a state where men are tempted still
To evil for a guard against worse ill,
And what in quality or act is best
Doth seldom on a right foundation rest,
He labors good on good to fix, and owes
To virtue every triumph that he knows:
—Who, if he rise to station of command,
Rises by open means; and there will stand
On honorable terms, or else retire,
And in himself possess his own desire;
Who comprehends his trust, and to the same
Keeps faithful with a singleness of aim;
And therefore does not stoop, nor lie in wait
For wealth, or honors, or for worldly state;
Whom they must follow; on whose head must fall,
Like showers of manna, if they come at all:
Whose power shed round him in the common strife,
Or mild concerns of ordinary life,
A constant influence, a peculiar grace;
But who, if he be called upon to face
Some awful moment to which Heaven has joined
Great issues, good or bad for human kind,
Is happy as a Lover; and attired
With sudden brightness, like a Man inspired;
And, through the heat of conflict, keeps the law
In calmness made, and sees what he foresaw;
Or if an unexpected call succeed,
Come when it will, is equal to the need:
—He who, though thus endued as with a sense
And faculty for storm and turbulence,
Is yet a Soul whose master-bias leans
To homefelt pleasures and to gentle scenes;
Sweet images! which, wheresoe'er he be,
Are at his heart; and such fidelity
It is his darling passion to approve;
More brave for this, that he hath much to love:—
'Tis, finally, the Man who lifted high,
Conspicuous object in a Nation's eye,
Or left unthought-of in obscurity,—
Who, with a toward or untoward lot,
Prosperous or adverse, to his wish or not—
Plays, in the many games of life, that one
Where what he most doth value msut be won:

Whom neither shape of danger can dismay,
Nor thought of tender happiness betray;
Who, not content that former worth stand fast,
Looks forward, persevering to the last,
From well to better, daily self-surpast;
Who, whether praise of him must walk the earth
Forever, and to noble deeds give birth,
Or he must fall, to sleep without his fame,
And leave a dead unprofitable name—
Finds comfort in himself and in his cause;
And, while the mortal mist is gathering, draws
His breath in confidence of Heaven's applause:
This is the happy Warrior; this is He
That every Man in arms should wish to be.

Bettmann

Ann Rutledge

EDGAR LEE MASTERS

*(Born August 23, 1869;
died March 5, 1950)*

Out of me unworthy and unknown
The vibrations of deathless music;
"With malice toward none, with charity for all."
Out of me the forgiveness of millions toward millions,
And the beneficent face of a nation
Shining with justice and truth.
I am Ann Rutledge who sleeps beneath these weeds,
Beloved in life of Abraham Lincoln,
Wedded to him, not through union,
But through separation.
Bloom forever, O Republic,
From the dust of my bosom!

From *Spoon River Anthology,* by Edgar Lee Masters, and
published by the Macmillan Company. Copyright 1916.
By special permission of the author and publisher.

Bettmann

Grass

CARL SANDBURG

(Born Galesburg, Illinois, 1872)

Pile the bodies high at Austerlitz and Waterloo.
Shovel them under and let me work—
        I am the grass; I cover all.

And pile them high at Gettysburg
And pile them high at Ypres and Verdun.
Shovel them under and let me work.
Two years, ten years, and passengers ask the conductor:
        What place is this?
        Where are we now?

        I am the grass.
        Let me work.

From *Cornhuskers*, by Carl Sandburg. Copyright 1918. Published by Henry Holt & Co. Special permission of the publisher.

Not in Vain

EMILY DICKINSON

(Born 1830; died 1886)

Reproduced by permission of Little, Brown & Company

If I can stop one heart from breaking,
I shall not live in vain:
If I can ease one life the aching,
Or cool one pain,
Or help one fainting robin
Unto his nest again,
I shall not live in vain.

Bettmann

Sheridan's Ride

THOMAS BUCHANAN READ

(Born March 12, 1822; died May 11, 1872)

Up from the South at break of day,
Bringing to Winchester fresh dismay,
The affrighted air with a shudder bore,
Like a herald in haste, to the chieftain's door,
The terrible grumble, and rumble, and roar,
Telling the battle was on once more,
    And Sheridan twenty miles away.

And wider still those billows of war
Thundered along the horizon's bar;
And louder yet into Winchester rolled
The roar of that red sea uncontrolled,
Making the blood of the listener cold,
As he thought of the stake in that fiery fray,
    With Sheriran twenty miles away.

But there is a road from Winchester town,
A good, broad highway leading down;
And there, through the flush of the morning light,
A steed as black as the steeds of night
Was seen to pass, as with eagle flight;
As if he knew the terrible need,
He stretched away with his utmost speed;
Hills rose and fell; but his heart was gay,
    With Sheridan fifteen miles away.

Still sprung from those swift hoofs, thundering South,
The dust, like smoke from the cannon's mouth;
Or the trail of a comet, sweeping faster and faster.
Foreboding to traitors the doom of disaster,
The heart of the steed and the heart of the master
Were beating like prisoners assaulting their walls,
Impatient to be where the battlefield calls;
Every nerve of the charger was strained to full play,
    With Sheridan only ten miles away.

Under his spurning feet the road
Like an arrowy Alpine river flowed,
And the landscape sped away behind
Like an ocean flying before the wind,
And the steed, like a barque fed with furnace ire,
Swept on, with his wild eye full of fire.
But lo! he is nearing his heart's desire;
He is snuffing the smoke of the roaring fray,
    With Sheridan only five miles away.

The first that the general saw were the groups
Of stragglers, and then the retreating troops;
What was done? What to do? A glance told him both,
Then, striking his spurs, with a terrible oath,
He dashed down the line 'mid a storm of huzzas,
And the wave of retreat checked its course there, because
The sight of the master compelled it to pause.
With foam and with dust the black charger was gray;
By the flash of his eye, and the red nostril's play,
He seemed to the whole great army to say,
"I have brought you Sheridan all the way
    From Winchester down to save the day!"

Hurrah! Hurrah for Sheridan!
Hurrah! Hurrah for horse and man!
And when their statues are placed on high,
Under the dome of the Union sky,
The American soldier's Temple of Fame;
Their with the glorious general's name,
Be it said, in letters both bold and bright,
    "Here is the steed that saved the day,
By carrying Sheridan into the fight,
    From Winchester, twenty miles away!"

Courtesy J. B. Lippincott Company.

Bettmann

The Present Crisis

JAMES RUSSELL LOWELL
(Born February 22, 1819; died August 12, 1891)

When a deed is done for Freedom, through the broad
  earth's aching breast
Runs a thrill of joy prophetic, trembling on from east to
  west,
And the slave, where'er he cowers, feels the soul within
  him climb
To the awful verge of manhood, as the energy sublime
Of the century bursts full-blossomed on the thorny stem of
  Time.

Through the walls of hut and palace shoots the instantane-
  ous throe,
When the travail of the Ages wrings earth's systems to
  and fro;
At the birth of each new Era, with a recognizing start,
Nation wildly looks at nation, standing with mute lips
  apart,
And glad Truth's yet mightier man-child leaps beneath
  the Future's heart.

So the Evil's triumph sendeth, with a terror and a chill,
Under continent to contient, the sense of coming ill,
And the slave, where'er he cowers, feels his sympathies
  with God
In hot tear-drops ebbing earthward, to be drunk up by
  the sod,
Till a corpse crawls round unburied, delving in the nobler
  clod.

For mankind are one in spirit, and an instinct bears
  along,
Round the earth's electric circle, the swift flash of right
  or wrong;

33

Whether conscious or unconscious, yet Humanity's vast
    frame
Though its ocean-sundered fibres feels the gush of joy or
    shame;—
In the gain or loss of one race all the rest have equal
    claim.

Once to every man and nation comes the moment to
    decide;
In the strife of Truth with Falsehood, for the good or evil
    side;
Some great cause, God's new Messiah, offering each the
    bloom or blight,
Parts the goats upon the left hand and the sheep upon
    the right,
And the choice goes by forever 'twixt that darkness and
    that light.

Hast thou chosen, O my people, on whose party thou
    shalt stand,
Ere the Doom from its worn sandals shakes the dust
    against our land?
Though the cause of Evil prosper, yet 'tis Truth alone is
    strong,
And, albeit she wander outcast now, I see around her
    throng
Troops of beautiful, tall angels, to enshield her from all
    wrong.

Backward look across the ages and the beacon-moments
    see,
That, like peaks of some sunk continent, jut through
    Oblivion's sea;
Not an ear in court or market for the low foreboding cry
Of those Crises, God's stern winnowers, from whose feet
    earth's chaff must fly;
Never shows the choice momentous till the judgment
    hath passed by.

Careless seems the great Avenger; history's page but record
One death- grapple in the darkness 'twist old system and
    the Word;
Truth forever on the scaffold, Wrong forever on the
    throne,—

Yet that scaffold sways the future, and, behind the dim
    unknown,
Standeth God within the shadow, keeping watch above
    his own.

We see dimly in the Present what is small and what is
    great,
Slow of faith how weak an arm may turn the iron helm
    of fate,
But the soul is still oracular; amid the market's din,
List the omnious stern whisper from the Delphic cave
    within,—
"They enslave their children's children who make com-
    promise with sin."

Slavery, the earth-born Cyclops, fellest of the giant brood,
Sons of brutish Force and Darkness, who have drenched
    the earth with blood,
Famished in his self-made desert, blinded by our purer
    day,
Gropes in yet unblasted regions for his miserable prey;
Shall we guide his gory fingers where our helpless children
    play?

Then to side with Truth is noble when we share her
    wretched crust,
Ere her cause bring fame and profit, and 'tis prosperous
    to be just;
Then it is the brave man chooses, while the coward
    stands aside,
Doubting in his abject spirit, till his Lord is crucified,
And the multitude make virtue of the faith they had
    denied.

Count me o'er earth's chosen heroes,—they were souls
    that stood alone,
While the men they agonized for hurled the contumelious
    stone,
Stood serene, and down the future saw the golden beam
    incline
To the side of perfect justice, mastered by their faith
    divine,
By one man's plain truth to manhood and to God's
    supreme design.

By the light of burning heretics Christ's bleeding feet I
  track,
Toiling up new Calvaries ever with the cross that turns
  not back,
And these mounts of anguish number how each generation learned
One new word of that grand *Credo* which in prophet-
  hearts hath burned
Since the first man stood God-conquered with his face to
  heaven upturned.

For humanity sweeps onward: where today the martyr
  stands,
On the morrow crouches Judas with the silver in his hands;
Far in front the cross stands ready and the crackling fagots
  burn,
While the hooting mob of yesterday in silent awe return
To glean up the scattered ashes into History's golden urn.

'Tis as easy to be heroes as to sit the idle slaves
Of a legendary virtue carved upon our father's graves,
Worshippers of light ancestral make the present light a
  crime;
Was the Mayflower launched by cowards, steered by men
  behind their time?
Turn those tracks toward Past or Future, that make Ply-
  mouth Rock sublime?

They were men of present valor, stalwart old iconoclasts,
Unconvinced by axe or gibbet that all virtue was the Past's;
But we make their truth our falsehood thinking that hath
  made us free,
Hoarding it in mouldy parchments, while our tender spirits
  flee
The rude grasp of that great Impulse which drove them
  across the sea.

They have rights who dare maintain them; we are traitors
  to our sires,
Smothering in their holy ashes Freedom's new-lit altar-fires;
Shall we make their creed our jailor? Shall we, in our haste
  to slay,

From the tombs of the old prohpets steal the funeral lamps
    away
To light up the martyr-fagots round the prophets of today?

New occasions teach new duties; Time makes ancient good
    uncouth;
They must upward still, and onward, who would keep
    abreast of Truth;
Lo, before us gleam her camp-fires! we ourselves must
    Pilgrims be,
Launch our Mayflower, and steer boldly through the des-
    perate winter sea,
Nor attempt the Future's portal with the Past's blood-
    rusted key.

Be Strong

MALTBIE DAVENPORT BABCOCK
(Born August 3, 1858; died May 18, 1901)

Photographed from portrait hanging in the lecture room of the
Brick Presbyterian Church, New
York, of which Dr. Babcock was
formerly pastor

Be strong!
We are not here to play, to dream, to drift;
We have hard work to do, and loads to lift;
Shun not the struggle—face it; 'tis God's gift.

Be strong!
Say not, "The days are evil. Who's to blame?"
And fold the hands and acquiesce—oh shame!
Stand up, speak out, and bravely, in God's name.

Be strong!
It matters not how deep intrenched the wrong,
How hard the battle goes, the day how long;
Faint not—fight on! To-morrow comes the song.

Bettmann

Columbus

CINCINNATUS HINER MILLER
Known as JOAQUIN MILLER

(Born November 10, 1841; died February, 17, 1913)

Behind him lay the gray Azores,
    Behind the Gates of Hercules;
Before him not the ghost of shores,
    Before him only shoreless seas.
The good mate said: "Now must we pray,
    For lo!the very stars are gone.
Brave Adm'r'l, speak; what shall I say?"
    "Why, say: "Sail on! sail on! and on!' "

"My men grow mutinous day by day;
    My men grow ghastly wan and weak."
The stout mate thought of home; a spray
    Of salt wave washed his swarthy cheek.
"What shall I say, brave Adm'r'l, say,
    If we sight naught but seas at dawn?"
"Why, you shall say, at break of day:
    'Sail on! sail on! sail on! and on!' "

They sailed and sailed, as winds might blow,
    Until at last the blanched mate said:
"Why, now not even God would know
    Should I and all my men fall dead.
These very winds forget their way,
    For God from these dread seas is gone.
Now speak, brave Adm'r'l; speak and say"—
    He said: "Sail on! sail on! and on!"

They sailed. They sailed. Then spake the mate:
    "This mad sea shows his teeth to-night;
He curled his lips, he lies in wait,
    With lifted teeth, as if to bite:
Brave Adm'r'l, say but one good word;
    What shall we do when hope is gone?"
The words leapt like a leaping sword:
    "Sail on! sail on! sail on! and on!"

38

Then, pale and worn, he kept his deck,
    And peered through darkness. Ah, that night
Of all dark nights! And then a speck—
    A light! a light! a light! a light!
It grew, a starlit flag unfurled!
    It grew to be Time's burst of dawn.
He gained a world; he gave that world
    Its grandest lesson: "On! sail on!"

From *Complete Poetical Works of Joaquin Miller*. By permission of Whitaker & Ray-Wiggin Co. Copyrighted.

Trees

SERGEANT JOYCE KILMER
165th Infantry (69th New York), A.E.F.
*(Born December 6, 1886; killed in action
near Ourcy, July 30, 1918)*

I think that I shall never see
A poem lovely as a tree.

A tree whose hungry mouth is prest
Against the earth's sweet flowing breast;

A tree that looks at God all day,
And lifts her leafy arms to pray;

A tree that may in Summer wear
A nest of robins in her hair;

Upon whose bosom snow has lain;
Who intimately lives with rain.

Poems are made by fools like me,
But only God can make a tree.

Reprinted from *Trees and Other Poems*, by Joyce Kilmer, by permission of George H. Doran Company, publishers. Copyright, 1914.

The Spires of Oxford
(As seen from the train)

WINIFRED M. LETTS

I saw the spires of Oxford
  As I was passing by,
The grey spires of Oxford
  Against a pearl-grey sky;
My heart was with the Oxford men
  Who went abroad to die.

The years go fast in Oxford,
  The golden years and gay;
The hoary colleges look down
  On careless boys at play,
But when the bugles sounded—War!
  They put their games away.

They left the peaceful river,
  The cricket field, the quad,
The shaven lawns of Oxford,
  To seek a bloody sod.
They gave their merry youth away
  For country and for God.

God rest you, happy gentlemen,
  Who laid your good lives down,
Who took the khaki and the gun
  Instead of cap and gown.
God bring you to a fairer place
  Then even Oxford town.

By permission from *The Spires of Oxford and Other Poems,* by W. M. Letts. Published by E. P. Dutton & Company.

Bettmann

Recessional

RUDYARD KIPLING

(Born December 30, 1865; died January 17, 1936)

God of our fathers, known of old—
  Lord of our far-flung battle line—
Beneath whose awful hand we hold
  Dominion over palm and pine—
Lord God of Hosts, be with us yet,
Lest we forget—lest we forget!

The tumult and the shouting dies—
  The Captains and the Kings depart—
Still stands Thine ancient sacrifice,
  An humble and a contrite heart.
Lord God of Hosts, be with us yet,
Lest we forget—lest we forget!

Far-called, our navies melt away—
  On dune and headland sinks the fire—
Lo, all our pomp of yesterday
  Is one with Nineveh and Tyre!
Judge of the Nations, spare us yet,
Lest we forget—lest we forget!

If, drunk with sight of power, we loose
  Wild tongues that have not Thee in awe—
Such boasting as the Gentiles use,
  Or lesser breeds without the Law—
Lord God of Hosts, be with us yet,
Lest we forget—lest we forget!

For heathen heart that puts her trust
  In reeking tube and iron shard—
All valiant dust that builds on dust,
  And guarding, calls not Thee to guard,
For frantic boast and foolish word,
Thy Mercy on Thy People, Lord! Amen!

Bettmann

The Cloud

PERCY BYSSHE SHELLEY
(Born August 4, 1792; died July 8, 1822)

I bring fresh showers for the thirsting flowers,
 From the seas and the streams;
I bear light shade for the leaves when laid
 In their noonday dreams.
From my wings are shaken the dews that waken
 The sweet buds every one,
When rocked to rest on their mother's breast,
 As she dances about the sun.
I wield the flail of the lashing hail,
 And whiten the green plains under;
And then again I dissolve it in rain,
 And laugh as I pass in thunder.

I sift the snow on the mountains below,
 And their great pines groan aghast;
And all the night 'tis my pillow white,
 While I sleep in the arms of the blast.
Sublime on the towers of my skyey bowers,
 Lightning, my pilot, sits;
In a cavern under is fettered the thunder,
 It struggles and howls at fits;
Over earth and ocean, with gentle motion,
 This pilot is guiding me,
Lured by the love of the genii that move
 In the depths of the purple sea;
Over the rills and the crags and the hills,
 Over the lakes and the plains,
Wherever he dream, under mountain or stream,
 The Spirit he loves remains;
And I all the while bask in heaven's blue smile,
 Whilst he is dissolving in rains.

The sanguine sunrise, with his meteor eyes,
 And his burning plumes outspread,
Leaps on the back of my sailing rack,
 When the morning star shines dead:
As on the jag of a mountain crag
 Which an earthquake rocks and swings,

An eagle alit one moment may sit
    In the light of its golden wings.
And when sunset may breathe from the lit sea beneath,
    Its ardors of rest and of love,
And the crimson pall of eve may fall
    From the depth of heaven above,
With wings folded I rest on mine airy nest,
    As still as a brooding dove.

That orbed maiden with white fire laden,
    Whom mortals call the moon,
Glides glimmering o'er my fleecelike floor,
    By the midnight breezes strewn;
And wherever the beat of her unseen feet,
    Which only the angels hear,
May have broken the woof of my tent's thin roof,
    The stars peep behind her and peer.
And I laugh to see them whirl and flee
    Like a swarm of golden bees,
When I widen the rent in my wind-built tent,—
    Till the calm rivers, lakes, and seas,
Like strips of the sky fallen through me on high
    Are each paved with the moon and these.

I bind the sun's throne with a burning zone,
    And the moon's with a girdle of pearl;
The volcanoes are dim, and the stars reel and swim,
    When the whirlwinds my banner unfurl.
From cape to cape, with a bridge-like shape,
    Over a torrent sea,
Sunbeam-proof, I hang like a roof,—
    The mountains its columns be.
The triumphal arch through which I march
    With hurricane, fire, and snow,
When the powers of the air are chained to my chair,
    Is the million-colored bow;
The sphere-fire above its soft colors wove,
    While the moist earth was laughing below.

I am the daughter of earth and water,
    And the nursling of the sky;
I pass through the pores of the ocean and shores;
    I change, but I cannot die.
For after the rain, when, with never a stain,
    The pavilion of heaven is bare,
And the winds and sunbeams, with their convex gleams,
    Build up the blue dome of air,
I silently laugh at my own cenotaph,
    And out of the caverns of rain,
Like a child from the womb, like a ghost from the tomb,
    I arise and unbuild it again.

How Did You Die?

EDMUND VANCE COOKE

*(Born June 5, 1866;
died December 18, 1932)*

Did you tackle that trouble that came your way
    With a resolute heart and cheerful?
Or hide your face from the light of day
    With a craven soul and fearful?
Oh, a trouble's a ton, or a trouble's an ounce,
    Or a trouble is what you make it.
And it isn't the fact that you're hurt that counts,
    But only how did you take it?

You are beaten to earth? Well, well, what's that?
    Come up with a smiling face.
It's nothing against you to fall down flat,
    But to lie there—that's disgrace.
The harder you're thrown, why the higher you bounce;
    Be proud of your blackened eye!
It isn't the fact that you're licked that counts;
    It's how did you fight and why?

And though you be done to death, what then?
    If you battled the best you could;
If you played your part in the world of men,
    Why, the Critic will call it good.
Death comes with a crawl, or comes with a pounce,
    And whether he's slow or spry,
It isn't the fact that you're dead that counts,
    But only, how did you die?

From *Impertinent Poems* by permission. Copyright 1903 by E. V. Cooke. 1907 by Dodge Publishing Company.

Bettmann

From a portrait in possession
of the Earl of Clarendon
(Courtesy *The Outlook*)

Wolsey's Farewell to His Greatness

From "Henry VIII"

This soliloquy of Wolsey occurs in the latter half of
Act 3, Scene 2, of "Henry VIII." a play now agreed
to be in some sense the joint work of Shakespeare
and Fletcher. The soliloquy is generally accepted as
Fletcher's writing.

JOHN FLETCHER

*(Born December 20, 1579; died August
28 [?], 1625)*

Farewell! a long farewell to all my greatness!
This is the state of man: today he puts forth
The tender leaves of hope, to-morrow blossoms,
And bears his blushing honors thick upon him;
The third day comes a frost, a killing frost;
And—when he thinks, good easy man, full surely
His greatness is a-ripening—nips his root,
And then he falls, as I do. I have ventur'd,
Like little wanton boys that swim on bladders,
This many summers in a sea of glory,
But far beyond my depth my high blown pride
At length broke under me, and now has left me,
Weary and old with service, to the mercy
Of a rude stream that must forever hide me.
Vain pomp and glory of this world, I hate ye!
I feel my heart new-opened. Oh! how wretched
Is that poor man that hangs on princes' favors!
There is, betwixt that smile we would aspire to,
That sweet aspect of princes, and their ruin,
More pangs and fears than wars or women have;
And when he falls, he falls like Lucifer,
Never to hope again.

Bettmann

The Blessed Damozel

DANTE GABRIEL ROSSETTI
(Born May 12, 1828; died April 9, 1882)

The blessed damozel leaned out
    From the gold bar of heaven;
Her eyes were deeper than the depth
    Of waters stilled at even;
She had three lilies in her hand,
    And the stars in her hair were seven.

Her robe, ungirt from clasp to hem,
    No wrought flowers did adorn,
But a white rose of Mary's gift,
    For service meetly worn;
Her hair that lay along her back
    Was yellow like ripe corn.

Her seemed she scarce had been a day
    One of God's choristers;
The wonder was not yet quite gone
    From that still look of hers;
Albeit, to them she left, her day
    Had counted as ten years.

(To one, it is ten years of years
    . . . Yet now, and in this place,
Surely she lean'd o'er me—her hair
    Fell all about my face. . . .
Nothing: the autumn fall of leaves
    The whole year sets apace.)

It was the rampart of God's house
    That she was standing on;
By God built over the sheer depth
    The which is Space begun;
So high, that looking downward thence
    She scarce could see the sun

It lies in heaven, across the flood
  Of ether, as a bridge.
Beneath, the tides of day and night
  With flame and darkness ridge
The void, as low as where this earth
  Spins like a fretful midge.

Around her, lovers, newly met
  'Mid deathless love's acclaims
Spake evermore among themselves
  Their heart-remember'd names;
And the souls mounting up to God
  Went by her like thin flames.

And still she bowed herself and stooped
  Out of the circling charm;
Until her bosom must have made
  The bar she leaned on warm,
And the lilies lay as if asleep
  Along her bended arm.

From the fixed place of heaven she saw
  Time like a pulse shake fierce
Through all the worlds. Her gaze still strove
  Within the gulf to pierce
The path; and now she spoke as when
  The stars sang in their spheres.

The sun was gone now; the curled moon
  Was like a little feather
Fluttering far down the gulf; and now
  She spoke through the still weather.
Her voice was like the voice the stars
  Had when they sang together.

(Ah, sweet! even now, in that bird's song,
  Strove not her accents there,
Fain to be hearkened? When those bells
  Possessed the mid-day air,
Strove not her steps to reach my side
  Down all the echoing stair?)

"I wish that he were come to me
  For he will come," she said.
"Have I not prayed in heaven?—on earth,
  Lord, Lord, has he not prayed?
Are not two prayers a perfect strength?
  And shall I feel afraid?

"When round his head the aureole clings,
    And he is clothed in white,
I'll take his hand and go with him
    To the deep wells of light;
As unto a stream we will step down,
    And bathe there in God's sight.

"We two will stand beside that shrine,
    Occult, withheld, untrod,
Whose lamps are stirred continually
    With prayer sent up to God;
And see our old prayers, granted, melt
    Each like a little cloud.

"We two will lie i' the shadow of
    That living mystic tree,
Within whose secret growth the Dove
    Is sometimes felt to be,
While every leaf that His plumes touch
    Saith His Name audibly.

"And I myself will teach to him
    I myself, lying so,
The songs I sing here; which his voice
    Shall pause in, hushed and slow,
And find some knowledge at each pause,
    Or some new thing to know.'

(Alas! We two, we two, thou say'st!
    Yea, one wast thou with me
That once of old. But shall God lift
    To endless unity
The soul whose likeness with thy soul
    Was but its love for thee?)

"We two," she said, "will seek the groves
    Where the Lady Mary is,
With her five handmaidens, whose names
    Are five sweet symphonies,
Cecily, Gertrude, Magdalen
    Margaret, and Rosalys.

"Circlewise sit they, with bound locks
    And foreheads garlanded;
Into the fine cloth, white like flame,
    Weaving the golden thread,
To fashion the birth-robes for them
    Who are just born, being dead.

"He shall fear, haply, and be dumb;
  Then will I lay my cheek
To his, and tell about our love,
  Not once abashed or weak:
And the dear Mother will approve
  My pride, and let me speak.

"Herself shall bring us, hand in hand,
  To Him round whom all souls
Kneel, the clear-ranged unnumbered heads
  Bowed with their aureoles:
And angels meeting us shall sing
  To their citherns and citoles.

"There will I ask of Christ the Lord
  Thus much for him and me:—
Only to live as once on earth
  With Love—only to be,
As then awhile, for ever now
  Together, I and he."

She gazed and listened, and then said,
  Less said of speech than mild—
"All this is when he comes." She ceased.
  The light thrilled towards her, filled
With angels in strong level flight.
  Her eyes prayed, and she smiled.

(I saw her smile.) But soon their path
  Was vague in distant spheres:
And then she cast her arms along
  The golden barriers,
And laid her face between her hands
  And wept. (I heard her tears.)

America for Me

HENRY VAN DYKE

(Born November 10, 1852; died April 10, 1933)

'Tis fine to see the Old World, and travel up and down
Among the famous palaces and cities of renown,
To admire the crumbly castles and the statues of the kings,—
But now I think I've had enough of antiquated things.

So it's home again, and home again, America for me!
My heart is turning home again, and there I long to be,
In the land of youth and freedom beyond the ocean bars,
Where the air is full of sunlight and the flag is full of stars

Oh, London is a man's town, there's power in the air;
And Paris is a woman's town, with flowers in her hair;
And it's sweet to dream in Venice, and it's great to study
    Rome;
But when it comes to living there is no place like home.

I like the German fir-woods, in green battalions drilled;
I like the gardens of Versailles with flashing fountains filled;
But, oh, to take your hand, my dear, and ramble for a day
In the friendly western woodland where Nature has her way!

I know that Europe's wonderful, yet something seems to
    lack:
The Past is too much with her, and the people looking
    back.
But the glory of the Present is to make the Future free,—
We love our land for what she is and what she is to be.

Oh, it's home again, and home again, America for me!
I want a ship that's westward bound to plough the rolling sea,
To the blessed Land of Room Enough beyond the ocean bars,
Where the air is full of sunlight and the flag is full of stars.

Requiem

ROBERT LOUIS STEVENSON

(Born November 13, 1850; died December 3, 1894)

Under the wide and starry sky
   Dig the grave and let me lie:
Glad did I live and gladly die,
   And I laid me down with a will.

This be the verse you grave for me:
Here he lies where he long'd to be;
Home is the sailor, home from the sea,
   And the hunter home from the hill.

The Gods of the Copybook Headings

RUDYARD KIPLING

(Born December 30, 1865; died January 17, 1936)

As I pass through my incarnations in every age and race,
I make my proper prostrations to the Gods of the Market-
   Place.
Peering through reverent fingers I watch them flourish
   and fall,
And the Gods of the Copybook Headings, I notice, outlast
   them all.

We were living in trees when they met us. They showed
   us each in turn
That Water would certainly wet us, as Fire would certainly burn:
But we found them lacking in Uplift, Vision and Breadth
   of Mind,
So we left them to teach the Gorillas while we followed
   the March of Mankind.

We moved as the Spirit listed. *They* never altered their pace,
Being neither cloud nor wind-borne like the Gods of the Market-Place;
But they always caught up with our progress, and presently word would come
That a tribe had been wiped off its icefield, or the lights had gone out in Rome.

With the Hopes that our World is built on they were utterly out of touch.
They denied that the Moon was Stilton; they denied she was even Dutch.
They denied that Wishes were Horses; they denied that a Pig had wings.
So we worshipped the Gods of the Market Who promised these beautiful things.

When the Cambrian measures were forming, They promised perpetual peace.
They swore, if we gave them our weapons, that the wars of the tribes would cease.
But when we disarmed They sold us and delivered us bound to our foe,
And the Gods of the Copybook Headings said: *"Stick to the Devil you know."*

On the first Feminian Sandstones we were promised the Fuller Life
(Which started by loving our neighbour and ended by loving his wife)
Till our women had no more children and the men lost reason and faith,
And the Gods of the Copybook Headings said: *"The Wages of Sin is Death."*

In the Carboniferous Epoch we were promised abundance for all,
By robbing selected Peter to pay for collective Paul;
But, though we had plenty of money, there was nothing our money could buy,
And the Gods of the Copybook Headings said: *"If you don't work you die."*

Then the Gods of the Market tumbled, and their smooth-tongued wizards withdrew,
And the hearts of the meanest were humbled and began to believe it was true

That All is not Gold that Glitters, and Two and Two
    make Four—
And the Gods of the Copybook Headings limped up to
    explain it once more.

.   .   .   .   .

As it will be in the future, it was at the birth of Man—
There are only four things certain since Social Progress
    began—
That the Dog returns to his Vomit and the Sow returns
    to her Mire,
And the burnt Fool's bandaged finger goes wabbling back
    to the Fire;
And that after this is accomplished, and the brave new
    world begins
When all men are paid for existing and no man must pay
    for his sins,
As surely as Water will wet us, as surely as Fire will burn,
The Gods of the Copybook Headings with terror and
    slaughter return!

Mercy

From "Merchant of Venice"

WILLIAM SHAKESPEARE
*(Born April 23 [?], 1564; died April 23,
1616)*

The quality of mercy is not strained;
It droppeth as the gentle rain from heaven
Upon the place beneath: it is twice blest,—
It blesseth him that gives and him that takes:
'Tis mightiest in the mightiest; it becomes
The thronèd monarch better than his crown:
His sceptre shows the force of temporal power,
The attribute to awe and majesty,
Wherein doth sit the dread and fear of kings;
But mercy is above this sceptred sway,—
It is enthronèd in the hearts of kings,
It is an attribute to God himself;
And earthly power doth then show likest God's,
When mercy seasons justice.

Bettmann

Abraham Lincoln Walks at Midnight

In Springfield, Illinois

VACHEL LINDSAY

*(Born Springfield, Ill., November 10, 1879;
died December 5, 1931)*

It is portentous, and a thing of state
That here at midnight, in our little town
A mourning figure walks, and will not rest,
Near the old court-house pacing up and down,
Or by his homestead, or in shadowed yards
He lingers where his children used to play,
Or through the market, on the well-worn stones
He stalks until the dawn-stars burn away.

A bronzed, lank man! His suit of ancient black,
A famous high top-hat and plain worn shawl
Make him the quaint great figure that men love,
The prairie-lawyer, master of us all.

He cannot sleep upon his hillside now.
He is among us:—as in times before!
And we who toss and lie awake for long
Breathe deep, and start, to see him pass the door.

His head is bowed. He thinks on men and kings.
Yea, when the sick world cries, how can he sleep?
Too many peasants fight, they know not why,
Too many homesteads in black terror weep.

The sins of all the war-lords burn his heart.
He sees the dreadnaughts scouring every main.
He carries on his shawl-wrapped shoulders now
The bitterness, the folly and the pain.

He cannot rest until a spirit-dawn
Shall come;—the shining hope of Europe free:
The league of sober folk, the Workers' Earth,
Bringing long peace to Cornland, Alp and Sea.

It breaks his heart that kings must murder still,
That all his hours of travail here for men
Seem yet in vain. And who will bring white peace
That he may sleep upon his hill again?

From *The Congo and Other Poems* by Vachel
Lindsay and published by the Macmillan
Company. Copyright, 1914. By special per-
mission of the author and publisher.

Bettmann

The Man with the Hoe

Written after seeing Millet's
world-famous painting of
a brutalized toiler

EDWIN MARKHAM

*(Born Oregon City, Oregon, 1852;
died March 7, 1940)*

God made man in his own image,
in the image of God made He him.—*Genesis.*

Bowed by the weight of centuries he leans
Upon his hoe and gazes on the ground,
The emptiness of ages in his face,
And on his back the burden of the world.
Who made him dead to rapture and despair,
A thing that grieves not and that never hopes,
Stolid and stunned, a brother to the ox?
Who loosened and let down this brutal jaw?
Whose was the hand that slanted back this brow?
Whose breath blew out the light within this brain?

Is this the Thing the Lord God made and gave
To have dominion over sea and land;
To trace the stars and search the heavens for power;
To feel the passion of Eternity?
Is this the dream He dreamed who shaped the suns
And markt their ways upon the ancient deep?
Down all the caverns of Hell to their last gulf
There is no shape more terrible than this---
More tongued with censure of the world's blind greed—
More filled with signs and portents for the soul—
More packt with danger to the universe.

What gulfs between him and the seraphim!
Slave of the wheel of labor, what to him
Are Plato and the swing of Pleiades?
What the long reaches of the peaks of song,
The rift of dawn, the reddening of the rose?
Thru this dread shape the suffering ages look;
Time's tragedy is in that aching stoop;
Thru this dread shape humanity betrayed,
Plundered, profaned and disinherited,
Cries protest to the Judges of the World,
A protest that is also prophecy.

O masters, lords and rulers in all lands,
Is this the handiwork you give to God,
This monstrous thing distorted and soul-quencht?
How will you ever straighten up this shape;
Touch it again with immortality;
Give back the upward looking and the light;
Rebuild in it the music and the dream;
Make right the immemorial infamies,
Perfidious wrongs, immedicable woes?

O masters, lords and rulers in all lands,
How will the future reckon with this Man?
How answer his brute question in that hour
When whirlwinds of rebellion shake all shores?
How will it be with kingdoms and with kings—
With those who shaped him to the thing he is—
When this dumb Terror shall rise to judge the world,
After the silence of the centuries?

This poem has been called "The battle-cry of the next thousand years." It has been translated into thirty languages.

From *The Man with the Hoe, and Other Poems*, by Edwin Markham. Published by Doubleday, Page & Co. Copyright, 1899, by the author, and used by his permission.

Bettmann

The Duel

EUGENE FIELD

(Born September 3, 1850; died November 4, 1895)

The gingham dog and the calico cat
Side by side on the table sat;
'Twas half-past twelve, and (what do you think!)
Nor one nor t' other had slept a wink!
    The old Dutch clock and the Chinese plate
    Appeared to know as sure as fate
There was going to be a terrible spat.

    (I wasn't there; I simply state
    What was told to me by the Chinese plate!)

The gingham dog went "bow-wow-wow!"
And the calico cat replied "mee-ow!"
The air was littered, an hour or so,
With bits of gingham and calico,
    While the old Dutch clock in the chimney-place
    Up with its hands before its face,
For it always dreaded a family row!

      (Never mind: I'm only telling you
      What the old Dutch clock declares is true!)

The Chinese plate looked very blue,
And wailed, "Oh, dear! what shall we do!"
But the gingham dog and the calico cat
Wallowed this way and tumbled that,
    Employing every tooth and claw
    In the awfullest way you ever saw—
And, oh! how the gingham and calico flew!

      Don't fancy I exaggerate—
      I got my news from the Chinese plate!)

Next morning where the two had sat
They found no trace of dog or cat;
And some folk think unto this day
That burglars stole that pair away!
    But the truth about the cat and pup
    Its this: they ate each other up!
Now what do you really think of that!

      (The old Dutch clock it told me so,
      And that is how I came to know.)

From *The Poems of Eugene Field.*
Copyright 1911, Charles Scribner's Sons.

Song
of the Chattahoochee

SIDNEY LANIER

(Born February 3, 1842; died September 7, 1881)

Out of the hills of Habersham,
　　Down the valleys of Hall
I hurry amain to reach the plain,
Run the rapid and leap the fall,
Split at the rock and together again,
Accept my bed, or narrow or wide,
And flee from folly on every side
With a lover's pain to attain the plain
　　Far from the hills of Habersham,
　　Far from the valleys of Hall.

All down the hills of Habersham,
　　All through the valleys of Hall,
The rushes cried *Abide, abide,*
The willful waterweeds held me thrall,
The laving laurel turned my tide,
The ferns and the fondling grass said *Stay,*
The dewberry dipped for to work delay,
And the little reeds sighed *Abide, abide,*
　　Here in the hills of Habersham,
　　Here in the valleys of Hall.

High o'er the hills of Habersham,
　　Veiling the valleys of Hall,
The hickory told me manifold
Fair tales of shade, the poplar tall
Wrought me her shadowy self to hold,
The chestnut, the oak, the walnut, the pine,
Overleaning, with flickering meaning and sign,
Said, *Pass not, so cold, these manifold*
　　Deep shades of the hills of Habersham,
　　These glades in the valleys of Hall.

And oft in the hills of Habersham,
    And oft in the valleys of Hall,
The white quartz shone, and the smooth brook-stone
Did bar me of passage with friendly brawl,
And many a luminous jewel lone—
Crystals clear or a-cloud with mist,
Ruby, garnet and amethyst—
Made lures with the lights of streaming stone
    In the clefts of the hills of Habersham,
    In the beds of the valleys of Hall.

But oh, not the hills of Habersham,
    And oh, not the valleys of Hall
Avail: I am fain to water the plain.
Downward the voices of Duty call—
Downward, to toil and be mixed with the main;
The dry fields burn, and the mills are to turn,
And a myriad flowers motally yearn,
And the lordly main beyond the plain
    Calls o'er the hills of Habersham,
    Calls through the valleys of Hall.

From *Poems of Sidney Lanier.* Copyright 1884 and 1891. Published by Charles Scribner's Sons.

Ode on Intimations of Immortality

From Recollections of Early Childhood

WILLIAM WORDSWORTH

(Born April 7, 1770; died April 23, 1850)

Bettmann

The Child is father of the Man;
And I could wish my days to be
Bound each to each by natural piety.

There was a time when meadow, grove, and stream,
The earth, and every common sight,
    To me did seem
    Apparelled in celestial light,
The glory and the freshness of a dream.
It is not now as it hath been of yore;—
    Turn wheresoe'er I may,
        By night or day,
The things which I have seen I now can see no more.

The rainbow comes and goes,
And lovely is the rose;
The moon doth with delight
Look round her when the heavens are bare;
Waters on a starry night
Are beautiful and fair;
The sunshine is a glorious birth;
But yet I know, where'er I go,
That there hath past away a glory from the earth.

Now, while the birds thus sing a joyous song,
And while the young lambs bound
As to the tabor's sound,
To me alone there came a thought of grief:
A timely utterance gave that thought relief;
And I again am strong.
The cataracts blow their trumpets from the steep;—
No more shall grief of mine the season wrong:
I hear the echoes through the mountains throng,
The winds come to me from the fields of sleep,
And all the earth is gay;
Land and sea
Give themselves up to jollity,
And with the heart of May
Doth every beast keep holiday;—
Thou child of joy
Shout round me, let me hear thy shouts, thou happy
shepherd-boy!

Ye blessed Creatures, I have heard the call
Ye to each other make; I see
The heavens laugh with you in your jubilee;
My heart is at your festival,
My head hath its coronal,
The fullness of your bliss, I feel—I feel it all.
Oh evil day! if I were sullen
While Earth herself is adorning
This sweet May-morning;
And the children are culling
On every side
In a thousand valleys far and wide,
Fresh flowers; while the sun shines warm
And the babe leaps upon his mother's arm:—
I hear, I hear, with joy I hear!
—But there's a tree, of many, one,
A single field which I have look'd upon,
Both of them speak of something that is gone:

The pansy at my feet
Doth the same tale repeat:
Whither is fled the visionary gleam?
Where is it now, the glory and the dream?

Our birth is but a sleep and a forgetting;
The Soul that rises with us, our life's Star,
      Hath had elsewhere its setting
         And cometh from afar;
      Not in entire forgetfulness,
      And not in utter nakedness,
But trailing clouds of glory do we come
         From God, who is our home:
Heaven lies about us in our infancy!
Shades of the prison-house begin to close
         Upon the growing Boy,
But he beholds the light, and whence it flows,
         He sees it in his joy;
The Youth, who daily farther from the east
      Must travel, still is Nature's priest
         And by the vision splendid
         Is on his way attended;
At length the Man perceives it die away,
And fade into the light of common day.

Earth fills her lap with pleasures of her own;
Yearnings she hath in her own natural kind,
And, even with something of a mother's mind,
         And no unworthy aim,
      The homely nurse doth all she can
To make her foster-child, her inmate, Man,
         Forget the glories he hath known,
And that imperial palace whence he came.

Behold the Child among his new-born blisses,
A six years' darling of a pigmy size!
See, where 'mid work of his own hand he lies,
Fretted by sallies of his mother's kisses,
With light upon him from his father's eyes!
See, at his feet, some little plan or chart,
Some fragment from his dream of human life,
Shaped by himself with newly-learnèd art;
      A wedding or a festival,
      A mourning or a funeral;
         And this hath now his heart,
      And unto this he frames his song;
         Then will he fit his tongue

To dialogues of business, love, or strife;
        But it will not be long
        Ere this be thrown aside,
        And with new joy and pride
The little actor cons another part;
Filling from time to time his 'humorous stage'
With all the persons, down to palsied Age,
That Life brings with her in her equipage;
        As if his whole vocation
        Were endless imitation.

Thou, whose exterior semblance doth belie
        Thy soul's immensity;
Thou best philosopher, who yet dost keep
Thy heritage, thou eye among the blind,
That, deaf and silent, read'st the eternal deep,
Haunted forever by the eternal Mind,—
        Mighty Prophet! Seer blest!
        On whom those truths do rest
Which we are toiling all our lives to find
In darkness lost, the darkness of the grave;
Thou, over whom thy Immortality
Broods like the day, a master o'er a slave,
A Presence which is not to be put by;
Thou little child, yet glorious in the might
Of heaven-born freedom on thy being's height,
Why with such earnest pains dost thou provoke
The years to bring the inevitable yoke,
Thus blindly with thy blessedness at strife?
Full soon thy soul shall have her earthly freight,
And custom lie upon thee with a weight
Heavy as frost, and deep almost as life!

        O joy! that in our embers
        Is something that doth live,
        That nature yet remembers
        What was so fugitive!
The thought of our past years in me doth breed
Perpetual benediction: not indeed
For that which is most worthy to be blest,
Delight and liberty, the simple creed
Of Childhood, whether busy or at rest,
With new-fledged hope still fluttering in her breast:—
        Not for these I raise
        The song of thanks and praise;
        But for those obstinate questionings
        Of sense and outward things,
        Fallings from us, vanishings;
        Blank misgivings of a creature

Moving about in worlds not realized,
High instincts, before which our mortal nature
Did tremble like a guilty thing surprised:
    But for those first affections,
    Those shadowy recollections,
      Which, be they what they may,
Are yet the fountain-light of all our day,
Are yet a master-light of all our seeing;
      Uphold us, cherish, and have power to make
Our noisy years seem moments in the being
Of the eternal Silence: truths that wake,
      To perish never;
Which neither listlessness, no mad endeavour,
      Nor man nor boy
Nor all that is at enmity with joy,
Can utterly abolish or destroy!
      Hence in a season of calm weather,
      Though inland far we be,
Our souls have sight of that immortal sea
      Which brought us hither;
      Can in a moment travel thither,
And see the children sport upon the shore,
And hear the mighty waters rolling evermore.

Then sing, ye birds, sing, sing a joyous song!
    And let the young lambs bound
    As to the tabor's sound!
We in thought will join your throng
    Ye that pipe and ye that play,
    Ye that through your hearts today
    Feel the gladness of the May!
What though the radiance which was once so bright
Be now forever taken from my sight,
    Though nothing can bring back the hour
Of splendour in the grass, of glory in the flower;
    We will grieve not, rather find
    Strength in what remains behind;
    In the primal sympathy
    Which having been must ever be;
    In the soothing thoughts that spring
    Out of human suffering;
    In the faith that looks through death,
In years that bring the philosophic mind.

And O, ye Fountains, Meadows, Hills, and Groves,
Forbode not any severing of our loves!
Yet in my heart of hearts I feel your might;
I only have relinquished one delight
To live beneath your more habitual sway:

I love the brooks which down their channels fret
Even more than when I tripped lightly as they;
The innocent brightness of a new-born day
        Is lovely yet;
The clouds that gather round the setting sun
Do take a sober clouring from an eye
That hath kept watch o'er man's mortality;
Another race hath been, and other palms are won.
Thanks to the human heart by which we live
Thanks to its tenderness, its joys, and fears,
To me the meanest flower that blows can give
Thoughts that do often lie too deep for tears.

Bettmann

Sonnet
"The World Is Too Much With Us"

WILLIAM WORDSWORTH
(Born April 7, 1770; died April 23, 1850)

The World is too much with us; late and soon,
Getting and spending, we lay waste our powers;
Little we see in Nature that is ours;
We have given our hearts away, a sordid boon!
This sea that bares her bosom to the moon:
The winds that will be howling at all hours,
And are up-gathered now like sleeping flowers;
For this, for everything, we are out of tune;
It moves us not. —Great God! I'd rather be
A Pagan suckled in a creed outworn,
So might I, standing on this pleasant lea,
Have glimpses that would make me less forlorn;
Have sight of Proteus rising from the sea,
Or hear old Triton blow his wreathèd horn.

Bettmann

Letter to a Young Friend

ROBERT BURNS

(Born January 25, 1759; died July 21, 1796)

I lang hae thought, my youthfu' friend,
  A something to have sent you,
Tho' it should serve nae ither end
  Than just a kind memento:
But how the subject-theme may gang
  Let time and chance determine:
Perhaps it may turn out a sang;
  Perhaps, turn out a sermon.

Ye'll try the world fu' soon, my lad;
  And, Andrew dear, believe me,
Ye'll find mankind an unco squad,
  And muckle they may grieve ye:
For care and troubles set your thought,
  Ev'n when your ends' attained:
And a' your views may come to nought,
  Where every nerve is strainèd.

I'll no say, men are villains a':
  The real, harden'd wicked,
Wha hae nae check but human law,
  Are to a few restricked;
But, och! mankind are unco weak
  An' little to be trusted;
If Self the wavering balance shake,
  It's rarely right adjusted!

Yet they what fa' in Fortune's strife
  Their fate we should na censure;
For still, th' important end of life
  They equally may answer:
A man may hae an honest heart,
  Tho poortith hourly stare him:
A man may tak a neebor's part,
  Yet hae nae cash to spare him.

Ay free, aff han', your story tell,
    When wi' a bosom cronie;
But still keep something to yoursel
    Ye scarcely tell to onie:
Conceal yoursel as weel's ye can
    Frae critical dissection:
But keek thro' every other man
    Wi' sharpen'd, sly inspection.

The sacred lowe o'well-plac'd love,
    Luxuriantly indulge it;
But never tempt th' illicit rove,
    Tho' naething should divulge it:
I waive the quantum o' the sin,
    The hazard of concealing;
But, och! it hardens a' within,
    And petrifies the feeling!

To catch Dame Fortune's golden smile,
    Assiduous wait upon her;
And gather gear by every wile
    That's justify'd by honour:
Not for to hide it in a hedge,
    Nor for a train-attendant;
But for the glorious privilege
    Of being independent.

The fear o' Hell's a hangman's whip
    To haud the wretch in order;
But where ye feel your honour grip
    Let that ay be your border:
Its slightest touches, instant pause—
    Debar a' side-pretences;
And resolutely keep its laws,
    Uncaring consequences.

The great Creator to revere
    Must sure become the creature;
But still the preaching cant forbear
    And ev'n the rigid feature:
Yet ne'er with wits profane to range
    Be complaisance extended;
An atheist-laugh's a poor exchange
    For Deity offended!

When ranting round in Pleasure's ring,
    Religion may be blinded;
Or if she gie a random sting,
    It may be little minded;

But when on Life we're tempest-driv'n—
    A conscience but a canker—
A correspondence fix'd wi' Heav'n
    Is sure a noble anchor!

Adieu, dear, amiable youth!
    Your heart can ne'er be wanting!
May prudence, fortitude, and truth,
    Erect your brow undaunting!
In ploughman phrase, "God send you speed,"
    Still daily to grow wiser;
And may ye better reck the rede,
    Than ever did th' adviser!

The Deacon's Masterpiece
or "The One-Hoss Shay"

OLIVER WENDELL HOLMES
(Born August 29, 1809; died October 7, 1894)

Bettmann

Have you heard of the wonderful one-hoss shay,
That was built in such a logical way
It ran a hundred years to a day,
And then, of a sudden, it—ah, but stay,
I'll tell you what happened without delay,
Scaring the parson into fits,
Frightening people out of their wits,—
Have you heard of that, I say?

Seventeen hundred and fifty-five.
Georgius Secundus was then alive,—
Snuffy old drone from the German hive.
That was the year when Lisbon-town
Saw the earth open and gulp her down,
And Braddock's army was done so brown,
Left without a scalp to its crown.
It was on the terrible Earthquake-day
That the Deacon finished the one-hoss shay.

Now in building of chaises, I tell you what,
There is always *somewhere* a weakest spot,—
In hub, tire, felloe, in spring or thill,
In panel, or crossbar, or floor, or sill,
In screw, bolt, thoroughbrace,—lurking still,
Find it somewhere you must and will,—
Above or below, or within or without,—
And that's the reason, beyond a doubt,
A chaise *breaks down,* but doesn't *wear out.*

But the Deacon swore (as Deacons do,
With an "I dew vum," or an "I tell yeou")
He would build one shay to beat the taown
'N the keounty 'n' all the kentry raoun':
It should be so built that it *couldn'* break daown:
   "Fur," said the Deacon, " 't's mighty plain
Thut the weakes' places mus' stan' the strain;
'N' the way t' fix it, uz I maintain,
                              Is only jest
T' make that place uz strong uz the rest."

So the Deacon inquired of the village folk
Where he could find the strongest oak,
That couldn't be split nor bent nor broke,—
That was for spokes and floor and sills;
He sent for lancewood to make the thills;
The crossbars were ash, from the straightest trees;
The panels of white-wood, that cuts like cheese,
But lasts like iron for things like these;
The hubs of logs from the "Settler's ellum,"—
Last of its timber,—they couldn't sell 'em,
Never an axe has seen their chips,
And the wedges flew from between their lips,
Their blunt ends frizzled like celery-tips;
Step and prop-iron, bolt and screw,
Spring, tire, axle, and linchpin too,
Steel of the finest, bright and blue;
Thoroughbrace bison-skin, thick and wide;
Boot, top, dasher, from tough old hide
Found in the pit when the tanner died.
That was the way he "put her through."—
"There!" said the Deacon, "naow she'll dew!"

Do! I tell you, I rather guess
She was a wonder, and nothing less!
Colts grew horses, beards turned gray,
Deacon and deaconess dropped away,
Children and grandchildren—where were they?
But there stood the stout old one-hoss shay
As fresh as on Lisbon-earthquake-day!

EIGHTEEN HUNDRED;—it came and found
The Deacon's masterpiece strong and sound.
Eighteen hundred increased by ten;—
"Hahnsum kerridge" they called it then.
Eighteen hundred and twenty came;—
Running as usual; much, the same.
Thirty and forty at last arrive,
And then come fifty, and FIFTY-FIVE.

Little of all we value here
Wakes on the morn of its hundredth year
Without both feeling and looking queer.
In fact, there's nothing that keeps its youth,
So far as I know, but a tree and truth.
(This is a moral that runs at large;
Take it. You're welcome. No extra charge.)
FIRST OF NOVEMBER,—the Earthquake-day.—
There are traces of age in the one-hoss shay,
A general flavor of mild decay,
But nothing local as one may say.
There couldn't be,—for the Deacon's art
Had made it so like in every part
That there wasn't a chance for one to start.
For the wheels were just as strong as the thills,
And the floor was just as strong as the sills,
And the panels just as strong as the floor,
And the whippletree neither less nor more,
And the back-crossbar as strong as the fore,
And spring and axle and hub *encore*.
And yet, *as a whole*, it is past a doubt
In another hour it will be *worn out!*

First of November, 'Fifty-five!
This morning the parson takes a drive.
Now, small boys, get out of the way!
Here comes the wonderful one-hoss shay,
Drawn by a rat-tailed, ewe-necked bay.
"Huddup!" said the parson. Off went they.
The parson was working his Sunday's text,—
Had got to *fifthly,* and stopped perplexed
At what the—Moses—was coming next.
All at once the horse stood still,
Close by the meet'n'-house on the hill.
—First a shiver, and then a thrill,
Then something decidedly like a spill,—
And the parson was sitting up on a rock,
At half-past nine by the meet'n'-house clock,—
Just the hour of the Earthquake shock!
—What do you think the parson found,

When he got up and stared around?
The poor old chaise in a heap or mound,
As if it had been to the mill and ground!
You see, of course, if you're not a dunce,
How it went to pieces all at once,—
All at once, and nothing first,—
Just as bubbles do when they burst.

End of the wonderful one-hoss shay,
Logic is logic. That's all I say.

The Building of the Ship

HENRY WADSWORTH LONGFELLOW
(*Born February 27, 1807; died March 24, 1882*)

Bettmann

Then the Master,
With a gesture of command,
Waved his hand;
And at the word,
Loud and sudden there was heard,
All around them and below,
The sound of hammers, blow on blow,
Knocking away the shores and spurs.
And see! she stirs:
She starts—she moves—she seems to feel
The thrill of life along her keel,
And, spurning with her foot the ground,
With one exulting, joyous bound,
She leaps into the ocean's arms!

And lo! from the assembled crowd
There rose a shout, prolonged and loud,
That to the ocean seemed to say,
"Take her, O bridegroom, old and gray,
Take her to thy protecting arms,
With all her youth and all her charms!"

How beautiful she is! How fair
She lies within those arms, that press
Her form with many a soft caress
Of tenderness and watchful care!
Sail forth into the sea, O ship!
Through wind and wave, right onward steer.
The moistened eye, the trembling lip,
And not the signs of doubt or fear.

Sail forth into the sea of life,
O gentle, loving, trusting wife,
And safe from all adversity
Upon the bosom of that sea
Thy comings and thy goings be!
For gentleness and love and trust
Prevail o'er angry wave and gust;
And in the wreck of noble lives
Something immortal still survives!

Thou, too, sail on, O ship of State!
Sail on, O Union, strong and great!
Humanity with all its fears,
With all the hopes of future years,
Is hanging breathless on thy fate!
We know what Master laid thy keel,
What Workman wrought thy ribs of steel,
Who made each mast, and sail, and rope,
What anvils rang, what hammers beat,
In what a forge and what a heat,
Were shaped the anchors of thy hope!
Fear not each sudden sound and shock,
'Tis of the wave and not the rock;
'Tis but the flapping of the sail,
And not a rent made by the gale.
In spite of rock and tempest's roar,
In spite of false lights on the shore,
Sail on, nor fear to breast the sea!
Our hearts, our hopes, are all with thee,
Our hearts, our hopes, our prayers, our tears,
Our faith triumphant o'er our fears,
Are all with thee—are all with thee!

Bettmann

Solitude

ELLA WHEELER WILCOX

(Born November 5, 1855; died October 30, 1919)

Laugh, and the world laughs with you;
    Weep, and you weep alone.
For the sad old earth must borrow its mirth,
    But has trouble enough of its own.
Sing, and the hills will answer;
    Sigh, it is lost on the air.
The echoes bound to a joyful sound,
    But shrink from voicing care.

Rejoice, and men will seek you;
    Grieve, and they turn and go.
They want full measure of all your pleasure,
    But they do not need your woe.
Be glad, and your friends are many;
    Be sad, and you lose them all.
There are none to decline your nectared wine,
    But alone you must drink life's gall.

Feast, and your halls are crowded;
    Fast, and the world goes by.
Succeed and give, and it helps you live,
    But no man can help you die.
There is room in the halls of pleasure
    For a long and lordly train,
But one by one we must all file on
    Through the narrow aisles of pain.

Reprinted from *Poems of Passion* by Ella
Wheeler Wilcox. By special permission
W. B. Conkey Company, Hammond, Ind.

Knee-Deep in June

JAMES WHITCOMB RILEY

"On an early day in a memorable October, Reuben
A. Riley and his wife, Elizabeth Marine Riley, re-
joiced over the birth of their second son. They called
him James Whitcomb ————"
 From *The Complete Works of James Whitcomb
Riley.* Bobbs-Merrill Company (in 6 volumes).
Mr. Riley always replied when asked the direct
question as to his age, "I am this side of forty."
October 7, 1853, is the generally accepted date of his
birth.

(Died July 22, 1916)

Tell you what I like the best—
 'Long about knee-deep in June,
'Bout the time strawberries melts
 On the vine,—some afternoon
Like to jes' git out and rest,
 And not work at nothin' else!

Orchard's where I'd ruther be—
Needn't fence it in for me!—
 Jes' the whole sky overhead,
And the whole airth underneath—
Sorto' so's a man kin breathe
 Like he ort, and kindo' has
Elbow room to keerlessly
 Sprawl out len'thways on the grass
 Where the shadders thick and soft
As the kivvers on the bed
 Mother fixes in the loft
Allus, when they's company!

Jes' a-sorto' lazin' there—
 S'lazy, 'at you peek and peer
 Through the wavin' leaves above,
 Like a feller 'at's in love
And don't know it, ner don't keer!
Ever'thing you hear and see
 Got some sorto' interest—
 Maybe find a bluebird's nest
 Tucked up there conveenently
 Fer the boy 'at's ap' to be
 Up some other apple-tree!
Watch the swallers skootin' past
'Bout as peert as you could ast;
 Er the Bob-white raise and whiz
 Where some other's whistle is.

73

Ketch a shadder down below,
And look up to find the crow—
Er a hawk—away up there,
'Peerantly froze in the air!—
    Hear the old hen squawk, and squat
    Over ever' chick she's got,
Suddent-like—and she knows where
    That-air hawk is, well as you!—
You jes' bet yer life she do!—
    Eyes a-glitterin' like glass,
    Waitin' till he makes a pass!

Pee-wees' singin', to express
    My opinion, 's second class,
Yit you'll hear 'em more er less;
    Sapsucks gittin' down to biz,
Weedin' out the lonesomeness;
    Mr. Bluejay, full o' sass,
    In them base-ball clothes o' his,
Sportin' round the orchard jes'
Like he owned the premises!
    Sun out in the fields kin sizz,
But flat on yer back, I guess,
    In the shade 's where glory is!
That's jes' what I'd like to do
Stiddy fer a year er two!

Plague! ef they ain't somepin' in
Work 'at kindo' goes ag'in
    My convictions!—'long about
    Here in June especially!—
    Under some old apple-tree,
    Jes' a-restin' through and through,
I could git along without
    Nothin' else at all to do
    Only jes' a-wishin' you
Wuz a-gittin' there like me,
And June was eternity!

Lay out there and try to see
Jes' how lazy you kin be!—
    Tumble round and souse yer head
    In the clover-bloom, er pull
    Yer straw hat acrost yer eyes
    And peek through it at the skies,
Thinkin' of old chums 'at's dead;
    Maybe smilin' back at you
    I' betwixt the beautiful
    Clouds o' gold and white and blue!—
Month a man kin railly love—
June, you know, I'm talkin' of!

March ain't never nothin' new!—
Aprile's altogether too
  Brash fer me! and May—I jes'
  'Bominate its promises,—
Little hints o' sunshine and
Green around the timber-land—
  A few promises, and a few
  Chip-birds, and a sprout er two,—
    Drap asleep, and it turns in
    'Fore daylight and snows ag'in!—

But when June comes—Clear my throat
  With wild honey!—Rench my hair
In the dew! and hold my coat!
    Whoop out loud! and throw my hat!—
June wants me, and I'm to spare!
Spread them shadders anywhere,
I'll git down and waller there,
    And obleeged to you at that!

From *Afterwhiles*, by James Whitcomb Riley.
Copyright 1898. Used by special permission of
the publishers, The Bobbs-Merrill Company.

Bettmann

Opportunity

JOHN JAMES INGALLS

(Born December 29, 1833; died July 16, 1900)

Master of human destinies am I.
Fame, love, and fortune on my footsteps wait,
Cities and fields I walk; I penetrate
Deserts and seas remote, and, passing by
Hovel, and mart, and palace, soon or late
I knock unbidden, once at every gate!
If sleeping, wake—if feasting, rise before
I turn away. It is the hour of fate,
And they who follow me reach every state
Mortals desire, and conquer every foe
Save death; but those who doubt or hesitate,
Condemned to failure, penury and woe,
Seek me in vain and uselessly implore—
I answer not. and I return no more.

Bettmann

Waiting

JOHN BURROUGHS
(Born April 3, 1837; died March 29, 1921)

Serene, I fold my hands and wait,
    Nor care for wind nor tide nor sea;
I rave no more 'gainst time or fate,
    For lo! my own shall come to me.

I stay my haste, I make delays—
    For what avails this eager pace?
I stand amid the eternal ways
    And what is mine shall know my face.

Asleep, awake, by night or day,
    The friends I seek are seeking me,
No wind can drive my bark astray
    Nor change the tide of destiny.

What matter if I stand alone?
    I wait with joy the coming years;
My heart shall reap where it has sown,
    And garner up its fruit of tears.

The waters know their own, and draw
    The brook that springs in yonder height;
So flows the good with equal law
    Unto the soul of pure delight.

The stars come nightly to the sky;
    The tidal wave unto the sea;
Nor time, nor space, nor deep, nor high,
    Can keep my own away from me.

Bettmann

Paul Revere's Ride

HENRY WADSWORTH LONGFELLOW
(Born February 27, 1807; died March 24, 1882)

Listen, my children, and you shall hear
Of the midnight ride of Paul Revere,
On the eighteenth of April, in Seventy-five;
Hardly a man is now alive
Who remembers that famous day and year.

He said to his friend, "If the British march
By land or sea from the town to-night,
Hang a lantern aloft in the belfry arch
Of the North Church tower as a signal light,—
One if by land, and two if by sea;
And I on the opposite shore will be,
Ready to ride and spread the alarm
Through every Middlesex village and farm,
For the country folk to be up and to arm."

Then he said "Good-night!" and with muffled oar
Silently rowed to the Charlestown shore,
Just as the moon rose over the bay,
Where swinging wide at her moorings lay
The *Somerset*, British man-of-war;
A phantom ship, with each mast and spar
Across the moon like a prison bar,
And a huge black hulk, that was magnified
By its own reflection in the tide.

Meanwhile, his friend through alley and street
Wanders and watches, with eager ears,
Till in the silence around him he hears
The muster of men at the barrack door,
The sound of arms, and the tramp of feet,
And the measured tread of the grenadiers,
Marching down to their boats on the shore.

Then he climbed the tower of the Old North Church,
By the wooden stairs, with stealthy tread,
To the belfry chamber overhead,
And startled the pigeons from their perch
On the sombre rafters, that round him made
Masses and moving shapes of shade,—
By the trembling ladder, steep and tall,
To the highest window in the wall,
Where he paused to listen and look down
A moment on the roofs of the town
And the moonlight flowing over all.

Beneath, in the churchyard, lay the dead,
In their night encampment on the hill,
Wrapped in silence so deep and still
That he could hear, like a sentinel's tread,
The watchful night-wind, as it went
Creeping along from tent to tent,
And seeming to whisper, "All is well!"
A moment only he feels the spell
Of the place and the hour, and the secret dread
Of the lonely belfry and the dead;
For suddenly all his thoughts are bent
On a shadowy something far away,
Where the river widens to meet the bay,—
A line of black that bends and floats
On the rising tide like a bridge of boats.

Meanwhile, impatient to mount and ride,
Booted and spurred, with a heavy stride
On the opposite shore walked Paul Revere
Now he patted his horse's side,
Now he gazed at the landscape far and near,
Then, impetuous, stamped the earth,
And turned and tightened his saddle girth;
But mostly he watched with eager search
The belfry tower of the Old North Church,
As it rose above the graves on the hill,
Lonely and spectral and sombre and still.
And lo! as he looks, on the belfry's height
A glimmer, and then a gleam of light!
He springs to the saddle, the bridle he turns,
But lingers and gazes, till full on his sight
A second lamp in the belfry burns.

A hurry of hoofs in a village street,
A shape in the moonlight, a bulk in the dark,
And beneath, from the pebbles, in passing, a spark

Struck out by a steed flying fearless and fleet;
That was all! And yet, through the gloom and the light,
The fate of a nation was riding that night;
And the spark struck out by that steed, in his flight,
Kindled the land into flame with its heat.
He has left the village and mounted the steep,
And beneath him, tranquil and broad and deep,
Is the Mystic, meeting the ocean tides;
And under the alders that skirt its edge,
Now soft on the sand, now loud on the ledge,
Is heard the tramp of his steed as he rides.

It was twelve by the village clock
When he crossed the bridge into Medford town.
He heard the crowing of the cock,
And the barking of the farmer's dog,
And felt the damp of the river fog,
That rises after the sun goes down.

It was one by the village clock,
When he galloped into Lexington.
He saw the gilded weathercock
Swim in the moonlight as he passed,
And the meeting-house windows, black and bare,
Gaze at him with a spectral glare,
As if they already stood aghast
At the bloody work they would look upon.

It was two by the village clock,
When he came to the bridge in Concord town.
He heard the bleating of the flock,
And the twitter of birds among the trees,
And felt the breath of the morning breeze
Blowing over the meadow brown.
And one was safe and asleep in his bed
Who at the bridge would be first to fall,
Who that day would be lying dead,
Pierced by a British musket ball.

You know the rest. In the books you have read
How the British Regulars fired and fled,—
How the farmers gave them ball for ball,
From behind each fence and farmyard wall,
Chasing the redcoats down the lane,
Then crossing the fields to emerge again
Under the trees at the turn of the road,
And only pausing to fire and load.

So through the night rode Paul Revere;
And so through the night went his cry of alarm
To every Middlesex village and farm,—
A cry of defiance, and not of fear,
A voice in the darkness, a knock at the door,
And a word that shall echo for evermore!
For, borne on the night-wind of the Past,
Through all our history, to the last,
In the hour of darkness and peril and need,
The people will waken and listen to hear
The hurrying hoof-beats of that steed,
And the midnight message of Paul Revere.

Bettmann

That Time of Year

WILLIAM SHAKESPEARE

(Born April 23 [?], 1564; died April 23, 1616)

That time of year thou may'st in me behold
    When yellow leaves, or none, or few, do hang
Upon those boughs which shake against the cold,
    Bare ruin'd choirs, where late the sweet birds sang:

In me thou see'st the twilight of such day
    As after sunset fadeth in the west,
Which by and by black night doth take away,
    Death's second self, that seals up all in rest:

In me thou see'st the glowing of such fire
    That on the ashes of his youth doth lie,
As the death-bed whereon it must expire,
    Consum'd with that which it was nourish'd by:

—This thou perceiv'st, which makes thy love more
        strong,
To love that well which thou must leave ere long.

Bettmann

Plant a Tree

LUCY LARCOM

(Born March 5, 1824 [?]; died April 27, 1893)

He who plants a tree
   Plants a hope.
   Rootlets up through fibres blindly grope;
Leaves unfold into horizons free.
   So man's life must climb
   From the clods of time
   Unto heavens sublime.
Canst thou prophesy, thou little tree,
What the glory of thy boughs shall be?

He who plants a tree
   Plants a joy;
   Plants a comfort that will never cloy;
Every day a fresh reality,
   Beautiful and strong,
   To whose shelter throng
   Creatures blithe with song.
If thou couldst but know, thou happy tree,
Of the bliss that shall inhabit thee!

He who plants a tree,—
   He plants peace.
   Under its green curtains jargons cease.
Leaf and zephyr murmur soothingly;
   Shadows soft with sleep
   Down tired eyelids creep,
   Balm of slumber deep.
Never hast thou dreamed, thou blessed tree,
Of the benediction thou shalt be.

He who plants a tree,—
   He plants youth;
   Vigor won for centuries in sooth;
Life of time, that hints eternity!

Boughs their strength uprear:
New shoots, every year,
On old growths appear;
Thou shalt teach the ages, sturdy tree,
Youth of soul is immortality.

He who plants a tree,—
He plants love,
Tents of coolness spreading out above
Wayfarers he may not live to see.
Gifts that grow are best;
Hands that bless are blest;
Plant! life does the rest!
Heaven and earth help him who plants a tree,
And his work its own reward shall be.

Bettmann

Abou Ben Adhem

JAMES HENRY LEIGH HUNT

(Born October 19, 1784; died August 28, 1859)

Abou Ben Adhem (may his tribe increase!)
Awoke one night from a deep dream of peace,
And saw, within the moonlight in his room,
    Making it rich, and like a lily in bloom,
An Angel writing in a book of gold:
Exceeding peace had made Ben Adhem bold,
And to the Presence in the room he said,
"What writest thou?" The Vision raised its head,
And with a look made of all sweet accord
Answered, "The names of those who love the Lord."
"And is mine one?" said Abou. "Nay, not so,"
Replied the Angel. Abou spoke more low,
But cheerly still; and said, "I pray thee, then,
Write me as one that loves his fellow-men."

The Angel wrote, and vanished. The next night
It came again with a great wakening light,
And showed the names whom love of God had blessed,
And, lo! Ben Adhem's name led all the rest!

Bettmann

The Bells

 EDGAR ALLEN POE

(Born January 19, 1809; died October 7, 1849)

Hear the sledges with the bells—
Silver bells!
What a world of merriment their melody foretells!
How they tinkle, tinkle, tinkle,
In the icy air of night!
While the stars that oversprinkle
All the heavens, seem to twinkle
With a crystalline delight;
Keeping time, time, time,
In a sort of Runic rhyme,
To the tintinnabulation that so musically wells
From the bells, bells, bells, bells,
Bells, bells, bells,—
From the jingling and the tinkling of the bells.

Hear the mellow wedding bells,
Golden bells!
What a world of happiness their harmony foretells!
Through the balmy air of night
How they ring out their delight!
From the molten-golden notes,
And all in tune,
What a liquid ditty floats
To the turtle dove that listens, while she gloats
On the moon!
Oh, from out the sounding cells,
What a gush of euphony voluminously wells!
How it swells!
How it dwells
On the Future! how it tells
Of the rapture that impels
To the swinging and the ringing
Of the bells, bells, bells,
Of the bells, bells, bells, bells,
Bells, bells, bells,—
To the rhyming and the chiming of the bells!

Hear the loud alarum bells—
Brazen bells!
What a tale of terror now their turbulency tells!
In the startled ear of night
How they scream out their affright!
Too much horrified to speak
They can only shriek, shriek,
Out of tune,
In a clamorous appealing to the mercy of the fire,
In a mad expostulation with the deaf and frantic fire,
Leaping higher, higher, higher,
With a desperate desire,
And a resolute endeavor,
Now—now to sit or never,
By the side of the pale-faced moon.
Oh, the bells, bells, bells!
What a tale their terror tells
Of despair!
How they clang, and clash, and roar!
What a horror they outpour
On the bosom of the palpitating air!
Yet the ear it fully knows,
By the twanging,
And the clanging,
How the danger ebbs and flows;
Yet the ear distinctly tells,
In the jangling,
And the wrangling,
How the danger sink and swells,
By the sinking or the swelling in the anger of the bells—
Of the bells—
Of the bells, bells, bells, bells,
Bells, bells, bells,—
In the clamor and the clangor of the bells!

Hear the tolling of the bells—
Iron bells!
What a world of solemn thought their monody compels!
In the silence of the night,
How we shiver with affright
At the melancholy menace of their tone!
For every sound that floats
From the rust within their throats
Is a groan.
And the people—ah, the people—
They that dwell up in the steeple,
All alone,
And who tolling, tolling, tolling,
In that muffled monotone,

Feel a glory in so rolling
  On the human heart a stone—
They are neither man nor woman—
They are neither brute nor human—
  They are Ghouls:
And their king it is who tolls;
And he rolls, rolls, rolls,
        Rolls
  A paean from the bells!
And his merry bosom swells
  With the paean of the bells!
And he dances, and he yells;
Keeping time, time, time,
In a sort of Runic rhyme,
  To the paean of the bells—
      Of the bells:
  Keeping time, time, time,
In a sort of Runic rhyme,
  To the throbbing of the bells—
      Of the bells, bells, bells—
  To the sobbing of the bells;
Keeping time, time, time,
        As he knells, knells, knells,
In a happy Runic rhyme,
        To the rolling of the bells—
    Of the bells, bells, bells—
        To the tolling of the bells,
    Of the bells, bells, bells, bells—
        Bells, bells, bells—
To the moaning and the groaning of the bells!

Bettmann

From the picture by John G. Eccardt in the National Portrait Gallery Courtesy *The Academy*

Elegy Written in a Country Church Yar

THOMAS GRAY

(Born December 26, 1716; died July 30, 1771)

The curfew tolls the knell of parting day,
    The lowing herd winds slowly o'er the lea,
The ploughman homeward plods his weary way,
    And leaves the world to darkness and to me.

Now fades the glimmering landscape on the sight,
    And all the air a solemn stillness holds,
Save where the beetle wheels his droning flight,
    And drowsy tinklings lull the distant folds;

Save that, from yonder ivy-mantled tower,
    The moping owl does to the moon complain
Of such as, wandering near her secret bower,
    Molest her ancient, solitary reign.

Beneath those rugged elms, that yew-tree's shade,
    Where heaves the turf in many a mould'ring heap,
Each in his narrow cell forever laid,
    The rude forefathers of the hamlet sleep.

The breezy call of incense-breathing morn,
    The swallow twittering from the straw-built shed,
The cock's shrill clarion, or the echoing horn,
    No more shall rouse them from their lowly bed.

For them no more the blazing hearth shall burn,
    Or busy housewife ply her evening care;
No children run to lisp their sire's return,
    Or climb his knees the envied kiss to share.

Oft did the harvest to their sickle yield,
    Their furrow oft the stubborn glebe has broke;
How jocund did they drive their team afield!
    How bowed the woods beneath their sturdy stroke!

Let not ambition mock their useful toil,
    Their homely joys, and destiny obscure;
Nor grandeur hear with a disdainful smile
    The short and simple annals of the poor.

The boast of heraldry, the pomp of power,
    And all that beauty, all that wealth e'er gave
Awaits alike the inevitable hour:
    The paths of glory lead but to the grave.

Nor you, ye proud, impute to these the fault,
    If memory o'er their tomb no trophies raise
Where through the long-drawn aisle and fretted vault
    The pealing anthem swells the note of praise.

Can storied urn or animated bust
    Back to its mansion call the fleeting breath?
Can Honor's voice provoke the silent dust
    Or Flattery soothe the dull cold ear of Death?

Perhaps in this neglected spot is laid
    Some heart once pregnant with celestial fire:
Hands that the rod of empire might have swayed,
    Or wak'd to ecstasy the living lyre;

But Knowledge to their eyes her ample page,
    Rich with the spoils of time, did ne'er unroll;
Chill Penury repressed their noble rage,
    And froze the genial current of the soul.

Full many a gem of purest ray serene
    The dark, unfathomed caves of ocean bear:
Full many a flower is born to blush unseen,
    And waste its sweetness on the desert air.

Some village Hampden, that, with dauntless breast,
    The little tyrant of his fields withstood,
Some mute, inglorious Milton, here may rest;
    Some Cromwell guiltless of his country's blood.

The applause of list'ning senates to command,
    The threats of pain and ruin to despise,
To scatter plenty o'er a smiling land,
    And read their history in a nation's eyes,

Their lot forbade; nor circumscribed alone
    Their growing virtues, but their crimes confined;
Forbade to wade thro' slaughter to a throne,
    And shut the gates of mercy on mankind;

The struggling pangs of conscious truth to hide,
    To quench the blushes of ingenuous shame,
Or heap the shrine of Luxury and Pride
    With incense kindled at the Muse's flame.

Far from the madding crowd's ignoble strife,
    Their sober wishes never learned to stray;
Along the cool sequestered vale of life
    They kept the noiseless tenor of their way.

Yet even these bones from insult to protect,
    Some frail memorial still erected nigh,
With uncouth rhymes and shapeless sculpture decked,
    Implores the passing tribute of a sigh.

Their names, their years, spelt by the unlettered Muse,
    The place of fame and elegy supply:
And many a holy text around she strews
    That teach the rustic moralist to die.

For who, to dumb forgetfulness a prey,
    This pleasing anxious being e'er resigned,
Left the warm precincts of the cheerful day,
    Nor cast one longing, lingering look behind?

On some fond breast the parting soul relies,
    Some pious drops the closing eye requires;
Ev'n from the tomb the voice of Nature cries,
    Ev'n in our ashes live their wonted fires.

For thee who, mindful of the unhonor'd dead,
    Dost in these lines their artless tale relate;
If chance, by lonely contemplation led,
    Some kindred spirit shall inquire thy fate,—

Haply some hoary-headed swain may say:
    "Oft have we seen him, at the peep of dawn,
Brushing with hasty steps the dews away,
    To meet the sun upon the upland lawn.

"There at the foot of yonder nodding beech,
    That wreathes its old fantastic roots so high,
His listless length at noontide would he stretch,
    And pore upon the brook that babbles by.

"Hard by yon wood, now smiling as in scorn,
    Mutt'ring his wayward fancies, he would rove;
Now drooping, woeful-wan, like one forlorn,
    Or craz'd with care, or cross'd in hopeless love.

"One morn I missed him on the custom'd hill,
 Along the heath, and near his favorite tree;
Another came,—nor yet beside the rill,
 Nor up the lawn, nor at the wood was he:

"The next, with dirges due, in sad array,
 Slowly through the church-way path we saw him borne;—
Approach and read (for thou canst read) the lay
 Grav'd on the stone beneath yon aged thorn."

THE EPITAPH

Here rest his head upon the lap of earth,
 A youth to fortune and to fame unknown;
Fair Science frown'd not on his humble birth,
 And Melancholy mark'd him for her own.

Large was his bounty, and his soul sincere;
 Heaven did a recompense as largely send:
He gave to misery all he had, a tear;
 He gained from heaven ('twas all he wished) a friend.

No farther seek his merits to disclose,
 Or draw his frailties from their dread abode,—
(There they alike in trembling hope repose),
 The bosom of his Father and his God.

Cuddle Doon

ALEXANDER ANDERSON

(Born April 30, 1845; died July 11, 1909)

The bairnies cuddle doon at nicht
    Wi' muckle fash an' din.
"Oh, try and sleep, ye waukrife rogues;
    Your faither's comin' in."
They never heed a word I speak.
    I try to gie a froon;
But aye I hap them up, an' cry,
    "Oh, bairnies, cuddle doon!"

Wee Jamie wi' the curly heid—
    He aye sleeps next the wa'—
Bangs up an' cries, "I want a piece"—
    The rascal starts them a'.
I rin an' fetch them pieces, drinks—
    They stop awee the soun'—
Then draw the blankets up, an' cry,
    "Noo, weanies, cuddle doon!"

But ere five minutes gang, wee Rab
    Cries oot, frae 'neath the claes,
"Mither, mak' Tam gie ower at ance:
    He's kittlin' wi' his taes."
The mischief's in that Tam for tricks;
    He'd bother half the toon.
But aye I hap them up, an' cry,
    "Oh, bairnies, cuddle doon!"

At length they hear their father's fit;
    An', as he steeks the door,
They turn their faces to the wa',
    While Tam pretends to snore.
"Hae a' the weans been gude?" he asks,
    As he pits aff his shoon.
"The bairnies, John, are in their beds,
    An' lang since cuddled doon."

An' just afore we bed oorsels,
　　We look at oor wee lambs.
Tam has his airm roun' wee Rab's neck,
　　An' Rab his airm roun' Tam's.
I lift wee Jamie up the bed,
　　An, as I straik each croon,
I whisper, till my heart fills up,
　　"Oh, bairnies, cuddle doon!"

The bairnies cuddle doon at nicht
　　Wi' mirth that's dear to me;
But soon the big warl's cark an' care
　　Will quaten doon their glee.
Yet, come what will to ilka ane,
　　May He who rules aboon
Aye whisper, through their pows be bald,
　　"Oh, bairnies, cuddle doon!"

Sonnet
On His Blindness

JOHN MILTON

(Born December 9, 1608; died November 8, 1674)

Bettmann

When I consider how my light is spent
　　Ere half my days, in this dark world and wide,
　　And that one talent, which is death to hide,
Lodged with me useless, though my soul more bent
To serve therewith my Maker, and present
　　My true account, lest He, returning, chide:
　　"Doth God exact day labor, light denied?"
I fondly ask; but Patience, to prevent
　　That murmur, soon replies, "God doth not need
　　Either man's work, or His own gifts; who best
Bear His mild yoke, they serve Him best. His state
Is kingly. Thousands at His bidding speed,
　　And post o'er land and ocean without rest;
They also serve who only stand and wait."

91

Bettmann

Thanatopsis

WILLIAM CULLEN BRYANT

(Born November 3, 1794; died June 12 1878)

To him who, in the love of Nature, holds
Communion with her visible forms, she speaks
A various language: for his gayer hours
She has a voice of gladness, and a smile
And eloquence of beauty; and she glides
Into his darker musings, with a mild
And healing sympathy, that steals away
Their sharpness, ere he is aware. When thoughts
Of the last bitter hour come like a blight
Over thy spirit, and sad images
Of the stern agony, and shroud, and pall,
And breathless darkness, and the narrow house,
Make thee to shudder, and grow sick at heart,—
Go forth under the open sky, and list
To Nature's teachings, while from all around—
Earth and her waters, and the depths of air—
Comes a still voice:—Yet a few days, and thee
The all-beholding sun shall see no more
In all his course; nor yet in the cold ground,
Where thy pale form was laid, with many tears,
Nor in the embrace of ocean, shall exist
Thy image. Earth, that nourished thee, shall claim
Thy growth, to be resolved to earth again;
And, lost each human trace, surrendering up
Thine individual being, shalt thou go
To mix forever with the elements;
To be a brother to the insensible rock,
And to the sluggish clod, which the rude swain
Turns with his share, and treads upon. The oak
Shall send his roots abroad, and pierce thy mold.
Yet not to thine eternal resting place
Shalt thou retire alone—nor couldst thou wish
Couch more magnificent. Thou shalt lie down
With patriarchs of the infant world—with kings,
The powerful of the earth—the wise, the good,

Fair forms, and hoary seers of ages past,
All in one mighty sepulcher. The hills,
Rock-ribbed, and ancient as the sun; the vales
Stretching in pensive quietness between;
The venerable woods; rivers that move
In majesty, and the complaining brooks,
That make the meadows green; and, poured round all
Old ocean's gray and melancholy waste—
Are but the solemn decorations all
Of the great tomb of man! The golden sun,
The planets, all the infinite host of heaven,
Are shining on the sad abodes of death,
Through the still lapse of ages. All that tread
The globe are but a handful to the tribes
That slumber in its bosom. Take the wings
Of morning, pierce the Barcan wilderness,
Or lose thyself in the continuous woods
Where rolls the Oregon and hears no sound
Save his own dashings—yet the dead are there;
And millions in those solitudes, since first
The flight of years began, have laid them down
In their last sleep—the dead reign there alone!
So shalt thou rest, and what if thou withdraw
In silence from the living; and no friend
Take note of thy departure? All that breathe
Will share thy destiny. The gay will laugh
When thou art gone, the solemn brood of care
Plod on, and each one as before shall chase
His favorite phantom; yet all these shall leave
Their mirth and their employments, and shall come
And make their bed with thee. As the long train
Of ages glides away, the sons of men—
The youth in life's green spring, and he who goes
In the full strength of years, matron and maid,
And the sweet babe, and the gray-headed man—
Shall one by one be gathered to thy side,
By those, who in their turn shall follow them.

So live that when thy summons comes to join
The innumerable caravan that moves
To that mysterious realm, where each shall take
His chamber in the silent halls of death,
Thou go not, like the quarry-slave at night,
Scourged to his dungeon, but, sustained and soothed
By an unfaltering trust, approach thy grave
Like one who wraps the drapering of his couch
About him, and lies down to pleasant dreams.

By special permission of
D. Appleton & Company.

Bettmann

The Children's Hour

HENRY WADSWORTH LONGFELLOW
(Born February 27, 1807; died March 24, 1882)

Between the dark and the daylight,
    When the light is beginning to lower,
Comes a pause in the day's occupations
    That is known as the Children's Hour.

I hear in the chamber above me
    The patter of little feet,
The sound of a door that is opened,
    And voices soft and sweet.

From my study I see in the lamplight,
    Descending the broad hall stair,
Grave Alice and laughing Allegra,
    And Edith with golden hair.

A whisper, and then a silence;
    Yet I know by their merry eyes,
They are plotting and planning together
    To take me by surprise.

A sudden rush from the stairway,
    A sudden raid from the hall!
By three doors left unguarded
    They enter my castle wall!

They climb up into my turret,
    O'er the arms and back of my chair;
If I try to escape, they surround me;
    They seem to be everywhere.

They almost devour me with kisses,
    Their arms about me entwine,
Till I think of the Bishop of Bingen
    In his Mouse-Tower on the Rhine.

Do you think, O blue-eyed banditti,
   Because you have scaled the wall,
Such an old mustache as I am
   Is not a match for you all?

I have you fast in my fortress,
   And will not let you depart,
But put you down into the dungeon
   In the round-tower of my heart.

And there will I keep you forever,
   Yes, forever and a day,
Till the wall shall crumble to ruin,
   And moulder in dust away.

Bettmann

Invictus

WILLIAM ERNEST HENLEY
(Born August 23, 1849; died July 12, 1903)

Out of the night that covers me,
   Black as the Pit from pole to pole,
I thank whatever gods may be
   For my unconquerable soul.

In the fell clutch of circumstance
   I have not winced nor cried aloud.
Under the bludgeonings of chance
   My head is bloody, but unbowed.

Beyond this place of wrath and tears
   Looms but the horror of the shade,
And yet the menace of the years
   Finds, and shall find me, unafraid.

It matters not how strait the gate,
   How charged with punishments the scroll,
I am the master of my fate;
   I am the captain of my soul.

Bettmann

Sea Fever

JOHN MASEFIELD

(Born Ledbury, Here-
fordshire, England,
June 1, 1878)

I must go down to the seas again, to the
lonely sea and the sky,
And all I ask is a tall ship and a star to steer
her by;
And the wheel's kick and the wind's song and
the white sail's shaking,
And a grey mist on the sea's face, and a grey
dawn breaking.

I must go down to the seas again, for the call
of the running tide
Is a wild call and a clear call that may not be
denied;
And all I ask is a windy day with the white
clouds flying,
And the flung spray and the blown spume, and
the sea-gulls crying.

I must go down to the seas again, to the
vagrant gypsy life,
To the gull's way and the whale's way, where
the wind's like a whetted knife;
And all I ask is a merry yarn from a laughing
fellow-rover,
And quiet sleep and a sweet dream when the
long trick's over.

Bettmann

Horatius

THOMAS BABINGTON MACAULAY

(Born October 25, 1800; died December 28, 1859)

Lars Posena of Clusium,
　By the nine gods he swore
That the great house of Tarquin
　Should suffer wrong no more.
By the nine gods he swore it,
　And named a trysting day,
And bade his messengers ride forth,
East and west and south and north,
　To summon his array.

East and west and south and north
　The messengers ride fast,
And tower and town and cottage
　Have heard the trumpet's blast.
The horsemen and the footmen
　Are pouring in amain
From many a stately market-place,
　From many a fruitful plain;
　　*　*　*　*
And now hath every city
　Sent up her tale of men;
The foot are fourscore thousand
　The horse are thousands ten.
Before the gates of Sutrium
　Is met the great array,
A proud man was Lars Porsena
　Upon the trysting day.
　　*　*　*　*
But by the yellow Tiber
　Was tumult and affright:
From all the spacious champaign
　To Rome men took their flight.
A mile around the city,
　The throng stopped up the ways;
A fearful sight it was to see
　Through two long nights and days.
　　*　*　*　*

Now, from the rock Tarpeian,
  Could the wan burghers spy
The line of blazing villages
  Red in the midnight sky.
The Fathers of the City,
  They sat all night and day
For every hour some horseman came
  With tidings of dismay.

     *   *   *   *

They held a council standing
  Before the river-gate;
Short time was there, ye well may guess,
  For musing or debate.
Outspake the Consul roundly:
  "The bridge must straight go down;
For since Janiculum is lost
  Naught else can save the town."

Just then a scout came flying,
  All wild with haste and fear:
"To arms! to arms! Sir Consul;
  Lars Porsena is here."
On the low hills to westward
  The Consul fixed his eye,
And saw the swarthy storm of dust
  Rise fast along the sky.

And nearer, fast and nearer,
  Doth the red whirlwind come;
And louder still and still more loud,
From underneath that rolling cloud,
Is heard the trumpet's war-note proud,
  The trampling and the hum.
And plainly and more plainly
  Now through the gloom appears,
Far to left and far to right,
In broken gleams of dark-blue light,
The long array of helmets bright,
  The long array of spears.

     *   *   *   *

But the Consul's brow was sad,
  And the Consul's speech was low,
And darkly looked he at the wall,
  And darkly at the foe:
"Their van will be upon us
  Before the bridge goes down;
And if they once may win the bridge
  What hope to save the town?"

Then outspake brave Horatius.
    The captain of the gate:
"To every man upon this earth
    Death cometh soon or late.
And how can man die better
    Than facing fearful odds
For the ashes of his fathers
    And the temples of his gods?

"Hew down the bridge, Sir Consul,
    With all the speed ye may;
I, with two more to help me,
    Will hold the foe in play,—
In yon strait path a thousand
    May well be stopped by three.
Now who will stand on either hand,
    And keep the bridge with me?"

Then outspake Spurius Lartius,—
    A Ramnian proud was he:
"Lo, I will stand at thy right hand,
    And keep the bridge with thee."
And outspake strong Herminius,—
    Of Titan blood was he:
"I will abide on thy left side,
    And keep the bridge with thee."

"Horatius," quoth the Consul,
    "As thou sayest, so let it be."
And straight against that great array,
    Forth went the dauntless Three.
Now, while the Three were tightening
    Their harness on their backs,
The Consul was the foremost man
    To take in hand an axe;
And Fathers mixed with Commons
    Seized hatchet, bar, and crow,
And smote upon the planks above,
    And loosed the props below.

*   *   *   *

Meanwhile the Tuscan army,
    Right glorious to behold,
Came flashing back the noonday light,
Rank behind rank, like surges bright
    Of a broad sea of gold.
Four hundred trumpets sounded
    A peal of warlike glee,
As that great host, with measured tread,
And spears advanced, and ensigns spread,
Rolled slowly toward the bridge's head,
    Where stood the dauntless Three.

The Three stood calm and silent,
   And looked upon the foes,
And a great shout of laughter
   From all the vanguard rose;
And forth three chiefs came spurring
   Before that mighty mass;
To earth they sprag, their swords they drew,
And lifted high their shields, and flew
   To win the narrow pass.

Aunus, from green Tifernum,
   Lord of the hill of vines;
And Seius, whose eight hundred slaves
   Sicken in Ilva's mines;
And Picus, long to Clusium
   Vassal in peace and war.

Who led to fight his Umbrian powers
From that grey crag where, girt with towers,
The fortress of Nequinum towers
   O'er the pale waves of Nar.

Stout Lartius hurled down Aunus
   Into the stream beneath;
Herminius struck at Seius,
   And clove him to the teeth;
At Picus brave Horatius
   Darted one fiery thrust,
And the proud Umbrian's gilded arms
   Clashed in the bloody dust.

*   *   *   *

But now no sound of laughter
   Was heard amongst the foes.
A wild and wrathful clamor
   From all the vanguard rose.
Six spears' lengths from the entrance
   Halted that mighty mass,
And for a space no man came forth
   To win the narrow pass.

But, hark! the cry is Astur:
   And lo! the ranks divide;
And the great lord of Luna
   Comes with his stately stride.
Upon his ample shoulders
   Clangs loud the fourfold shield,
And in his hand he shakes the brand
   Which none but he can wield.

He smiled on those bold Romans,
    A smile serene and high;
He eyed the flinching Tuscans,
    And scorn was in his eye.
Quoth he, "The she-wolf's litter
    Stand savagely at bay;
But will ye dare to follow,
    If Astur clears the way?"

Then, whirling up his broadsword
    With both hands to the height,
He rushed against Horatius,
    And smote with all his might,
With shield and blade Horatius
    Right deftly turned the blow,
The blow, though turned, came yet to nigh;
It missed his helm, but gashed his thigh.
The Tuscans raised a joyful cry
    To see the red blood flow.

He reeled, and on Herminius
    He leaned one breathing-space,
Then, like a wild-cat mad with wounds,
    Sprang right at Astur's face.
Through teeth and skull and helmet
    So fierce a thrust he sped,
The good sword stood a handbreadth out
    Behind the Tuscan's head.

And the great lord of Luna
    Fell at that deadly stroke,
As falls on Mount Avernus
    A thunder-smitten oak.
Far o'er the crashing forest
    The giant arms lie spread;
And the pale augurs, muttering low,
    Gaze on the blasted head.

On Astur's throat Horatius
    Right firmly pressed his heel,
And thrice and four times tugged amain,
    Ere he wrenched out the steel.
"And see," he cried, "the welcome,
    Fair guests, that waits you here!
What noble Lucumo comes next
    To taste our Roman cheer?"

    *   *   *   *

But meanwhile axe and lever
   Have manfully been plied,
And now the bridge hangs tottering
   Above the boiling tide.
"Come back, come back, Horatius!"
   Loud cried the Fathers all;
"Back, Lartius! back, Herminius!
   Back, ere the ruin fall!"

Back darted Spurius Lartius;
   Herminius darted back;
And, as they passed, beneath their feet
   They felt the timbers crack;
But when they turned their faces,
   And on the further shore
Saw brave Horatius stand alone,
   They would have crossed once more.

But, with a crash like thunder,
   Fell every loosened beam,
And, like a dam, the mighty wreck
   Lay right athwart the stream;
And a long shout of triumph
   Rose from the walls of Rome,
As to the highest turret-tops
   Was splashed the yellow foam.

*   *   *   *

Alone stood brave Horatius,
   But constant still in mind,—
Thrice thirty thousand foes before,
   And the broad flood behind.
"Down with him!" cried false Sextus,
   With a smile on his pale face;
"Now yield thee," cried Lars Porsena,
   "Now yield thee to our grace!"

Round turned he, as not deigning
   Those craven ranks to see;
Naught spake he to Lars Porsena,
   To Sextus naught spake he;
But he saw on Palatinus
   The white porch of his home;
And he spake to the noble river
   That rolls by the towers of Rome:

"O Tiber! Father Tiber!
   To whom the Romans pray
A Roman's life, a Roman's arms,
   Take thou in charge this day!"

So he spake, and, speaking, sheathed
 The good sword by his side,
And, with his harness on his back,
 Plunged headlong in the tide.

No sound of joy or sorrow
 Was heard from either bank,
But friends and foes in dumb surprise,
With parted lips and straining eyes,
 Stood gazing where he sank;
And when above the surges
 They saw his crest appear,
All Rome sent forth a rapturous cry,
And even the ranks of Tuscany
 Could scarce forbear to cheer.

But fiercely ran the current,
 Swollen high by months of rain,
And fast his blood was flowing;
 And he was sore in pain,
And heavy with his armor,
 And spent with changing blows;
And oft they thought him sinking,
 But still again he rose.

   * * * *

And now he feels the bottom;—
 Now on dry earth he stands;
Now round him throng the Fathers
 To press his gory hands.
And, now, with shouts and clapping,
 And noise of weeping loud,
He enters through the River Gate,
 Borne by the joyous crowd.

Each in His Own Tongue

WILLIAM HERBERT CARRUTH

(Born April 5 1859; died December 15, 1924)

A fire-mist and a planet,
    A crystal and a cell,
A jelly-fish and a saurian,
    And caves where the cave-men dwell;
Then a sense of law and beauty
    And a face turned from the clod—
Some call it Evolution,
    And others call it God.

A haze on the far horizon,
    The infinite, tender sky,
The ripe rich tint of the cornfields,
    And the wild geese sailing high—
And all over upland and lowland
    The charm of the golden-rod—
Some of us call it Autumn
    And others call it God.

Like tides on a crescent sea-beach,
    When the moon is new and thin,
Into our hearts high yearnings
    Come welling and surging in—
Come from the mystic ocean,
    Whose rim no foot has trod,—
Some of us call it Longing,
    And others call it God.

A picket frozen on duty,
    A mother starved for her brood,
Socrates drinking the hemlock,
    And Jesus on the rood;
And millions who, humble and nameless,
    The straight, hard pathway plod,—
Some call it Consecration,
    And others call it God.

From *Each in His Own Tongue and Other Poems.* G. P. Putnam's Sons, New York.

Bettmann

The Eternal Goodness

John Greenleaf Whittier

*(Born December 17, 1807; died September
7, 1892)*

O friends! with whom my feet have trod
    The quiet aisles of prayer,
Glad witness to your zeal for God
    And love of man I bear.

I trace your lines of argument;
    Your logic linked and strong
I weigh as one who dreads dissent,
    And fears a doubt as wrong.

But still my human hands are weak
    To hold your iron creeds:
Against the words ye bid me speak
    My heart within me pleads.

Who fathoms the Eternal Thought?
    Who talks of scheme and plan?
The Lord is God! He needeth not
    The poor device of man.

I walk with bare, hushed feet the ground
    Ye tread with boldness shod;
I dare not fix with mete and bound
    The love and power of God.

Ye praise His justice; even such
    His pitying love I deem:
Ye seek a king; I fain would touch
    The robe that hath no seam.

Ye see the curse which overbroods
    A world of pain and loss;
I hear our Lord's beatitudes
    And prayer upon the cross.

More than your schoolmen teach, within
    Myself, alas! I know:
Too dark ye cannot paint the sin,
    Too small the merit show.

I bow my forehead to the dust,
    I veil mine eyes for shame,
And urge, in trembling self-distrust,
    A prayer without a claim.

I see the wrong that round me lies,
    I feel the guilt within;
I hear, with groan travail-cries,
    The world confess its sin.

Yet, in the maddening maze of things,
    And tossed by storm and flood,
To one fixed trust my spirit clings;
    I know that God is good!

Not mine to look where cherubim
    And seraphs may not see,
But nothing can be good in Him
    Which evil is in me.

The wrong that pains my soul below
    I dare not throne above,
I know not of His hate,—I know
    His goodness and His love.

I dimly guess from blessings known
    Of greater out of sight,
And, with the chastened Psalmist, own
    His judgments too are right.

I long for household voices gone,
    For vanished smiles I long,
But God hath led my dear ones on,
    And He can do no wrong.

I know not what the future hath
    Of marvel or surprise,
Assured alone that life and death
    His mercy underlies.

And if my heart and flesh are weak
    To bear an untried pain,
The bruised reed He will not break,
    But strengthen and sustain.

No offering of my own I have,
　Nor works my faith to prove;
I can but give the gifts He gave,
　And plead His love for love.

And so beside the Silent Sea
　I wait the muffled oar;
No harm from Him can come to me
　On ocean or on shore.

I know not where His islands lift
　Their fronded palms in air;
I only know I cannot drift
　Beyond His love and care.

O brothers! if my faith is vain,
　If hopes like these betray,
Pray for me that my feet may gain
　The sure and safer way.

And Thou, O Lord! by whom are seen
　Thy creatures as they be,
Forgive me if too close I lean
　My human heart to Thee!

Bettmann

Summum Bonum

ROBERT BROWNING

(Born May 7, 1812; died December 12, 1889)

All the breath and the bloom of the
　　year in the bag of one bee:
All the wonder and wealth of the mine in
　　the heart of one gem:
In the core of one pearl all the shade and the
　　shine of the sea:
　Breath and bloom, shade and shine,—wonder,
　　wealth, and—how far above them—
　　　Truth, that's brighter than gem,
　　　Trust, that's purer than pearl,—
Brightest truth, purest trust in the universe—
　　all were for me
　　　In the kiss of one girl.

Bettmann

If

RUDYARD KIPLING

(Born December 30, 1865; died January 17, 1936)

If you can keep your head when all about you
  Are losing theirs and blaming it on you;
If you can trust yourself when all men doubt you,
  But make allowance for their doubting too:
If you can wait and not be tired by waiting,
  Or, being lied about, don't deal in lies,
Or being hated don't give way to hating,
  And yet don't look too good, nor talk too wise;

If you can dream—and not make dreams your master;
  If you can think—and not make thoughts your aim,
If you can meet with Triumph and Disaster
  And treat those two impostors just the same:
If you can bear to hear the truth you've spoken
  Twisted by knaves to make a trap for fools,
Or watch the things you gave your life to, broken,
  And stoop and build 'em up with worn-out tools;

If you can make one heap of all your winnings
  And risk it on one turn of pitch-and-toss,
And lose, and start again at your beginnings,
  And never breathe a word about your loss:
If you can force your heart and nerve and sinew
  To serve your turn long after they are gone,
And so hold on when there is nothing in you
  Except the Will which says to them: "Hold on!"

If you can talk with crowds and keep your virtue,
  Or walk with Kings—nor lose the common touch,
If neither foes nor loving friends can hurt you,
  If all men count with you, but none too much:
If you can fill the unforgiving minute
  With sixty seconds' worth of distance run,
Yours is the Earth and everything that's in it,
  And—which is more—you'll be a Man, my son!

Bettmann

The Day Is Done

HENRY WADSWORTH LONGFELLOW

(Born February 27, 1807; died March 24, 1882)

The day is done, and the darkness
  Falls from the wings of Night,
As a feather is wafted downward
  From an eagle in his flight.

I see the lights of the village
  Gleam through the rain and the mist,
And a feeling of sadness comes o'er me
  That my soul cannot resist:

A feeling of sadness and longing,
  That is not akin to pain,
And resembles sorrow only
  As the mist resembles the rain.

Come, read to me some poem,
  Some simple and heartfelt lay,
That shall soothe this restless feeling,
  And banish the thoughts of day.

Not from the grand old masters,
  Not from the bards sublime,
Whose distant footsteps echo
  Through the corridors of Time.

For, like strains of martial music,
  Their mighty thoughts suggest
Life's endless toil and endeavor;
  And tonight I long for rest.

Read from some humbler poet,
  Whose songs gushed from his heart,
As showers from the clouds of summer,
  Or tears from the eyelids start;

Who, through long days of labor,
    And nights devoid of ease,
Still heard in his soul the music
    Of wonderful melodies.

Such songs have power to quiet
    The restless pulse of care,
And come like the benediction
    That follows after prayer.

Then read from the treasured volume
    The poem of thy choice,
And lend to the rhyme of the poet
    The beauty of thy voice.

And the night shall be filled with music
    And the cares, that infest the day,
Shall fold their tents, like the Arabs,
    And as silently steal away.

Bettmann

Love of Country
From "The Lay of the Last
Minstrel"

SIR WALTER SCOTT
*(Born August 15, 1771; died September 21,
1832)*

Breathes there the man with soul so dead
Who never to himself hath said:
    "This is my own, my native land"?
Whose heart hath ne'er within him burned
As home his footsteps he hath turned,
    From wandering on a foreign strand?
If such there breathe, go mark him well;
For him no minstrel raptures swell;
High though his titles, proud his name,
Boundless his wealth as wish can claim;
Despite those titles, power and pelf,
The wretch concentred all in self,
Living, shall forfeit fair renown,
And, doubly dying, shall go down
To the vile dust from whence he sprung,
Unwept, unhonored, and unsung.

Bettmann

Nobility

ALICE CARY

(Born April 26, 1820; died February 12, 1871)

True worth is in *being*, not *seeming*,—
   In doing, each day that goes by,
Some little good—not in dreaming
   Of great things to do by and by.
For whatever men say in their blindness,
   And spite of the fancies of youth,
There's nothing so kingly as kindness,
   And nothing so royal as truth.

We get back our mete as we measure—
   We cannot do wrong and feel right,
Nor can we give pain and gain pleasure,
   For justice avenges each slight.
The air for the wing of the sparrow,
   The bush for the robin and wren,
But always the path that is narrow
   And straight, for the children of men.

'Tis not in the pages of story
   The heart of its ills to beguile,
Though he who makes courtship to glory
   Gives all that he hath for her smile.
For when from her heights he has won her,
   Alas! it is only to prove
That nothing's so sacred as honor,
   And nothing so loyal as love!

We cannot make bargains for blisses,
   Nor catch them like fishes in nets;
And sometimes the thing our life misses
   Helps more than the thing which it gets.
For good lieth not in pursuing,
   Nor gaining of great nor of small,
But just in the doing, and doing
   As we would be done by, is all.

Through envy, through malice, through hating,
   Against the world, early and late,
No jot of our courage abating—
   Our part is to work and to wait.
And slight is the sting of his trouble
   Whose winnings are less than his worth;
For he who is honest is noble,
   Whatever his fortunes or birth.

Bettmann

The Minuet
MARY MAPES DODGE
(Born January 26, 1838; died August 21, 1905)

Grandma told me all about it,
Told me so I couldn't doubt it,
How she danced, my grandma danced; long ago—
How she held her pretty head,
How her dainty skirt she spread,
How she slowly leaned and rose—long ago.

Grandma's hair was bright and sunny,
Dimpled cheeks, too, oh, how funny!
Really quite a pretty girl—long ago.
Bless her! why, she wears a cap,
Grandma does, and takes a nap
Every single day: and yet
Grandma danced the minuet—long ago.

"Modern ways are quite alarming,"
Grandma says, "but boys were charming"
(Girls and boys she means, of course) "long ago."
Brave but modest, grandly shy;
She would like to have us try
Just to feel like those who met
In the graceful minuet—long ago.

From *Along the Way.* Copyright 1879.
Published by Charles Scribner's Sons.

Bettmann

Childe Harold's Farewell to England

GEORGE GORDON BYRON
(Sixth Lord)

(Born January 22, 1788; died April 19, 1824)

Adieu, adieu! my native shore
    Fades o'er the waters blue;
The night-winds sigh, the breakers roar,
    And shrieks the wild sea-mew.
Yon sun that sets upon the sea,
    We follow in his flight;
Farewell awhile to him and thee,
    My native land—Good-night.

A few short hours and he will rise
    To give the morrow birth;
And I shall hail the main and skies,
    But not my mother earth.
Deserted is my own good hall,
    Its hearth is desolate;
Wild weeds are gathering on the wall;
    My dog howls at the gate.

Come hither, hither, my little page!
    Why dost thou weep and wail?
Or dost thou dread the billow's rage,
    Or tremble at the gale?
But dash the tear-drop from thine eye;
    Our ship is swift and strong;
Our fleetest falcon scarce can fly
    More merrily along.

"Let winds be shrill, let waves roll high,
    I fear not wave nor wind:
Yet marvel not, Sir Childe, that I
    Am sorrowful in mind;
For I have from my father gone,
    A mother whom I love,
And have no friends, save these alone,
    But thee—and One above.

"My father blessed me fervently,
  Yet did not much complain;
But sorely will my mother sigh
  Till I come back again."—
Enough, enough, my little lad!
  Such tears become thine eye;
If I thy guileless bosom had,
  Mine own would not be dry.

*   *   *   *

God Save the Flag

OLIVER WENDELL HOLMES

(Born August 29, 1809; died October 7, 1894)

Bettmann

Washed in the blood of the brave and the blooming,
  Snatched from the altars of insolent foes,
Burning with star-fires, but never consuming,
  Flash its broad ribbons of lily and rose.

Vainly the prophets of Baal would rend it,
  Vainly his worshippers pray for its fall;
Thousands have died for it, millions defend it,
  Emblem of justice and mercy to all:

Justice that reddens the sky with her terrors,
  Mercy that comes with her white-handed train,
Soothing all passions, redeeming all errors,
  Sheathing the sabre and breaking the chain.

Borne on the deluge of old usurpations,
  Drifted our Ark o'er the desolate seas,
Bearing the rainbow of hope to the nations,
  Torn from the storm-cloud and flung to the breeze!

God bless the Flag and its loyal defenders,
  While its broad folds o'er the battle-field wave,
Till the dim star-wreath rekindle its splendors,
  Washed from its stains in the blood of the brave!

Bettmann

The Raven

EDGAR ALLEN POE

(Born January 19, 1809; died October 7, 1849)

Once upon a midnight dreary, while I pondered, weak
    and weary,
    Over many a quaint and curious volume of forgotten lore,
While I nodded, nearly napping, suddenly there came a
    tapping,
      As of someone gently rapping, rapping at my chamber
      door.
      " 'Tis some visitor," I muttered, "tapping at my cham-
      ber door;
          Only this, and nothing more."

Ah, distinctly I remember, it was in the bleak December,
    And each separate dying ember wrought its ghost upon
    the floor.
Eagerly I wished the morrow; vainly I had sought to borrow
    From my books surcease of sorrow, sorrow for the lost
    Lenore,
    For the rare and radiant maiden whom the angels name
    Lenore,
          Nameless here forevermore.

And the silken sad uncertain rustling of each purple curtain
    Thrilled me——filled me with fantastic terrors never felt
    before;
So that now, to still the beating of my heart, I stood
    repeating,
    " 'Tis some visitor entreating entrance at my chamber
    door,
    Some late visitor entreating entrance at my chamber door;
        This it is, and nothing more."

Presently my soul grew stronger; hesitating then no longer,
  "Sir," said I, "or madam, truly your forgiveness I implore;
But the fact is, I was napping, and so gently you came
    rapping,
    And so faintly you came tapping, tapping at my cham-
      ber door,
    That I scarce was sure I heard you." Here I opened
      wide the door;—
        Darkness there, and nothing more.

Deep into the darkness peering, long I stood there, won-
    dering, fearing,
    Doubting, dreaming dreams no mortals ever dare to
      dream before;
But the silence was unbroken, and the stillness gave no
    token,
And the only word there spoken was the whispered word,
    "Lenore?"
    This I whispered, and an echo murmured back the word,
      "Lenore!"
        Merely this, and nothing more.

Back into the chamber turning, all my soul within me
    burning,
    Soon again I heard a tapping, something louder than
      before,
"Surely," said I, "surely, that is something at my window
    lattice;
    Let me see, then, what thereat is, and this mystery explore;
    Let my heart be still a moment, and this mystery explore;
      'Tis the wind, and nothing more."

Open here I flung the shutter, when, with many a flirt and
    flutter,
    In there stepped a stately raven, of the saintly days of
      yore.
Not the least obeisance made he; not a minute stopped or
    stayed he;
    But with mien of lord or lady, perched above my cham-
      ber door;
    Perched upon a bust of Pallas, just above my chamber
      door,
        Perched, and sat, and nothing more.

Then this ebony bird beguiling my sad fancy into smiling,
    By the grave and stern decorum of the countenance it
      wore,

"Though thy crest be shorn and shaven, thou," I said, "art
    sure no craven,
    Ghastly, grim, and ancient raven, wandering from the
      nightly shore.
    Tell me what the lordly name is on the Night's Pluton-
      ian shore."
               Quoth the raven, "Nevermore."

Much I marvelled this ungainly fowl to hear discourse so
    plainly,
    Though its answer little meaning, little relevancy bore;
For we cannot help agreeing that no living human being
    Ever yet was blessed with seeing bird above his cham-
      ber door,
    Bird or beast upon the sculptured bust above his cham-
      ber door,
               With such name as "Nevermore."

But the raven, sitting lonely on that placid bust, spoke only
    That one word, as if his soul in that one word he did
      outpour.
Nothing further then he uttered; not a feather then he
    fluttered;
    Till I scarcely more than muttered, "Other friends have
      flown before;
    On the morrow *he* will leave me, as my hopes have flown
      before."
               Then the bird said, "Nevermore."

Startled at the stillness broken by reply so aptly spoken,
    "Doubtless," said I, "what it utters is its only stock and
      store,
Caught from some unhappy master, whom unmerciful
    disaster
    Followed fast and followed faster, till his songs one
      burden bore,—
    Till the dirges of his hope that melancholy burden bore
      Of "Never—nevermore."

But the raven still beguiling all my fancy into smiling,
    Straight I wheeled a cushioned seat in front of bird and
      bust and door;
Then, up on the velvet sinking, I betook myself to linking
    Fancy unto fancy, thinking what this ominous bird of
      yore,
    What this grim, ungainly, ghastly, gaunt, and ominous
      bird of yore
             Meant in croaking, "Nevermore."

Thus I sat engaged in guessing, but no syllable expressing
To the fowl, whose fiery eyes now burned into my
bosom's core;
This and more I sat divining, with my head at ease re-
clining
On the cushion's velvet lining that the lamplight gloated
o'er,
She shall press, ah, nevermore!

Then, methought, the air grew denser, perfumed from an
unseen censer
Swung by seraphim whose footfalls tinkled on the tufted
floor.
"Wretch," I cried, "thy God hath lent thee — by these
angels he hath sent thee
Respite—respite and nepenthe from thy memories of
Lenore!
Quaff, O quaff this kind nepenthe, and forget this lost
Lenore!"
Quoth the raven, "Nevermore!"

"Prophet!" said I, "thing of evil!—prophet still, if bird or
devil!
Whether tempter sent, or whether tempest tossed thee
here ashore,
Desolate, yet all undaunted, on this desert land enchanted—
On this home by horror haunted—tell me truly, I implore:
Is there—*is* there balm in Gilead?—tell me—tell me I im-
plore!"
Quoth the raven, "Nevermore."

"Prophet!" said I, "thing of evil—prophet still, if bird or
devil!
By that heaven that bends above us—by that God we
both adore—
Tell this soul with sorrow laden, if, within the distant
Aidenn,
It shall clasp a sainted maiden, whom the angels name
Lenore—
Clasp a rare and radiant maiden, whom the angels name
Lenore?
Quoth the raven, "Nevermore."

"Be that word our sign of parting, bird or fiend!" I shrieked,
upstarting—
"Get thee back into the tempest and the Night's Pluton-
ian shore!

Leave no black plume as a token of that lie thy soul hath
spoken!
Leave my loneliness unbroken! — quit the bust above
my door!
Take thy beak from out my heart, and take thy form
from off my door!"
Quoth the raven, "Nevermore."

And the raven, never flitting, still is sitting, still is sitting
On the pallid bust of Pallas just above my chamber door;
And his eyes have all the seeming of a demon's that is
dreaming;
And the lamplight o'er him streaming throws the shadow
on the floor;
And my soul from out that shadow that lies floating on
the floor
Shall be lifted—nevermore!

The Highwayman

ALFRED NOYES

(Born September 16, 1880; died June 29, 1958)

PART ONE

The wind was a torrent of darkness among the gusty trees,
The moon was a ghostly galleon tossed upon cloudly seas,
The road was a ribbon of moonlight over the purple moor,
And the highwayman came riding,
Riding, riding,
The highwayman came riding, up to the old inn-door.

He'd a French cocked-hat on his forehead, a bunch of lace
at his chin,
A coat of the claret valvet, and breeches of brown doe-skin;
They fitted with never a wrinkle: his boots were up to the
thigh!
And he rode with a jeweled twinkle,
His pistol butts a-twinkle,
His rapier hilt a-twinkle, under the jeweled sky.

Over the cobbles he clattered and clashed in the dark inn-
yard,
And he tapped with his whip on the shutters, but all was
locked and barred;
He whistled a tune to the window, and who should be
waiting there
But the landlord's black-eyed daughter,
Bess, the landlord's daughter,
Plaiting a dark red love-knot into her long black hair.

And dark in the dark old inn-yard a stable-wicket creaked
Where Tim the ostler listened, his face was white and
peaked;
His eyes were hollows of madness, his hair like mouldy hay,
But he loved the landlord's daughter,
The landlord's red-lipped daughter,
Dumb as a dog he listened, and he heard the robber say:

"One kiss, my bonny sweetheart, I'm after a prize tonight,
But I shall be back with the yellow gold before the morn-
ing light;
Yet, if they press me sharply, and harry me through the day,
Then look for me by moonlight,
Watch for me by moonlight,
I'll come to thee by moonlight, though hell should bar the
way."

He rose upright in the stirrups; he scarce could reach her
hand,
But she loosened her hair i' the casement! His face burnt
like a brand
As the black cascade of perfume came tumbling over his
breast;
And he kissed its waves in the moonlight,
(Oh, sweet black waves in the moonlight!)
Then he tugged at his rein in the moonlight, and galloped
away to the West.

PART TWO

He did not come in the dawning: he did not come at noon;
And out o' the tawny sunset, before the rise o' the moon,
When the road was a gypsy's ribbon, looping the purple
moor,
A red-coat troop came marching,
Marching, marching,
King George's men came marching, up to the old inn-door.

120

They said no word to the landlord, they drank his ale instead,
But they gagged his daughter and bound her to the foot
of her narrow bed;
Two of them knelt at her casement, with muskets at their
side!
> There was death at every window;
> And hell at one dark window;
For Bess could see, through her casement, the road that *he*
would ride.

They had tied her up to attention, with many a sniggering
jest;
They had bound a musket beside her, with the barrel be-
neath her breast!
"Now keep good watch!" and they kissed her.
She heard the dead man say—
> *Look for me by moonlight;*
> *Watch for me by moonlight;*
I'll come to thee by moonlight, though hell should bar the way!

She twisted her hands behind her; but all the knots held
good!
She writhed her hands till her fingers were wet with sweat
or blood!
They stretched and strained in the darkness, and the hours
crawled by like years,
> Till, now, on the stroke of midnight,
> Cold, on the stroke of midnight,
The tip of one finger touched it! The trigger at least was
hers!

The tip of one finger touched it; she strove no more for
the rest!
Up, she stood up to attention, with the barrel beneath her
breast,
She would not risk their hearing! she would not strive
again;
> For the road lay bare in the moonlight,
> Blank and bare in the moonlight;
And the blood of her veins in the moonlight throbbed to
her love's refrain.

Tlot-tlot, tlot-tlot! Had they heard it? The horse-hoofs ringing clear;
Tlot-tlot, tlot-tlot, in the distance? Were they deaf that they
did not hear?
Down the ribbon of moonlight, over the brow of the hill,
> The highwayman came riding,
> Riding, riding!
The red-coats looked to their priming! She stood up,
straight and still!

Tlot-tlot, in the frosty silence! *Tlot-tlot,* in the echoing night!
Nearer he came and nearer! Her face was like a light!
Her eyes grew wide for a moment! she drew one last deep
breath,
Then her finger moved in the moonlight,
Her musket shattered the moonlight,
Shattered her breast in the moonlight and warned him—
with her death.

He turned; he spurred to the West; he did not know she
stood
Bowed, with her head o'er the musket, drenched with her
own red blood!
Not till the dawn he heard it; his face grew grey to hear
How Bess, the landlord's daughter,
The landlord's black-eyed daughter,
Had watched for her love in the moonlight, and died in
the darkness there.

Back, he spurred like a madman, shrieking a curse to the
sky,
With the white road smoking behind him and his rapier
brandished high!
Blood-red were his spurs i' the golden noon; wine-red was
his velvet coat,
When they shot him down on the highway,
Down like a dog on the highway,
And he lay in his blood on the highway, with the bunch
of lace at his throat.

*And still of a winter's night, they say, when the wind is in the
trees,*
When the moon is a ghosly galleon tossed upon cloud seas,
When the road is a ribbon of moonlight over the purple moor,
A highwayman comes riding,
Riding, riding,
A highwayman comes riding, up to the old inn-door.

Over the cobbles he clatters and clangs in the dark inn-yard;
*He taps with his whip on the shutters, but all is locked and
barred;*
*He whistles a tune to the window, and who should be waiting
there*
But the landlord's black-eyed daughter,
Bess, the landlord's daughter,
Plaiting a dark red love-knot into her long black hair.

Bettmann

A Psalm of Life

HENRY WADSWORTH LONGFELLOW

(Born February 27, 1807, died March 24, 1882)

Tell me not, in mournful numbers,
　　Life is but an empty dream!—
For the soul is dead that slumbers
　　And things are not what they seem.

Life is real! Life is earnest!
　　And the grave is not its goal;
Dust thou art, to dust returnest,
　　Was not spoken of the soul.

Not enjoyment, and not sorrow,
　　Is our destined end or way;
But to act, that each tomorrow
　　Find us farther than today.

Art is long, and Time is fleeting,
　　And our hearts, though stout and brave,
Still, like muffled drums, are beating
　　Funeral marches to the grave.

In the world's broad field of battle,
　　In the bivouac of life,
Be not like dumb, driven cattle!
　　Be a hero in the strife!

Trust no Future, howe'er pleasant!
　　Let the dead Past bury its dead!
Act,—act in the living Present!
　　Heart within, and God o'erhead!

Lives of great men all remind us
　　We can make our lives sublime,
And, departing, leave behind us
　　Footprints on the sands of time.

Footprints, that perhaps another,
　　Sailing o'er life's solemn main,
A forlorn and shipwrecked brother,
　　Seeing, shall take heart again.

Let us then be up and doing,
　　With a heart for any fate;
Still achieving, still pursuing,
　　Learn to labor and to wait.

Bettmann

For A' That
and A' That
ROBERT BURNS

(Born January 25, 1759; died July 21, 1796)

Is there for honest poverty
That hings his head, and a' that?
The coward slave, we pass him by;
We dare be poor for a' that!
For a' that, and a' that,
Our toils obscure, and a' that;
The rank is but the guinea stamp—
The man's the gowd for a' that!

What tho' on hamely fare we dine,
Wear hodden gray, and a' that?
Gie fools their silks, and knaves their wine—
A man's a man for a' that!
For a' that, and a' that,
Their tinsel show, and a' that;
The honest man, though e'er sae poor,
Is king o'men, for a' that!

Ye see yon birkie ca'd a lord,
Wha struts, an' stares, an' a' that—
Tho' hundreds worship at his word,
He'd but a coof for a' that;
For a' that, and a' that,
His riband, star, and a' that;
The man of independent mind,
He looks an' laughs at a' that.

A prince can mak a belted knight,
A marquis, duke, and a' that;
But an honest man's aboon his might—
Gude faith, he mauna fa' that!
For a' that, and a' that,
Their dignities, an' a' that;
The pith o' sense, and pride o' worth,
Are higher rank than a' that.

Then let us pray that come it may,—
As come it will for a' that,—
That sense and worth, o'er a' the earth,
May bear the gree, an' a' that.
For a' that, and a' that,
It's comin' yet, for a' that—
That man to man, the warld o'er,
Shall brithers be for a' that.

Bettmann

Jest 'Fore Christmas
EUGENE FIELD
(Born September 3, 1850; died November 4, 1895)

Father calls me William, sister call me Will,
Mother calls me Willie, but the fellers call me Bill!
Mighty glad I ain't a girl—ruther be a boy,
Without them sashes, curls, an' things that's worn by
    Fauntleroy!
Love to chawnk green apples an' go swimmin' in the lake—
Hate to take the castor-ile they give for belly-ache!
Most all the time, the whole year round, there ain't no
    flies on me,
But jest 'fore Christmas I'm as good as I kin be!

Got a yeller dog named Sport, sick him on the cat;
First thing she knows she doesn't know where she is at!
Got a clipper sled, an' when us kids goes out to slide,
'Long comes the grocery cart, an' we all hook a ride!
But sometimes when the grocery man is worrited an' cross,
He reaches at us with his whip, an' larrups up his hoss,
An' then I laff an' holler, "Oh, ye never teched *me!*"
But jest 'fore Christmas I'm as good as I kin be!

Gran'ma says she hopes that when I git to be a man,
I'll be a missionarer like her oldest brother, Dan,
As was et up by the cannibals that live in Ceylon's Isle,
Where every prospeck pleases, an' only man is vile!
But gran'ma she has never been to see a Wild West show
Nor read the life of Daniel Boone, or else I guess she'd kno
That Buff'lo Bill an' cowboys is good enough for me!
Excep' jest 'fore Christmas, when I'm as good as I kin b

And then old Sport he hangs around, so solemn-like an' st
His eyes they seem a-sayin': "What's the matter, little Bil
The old cat sneaks down off her perch an' wonders what
    become
Of them two enemies of hern that used to make things hur
But I am so perlite an' tend so earnestly to biz,
That mother says to father: "How improved our Willie is!
But father, havin' been a boy hisself, suspicions me
When, jest 'fore Christmas, I'm as good as I kin be!

For Christmas, with its lots an' lots of candies, cakes a
    toys,
Was made, they say, for proper kids an' not for naught
    boys;
So wash yer face an' bresh yer hair, an' mind yer p's and q
And don't bust out yer pantaloons, and don't wear ou
    yer shoes;
Say "Yessum" to the ladies, and "Yessur" to the men,
An' when they's company, don't pass yet plate for pie agai
But, thinkin' of the things yer'd like to see upon that tre
Jest 'fore Christmas be as good as yer kin be!

From *The Poems of Eugene Field.* 19
Published by Charles Scribner's So

Bettmann

Gradatim

JOSIAH GILBERT HOLLAND
(Born July 24, 1819; died October 12, 1881)

Heaven is not gained at a single bound;
　But we build the ladder by which we rise
　From the lowly earth to the vaulted skies,
And we mount to its summit round by round.

I count this thing to be grandly true,
　That a noble deed is a step toward God—
　Lifting the soul from the common sod
To a purer air and a broader view.

We rise by things that are 'neath our feet;
　By what we have mastered of good and gain;
　By the pride deposed and the passion slain,
And the vanquished ills that we hourly meet.

We hope, we aspire, we resolve, we trust,
　When the morning calls us to life and light,
　But our hearts grow weary, and, ere the night,
Our lives are trailing the sordid dust.

We hope, we resolve, we aspire, we pray,
　And we think that we mount the air on wings
　Beyond the recall of sensual things,
While our feet still cling to the heavy clay.

Wings for the angels, but feet for men!
　We may borrow the wings to find the way—
　We may hope, and resolve, and aspire, and pray,
But our feet must rise, or we fall again.

Only in dreams is a ladder thrown
　From the weary earth to the sapphire walls;
　But the dream departs, and the vision falls,
And the sleeper wakes on his pillow of stone.

Heaven is not reached at a single bound:
　But we build the ladder by which we rise
　From the lowly earth to the vaulted skies,
And we mount to its summit round by round.

Bettmann

The Barefoot Boy

JOHN GREENLEAF WHITTIER
(Born December 17, 1807; died September 7, 1892)

Blessings on thee, little man,
Barefoot boy, with cheek of tan!
With thy turned-up pantaloons,
And thy merry whistled tunes;
With thy red lip, redder still,
Kissed by strawberries on the hill;
With the sunshine on thy face,
Through thy torn brim's jaunty grace,
From my heart I give thee joy,—
I was once a barefoot boy.
Prince thou art,—the grown-up man
Only is republican,
Let the million-dollared ride!
Barefoot, trudging at his side,
Thou hast more than he can buy,
In the reach of ear and eye—
Outward sunshine, inward joy;
Blessings on thee, barefoot boy!

Oh, for boyhood's painless play,
Sleep that wakes in laughing day,
Health that mocks the doctor's rules,
Knowledge never learned of schools,
Of the wild bee's morning chase,
Of the wild flower's time and place,
Flight of fowl and habitude
Of the tenants of the wood;
How the tortoise bears his shell,
How the woodchuck digs his cell,
And the groundmole sinks his well;
How the robin feeds her young,
How the oriole's nest is hung,
Where the whitest lilies grow,
Where the freshest berries grow,
Where the ground-nut trails its vine,
Where the wood-grape's clusters shine,

Of the black wasp's cunning way,—
Mason of his walls of clay,—
And the architectural plans
Of gray-hornet artisans!—
For, eschewing books and tasks,
Nature answers all he asks,
Hand in hand with her he walks,
Face to face with her he talks,
Part and parcel of her joy,—
Blessings on the barefoot boy!

Oh, for boyhood's time of June,
Crowding years in one brief moon,
When all things I heard or saw,
Me, their master, waited for.
I was rich in flowers and trees,
Humming-birds and honeybees,
For my sport the squirrel played,
Plied the snouted mole his spade;
For my task the blackberry cone
Purpled over hedge and stone;
Laughed the brook for my delight
Through the day and through the night,—
Whispering at the garden wall,
Talked with me from fall to fall;
Mine the sand-rimmed pickerel pond,
Mine the walnut slopes beyond,
Mine, on bending orchard trees,
Apples of Hesperides!
Still, as my horizon grew,
Larger grew my riches too;
All the world I saw or knew
Seemed a complex Chinese toy
Fashioned for a barefoot boy.

Oh, for festal dainties spread,
Like my bowl of milk and bread,—
Pewter spoon and bowl of wood,
On the doorstone, gray and rude!
O'er me, like a regal tent,
Cloudy-ribbed, the sunset bent,
Purple-curtained, fringed with gold,
Looped in many a wind-swung fold.
While for music came the play
Of the pied frog's orchestra,
And, to light the noisy choir,
Lit the fly his lamp of fire.
I was monarch: pomp and joy
Waited on thee, barefoot boy!

Cheerily, then, my little man,
Live and laugh as boyhood can!
Though the flinty slopes be hard,
Stubble-speared the new-mown sward,
Every morn shall lead thee through
Fresh baptisms of the dew;
Every evening from thy feet
Shall the cool wind kiss the heat;
All too soon these feet must hide
In the prison cells of pride,
Lose the freedom of the sod,
Like a colt's for work be shod,
Made to tread the mills of toil,
Up and down in ceaseless moil;
Happy if their track be found
Never on forbidden ground;
Happy if they sink not in
Quick and treacherous sands of sin,
Ah! that thou couldst known thy joy,
Ere it passes, barefoot boy!

Polonius' Advice to Laertes
From "Hamlet"

WILLIAM SHAKESPEARE

(Born April 23 [?], 1564; died April 23, 1616)

There,—my blessing with you!
And these few precepts in thy memory
See thou character.—Give thy thoughts no tongue,
Nor any unproportion'd thought his act.
Be thou familiar, but by no means vulgar.
The friends thou hast, and their adoption tried,
Grapple them to thy soul with hoops of steel;
But do not dull thy palm with entertainment
Of each new-hatched, unfledged comrade. Beware
Of entrance to a quarrel; but being in,
Bear't that the opposed may beware of thee.
Give every man thine ear, but few thy voice:
Take each man's censure, but reserve thy judgment.
Costly thy habit as thy purse can buy,
But not expressed in fancy; rich, not guady:
For the apparel oft proclaims the man.
Neither a borrower nor a lender be,
For loan oft loses both itself and friend,
And borrowing dulls the edge of husbandry.
This above all: to thine own self be true,
And it must follow, as the night the day,
Thou canst not then be false to any man.

The Flag Goes By

HENRY HOLCOMB BENNETT

*(Born December 5, 1863;
died April 30, 1924)*

Hats off!
Along the street there comes
A blare of bugles, a ruffle of drums,
A flash of color beneath the sky:
    Hats off!
The flag is passing by!

Blue and crimson and white it shines,
Over the steel-tipped, ordered lines.
    Hats off!
The colors before us fly;
But more than the flag is passing by.

Sea-fights and land-fights, grim and great,
Fought to make and to save the State:
Weary marches and sinking ships;
Cheers of victory on dying lips;

Days of plenty and years of peace;
March of a strong land's swift increase;
Equal justice, right and law,
Stately honor and reverend awe;

Sign of a nation, great and strong
To ward her people from foreign wrong:
Pride and glory and honor,—all
Live in the colors to stand or fall.

Hats off!
Along the street there comes
A blare of bugles, a ruffle of drums;
And loyal hearts are beating high:
    Hats off!
The flag is passing by!

"The Things That Are More Excellent"

WILLIAM WATSON

(Born August 2, 1858; died 1935)

As we wax older on this earth,
    Till many a toy that charmed us seems
Emptied of beauty, stripped of worth,
    And mean as dust and dead as dreams,—
For gauds that perished, shows that passed,
    Some recompense the Fates have sent:
Thrice lovelier shine the things that last,
    The things that are more excellent.

Tired of the Senate's barren brawl,
    An hour with silence we prefer,
Where statelier rise the woods than all
    Yon towers of talk at Westminster.
Let this man prate and that man plot,
    On fame or place or title bent:
The votes of veering crowds are not
    The things that are more excellent.

Shall we perturb and vex our soul
    For "wrongs" which no true freedom mar,
Which no man's upright walk control,
    And from no guiltless deed debar?
What odds though tonguesters heal, or leave
    Unhealed, the grievance they invent?
To things, not phantoms, let us cleave—
    The things that are more excellent.

Nought nobler is, than to be free:
    The stars of heaven are free because
In amplitude of liberty
    Their joy is to obey the laws.
From servitude to freedom's *name*
    Free thou thy mind in bondage pent;
Depose the fetich, and proclaim
    The things that are more excellent.

And in appropriate dust be hurled
   That dull, punctilious god, whom they
That call their tiny clan the world,
   Serve and obsequiously obey:
Who con their ritual of Routine,
   With minds to one dead likeness blent,
And never ev'n in dreams have seen
   The things that are more excellent.

To dress, to call, to dine, to break
   No canon of the social code,
The little laws that lacqueys make,
   The futile decalogue of Mode,—
How many a soul for these things lives,
   With pious passion, grave intent!
While Nature careless-handed gives
   The things that are more excellent.

To hug the wealth ye cannot use,
   And lack the riches all may gain,—
O blind and wanting wit to choose,
   Who house the chaff and burn the grain!
And still doth life with starry towers
   Lure to the bright, divine ascent!—
Be yours the things ye would: be ours
   The things that are more excellent.

The grace of friendship—mind and heart
   Linked with their fellow heart and mind;
The gains of science, gifts of art;
   The sense of oneness with our kind;
The thirst to know and understand—
   A large and liberal discontent:
These are the goods in life's rich hand,
   The things that are more excellent.

In faultless rhythm the ocean rolls,
   A rapturous silence thrills the skies;
And on this earth are lovely souls,
   That softly look with aidful eyes.
Though dark, O God, Thy course and track,
   I think Thou must at least have meant
That nought which lives should wholly lack
   The things that are more excellent.

From *The Poems of William
Watson.* Copyright by John
Lane Co., Publishers, New York.

Bettmann

Concord Hymn
Sung at the completion of the Battle Monument, April 19, 1886

RALPH WALDO EMERSON
(Born May 25, 1803; died April 27, 1882)

By the rude bridge that arched the flood,
  Their flag to April's breeze unfurled,
Here once the embattled farmers stood,
  And fired the shot heard round the world.

The foe long since in silence slept;
  Alike the conqueror silent sleeps;
And Time the ruined bridge has swept
  Down the dark stream which seaward creeps.

On this green bank, by this soft stream,
  We set today a votive stone;
That memory may their deed redeem,
  When, like our sires, our sons are gone.

Spirit, tnat made those spirits dare
  To die, and leave their children free,
Bid Time and Nature gently spare
  The shaft we raise to them and thee.

Keep a-Goin'

FRANK L. STANTON
*(Born February 22, 1857; died
January 7, 1927)*

If you strike a thorn or rose,
 Keep a-goin'!
If it hails or if it snows,
 Keep a-goin'!
'Taint no use to sit an' whine
When the fish ain't on your line;
Bait your hook an' keep a-tryin'—
 Keep a-goin'!

When the weather kills your crop,
 Keep a-goin'!
Though 'tis work to reach the top,
 Keep a-goin'!
S'pose you're out o' ev'ry dime,
Gittin' broke ain't any crime;
Tell the world you're feelin' *prime*—
 Keep a-goin'!

When it looks like all is up,
 Keep a-goin'!
Drain the sweetness from the cup,
 Keep a-goin'!
See the wild birds on the wing,
Hear the bells that sweetly ring,
When you feel like sighin', sing—
 Keep a-goin'!

Life Sculpture

GEORGE WASHINGTON DOANE

(Born May 27, 1799; died April 27, 1859)

Chisel in hand stood a sculptor boy
    With his marble block before him,
And his eyes lit up with a smile of joy,
    As an angel-dream passed o'er him.

He carved the dream on that shapeless stone,
    With many a sharp incision;
With heaven's own light the sculpture shone,—
    He'd caught that angel-vision.

Children of life are we, as we stand
    With our lives uncarved before us,
Waiting the hour when, at God's command,
    Our life-dream shall pass o'er us.

If we carve it then on the yielding stone,
    With many a sharp incision,
Its heavenly beauty shall be our own,—
    Our lives, that angel-vision.

Bettmann

The Choir Invisible

GEORGE ELIOT (MARY ANN EVANS)

(Born November 22, 1819; died December 22, 1880)

Oh, may I join the choir invisible
Of those immortal dead who live again
In minds made better by their presence; live
In pulses stirred to generosity,
In deeds of daring rectitude, in scorn
For miserable aims that end with self,
In thoughts sublime that pierce the night like stars,
And with their mild persistence urge men's search
To vaster issues. So to live is heaven:
To make undying music in the world,
Breathing a beauteous order that controls
With growing sway the growing life of man.
So we inherit that sweet purity
For which we struggled, failed, and agonized
With widening retrospect that bred despair.
Rebellious flesh that would not be subdued,
A vicious parent shaming still its child,
Poor anxious penitence, is quick dissolved;
Its discords, quenched by meeting harmonies,
Die in the large and charitable air.
And all our rarer, better, truer self,
That sobbed religiously in yearning song,
That watched to ease the burden of the world,
Laboriously tracing what must be,
And what may yet be better,—saw within
A worthier image for the sanctuary,
And shaped it forth before the multitude,
Divinely human, raising worship so
To higher reverence more mixed with love,—
That better self shall live till human Time
Shall fold its eyelids, and the human sky
Be gathered like a scroll within the tomb
Unread forever. This is life to come,—
Which martyred men have made more glorious
For us who strive to follow. May I reach

That purest heaven,—be to other souls
The cup of strength in some great agony,
Enkindle generous ardor, feed pure love,
Beget the smiles that have no cruelty,
Be the sweet presence of a good diffused,
And in diffusion ever more intense!
So shall I join the choir invisible
Whose music is the gladness of the world.

Bettmann

Marmion and Dougla
From "Marmion"

SIR WALTER SCOTT
(Born August 15, 1771; died September 21, 1832)

The train from out the castle drew,
But Marmion stopped to bid adieu:—
    "Though something I might plain," he said
"Of cold respect to stranger guest,
Sent hither by your king's behest,
    While in Tantallon's towers I stayed,
Part we in friendship from your land,
And noble Earl, receive my hand."—

But Douglas round him drew his cloak,
Folded his arms, and thus he spoke:—
"My manors, halls, and bowers shall still
Be open, at my sovereign's will
To each one whom he lists, howe'er
Unmeet to be the owner's peer.
My castles are my king's alone
From turret to foundation-stone,—
The hand of Douglas is his own;
And never shall in friendly grasp
The hand of such as Marmion clasp."—

Burned Marmion's swarthy cheek like fire,
And shook his very frame for ire,
    And—"This to me!" he said,—

"An't were not for thy hoary beard,
Such hand as Marmion's had not spared
   To cleave the Douglas' head!
And first I tell thee, haughty Peer,
He who does England's message here,
Although the meanest in her state,
May well, proud Angus, be thy mate:
And, Douglas, more I tell thee here,
   Even in thy pitch of pride,
Here in thy hold, thy vassals near,
(Nay, never look upon your lord,
And lay your hands upon your sword,)
   I tell thee, thou'rt defied!
And if thou said'st I am not peer
To any lord in Scotland here,
Lowland or Highland, far or near,
   Lord Angus, thou hast lied!"—
On the Earl's cheek the flush of rage
O'ercame the ashen hue of age;
Fierce he broke forth,—"And dar'st thou then
To beard the lion in his den,
   The Douglas in his hall?
And hop'st thou hence unscathed to go?
No, by St. Bride of Bothwell, no!
Up drawbridge, grooms,—what, Warder, ho!
   Let the portcullis fall."—

Lord Marmion turned,—well was his need!—
And dashed the rowels in his steed,
Like arrow through the archway sprung;
The ponderous gate behind him rung:
To pass there was such scanty room,
The bars, descending, razed his plume.

The steed along the drawbridge flies,
Just as it trembled on the rise;
Not lighter does the swallow skim
Along the smooth lake's level brim;
And when Lord Marmion reached his band
He halts, and turns with clenched hand,
And shout of loud defiance pours,
And shook his gauntlet at the towers.

Bettmann

Ode on a Grecian Urn

JOHN KEATS

(Born October 31, 1795; died February 23, 1821)

Thou still unravished bride of quietness,
  Thou foster child of Silence and slow Time,
Sylvan historian, who canst thus express
  A flowery tale more sweetly than our rhyme:
What leaf-fring'd legend haunts about thy shape
  Of deities or mortals, or of both,
    In Tempe or the dales of Arcady?
What men or gods are these? What maidens loath?
  What mad pursuit? What struggle to escape?
    What pipes and timbrels? What wild ecstasy?

Heard melodies are sweet, but those unheard
  Are sweeter; therefore, ye soft pipes, play on;
Not to the sensual ear, but more endeared,
  Pipe to the spirit ditties of no tone;
Fair youth, beneath the trees, thou canst not leave
  Thy song, nor ever can those trees be bare;
    Bold Lover, never, never canst thou kiss,
Though winning near the goal—yet, do not grieve;
  She cannot fade, though thou hast not thy bliss,
    For ever wilt thou love, and she be fair!

Ah, happy, happy boughs! that cannot shed
  Your leaves, nor ever bid the Spring adieu;
And, happy melodist, unweariéd,
  For ever piping songs for ever new;
More happy love! more happy, happy love!
  For ever warm and still to be enjoy'd,
    For ever panting, and for ever young;
All breathing human passion far above,
  That leaves a heart high-sorrowful and cloy'd,
    A burning forehead, and a parching tongue.

Who are these coming to the sacrifice?
  To what green altar, O mysterious priest,
Lead'st thou that heifer lowing at the skies,
  And all her silken flanks with garlands drest?
What little town by river or seashore,
  Or mountain-built with peaceful citadel,
  Is emptied of this folk, this pious morn?
And, little town, thy streets for everymore
  Will silent be; and not a soul to tell
  Why thou are desolate, can e'er return.

O Attic shape! Fair attitude! with brede
  Of marble men and maidens overwrought,
With forest branches and the trodden weed;
  Thou, silent form, dost tease us out of thought
As doth eternity: Cold Pastoral!
  When old age shall this generation waste,
  Thou shalt remain, in midst of other woe
Than ours, a friend to man, to whom thou say'st,
  "Beauty is truth, truth beauty,"—that is all
  Ye know on earth, and all ye need to know.

The Heart of the Tree

HENRY CUYLER BUNNER
(Born August 3, 1855; died May 11, 1896)

What does he plant who plants a tree?
  He plants a friend of sun and sky;
He plants the flag of breezes free;
The shaft of beauty, towering high;
He plants a home to heaven anigh
  For song and mother-croon of bird
  In hushed and happy twilight heard—
The treble of heaven's harmony—
These things he plants who plants a tree.

What does he plant who plants a tree?
  He plants cool shade and tender rain,
And seed and bud of days to be,
And years that fade and flush again;
He plants the glory of the plain;
  He plants the forest's heritage;
  The harvest of a coming age;
The joy that unborn eyes shall see—
These things he plants who plants a tree.

What does he plant who plants a tree?
    He plants, in sap and leaf and wood,
  In love of home and loyalty
And far-cast thought of civic good—
  His blessings on the neighborhood
    Who in the hollow of His hand
    Holds all the growth of all our land—
A nation's growth from sea to sea
Stirs in his heart who plants a tree.

By special arrangement with
Charles Scribner's Sons, Publishers.

Bettmann

Crossing the Bar

ALFRED TENNYSON

*(Born August 6, 1809; died October
1892)*

Sunset and evening star,
  And one clear call for me,
And may there be no moaning of the bar,
  When I put out to sea.

But such a tide as moving seems asleep,
  Too full for sound and foam,
When that which drew from out the boundless deep
  Turns again home.

Twilight and evening bell,
  And after that the dark!
And may there be no sadness of farewell,
  When I embark;

For tho' from out our bourne of time and place
  The flood may bear me far,
I hope to see my Pilot face to face
  When I have crossed the bar.

Bettmann

Soliloquy from "Hamlet"

WILLIAM SHAKESPEARE

(Born April 23 [?] 1564; died April 23, 1616)

To be, or not to be; that is the question;
Whether 'tis nobler in the mind to suffer
The slings and arrows of outrageous fortune,
Or to take arms against a sea of troubles,
And by opposing end them. To die: to sleep:
No more; and by a sleep to say we end
The heart-ache and the thousand natural shocks
That flesh is heir to; 'tis a consummation
Devoutly to be wished.   To die; to sleep;
To sleep: perchance to dream: aye, there's the rub;
For in that sleep of death what dreams may come,
When we have shuffled off this mortal coil,
Must give us pause: there's the respect
That makes calamity of so long life;
For who would bear the whips and scorns of time,
The oppressor's wrong, the proud man's contumely,
The pangs of despis'd love, the law's delay,
The insolence of office, and the spurns
That patient merit of the unworthy takes,
When he himself might his quietus make
With a bare bodkin? Who would fardels bear,
To grunt and sweat under a weary life,
But that the dread of something after death—
The undiscover'd country from whose bourn
No traveler returns—puzzles the will
And makes us rather bear those ills we have
Than fly to others that we know not of?
Thus conscience does make cowards of us all,
And thus the native hue of resolution
Is sicklied o'er with the pale cast of thought,
And enterprises of great pith and moment
With this regard their currents turn awry,
And lose the name of action.

Bettmann

She Was a Phantom of Delight

WILLIAM WORDSWORTH

(Born April 7, 1770; died April 23, 1850)

She was a phantom of delight
When first she gleamed upon my sight;
A lovely apparition, sent
To be a moment's ornament;
Her eyes as stars of twilight fair;
Like twilight's, too, her dusky hair;
But all things else about her drawn
From May-time and the cheerful dawn;
A dancing shape, an image gay,
To haunt, to startle, and waylay.

I saw her upon nearer view,
A spirit, yet a woman too!
Her houshold motions light and free,
And step of virgin liberty;
A countenance in which did meet
Sweet records, promises as sweet;
A creature not too bright or good
For human nature's daily food,
For transient sorrows, simple wiles,
Praise, blame, love, kisses, tears, and smiles.

And now I see with eye serene
The very pulse of the machine;
A being breathing thoughtful breath,
A traveler between life and death;
The reason firm, the temperate will,
Endurance, foresight, strength, and skill;
A perfect woman, nobly planned
To warn, to comfort, and command;
And yet a spirit still, and bright
With something of angelic light.

Bettmann

The Spider and the Fly
A Fable

MARY HOWITT

(Born March 12, 1799; died January 30, 1888)

"Will you walk into my parlor?" said the spider to the fly;
" 'Tis the prettiest little parlor that ever you did spy.
The way into my parlor is up a winding stair,
And I have many pretty things to show when you are there."
"O no, no," said the little fly, "to ask me is in vain,
For who goes up your winding stair can ne'er come down
    again."

"I'm sure you must be weary, dear, with soaring up so high;
Will you rest upon my little bed?" said the spider to the fly.
"There are pretty curtains drawn around, the sheets are
    fine and thin,
And if you like to rest awhile, I'll snugly tuck you in."
"O no, no," said the little fly, "for I've often heard it said,
They *never, never wake* again, who sleep upon *your* bed."

Said the cunning spider to the fly, "Dear friend, what shall
    I do,
To prove the warm affection I've always felt for you?
I have within my pantry good store of all that's nice;
I'm sure you're very welcome; will you please to take a
    slice?"
"O no, no," said the little fly, "kind sir, that cannot be;
I've heard what's in your pantry, and I do not wish to see."

"Sweet creature!" said the spider, "you're witty and you're
    wise,
How handsome are your gauzy wings, how brilliant are
    your eyes!
I have a little looking-glass upon my parlor shelf.

If you'll step in one moment, dear, you shall behold
    yourself."
"I thank you, gentle sir," she said, "for what you're pleased
    to say,
And bidding you good-morning *now,* I'll call *another* day."

The spider turned him round about, and went into his den,
For well he knew the silly fly would soon be back again:
So he wove a subtle web, in a little corner sly,
And set his table ready to dine upon the fly.
Then he came out to his door again, and merrily did sing,
"Come hither, hither, pretty fly, with the pearl and silver
    wing:
Your robes are green and purple; there's a crest upon your
    head;
Your eyes are like the diamond bright, but mine are dull as
    lead."

Alas, alas! how very soon this silly little fly,
Hearing his wily flattering words, came slowly flitting by.
With buzzing wings she hung aloft, then near and nearer
    drew,
Thinking only of her brilliant eyes, and green and purple
    hue;
Thinking only of her crested head—*poor foolish thing!*
    At last,
Up jumped the cunning spider, and fiercely held her fast.
He dragged her up his winding stair, into his dismal den,
Within his little parlor; but she ne'er came out again!

And now, dear little children, who may this story read,
To idle, silly, flattering words, I pray you ne'er give heed;
Unto an evil counselor close heart, and ear, and eye,
And take a lesson from this tale of the Spider and the Fly.

Bettmann

Maud Muller

JOHN GREENLEAF WHITTIER

(Born December 17, 1807; died September 7, 1892)

Maud Muller, on a summer's day,
Raked the meadow sweet with hay.
Beneath her torn hat glowed the wealth
Of simple beauty and rustic health.
Singing, she wrought, and her merry glee
The mock-bird echoed from his tree.

But when she glanced to the far-off town,
White from its hill-slope looking down,
The sweet song died, and a vague unrest
And a nameless longing filled her breast;
A wish, that she hardly dared to own,
For something better than she had known.

The Judge rode slowly down the lane,
Smoothing his horse's chestnut mane:
He drew his bridle in the shade
Of the apple-trees, to greet the maid,
And asked a draught from the spring that flowed
Through the meadow across the road.

She stooped where the cool spring bubbled up,
And filled for him her small tin cup,
And blushed as she gave it, looking down
On her feet so bare, and her tattered gown.
"Thanks!" said the Judge, "a sweeter draught
From a fairer hand was never quaffed."

He spoke of the grass, and flowers, and trees,
Of the singing birds and the humming bees;
Then talked of the haying, and wondered whether
The cloud in the west would bring foul weather.
And Maud forgot her brier-torn gown,
And her graceful ankles bare and brown,
And listened, while a pleased surprise
Looked from her long-lashed hazel eyes.

At last, like one who for delay
Seeks a vain excuse, he rode away.
Maud Muller looked and sighed: "Ah, me!
That I the Judge's bride might be!
He would dress me up in silks so fine,
And praise and toast me at his wine.

"My father should wear a broadcloth coat;
My brother should sail a painted boat;
I'd dress my mother so grand and gay,
And the baby should have a new toy each day;
And I'd feed the hungry and clothe the poor,
And all should bless me who left our door."

The Judge looked back as he climbed the hill,
And saw Maud Muller standing still.
"A form more fair, a face more sweet,
Ne'er has it been my lot to meet;
And her modest answer and graceful air
Show her wise and good as she is fair.

"Would she were mine, and I to-day,
Like her, a harvester of hay;
No doubtful balance of rights and wrongs,
Nor weary lawyers with endless tongues;
But low of cattle and song of birds,
And health, and quiet, and loving words."

But he thought of his sisters, proud and cold,
And his mother, vain of her rank and gold;
So, closing his heart, the Judge rode on,
And Maud was left in the field alone.
But the lawyers smiled that afternoon,
When he hummed in court an old love-tune;
And the young girl mused beside the well,
Till the rain on the unraked clover fell.

He wedded a wife of richest dower,
Who lived for fashion, as he for power;
Yet oft, in his marble hearth's bright glow,
He watched a picture come and go;
And sweet Maud Muller's hazel eyes,
Looked out in their innocent surprise.

Oft when the wine in his glass was red,
He longed for the wayside well instead;
And closed his eyes on his garnished rooms,
To dream of meadows and clover-blooms.

And the proud man sighed, with a secret pain,
"Ah, that I were free again!
Free as when I rode that day,
Where the barefoot maiden raked her hay."

She wedded a man unlearned and poor,
And many children played round her door;
But care and sorrow and wasting pain
Left their traces on heart and brain.
And oft when the summer sun shone hot
On the new-mown hay in the meadow lot,
And she heard the little spring brook fall
Over the roadside, through the wall,
In the shade of the apple-tree again
She saw a rider draw his rein,
And, gazing down with timid grace,
She felt his pleased eyes read her face.

Sometimes her narrow kitchen walls
Stretched away into stately halls;
The weary wheel to a spinet turned;
The tallow candle an astral burned;
And for him who sat by the chimney lug,
Dozing and grumbling o'er pipe and mug,
A manly form at her side she saw,
And joy was duty, and love was law.
Then she took up her burden of life again,
Saying only, "It might have been!"

Alas for maiden, alas for Judge,
For rich repiner and household drudge!
God pity them both! and pity us all,
Who vainly the dreams of youth recall;
For of all sad words of tongue or pen
The saddest are these: "It might have been!"
Ah, well! for us all some sweet hope lies
Deeply buried from human eyes;
And in the hereafter angels may
Roll the stone from its grave away!

The Night Before Christmas

CLEMENT CLARKE MOORE

(Born July 15, 1779; died July 10, 1863)

Bettmann

Courtesy *Collier's Weekly*

'Twas the night before Christmas, when all through the
    house
Not a creature was stirring, not even a mouse;
The stockings were hung by the chimney with care,
In hopes that St. Nicholas soon would be there;
The children were nestled all snug in their beds,
While visions of sugar-plums danced in their heads;
And Mamma in her kerchief, and I in my cap,
Had just settled our brains for a long winter's nap,
When out on the lawn there arose such a clatter,
I sprang from my bed to see what was the matter.
Away to the window I flew like a flash,
Tore open the shutters and threw up the sash.
The moon, on the breast of the new-fallen snow,
Gave a luster of mid-day to objects below;
When, what to my wandering eyes should appear,
But a miniature sleigh, and eight tiny reindeer,
With a little old driver, so lively and quick,
I knew in a moment it must be St. Nick.
More rapid than eagles his coursers they came,
And he whistled, and shouted, and called them by name:
"Now, Dasher! now, Dancer! now, Prancer and Vixen!
On, Comet! on, Cupid! on, Donder and Blitzen!
To the top of the porch, to the top of the wall!
Now, dash away, dash away, dash away, all!"
As dry leaves that before the wild hurricane fly,
When they meet with an obstacle, mount to the sky,
So, up to the house-top the coursers they flew,
With the sleigh full of toys—and St. Nicholas, too.
And then in a twinkling I heard on the roof
The prancing and pawing of each little hoof.
As I drew in my head, and was turning around,
Down the chimney St. Nicholas came with a bound.
He was dressed all in fur from his head to his foot,

And his clothes were all tarnished with ashes and soot;
A bundle of toys he had flung on his back,
And he looked like a peddler just opening his pack.
His eyes how they twinkled! his dimples how merry!
His cheeks were like roses, his nose like a cherry;
His droll little mouth was drawn up like a bow,
And the beard on his chin was as white as the snow.
The stump of a pipe he held tight in his teeth,
And the smoke it encircled his head like a wreath;
He had a broad face and a little round belly
That shook, when he laughed, like a bowlful of jelly.
He was chubby and plump—a right jolly old elf;
And I laughed when I saw him, in spite of myself.
A wink of his eye, and a twist of his head,
Soon gave me to know I had nothing to dread.
He spoke not a word, but went straight to his work,
And filled all the stockings; then turned with a jerk,
And laying his finger aside of his nose,
And giving a nod, up the chimney he rose.
He sprang to his sleigh, to his team gave a whistle,
And away they all flew like the down of a thistle;
But I heard him exclaim, ere he drove out of sight,
"Happy Christmas to all, and to all a goodnight!"

Home
EDGAR A. GUEST
(Born August 20, 1881; died August 5, 1959)

It takes a heap o' livin' in a house t' make it
    home,
A heap o' sun an' shadder, an' ye sometimes
    have t' roam
Afore ye really 'preciate the things ye lef'
    behind,
An' hunger fer 'em somehow, with 'em allus
    on yer mind.
It don't make any differunce how rich ye get
    t' be,
How much yer chairs an' tables cost, how great
    yer luxury;
It ain't home t' ye, though it be the palace of a
    king,
Until somehow yer soul is sort o' wrapped 'round
    everything.

Home ain't a place that gold can buy or get up
    in a minute;
Afore it's home there's got t' be a heap o' livin'
    in it;
Within the walls there's got t' be some babies
    born, and then
Right there ye've got t' bring 'em up t' women
    good, an' men;
And gradjerly, as time goes on, ye find ye
    wouldn't part
With anything they ever used—they're grown
    into yer heart:
The old high chairs, the playthings, too, the
    little shoes they wore
Ye hoard; an' if ye could ye'd keep the thumb-
    marks on the door.

Ye've got t' weep t' make it home, ye've got t'
    sit an' sigh
An' watch beside a loved one's bed, an' know
    that Death is nigh;
An' in the stillness o' the night t' see Death's
    angel come,
An' close the eyes o' her that smiled, an' leave
    her sweet voice dumb.
Fer these are scenes that grip the heart, an'
    when yer tears are dried,
Ye find the home is dearer than it was, an'
    sanctified;
An' tuggin' at ye always are the pleasant
    memories
O' her that was an' is no more—ye can't escape
    from these.

Ye've got t' sing an' dance fer years, ye've got
    t' romp an' play,
An' learn t' love the things ye have by usin' 'em
    each day;
Even the roses 'round the porch must blossom
    year by year
Afore they 'come a part o' ye, suggestin'
    someone dear
Who used t' love 'em long ago, an' trained 'em
    jes' t' run
The way they do, so's they would get the early
    mornin' sun;
Ye've got t' love each brick an' stone from
    cellar up t' dome:
It takes a heap o' livin' in a house t' make it
    home.

Reprinted from *A Heap o' Livin'* by Edgar
A. Guest, by permission of The Reilly
& Lee Co., publishers. Copyright 1916.

Bettmann

My Kate

ELIZABETH BARRETT BROWNING

(Born March 6, 1806; died June 30, 1861)

She was not as pretty as women I know,
And yet all your best made of sunshine and snow
Drop to shade, melt to nought in the long-trodden ways,
While she's still remembered on warm and cold days—
My Kate.

Her air had a meaning, her movements a grace;
You turned from the fairest to gaze on her face;
And when you had once seen her forehead and mouth,
You saw as distinctly her soul and her truth—
My Kate.

Such a blue inner light from her eyelids outbroke,
You looked at her silence and fancied she spoke;
When she did, so peculiar yet soft was the tone,
Though the loudest spoke also, you heard her alone—
My Kate.

I doubt if she said to you much that could act
As a thought or suggestion; she did not attract
In the sense of the brilliant or wise; I infer
'Twas her thinking of others made you think of her—
My Kate.

She never found fault with you, never implied
Your wrong by her right; and yet men at her side
Grew nobler, girls purer, as through the whole town
The children were gladder that pulled at her gown—
My Kate

None knelt at her feet confessed lovers in thrall;
They knelt more to God than they used—that was all;
If you praised her as charming, some asked what you meant,
But the charm of her presence was felt when she went—
My Kate.

The weak and the gentle, the ribald and rude,
She took as she found them, and did them all good;
It always was so with her—see what you have!
She has made the grass greener even here with her grave—
My Kate.

Bettmann

Lincoln, the Man of the People
EDWIN MARKHAM

(Born Oregon City, Oregon, 1852; died March 7, 1940)

When the Norn Mother saw the Whirlwind Hour
Greatening and darkening as it hurried on,
She left the Heaven of Heroes and came down
To make a man to meet the mortal need.
She took the tried clay of the common road—
Clay warm yet with the genial heat of Earth,
Dasht through it all a strain of prophecy;
Tempered the heap with thrill of human tears;
Then mixt a laughter with the serious stuff.
Into the shape she breathed a flame to light
That tender, tragic, ever-changing face;
And laid on him a sense of the Mystic Powers,
Moving—all husht—behind the mortal vail.
Here was a man to hold against the world,
A man to match the mountains and the sea.

The color of the ground was in him, the red earth;
The smack and tang of elemental things:
The rectitude and patience of the cliff;
The good-will of the rain that loves all leaves;
The friendly welcome of the wayside well;
The courage of the bird that dares the sea;
The gladness of the wind that shakes the corn;
The pity of the snow that hides all scars;
The secrecy of streams that make their way
Under the mountain to the rifted rock;
The tolerance and equity of light
That gives as freely to the shrinking flower
As to the great oak flaring to the wind—
To the grave's low hill as to the Matterhorn
That shoulders out the sky. Sprung from the West,
He drank the valorous youth of a new world.
The strength of virgin forests braced his mind,
The hush of spacious prairies stilled his soul.
His words were oaks in acorns; and his thoughts
Were roots that firmly gript the granite truth.

155

Up from log cabin to the Capitol,
One fire was on his spirit, one resolve—
To send the keen ax to the root of wrong,
Clearing a free way for the feet of God,
The eyes of conscience testing every stroke,
To make his deed the measure of a man.
He built the rail-pile as he built the State,
Pouring his splendid strength through every blow:
The grip that swung the ax in Illinois
Was on the pen that set a people free.

So came the Captain with the mighty heart;
And when the judgment thunders split the house,
Wrenching the rafters from their ancient rest.
He held the ridgepole up, and spikt again
The rafters of the Home. He held his place—
Held the long purpose like a growing tree --
Held on through blame and faltered not at praise.
And when he fell in whirlwind, he went down
As when a lordly cedar, green with boughs,
Goes down with a great shout upon the hills,
And leaves a lonesome place against the sky.

This revised version was chosen out of 250 Lincoln poems
by the committee headed by Chief Justice Taft — was
chosen to be read at the dedication of the great Lincoln
Memorial erected by the Government in Washington,
D. C. This was in 1922. There were 100,000 listeners
on the ground and two million over the radio. President
Harding delivered the address, and Edwin Markham
read the poem. It is taken from his volume, *Lincoln and
Other Poems*, published by Doubleday, Page and Company—copyrighted 1900, by the author, and used by his
permission.

On the Building of Springfield

Vachel Lindsay

*(Born Springfield, Ill., November 10, 1879;
died December 5, 1931)*

Bettmann

Let not our town be large, remembering
    That little Athens was the Muses' home,
That Oxford rules the heart of London still,
    That Florence gave the Renaissance to Rome.

Record it for the grandson of your son—
    A city is not builded in a day:
Our little town cannot complete her soul
    Till countless generations pass away.

Now let each child be joined as to a church
  To her perpetual hopes, each man ordained:
Let every street be made a reverent aisle
  Where Music grows and Beauty is unchained.

Let Science and Machinery and Trade
  Be slaves of her, and make her all in all,
Building against our blatant, restless time
  An unseen, skilful, medieval wall.

Let every citizen be rich toward God.
  Let Christ, the beggar, teach divinity.
Let no man rule who holds his money dear.
  Let this, our city, be our luxury.

We should build parks that students from afar
  Would choose to starve in, rather than go home,
Fair little squares, with Phidian ornament.
  Food for the spirit, milk and honeycomb.

Songs shall be sung by us in that good day,
  Songs we have written, blood within the rhyme
Beating, as when Old England still was glad,—
  The purple, rich Elizabethan time.

Say, is my prophecy too fair and far?
  I only know, unless her faith be high,
The soul of this, our Nineveh, is doomed,
  Our little Babylon will surely die.

Some city on the breast of Illinois
  No wiser and no better at the start
By faith shall rise redeemed, by faith shall rise
  Bearing the western glory in her heart.

The genius of the Maple, Elm and Oak,
  The secret hidden in each grain of corn,
The glory that the prairie angels sing
  At night when sons of Life and Love are born,

Born but to struggle, squalid and alone,
  Broken and wandering in their early years;
When will they make our dusty streets their goal,
  Within our attics hide their sacred tears?

When will they start our vulgar blood athrill
  With living language, words that set us free?
When will they make a path of beauty clear
  Between our riches and our liberty?

We must have many Lincoln-hearted men—
  A city is not builded in a day—
And they must do their work, and come and go
  While countless generations pass away.

From *Collected Poems* by Vachel Lindsay and
published by The Macmillan Co. Copyright
1923. By permission of the author and publisher.

Bettmann

Mending Wall

ROBERT FROST

(Born San Francisco, March 26, 1875)

Something there is that doesn't love a wall,
That sends the frozen-ground-swell under it,
And spills the upper boulders in the sun;
And makes gaps even two can pass abreast.
The work of hunters is another thing:
I have come after them and made repair
Where they have left not one stone on a stone,
But they would have the rabbit out of hiding,
To please the yelping dogs. The gaps I mean,
No one has seen them made or heard them made,
But at spring mending-time we find them there.
I let my neighbour know beyond the hill;
And on a day we meet to walk the line
And set the wall between us once again.
We keep the wall between us as we go.
To each the boulders that have fallen to each.
And some are loaves and some so nearly balls
We have to use a spell to make them balance:
"Stay where you are until our backs are turned!"
We wear our fingers rough with handling them.
Oh, just another kind of out-door game,
One on a side. It comes to little more:
There where it is we do not need the wall:
He is all pine and I am apple orchard.
My apple trees will never get across
And eat the cones under his pines, I tell him.
He only says, "Good fences make good neighbours."
Spring is the mischief in me, and I wonder
If I could put a notion in his head:
"*Why* do they make good neighbours? Isn't it
Where there are cows? But here there are no cows.

Before I built a wall I'd ask to know
What I was walling in or walling out,
And to whom I was like to give offense.
Something there is that doesn't love a wall,
That wants it down." I could say "Elves" to him,
But it's not elves exactly and I'd rather
He said it for himself. I see him there
Bringing a stone grasped firmly by the top
In each hand, like an old-stone savage armed.
He moves in darkness as it seems to me,
Not of woods only and the shade of trees.
He will not go behind his father's saying,
And he likes having thought of it so well
He says again, "Good fences make good neighbours."

From *North of Boston*, by Robert Frost.
Copyright 1915. Permission by Henry Holt &
Co. Special permission of the publisher.

Bettmann

The Fool's Prayer

EDWARD R. SILL

*(Born April 29, 1841; died February 27,
1887)*

The royal feast was done; the King
    Sought some new sport to banish care,
And to his jester cried: "Sir Fool,
    Kneel now, and make for us a prayer!"

The jester doffed his cap and bells,
    And stood the mocking court before;
They could not see the bitter smile
    Behind the painted grin he wore.

He bowed his head, and bent his knee
    Upon the monarch's silken stool;
His pleading voice arose: "O Lord,
    Be merciful to me, a fool!

"No pity, Lord, could change the heart
  From red with wrong to white as wool;
The rod must heal the sin: but, Lord,
  Be merciful to me, a fool!

" 'Tis not by guilt the onward sweep
  Of truth and right, O Lord, we stay;
'Tis by our follies that so long
  We hold the earth from heaven away.

"These clumsy feet, still in the mire,
  Go crushing blossoms without end;
These hard, well-meaning hands we thrust
  Among the heart-strings of a friend.

"The ill-timed truth we might have kept—
  Who knows how sharp it pierced and stung?
The word we had not sense to say—
  Who knows how grandly it had rung?

"Our faults no tenderness should ask,
  The chastening stripes must cleanse them all;
But for our blunders—oh, in shame
  Before the eyes of heaven we fall.

"Earth bears no balsam for mistakes;
  Men crown the knave, and scourge the tool
That did his will; but Thou, O Lord,
  Be merciful to me, a fool!"

The room was hushed; in silence rose
  The King, and sought his gardens cool,
And walked apart, and murmured low,
  "Be merciful to me, a fool!"

Bettmann

To a Waterfowl

WILLIAM CULLEN BRYANT

(Born November 3, 1794; died June 12,
1878)

Whither, 'midst falling dew,
　While glow the heavens with the last steps of day,
Far, through their rosy depths, dost thou pursue
　Thy solitary way?

Vainly the fowler's eye
　Might mark thy distant flight to do thee wrong,
As, darkly painted on the crimson sky,
　Thy figure floats along.

Seek'st thou the plashy brink
　Of weedy lake, or marge of river wide,
Or where the rocking billows rise and sink
　On the chafed ocean's side?

There is a Power whose care
　Teaches thy way along pathless coast—
The desert and illimitable air—
　Lone wandering, but not lost.

All day thy wings have fanned,
　At that far height, the cold, thin atmosphere,
Yet stoop not weary, to the welcome land,
　Though the dark night is near.

And soon that toil shall end;
　Soon shalt thou find a summer home, and rest,
And scream among thy fellows; reeds shall bend,
　Soon, o'er thy sheltered nest.

Thou'rt gone! the abyss of heaven
　Hath swallowed up thy form; yet on my heart
Deeply hath sunk the lesson thou hast given,
　And shall not soon depart.

He who, from zone to zone,
    Guides through the boundless sky thy certain flight,
In the long way that I must tread alone
    Will lead my steps aright.

By special permission of
D. Appleton & Company.

I Shall Not Pass This Way Again
A Symphony

EVA ROSE YORK
(Born December 22, 1858)

I shall not pass this way again—
    Although it bordered be with flowers,
    Although I rest in fragrant bowers,
        And hear the singing
        Of song-birds winging
To highest heaven their gladsome flight;
Though moons are full and stars are bright,
And winds and waves are softly sighing,
While leafy trees make low replying;
Though voices clear in joyous strain
Repeat a jubilant refrain;
Though rising suns their radiance throw
On summer's green and winter's snow,
In such rare splendor that my heart
Would ache from scenes like these to part;
        Though beauties heighten,
        And life-lights brighten,
And joys proceed from every pain,—
I shall not pass this way again.

Then let me pluck the flowers that blow,
And let me listen as I go
        To music rare
        That fills the air;
        And let hereafter
        Songs and laughter
Fill every pause along the way;
And to my spirit let me say:

"O soul, be happy; soon 'tis trod,
The path made thus for thee by God.
Be happy, thou, and bless His name
By whom such marvellous beauty came."
And let no chance by me be lost
To kindness show at any cost.
I shall not pass this way again;
Then let me now relieve some pain,
Remove some barrier from the road,
Or brighten some one's heavy load;
A helping hand to this one lend,
Then turn some other to befriend.

O God, forgive
That now I live
As if I might, sometime, return
To bless the weary ones that yearn
For help and comfort every day,—
For there be such along the way.
O God, forgive that I have seen
The beauty only, have not been
Awake to sorrow such as this;
That I have drunk the cup of bliss
Remembering not that those there be
Who drink the dregs of misery.

I love the beauty of the scene,
Would roam again o'er fields so green;
But since I may not, let me spend
My strength for others to the end,—
For those who tread on rock and stone,
And bear their burdens all alone,
Who loiter not in leafy bowers,
Nor hear the birds nor pluck the flowers.
A larger kindness give to me,
A deeper love and sympathy;
Then, O, one day
May someone say—
Remembering a lessened pain—
"Would she could pass this way again."

Taken by permission from
A Treasury of Canadian Verse.
Published by E. P. Dutton & Co.

Bettmann

Apostrophe to the Ocean

From "Childe Harold's Pilgrim

GEORGE GORDON BYRON
(Sixth Lord)

(Born January 22, 1788; died April 19, 1824)

There is a pleasure in the pathless woods,
　There is a rapture on the lonely shore,
There is society where none intrudes,
　By the deep sea, and music in its roar.
　I love not man the less, but Nature more,
From these our interviews, in which I steal
　From all I may be, or have been before,
To mingle with the universe, and feel
What I can ne'er express, yet can not all conceal.

Roll on, thou deep and dark blue ocean, roll!
　Ten thousand fleets sweep over thee in vain;
Man marks the earth with ruin, his control
　Stops with the shore; upon the watery plain
　The wrecks are all thy deed, nor doth remain
A shadow of man's ravage, save his own,
　When for a moment, like a drop of rain,
He sinks into thy depths with bubbling groan,
Without a grave, unknelled, uncoffined, and unknown.

His steps are not upon thy paths, thy fields
　Are not a spoil for him,—thou dost arise
And shake him from thee; the vile strength he wields
　For earth's destruction thou dost all despise,
　Spurning him from thy bosom to the skies,
And send'st him, shivering in thy playful spray
　And howling, to his gods, where haply lies
His pretty hope in some near port or bay,
And dashest him again to earth:—there let him lay.

The armaments which thunder-strike the walls
　Of rock-built cities, bidding nations quake,
And monarchs tremble in their capitals;
　The oak leviathans, whose huge ribs make
　Their clay creator the vain title take

Of lord of thee, and arbiter of war;—
   These are thy toys, and, as the snowy flake,
They melt into the nest of waves, which mar
Alike the Armada's pride or spoils of Trafalgar.

Thy shores are empires, changed in all save thee;
   Assyria, Greece, Rome, Carthage—what are they?
Thy waters wasted them while they were free,
   And many a tyrant since; their shores obey
   The stranger, slave, or savage; their decay
Has dried up realms to deserts: not so thou,
   Unchangeable save to thy wild waves' play;
Time writes no wrinkle on thy azure brow;
Such as creation's dawn beheld, thou rollest now.

Thou glorious mirror, where the Almighty's form
   Glasses itself in tempests; in all time,
Calm or convulsed; in breeze, or gale, or storm,
   Icing the pole, or in the torrid clime,
   Dark-heaving; boundless, endless, and sublime;—
The image of Eternity, the throne
   Of the Invisible; even from out thy slime
The monsters of the deep are made; each zone
Obeys thee; thou goest forth, dread, fathomless, alone.

And I have loved thee, Ocean! and my joy
   Of youthful sports was on thy breast to be
Borne, like thy bubbles, onward: from a boy
   I wanton'd with thy breakers—they to me
   Were a delight; and if the freshening sea
Made them a terror—'twas a pleasing fear,
   For I was as it were a child of thee,
And trusted to thy billows far and near,
And laid my hand upon thy mane—as I do here.

Bettmann

Renascence

EDNA ST. VINCENT MILLAY
A.B. Vassar College 1917

*(Born February 22, 1892;
died October 19, 1950)*

All I could see from where I stood
Was three long mountains and a wood;
I turned and looked the other way,
And saw three islands in a bay.
So with my eyes I traced the line
Of the horizon, thin and fine,
Straight around till I was come
Back to where I'd started from;
And all I saw from where I stood
Was three long mountains and a wood.
Over these things I could not see:
These were the things that bounded me;
And I could touch them with my hand,
Almost, I thought, from where I stand.
And all at once things seemed so small
My breath came short, and scarce at all.
But, sure, the sky is big, I said:
Miles and miles above my head;
So here upon my back I'll lie
And look my fill into the sky.
And so I looked, and, after all,
The sky was not so very tall.
The sky, I said, must somewhere stop,
And—sure enough!—I see the top!
The sky, I thought, is not so grand;
I 'most could touch it with my hand!
And reaching up my hand to try,
I screamed to feel it touch the sky.
I screamed, and—lo!—Infinity
Came down and settled over me;
Forced back my scream into my chest,
Bent back my arm upon my breast,
And, pressing of the Undefined
The definition on my mind,
Held up before my eyes a glass

Through which my shrinking sight did pass
Until it seemed I must behold
Immensity made manifold;
Whispered to me a word whose sound
Deafened the air for worlds around,
And brought unmuffled to my ears
The gossiping of friendly spheres,
The creaking of the tented sky,
The ticking of Eternity.

I saw and heard and knew at last
The How and Why of all things, past,
And present, and forevermore.
The Universe; cleft to the core,
Lay open to my probing sense
That, sick'ning, I would fain pluck thence
But could not,—nay! But needs must suck
At the great wound, and could not pluck
My lips away till I had drawn
All venom out.—Ah, fearful pawn!
For my omniscience paid I toll
In infinite remorse of soul.
All sin was of my sinning, all
Atoning mine, and mine the gall
Of all regret. Mine was the weight
Of every brooded wrong, the hate
That stood behind each envious thrust,
Mine every greed, mine every lust.
And all the while for every grief,
Each suffering, I craved relief
With individual desire,—
Craved all in vain! And felt fierce fire
About a thousand people crawl;
Perished with each,—then mourned for all!
A man was starving in Capri;
He moved his eyes and looked at me;
I felt his gaze, I heard his moan,
And knew his hunger as my own.
I saw at sea a great fog bank
Between two ships that struck and sank;
A thousand screams the heavens smote;
And every scream tore through my throat.
No hurt I did not feel, no death
That was not mine; mine each last breath
That, crying, met an answering cry
From the compassion that was I.
All suffering mine, and mine its rod;
Mine, pity like the pity of God.
Ah, awful weight! Infinity

Pressed down upon the finite Me!
My anguished spirit, like a bird,
Beating against my lips I heard;
Yet lay the weight so close about
There was no room for it without.
And so beneath the weight lay I
And suffered death, but could not die.

Long had I lain thus, craving death,
When quietly the earth beneath
Gave way, and inch by inch, so great
At last had grown the crushing weight,
Into the earth I sank till I
Full six feet under ground did lie,
And sank no more,—there is no weight
Can follow here, however great.
From off my breast I felt it roll,
And as it went my tortured soul
Burst forth and fled in such a gust
That all about me swirled the dust.

Deep in the earth I rested now;
Cool is its hand upon the brow
And soft its breast beneath the head
Of one who is so gladly dead.
And all at once, and over all
The pitying rain began to fall;
I lay and heard each pattering hoof
Upon my lowly, thatchèd roof.
And seemed to love the sound far more
Than ever I had done before.
For rain it hath a friendly sound
To one who's six feet under ground;
And scarce the friendly voice or face:
A grave is such a quiet place.

The rain, I said, is kind to come
And speak to me in my new home.
I would I were alive again
To kiss the fingers of the rain,
To drink into my eyes the shine
Of every slanting silver line,
To catch the freshened, fragrant breeze
From drenched and dripping apple-trees.
For soon the shower will be done,
And then the broad face of the sun
Will laugh above the rain-soaked earth
Until the world with answering mirth

Shakes joyously, and each round drop
Rolls, twinkling, from its grass-blade top
How can I bear it; buried here,
While overhead the sky grows clear
And blue again after the storm?
O, multi-colored, multiform,
Beloved beauty over me,
That I shall never, never see
Again! Spring-silver, autumn-gold,
That I shall never more behold!
Sleeping your myriad magics through,
Close-sepulchred away from you!
O God, I cried, give me new birth,
And put me back upon the earth!
Upset each cloud's gigantic gourd
And let the heavy rain, down-poured
In one big torrent, set me free,
Washing my grave away from me!

I ceased; and through the breathless hush
That answered me, the far-off rush
Of herald wings came whispering
Like music down the vibrant string
Of my ascending prayer, and—crash!
Before the wild wind's whistling lash
The startled storm-clouds reared on high
And plunged in terror down the sky
And the big rain in one black wave
Fell from the sky and struck my grave.
I know not how such things can be;
I only know there came to me
A fragrance such as never clings
To aught save happy living things;
A sound as of some joyous elf
Singing sweet songs to please himself,
And, through and over everything,
A sense of glad awakening.
The grass, a-tiptoe at my ear,
Whispering to me I could hear;
I felt the rain's cool finger-tips
Brushed tenderly across my lips,
Laid gently on my sealèd sight,
And all at once the heavy night
Fell from my eyes and I could see,—
A drenched and dripping apple-tree,
A last long line of silver rain,
A sky grown clear and blue again.
And as I looked a quickening gust
Of wind blew up to me and thrust

Into my face a miracle
Of orchard breath, and with the smell,—
I know how such things can be!—
I breathed my soul back into me.
Ah! Up then from the ground sprang I
And hailed the earth with such a cry
As is not heard save from a man
Who has been dead, and lives again.

About the trees my arms I wound;
Like one gone mad I hugged the ground;
I raised my quivering arms on high;
I laughed and laughed into the sky,
Till at my throat a strangling sob
Caught fiercely, and a great heart-throb
Sent instant tears into my eyes;
Oh God, I cried, no dark disguise
Can e'er hereafter hide from me
Thy radiant identity!
Thou canst not move across the grass
But my quick eyes will see Thee pass,
Nor speak, however silently,
But my hushed voice will answer Thee.
I know the patch that tells Thy way
Through the cool eve of every day;
God, I can push the grass apart
And lay my finger on Thy heart!

The world stands out on either side
No wider than the heart is wide;
Above the world is stretched the sky,—
No higher than the soul is high.
The heart can push the sea and land
Farther away on either hand;
The soul can split the sky in two,
And let the face of God shine through.
But East and West will pinch the heart
That can not keep them pushed apart;
And he whose soul is flat—the sky
Will cave in on him by and by.

Reprinted by special permission of the publisher, Mitchell Kennerley. Copyright, 1912.

Bettmann

Epilogue
to Asolando

ROBERT BROWNING

(Born May 7, 1812; died December 12, 1889)

At the midnight in the silence of the sleep-time,
   When you set your fancies free,
Will they pass to where—by death, fools think, imprisoned—
Low he lies who once so loved you, whom you loved so,
     —Pity me?

Oh to love so, be so loved, yet so mistaken!
   What had I on earth to do
With the slothful, with the mawkish, the unmanly?
Like the aimless, helpless, hopeless, did I drivel
     —Being—who?

One who never turned his back but marched breast forward,
   Never doubted clouds would break,
Never dreamed, though right were worsted, wrong would
    triumph,
Held we fall to rise, are baffled to fight better,
     Sleep to wake.

No, at noonday in the bustle of man's work-time
   Greet the unseen with a cheer!
Bid him forward, breast and back as either should be,
"Strive and thrive!" cry "Speed,—fight on, fare ever
    There as here!"

By special permission of
the Houghton-Mifflin Co.

In regard to the third stanza of this poem the
Pall Mall Gazette of February 1, 1890, related this
incident: "One evening, just before his death-ill-
ness, the poet was reading this from a proof to
his daughter-in-law and sister. He said: 'It almost
looks like bragging to say this, and as if I ought
to cancel it; but it's the simple truth; and as it's
true, it shall stand.'"

Bettmann

L'Envoi

RUDYARD KIPLING

(Born December 30, 1865; died January 17, 1936)

When earth's last picture is painted, and the tubes are
    twisted and dried,
When the oldest colors have faded, and the youngest critic
    has died,
We shall rest, and, faith, we shall need it—lie down for
    an aeon or two,
Till the Master of All Good Workmen shall set us to work
    anew!

And those that were good will be happy: they shall sit in
    a golden chair;
They shall splash at a ten-league canvas with brushes of
    comets' hair;
They shall find real saints to draw from — Magdalene,
    Peter and Paul;
They shall work for an age at a sitting and never be tired
    at all!

And only the Master shall praise us, and only the Master
    shall blame;
And no one shall work for money, and no one shall work
    for fame;
But each for the joy of the working, and each, in his sepa-
    rate star,
Shall draw the Thing as he sees It for the God of Things
    as They Are!

Bettmann

Gettysburg Address

Speech at the Dedication of the National Cemetery
at Gettysburg November 19, 1863

ABRAHAM LINCOLN

Fourscore and seven years ago our fathers brought
forth upon this continent a new nation, conceived in liberty, and dedicated to the proposition that all men are
created equal. Now we are engaged in a great civil war,
testing whether that nation, or any nation so conceived
and so dedicated, can long endure. We are met on a great
battlefield of that war. We have come to dedicate a portion of that field as a final resting-place for those who here
gave their lives that that nation might live. It is altogether
fitting and proper that we should do this. But in a larger
sense we cannot dedicate, we cannot consecrate, we cannot hallow this ground. The brave men, living and dead,
who struggled here, have consecrated it far above our poor
power to add or detract. The world will little note, nor
long remember, what we say here; but it can never forget
what they did here. It is for us, the living, rather to be
dedicated here to the unfinished work which they who
fought here have thus far so nobly advanced. It is rather
for us to be here dedicated to the great task remaining
before us, that from these honored dead we take increased
devotion to that cause for which they gave the last full
measure of devotion; that we here highly resolve that
these dead shall not have died in vain; that this nation,
under God, shall have a new birth of freedom, and that
government of the people, by the people, and for the people, shall not perish from the earth.

Executive Mansion
Washington, Nov 21, 1864

To Mrs Bixby, Boston, Mass,

Dear Madam.

I have been shown in the files of the War Department a statement of the Adjutant General of Massachusetts that you are the mother of five sons who have died gloriously on the field of battle. I feel how weak and fruitless must be any word of mine which should attempt to beguile you from the grief of a loss so overwhelming. But I cannot refrain from tendering you the consolation that may be found in the thanks of the republic they died to save. I pray that our Heavenly Father may assuage the anguish of your bereavement, and leave you only the cherished memory of the loved and lost, and the solemn pride that must be yours to have laid so costly a sacrifice upon the altar of freedom

Yours very sincerely and respectfully
A. Lincoln

On the walls of Brasenose College, Oxford University, England, this letter of the "rail-splitter" President hangs as a model of purest English, rarely, if ever, surpassed.

The Ten Commandments

I

I am the Lord thy God, which have brought thee out of the land of Egypt, out of the house of bondage.

Thou shalt have no other gods before me.

II

Thou shalt not make unto thee any graven image, or any likeness of any thing that is in heaven above, or that is in the earth beneath, or that is in the water under the earth:

Thou shalt not bow down thyself to them, nor serve them: for I the Lord thy God am a jealous God, visiting the iniquity of the fathers upon the children unto the third and fourth generation of them that hate me;

And shewing mercy unto thousands of them that love me, and keep my commandments.

III

Thou shalt not take the name of the Lord thy God in vain; for the Lord will not hold him guiltless that taketh his name in vain.

IV

Remember the Sabbath day to keep it holy:

Six day shalt thou labor, and do all thy work:

But the seventh day is the Sabbath of the Lord thy God; in it thou shalt not do any work, thou, nor thy son, nor thy daughter, thy man-servant, nor thy maid-servant, nor thy cattle, nor the stranger that is within thy gates:

For in six days the Lord made heaven and earth, the sea, and all that in them is, and rested the seventh day: wherefore the Lord blessed the Sabbath day, and hallowed it.

V

Honor thy father and thy mother: that thy days may be long upon the land which the Lord thy God giveth thee.

VI

Thou shalt not kill.

VII

Thou shalt not commit adultery.

VIII

Thou shalt not steal.

IX

Thou shalt not bear false witness against thy neighbor.

X

Thou shalt not covet thy neighbor's house, thou shalt not covet thy neighbor's wife, nor his man-servant, nor his maid-servant, nor his ox, nor his ass, nor anything that is thy neighbor's.

Magna Charta

Bettmann

Engraved for Sydney's *History of England*

On June 15, 1215, King John met the barons near Runnymeade on the Thames, and granted them the charter which they laid before him.

This charter contains sixty-three articles, some of which were merely temporary; the principles upon which the whole English judicial system is based are these:

"No freeman shall be taken or imprisoned, or disseised*, or outlawed, or banished ... unless by the lawful judgment of his peers, or by the law of the land."

"We will sell to no man, we will not deny to any man, either justice or right."

Among the most important articles were the two which limited the power of the king in maters of taxation:

"No scutage or aid shall be imposed in our kingdom unless by the general council of our kingdom;" and

"For the holding of the general council of the kingdom . . . we shall cause to be summoned the archbishops, bishops, abbots, earls, and the greater barons of the realm, singly, by our letters. And furthermore we shall cause to be summoned generally by our sheriffs and bailiffs, all others who hold of us in chief."

*Dispossessed of land.

The War Inevitable, March, 1775

PATRICK HENRY

Bettmann

They tell us, Sir, that we are weak — unable to cope with so formidable an adversary. But when shall we be stronger? Will it be the next week, or the next year? Will it be when we are totally disarmed, and when a British guard shall be stationed in every house? Shall we gather strength by irresolution and inaction? Shall we acquire the means of effectual resistance by lying supinely on our backs, and hugging the delusive phantom of hope, until our enemies shall have bound us hand and foot? Sir, we are not weak, if we make a proper use of those means which the God of nature hath placed in our power.

Three millions of People, armed in the holy cause of liberty, and in such a country as that which we possess. are invincible by any force which our enemy can send against us. Beside, Sir, we shall not fight our battles alone. There is a just God who presides over the destinies of Nations, and who will raise up friends to fight our battles for us. The battle, Sir, is not to the strong alone; it is to the vigilant, the active, the brave. Besides, Sir, we have no election. If we were base enough to desire it, it is now too late to retire from the contest. There is no retreat but in submission and slavery! Our chains are forged! Their clanking may be heard on the plains of Boston! The war is inevitable; and let it come! I repeat, Sir, let it come!

It is in vain, Sir, to extenuate the matter. Gentlemen may cry, Peace, Peace!—but there is no peace. The war is actually begun! The next gale that sweeps from the North will bring to our ears the clash of resounding arms! Our brethren are already in the field! Why stand we here idle? What is it that Gentlemen wish? What would they have? Is life so dear, or peace so sweet, as to be purchased at the price of chains and slavery? Forbid it, Almighty God! I know not what course others may take; but as for me, give me liberty or give me death!

177

The Declaration of Independence

In Congress, July 4th, 1776

The Unanimous Declaration of the Thirteen United States of America

When, in the course of human events, it becomes necessary for one people to dissolve the political bands which have connected them with another, and to assume, among the powers of the earth, the separate and equal station to which the laws of nature and of nature's God entitle them, a decent respect to the opinions of mankind requires that they should declare the causes which impel them to the separation.

We hold these truths to be self-evident: that all men are created equal; that they are endowed by their Creator with certain inalienable rights; that among these are life, liberty, and the pursuit of happiness. That to secure these rights, governments are instituted among men, deriving their just powers from the consent of the governed; that whenever any form of government becomes destructive of these ends it is the right of the people to alter or to abolish it, and to institute a new government, laying its foundation on such principles, and organizing its powers in such form, as to them shall seem most likely to effect their safety and happiness. Prudence, indeed, will dictate, that governments long established should not be changed for light and transient causes; and accordingly all experience hath shown, that mankind are more disposed to suffer, while evils are sufferable, than to right themselves by abolishing the forms to which they are accustomed. But when a long train of abuses and usurpations, pursuing invariably the same object, evinces a design to reduce them under absolute despotism, it is their right, it is their duty, to throw off such government, and to provide new guards for their future security. Such has been the patient sufferance of these colonies; and such is now the necessity which constrains them to alter their former system of government. The history of the present king of Great Britain is a history of repeated injuries and usurpations, all having in direct object the establishment of an absolute tyranny over these states. To prove this, let facts be submitted to a candid world.

He has refused his assent to laws the most wholesome and necesary for the public good.

He has forbidden his governors to pass laws of immediate and pressing importance, unless suspended in their operation till his assent should be obtained; and when so suspended, he has utterly neglected to attend to them.

He has refused to pass other laws for the accommodation of large districts of people, unless those people would relinquish the right of representation in the legislature —a right inestimable to them, and formidable to tyrants only.

He has called together legislative bodies at places unusual, uncomfortable, and distant from the depository of their public records, for the sole purpose of fatiguing them into compliance with his measures.

He has dissolved representative houses repeatedly, for opposing, with manly firmness, his invasions on the rights of the people.

He has refused, for a long time after such dissolutions, to cause others to be elected; whereby the legislative powers, incapable of annihilation, have returned to the people at large, for their exercise, the state remaining in the meantime exposed to all the dangers of invasion from without, and convulsions within.

He has endeavored to prevent the population of these states; for that purpose obstructing the laws for naturalization of foreigners; refusing to pass others to encourage their migration hither, and raising the conditions of new appropriations of lands.

He has obstructed the administration of justice, by refusing his assent to laws for establishing judiciary powers.

He has made judges dependent on his will alone, for the tenure of their offices, and the amount and payment of their salaries.

He has erected a multitude of new offices, and sent hither swarms of officers, to harass our people, and eat out their substance.

He has kept among us, in times of peace, standing armies, without the consent of our legislature.

He has affected to render the military independent of, and superior to, the civil power.

He has combined with others to subject us to a jurisdiction foreign to our constitution, and unacknowledged by our laws; giving his assent to their acts of pretended legislation:

For quartering large bodies of armed troops among us:

For protecting them, by a mock trial, from punishment for any murders which they should commit on the inhabitants of these states:

For cutting off our trade with all parts of the world:

For imposing taxes on us without our consent:

For depriving us, in many cases, of the benefits of trial by jury:

For transporting us beyond seas to be tried for pretended offences:

For abolishing the free system of English laws in a neighboring province, establishing therein an arbitrary government, and enlarging its boundaries, so as to render it at once an example and fit instrument for introducing the same absolute rule into these colonies:

For taking away our charters, abolishing our most valuable laws, and altering, fundamentally, the forms of our governments:

For suspending our own legislatures, and declaring themselves invested with power to legislate for us in all cases whatsoever.

He has abdicated government here, by declaring us out of his protection and waging war against us.

He has plundered our seas, ravaged our coasts, burnt our towns and destroyed the lives of our people.

He is at this time transporting large armies of foreign mercenaries to complete the works of death, desolation, and tyranny, already begun with circumstances of cruelty and perfidy scarcely paralleled in the most barbarous ages, and totally unworthy the head of a civilized nation.

He has constrained our fellow-citizens, taken captive on the high seas, to bear arms against their country, to become the executioners of their friends and brethren, or to fall themselves by their hands.

He has excited domestic insurrections among us, and has endeavored to bring on the inhabitants of our frontiers the merciless Indian savages, whose known rule of warfare is an undistinguished destruction of all ages, sexes, and conditions.

In every stage of these oppressions we have petitioned for redress in the most humble terms; our repeated petitions have been answered only by repeated injury. A prince whose character is thus marked by every act which may define a tyrant is unfit to be the ruler of a free people.

Nor have we been wanting in attentions to our British brethren. We have warned them, from time to time, of attempts by their legislature to extend an unwarrantable jurisdiction over us. We have reminded them of the circumstances of our emigration and settlement here. We have appealed to their native justice and magnanimity, and we have conjured them by the ties of our common kindred to disavow these usurpations, which would inevitably interrupt our connections and correspondence. They, too, have been deaf to the voice of justice and consanguinity. We must, therefore, acquiesce in the necessity which denounces our separation, and hold them, as we hold the rest of mankind, enemies in war, in peace friends.

We, therefore, the representatives of the United States of America, in General Congress assembled, appealing to the Supreme Judge of the world for rectitude of our intentions, do, in the name and by the authority of the good people of these colonies, solemnly publish and declare that these United Colonies are, and of right ought to be, free and independent States; that they are absolved from all allegiance to the British crown, and that all political connection between them and the State of Great Britain is, and ought to be, totally dissolved; and that, as free and independent States, they have full power to levy war, conclude peace, contract alliances, establish commerce, and to do all other acts and things which independent States may of right do. And for the support of this declaration, with a firm reliance on the protection of Divine Providence, we mutually pledge to each other our lives, our fortunes, and our sacred honor.

Signed by order and in behalf of the Congress.

JOHN HANCOCK, President.

Attested, CHARLES THOMPSON, Secretary.

NEW HAMPSHIRE.
Josiah Bartlett,
William Whipple,
Matthew Thornton.

RHODE ISLAND.
Stephen Hopkins,
William Ellery.

NEW YORK.
William Floyd,
Phillip Livingston,
Francis Lewis,
Lewis Morris.

MASSACHUSETTS BAY.
Samuel Adams,
John Adams.
Robert Treat Paine,
Eldridge Gerry.

CONNECTICUT.
Roger Sherman,
Samuel Huntington,
William Williams.
Oliver Wolcott

NEW JERSEY.
Richard Stockton,
John Witherspoon,
Francis Hopkinson,
John Hart,
Abraham Clark.

PENNSYLVANIA.
Robert Morris,
Benjamin Rush,
Benjamin Franklin,
John Morton,
George Clymer,
James Smith,
George Taylor,
James Wilson,
George Ross.

DELAWARE.
Caesar Rodney,
George Read,
Thomas M'kean.

MARYLAND.
Samuel Chase,
William Paca,
Thomas Stone,
Charles Carroll of Carrollton.

VIRGINIA.
George Wythe,
Richard Henry Lee,
Thomas Jefferson,
Benjamin Harrison,
Thomas Nelson, Jr.,
Francis Lightfoot Lee,
Carter Braxton.

NORTH CAROLINA.
William Hooper,
Joseph Hewes,
John Penn.

SOUTH CAROLINA.
Edward Rutledge,
Thomas Heyward, Jr.,
Thomas Lynch, Jr.,
Arthur Middleton.

GEORGIA.
Dutton Gwinnett,
Lyman Hall,
George Walton.

I N choosing books for children these rules, recently laid down by an author of books for boys, are worth the consideration of parents:

"Read your children's books yourself. Or better still, get your boy or girl to read them aloud to you. Ask yourself during the reading:

'Does this book lay stress on villainy, deception or treachery?'

'Are all the incidents wholesome, probable and true to life?'

'Does it show young people contemptuous toward their elders and successfully opposing them?'

'Do the young characters in the book show respect for teachers and others in authority?'

'Are these characters the kind of young people you wish your children to associate with?'

'Does the book speak of and describe pranks, practical jokes and pieces of thoughtless and cruel mischief as though they were funny and worthy of imitation?'

'Is the English good and is the story written in good style?' "

Index

Index of Authors